Whitemarsh
Information Systems Corporation

Enterprise Governance Community of Interest Handbook

Michael M. Gorman

Whitemarsh Information Systems Corporation
2008 Althea Lane
Bowie, Maryland 20716
Tele: 301-249-1142
Email: Whitemarsh@wiscorp.com
Web: www.wiscorp.com

ISBN 978-0-9789968-7-1

Printed in the United States of America

Table of Contents

Figures

Tables

Preface

Why was this book necessary? Governance within enterprises almost always involves large collections of sometimes-integrated and/or sometimes-interoperable work products. Governance is almost always multi-functional. Hence, governance, as an enterprise discipline, has always been a cross-functional community effort.

The work products are the specifications of the databases, the missions, organizations, functions within which the databases operate, and addresses also the specifications of the business information systems.

Communities of Interest are not just the right approach for these efforts. They have been the only approach for the past 50+ years. Highly efficient, and broadly successful Communities of Interest are work-product centric, author-anonymous organizations. Individual contributions are subservient to the work products produced.

The cost for a Community of Interest approach over the Stove Pipe approach is 50% less. Additionally, it is almost 10 times less when adding an additional system/member than the Stove Pipe approach. That alone should be sufficient justification for the Governance Community of Interest approach.

This is a handbook for successful Governance Communities of Interest. That is, those that are work-product centric, and author-anonymous. To be successful, Governance Communities of Interest operate under a formal set of rules and produce highly engineered, thoroughly-integrated work products.

Simply put, this book is a "battle plan" for governance across the enterprise. This book is highly engineered, thoroughly planned, and read to execute, "right out of the box." Everything implied by the book already exists and is 100% operational.

The Congress of the United States (a Community of Interest for America) operates under an elaborate set of rules. These rules were adapted for members of ordinary societies by GEN Henry M. Robert in 1915. These are now commonly called *Robert's Rules*. Notwithstanding they also require a "Sergeant of Arms." For sure not to shoot members, but to enforce good order. From the United States Senate website[1], "The Sergeant at Arms and Doorkeeper, elected by the members, serves as the protocol and chief law enforcement officer and is the principal administrative manager for most

---

[1] The website address is:
<http://www.senate.gov/reference/office/sergeant_at_arms.htm>

support services in the United States Senate." Even with such an individual, some sessions in both houses of the U.S. Congress seem not to be in good order.

Over the years, I have participated in a number of Governance Communities of Interest. These range from committees to develop programs for Boy Scout Troops, to informal groups within various employments, and a number of times during Whitemarsh consulting assignments. As the years have passed, the financial impacts of decisions made by Communities of Interest have become greater. Such decisions should be made not only with the utmost technical precision but also with the utmost bureaucratic care. Proper formulation, notice, discussion, voting, and on some occasions, appeals are all absolutely essential.

Some Governance Communities of Interest seem like "professional" hockey games: Three 20 minute periods of continuous fighting interrupted by short intervals of skating around the rink. When serious Governance Community of Interest discussions and decisions need to take place, consuming 50% of the time settling who votes, how votes are taken, what determines success or failure, if or when you can abstain, when papers are produced, and how minutes are is clearly a waste of time and effort. All of that should be predetermined by the rules and procedures of good order.

This book sets down a set of bureaucratic and procedural rules for accomplishing the scope and program of work of Governance Communities of Interest as well as clear procedures for technical work. Finally, this book provides the technical policies, procedures and product specifications needed. They are provided in this book and are very much further detailed in other materials from the Whitemarsh website[2].

I hope this book brings value to your Governance Community of Interest efforts. Suggestions for revision are always welcome. Send me email.[3]

Michael M. Gorman
June 2017

[2] www.wiscorp.com

[3] The email address is: Whitemarsh@wiscorp.com

Acknowledgments

There were four main sources for the material in this book. First is the Multi-Lateral Interoperability Program[4]. This is a military Command and Control (C2) community of interest exclusively focused on governance that was founded within NATO (North Atlantic Treaty Organization). The MIP organization has been operational for more than 20 years across 26 nations. Simply stated, this organization has created a first class Transaction Data Staging Area Data Model for Command and Control. Not surprisingly, it is called C2IEDM. The scope and the purpose of the MIP organization are set down in the opening section of Chapter 1 of this book. Only very minor edits were performed on their text. If the text is compelling as to its mission and goals, it is because the need for and concepts surrounding governance transcend organizations and nations. The most significant contribution of these materials has been the engineering of this style of community of interest. While the MIP material has been edited for use in this book, the intention was to remain true to their Governance Community of Interest engineering.

The second source for material is an even older community of interest: The International Committee of Information Technology Standards (INCITS, www.incits.org). This organization is at least 40 years old and operates under the auspices of the American National Standards Institute (ANSI). This uniquely American, volunteer-based, organization is responsible for developing IT standards for SQL, COBOL, FORTRAN, Optical Digital Data Disks, C, C++, Metadata, Radio Frequency Identification (RAID), and the like. The INCITS organization operates almost exclusively through Communities of Interest. The author of this book has been the Secretary of the Database Languages Committee, DM32.2, since its very first meeting in April 1978. The organizational and operational materials from INCITS have been invaluable in the construction of the "bureaucratic" component of this book. Similarly, while the INCITS material has been edited for use in this book, the intention was to remain true to its information technology standard's Communities of Interest engineering. Thus, similarity to the original text is no accident.

Just having a complete policies and procedures manual to govern meetings, documents, decisions and appeals to decisions does not automatically bring peace, order, and harmony. That is achieved by a chair who understands that

---

[4] The MIP website is located at: https://www.mimworld.org

his role is to progress the standard and doing that requires peace, order and harmony. For 36 of the 38 years, the chair of DM32.2 (previously known as H2 and X3H2) has been Dr. Donald Deutsch. The DM32.2 standards are clearly the most accepted IT standards in the world is due to his firm hand and calm demeanor. Don, my "ANSI boss," and a close friend for more than 50 years is therefore great fully acknowledged. Because the engineering and operations of DM32.2 are excellent, a number of DM32.2 documents have been employed to construct key content in several chapters.

The ANSI and ISO organizations have developed two key standards that greatly assist in the development of data management language standards. These are the SQL standards that are managed by the ANSI INCITS DM32.2 Technical Committee on Database Languages, and the ISO 11179 Standard for Data Element Registries. The U.S. Committee for the ISO 11179 Standard is ANSI INCITS DM32.8 Technical Committee on Metadata. Information about both these standards and organizations can be obtained from INCITS[5].

The third source of material has been the Office of the CIO of the United States Army. During the time, September 2003 through December 2004, this author, and two other individuals, Bruce Haberkamp and Jim Blalock worked almost continuously on building an enterprise[6]-wide Data Management Program that could achieve governance across the U.S. Army. A workshop based on a prototype of these efforts was conducted in December 2003. It was very successful. Dr. Edward Siomacco (COL, U.S. Army Ret) authorized and encouraged the workshop. These efforts resulted in sections within two Army documents. The data management paragraphs of Army Regulation 25-1, and an entire data management chapter in the Department of Army Pamphlet

---

[5]. The INCITS website is: www.incits.org.

[6]. As defined within this book, an enterprise is merely a term to relate to a collection of organization units that have common collections of data, processes, activities within a business or a company and sometimes beyond corporate affiliations as in the case of governance. Ideally, there is also a common governance of these items. An enterprise is therefore not just a synonym for business or a company. Rather, it is intended to convey a common data, process, and activity view across the organizational units sharing that view. A Governance Program is presumed to work across enterprises. Specific Communities of Interest work within enterprises and with respect to governance work products. Some Communities of Interest work across corporate boundaries as in the case of the ANSI committee of the U.S. State Motor Vehicle Departments. Maryland drivers who speed in Nebraska see notations on their Maryland driving record.

(DA PAM 25-1-1). These materials provided the three distinct levels to the Data Management Program: Program, Project, and Community of Interest.

The fourth sets of materials have been from the Whitemarsh Corporation's extensive development of data management related methodologies, metadata engineering, and a metadata repository that can accomplish the program and scope of work for a Community of Interest. These materials have been in constant use and refinement since the middle 1970s. Organizations that have employed these materials are listed under Clients on the Whitemarsh website. During 2005 and 2006 Whitemarsh constructed the materials necessary for a Data Interoperability Community of Interest. This book is a "Governance" adaption of these materials.

Collectively then, the organizational engineering from the MIP program, the bureaucratic structures and processes from INCITS, the firm and guiding hand of a "Don Deutsch," the programmatic levels from the U.S. Army, and the technical materials from Whitemarsh have been brought together to create this book. All during the engineering and construction of this book, Hank Lavender, a retired USAF Colonel and graduate of the Air Force Academy, and also a senior database management consultant to the U.S. Department of Logistics's Defense Logistics Standards Management Office, and a long time friend and a professional colleague, has been ever ready to read a chapter, and even whole manuscripts and provide back immediate and very constructive comments.

Within the MIP program thanks goes to Gene Simaitis and Francisco Loaiza both retired from the Institute for Defense Analysis, to COL Stuart Whitehead, and to Mike Morris. These four along with countless others have made the MIP data model, the C2IEDM, the premiere Command and Control data model throughout the world.

A common thread to all of these Army governance initiatives has been the Office of the CIO formerly under the command of LTG Stephen Boutelle. It was his program actions that funded the development of the data management materials within the Army regulations, and that funded the workshop that demonstrated that the guidance in this book works efficiently and effectively.

It is largely because of the hundreds of staff years from all these four acknowledged organizations and all the individuals who reviewed this book represents an integration, editing, and publication effort rather than an original creation effort. In short because of all these efforts, this book is equivalent to a book you would read after it has been continuously revised over many years.

1

The Demand for Governance

The application of IT in the early 21st century is demanding. It covers a wide spectrum of scenarios that range from conventional to crises responses, and to asymmetric operations. Unilateral capability is important but most planning is made on the assumption of scenarios that are difficult to predict and which often arise at short notice. Thus, the nature and composition of IT to meet requirements may be quite specific but should be based upon general and flexible capabilities.

To achieve this, an assured capability for governance is essential. The successful executions of fast-moving operations needed an accelerated decision-action cycle, increased tempos of operations, and the ability to conduct operations. Executives require timely and accurate information. Also, supporting business information systems[7] need to pass information within and across many boundaries. Moreover, tactical information must be provided to the operational and strategic levels of command.

The aim of a Governance Community of Interest, hereafter referred to just by Community of Interest, is to achieve governance at all levels in support of operations. Because governance is almost always cross-functional, and cross-organizational, achievement of the highest level of governance requires institutionalized, cross-functional, and cross-organizational semantics.

In other Whitemarsh books and all throughout all the Whitemarsh Metabase System Modules and user guides, the key effort is to create IT work products from across the enterprise in an integrated, interoperable, non-Redundant

[7]. In the context of this book, a Business Information System is generic term for an information system that most commonly employs a database management system and a database. Simply put, a business information system is an application of IT technology in support of a collection of end users. The term is thus distinguished for example, from a computer's Operating System such as Windows or Unix, or a Database Management System such as Oracle, or "office" systems like Microsoft's Word, Power Point or Excel.

manner. In contrast, Governance is focused on the integrity and correctness of work products. The Whitemarsh Metabase System's Governance module focuses on recording the personal identity including organization and functional context responsible for governance.

This book's focus is on the architecture and engineering of governance across the enterprise. The process of actually recording Governance architecture and engineering is managed through the Whitemarsh Project Management functional module. Together, the Whitemarsh Metabase Governance and Project Management modules enable the complete accomplishment of enterprise-wide governance.

The catch phrase for this within the U.S. DoD for accomplishing enterprise-wide governance integration and interoperability is *factory to foxhole.* Specialized, parochial semantics however, are direct inhibitors to governance.

The concept for the overall end state is to have multiple and disparate organizations operate as a single, synchronized team in accomplishing its assigned mission. In order to achieve that synergy, a common understanding is required. Governance's contribution to this end-state facilitates the timely flow of commonly-understood, accurate and relevant information.

The perspective of this book is that there is a collection of operational Communities of Interest within an enterprise's Governance Program, and this book is a component of day-to-day operations of all the subgroups[8] within the Governance Program. If it is the case that there is only one community of interest, the entire organizational structure could consist solely of that community of interest and its contained technical committees. Consequentially, there would be no need for a Governance Program Committee and any of its contained subgroups. Other areas of this book could be similarly organizationally collapsed and/or streamlined in such a case.

[8]. Within the context of this document, *subgroup* is a generic term that refers to any constituted governance program organizational entity including the Governance Program committee, its contained boards, Communities of Interest, its contained technical committees. This term is employed within the context in question, and applies universally to all governance program organizational entities.

1.1 Formal Interpretation of this Book

The perspective of this book is not "Whitemarsh to reader," but from an organization that has adopted and promulgated this book within its governance community of interest. Consequently, the presumed reader is someone who is using the book as their day-to-day governance operating handbook. Because of this perspective, formal interpretation of this book may be obtained upon request to the Governance Program Committee[9]. It is their responsibility to determine the meaning of any content and to render decisions about the effect of such interpretation. Any request for interpretation should be addressed by Procedures Board Committee at the first meeting following receipt of the request.

The Governance Program Committee maintains a record of all requests including the substance of the request and the interpretation provided. This record of interpretation should be periodically distributed to all members of the Governance Program Committee as well as all subgroup officers, and will serve as a basis for future revisions of this document.

Appeals to any interpretation made under this procedure may be made directly to the Community of Interest by requesting in writing that the issue be reviewed at its next scheduled meeting of the Governance Program Committee.

1.2 Objective of this Book

The objective of this book is to facilitate the identification, development, and evolution of Governance Assessments. These Governance Assessment are produced within Communities of Interest that, in turn, operate within an enterprise's Governance Program. Governance Assessment from one Community of Interest are themselves almost always semantically

9. From the publishing perspective of this book, if a reader of this book finds that content is missing, misstated, or could be stated or described differently, suggestions are always welcome. Send them to Whitemarsh@Wiscorp.com. The ultimate goal of this book is to assist in the engineering of Communities of Interest that operate efficiently and effectively. Feedback will enhance future editions.

interrelated with other Governance Assessments from other Communities of Interest.

A key function of certain subgroups within the overall Governance Program is semantic harmonization across Governance Assessments. Without harmonization Governance Assessments ultimately become the specifications of the governance of just one "stovepipe" database. The centerpiece product in a Governance Assessment is the Metabase System database. Within this software and database there exist multiple classes of metadata across the entire enterprise that should be integrated, interoperable, non-redundant and of common meaning.

1.3 Communities of Interest

From the Wikipedia, "a Community of interest is a community of people who share a common interest or passion, such as rugby fans on Rugby365.com, or music lovers on MP3.com. These people exchange ideas and thoughts about the given passion, but may know (or care) little about each other outside of this area. Participation in a community of interest can be compelling, entertaining and create a 'sticky' community where people return frequently and remain for extended periods."

Within the context of this book, a Community of Interest is the organizational implementing mechanism through which governance is achieved across collections of data. In almost all organizations, data is cross functional. Consequently, governance communities of interest under whatever names they have been called have existed for 30 or more years.

Within information technology, Communities of Interest is really a new name for an old concept. Charles Betz indicates that these groups have been called Communities of Practice, Consortia, Steering Committees, Advisory Committees/Councils, Coordinating Committees, or Interest Groups.

Communities of Interest exist within the context of an organization's governance program. Each community of interest is likely focused on a particular functional area or a collection of functional areas. For example, if there is a governance community of interest for Order Processing, then while functionally narrow, it may embrace a collection of organizations and individuals that deal with creating interoperable order processing data. Such a community might exist because each participating organization has a different order processing system.

Other more naturally existing governance communities of interest exist with data operational data store (ODS) a database and data warehouse (both wholesale and retail) projects, or master data projects (including reference data). These classes of projects have always been cross functional, and thus, the groups of individuals from the different participating organizations have always functioned as communities of interest.

This book then is really a new book about an old concept. The objective is to provide a formalization to these cross-functional governance groups so that when these groups come into existence they can operate more smoothly, efficiently, and effectively. Less smoke and mirrors: more real work.

1.4 Organization of the Book

The overall organization of this book is in Parts and Chapters.

- Part I, Introduction and Rationale, Chapter 1 and 2 introduce and provide an overall rationale for governance.

- Part II, Governance Infrastructure, Chapters 3 through eight, are the infrastructures chapters for establishing governance programs and their communities of interest.

- Part III, Governance Bureaucracy, Chapters 9 through 13, set out the policies, procedures, organizations, and rules under which a governance program is executed.

The parts, chapters and descriptions are provided in Table 1. Every chapter concludes with a set of questions that represent exercises for the reader.

Governance Community of Interest Handbook Organization		
Part	**Chapter**	**Description**
I. Governance Introduction and Rationale	1.Demand for Governance	This chapter presents the overall rationale for the demand for governance, a description of Communities of Interest, the Knowledge Worker Framework, Governance' s value proposition, the objective of the book and its organizational framework.
	2. Rationale for Governance	This chapter presents the rationale for a community of interest. Included in the rationale are its key reasons for existence, the role of shared policy, and the need to focus on work products and governance identified process specifications.
II. Governance Infrastructure	3. Required Governance Metadata Infrastructure	This chapter sets forth the requirements for metadata with the objective that the reader concludes that to have any reasonable hope of being successful in governance there must first be success with the metadata appropriate for governance.
	4. Mission of Governance	Chapter 4 presents the overall mission of governance. Missions describe the objective in idealized terms without the "who" (Positions and Organization), or the "how" (functions).
	5. Governance Work Products	Chapter 5 present the "what." That is, the metadata products that need to be created during the existence of a governance project. In this case these products are the specifications necessary to then implement so as to enable governance throughout an enterprise's operations.
	6. Governance Process Management	Chapter 6 describes and enumerates the processes, which, in the case of a Governance Program are the audits and evaluation processes used by members of the various Governance Programs to determine the integrity and correctness of the work products set out in Chapter 5. The actual processes are contained in the appendix.
	7. Governance Events	Chapter 7 presents the business events that occur along the road to creating the metadata-based products of Chapter 5 that are assessed in Chapter 6. Also presented are the bureaucratic business events

Governance Community of Interest Handbook Organization		
Part	**Chapter**	**Description**
		that occur while carrying out the scope and program of work of a Governance Program.
	8. Governance Functions	This chapter presents the business functions, that is, the processes that are to be undertaken by the positions within the organizations to build the products necessary for a successful governance mission. Of necessity, these processes are not completely detailed. Additional detail is available from various methodology products from the Whitemarsh website.
III. Governance Bureaucracy	9. Governance Organizations	This chapter presents the various organizations that should exist for a robust Governance Program. If your program is merely a single Community of Interest, the organizational structure should be collapsed into just the organization, Community of Interest. The chair and officers of that one Community of Interest would necessarily have to assume the responsibilities, authorities and duties of the total program. If thereafter additional Communities of Interest emerge, then the additional layers within the organization should be created and set into place.
	10. Governance Positions	This chapter presents the various positions that should exist across the subgroup organizations. In this book "position" applies to members as well as functional positions such as officers, editors, and the like. Included as well in this chapter are the processes for applying for membership, withdrawal of membership, and member status review.
	11. Governance Documents and Guidance	This chapter presents a sketch of the kinds of documents or "large" products that are built from the collections of metadata products set out in Chapter 5 over which governance is to be exercised. These were drawn from the Whitemarsh database project methodology and are identified work products within the Metabase System database. Every other enterprise that has an IT methodology would need to examine, retain, or replace the set of documents described in this Chapter.

Governance Community of Interest Handbook Organization		
Part	**Chapter**	**Description**
	12. Governance Projects	This chapter presents the various projects involved in Governance Programs and Communities of Interest. A project is creation, evolution, or employment of a collection of metadata products accomplished through a set of functions performed by one or more positions within one or more organizations in support of the governance mission. Projects must be identified, staffed, allocated resources, and monitored for both timeliness and quality.
	13. Governance Rules	This chapter contains a detailed set of rules that govern the operation of any subgroup within a Governance Program. Rules are needed because the consequences of decisions from any Community of Interest decision are likely to have significant monetary and other resource effects.

Table 1. Chapters Organization by Part Sequence.

Now, if all of this sounds like a lot of work, it really is and isn't. It is a lot of work if you and your organization are not accomplishing it now. But it isn't a lot of work when you compare it to the collective set of activities that are performed and products that are built to remedy governance chaos.

Accomplished well, these activities have a negative real-dollar cost and a negative time expenditure. At first, there will be more time and money spent ramping up the effort. But once done, the time and money expenditures that were formerly budgeted can be reduced well in excess of this ramp-up cost.

Has this been proven? Of course it has. Chapter 3 contains just a few examples. In one 1980s example, multiple versions of a particular class of business information system were being built, individually, for a cost of about $400,000. After these practices were put into place, these same systems were being created for about $100,000. The cost for the ramp up was about $125,000. So, the first use of these policies and procedure was projected to cost about $525,000. But the second was to cost 60% (of the $400,00), and there after, 40% (of the $400,00). Because of rigorous metadata, excellent systems engineering, and overarching governance over all the work products across the business information system implementation projects, the first system came in at 80% of the $525,000; the second system came in at 40%; and thereafter, the systems came in at 20%. That actually meant that there was almost a positive ROI on the first use. Actually, the cost was just $20,000 over the custom system cost.

Has this strategy and fundamental organization been used outside of IT? Of course it has. Just look at the organization, operating procedures, and results from any well run fire department. Within these departments there are well-defined missions for each class of fire or emergency; clearly identified objects that are employed and interrelated one with another; clearly delineated systems that are employed to report fires, dispatch equipment, manage fire suppression, and report and evaluate on results; well-defined events that are the consequence of functions and that employ systems; all manner of human functions that are performed, and finally, detailed and experience honed organizations to perform all manners of fire activities.

Similar examples abound for almost every highly organized complex activity. In virtually 100% of these organizations chaos occurs only when the missions through to organizations are not well engineered and rigorously followed. Chaotically engineered and organized activities that produce quality, efficient and cost-effective results are almost always only accidental.

1.4 Knowledge Worker Framework

The book begins with this chapter. Chapter 2 explains the need of governance environments. The overall architecture for the book is the Knowledge Worker Framework. Frameworks are merely mechanisms for depicting, understanding, and explaining a complex subject. Some frameworks are durable and persistent while others are temporal. A framework for the Knowledge Worker, initially described in the early 1980s by Matthew Flavin, is throughly explained in materials from the Whitemarsh website. This framework is for the knowledge worker rather than for the process worker. The columns for the framework and how they are accomplished within the context of Governance are set out and briefly described in Table 2.

Knowledge Worker Framework		
Column	**Chapter**	**Description**
Mission	Chapter 4, Mission of Governance	The set of work products that address the enterprise itself. Every work product across the framework is able to be described in terms of what aspect of the enterprise's mission it accomplishes or supports. Simply put, all work products are essential, not accidental attributes of the enterprise's mission
Database Object	Chapter 5, Governance Work Products	The set of products to be audited and evaluated through integrity and correctness assessments.
Business Information System	Chapter 6, Governance Process Management	The identification, architecture, and specification of work product-based processes necessary to achieve the enterprise's required integrity and correctness.
Business Event	Chapter 7, Governance Events	The set of events that are the triggering mechanisms for the business information system column's work products. The activation of the triggers is set out through the various business functions performed by persons within the enterprise.
Business Function	Chapter 8, Governance Functions	The set of human activities performed by persons within the context of their enterprise organizations.
Business Organization	Chapter 9, Governance Organizations	The enterprise's bureaucratic structures within which enterprise work are identified, planned, and managed.

Table 2. Knowledge Worker Framework Columns.

The rows of the Knowledge Worker Framework are the same as those in the Zachman Framework for Information Systems Architecture. These are set out and briefly described in Table 3. Each cell across the six-column rows identifies the work products that need to be created, updated, used, and of course, governed.

Knowledge Worker Framework	
Row	Description
Scope	Work products that set out the overall scope and objective of each of the six columns, which collectively describe the entire architecture and engineering of the enterprise.
Business	Work products that describe, at a business level, the work products that describe, how the various Knowledge Worker Framework columns are accomplished.
System	Work products that describe, at a system level, the work products that form the systematic architecture and design of the approach undertaken to achieve the accomplishments required from within the business row.
Technology	Work products that describe, at a technology level, the work products that set out in a technology-specific manner just how the various system-row-based work products are implemented across the enterprise.
Deploy-ment	Work products that describe, at a deployment level, the work products that identify just how and in what manner the required technologies are actually implemented and are then to be used by the enterprise.
Operations	Work products that describe, at an operational level, the work products being actually used by the enterprise through its organizations and persons to accomplish enterprise missions.

Table 3. Knowledge Worker Framework Rows.

The Knowledge Work Framework (KWF) was established in response to a detailed analysis of eight multi $100 million Federal business information system failures. The KWF is presented in Table 4. The allocation of U.S. General Accountability Office failures (in percent values) is presented in Table 5.

The items in each of the 36 cells are the enterprise, database, and business information system work products that the Metabase System captures, stores, integrates, interrelates, updates and reports across the enterprise in a non-redundant manner. 100% of the work products are based on published and well known IT techniques and disciplines.

The following are findings resulting from the analysis of GAO information technology failures from within Table 4.

- 41% of all database and business information system errors occur in the first two rows.
- 50% of all the errors occur after the effort is completed (columns 5 and 6, rows 3 thru 6).
- 5% of all the errors are the direct cause of Information Technology.

The conclusion is clear and compelling. The scope and domain of the Metabase Systems must be the entire KWF's work products for there to be a greater than 5% chance of database and business information system success across the enterprise.

Whitemarsh Knowledge Worker Framework							
		Man-Machine Interface					
		Machine		Interface	Man		
View Points	**Mission**	**Database Object**	**Business Informati on System**	**Business Event**	**Business Function**	**Organ-ization**
Scope	List of Business Missions	List of Major Database Domains	List of Business Informa-tion Systems	List of Interface Events	List of Major Business Scenarios	List of Organ-izations
Bus-iness	Mission Hierarchies and Resource Definitions	Database Domain Specifi-cations	Informa-tion Sequencing and Hierarchies	Event Se-quencing and Hierarchies	Business Scenario Sequencing and Hierarchies	Organiza-tion Charts, Jobs and Descrip-tions

Whitemarsh Knowledge Worker Framework							
		Man-Machine Interface					
		Machine		Interface	Man		
View Points	**Mission**	**Database Object**	**Business Informati on System**	**Business Event**	**Business Function**	**Organ-ization**
System	Resource Life Cycles and Mappings to Database Objects and Business Information Systems	Data Ele-ments Specified Data Mod-els and Identified Database Objects	Business Information System Designs	Invocation Protocols, Input and Output Data, and Messages	Best Practices, Quality Measures and Accom-plishment Assess-ments	Job Roles, Respon-sibilities, and Activity Schedules
Tech-nology	Implemented Resource Life Cycle Nodes as Business Information Systems	Imple-mented Database Models and Detailed Database Objects	Business Information Systems Designs	Presenta-tion Layer Business Information System Instigators	Activity Sequences to Accomplish Business Scenarios	Procedure Manuals, Task Lists, Quality Measures and Assess-ments
De-ploy-ment	Resource Life Cycle Nodes as Business Information Systems	Operational Database Models	Implemente d Business Informa-tion Systems	Client & Server Windows And/or Batch Execution Mech-anisms	Office Policies and Procedures to Accomplish Activities	Daily Schedules, Shift and Personnel Assign-ments
Oper-ations	Operating Resource Life Cycle Nodes Business Information Systems	View Data Models	Operating Informa-tion Systems	Start, Stop, and Mes-sages	Detailed Procedure Based Instructions	Daily Activity Executions, and Assess-ments

Table 4. Knowledge Worker Framework

Knowledge Worker Framework							Row Totals of GAO Allocated Errors in Percent
		Man-Machine Interface					
		Machine		Interface	Man		
Deliverables	Mission	Database Object	Business Information System	Business Event	Business Function	Organization	
Scope	5	2	3	1	3	4	18
Business	5	3	2	1	6	6	23
System	3	2	2	1	12	8	28
Technology	1	0	0	0	8	6	15
Deployment	0	0	0	0	5	5	10
Operations	0	0	0	0	3	3	6
Col. Totals	14	7	7	3	37	32	100

Table 5. U.S. Government Accountability Office Business Information System Errors in Percent values.

Note: All numbers expressed as Percent allocations of all errors to the cells ...12 Gray cells are Information Technology cells

Figure 1 depicts the Knowledge Worker Framework. Explained in a left-to-right fashion, every enterprise has a mission, and without a mission there is no reason for the enterprise. Database object classes and the resulting database objects represent the "data proof" that the mission is accomplished. Business information systems are the "IT mechanisms" through which the mission-based data is collected and stored in databases. Business events are the business information system triggering mechanisms that are set within calendar and business cycles. Functions, often called in this book, Business Functions, are the human-centric processes that are performed and that on

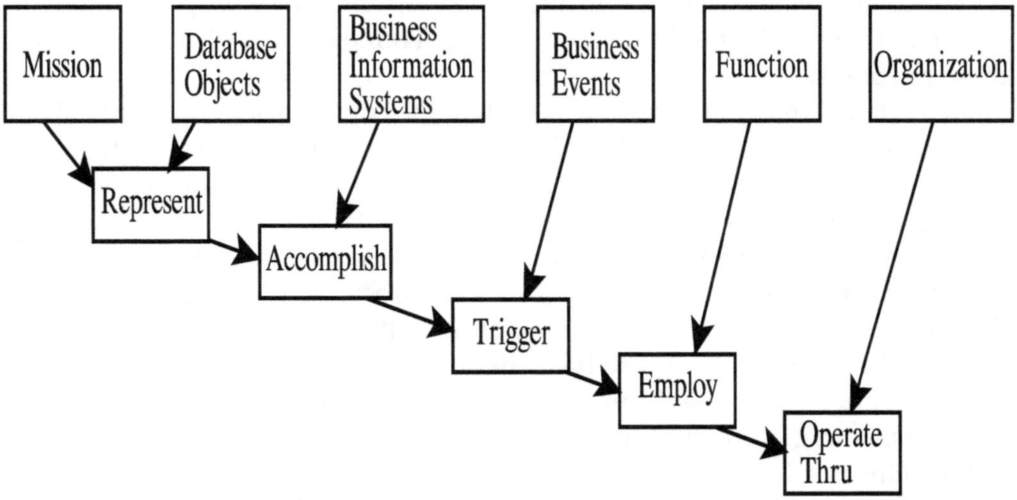

Figure 1. Interrelationships among Knowledge Worker Framework components.

occasion trigger the business events. Finally, organization, also called Business Organizations in this book, are the bureaucratic constructs of collections of persons who perform business functions.

The order, left to right, represents the least political to the most political. "Where," that is, location is not in the framework because in today's network environments, "where" can be anywhere and often is virtual.

This book's mission is to build governed data environments. As this mission is accomplished, work products are constructed in the form of metadata-based work products, known here as Database Objects. To instantiate these database objects, business information systems are executed. These too are metadata-based. These metadata-based business information systems are, in turn, activated through the accomplishment of business functions, which too, are in the form of metadata. Finally, the business functions are accomplished by persons operating within positions of the organizations participating in the communities of interest.

Stated from right to left, organizations operate through functions which, when performed, trigger business events that activate business information systems that add, delete, or modify the data of the database objects in the fulfillment of governance missions.

It is because well-governed environments are needed, are specified, exist within organizations, and are employed by persons as they perform their functions in support of accomplishing some aspect of the enterprise's mission that this framework, the Knowledge Worker Framework, is ideally suited to these purposes.

The metadata repository that is to contain the complete specifications of governance environments is described in Chapter 3. Its high-level data model and is further specified in Chapter 5. The governance data model's corresponding process model is specified in Chapter 6.

The positions that should be established are described in Chapter 10. Chapter 11 provides the specifications for key documents and guidance for document creation. Chapter 12 enumerates the types of governance projects that should be undertaken. The final chapter, Chapter 13, provides a set of rules that govern the establishment of communities of interest, the conduct of meetings, voting, the collection of fees and other necessary activities that reduced the need for a real Sergeant of Arms.

In general, Chapters 4 through 13 represent the policies, products, processes, projects, procedures, positions, organizations, and rules for instituting and operating a Governance Program through its contained Communities of Interest.

This book is intended to be a day-to-day cookbook for any subgroup within a Governance Program. The form of the book's content is sometimes narrative paragraphs, and other times hierarchal lists and/or specifications. The intention was to create the material in best use-form. In short, this book contains: the what, the when, and the how to accomplish governance's specification, implementation, and evolution.

1.5 The Metabase System

The executing and/or accomplishment mechanism of this book can either be through manually constructed forms or through a sophisticated metadata management system that supports the integration, interoperability and non-redundancy of all the work products from within the Knowledge Worker Framework that must be Governed.

To achieve that end, Whitemarsh has constructed a Metabase (metadata database) System which is a sophisticated metadata management system.

The concept surrounding the creation a metadata management system, which is now called the Metabase System, was created for the Council of Great City Schools in support of a project, PMIS (Planning and Management

Information System) for the Dallas Texas Independent School District in 1972. The developed database and system captured, stored, interrelated, and reported the architecture, design, and specifications of PMIS as it was created and employed. The database management system (DBMS) employed for both PMIS and the metadata management system was System 2000 from MRI Systems Corporation in Austin, Texas.

A larger and more sophisticated version of the metadata management system concept was based on a design created at Yourdon, Inc of New York City. It was implemented through Information Builder's Focus at the Hartford Insurance Company in the late 1970s.

The name, Metabase System, was created within the Whitemarsh book, *Managing Database: Four Critical Factors,* which set out an even more comprehensive design in the early 1980s. The book's design of the Metabase System was employed for Metabase System implementations at Hershey, Freddie Mac, and the Social Security Administration.

Common across all the implementations was the Metabase System's concept, that is, to capture, store, integrate, interrelate, update and report the architecture, design, and specifications of the enterprise and its databases and business information systems, and the use of a DBMS as the Metabase System's engine. The Metabase System's design was expanded and was featured throughout the book, *Enterprise Database in a Client-Server Environment.*

A very robust production version of the Metabase System was created for the U.S. Army's Tank Automotive Command (TACOM) in the middle 1980s. One of TACOM's business information systems focused on knowing what repair parts were needed and where repair depots had to be located to ensure 100% readiness of the U.S. Army around the world. Fundamentally, every weapon system was conceptually similar, but each had unique characteristics and different components; for example, the M1A1 Abrams tank and a Humvee.

Under the existing development environment, an IT contractor built, a new-from-scratch, IT system for each weapon system. These, at the time, were costing about $400K. Two such systems were built over a three-year period. The Army wanted 10 more in one year. The existing architecture, design, and implementation process clearly would not scale.

Whitemarsh was brought in to invent two IT factories using the Metabase System concept as the core: One for design and the second for construction. The design factory was engineered around the Metabase System core and was built using the Computer Systems Corporation's DBMS Manage. The construction factory was developed through what is now Object Oriented techniques and the Fortran language. The factory, which drew specifications from the Metabase System in order to manufacture the needed TACOM business information systems from libraries of pre written processes.

The effort was proposed to be $488K (about 22% more than a single custom-developed system) for the first new system including building the factories. The second system was to be 60%, and thereafter the systems were to cost about 40%. ROI was to be achieved by the second system. However, the first system cost 80% of the $525K, that is, $488K. The second cost 40% (not 60%) and thereafter they cost only 20% (not 40%). The reasons for delivering under budget and ahead of schedule were two: Standardized methodology, and standardized factories (design and construction).

In the early 1990s, the MITRE Corporation used the Metabase System's architecture and design to modify and expand the Oracle Corporation's CASE (Computer Aided System Engineering) tool-set in order to scope and set out the architecture for MITRE's own suites of infrastructure business information systems.

MITRE then employed a different architecture subset of the Metabase System for the State of California. Arthur Andersen had spent significant State funds to build a fiscal management and patient tracking system for the developmentally disadvantaged. The effort was hallmarked by many overruns and broken schedules. Ultimately, the system was finished and turned over to the State. However, no documentation beyond that of the original Arthur Andersen proposal existed.

The MITRE Corporation had been retained to design a significant extension to the State's system which would be used by an implementation contractor. Three staff from MITRE went to Sacramento. Because no documentation of the existing system existed, a version of the Metabase System was created through Information Builders, Focus, to contain the inductively derived specifications of the existing system.

The California agency's staff were the ones with the knowledge. Once an inventory of system artifacts was developed, work proceeded to build the lower and upper levels of database and business information system understanding. While that occurred, other MITRE staff developed an understanding of all the system components that needed to be changed. Once the Metabase database was built, the changes were mapped, and a development contractor was secured. The Metabase System and its database remained with the State of California.

Subsequent to the California Metabase System effort, different versions of the Metabase System were created for the States of Ohio and Delaware, the U.S. Department of Commerce, the U.S. Marshals Service, the Office of Personnel Management, and the U.S. DoD Inspector General for Audits.

Three characteristics are common across all Metabase System versions:

- Its core engine is a DBMS as metadata management is "data-centric."
- Its design is tailored for the specific organization within which it is employed.
- Its purpose and intent are the capture, storage, integration, interrelationship, update and reporting of the architecture, design, and specifications of the enterprise and its databases and business information systems.

As the Metabase System implementations progressed over its first 25+ years, fewer and fewer core changes were needed. Central, however, to the Metabase System's architecture, design, and implementation is that it must satisfy the following requirements:

- The domain of its metadata needs to address the enterprise and to span the life cycle of databases and business information systems in an integrated, interoperable, and a non-redundant manner.
- The Metabase System has to be inherently multi-user.
- The Metabase System must concurrently operate within client-server and over the Internet.
- Metabase System's architecture and domain have to be able to expand and change in a cost-effective way as the need arises.

The current version of the Metabase System as a product of Whitemarsh Information Systems Corporation, was started in the late 1990s. It has SQL engines at its core, has a metadata table-based database of more than 400 tables, and has a GUI layer that operates over client-server and the Internet in a multi-user fashion. There are currently more than 300 users worldwide of its freely downloadable version. The Metabase System is implemented through the business information system generator, Clarion, a continuously developed product over the past 30 years by the *SoftVelocity Corporation*. Consequently, the Metabase System is able to be expanded and changed through traditional data-centric information technology techniques for about 15% of normal business information system effort and costs.

1.6 Executing this Book

The chapters of this book, as illustrated through the Knowledge Worker Framework depicted in Figure 1, are set out as a way to engineer and constitute a governance program, to establish communities of interest, and to establish governance projects. This stands in stark contrast to the planning and executing the everyday activities to actually build the IT environments. So, if you are not part of the engineering and construction crew but part of the using-crew, this section is for you.

Consider a house. You do not start by building the front door, then the hallway, then the dining room or living room, and then the downstairs half-bath, the kitchen, rec-room, and backdoor. And then, build the stairs, the upstairs hallway, the bedrooms, and the bathrooms. Rather, these are "use-ways" once the house is built.

Consequently, either an entirely different book would have had to be created or an alternative manner of executing the contents of this book had to be set out. The latter were chosen.

Section 1.4 identifies the engineering and construction process through the Knowledge Worker Framework. This section identifies the use-sequence. Sometimes the sequence is the same. Other times it is different. Represented here is the day-to-day execution of governance programs, organizations, and projects once instituted. As Figure 1 depicts the engineering sequence of the Knowledge Worker Framework for the key chapters, Figure 2 depicts the "execution sequence" for the chapters. Rules, Chapter 13 is missing from this figure because rules are "called" from many if not all the other chapters. In actuality, "rules" are invoked when decisions cannot be made except through the application of a precise rule set.

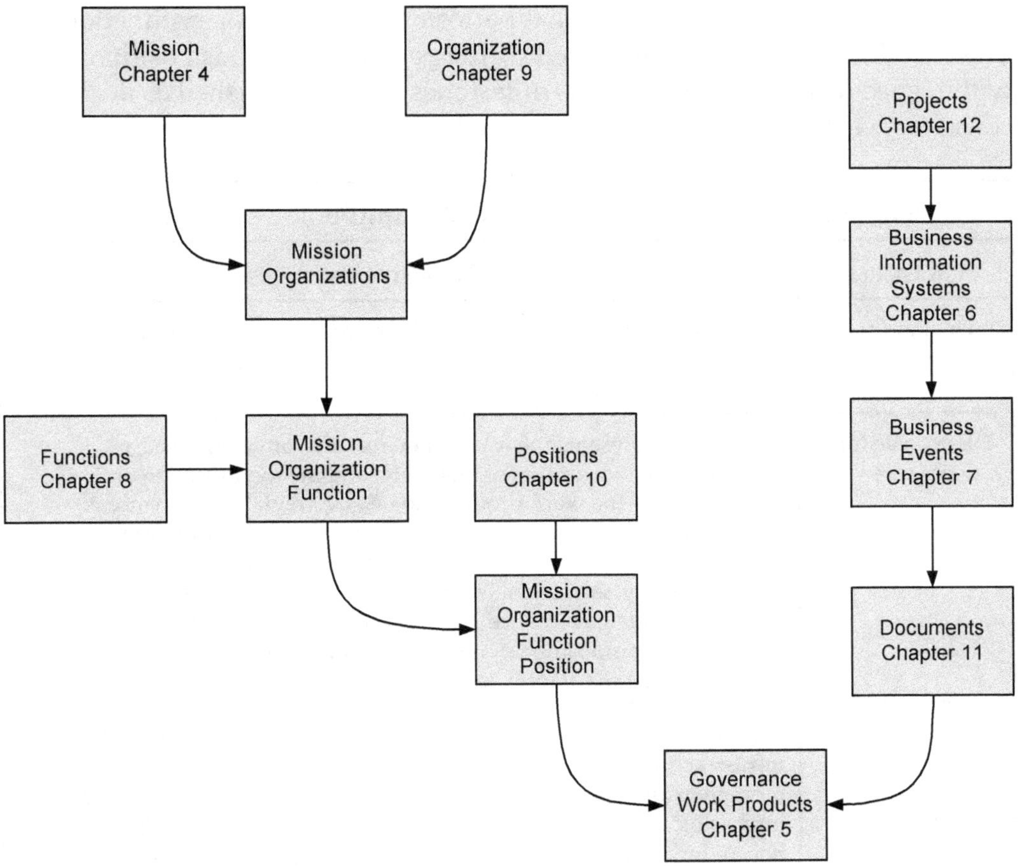

Figure 2. Enterprise Governance Specification Build Sequence.

The suggested way to read and use this book is set out in Table 6. Each description cell contains guidance as to the reading of the chapter and also a use-based description of the chapter. The first three rows of Table 6, Demand, Rationale, and Metadata represent all that is needed to be read, accepted, and in the case of the metadata repository, deployed. Row 4, Mission, when accomplished produces the metadata that is stored in row 3's metadata repository.

In the execution sequence, missions are first specified through a bootstrap ad hoc organization. If there is a go-ahead for a governance program, the organizations are created as necessary. It may be a full governance program and its subcommittees along with several communities of interest, or it may be a single community of interest that performs all the necessary functions. Then, as the functions are performed by the persons in various positions within specific projects, the various milestones are accomplished as a consequence of building the various metadata products.

Governance Community of Interest Handbook Use Sequence

Chapters	Description
1. Demand for Governance	This chapter provides the overall objective of the book and the use of communities of interest to achieve governance then you should not proceed to Chapter 2.
2. Rationale for Governance	This chapter presents the overall key reasons for governance, a comprehensive definition of metadata, and the identification and engineering of the work products to be governed. If governance is merely viewed as vast seas of ad hoc, unintegrated, redundant and semantically conflicting work product specifications, you will never achieve enterprise success. In contrast, there is a value proposition for enterprise-wide governance. If however, there is not general agreement on this value proposition or an analogous value proposition, stop and do not proceed to Chapter 3.
3. Required Governance Metadata Infrastructure	This chapter presents the value from having the appropriate metadata infrastructure. If that metadata infrastructure is not achieved, having more than just point-to-point interfaces between systems is largely impossible. If an organization does not have an integrated, end-to-end, non-redundant metadata infrastructure, even if all the collections of point-to-point interfaces are centrally managed, they will just be another server-farm of stand-alone databases, but this time of metadata. If there is any improvement, it's marginal. Centralized defined collections of point-to-point interfaces are not the mission of a quality Governance Program. Rather, the goal must be first an end-to-end integrated metadata model. Second, the loading into a Metabase System database the appropriate metadata from all systems and databases participating in a non-redundant and integrated manner so that true semantic harmony including precision and granularity can be achieved. If you cannot agree on the engineering and organization of metadata, or on the creation of formal policies, procedures, and organizations for the creation, maintenance and use of metadata, stop and do not proceed to Chapter 4.

Governance Community of Interest Handbook Use Sequence	
Chapters	**Description**
4. Mission of Governance	This chapter presents the missions that must be accomplished in any Governance Program. These missions should be reviewed and if necessary be refined before any other real work is attempted. Missions are hierarchically organized descriptions of the idealized target or objective of the effort. If you cannot agree on the destination, then do not start the journey. When a governance project is actually started, the missions related to the areas involved are created. These too are reviewed and revised. Agreement by participants is critical as these become the basis for governance. Shared missions beget shared work product specifications. Once you have identified shared missions, proceed to create the necessary organizations that support the information systems that feed and/or retrieve data from the shared spaces.
9. Governance Organization	This chapter presents the types and kinds of organizations that should be established to be successful. Each organization is defined and the types of positions that should be established are identified. As stated above, if there is only a single Community of Interest, then these organizations do not have to be established. Rather, each organization type should be reviewed and the key functions and duties of the organization should be reflected, if appropriate, in the single Community of Interest. Each of these organizations should be reviewed and modified to make sure they fit into your overall organizational structure. When a governance project starts and after the missions are created, you can know whether this is a single Community of Interest effort or whether there has to be a Governance Program infrastructure created as well. Each organization has to be established, chartered, and staffed. A metadata management support infrastructure has to be procured or activated. Staff has to be obtained, assigned, and trained. Once the Community of Interest is set into place then the first meetings can start.
10. Governance Positions	This chapter presents the positions that must be established in any of the organizations that are created via Chapter 9. Each position and its duties are generally described. Given your organization, are the positions properly named? Should their duties be enhanced or streamlined? These are all-important issues that should be addressed. Along with the organizations the various positions have to be created and staff assigned to the positions. The actual skills required are implied

Governance Community of Interest Handbook Use Sequence	
Chapters	**Description**
	by the missions, functions, organizations, and positions. All the activities within these positions are common, every day IT activities that should be readily known or learned by professionals. Detailed process specifications, training courses and the like are all contained on the Whitemarsh website.
8. Governance Functions	This chapter presents the functions, but at a high level that needs to be performed by each of the organizations set out in Chapter 9 in support of achieving either the overall Governance Program and/or any of the Communities of Interest. The functions that are to be performed are every day IT tasks and are fully defined and described in any number of university courses on data modeling, software development, configuration management, unit and system testing and documentation.
12. Governance Projects	This chapter identifies and describes the types of projects to be accomplished in the development of any Governance Assessment. Each of these project types should be examined and evaluated to ensure that it is complete. Missing components should be added. Unnecessary components should be deleted. Each project should identify the appropriate milestones and the required metadata products, and ultimately the functions that need to be performed by the positions within organizations to achieve the governance mission. Once missions are done, organizations created, positions filled, and staffs are ready to perform tasks, the governance projects can be instituted and accomplished. Each project has its own process model implied in the various sections. Chapter 4 builds the products identified in Chapter 5 according to the specialized work breakdown structures set out in Chapter 8. The level of governance achieved depends on the level of the enterprise on which it is focused. The higher the level the higher the level of governance, the more useful the work products.
6. Governance Processes	This chapter presents the processes to be used to audit and evaluate the integrity and correctness of the work products. You need to assess that you have the complete set of work products and the right processes. Because many of the work products involve other work products, when the governance processes are completed, there will be an end-to-end set of work products that have been assessed for integrity and correctness.
7. Governance Events	This chapter presents the milestones that are to be accomplished in the achievement of the program and scope of work of the Governance

Governance Community of Interest Handbook Use Sequence	
Chapters	**Description**
	Program and of any Community of Interest. Are these the right milestones for Governance Assessments in your organization? If not, then change them so that you can ensure that Governance Assessments are properly constructed so as to gain maximum acceptance. Each of these milestones should be accomplished through the application of the functions outlined in Chapter 8. The resource assignment strategies should be set into place to ensure that the right quantity of staff is assigned to the functions, positions, and organizations to achieve the milestones.
11. Governance Documents	This chapter provides a strawman set of documents or products from the Whitemarsh database project methodology that represent collections of metadata products from Chapter 5. Each product should be examined to determine if it is appropriate for your IT organization. If there are different ones, then make modifications accordingly. The goal is to have a complete set of products across all the critical IT dimensions. It is clear that a given metadata product from Chapter 5 is employed multiple times and serves different rolls in the development of complete IT specifications for a complete governance solution. As Community of Interest projects are accomplished, certain "bureaucratic" documents such as progress reports, annual reports, finance reports have to be created. These reports will take time to accomplish. If there is a robust infrastructure of metadata, these reports will mainly be processes of metadata extraction and formulation into the sections of the different administrative reports.
5. Governance Work Products	This chapter identifies and describes the actual metadata products that are to be built in order to achieve the governance milestones. Examine each product and determine if you know how to build it. Do you have the proper metadata tools in place to ensure that not only are the metadata products built but that you know how to build the products? There are copious materials on the Whitemarsh website that assist in this regard. Creating the governance metadata objects is a critical step. Short cuts should not be taken, for example, not creating missions, organizations, etc. and proceeding directly to data models. It is within the context of the enterprise metadata and the information systems metadata that the entirety of the governance metadata models have real life and value.

Governance Community of Interest Handbook Use Sequence	
Chapters	**Description**
	Experience has shown that when metadata is built at the enterprise and information systems levels there is an increased level on the maturity scale.
13. Governance Rules	This chapter provides the individual set of rules that should be observed by the various positions within the different organizations. As stated above, every decision by a community of interest has 10s of thousands of dollars of implications. Some decisions will cost millions of dollars. Each such decision, therefore, should be made with the maximum precision and good-order. Delivery of documents that form the basis for decision making, sufficient review time, proper motions, questions, discussions, and votes are all critical for a well engineered and operating organization with such an important mission. Hopefully, this chapter will never have to be accessed because there is a 100% consensus on every issue. But just in case there isn't, this chapter contains the necessary rules through which decisions can be made.

Table 6. Chapters and Description by Execution Sequence.

Supplementing all the material in this book is a large quantity of books, courses, methodologies, and also a metadata repository software system from Whitemarsh. This book, in conjunction with these materials should make the creation and operation of Governance Communities of Interest a practical, rational, and accomplishable set of activities.

This book does not contain "the only way" to accomplish governed environments. Rather, it is "a way." The data and process chapters contain detailed specifications. Again, these detailed specifications represent "a way," not "the way." There is a similar quantity of detail in the mission, organization, function, and position chapters. These too represent "a way," not "the way." The ultimate goal of the book is to convey a sufficiently detailed strategy such that, if followed, would lead to success. Alternatively, if another approach is desired, then the detail in this book provides good benchmarks for testing comprehensiveness and completeness.

1.7 Questions and Exercises

1. What is the "state" of governance in your enterprise? Rate it from "fantastic" to "sad." Why do you think it is one rating or the other? How do you really know? What are your measures for computing your rating?

2. How much time, effort, and energy of your organization is expended creating the policies, procedures and rules that govern COIs versus accomplishing the real work of COIs? How much COI start-up time does your organization consume? If this time were "close to zero," how would that help get real work accomplished?

3. How have the bureaucratic organizational activities that have occurred at the start of COIs affected the quantity and quality of the work accomplished? Has the lack of "getting out of the gates fast" dampened enthusiasm, negatively impacted your budgets, and lost credibility in your COI's mission?

4. If this book was adopted "as-is," would this book's strategies regarding organizations, policies, and procedures affect the time, effort and energy that are able to be expended to achieve governance? How could having all the "bureaucracy" engineered and ready to go before you start help?

5. Have you tried COIs in your enterprise regardless of what they are called? Have they worked? Why and why not? Have they brought benefits? What are they and how have they affected the "bottom line" of your organization?

6. Given that you are going to embark on the development of a reasonable quantity of governed databases and business information systems, what would the effect likely be on your current IT environment?

7. How much time and money are you likely to save from a reasonable quantity of governed databases and business information systems? How will you know and measure it?

8. What are the management decisions, strategies and plans that are likely to be affected by having a reasonable quantity of governed databases and business information systems?

9. What would be the benefits of just "adopting" this book's COI organizational structures, policies, procedures, offices, roles, responsibilities, and products at the very start of a COI and then modifying this adopted way of running the COI after the first six months or a year? Would such a move stifle or enable the real work of a COI?

2

Rationale for Governance

2.1 Key Reasons for Governance

In order to put forward a good rationale, the purpose or value of a Community of Interest has to be set down. From the point of view of this book the reasons are to:

- Increase the level of conflict-free policy execution.
- Increase the level of confidence in decision making.
- Reduce the risk in decision making.
- Reduce the cost of preparation and research prior to decision making.

The first section of Chapter 1 clearly states the mission of governance: the ability to make collective decisions faster and with greater confidence. This Chapter, also states that there is a need for governance because of shared missions. Chapter 2 also presents the metadata models necessary to capture the complete specifications necessary to know exactly what data can and should be shared. Simply put, the data subset representations of shared missions need to be exchanged. Since mission descriptions can be 50 pages or more in length, a more precise identification of what is to be shared and the basis for sharing needs to be specified.

Chapter 1 also clearly infers that it is not the fixed, random, or even ad hoc exchanges of data between business information systems, or between end-users and business information systems that ultimately are critical and important. Rather, it is the common, shared, and consensus-based understanding of data that has to be set out in each of the systems that ultimately control the data that is captured, stored in databases, and then shared. Achieving that requires governance. If such an environment exists, not only will the routine business process drive data exchanges be improved but so also will be the random and ad hoc access of data through business information systems because semantics and value domains will be reliable and repeatable.

Given common, shared and integrated metadata, business managers and decision makers can integrate databases with the confidence that the responses come from a network of non-redundant, integrated, synchronized, and semantically homogeneous databases and business information systems. Such products are the result of governance.

2.2 Shared Policy is Basis for Common Understanding

The basis for the common, shared, and consensus-based understanding of data is policy. After all, data is the "what" that remains after *policy* is executed. Thus, *Data is Executed Policy*. When an organization creates policies, it necessarily creates as its companion, procedures. Together, policy and procedures are set into place to the run the business. As the business runs, data, the consequence of policy execution, is created and stored in databases. These databases become the persistent memory of the organization.

"Data" specifications are thus policy definitions. Similarly, process specifications are procedure definitions. Consequently, all data (i.e., policy) specifications are metadata. All process (i.e., procedure) specifications are also metadata. A metadata database (e.g., Whitemarsh Metabase) is a database within which for all enterprise Policy and Procedure Specifications are captured, stored, and managed. The metadata model diagrams in Figures 7 through 27 are high level graphical depictions of shared policies and procedures.

Any policies and procedures that are not specified or transformed to metadata, and that do not result in database data, are not only just anecdotes, they also cannot lead to trustworthy enterprise persistent memory. Similarly, these non specified policies and procedures cannot lead to trustworthy governance.

Policies exist in meaningful configurations that map onto the common sense-based transactions of the business. These transactions are all tied to one or more of the resource life cycle nodes. The processes that support the capture, storage, modification, and access of the data are accomplished by the business information systems.

2.3 Comprehensive Definition of Metadata

A quick response to the question, What is Metadata, is that it is *data about data.* However, that's too cute. More formally, the string, metadata, is divided into *meta* and *data.* "Meta" in the Oxford Dictionary means, "something of a higher or second-order kind." The word, data, however is not employed within this book in its strictest sense, that is, a data item like *Birth date* and the data item's value of *03/22/1941*, but in more general sense so as to include unstructured data like text and diagrams.

For the purposes of this book, the scope of metadata is set within the entire context of the enterprise. Consequently, metadata are the materialized artifacts that define the enterprise and also the requirements for, the specifications of, design of, or even executing characteristics of an IT system, or component of that system. "System" here is used in a very broad context. Thus, included within the scope of systems are databases, business information systems, and their technology environments. Therefore, metadata is what is one or more levels of abstraction removed from the actual databases, business information systems, or their technology environments. In a computing environment, this type of metadata includes:

- Requirements.
- Functional descriptions.
- Work plans.
- Database designs through to schema DDL (data definition language).
- Business information system designs possibly through to computer program source code libraries.
- Technology environment designs through to actual installation artifacts.

But within this context, metadata does not include:

- Actual databases with data records of employees, invoices, products, and customers.

- Executing business information systems.
- Operating systems and other systems software such as DBMS and Web browsers.
- Telecommunications Networks.
- Computers.

These are not metadata because they are from the "reality domain," while the previous list represents artifacts in the "about the reality" domain. But once the business information system is executing, metadata may be created that describes the characteristics of the operating environment. That class of metadata includes for example:

- Computer system execution schedules.
- Computing resource consumption requirements.
- Quantity of records in particular files.
- Quantity of users by time of day for particular processes.
- Job completion and/or error messages.

2.4 Database Objects: Governance Foundation Stones

The data specifications within which business transactions are created and exist are database object classes. The domain of data of a database object class should relate perfectly to the domain of data of a coherent policy existing within the enterprise. It is on the foundation of quality-database that there can be quality shared data. That is because:

- Each database object class's data structure (typically database tables) is the data representation of a policy's definition.
- The database object class's processes through which data rows are added, deleted, and modified are the mechanisms necessary for policy execution, that is, the policy's procedures through which database objects are transformed from one valid state to another.

- A fully defined policy that includes both its complete definition and its necessary steps for coherent execution.
- Interrelated collections of rows across multiple tables of one database object class and across multiple collections of rows across multiple database object classes form more comprehensive policies.

When data is seen as executed policy, and is realized through database objects, then quality databases support the following within the enterprise:

- Business information systems that are a coherent union of the policy that, in turn, support the execution of procedures that represent the accomplishment of the policy. Because of shared policy, data can be more easily shared across systems whether in scheduled or ad hoc manners.
- Consistent collection and/or modification of policy instances through the life cycle of the policy. These policies, applied enterprise-wide, ensure that all systems and databases participating in a community of interest are similarly updated.
- Consistent execution of policies whenever, wherever, and however deployed as the essence of the policy, and the totality of its critical procedures are encapsulated within the database object class itself.
- Minimized redundancy and consistent policy implementations across distributed environments as the database object class can be distributed through encapsulated strategies.
- Comparable instances of deployed policies that are independent of hardware architectures and operating systems.

2.5 Engineering Database Objects

What forms the basis of a database object? Simply, it is a business' policies and procedures. While policies can exist without procedures, the converse is not true. This ontological priority dictates that procedure is dependent on policy. They go together like hand and glove. The glove (procedure) serves no useful purpose without the hand (policy).

A database object is an instance of a person, place, or thing that has internal consistency, and can be transformed from one valid, predefined state to another through well-defined rules. The minimum value states are null and valued. The internal behavior of a database object class as its objects transform from one state to another is immaterial to its user. Database object classes conform to the requirements of business rather than the converse. Database objects are the corporate memory of the enterprise. All the rest are anecdotes.

Policies and procedures, that is, database object classes, bring order, consistency, and predictability. The larger the enterprise, the greater the dependence on policies and procedures. Data is the evidence of policy execution. An employee's record is proof that policies have been carried out. Procedures are the techniques, methods, or processes by which policies are carried out. For example, if an enterprise's policy is to be profitable, then its balance statement, produced by processing all the general and subsidiary journals are the measure of adherence to the policy. If policy is met, the enterprise must be profitable.

The procedures are named, and their data actions are associated with specific subsets of the named data structure. The names of the procedure sets represent data structure transformations from one recognizable state to another. Each state represents a determined value set within the business. Procedures include, for example: establishing an employee requisition, accomplishing employee hiring, and performing employee assignment.

Enterprise-database is an organizational operating condition in which there are both defined policy coherence and integrity, as well as consistency in policy transformations throughout the enterprise irrespective of functional and organizational style and irrespective of policy transformation technology (that is, computers, operating systems, programming languages, and database management systems).

Enterprise-database is the expression, population, use, and manipulation of all database objects. Enterprise-database begins first with quality-database object classes founded upon the policies and procedures surrounding their specification, implementation and evolution.

Value proceeds not first from the database object, but from the database object class. The consequences of quality-database object classes are "real" database objects. The information technology assets of the enterprise are both its database objects and its database object classes.

Finally, an enterprise is interoperable only to the extent to which its metadata is non-redundant, not conflicting, and integrated. In short, governed. To believe otherwise or to believe that, for example, the only thing that has to happen to database objects is that they are transformed to XML in order for an enterprise to be interoperable. This flies in the face of common sense and simple logic. Is it "record" or "record?" Is it seam or seem? Is it 2.79 MPH or 2.79 KPH? Is it rounded or precise? Is it a running total or an amount at that instant? Data alone doesn't provide the answer. Data and semantics do, but only in context in an integrated, non-conflicting, and a non-redundant manner.

2.6 Impact of Governance

As stated above, governance is all about establishing and effecting integrity and correctness. While that is important within a single database and business information system, it is critical across an enterprise's functionally-wide set of databases and business information systems.

There are two approaches to governance: Stovepipe and Community of Interest. The stovepipe approach accomplishes governance completely within the context of a single database and business information system. Here, governance is defined, implemented, and maintained for each database and business information system and for each different interface across the databases and business information systems.

In contrast, community of interest governance accomplishes governance across the whole community of databases and business information systems.

While stovepipe governance would be cheaper for one specific database and business information system, the sum total of all the stovepipe governances across all the databases and business information systems would greatly exceed the cost of community of interest governance.

There are a number of reasons for that. First, governances for each of the databases and business information systems must be created and managed. Second, an additional governance effort must exist to resolve the data semantic disparities across the individually governed databases and business information systems. And third, and possibly the most expensive, governance efforts must be undertaken for each of the different shared data interfaces. And for these, there must be a governance effort for each side of the data exchanges.

In contrast, a community of interest for governance enables shared missions et al to be defined once and implemented many times wherever used within the individual databases and business information systems.

2.7 Value Proposition for Governance

Many arguments can be made for governance including increased consistency, data quality, timeliness and the reasons cited in Chapter 1. While these are all important, they are very difficult to measure mainly because databases and business information systems are too expensive to set up in controlled experiment modes: One clearly bad, another clearly good. The one argument that can be made very clear and compelling and one that "management" can readily see is the cost argument.

A general rule of thumb for estimating the cost of a business information system is to first develop a third normal form data model for business information system's domain, and then multiple the count of tables by 80 to get a rough estimate of the quantity of function points of information technology capability to be created and implemented. Function points can range from $200 for "commercial" business information systems to $400 for a high precision "military" command and control business information systems. Thus, for a 1,000 table database, the cost would be 1,000 x 80 x $200 ($10 million) at the minimum and 1,000 x 80 x $400 at the maximum ($20 million).

From a study done about the U.S. Department of Defense's STRATCOM (Strategic Command) standardization initiative, a collection of business information systems and databases were identified. They were examined for redundancy, conflict, and overlap. The goal was to minimize these characteristics. The result was that 35 systems were reduced to just six. The quantity of lines of code was reduced from 20 million to just 12 million, and the quantity of databases were reduced from 23 to just 12. The total quantity of database columns was reduced from 18,000 to just 2,200. As to costs, there was a reduced operational cost of 20% and there was a redirection of 26% of all staff billets.

In 1995, another study performed at the U.S. DoD's Air Force showed that the average cost of a data interface between two systems costs about $350,000 per year. Extrapolated to the Air Force as a whole, the cost was $167 million per year.

A general approach to creating a governance environment is to first enact governance for each database and business information system and second, to enact Governance to each of the interfaces between two different systems. If each system exchanges data with the other, that's two interfaces, and the organization owner of each system needs to budget $350,000 each year. Reduced to an interface table count, it comes to about 10 tables for each interface specification ($350K / 80 / $400). When the quantity of systems rises to 15, the quantity of one-way interfaces of every system to every other system rises according to the formula: N*(N-1)/2 or 105. If every interface is two-way, there would be 210 interfaces. That is about $80 million per year. Now, not every system interfaces with every other system, nor are all the interfaces two way. So, the $80 million cost is the outside estimate.

The inside cost number would be that every system has just one interface with its successor system. That would be 14 interfaces for a yearly cost of about $5 million. Assuming an average between the two, the cost would be about $37.5 million per year. If, in this example, there was a common Transaction Data Staging Area Data Model, there would be just 15 one-way or 30 two-way interfaces. Assuming the average, that is, 23 total interfaces, then the cost would be about $8 million per year. That's a savings of about $30 million per year in just interface development and maintenance costs.

In a mid 1990s study of an entire collection of databases, supporting systems and the exchange of data among systems, it was determined that about 200 individual databases all contained data that could be traced to just four original source databases. Instead of different systems sourcing their data from 200, just four data sourcing strategies need to be created. Since this potential disaster was discovered before all interfaces were created to the 200 data sources, there were no real savings, just a large cost overrun avoided.

Using typical metrics for a management information system, the savings by totally eliminating one system is significant. Table 7 tabulates the savings.

Cost Avoidance by Eliminating one System in an Information Exchange	
Characteristic	**Value**
Average MIS is 200 Tables	200
Function points of software per table	80
Each function point costs	$400

Cost Avoidance by Eliminating one System in an Information Exchange	
Characteristic	**Value**
Initial MIS Cost (200 * 80 * 400)	$6.4 million
Life cycle costs for evolution & maintenance 5x more	$32 million
Total Life Cycle Cost	$38.4 million

Table 7. Cost Avoidance by Eliminating one System in an Information Exchange.

The only real way to get a handle on the costs of an existing network of databases and business information systems is to identify and capture the entire set of work products implied by the meta models contained in Figures 7 through 27. This metadata will provide a rough network topology of what resource life cycle nodes are addressed by which business information systems and databases. Clearly, if through this analysis, a given database is being created by more than one business information system, there is a consolidation opportunity. Additionally, if systems and database object classes are mapped to multiple resource life cycle nodes, there are partitioning opportunities that enable simplification and possibly eventual consolidation of partitioned business information systems allocated to the same resource life cycle node.

A second example for the financial justification creating a governance community of interest is provided in Tables 8 through 11. These examples are clearly more specific to two different methods of achieving governance: The Community of Interest Approach, and the Stove Pipe approach. Included in these two examples is not only the cost of business information system development but also the cost of the "bureaucracy." That is, meetings, travel and the like. The COI cost numbers are all based on the strategies put forth in this book. The Stove-pipe numbers are based on actual experience of the years on the part of the author and of colleagues who read and commented on this book. The conclusion drawn from these tables is very clear: The Governance Community of Interest approach is both half the price of the Stove Pipe approach, and also close to 10x cheaper to add another community member.

Community of Interest Approach Cost		
Ite m	**Description**	**Cost**
1	COI Term. 2 years. 6 meetings per year. Each meeting is 1 staff week. Staff time cost per meeting is $100 per hour. (2 x 6 x 40 x $100 x 25 staff)	$1,200,000
	Meeting Room costs $4000 per meeting (room plus facilities charges and refreshments is $800 per day. (4,000 x 12)	$48,000
	Travel, Hotel, and Per Diem cost per attendee per meeting, $1500. (25 x 12 x $1500)	$450,000
2	Full Time Chair. Salary and Benefits $300K. Travel et al, $100K. For two years.	$800,000
3	Full Time Editor. Salary and Benefits $225K. Travel et al, $100K.	$650,000
4	25% Part Time COI Secretary. Salary and Benefits $160K. Travel et al, $100K.	$280,000
5	Membership 25. Non meeting participation time. 2000 hours over two years at $100 per hour (25 x 2000 hours x $100 per hour)	$5,000,000
6	Computing resources for website, standard, software, and information sharing over two years.	$25,000
7	• Business Information System modification to accommodate Governance Standard. • 6 database objects (5 tables each) per system. 80 Function Points per table at $200 per function point • (6 x 5 x 80 x 200 x 10)	$4,800,000
	Total COI Cost	$13,253,000

Table 8. Community of Interest Approach to Governance.

Stove Pipe Interoperability Approach Costs		
Item	**Description**	**Cost**
1	10 Systems are to be interfaced. Quantity of Interfaces is (n x (n-1)/2 = 45.	n/a
2	Each Interface consists of 4 database objects with 5 tables per database object.	n/a
3	Interface Discovery Meetings. 4 meetings. Each meeting is 2 staff days. Term four months. 3 staff per interface organization. Staff time cost per meeting is $100. 45 Interfaces. (4 meetings x 2 days x 2 organizations x 3 person per organization x 8 hours per day x $100 per hour x 45 Interfaces)	$1,728,000
	Meeting Room costs $1600 per meeting (room plus facilities charges and refreshments is $800 per day. ($1600 x 4 x 45)	$288,000
	Travel, Hotel, and Per Diem cost per attendee per meeting, $1000. (6 staff x 4 meetings x $1000 per meeting x 45)	$1,080,000
4	Interface Management. Non meeting participation time. 50% over four months, and 50% time over next six months to manage interface implementation. 2 persons per organization per interface. 10 months x 50% x 2 x 4.33 x 40 x $100 x 45 interfaces.	$7,794,000
5	Interface Implementation. Computing resources per interface. Server, 10 terminals, website over two years $5,000 per interface.	$225,000
6	Per Interface Cost: 4 database objects per interface (5 tables each) per Interface. Each Interface is 20 tables x 80 function points per table x $200 per function point. (4 x 5 x 80 x 200 x 45)	$14,400,000
	Total Interface Costs	$25,515,000

Table 9. Stove Pipe approach to governance development.

Incremental Cost to add an 11th Member's System to the Community of Interest		
Item	**Description**	**Cost**
1	Meet with Chair, Editor and Secretary. 2 staff weeks. 5 persons from new Interfacing Organization. \$100 per hour. Chair (1 day) (1 x 8 x \$200 per hour = \$1600) Editor (10 days) (1 x 10 x 8 x \$150 per hour = \$12,000) Secretary (5 days) (1 x 5 x 8 x \$75 per hour = \$3,000) Interfacing Organization (5 x 10 x 8 x \$100 per hour = \$40,800	\$57,600
	Meeting Room costs \$8000 per meeting (room plus facilities charges and refreshments is \$800 per day. (\$8000 x 1)	\$8,000
	Travel, Hotel, and Per Diem cost per attendee per meeting, \$2500. (8 staff x 1 meetings x \$2500 per meeting)	\$20,000
2	Non meeting participation time. 500 hours over six months at \$100 per hour (1 x 500 hours x \$100 per hour)	\$50,000
3	Business Information System modification to accommodate Governance Assessment. 6 database objects (5 tables each) per system. 80 Function Points per table at \$200 per function point (6 x 5 x 80 x 200 x 1)	\$480,000
Incremental Cost to add one additional Business Information System		\$615,600

Table 10. Incremental Costs Associated with Adding an 11th Community Member.

Incremental Cost to add an 11th System with Stove-Pipe Approach		
Item	**Description**	**Cost**
1	Interface Discovery Meetings. 4 meetings. Each meeting is 2 staff days. Term four months. 3 staff per interface organization. Staff time cost per meeting is \$100. 10 Interfaces. (4 meetings x 2 days x 2 organizations x 3 person per organization x 8 hours per day x \$100 per hour x 10 Interfaces)	\$384,000.00

Incremental Cost to add an 11th System with Stove-Pipe Approach		
Item	**Description**	**Cost**
	Meeting Room costs $1600 per meeting (room plus facilities charges and refreshments is $800 per day. ($1600 x 4 x 10)	$64,000
	Travel, Hotel, and Per Diem cost per attendee per meeting, $1000. (6 staff x 4 meetings x $1000 per meeting x 10)	$240,000
2	Interface Management. Non meeting participation time. 50% over four months, and 50% time over next six months to manage interface implementation. 2 persons per organization per interface. 10 months x 50% x 2 x 4.33 x 40 x $100 x 10 interfaces.	$1,732,000
3	Interface Implementation. Computing resources per interface. Server, 2 terminals, website over two years $5,000 per interface.	$50,000
4	Per Interface Cost: 4 database objects per interface (5 tables each) per Interface. Each Interface is 20 tables x 80 function points per table x $200 per function point. (4 x 5 x 80 x 200 x 10)	$3,200,000
Incremental Cost to add one additional Business Information System		$5,670,000

Table 11. Incremental costs for the Stove Pipe approach to add an 11th system.

One final example of the value of community of interest governance involves a $1B IT failure from the United States Air Force. A study was undertaken to identify the key root causes of the United States Air Force's failure to successfully develop a $1 Billion Expeditionary Combat Support System. The audit, developed through a special USAF effort, was required by and submitted in 2013 to the senior staff of the Air Force and to Congress. The root-cause failure findings, taken from the Acquisition Incident Review Team's Executive Summary, were:

Understanding the Data. The Air Force must thoroughly understand its data. It didn't in the Expeditionary Combat Support System. All of the data must be understood, not just the data we thought we had, and not just the data we wanted to address, but all of it. This matter cannot be solved by doing

Legacy Deconstruction at the same time as blueprinting, at the same time as building the new "To-Be" solution. It needs to be done first. It needs to be a coordinated effort combined with an understanding that accomplishing this will take time

Understanding the "As-is" and "To-be" Architectures: The Air Force didn't understand the "As-Is" or the "To-Be" architectures. After exposing and understanding all the data, knowledge is needed on how it is connected or put together. This allows a better assessment on whether the "To-Be" architecture is complete. With Expeditionary Combat Support System, the lack of a detailed knowledge of the "As-Is" resulted in an incomplete assessment of what the 'To-Be" represented for Expeditionary Combat Support System. As of the date of this report, the number of systems Expeditionary Combat Support System was to replace is unknown. Unlike traditional weapon system acquisition, which focuses primarily on the "To-Be" and increasing capability, in business systems, one must understand the "As-Is," since much of it is critical in order for the field to accomplish the logistics mission.

A Transition Plan from "As-is" to "To-be:" The Air Force lacked a transition plan for resolving the differences between the "As-Is" and 'To Be." This resulted in an inability for Expeditionary Combat Support System to successfully accomplish its goal. As referenced in the report, the process is similar to a construction project where temporary structures must be built, then later torn down in order to make way for the new road. This transition is the heart of the effort, and takes time. However, since the Air Force did not understand the "As-Is" or "To Be" architectures, arriving at a transition plan was impossible.

The Right Execution Plan: Even if the Air Force had a transition plan from the "As-Is" to the "To-Be" architecture, it lacked a way to properly execute it. The Air Force needed to obtain a software package that could accomplish the "To-Be," however, the Air Force knew from market research that no single, stand-alone product could satisfy its need (the AF permitted "bolt on" applications), but there existed no follow through on exactly how Expeditionary Combat Support System would achieve the "To-Be" utilizing a software product requiring bolt-ons that increased the number of interfaces. The detailed execution plan did not exist. Additionally, the Systems Integrator needed to have the ability to code the vision as described through the blueprinting process, and the Air Force needed a way to articulate how to execute from the "As-Is" to the "To-Be." While the Air Force, as part of the Systems Integrator contract arrangement, provided hundreds of Subject Matter Experts to assist in this endeavor, the Subject Matter Experts had no single vision on how to accomplish this. All the Subject Matter Experts from the field had different processes they utilized, and yet these same individuals were asked to communicate a single vision to the Systems Integrator on how the transition would occur.

The Right Development Environment: Expeditionary Combat Support System was trying to be developed in an unrealistic environment; one that did not mirror the reality of the operational environment. Although this issue doesn't get much play with Expeditionary Combat Support System alumni, it would have been a root cause to the program failure even if they made it through all of the other challenges. The software has to work in the expected environment.

The Right Culture: The culture would have had to accept the new vision as designed into the code. That means that everyone would have had to understand the vision of Expeditionary Combat Support System and been convinced their equities were being taken care of in this program. There was universal agreement during interviews that this was not going to happen, but there was very little understanding as to why.

2.8 Measuring the Level of Governance

A very critical question regarding the specifications associated with the development of shared data is the level of interoperability that should be represented by a Governance Assessment. The cost of not having governance can be quite significant.

For example, in a mid 1990s study by the United States Air Force, they determined that a lack of governance was costing it approximately $167 million per year in expenses to develop and maintain system interfaces.

The stories regarding the U.S. Gulf War I during 1991 are legend. Battle plans had to be stored on 3.5 inch disks and then flown by helicopter to different military organizations so they can be read, transformed and used.

In the early 1990s, the C4ISR architecture working group began to address the interoperability issue in earnest. C4ISR stands for Command, Control, Communications, Computers, Intelligence Surveillance, and Reconnaissance. A key deliverable from this architecture working group was LISI (Levels of Information Systems Interoperability).

The Levels of Information Systems Interoperability is model, generated in 1998, has five levels (zero as worst, and four as best) as is provided in Table 12.

Levels of Information Systems Interoperability	
Level	**Description**
4	Distributed global information and business information systems. Simultaneous interactions with complex data. Advanced collaboration, e.g., interactive Common Operational Picture updates, and event-triggered global database updates.
3	Sophisticated collaboration, e.g., Common Operational Picture.
2	Heterogeneous product exchange. Basic collaboration Group Collaboration, e.g., exchange of annotated imagery, maps with overlays.
1	Homogeneous product exchange e.g., FM voice, tactical data links, text files, transfers, messages, e-mail.
0	Manual Gateway, e.g., diskette, tape, hard copy exchange.

Table 12. Levels of Information Systems Interoperability.

From the 1998 report,

> The LISI Interoperability Maturity Model provides a common basis for requirements definition and for incremental system improvements. The LISI Interoperability Maturity Model identifies the stages through which systems should logically progress, or "mature," in order to improve their capabilities to interoperate. LISI considers five increasing levels of sophistication regarding system interaction and the ability of the system to exchange and share information and services. Each higher level represents a demonstrable increase in capabilities over the previous level of system-to-system interaction.

In the eight years since the release of the LISI process, its goals and objectives have largely been unrealized despite recommendations by the C4ISR Working group.

Rather than let the underlying concepts from this valuable approach disappear, Andreas Tolk formerly at Virginia Modeling Analysis & Simulation Center (VMASC), Old Dominion University along with members of that center has extended the LISI into an LCIM (Levels of Conceptual Interoperability Model). While the LISI model focuses on the system view within an enterprise, the Levels of Conceptual Interoperability Model (LCIM) presented in Table 13 was developed to focus on the importance of data and their exchange between systems regarding interoperability. As such, it is applicable in various domains, from ontological applications via web services to data model replications. The LCIM model has an analogous but different set of levels. These are depicted in Figure 3.

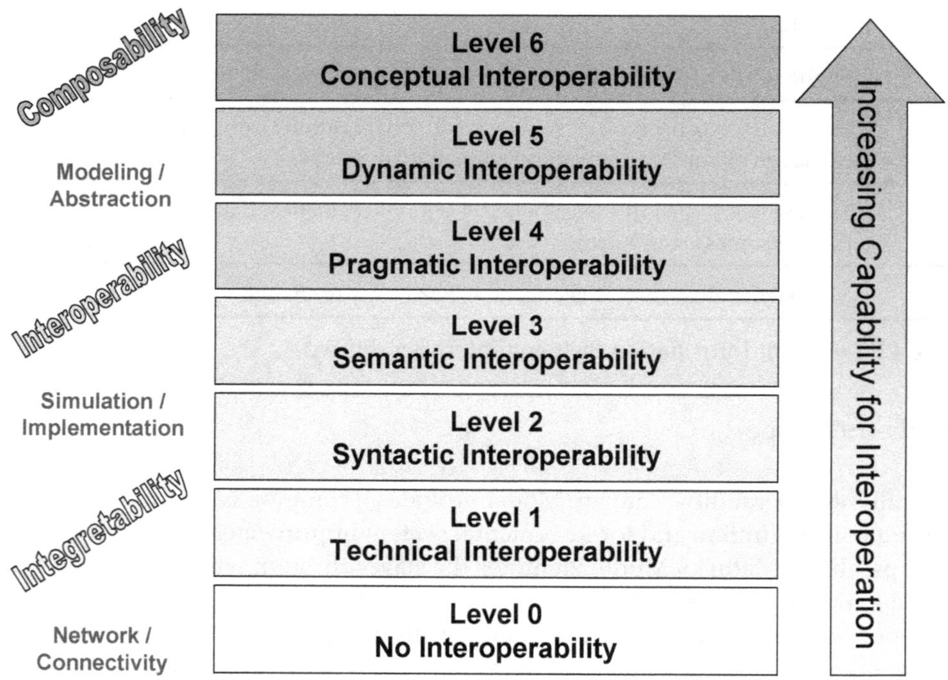

Figure 3. Levels of Conceptual Interoperability Model.

Specifically, the level, where again zero is the lowest and six is the highest, are described in Table 9.

Levels of Conceptual Interoperability Model	
Level	**Description**
6	The conceptual data models underlying the data across systems are aligned. This requires that conceptual models be documented as "fully specified but implementation independent models," enabling their interpretation and evaluation by other engineers.
5	Systems are able to comprehend the state changes that occur in each other system's assumptions and constraints over time; thus, the effect of the information exchange is unambiguously defined.
4	The meaning of the data and the context of its use are "understood" by the participating systems, and the context in which it is exchanged is unambiguously defined.
3	The meaning of the data is shared through the use of a common reference model and the content of the information exchange requests are unambiguously defined.
2	A common protocol to structure the data is used; the format of the information exchange is unambiguously defined.
1	A communication infrastructure is established, underlying networks and communication protocols are unambiguously defined.
0	Stand-alone systems have no shared data.

Table 13. Levels of Conceptual Interoperability.

A brief comparison was conveyed at the September 2006, Fall Simulation Interoperability Workshop in Orlando, FL. Leslie Winters of the U.S. DoD Joint Forces Command wrote in the paper, "Next Generation Governance: It's all About the Metadata" that:

> There is a relationship between the LISI and LCIM. The conclusion one may draw is that enterprise level systems interoperability with conceptual interoperability of data can support and promote unified interoperability of an organization. This is because high levels of interoperability from a systems and data perspective will lead to the shared understanding that is required from the organizational perspective in an organization that is dependent on IT.

This interrelationship is shown in Figure 4. In general, the missions, organizations, function, database objects, and business events metadata that are recommended to be collected, along with the engineering of the governance program and its subgroups, and the Communities of Interest and its subgroups are all geared to create interoperable data environments that are very high on the LCIM scale. The specific LCIM questionnaire and evaluation strategies are not included in this version of the book.

2.9 Summary

The key point in all these analyses and strategies is that there has to be common-mission-based Communities of Interest from multiple organizational areas. Once enterprise missions are discovered and the organizations allocated, the Communities of Interest are readily apparent. The initial objective of these Communities of Interest is to identify the appropriate resources, their life cycles, and to discover and allocate database object classes and business information systems.

All the Communities of Interest need to consolidate their findings and present an enterprise-wide picture of the overall topology of database object classes and business information systems. From that basis, the real work of the community of interest can begin. That is, configuring the most efficient and effective set of governance specifications that:

- Increase the level of conflict free policy execution.
- Increase the level of confidence in decision making.
- Reduce the risk in decision making.
- Reduce the cost of preparation and research prior to decision making.

The sections on the levels of conceptual interoperability are very important. They provide ways to assess the level of interoperability that can be expected from any governance implementation strategy. If the target is tactical or syntactic level, then, while that may be achieved, it would likely be a surprise if levels higher than that are also accomplished. While lower levels seem easier and less costly to achieve, that is, in the long term, a false conclusion. If an integrated metadata environment is already installed and operating, creating a new interoperable data and system is easier and quicker if these are based on the already defined and reusable semantics and processes.

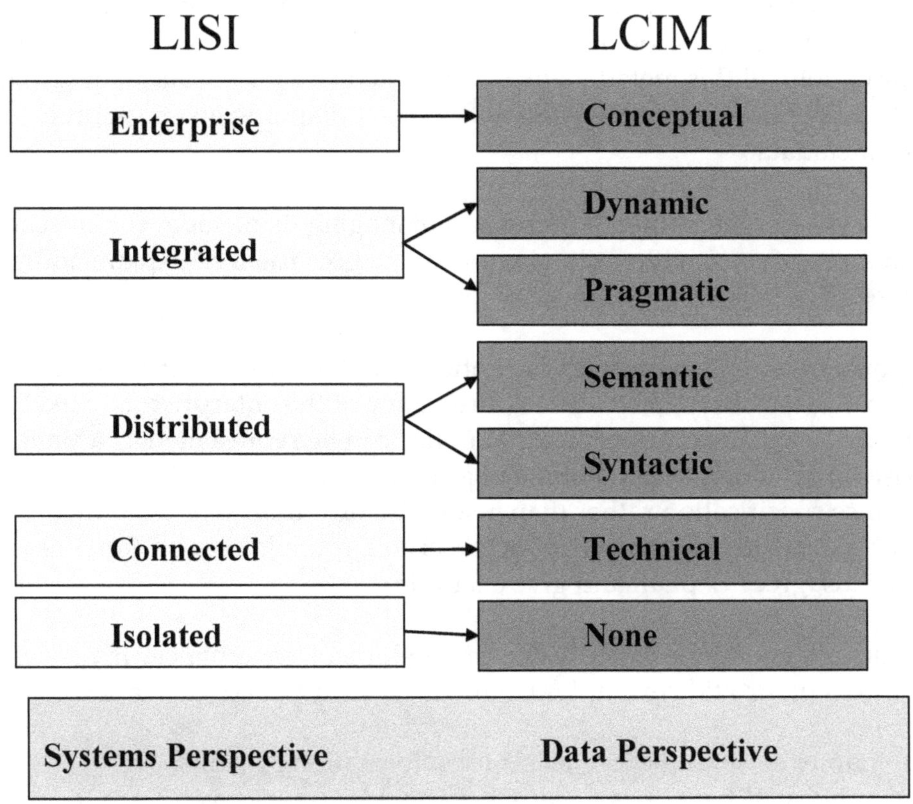

Figure 4. Interrelationship between LISI and LCIM.

2.10 Questions and Exercises

1. Do you fundamentally agree with the key reasons for having Governance? How are these governance key reasons manifest in your organization?

2. Do you agree that shared data is fundamentally a reflection of shared policy? If yes, why? If no, then why not? The book holds that "Data is executed policy." Agree or disagree? If agree, then can you have shared data without shared policy?

3. This chapter has an expansive definition of Metadata? Do you agree? If yes, why? If no, why not? If you agree, then shouldn't the metadata database (i.e., Metabase) hold all this metadata in an integrated and non-redundant fashion? Wouldn't all the artifacts associated with project planning just be another form of metadata?

4. How is your organization defining and managing its metadata? How can you have governance without having metadata governance? Explain and give examples.

5. Do you agree or disagree with the notion of a database object class? If a database object class represents an entire policy of the enterprise, is it likely that the data structure supporting that policy can be represented as a single database table? If not, then database object classes have to be the focus of governance specification rather than just tables of columns or individual columns so as to assure agreement on precision, granularity and timeliness. Agree or disagree? Explain and give examples.

6. Do you agree with the stated value proposition of governance? If yes, why? If not, why not. Provide examples from within your own organization.

7. This chapter sets out the five levels for Information Systems Interoperability. Where does governance fit within these levels? Are there parallel levels for governance? If yes, why? If not, why not? Provide examples from within your own organization.

8. This chapter sets out six levels of Conceptual Interoperability. How do these levels relate to the five levels of Business Information System Interoperability? Do you agree with the relationships shown in Figure 4? If yes, why? If not, why not? Provide examples from within your own organization.

9. In this Chapter's Summary there are four bullet points. Do you agree that these four mechanisms are measurements of governance achievement? If yes, why? If not, why not. Provide examples from within your own organization.

3

Required Governance Metadata Infrastructure

3.1 Scope, Meaning, and Value of Metadata

No one would ever question why a business needs highly organized and correctly maintained finance books. Analogously, a metadata infrastructures is the business's information technology's books. If you cannot run a good business without the former, you cannot run good enterprise IT without the latter. The overall bureaucratic process of defining, effecting, and managing shared data and process semantics is enterprise governance.

Organizations are increasingly distributed. That is, there are multiple companies and business units. Each of these has its own financial set of books. Ultimately, however all these books have to be brought together so that a consolidated balance sheet can be produced. To have financial interoperability, that is, the ability to produce a consolidated balance sheet, there must first be consistency and common definitions on the meaning, granularity, and precision of financial information.

Similarly, there needs to be governance across many IT organizational units within the enterprise to have consolidated inventories, sales, staffing statistics, distribution systems, and other forms of corporate assets. And again, the collection of common meanings and the specifications of granularity and precision of all this corporate data are represented as metadata, which, coupled with special processes becomes the enterprise's governance. Thus, you cannot have shared data without first having a good foundation of metadata. The two go hand and glove: quality metadata precedes quality data. And quality metadata across the enterprise precedes efficient and effective governance.

A significant portion of the time and costs associated with resolving the Year 2000 (Y2K) problem can be directly attributed to a lack of a quality metadata environment within business information system organizations. The fact that one business information systems organization within an enterprise had virtually no Y2K problem while another organization within that same enterprise was running their business information systems shop "24x7" to fix the Y2K problem was no accident. The former had a long history of metadata management and the latter believed that metadata was a wasted overhead expense.

Vital to governance is control over semantics. The controls are mainly in the area of the definitions that form the basis of the interfaces to Governance Assessment processes (e.g., computing net profit) and the standard data definitions (e.g., the meaning of profit).

It is not necessary, however, to control the interfaces to the end user. Just how a data entry screen or report looks to different people is immaterial so long as the enforced semantics (rules of meaning and usage) are the same.

Semantics can either be created, stored and updated/evolved during the very process of business information systems and database development or afterwards as a hindsight remembrance effort. In the development of large information technology projects dealing with enterprise-wide, indispensable business functions, hindsight remembrance efforts, that is, the documentation of the design requirements and resulting business information system specifications are seldom accomplished such that they are timely, accurate, or complete. That is disastrous for the following three reasons:

- Only the momentous facts that are remembered are recorded.
- As systems are specified, the lower-level design details are redundantly developed, often in conflicting manners.
- As system components are maintained, the efforts are crippled because of the undocumented business knowledge that is essential to understanding.

More important than when to create and capture the metadata that comprise the complete semantics of databases and business information systems are the orientation employed during the creation and capture process. If the orientation is IT-system centric, metadata stovepipes are the most likely consequence. All the semantics will have been defined with the IT system as the outer scope. If, however, there is an enterprise-wide viewpoint in place such that data and process definitions are defined with the enterprise in mind, the inevitable efforts required to make data interoperable will be greatly lessened.

As is often the case, in the event that stove-pipe systems already exist that are now being required to share data, it is very critical to have an enterprise-view of semantics under which the existing systems are analyzed, mapped, and enabled for governance. If only the semantics of the interchanges are captured, the effort is just another set of creating more stovepipes. But in this case, virtual stovepipes.

Systems are required to interoperate because they share an aspect of one or more missions. Data from one system is required to support the inferred mission being accomplished by the other system. Whole collections of systems that are required to share data must therefore have broadly shared missions. Missions are detailed in terms of both data and functions. Organizations perform functions that access, create, update, or delete the data. Common mission areas are the outer boundaries of the shared data. To only collect the semantics of the shared data without first identifying the shared mission, functions, and organizations is to greatly short change the effort. If through analysis there is no shared mission, then there cannot be shared data.

A shared mission does not require shared and/or simultaneously occurring activities. For example, a sales organization that has staff in the field who meet with customers, determine customer product needs, deliver requirements, their purchasing and payment habits, their level of required customer support and the like are likely to be performed by organizations outside the direct mission of Sales and Marketing. Notwithstanding, Sales and Marketing needs up to date data from all these areas. Consequently, there is a shared mission: Total Customer Management. Because of this shared mission, there needs to be shared semantics. Shared data can cross multiple mission areas especially if missions are hierarchically defined.

Without fully knowing the shared mission, functions, and data, the likelihood of having productive data sharing is greatly reduced. If the determination of the scope and domain of the shared missions occurs after all the systems are built, the effort will take longer, and more work will be required to resolve the differences and redundancies that occurred because the IT systems were created within stovepipes. Well-engineered governance ensures shared missions.

3.2 Metabase System and the Knowledge Worker

Knowledge workers require policies and procedures to effectively accomplish their work. Policies are specifications of what is done. Procedures are specifications of how something is done. Both classes of specifications are metadata because they are specifications of the thing being accomplished and the way it is actually accomplished. Policies and procedures are often supported by business information systems and databases.

All this metadata, that is, the specifications of policies (things) and procedures (the way things are done), must be set within a metadata infrastructure for the knowledge worker. This infrastructure must accommodate both top-down and bottom up efforts. Eventually, if accomplished bottom-up, but with a goal of building all the metadata that would have occurred had the effort been top-down, the future efforts of building new systems, eliminating redundant systems, or evolving systems will become much easier, faster, and more cost-effective because there will already be an over arching set of shared missions, data, functions and organizations.

The set of metadata, eventually resulting across the six Knowledge Worker Framework columns is captured by the various functional modules of the Metabase System. The interrelationship of the Knowledge Worker Framework and the Metabase System's functional modules are set out in Table 14. Rather than only listing the names of the Metabase System Modules, the "Questions" that the various Metabase System modules enable to be answered are also provided. The Metabase System's modules are listed in alphabetical order, not accomplishment order.

Business Questions Addressed by the Metabase Modules Within the Knowledge Worker Framework						
	Knowledge Worker Framework Columns					
Metabase Software Module Scope	Mission	Database Objects	Business Information Systems	Business Event	Business Function	Business Organization
Business Event Management: *What are the business events, where are they, how are they related to both the overall business's process model and calendar models, and then now are these events related to 1) mission, organization, function, 2)business information systems, 3) business event cycles, and 4) calendar cycles. What is the impact on these business events when policy (a.k.a., data) is required or changed.*				✔		
Business Information Systems: *What are the business information systems, where are they, how are they related to mission, organization, function, and databases. What is the impact on these business information systems when policy (a.k.a., data) is required or changed.*			✔			

Business Questions Addressed by the Metabase Modules Within the Knowledge Worker Framework						
	Knowledge Worker Framework Columns					
Metabase Software Module Scope	Mission	Database Objects	Business Information Systems	Business Event	Business Function	Business Organization
Data Element Model: *What are the context independent business facts and their specifications that can be deployed to fully define the semantics that define these business facts, or that form the basis for these business facts as they are refined through the allocation of semantic and data use modifiers. Where are these data element semantics deployed throughout the various data models whose facts (attributes, columns, DBMS columns, and View columns are based on these facts.*		✔				
Data Integrity Rule Specification and Binding: *What are the rules that govern the integrity of data that is specified across all the deployed uses of that data. How are these rules defined and where are they bound such they are defined once and bound where appropriate? What are the processes and how are these processes executed that ensure data integrity during all data object operations?*		✔	✔			

Business Questions Addressed by the Metabase Modules Within the Knowledge Worker Framework

Metabase Software Module Scope	Knowledge Worker Framework Columns: Mission	Database Objects	Business Information Systems	Business Event	Business Function	Business Organization
Database Objects: *What are the major data-based object classes and objects that form enterprise databases. What are the state-based process life cycles for these data-based object classes? What are the database record (i.e., table-based) processes that control the fundamental integrity of individual database records. What are the data-based object class business information systems that transform database objects from one predefined value-state to another?*		✔	✔			
Document and Form: *What documents and forms provide critical information about the enterprise? How are those documents and forms interrelated one with the other? How are these materials subdivided and then properly related to specific functions performed by organizations in the accomplishment of missions? How are these able to be related to certain View columns?*	✔	✔	✔	✔	✔	✔

Business Questions Addressed by the Metabase Modules Within the Knowledge Worker Framework						
	Knowledge Worker Framework Columns					
Metabase Software Module Scope	Mission	Database Objects	Business Information Systems	Business Event	Business Function	Business Organization
Enterprise Architecture Management: *What are the five distinct architectures that comprise the over set within the enterprise, and how are these architectures intersected and mapped to the Knowledge Worker Framework in support of projects that contribute to the build rationale and sequence of an overall Information Systems Plan?*	✔	✔	✔	✔	✔	✔
Functions: *What are the human-based processes performed by groups in their achievement the various missions of the enterprise from within different enterprise organizations? What human processes are common across and within organizations, business events and by indirection, business information systems and databases?*					✔	

Business Questions Addressed by the Metabase Modules Within the Knowledge Worker Framework						
	Knowledge Worker Framework Columns					
Metabase Software Module Scope	Mission	Database Objects	Business Information Systems	Business Event	Business Function	Business Organization
Governance: *Who are the persons, and what is their enterprise context, that is, their Mission, Organization, Function, and Position who are currently responsible for the integrity and correctness of a large collection of work products that are developed within the scope of the various Metabase System Functional modules.*	✔	✔	✔	✔	✔	✔
Implemented Data Model: *What are the database models that are able to be employed as the basis of operational databases that can be employed by business information systems? What are the database implementations of data-based concepts contained in the specified data models? What are the various columns, including value domains, data integrity processes, and data types that are an implementation of various data elements and/or attributes from specified data models that defined concepts?*		✔				

Business Questions Addressed by the Metabase Modules Within the Knowledge Worker Framework						
	Knowledge Worker Framework Columns					
Metabase Software Module Scope	Mission	Database Objects	Business Information Systems	Business Event	Business Function	Business Organization
Information Needs Analysis: *What information (a.k.a. query results or reports) is needed by various organizations in their functional accomplishment of missions and what databases and information systems provide this information?*		✔	✔			
Missions: *What are the essential missions that define the very existence of the enterprise, and that are the ultimate goals and objectives that measure enterprise accomplishment from within different business functions and organizations?*	✔				✔	✔

Business Questions Addressed by the Metabase Modules Within the Knowledge Worker Framework						
	Knowledge Worker Framework Columns					
Metabase Software Module Scope	Mission	Database Objects	Business Information Systems	Business Event	Business Function	Business Organization
Operational Data Model: *What are the actual databases and models that are employed by business information systems? What are the databases and models that operationally specify data-based specifications from DBMS independent database models? What are the various DBMS columns, including value domains, data integrity processes, and data types that are an implementation of various data elements and/or attributes from specified data models that defined concepts?*	✔	✔	✔	✔	✔	✔
Organizations: *Which organizations are accomplishing what aspects of missions with what databases, information systems and through which functions?*	✔			✔	✔	✔

Business Questions Addressed by the Metabase Modules Within the Knowledge Worker Framework						
	Knowledge Worker Framework Columns					
Metabase Software Module Scope	Mission	Database Objects	Business Information Systems	Business Event	Business Function	Business Organization
Project Management. *What are the various knowledge worker projects that address one or more collections of activities that create an IT work product that supports the enterprise? What are the detailed deliverables, collections of tasks, assigned staff, work accomplishment resources, and work environment factors that affect the accomplishment of project work. What are all the different projects by IT work product.*	✔	✔	✔	✔	✔	✔
Reports. *What are the specifications of the reports that are to be generated by business information systems and/or DBMS ad hoc query language or package report writers. What are the various view columns or directly connected database columns involved in the database?*			✔	✔		

Business Questions Addressed by the Metabase Modules Within the Knowledge Worker Framework						
	Knowledge Worker Framework Columns					
Metabase Software Module Scope	Mission	Database Objects	Business Information Systems	Business Event	Business Function	Business Organization
Requirements: *What are the requirements that in total support the development of key enterprise database components? How these requirements are interrelated, subdivided, and then related to the various metadata components that are "required" as a consequence? How can the complete set of effects can be known and interrelated?*	✔	✔	✔	✔	✔	✔
Resource Life Cycles: *What are the key Resources (facilities, materiel, staff, etc.)?How are they sequenced, interrelated, and how are they supported through databases and information systems?*		✔	✔			

Business Questions Addressed by the Metabase Modules Within the Knowledge Worker Framework						
	Knowledge Worker Framework Columns					
Metabase Software Module Scope	Mission	Database Objects	Business Information Systems	Business Event	Business Function	Business Organization
Screens/GUIs: *What are the end-user graphical user interface specifications that enable end-users to interact with business information systems for data entry, formatted reports, ad hoc reporting, and for navigating through defined features of the business information systems? What are the various screens that are affected by specific view-column database interfaces with business information systems? What are the various processes that affect either the data presented through the wire frames or are stored in the databases? What are the various controls and invoked processes evident through the screens?*		✔	✔			
Specified Model: *What are the data model specifications that represent concepts that are to be included in database models? What are the data elements that are represented as subject-entity-attributes across the specified concept data models? What are the various attribute-bound value domains, data integrity processes, and data types that are an implementation of various data elements?*		✔				

Business Questions Addressed by the Metabase Modules Within the Knowledge Worker Framework						
	Knowledge Worker Framework Columns					
Metabase Software Module Scope	Mission	Database Objects	Business Information Systems	Business Event	Business Function	Business Organization
Use Cases: *What are the detailed business process scenarios required to accomplish the necessary work of the enterprise? What are the interrelationships among use cases? How are the use cases subdivided into certain events? What are the pre-, post-, and special-conditions of these use cases? What are the business facts that are read, selected, updated, and reported within use cases? What are the relationships between use case facts and database view columns?*	✔	✔	✔	✔	✔	✔
User Acceptance Tests: *What are the requirements-based accepted tests deemed appropriate and necessary to determine the adequacy of a business information system before it is released? What are the requirements that are being validated as being completed? What are the business information system components that are being tested?*		✔	✔			

Business Questions Addressed by the Metabase Modules Within the Knowledge Worker Framework						
	Knowledge Worker Framework Columns					
Metabase Software Module Scope	Mission	Database Objects	Business Information Systems	Business Event	Business Function	Business Organization
View Model: *What are the data interface specifications between databases and business information systems? What are the various business information systems that are supported by specific databases? What are the various databases that are accessed by business information systems. What are the data-based mappings between views that support database interoperability? What are the data-based processes that transform data via one view to the data specifications of a different view?*		✔	✔			

Table 14. Business Metadata Domains within the Knowledge Worker Framework.

3.3 Governance Framework

The set of metadata models, components within those models, and processes that cause those models to materialize exist within an overall framework for governance. Figure 5 depicts the key components in that framework.

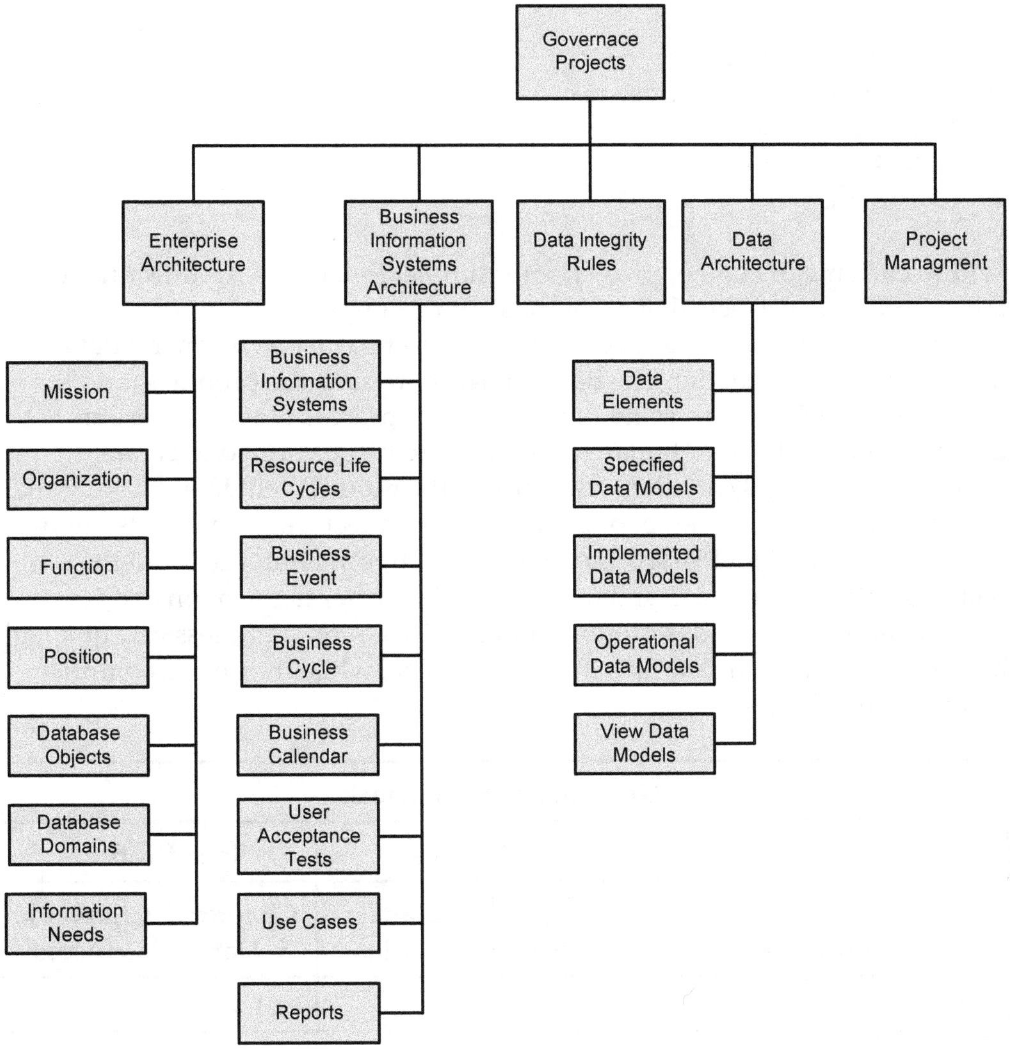

Figure 5. Governance Framework.

Fundamentally, Figure 5 illustrates that all governance activities are accomplished through projects. That means that every governance activity should be planned, budgeted, has deliverables, and is able to be audited, reviewed, and as necessary executed again. Broadly there are five classes of projects, And within the five governance project classes there are 20 subordinate governance projects.

- Enterprise Architecture
- Business Information Systems
- Data Integrity Rules
- Data Architecture
- Governance

Within each major class of project, for example, Enterprise Architecture, there are subordinate projects that accomplish, for example, missions or organizations, or functions. Each class of project has its own general data model and process model. The data model represents the products, and the specifications of the constructed products. The process model represents the activities (manual and automated) that need to be performed to create, updated, delete, and/or otherwise employ the represented data.

Table 15 identifies the set of governance architecture components, high-level and a more detailed-level set of diagram figure references, and the sections within Chapters 5 and 6 that provide further description and/or specification. All these descriptions and specifications are necessarily at a high level because the complete specifications, which, while they exist, comprise many more of pages.

Governance Framework					
Governed Work Product		**Figures**		**Specifications**	
		High Level	**Metadata Entities**	**Chapter 5, Data**	**Chapter 6, Process**
Enterprise Architecture	Mission	7	29	5.2.1	6.1.1
	Organization	7	29	5.2.2	6.1.1
	Function	7	29	5.2.3	6.1.1
	Position	7	29	5.2.4	6.1.2

Governance Framework					
Governed Work Product		Figures		Specifications	
		High Level	Metadata Entities	Chapter 5, Data	Chapter 6, Process
	Information Needs	8	30	5.2.5	6.1.3
	Resource Life Cycle Analysis	9	31	5.2.6	6.1.4
	Database Domains	7	29	5.2.7	6.1.6
	Database Objects	10	32	5.2.8	6.1.5
	Documents & Forms	11	33	5.5.9 & 5.5.10	6.1.7
	Requirements	12	34	5.2.11	6.1.8
Business Information Systems Architecture	Business Information Systems	13	35	5.3.1	6.2.1
	Business Events	14	36	5.3.2	6.2.2
	Business Cycle	14	36	5.3.3	6.2.3
	Business Calendar	14	36	5.3.4	6.2.4
	User Acceptance Test	15	37	5.3.5	6.2.5
	Use Cases	16	38	5.3.6	6.2.6
	Reports	17	39	5.3.7	6.2.7
	External File Interface	n/a	n/a	5.3.8	6.2.8
Data Integrity Rules	Data Integrity Rules	18	40	5.4	6.3

<table>
<tr><th colspan="6">Governance Framework</th></tr>
<tr><th colspan="2" rowspan="2">Governed Work Product</th><th colspan="2">Figures</th><th colspan="2">Specifications</th></tr>
<tr><th>High Level</th><th>Metadata Entities</th><th>Chapter 5, Data</th><th>Chapter 6, Process</th></tr>
<tr><td rowspan="6">Data Architecture</td><td>Data Elements</td><td>21</td><td>41</td><td>5.5.1</td><td>6.4.1</td></tr>
<tr><td>Business Domain</td><td>21</td><td>41</td><td>5.5.2</td><td>6.4.2</td></tr>
<tr><td>Specified Data Model</td><td>22</td><td>42</td><td>5.5.3</td><td>6.4.3</td></tr>
<tr><td>Implemented Database Model</td><td>23</td><td>43</td><td>5.5.4</td><td>6.4.4</td></tr>
<tr><td>Operational Database Model</td><td>24</td><td>44</td><td>5.5.5</td><td>6.4.5</td></tr>
<tr><td>View Data Model</td><td>25</td><td>45</td><td>5.5.6</td><td>6.4.6</td></tr>
<tr><td>Project Management</td><td>Project Management</td><td>26</td><td>46</td><td>5.6</td><td>6.5</td></tr>
<tr><td>Governance</td><td>Governance</td><td>27</td><td>47</td><td>5.7</td><td>6.6</td></tr>
</table>

Table 15. Cross Reference among Architecture Components, Figures, and References in Chapters 5 and 6.

3.4 Required Metadata Models

The high-level meta models, which enable the collection of the metadata necessary to support efficient and cost-effective governance, are presented here. Each subsection contains the rationale why this class of metadata is required for governance. These models are:

- Enterprise Architecture
  - Mission, Organization, Function and Position (Figure 7)
  - Information Needs (Figure 8)

- Resource Life Cycle Management (Figure 9)
- Database Object Specifications (Figure 10)
- Document & Forms (Form 11)
- Requirements (Figure 12)

- Business Information Systems Architecture
  - Business Information Systems (Figure 13)
  - Business Events (Figure 14)
  - User Acceptance Tests (Figure 15)
  - Use Cases (Figure 16)
  - Reports (Figure 17)
- Data Integrity Rules (Figure 18)
- Data Architecture
  - Database Architecture Classes (Figure 20)
  - Data Element Model (Figure 21)
  - Specified Data Model (Figure 22)
  - Implemented Database Model (Figure 23)
  - Operational Database Model (Figure 24)
  - View Data Model (Figure 25)
- Project Management (Figure 26)
- Governance Management (Figure 27)

Third normal form versions of these models are provided at the end of Chapter 5. The identification of governance process models are provided in Chapter 6. Detailed processes for these governance processes are provided in the Appendix. In the Figures 29 through 47 the lines with crow's-feet (circle with a three-toed foot) at one or both ends to represent relationships lines.

In all these diagrams, a line with a single crow's foot is a one-to-many relationship with the crow's foot resting on the "many" end. If the line has a crow's foot at both ends that is a many-to-many relationship. If the line is circular that is a recursive or hierarchical relationship. Finally, if there are two one-to-many relationship lines between two entities, that signifies a network relationship that serves to represent bills-of-materials.

3.5 Governed Work-Product Integration

The entire set of "nouns" in the cells of Table 4's depiction of the Knowledge Worker Framework are all work products. Accomplishing them in isolation only results in a forest of stovepipe silos. These work products are engineered to be integrated, and must be accomplished in context with one another.

A depiction of the interrelationships of the work products for business information systems is presented in Figure 6. Table 16 also shows the cross reference between the Data Architecture reference model data models and the typical work products of a business information system effort.

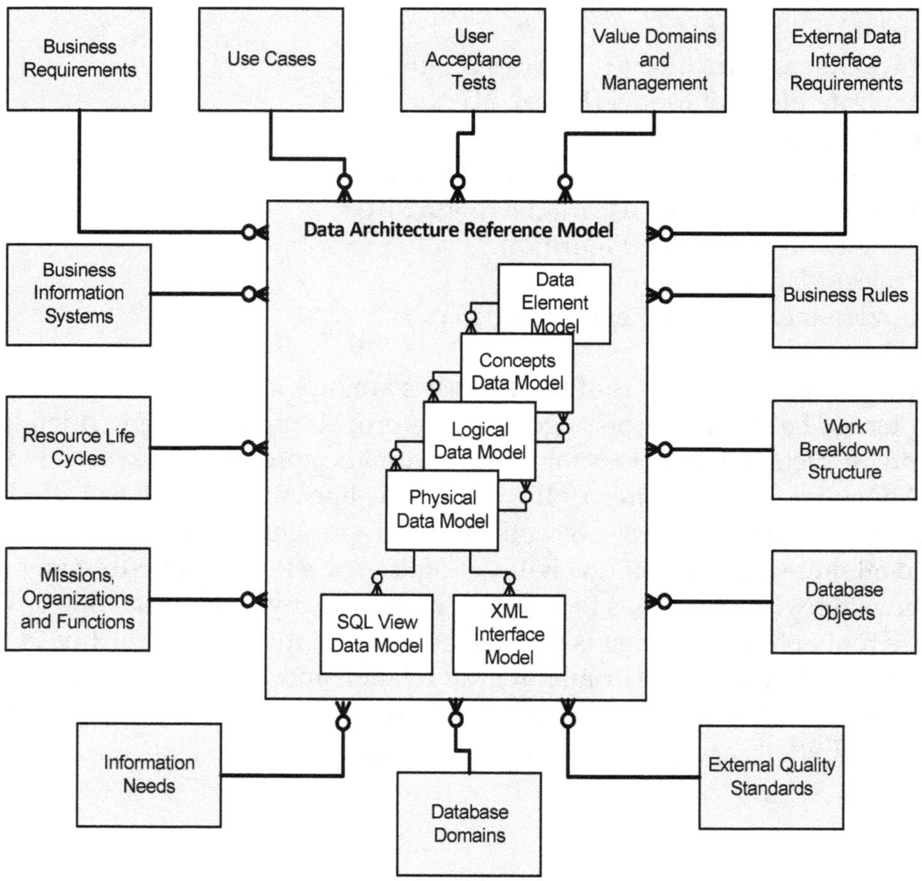

Figure 6. Cross Reference between Data Architecture Models and Business Information System Work Products.

Business Information System Work Products, for example, Business Requirements, shown in Figure 6 can have a one-to-many relationship between one or more different business information system work products and zero, one or more of the data models. When two or more business information system work products are interrelated with one or more of the data models, there may exist relationship between those two business information system work products through artifacts contained in the data models.

For example, there is a business requirement to capture student addresses. Additionally, there would be a Use Case through which a student's address is captured. Apart from the obviousness of the interrelationship, the fact that there is a common data structure, Student Address, there is an implicit interrelationship between the two business information system work products, business requirements and use cases. When both work products and the data models are stored in a Metabase System, the exposition of the business information system work product traceability of one work product to the other is a simple report request.

Table 16 identifies each of the business information system work products from Figure 6. Here they are in alphabetical order. These are cross referenced with the data models from the Data Architecture Reference model that is at the center of Figure 6. In Table 16, these work products are listed in column 1.

The data models from Figure 6 identified in Table 16 are not accomplished in isolation. They result from an initial and then ongoing analysis of the various business information system work products. That is, Business Requirements, Business Rules, and the like. As each of these business information system work products is developed, reviewed, and evolved, the effect of those activities must be reflected in one or more of the data models depicted in Figure 6 and identified in Table 16.

Work Products	Data Architecture Reference Model Component					
	Data Ele-ment	Con-cepts Data Model	Implem ented data-base model	Oper-ation-al data-base model	View Data Model	XML Data Mo-del
Business Information Systems				✔	✔	✔
Business Requirements		✔	✔	✔		✔
Business Rules	✔		✔	✔	✔	✔
Database Domains			✔			
Database Objects			✔			
External Data Interface Requirements				✔	✔	✔
Eternal Quality Standards	✔	✔	✔	✔	✔	✔
Information Needs	✔		✔			
Mission Organization Functions			✔			
Resource Life Cycles			✔			
Use Cases			✔	✔	✔	✔
User Acceptance Tests				✔	✔	✔
Value Domains and Management	✔	✔	✔	✔	✔	✔
Work Breakdown Structure (WBS)	✔	✔	✔	✔	✔	✔

Table 16. Cross Reference Between Work Products and Data Architecture Reference Model Components.

Each of the business information system work products from the first column of Table 16 is described in Table 17. The last column of Table 17 enumerates the key data model artifacts associated with each work product.

This book does not address how to create each of these business information system work products because the creation process is more than adequately addressed within other Whitemarsh books, courses, seminars, and methodology documents and Metabase System user guides. Rather, the focus of this book is the necessary and sufficient governance that must exist among all the enterprise work products.

Business Information System Life Cycle Work Products		
Component	**Description**	**Data Model Components**
Business Requirements	Business Requirements are the identification, specification, and definition of the components that must exist in the ultimate solution delivered by the contractor. Business Requirements form the foundation upon which all components of are engineered, implemented, and maintained. Business requirements will evolve over time. Thus, it is important to be able to track the initial and evolved requirements. It is unrealistic to initially have all requirements because new and/or revised requirements are discovered all during the project's architecture, engineering, and implementation.	Subjects, Entities Attributes Data Elements Database Domains Database Objects
Business Rules	Business Rules are assertions of truth-states in the database. Each business rule includes the identification, name, description, and exact specification of data-based rules that must be either true or that, after the execution of an information system process, results in a state of truth. There are two classes of Business Rules: data and process. Almost invariably, business rules depend on existing data, reference or control data, or data that is determined as a consequence of a process's execution. Almost all business rules are mappable to data, whether persistent or temporary.	Schema Tables Columns DBMS Schema DBMS Tables DBMS Columns Value Domains

Business Information System Life Cycle Work Products		
Component	**Description**	**Data Model Components**
	Business rules are almost always discovered during design sessions, and use-case walkthroughs. As business rules are discovered, the various data models need to be concurrently examined to determine whether the database can support the rules. Since every business rule has a process component, a key component of each rule is the specification of the process and a determination of where that rule is bound. That is, bound into the data model component (e.g., Data Element, or DBMS column), a low-level application component, a mid-level application process, or in the user presentation layer. Because of this multiplicity of possible bindings, business rules need to be centrally defined and managed, but bound only into the data model or business information system work product within which it is accomplished.	
Work Breakdown Structure (WBS)	Work Breakdown Structures are hierarchical representations of two classes of effort: What, and How. The "what" type of WBS contains an action phrase and a noun phrase that together describe what is to be done, and the name of the work product creation or evolution. The second class of WBS, the "how WBSs" are tuned to deliverables but to the actual techniques employed to accomplish the data model or business information system work product. Both the "What" WBS and the "How" WBSs need to be interlinked. Well developed metadata management systems include complete project management so that work plans and progress against work plans can be directly tied to and integrated with accomplishments.	Subjects, Entities Attributes Data Elements Database Domains Database Objects Schema Tables Columns DBMS Schema DBMS Tables DBMS Columns

Business Information System Life Cycle Work Products		
Component	**Description**	**Data Model Components**
External data interface Data Requirements	External data interface Requirements are the specifications of an interface between an internal database data structure and some external data source. Each interface essentially consists of a fully defined data model that defines every field in the interface to the extent that a software module can be created to read the records represented by the interface and take appropriate action against the database. Such actions can be to insert, delete, or modify database records.	DBMS Schemas DBMS Tables DBMS Columns DBMS Relationships Value Domains Views View Columns Relationships XML Schemas XML Elements XML Attributes
External Quality Standards	External Quality Standards are de jure and de facto standards through which data management products and/or processes can be judged. The ISO Standard 11179 enables assessment of the adequacy and completeness of the metadata associated with data elements. Included in this class of assessment are Concepts, Conceptual Value Domains, Data Element Concepts, Value Domains including mapping among equivalent values, Data Element Classifications, and Administrative Information (for Stewardship). The ISO/ANSI SQL standard enables the assessment of SQL data structures and languages employed in database designs and application program access. WC3 XML standards enable an analysis of the names and engineering of XML schemas and XML data streams so as to ensure maximum interoperability conformity to existing sets of XML schema models.	Schemas Tables Columns Relationships Views View Columns Relationships XML Schemas XML Elements XML Attributes

Business Information System Life Cycle Work Products		
Component	**Description**	**Data Model Components**
Business Information Business Information Systems	Business Information Systems are the broad characterizations of the application systems that capture, update, and report data. Business Information Systems are additionally detailed into their specific components, and those that deal with database data are mapped to the appropriate data model component.	Views View Columns Relationships XML Schemas XML Elements XML Attributes
Use Cases	Use Cases are highly engineered pseudo-process models that clearly define the behavior of the users and business information systems, and also the responses provided from the databases as they take in, modify, or provide data to users. Use-cases are detailed to the level such that a programmer can interpret the process intent and write an application system module without semantic and/or process misunderstanding. Use Cases present behavior-based scenarios of the use of the database to accomplish the requirements. Because use-cases directly identify database data, mappings can be created between one use-case and another to identify redundancy and possible conflict. Mappings can also be made between the detailed data and process aspects of use-cases and business requirements, deployments of use-cases in software and hardware, value domains, business rules, and WBS.	Schemas Tables Columns Relationships Value Domains DBMS Schemas DBMS Tables DBMS Columns DBMS Relationships Views View Columns Relationships XML Schemas XML Elements XML Attributes
User Acceptance Tests	User Acceptance Tests are stylized user-application system interaction scripts that can be exercised to the extent that fully informed users can determine that all the requirements have been met and all use-cases are satisfactorily performed. User Acceptance Tests (UAT) are the ultimate mechanisms through which organizations determine that it has received the business information system that was specified. Because of all the different data	DBMS Schemas DBMS Tables DBMS Columns DBMS Relationships Value Domains Views View Columns Relationships XML Schemas

Business Information System Life Cycle Work Products		
Component	**Description**	**Data Model Components**
	models, and work products, the User Acceptance tests can be very comprehensive and very telling.	XML Elements XML Attributes
Value Domains	Value domains relate to the allowed, disallowed, or other defined collections of values and interconnection of values that represent discrete choices (Gender = Male, Female, unknown), or sequenced states such as Applied, Reviewed, Accepted, Rejected, or Appealed. Included as well are the mappings across time of evolved and/or changed value domains. Value domains commonly stand alone and are allocated to data elements, or to attributes, columns, or DBMS columns. In all cases of value domain allocation, the allocations must be such that semantics conflicts are prohibited.	DBMS Schemas DBMS Tables DBMS Columns DBMS Relationships Value Domains Views View Columns Relationships XML Schemas XML Elements XML Attributes
Resource Life Cycle Analyses	Resource Life Cycle of Analysis identifies, defines, and sets out the resources of the enterprises, the life cycles that represent their accomplishments, and the interrelationships among the different enterprise resource life cycles. Resource life cycle nodes represent the end-state data resulting from the execution of business information systems. The end-state data is represented through database object classes.	Schemas Tables Columns Relationships
Missions Organizations and Functions	Missions, organizations, functions, and position assignments represent the identification, definition, and interrelationships among the persons who, through their positions, perform functions within their organizations that accomplish enterprise missions. Missions define the very existence of the enterprise, and that are the ultimate goals and objectives that measure enterprise accomplishment from within different business functions and organizations. Functions represent the procedures performed by enterprise organization groups as they achieve the various missions of the enterprise from within different enterprise organizations. Organizations represent the bureaucratic units	Schemas Tables Columns Relationships

Business Information System Life Cycle Work Products		
Component	**Description**	**Data Model Components**
	created to perform through their functions the mission of the enterprise.	
Information Needs	Information needs represent the identification, definition, and interrelationship of the information needed by various organizations in their functional accomplishment of missions and what databases and information systems provide this information?	Schemas Tables Columns Relationships
Database Domains	Database domains are the data-intensive bridge between mission descriptions and database object classes. While database object classes are non redundant, they may be referenced by several database domains.	Schemas Tables Columns Relationships
Database Object Classes	Database object classes represent the identification of 1) the critical data structures, 2) the processes ensure high quality and integrity data within these data structures, 3) the value-based states represented by these data structures, and 4) the database object centric information systems that value and transform database objects from one state to the next. Database Objects are transformed from one valid state to another in support of fulfilling the information needs of business information systems as they operation within the business functions of organizations.	Schemas Tables Columns Relationships

Table 17. Data Management Components and affected Data Models.

3.6 Enterprise Architecture Metadata

Enterprise Architecture metadata includes metadata from:

- Missions, Organizations, Functions, Positions and Persons
- Information Needs
- Resource Life Cycle Analysis

- Database Objects
- Documents and Forms
- Requirements

All the work products set out in the sections below are described at a high-level in Table 17. In the last column of Table 17 are the specific work products that must be created to fairly present a completed work product.

In Figures 7 through 27 are all "high-level" data models. Figures 29 to 47 are more detailed versions of these data models.

3.6.1 Mission, Organization, Function and Position

Missions, organizations, functions, positions, and database domains metadata interrelationships are depicted in Figure 7. This collection of metadata to represent the context into which all data models and process models are placed.

Missions are multi-level network-based models and are needed to identify the joint domains under which data is to be shared. Shared missions imply shared data. If there are shared missions but no shared data, the nonshared data necessarily exists in stove-pipe data structures.

In environments where data sharing is not possible, the data should at least exhibit shared semantics. As an extension to the Sales and Marketing example from above, the salesmen in the field may have locally loaded, stored, and processed databases through which customer management occurs. If that local data has its own stovepipe semantics versus the shared data semantics, then, when the salesman needs a data refresh, there will have to be downloading, transformation, and then loading of the salesman's database. Or, if the salesman needs a question answered from the home office, most likely the salesman will ask the question in terms of the data structures, names and value domains from the laptop's databases. Confusion would certainly occur if the semantics are all stovepipe-based semantics versus the shared-data semantics. In all these situations, governance needs to occur to occur to ensure shared semantics.

Organizations are also multi-level network-based models and are cross-referenced with missions. If certain missions are shared, there should also be joint organizations that administer the shared missions. Positions, within the context of organizations are needed to know what activities have to be

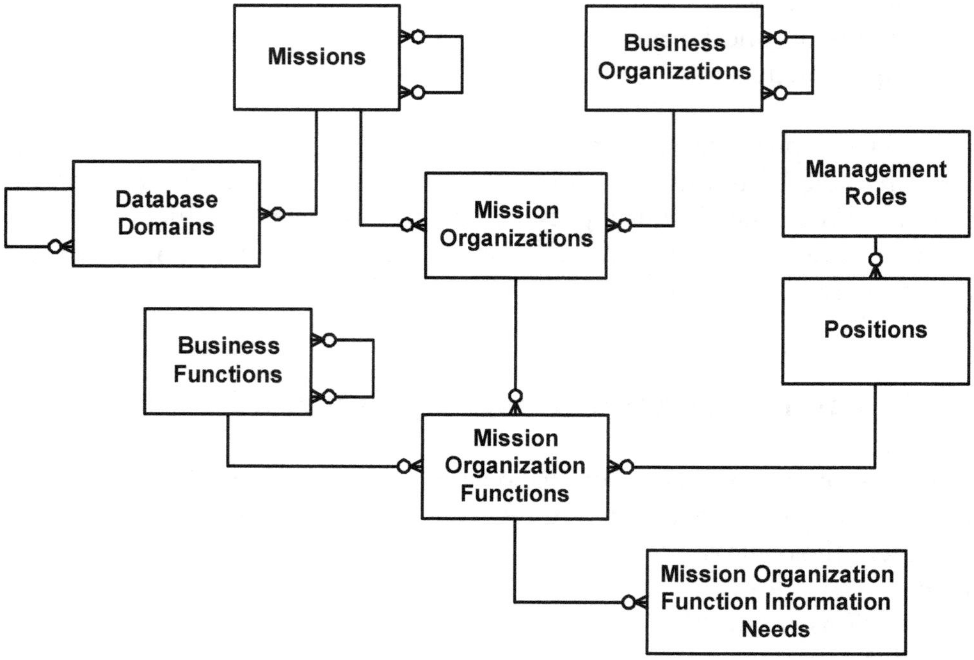

Figure 7. Missions, Organizations, Functions, Positions & Database Domains.

performed to accomplish the shared missions. Finally, functions are needed so that it can be known what activities are affected by the shared data that exist across organizations within their common missions.

Functions represent the human activities that are performed by individuals acting in certain positions. These functions can be performed within the context of multiple sets of mission-organization pairs.

Positions are categories of work activities performed by persons. A position may exist within multiple mission-organization pairs within the context of those organizations.

The Governance Metabase System module identifies persons charged with governance across the list of work products managed within Metabase System databases. This module also identifies and describes specific positions appropriate for governance.

3.6.2 Information Needs

Information needs, depicted in Figure 8, are required because these spell out the specifications required for shared data across the functions performed by the organizations, in accomplishing the common missions.

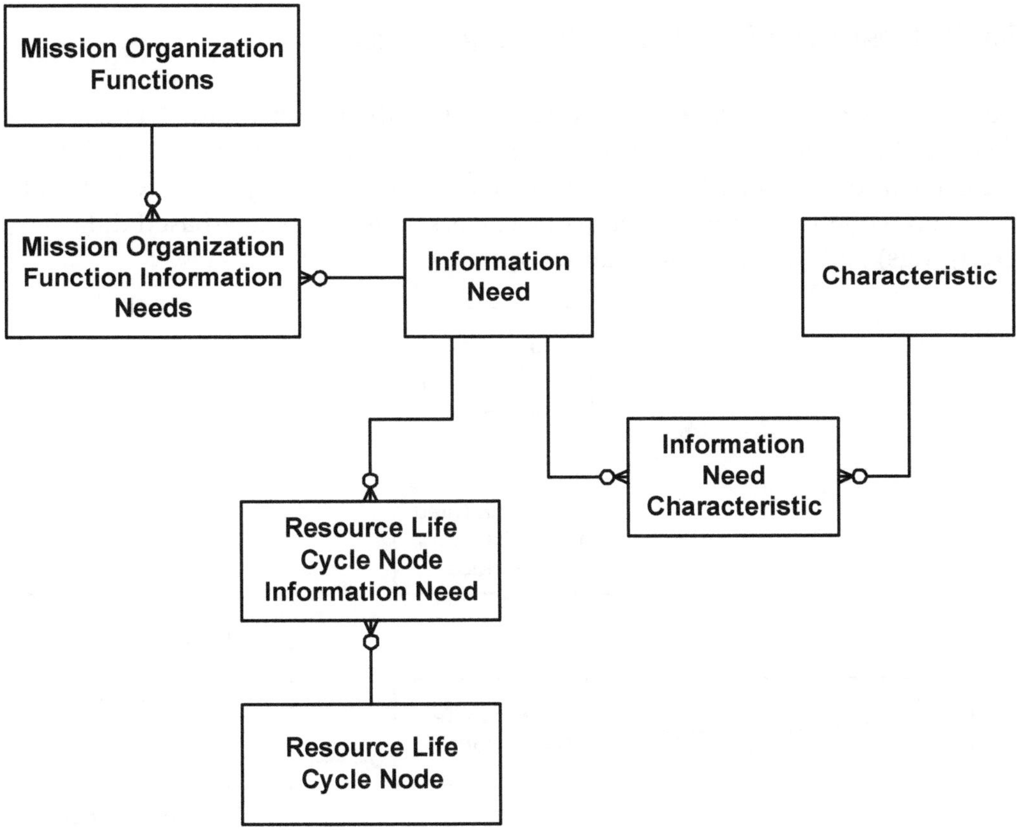

Figure 8. Information Needs.

Specifying information need requirements is the first step in determining the information needed by the enterprise to be supported by Resource Life Cycle Analysis models and by inference business information systems and database objects. Database objects, in turn, imply shared data requirements on databases. Without knowing the common information needs there is no basis for the information sharing. Information need's information also includes the initial characteristics of the needs such as the granularity, frequency, and form of the shared data requirement.

3.6.3 Resource Life Cycle Management

Resources, see Figure 9, (e.g., facilities, assets, staff, and programs), and resource life cycles (major state changes in the life of a resource), and resource life cycle intersections (Resource Life Cycle Node Structure) are needed to set the overall context of the database object classes (major policy-based data groupings) and business information systems.

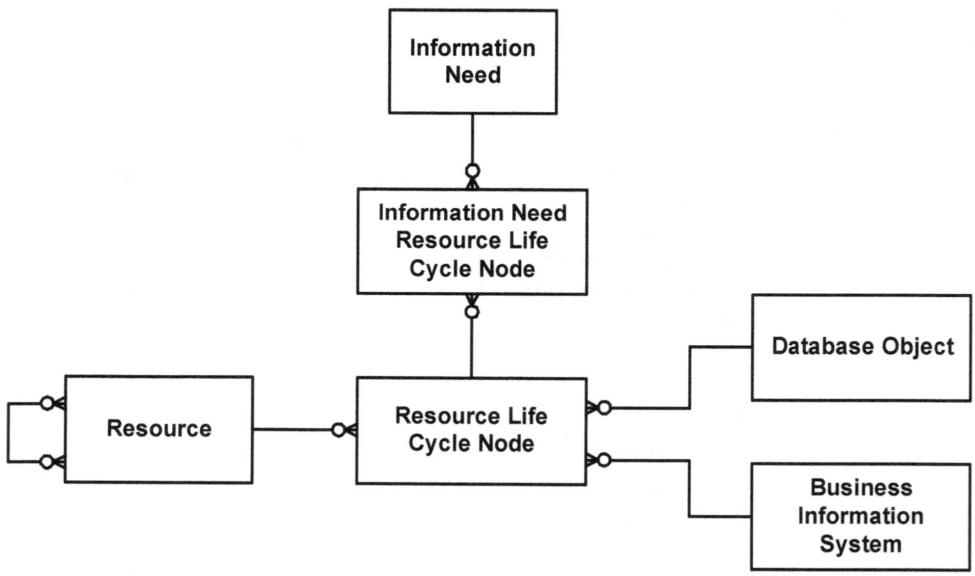

Figure 9. Resource Life Cycle.

Resources and their life cycles are mapped to information needs that are made available to the functions performed by organizations in the pursuit of missions. Without resources there is no unifying focus for data creating evolution and sharing across the enterprise. Additionally, resource life cycles enable the identification of redundant, conflicting, and missing database object classes and business information systems. Finally, these provide a cross check on the adequacy of the information needs.

3.6.4 Database Objects

Database object classes, see Figure 10, are required because each represents the complete specification of a major policy area represented within the domain of the enterprise and also one or more database. Each database object class is supported by its state changes, its table-based transformation processes to ensure integrity of change, and finally by the database object information systems that cause the database object to be changed from one valid state to another.

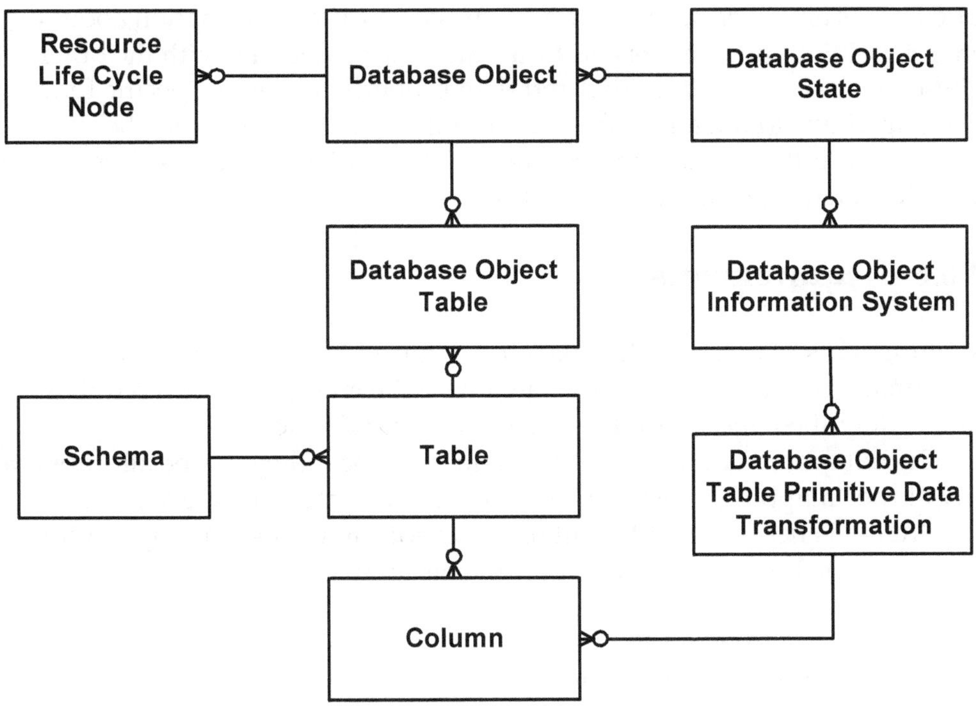

Figure 10. Database Object Classes.

It is necessary that database object classes be completely specified prior to being implemented so that the policies that the database objects are correct with respect to granularity and precision. Databases that contain database objects from database object classes must do so in a semantically correct manner.

Otherwise, subsets of database objects cannot represent shared data, which, in turn, cannot be exchanged in a meaningful way. If some databases contain database objects at a different level of granularity and precision, the transformation from the base granularity and precision must be specified so that value transformations can be determined to be correct. If this contextual setting is not accomplished, creating shared data environments is difficult, time-consuming, and expensive.

3.6.5 Documents & Forms

Documents and Forms, see Figure 11, provide critical information about the enterprise. Both documents and forms are interrelated one with the other. These materials are subdivided and then properly related to specific functions performed by organizations in the accomplishment of missions. The documents and forms are both related to Mission-Organization-Forms. Forms are additionally related to View Volumes.

3.6.6 Requirements

Requirements Management, depicted in Figure 12, enables the creation and assignment of requirements associated with the enterprise. Each requirement can be described and interrelated with other requirements.

Once requirements are identified and described, they can be allocated to any of the "mapping" items above. This permits enterprises to know the requirements needed by different organizations in the performance enterprise missions. The broad classes of requirements are:

- Enterprise Architecture
- Business Information Systems
- Data Integrity Rules
- Data Architectures
- Project Management
- Governance

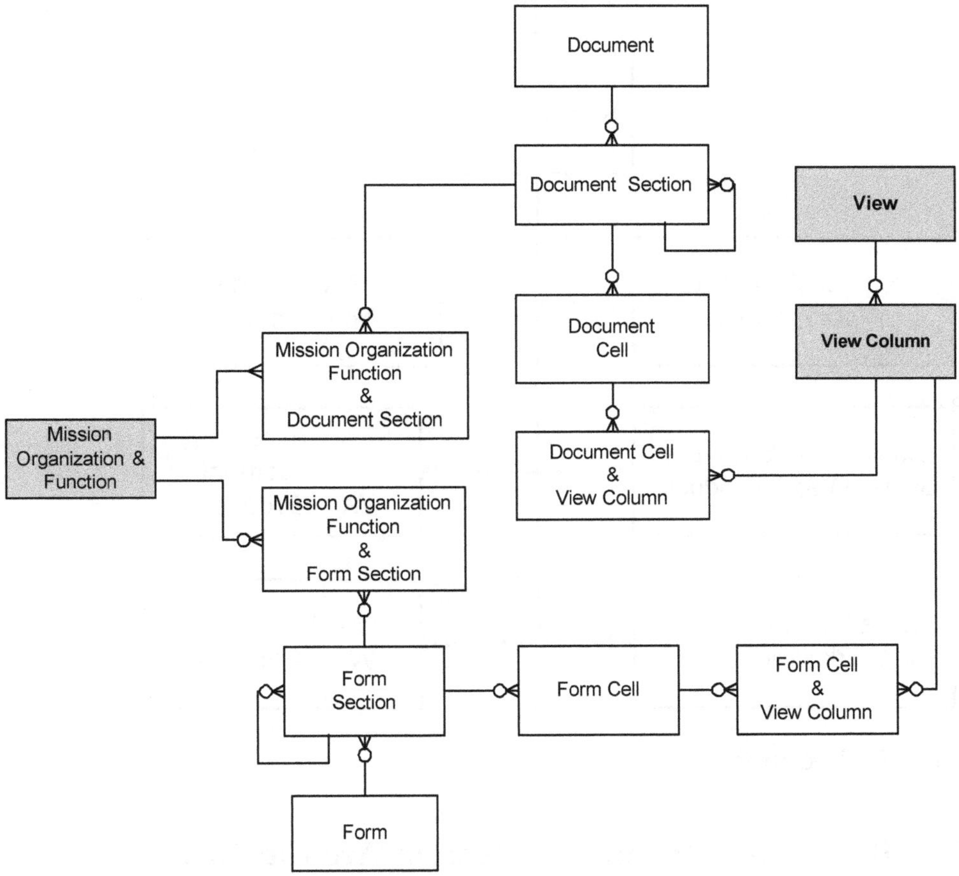

Figure 11. Documents and Forms.

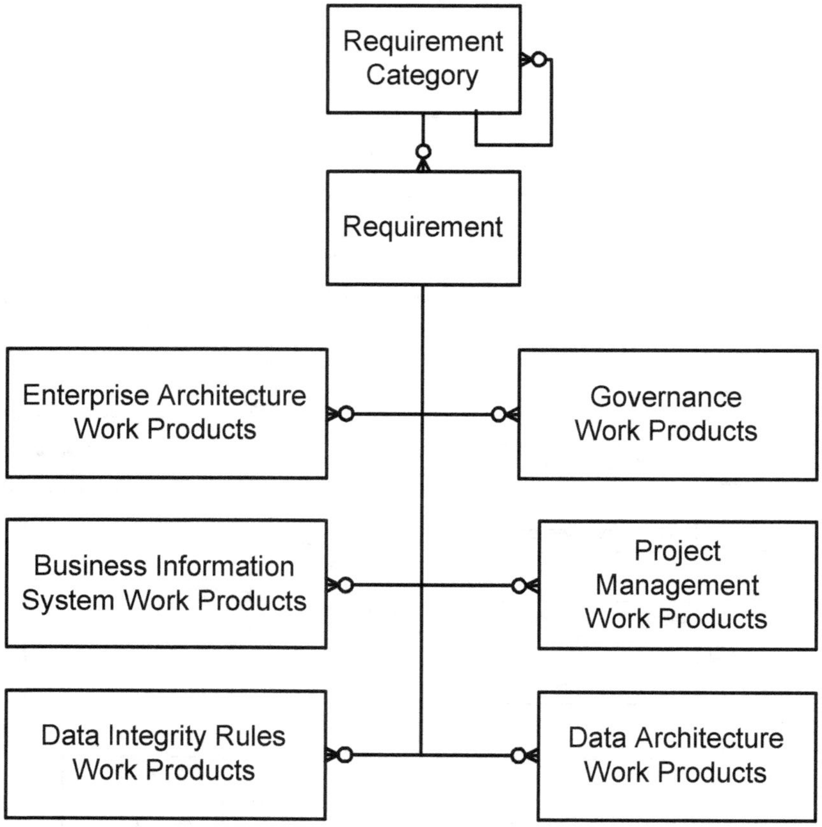

Figure 12. Requirements.

3.7 Business Information System Architecture

Business Information Systems Architecture includes metadata from:

- Business Information Systems
- Business Events
- User Acceptance Tests
- Use Cases
- Reports

3.7.1 Business Information Systems

Business information systems, depicted in Figure 13, are set within resource life cycle nodes of resources. The goal of business information systems is to collect enterprise data that transforms database objects from one state to another in support of the accomplishment of enterprise missions.

Business information systems, when executed, cause the execution of the database object information systems, which, in turn, cause the state changes of database objects.

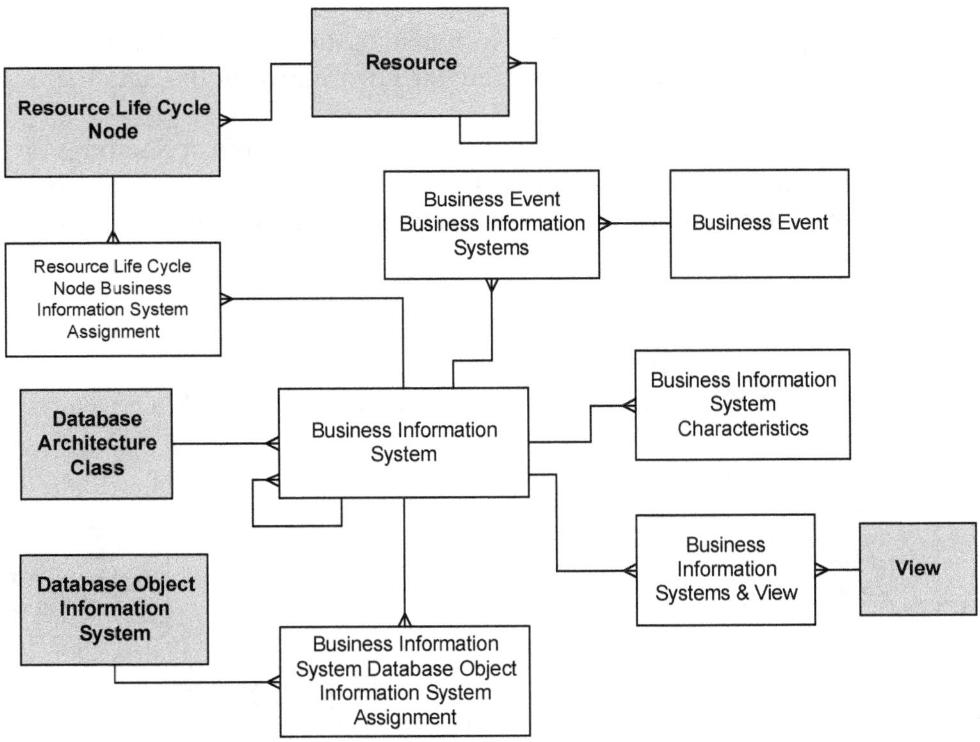

Figure 13. Business Information Systems.

3.7.2 Business Events

Business events, depicted in Figure 14, along with calendar cycles need to be determined to know when data is collected, which business information system performs the collection, and how the collections are set within calender and/or business cycles. Here, a calendar cycle takes on its common meaning.

A business cycle can be seasons such as the holiday season, the school year, and the like. Or a business cycle could be its financial year, tax year, or in the cases of some businesses where its year is thirteen 4-week months. Business information systems are triggered by their corresponding calender and business event cycles. Each such triggering is known as a business event. Without setting business information system activities within calendars and business cycles it will be difficult to know the currentness of the data that has been collected or to be accessed.

Business information systems are set within resource life cycle nodes of resources. Business information systems, when executed, cause the execution of the database object information systems, which, in turn, cause the state changes of database objects.

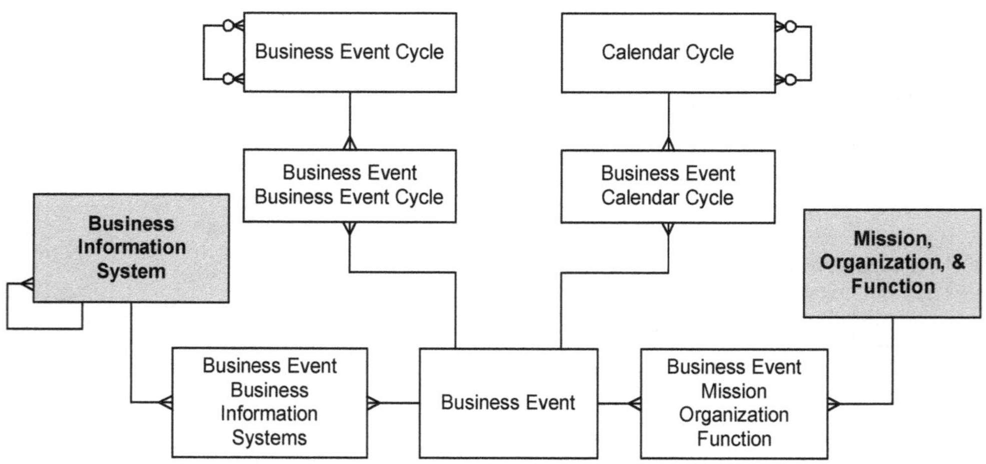

Figure 14. Business Events.

3.7.3 User Acceptance Test

User Acceptance Tests, depicted in Figure 15, are based on network structured collections of processes invoked within Use Case Events are mapped to View Columns. User Acceptance Test Steps are related to one or more Requirements.

User Acceptance Tests are requirements-based accepted tests that are deemed appropriate and necessary to determine the adequacy of a business information system. The requirements of Use Cases must be validated to be considered complete. User Acceptance Tests are related both to Use Cases and also to the View Columns that are employed to verify test accomplishment. View Columns are, in turn, mapped to the Operational Database and as appropriate to both compound and derived data elements.

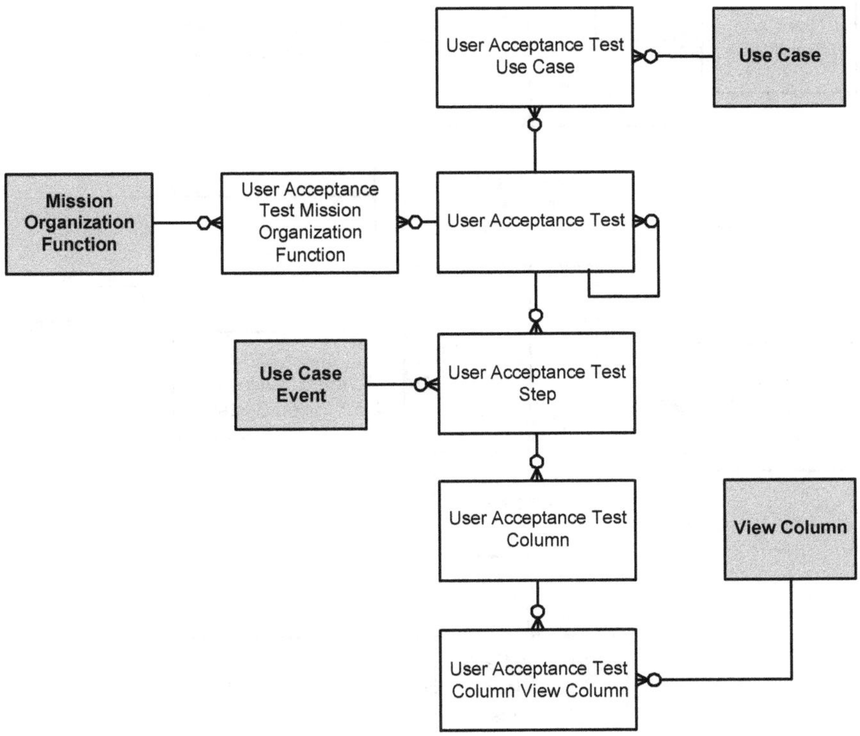

Figure 15. User Acceptance Tests.

3.7.4 Use Cases

Use Cases, depicted in Figure 16, enable the creation, updating, and interrelationships of detailed function model specifications. The use cases contain use case network structures, use case events, pre conditions, post conditions, special conditions, use case facts, and use case actors. These use case components are able to be interrelated with business information systems, database table columns, and Mission-Organization-Functions, and through those to Persons functioning within Positions.

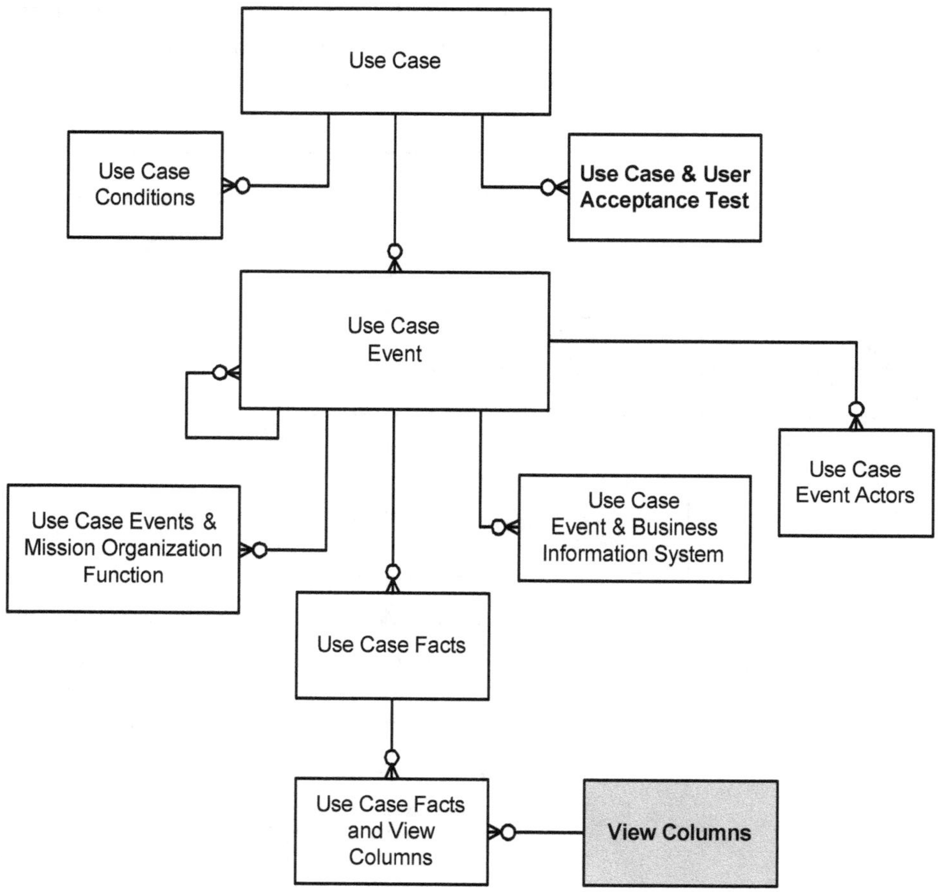

Figure 16. Use Cases.

3.7.5 Reports

The Reports Management, depicted in Figure 17, enables the specification of reports to be produced by the business information system. The reports consist of a report that can be contained in a network of report blocks. Each report can be hierarchically organized into report sections. Each report section can be mapped to serve the needs of one or more Mission-Organization-Function combinations. Report sections then contain report cells which are then mapped to view columns.

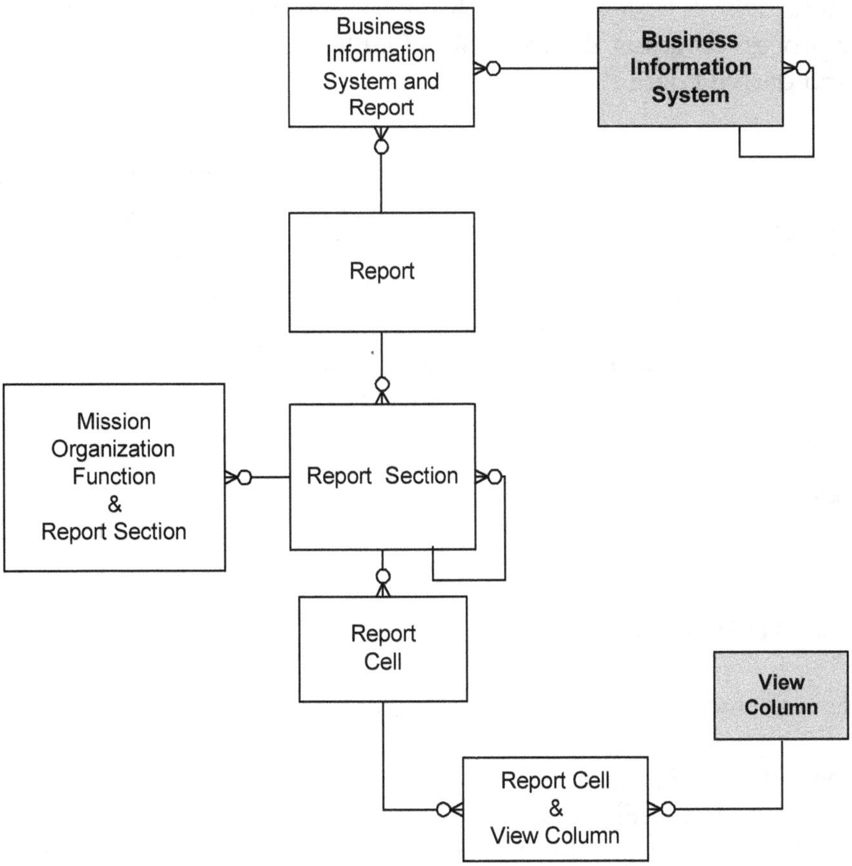

Figure 17. Reports.

3.8 Data Integrity Rules

Data Integrity Rules, depicted in Figure 18 exists in two parts: Specification and Binding. The rules are specified generically and can exist in network and/or hierarchical structured collections. The individual components of each data integrity rule actually consist of four classes of rules: Input, Select, Validate, and Action. Each rule is then mapped to the Implemented Database Model metadata object, Column.

The binding of each specified rule is to the closest of the data integrity rule's actual validation of the overall metadata component within which the data integrity rule exists. Included are: data elements, entities, attributes, tables, columns, DBMS tables, DBMS columns, views, view columns, database object table process columns, database object table processes, compound data elements, and derived data elements.

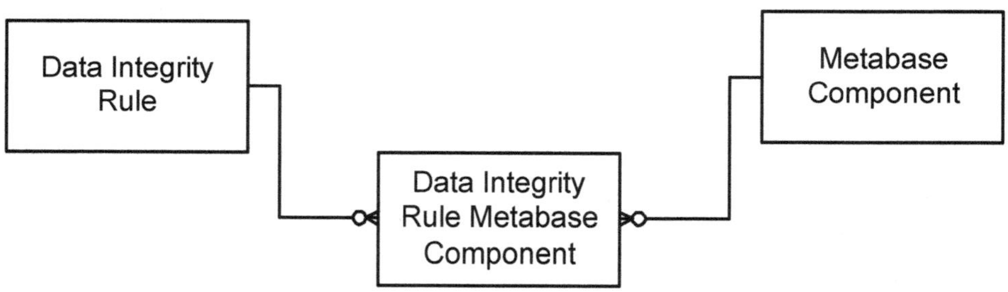

Figure 18. Data Integrity Rules.

3.9 Data Architecture

Data Architecture includes metadata from the following:

- Data Element Model (Figure 21)
- Specified Data Model (Figure 22)
- Implemented Database Model (Figure 23)
- Operational Database Model (Figure 24)
- Views (Figure 25)

Data model specifications, illustrated in Figure 19, are organized into five levels. At the highest level are the ISO 11179 data elements. At the lowest level are the View models that intersect business information systems.

The reason there are three levels of data models as well as a view model and the ISO 11179 data element model is to support an efficient and effective data sharing environment. Without all these five interrelated data models, the database designers and analysts will have to rely on memory, note cards, Visio diagrams, or other devices to know the precise details of data sharing specifications.

Even more important, these interrelated data models must exist within a multi-user, federated and distributed metadata repository system such as the Metabase System that, in turn, supports a universal source of quality data semantics. Without these models, data sharing specifications is more expensive, redundant, conflicting, and leads to more stove pipes. This time,

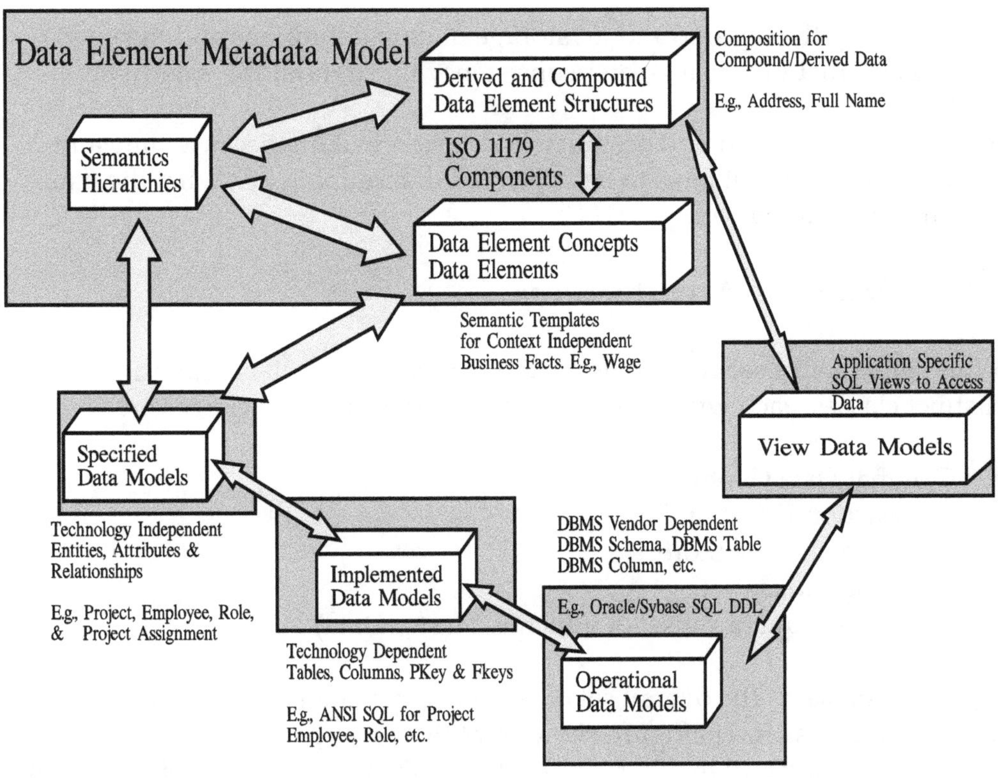

Figure 19. Five Data Model Levels.

however, the stove pipes are metadata stove pipes.
The key benefits associated with metadata management include:

- Assist top management in identifying the resources required to build a business information system.
- Provide discipline and control for the design process.
- Provide a structured approach to data model manufacturing.
- Enhance the business information system development process through the utilization of prior work.
- Provide a management facility for monitoring database projects.
- Allow for the non-redundant storage of data definitions and business policies that produce greater consistency throughout the enterprise.
- Increase the speed and accuracy in decision making because time and resources will not have to be expended determining just what the data and processes mean.

3.9.1 Database Architectures

While this should seem obvious, all databases are not alike. There are five distinct classes, each with their own characteristics. These classes are:

- Original Data Capture
- Transaction Data Staging Area
- Operational Data Store
- Data warehouse
- Reference Data (a subset of which is Master Data)

Figure 20 presents the overall set of relationships among these database architecture classes. The figure shows that the data proceeds from the left to the right, and over all the first four of the database classes, the reference data database classes crosses all four manages all commonly accessible data as well as data with restricted value domains.

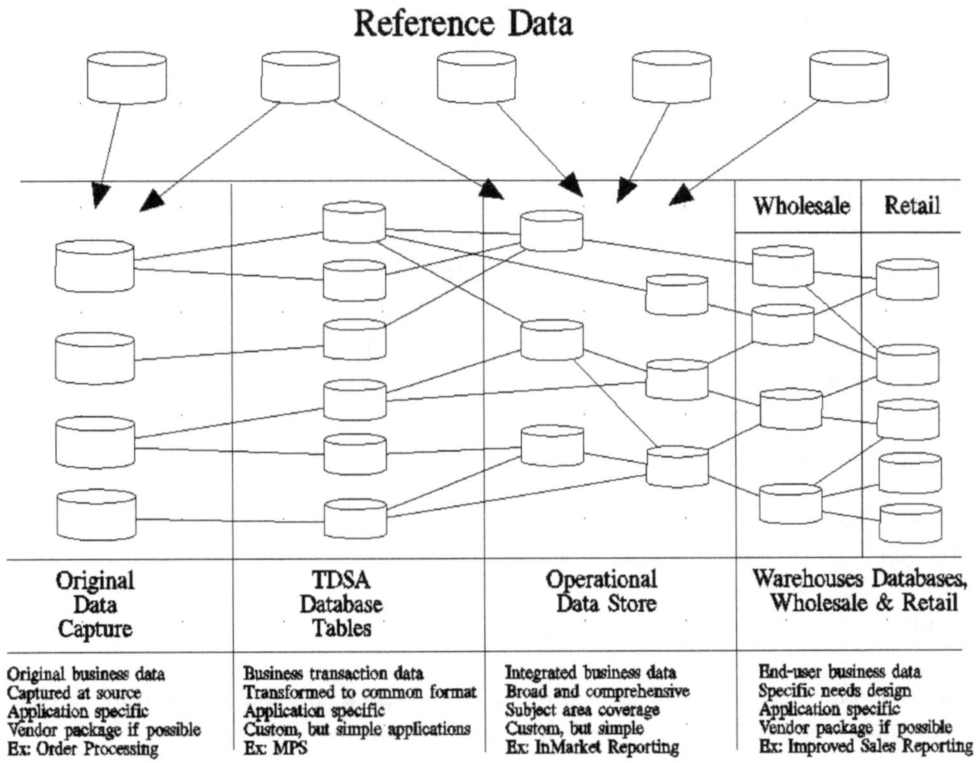

Figure 20. Database Architecture Classes.

3.9.1.1 Reference Data

Reference data, depicted across the top of Figure 20, is that set of data that is commonly employed across the other different classes of data. Examples of reference data include sets of data such as:

- Gender codes and names
- State codes and names
- Country codes and names
- Units of measure and names
- Currency codes, denominations, and names
- Standard address parts such as street (ST), road (RD), etc.
- Manufacturing parts, names, and descriptions

Reference data has distinct characteristics such as:

- Persistence
- Employed in longitudinal policy formulation
- Impacts multiple policy areas
- Enables fact discrimination and/or selection
- Break points for fact aggregation and statistical analysis
- Requires higher level of management approval
- Causes multiple negative impacts when changed
- Is not easily melded with other strategic data (zip | telephone = ???)
- Gives meaning to quantities (physical dimension, time dimensions)

There are six classes of reference data that must be addressed. These are:

- **Single Content Column**. A single column of reference data such as a person Gender (e.g., female and male), Gender. See current practice above.

- **Multiple Content Column**. Multiple columns that should be treated together.

- **Sequenced**. Single or multiple columns of reference data that proceed in a strict sequence. For example, Proposed, Draft, Final, and Revised.

- **Mapped Values**. Single or multiple columns of reference data that have changed values and/or meanings across time, or that represent a "transformed in" value from a set of inward interface processes or "transformed out" value for a set out outward interface processes. Mapped values may also represent a reduction in the quantity of "mapped to" values from a set of "mapped from" values. The converse is also possible.

- **Discrete Values**. Specific enumerated values that can be additionally allowed or disallowed. There can be multiple sets of discrete values, some allowed and other disallowed.

- **Range Of Values.** Specific ranges of values that can be additionally allowed or disallowed. There can be multiple sets of value ranges, some allowed and other disallowed.

Reference data is established through formally created projects that cause the reference data to be created, stored, reported and maintained. Reference data projects are critical to the business in that the business' fact data stored in the

Original Data Capture databases is categorized, summarized, validated, and reported by means of the reference data.

3.9.1.2 Original Data Capture

Original Data Capture databases, depicted on the left side of Figure 20, are those that capture all business facts. Prior to being stored in an Original Data Captures database, either the business data is manual, that is, customer orders, employment applications, hours worked but not yet recorded, and the like, or it is automated but resides in an external source. The characteristics of this operational data are that it's detailed atomic data rather than summarized. The data is accurate as of the last update. The databases that contain this type of data are stable and long lasting with normalized data structures. These databases make heavy use of reference data to ensure that it is understood across all users. Because of reference data and because of very extensive integrity checking no invalid data should ever be allowed.

Original Data Capture databases are generally tuned for the transaction capture, storage and update of data. Correctness and integrity are of paramount importance. Performance is clearly secondary. The databases are specifically oriented toward specific applications such as order capture, order processing, staff time recording and reporting, and payroll. Because these applications are very narrow in scope, they are commonly acquired as commercial off the shelf (COTS) packages.

3.9.1.3 Transaction Data Staging Area

Transaction data staging area (TDSA) databases, depicted to the immediate right of Original Data Capture, are the beginning of integrated data semantics for the entire enterprise. The individual Original Data Capture database applications may have both specialized and localized semantics. These localized semantics may exist throughout the enterprise because of different languages, laws, and existing sets of application packages that existed prior to migrating to an enterprise wide data architecture.

To handle all these situations, data translators/transformers are created that take localized data values and meanings and translate/transform them to enterprise-wide values and meanings. The transaction data, now understood through enterprise-wide semantics is placed in a staging area for a specific period of time. At the end of the specified time period, the data is dropped from the staging area. Applications requiring data from the staging area only have to know where it is and the set of semantics that govern it.

The fundamental role of data within the TDSA is to relieve the individual Original Data Capture databases from having to contain enterprise wide semantics and to relieve the Operational Data Store databases from having to know the location of the individual Original Data Capture database applications and from having to know the values and semantics for each Original Data Capture database.

3.9.1.4 Operational Data Store

An Operational Data Store (ODS) database, depicted in the middle of Figure 20, embraces a wide area of a business such as all finance, all human resources, all sales, orders and marketing. The data for these integrated databases is taken from the various TDSA databases and is combined into one overall database. There may be a database in ODS database class that contains sales and customer management that ODS database may well be an amalgamation of data from the following databases:

- Sales organization management that defines and manages all sales regions, districts and territories

- Human resources that provide the proper information about each salesperson who is assigned to a territory

- Customer management who ensures that all the customers are properly identified, classified, and managed

- Order processing that receives, tracks, and performs all order management through to actual shipment.

- Product inventory management that receives product into product warehouses, fills orders, and begins the process of product distribution

- Manufacturing which transforms raw products into finished goods

- Product distribution which receives filled orders from inventory and delivers them to the customers.

- Accounts payable and receivable which financially accounts for orders and invoicing

These Original Data Capture database systems provide transaction data to the enterprise TDSA which are represented in Figure 20 through the "lines" that connect the Original Data Capture databases through the TDSA databases to the ODS databases. The data loading and update systems that feed the ODS databases take data from the TDSA and load and/or update the ODS databases.

In addition to the data integration route, some data from one database may certainly be required in others. For example, sales organization management assigns customers and sales persons to specific sales organizations such as regions, districts and territories. The data from these "cousin" applications would be available in a read-only manner. Whether the references from one sales organization management database that lists the current district manager as Bruce Baine does so through a "hotlink" or through a week integrity check routine is a matter of technology, not of fundamental design.

3.9.1.5 Data Warehouses

Data warehouse databases, depicted on the right side of Figure 20, are a special class of databases for two reasons:

- No updating other than summarization occurs
- All data has its units and granularities synchronized

Simply put, data, as a warehouse item represents a finished good. No more "manufacturing" or "finishing" is going on. In the case of data that means no updating. The data (warehouse item) may be selected according to a specific order and may even be palletized with other items of the same or different types and sent to a more localized distribution point. Because of these similarities with the concept of product warehouse the concept of a data warehouse arose.

A very early proponent of data warehouses, Bill Inmon (Prism Solutions of Littleton, Colorado) defines it to be a collection of integrated, subject-oriented databases designed to support the decision support function, where each unit of data is relevant to some moment in time. The data warehouse thus contains atomic and lightly summarized data.

Ron Ross, another data warehouse proponent defines a data warehouse to be a structured database that stores consolidated data for decision support from production-level files or databases.

Another definition for warehouse comes from Vidette Poe who defines a data warehouse as the [data] foundation of a decision support system (Building a Data Warehouse, Prentice Hall, 1996).

Starting in the early 2000s, there has been a data modeling "battle" within the data warehouse community. The proponent of traditional modeling, commonly called E-R modeling has been Bill Inmon. A very different data warehouse modeling technique is called "Star Schemas," and its proponent is Ralph Kimball. The traditional technique results in data warehouse databases that are large collection of SQL tables interrelated through primary-to-foreign key relationships.

The Star Schema data warehouse modeling technique has a "fact" table at the center of each "star" and a series of slowly changing dimensions radiating out from the fact-table center.

Data warehouses come in two flavors: wholesale and retail. The critical difference between the two is in the area of size and scope. A retail data warehouse is clearly smaller because it contains less data. For example, there may be a customer profile retail data warehouse that contains all relevant customer information for the Yellow Knife sales territory. The wholesale data warehouse might be the one that contains all the customer sales information for all the Northwest Territories of Canada.

A retail data warehouse also differs in scope in that its focus may be narrower than that of its source wholesale warehouse. For example, all the customer profile information for hospital customers for a particular segment of a product line versus all the customers for all the product lines.

3.9.2 Data Element Model

Data Element metadata, depicted in Figure 21, contains the semantics for business facts. These facts are set within ISO 11179 data element metadata standard. The ISO 11179 architecture starts with Concepts that are to be represented through data. Defined as well are Conceptual Value Domains for these Concepts. Concepts and Conceptual Value Domains are brought together resulting in Data element Concepts, which are, in turn, are set within contexts of Concepts and Conceptual Value Domains.

Names of the data element concepts, data elements, and down through to attributes of entities and columns of databases need to be established within taxonomies of well-developed words that set out semantics. Once set out, the semantic hierarchies enable automatically constructed names, definitions, and abbreviations. While the automatic nature is of value, even more valuable is all the business fact semantics that is now controlled and managed.

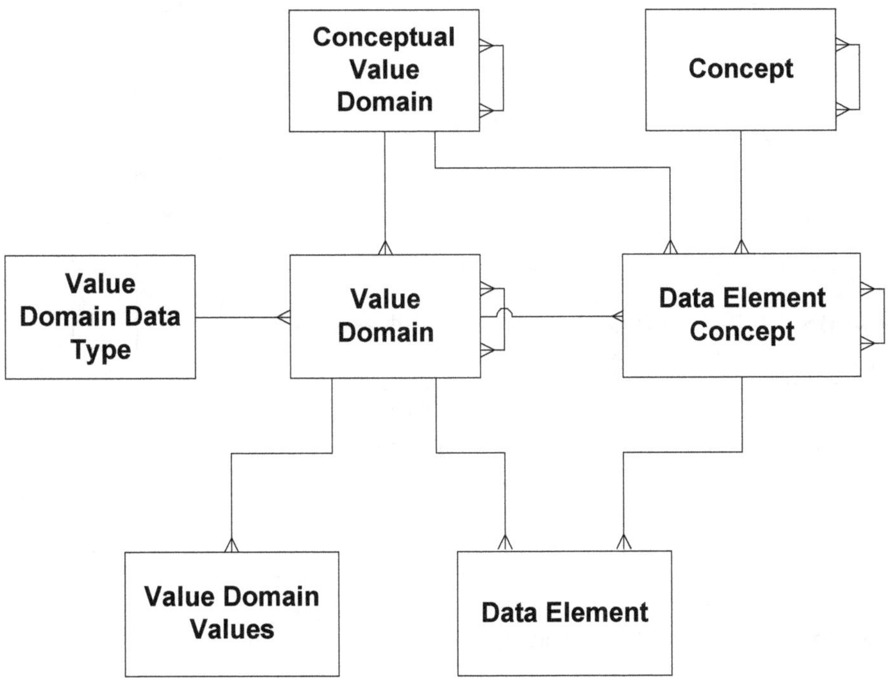

Figure 21. Data Element Metadata Model.

3.9.3 Specified Data Model

Specified Data Model metadata, depicted in Figure 22, represent standardized templates through which actual data models can be manufactured. Constructed this way, along with all the attributes of the Specified Data Model entities are mapped to ISO 11179 data elements, there is an umbrella of enterprise-wide data semantics to support high quality database schemas for data collection, evolution, management, and sharing.

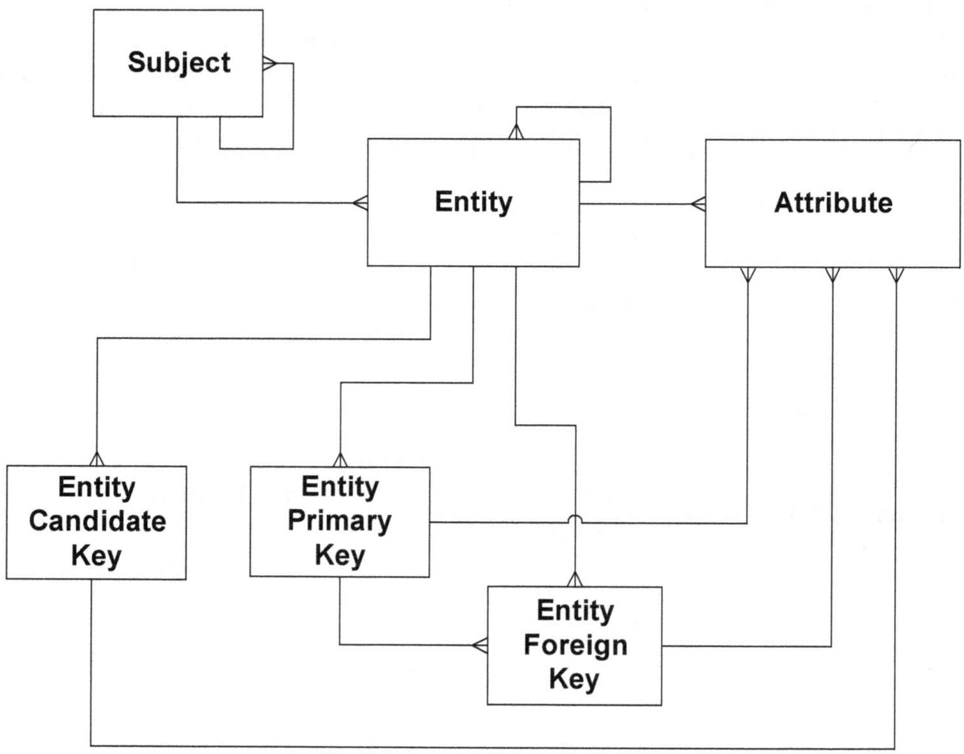

Figure 22. Specified Metadata Model.

3.9.4 Implemented Database Model

Implemented database models, depicted in Figure 23 define the database schema models of tables and columns. Each collection of tables and columns is mapped to a database object class, and is either an entire database object class or a proper subset of one. Implemented database models are mapped back to their ancestors' data model templates of subjects, entities and attributes. The relationship between implemented and specified data models is through the mapping of an attribute to a column. This enables the multiple

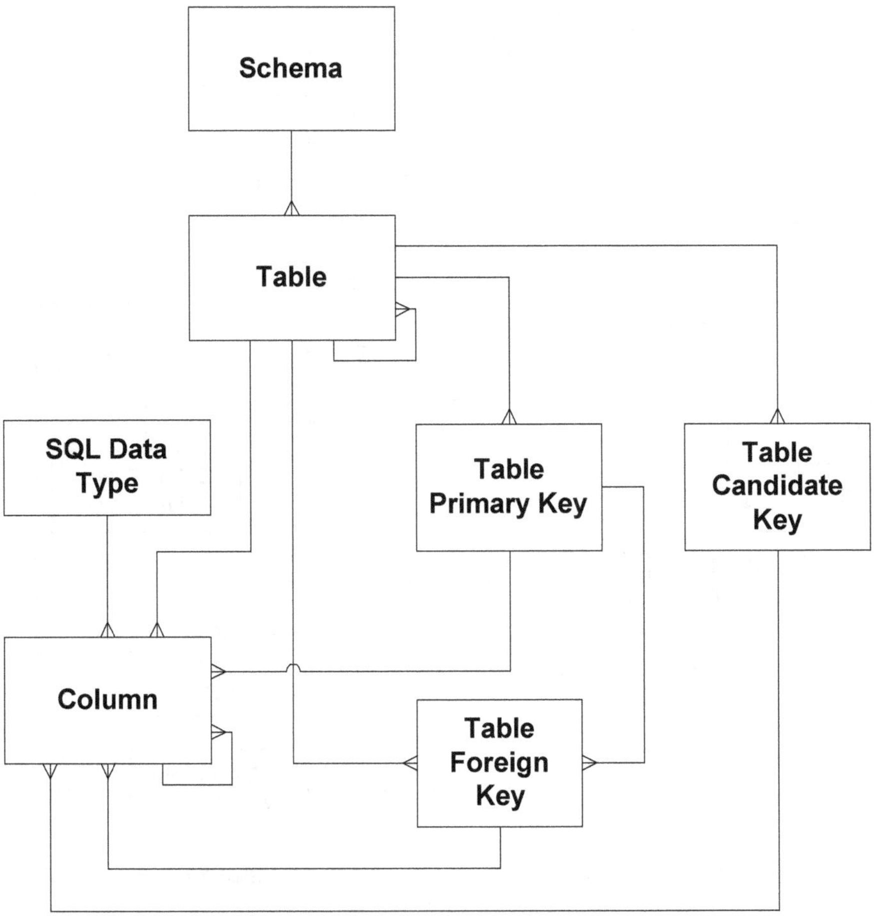

Figure 23. Implemented Database Metadata Model.

use of a whole or partial entity within the same Implemented Database Model table, and across multiple Implemented Database Model schemas.

3.9.5 Operational Database Model

Operational database models, depicted in Figure 24, are the database schema models of shared operational data. Rows of data from one or more Operational Database Model tables (called DBMS Tables) are exchanged

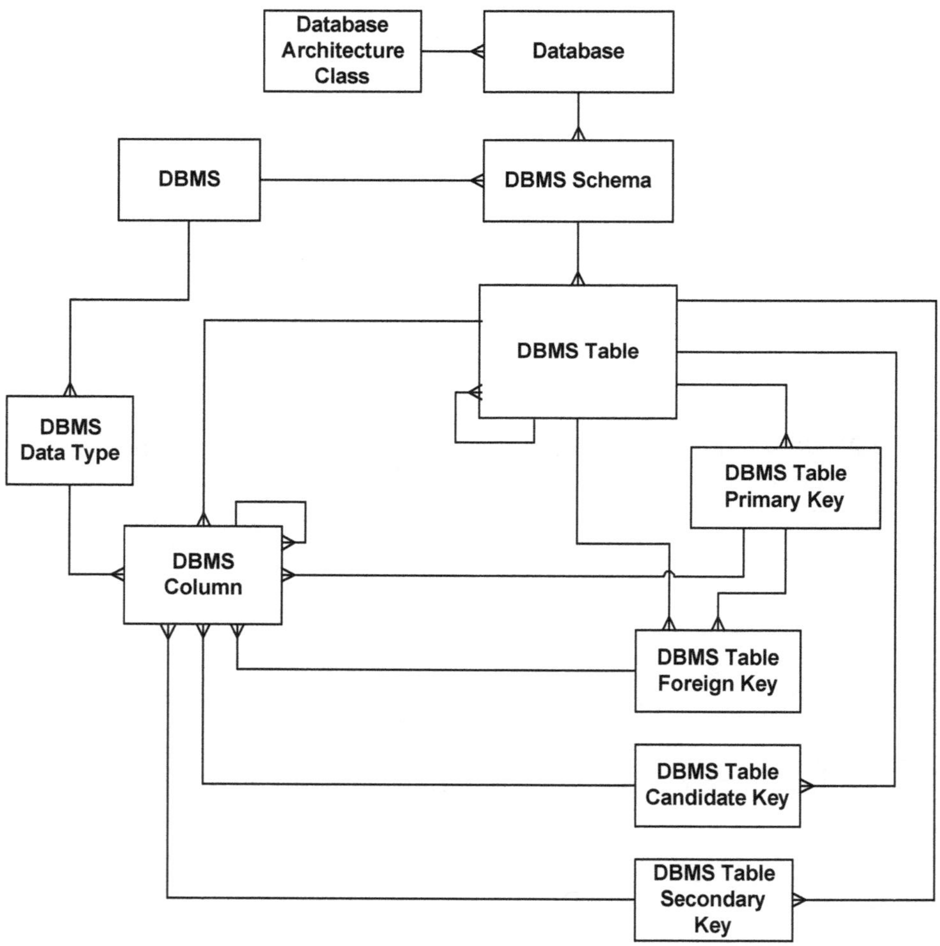

Figure 24. Operational Database Metadata Model.

between and among business information systems. The relationship between operational and implemented data models is through the mapping of an Implemented Database Schema Table column to a DBMS column. This enables the multiple use of a whole or partial table specifications within the same Operational Database Model tables, and across multiple Operational Database Model schemas.

3.9.6 View Model

View models, depicted in Figure 25, represent the specification of the data exchange between a database through the database management system to the business information system.

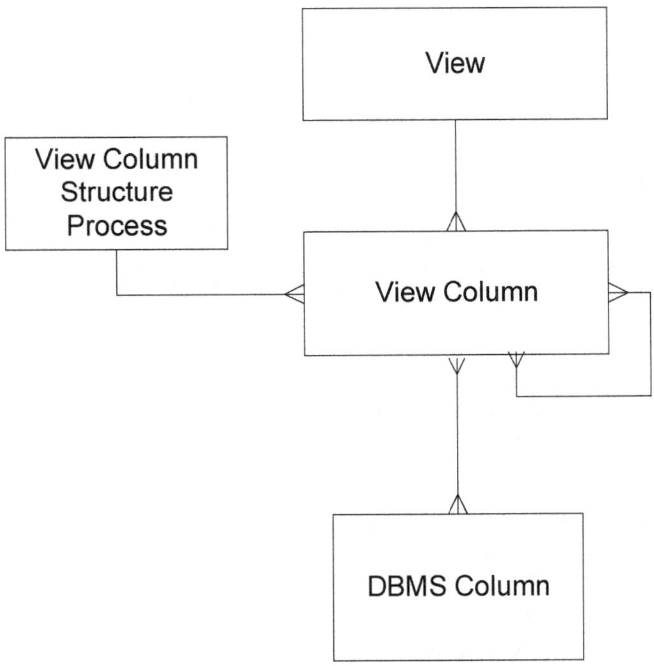

Figure 25. View Metadata Model.

3.10 Project Management

Project Management, depicted in Figure 26, is founded on the principal that project management data is just another form of metadata, and that all the other metadata model metadata can be appropriately integrated with project management metadata.

The Project Management module is founded on templates. These exist for: project, deliverable, and task. Once a project template is picked project deliverables and project tasks are generated form their corresponding templates and set up for full specification. That is, the adding of work environment factors, skill levels of assigned staff, and the identification of the

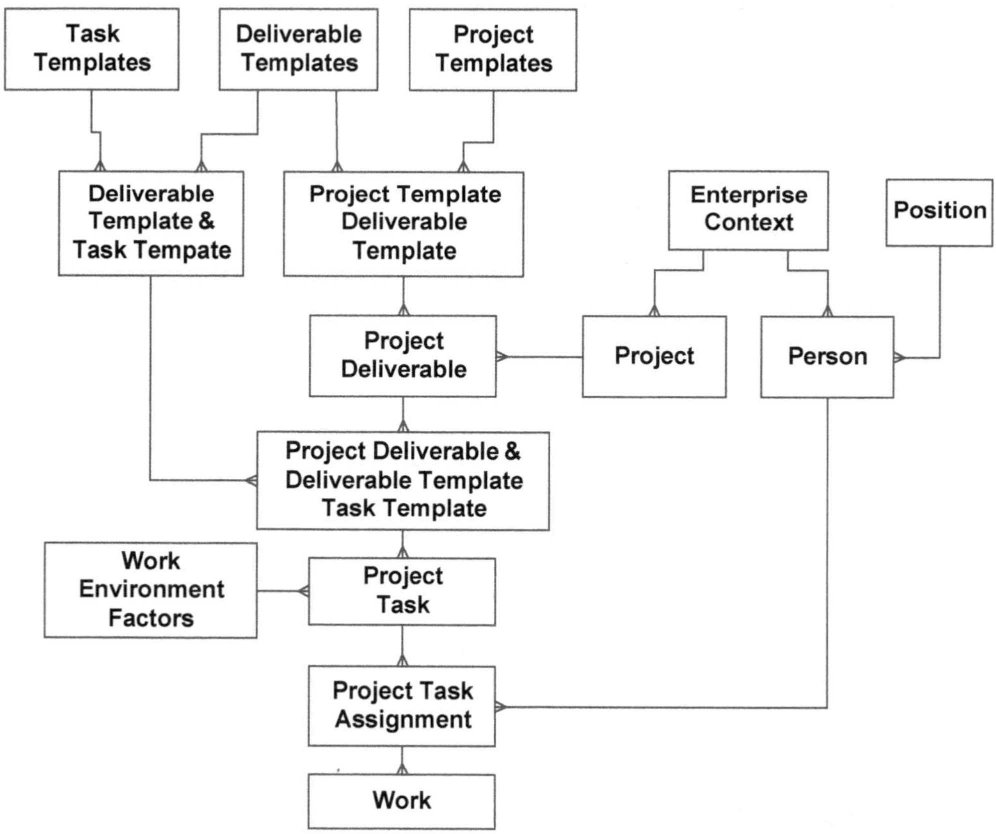

Figure 26. Project Management.

particular Resource Life Cycle node that is the target of the project. As the project progresses, work-accomplishments records are stored so that earned-value reporting can be generated.

3.11 Governance

Governance, depicted in Figure 27, enables the allocation of a specific person within the context of a Mission-Organization-Function-Position to be directly responsible for the integrity and correctness of one or more specific work product instances. An example might be a specifically named Implemented Data Model Schema for Inventory Management. By that assignment, that person is also responsible for all the work products related to that specific schema, including all the Inventory Management's tables, columns, keys, and relationships. That extended responsibility extends even further for all column semantic modifiers, data use modifiers and value domains.

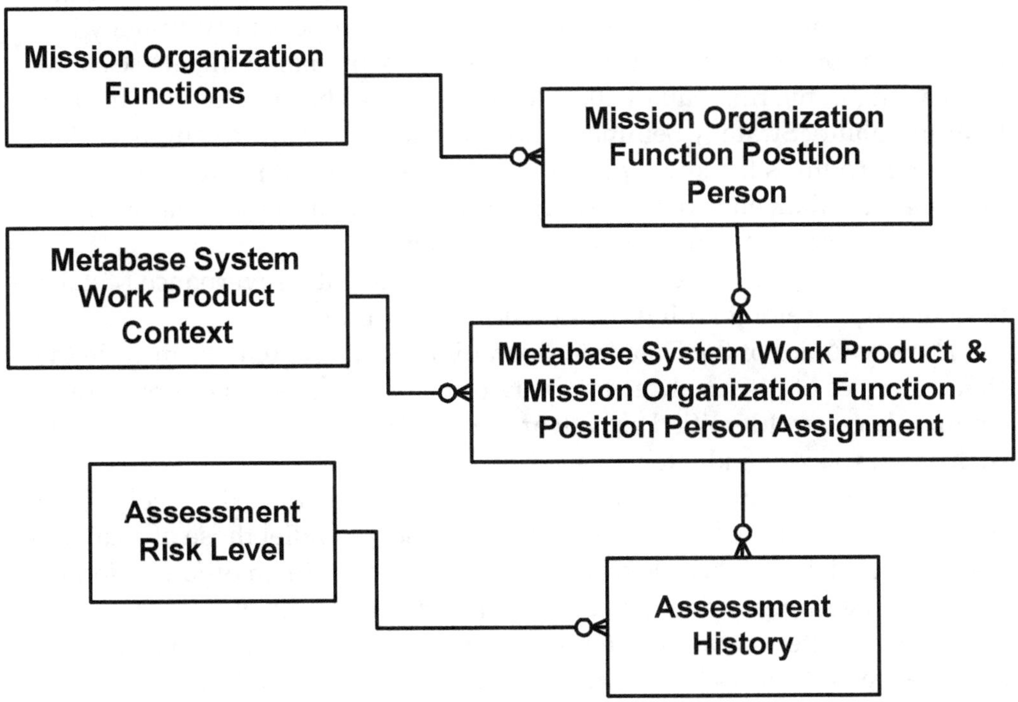

Figure 27. Governance Management.

Some of the governance assignments are assigned multiple times. For example, semantic modifiers and data use modifiers can be directly assigned to another person. Because of this, whenever there is a question about the meaning of a semantic modifier and data use modifier assigned to a given column, that person should be consulted as well. Because of this, many Governance work product assignments are actually accomplished by governance teams.

The Metabase System assignment strategy allows for the history of those assignments.

3.12 Governance Summary

The goal of Whitemarsh efforts over the past 35+ years has been to assist clients in the development of quality database environments. That is, environments where data sharing is common, efficient, and effective. To this end, Whitemarsh, starting in late 2003, began a formal definition of a strategy for achieving data sharing. Whitemarsh's data interoperability strategy is manifest in courses, seminars, workshops, the Whitemarsh Metabase System.

Starting in the first half of 2006 Whitemarsh has been delivering a Data Interoperability Strategy Seminar. This seminar about how to engineer data sharing introduces the key topics and scenarios involved in creating interoperable data environments. The ultimate goal of the seminar is to teach the steps necessary to build shared data systems.

In the second half of 2016, Whitemarsh released its Governance Metabase System module along with its companion user guide.

The key topics of the Data Interoperability Strategy seminar include the characteristics of governance and the two classes of governance errors that commonly occur. Identified as well are the problems that commonly occur such as complexity and latency.

Also presented in this data interoperability seminar are the levels of data sharing than can be achieved. These levels closely parallel those of a capability maturity model, and these levels can be assessed within an organization in generally the same manner as can software or data maturity.

The Data Interoperability seminar presents an overall framework for governance and shows how common frameworks such as Zachman, Enterprise Architecture, and the Knowledge Worker affect the achievement of governance.

The seminar describes the key technological components of any really first-class interoperable data environment and provides examples of each including why these technological components are so important.

The seminar presents the overall contract and construction of a metadata repository environment critical component to a success strategy. Described as well is the necessary governance environment including an infrastructure, Communities of Interest, key processes, success measures and the necessary training and tools.

The seminar then details the various scenarios that must occur to achieve a governance environment including enterprise architectures, business information systems plans, data model engineering, and, then both reverse and forward engineering. Collectively these scenarios cause the creation of and enable the maintenance and evolution of governance environments.

The seminar concludes with the key measures and returns on investment, and an overall summary and "way ahead," and most important, a questionnaire that polls the attendees on the strategies covered and the level of importance these concepts should receive in their corporate homes. The questionnaire is provided in Table 18. Shown in the table is a tabulation of 14 data management issues presented during the seminar. The percent values indicate the level of agreement the respondents expressed about the issue. As can be inferred, governance over these issues is quite important. The companies that had attendees at the seminar are listed in Table 18.

The high level metadata models enable IT organizations to have their own governance infrastructure. With this governance infrastructure, an IT executive can know that the data being used comes from a given system is high quality and is linked via metadata mappings to other systems that, for example run every night.

The Metabase System's data models enable integration and non-redundancy across the complete set of Enterprise Architecture, and IT specifications that ultimately drive the construction of databases and business information systems. These data models include enterprise missions, organizations, functions, and the database business information systems metadata used to represent state transforms of critical enterprise resources. These data models also enable the discovery of which resources are "naked," and which are updated by redundant and semantically conflicted systems and/or databases, etc.

Data Interoperability Strategy Survey. Responses from about 20% of attendees.				
	Percent			
Questions	Strongly Agree	Agree	Disagree	Strongly Disagree
Organizations would benefit from a comprehensive data management program including courses, methodologies, workshops, etc.	68	30	2	0
Organizations would benefit if databases (not DBMS) had consistent semantics for names for table columns across schemas.	78	20	0	2
Organizations would benefit from automatic Data Element, Attribute and Column naming and abbreviations built with consensus-based word lists and phrases (taxonomies).	53	47	0	0
Organizations would benefit from automatic Data Element, Attribute and Column definitions derived from contexts, value domains, etc.	50	42	8	0
Organizations would benefit if databases (not DBMS) had consistent semantics for value domains.	69	29	2	0
Semantics should be inheritable from ISO 11179 Data elements to attributes, and from attributes to columns.	33	67	0	0
There is value in having data model templates that can be used in defining column collections within tables.	53	47	0	9
XML Schemas should be generated from a foundation of well designed and integrated data models.	51	45	4	0
Organizations would benefit from metadata repositories that support metadata integration and non-redundancy across projects, departments, etc. That is, define-once and use many-	82	18	0	0

Data Interoperability Strategy Survey. Responses from about 20% of attendees.				
	Percent			
Questions	Strongly Agree	Agree	Disagree	Strongly Disagree
times.				
Organizations would benefit from metadata repositories that are part of the everyday work process rather than a post implementation documentation effort.	86	12	2	0
End-users would benefit if they had access to metadata repositories for names, definitions, and the like.	82	16	2	0
Organizations would benefit from metadata repositories if the repositories could capture, report and support update of analysis and design work products in an integrated non-redundant manner.	64	36	0	0
Project quality and work-speed would likely benefit if supported by comprehensive metadata repositories.	71	29	0	0
Organizations would benefit from metadata management strategies supported by both bottom-up reverse engineering, and top-down new database (not DBMS) manufacturing.	57	41	2	0
Average of Percent	64	34	1	1

Table 18. Survey Questions and Percent Results from Data Management Strategy Seminars.

Governance Strategy Seminar Participant Organizations

Allstate Insurance
American Airlines
Bank of Montreal
Bill Chadwick Consulting
Blue Cross Blue Shield of Texas
BOM Financial Group
BTE Architects
Canadian Tire
Cap Gemini Energy
Caremark
CCC Information Systems
Chartwell, Inc.
Chevron Texaco
CIBC
Cingular
Citi Group
City of Toronto
CNA Insurance
Country Wide
Coventry Health Care
CUNA Mutual Group
Discover Financial Services
DOFASCO, Inc
East Neuk Associates
Elkay Manufacturing
Essential Futures
FedEx Services
Great Lakes Education Loan Services
HBC
HesselLink & Company
IBM Global Services
IESO (Independent Electrical System Operator)
J.P. Morgan Chase
Kohls Department Stores
Northern Trust
Railroad Retirement Board
RBC Financial Group
RR Donnelley
SentientPoint, Inc
Signma Systems
Solucient, LLC
Southwest Airlines
The Economical Insurance Group
The Burlington Northern and Santa Fe Railroad Company
U.S. Department of Homeland Security
United Airlines
Wallstreet Consulting
WEA Trust
WIS DoT
WPS Insurance

The high level metadata models enable IT organizations to have their own governance infrastructure. With this governance infrastructure, an IT executive can know that the data being used comes from a given system is high quality and is linked via metadata mappings to other systems that, for example run every night.

The Metabase System's data models enable integration and non-redundancy across the complete set of Enterprise Architecture, and IT specifications that ultimately drive the construction of databases and business information systems. These data models include enterprise missions, organizations, functions, and the database business information systems metadata used to represent state transforms of critical enterprise resources. These data models also enable the discovery of which resources are "naked," and which are updated by redundant and semantically conflicted systems and/or databases, etc.

Because of the set of meta entities that comprise Business Events, Business Event Calendars, and Calendars, the processes including their sequence and updated databases can be known. For example that feeder systems are run every day but the sales forecast is run Quarterly. Where are the most current numbers? The Metabase System supports answers to those types of questions.

Because of the ISO 11179 Data element metadata meta-entities, you can trace data types and precision. If one column is "99" and another is "99v99" and if the "99v99" is rolled into the "99", then what happened to the "cents?"

Because of the Specified Data Model meta entities (subject-entity-attribute) you can trace granularity to make sure that the granularity is synchronized. Suppose one table has a primary key component of Year and Month. But another has Year, Month, and Day? Which is more precise? When you extract-transform-and-load (ETL) data from the YMD rows into the YM table, does the YM table represent last, rolling, highest, lowest, who knows?

All of this must be wrapped within a Governance Architecture that includes 1) personal assignment responsibility, 2) the generation of appropriate governance managed projects, and 3) access to the specific Metadata system stored metadata for the work products that is the target of governance.

3.13 Questions and Exercises

1. Metadata are the "business records" of Information Technology support of the enterprise. Do you have a metadata database, that is, a Metabase? If so, does it address the full spectrum of metadata set out in Chapter 2? If yes, is it integrated and non-redundant? If yes, what has been the effect on the creation, use, and maintenance of "IT's books?" Have you reduced costs? Increased productivity? Decreased the risk of maintenance? Have you increased the quality (i.e., interoperability) of your data? Can it be used concurrently Client/Server and over the Internet? If no, why not?

2. Is your metadata too narrow in scope? "Technical" only? "Technical," here means metadata of only operational databases and systems. If technical only, how do you define enterprise architectures, business information systems planning, data models or business information systems?

3. Has there been a "my way or highway" solution and approach as opposed to an enterprise-wide multi-level approach for metadata management that is enterprise-wide and is wrapped in a governance architecture? Provide examples from within your own organization.

4. In Section 3.1, do you agree with the characterization of the problems associated with a lack of comprehensive metadata? If yes, why? If not, why not? Provide examples from within your own organization.

5. The point of Section 3.2 is that all metadata must exist in a framework. It illustrates the use of the Knowledge Worker Framework as a mechanism of metadata characterization and organization. What are the good and bad points of having a framework? Can there be multiple frameworks? Can there, or "must" there be shared metadata across frameworks? How else can multiple frameworks be interrelated? Aren't frameworks just "windows" into enterprise-wide metadata databases? Provide examples from within your enterprise of integrated frameworks and common metadata. What has been the benefit? Have such frameworks enabled the avoidance of "stove-pipes" of data and business information systems?

6. Section 3.3 describes a Governance Framework. It further identifies six contained architectures. How are these three architectures interrelated? Can these architectures stand alone? Should they? How should they be done, one after the other or independently? What are the advantages and drawbacks to the different approaches?

7. Do you agree with the interrelationships among the figures of this chapter, and those in Chapters 5 and 6 that depict data and process models? If you agree, how would you organize development teams? What should be the key positions, roles, duties, and responsibilities? What should be the work products?

8. Sections 3.4 through 3.9 describe and outline the various contained metadata models for achieving shared data across the enterprise. Do you agree with the high level depictions of these models? Do they convey a coherent story? If you agree with the approach, why? If not, why not? Provide examples from within your own organization.

9. Section 3.10 describes the project management approach that enables complete integration of projects, deliverables, tasks, skills and work environment factors. If there is only a stand-alone project management system how can this level of integration be achieved?

10. Section 3.11 describes the overall process for instigation and recording the assigned responsibilities for governance across the enterprise. If governance is not integrated within all the work products, how can it be managed? How can all the work products that are be interrelated be discovered and integrated in unison?

11. Section 3.12 sets out questions regarding metadata development and management. Are these the right questions? If you took an informal survey within your organization, what would your tallies for "Strongly Agree" through "Strongly Disagree" be? Do this survey and the tallies make the case for metadata management? If you agree, why? If not, why not? Provide examples from within your own organization.

4

Governance Mission

4.1 Governance Mission

Governance not only manages the auditing and evaluation of necessary metadata specifications of the enterprise to insure integrity and correctness, but also the governance of shared databases and business information systems so as to achieve maximum data sharing. In support of that mission there are two overall subordinate missions:

- Governance Program Management.
- Governance Assessments Development Management.

4.2 Governance Program Management

Governance Program Management involves the policies and procedures associated with engineering and operating the overall governance program within the enterprise. Included within the overall program management are:

- The governance program itself.
- Project and community of interest engineering and management.
- The identification, specification, and management of the various metadata products that are contained in various metadata development projects.
- The set of business events that track the progress of building Governance Assessments.
- The organizations and positions within the organizations involved in

managing the Governance Program and in managing the metadata products.

- The functions necessary for accomplishing Governance Program activities.
- The overall IT deliverables that contain the metadata product specifications.
- The rules that govern the correct operation of the Governance Program.

Involved also are the creation and management of all Governance Assessments that are identified and developed.

The overall goal of the Governance Program is to instigate and manage shared governance projects. While each shared data project must stand on its own, the collections of shared data projects need to fit within a broader scope of enterprise shared data. Some projects rely on data that is created by multiple governance projects. To ensue maximum shared data across these multiple sets of shared data, one or more Communities of Interest have as their domain the collective-shared domain of other Communities of Interest.

The Governance Assessments Development Board within the Governance Program committee ensures that the operations of the various Communities of Interest are in accordance with the Governance Program's scope and program objectives. Included in this are the creation and management of Governance Program master schedules, lists of Governance projects, adherence to schedules, and other programmatic administrative matters such as a central document register and databases, websites, budgets, financial reports, and completeness, and quality evaluations of Community of Interest developed and maintained Governance Assessments.

4.3 Governance Assessments Development Management

Governance Assessments within the Governance Program are developed by a series of technical committees within its overall Community of Interest. Each technical committee builds metadata products that contain the specifications of the enterprise along with its IT databases and business information systems that must be built, tested, and managed as they operate to achieve the mission of enterprise-wide governance. Rigor is maintained through all these recognized system engineering practices. The technical committees over which governance must exist are:

- Enterprise Architecture
- Operations
- Systems Engineering and Architecture
- Data Modeling
- Test and Evaluation
- Configuration Control

4.3.1 Enterprise Architecture Technical Committee

The purpose of the Enterprise Architecture Technical Committee is to model the enterprise as a whole. The Enterprise Architecture Technical Committee provides advice to all other technical committees as it is within the context of the enterprise's overall architecture that governance is defined and managed. The key components included in enterprise architecture that require governance are:

- Missions
- Organizations
- Functions
- Information Needs Analysis
- Resource Life Cycle Analysis
- Database Objects
- Documents & Forms
- Requirements

Governed specifically, the Enterprise Architecture Technical Committee:

- Identifies and describes the enterprise missions that are the essence of the enterprise.

- Identifies and describes the enterprise organizations that enable the work of the enterprise to be accomplished.

- Identifies the relationships between missions and organizations.

- Identifies and describes the enterprise functions that are performed by persons within positions in support of the enterprise.

- Identifies and describes the relationships between mission-organizations and functions.

- Identifies and describes the enterprise information needs required by functions within organizations that fulfill missions.

- Identifies and describes the key characteristics of information needs.

- Identifies and describes the relationships between enterprise information needs and mission-organization-functions.

- Identifies and describes the resources that define the scope of the work of then enterprise

- Identifies and describes the resource life cycle nodes that represent the states transformations of a resource.

- Identifies and describes the relationships between enterprise information needs and resource life cycle nodes.

- Identifies and describes the relationships between resources through enablement vectors between a source Resource Life Cycle Node and a target Resource Life Cycle Node.

- Identifies and describes the relationship between a Resource Life Cycle Node and the database objects within databases that serve to achieve the state represented by the Resource Life Cycle Node.

- Identifies and describes the relationship between a Resource Life Cycle Node and the business information system that serve to achieve the state represented by the Resource Life Cycle Node.

- Identifies and describes the scope, purpose, and nature of database object classes and how they are to be used to accomplish significant policies of the enterprise.

- Identifies and describes the data structures necessary for each database object class including the specific table-based data structures, the specification of the processes that ensure correct database object table record inserts, deletes, and modifications.

- Identifies and describes the states though which database objects proceed in the initiation and life cycle of database objects that reflect the achievement of the purpose of database object classes.

- Identifies and describes the database object information systems that move a database object from one state to the next in a coherent and stage-based correctness process.

- Identifies and describes the various documents and forms that are necessary to fully represent the accomplishment of missions across the enterprise.

- Identifies and describes the specification and intended content of documents that need to exist and be allocated to Metabase System created metadata, and if appropriate to various View Columns of data that is captured and managed by Business Information Systems.

- Identifies and describes the specification and intended content of forms that need to exist as they represent the initial source of data that would be stored in the Metabase System created metadata, and the various View Columns of data that is captured and managed by Business Information Systems.

- Identifies and describes the various requirements that are known at the start of a metadata-based component of the Metabase System including for example, Missions, Organizations, Functions, Business Events, databases and Business information Systems.

- Identifies and describes the various requirements that are discovered during the creation and maintenance of metadata-based components of the Metabase System including for example, Missions, Organizations, Functions, Business Events, databases and Business information Systems.

- Identifies and describes the detailed specifications of requirements and exactly the identifications of the various metadata-based components that represent the accomplishment of or adherence to the requirements.

4.3.2 Operations Technical Committee

The purpose of operations is to model the relevant aspects of the Business Information Systems (operation's perspective) to the Community of Interest solution. The operational modeling discipline is concerned with understanding the program and doctrinal context within the Community of Interest solution, developing the operational requirements, developing the Community of Interest solution's operational structure, behavior and performance, identifying and modeling the operational information needs, and developing the operational test cases that will be used to validate the Community of Interest solution. The Operations Technical Committee provides operational advice to all other technical committees and operational support to technical groups on an as required basis. Governed specifically, the Operations Technical Committee:

- Identifies user/operational aspects of the work products that visibly show adherence to Governance Assessments requirements throughout the appropriate organizational levels.

- Identifies and prioritizes data models in order to achieve both horizontal and vertical implementation and adherence to Governance Assessments.

- Identify and develop possible new governance projects and recommend change proposals on existing governance projects.

- Validate governance adherence to data integrity rules that supports horizontal and vertical information exchanges.

- Analyzes governance aspects of operational processes to ensure enterprise-wide adherence.

- Identifies and takes heed of lessons learned from other governance initiatives and deployments.

- Provides user and operational guidance to other the Community of Interest technical committees in the development and/or execution of work plans, and ensures that the governance solution meets operational requirements.
- Validates operational aspects of the implemented governance efforts.
- Develops detailed work plans to ensure the accomplishment of the Governance Program objectives.
- Defines the overall operational architecture for the Governance Program.
- Defines measures of success (effectiveness and performance) for Governance Assessments operational tests and validation.
- Defines operational test cases and scenarios for operational tests and validation.
- Integrates with other Community of Interest technical committees, and other Communities of Interest as necessary.

4.3.3 Systems Engineering & Architecture Technical Committee

The purpose of the system modeling discipline is to model the relevant governance aspects of the Business Information Systems (system's perspective). The system modeling discipline is concerned with: understanding the governance context for the system, developing the system's requirements, developing the system's governance structure, required governance behavior and performance, management and operating procedures, modeling the data, defining data integrity rules, and developing the technical and system test cases that will be used to verify the Community of Interest governance solutions.

The main task of the System Engineering and Architecture Technical Committee is creating the high level Community of Interest governance requirements in response to the Business Information System information requirements, and allocating them to appropriate component of the solution.

These system level governance requirements are derived from the evolving operational requirements. All of this is in support of a properly governed data architecture for semantics, data structures, value domains and restricted value sets necessary to support common and consensus-based understanding across the user community of shared missions.

It is the task of the System Engineering and Architecture Technical Committee to explore emerging technology and evolving Governance Assessments for application to future governance implementation specifications. In this regard the System Engineering and Architecture Technical Committee may recommend and conduct experimentation as required, subject to approval by Communities of Interest. Governed specifically, the Systems Engineering & Architecture Committee:

- Develops and maintains the governance requirements on shared data architecture in response to the business information system requirements and by allocating them to an appropriate component of the governance architecture.

- Derives these system requirements from the evolving operational governance requirements.

- Defines technical solutions to address operational and procedural governance requirements.

- Derives the detailed requirements from systems level governance requirements and for the evolution of the Governance Program.

- Derives the management and operating procedures for Governance.

- Derives data integrity rules for the use of Governance.

- Explores emerging technologies and evolving Governance Assessments for application to future governance specifications.

- Validates Governance implementation and system level test specifications.

- Develops, in collaboration with the Governance Project Committee, and under the guidance of the Governance Program Committee, an integrated system's engineering framework describing the engineering phases, milestones, artifacts and tools for governed projects.

- Integrates with other Community of Interest technical committees, and other Communities of Interest as necessary.

4.3.4 Data Modeling Technical Committee

The purpose of data modeling is to transform stakeholders' governance needs into appropriate needs within data models. Data modeling is concerned with information modeling, data modeling, data management, and providing guidance for the actual implementation.

The main task of the Data Modeling Technical Committee is to take the governance requirements for the shared data models identified by the Operational Technical Committee as well as other requirements allocated by the System Engineering and Architecture Technical Committee, and define the appropriate governance requirements that must be present within each data model. The Data Modeling Technical Committee is also responsible for the governance aspects of data management and maintenance of the appropriate government requirements for all shared data models.

The Data Modeling Technical Committee is the custodian for the common reference data, and for test and demonstration data needed to test and validate governance. The Data Modeling Technical Committee provides data modeling advice to all other technical committees and data modeling support to technical groups on an as required basis. Governed specifically, the Data Modeling Committee:

- Define the governance requirements that are imposed over data architecture models including the data element model, specified data models, implemented database models and the operational database models.

- Ensures that there is maximum and common use of data element and specified data models across all implemented and operational data models so as to ensure maximum governance across the shared data models created by each Community of Interest.

- Provides data modeling advice to all other technical committees on an as required basis.

- Integrates with other Community of Interest technical committees, and other Communities of Interest as necessary.

4.3.5 Test and Evaluation Technical Committee

The test engineering discipline is concerned with the overall test philosophy and critical test issues related to validating governance. The objective is that, after the conduct of the collection of these activities, confidence will have been provided that the Community of Interest solution to validate enterprise-wide governance requirements. The Operational Technical Committee, System Engineering and Architecture Technical Committee and Data Modeling Technical Committees all perform aspects of the test engineering discipline; nevertheless, the Test and Evaluation Technical Committee has the overarching responsibility. Governed specifically, the Test and Evaluation Committee:

- Ensures that the test engineering discipline properly includes governance requirements and is performed in a consistent, complete and coherent manner.

- Produces and maintains an overall the Test and Evaluation Master Plan, including a Test and Evaluation Strategy, and a test schedule.

- Coordinates all aspects of Implementation Level Tests, System Level Tests, Operational Level Tests, demonstrations and exercises, and, if needed, during other exercises and demonstrations.

- Produces test specifications for the Implementation Level Tests, System Level Tests and Operational Level Tests.

- Ensures that the Implementation Level Tests, System Level Tests and Operational Level Tests verify and validate governance among the organizations involved and the satisfaction of the requirements.

- Provides guidelines for organizations to execute the Implementation Level Tests and validate the test results of the Implementation Level Tests.

- Plans, conducts, monitors, assesses, evaluates and reports on all aspects of the System Level Tests with the assistance of the other technical committees.

- Plans, conducts, monitors, assesses, evaluates and reports on all aspects of the Operational Level Tests, with the assistance of the Operations Technical Committee.

- Develops a data collection and evaluation plan for System Level Tests and Operational Level Tests.

- Records data collection and evaluation results into the test-results database.

- Maintains problem reports with appropriate metrics required for a continuous assessment and resolution.

- Maintains system management and test metrics.

- Acts as custodian for governance test data.

- Proposes changes to the Governance Assessments as a result of the test analysis.

- Coordinates, conducts and supports the governance adherence tests and demonstration.

- Integrates with other Community of Interest technical committees, and other Communities of Interest as necessary.

4.3.6 Governance Configuration Control Technical Committee

The Configuration Control Technical Committee specifies a common set of procedures, methods and processes for controlling the Governance Assessment's configuration. The Configuration Control Technical Committee also provides configuration control advice to all other technical committees on an as required basis. Configuration control must extend to all aspects of Governance Assessments including all its metadata, generated DBMS schemas, and all attendant software. Governed specifically, the Configuration Control Technical Committee:

- Defines a common set of governance procedures and mechanisms upon which all the Governance Program baseline products will be managed.
- Implements the procedures defined in the Configuration Management Plan.
- Records and reports the status of configuration controlled items.
- Coordinates the change implementation process of the products.
- Processes requests for waivers and requests for deviation.
- Prepares and reports activities to the Governance Project Committee.
- Controls distribution of all Governance Committee products.
- Maintains a current glossary.
- Integrates with other Community of Interest technical committees, and other Communities of Interest as necessary.

4.4 Governance Mission Summary

Missions are the hierarchical or network organized text-based statements of the idealized outcomes. Missions are the ultimate targets or objectives. Mainly, missions are never achieved in any final form. Missions serve as the contexts for both organizations and functions. When missions are set down, and then when organizations and functions are also set down, there should be even coverage among them all. There should be no organization without a mission.

There should be no function without an organization to accomplish it and a mission that is addressed. If there are any discrepancies between missions, organizations, and functions then these have to be resolved before proceeding.

It is much easier, cheaper, and faster to fix these problems before any detailed specifications such as those contained in Chapters 5 and 6 are set out and employed within the Metabase System, or are turned into a metadata repository designs and metadata repository system implementation.

Careful review of reports by the U.S. General Accountability Office clearly show that almost 95% of all the errors in IT systems are cause by factors outside of IT. Chief among these factors are missions, organizations, and functions. It is therefore critical that missions be properly specified. In addition to comparing missions against existing organizations and functions, a key indicator of completeness is to review the missions and then attempt to conclude whether the enterprise has been completely and comprehensively described. If not there is likely something missing in mission specification. A similar review should then be done with respect to organizations, and then finally functions.

4.5 Questions and Exercises

1. *If you don't know where you're going, it doesn't matter much which road you take.* That's the essence of the exchange between Alice and the Cheshire cat in Alice and Wonderland. Mission models are the "Where you are going." Missions are highly organized textual expositions of the idealized outcomes. How important is it to have clear, comprehensive, and consensus-based missions before you start any metadata management effort?

2. Mission models can be 20-30 pages of text, so isn't it valuable to focus on just one well-defined subset of the overall enterprise mission versus the whole enterprise mission? Doesn't that increase the change of success? What have your experiences been trying to tackle too large of a mission area? What have your experiences been when the areas you've tackled have been defined in isolation without regard to the overall enterprise? Explain and provide examples.

3. Shouldn't there be a mission for Governance? Where would that mission area fall within the overall enterprise mission? What aspects of the Governance mission overlap with other mission area? Does that mean there should be shared data across those overlapping mission areas? What would be the likely result if the shared-data areas were defined in isolation? Explain and provide examples.

4. Section 4.2 sets out the mission for the overall governance program. Do you agree with this missions? Should it be more, less, different? How does this overall program mission compare with what your organization has for its governance mission? Is this mission different enough from what should be done that you should expend resources re-doing it before starting? If yes, why? If no, then how much time would be saved by just accepting it and moving on?

5. Section 4.3 briefly sets out the mission for developing individual Governance Assessments. Is yours different enough from what should be done that you should expend resources re-doing it before starting? If yes, why? If no, then how much time would be saved by just accepting it and moving on?

6. Section 4.3.1 through 4.3.6 sets out the missions for all the different groups within a governance community of interest. Is yours different enough from what should be done that you should expend resources re-doing it before starting? If yes, why? If no, then how much time would be saved by just accepting it and moving on?

7. After a review of the mission sections, are they worth adopting, "right out of the box," or would there be real "progress value" in taking two or months from the start of an effort to redevelopment these from scratch? What

significant increase in value would there be from such a re-defines effort? Wouldn't there be more value by adopting these, as is, and then revisiting them in six months to a year?

5

Governance Work Products

There is a high degree of integration among the work products that are governed within and across the Metabase System's functional modules. Figure 28 illustrates these interrelationships in at a high level. Each "box" represents a Metabase System functional module. Table 19 sets out the Metabase System modules and the names of the specific work products within each module that are governed.

The governed work products are drawn directly from Figures 29 through 47. That is, once valued, these metadata components are the specifications of products to be governed. These are not actual work products, but the specifications of the work products. These specifications, when turned into actual work products, that is, when actual databases and business information systems are constructed, there exists an environment to be governed across the enterprise.

This book contains the specifications of these metadata components. Users of this book should take these specifications and use them to either construct a Metabase System, or to procure one. A free version of the Metabase System can be obtained from the Whitemarsh website.[10]

Once the Metabase System is obtained and installed, its use enables the creation of "actual" governance specification that, in turn, can be implemented to cause enterprise-wide governance environments to exist. The entity-relationship data models for each of these database object classes is

[10]. The Whitemarsh metadata management systems is called the Metabase System. It was first designed in the late 1970s, and has been deployed through a number of large scale database management systems. The Metabase System is almost always used in conjunction with database-centric projects. Employing the Metabase System in a Governance Community of Interest is ideal because it is inherently multi-user, able to be used Client/Server and over the Internet, and it is especially designed to be represent enterprise-wide metadata in an integrated, interrelated, and non-redundant fashion.

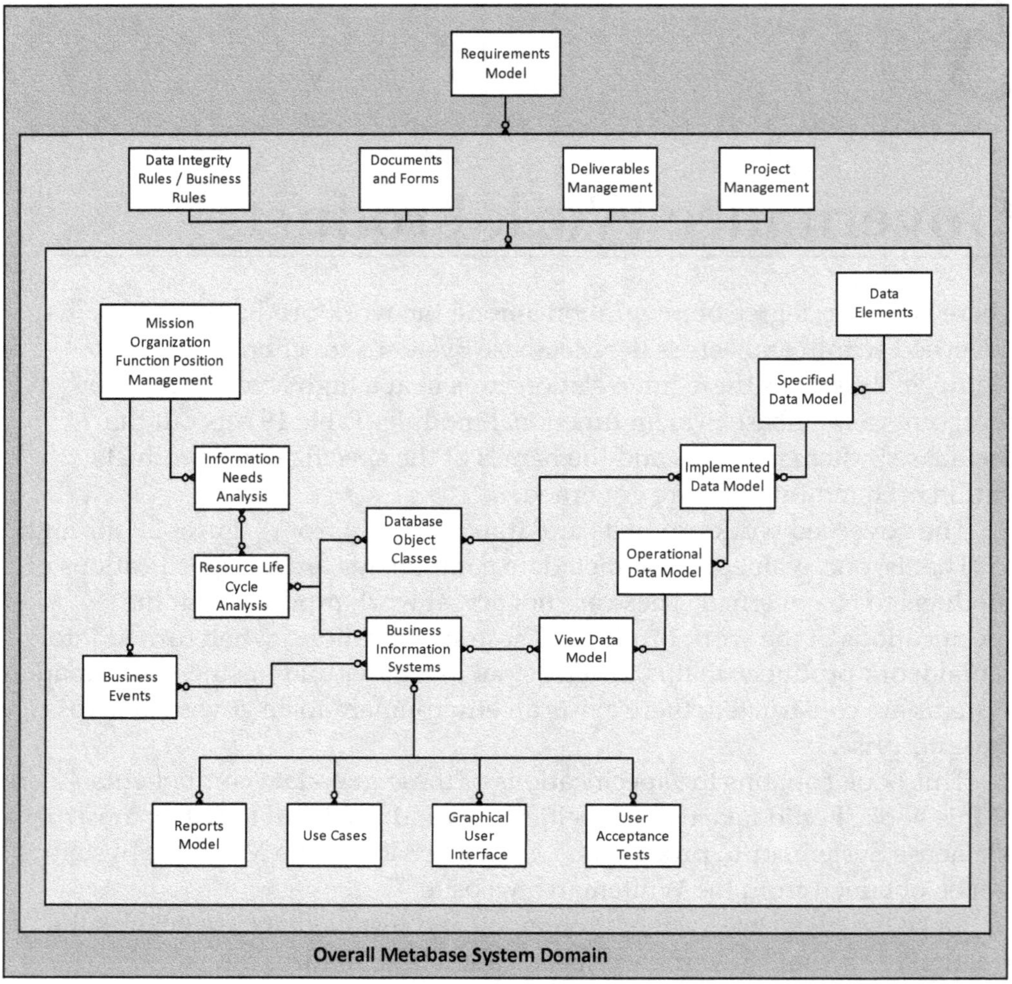

Figure 28. Enterprise Governance Metabase System Domain

provided in Figures 29 through 47 at the end of this chapter. Each of these figures represents the metadata for a discrete functional area. In each of these figures, some of the tables are shaded gray. That means that the data is entered through a different functional area from a Metabase System Module. For example, Resource, shaded gray in Figure 35, Business Information Systems, is created in the Resource Life Cycle Analysis functional area which is depicted in Figure 31.

In the Figures 29 through 47, a line with a single crow's foot is a one-to-many relationship with the crow's foot resting on the "many" end. If the line has a crow's foot at both ends, which is a many-to-many relationship. If the line is circular, which is a recursive or hierarchical relationship. Finally, if there are two one-to-many relationship lines between two entities, which signifies a network relationship that serves to represent bills-of-materials

This chapter contains the data structures of these work products. Chapter 6 sets out their governance processes in a high-level form. The Appendix sets out the processes in detail.

The Governance module processes record the assignment of the governing persons, their contextual mission-organization-function-positions and the specific work product instances over which they exercise governance. In addition to who is assigned to accomplish the work, the results and a history of all assessments is also stored.

Each of the process models also references Figures 29 through 47. Some figures contain multiple database object classes. In the Metabase System, each of these figures represents a Metabase System functional module.

<table>
<tr><th>Metabase System Module</th><th colspan="2">Governed Work Products</th></tr>
<tr><td>Business Events</td><td colspan="2">Business Event, Business Cycle, Calendar Cycle</td></tr>
<tr><td>Business Information Systems</td><td colspan="2">Business Information Systems</td></tr>
<tr><td>Database Objects</td><td colspan="2">Database Objects, Database Primitive Data Transformations, Database Object States, Database Objects Information Systems</td></tr>
<tr><td>Data Integrity Rules</td><td colspan="2">Data Integrity Rules</td></tr>
<tr><td rowspan="3">Data Modeling</td><td>Data Elements</td><td>Business Domains, Concepts, Conceptual Value Domains, Data Elements, Data Element Concepts, Data Types, Meta Category Value Types, Value Domains</td></tr>
<tr><td>Specified Data Model</td><td>Subjects (and implied entities, attributes and relationships)</td></tr>
<tr><td>Implemented Data Model</td><td>Schemas (and implied Tables, columns, and relationships)</td></tr>
</table>

Metabase System Module	Governed Work Products	
	Operational Data Model	DBMS Schemas (and implied DBMS tables, DBMS Columns, and relationships) plus Database Architectures, Databases, and DBMS
	View Data Model	View Data Models (and implied view model components)
Documents and Forms	Documents and Forms	
Governance	Governed work product assignment, Governance Assessment Results and History	
Information Needs Analysis	Information Needs, Information Need Characteristics	
Missions, Organizations & Functions	Mission, Organization, Mission-Organizations, Function, Mission Organization Function, Positions, Persons, and Database Domains	
Project Management	Project Templates, Deliverable Templates, Task Templates, Skills, and Work Environment Factors	
Reports	Reports	
Requirements	Requirements	
Resources & Life Cycles	Resources and Life Cycle Nodes	
User Acceptance Tests	User Acceptance Tests	
Use Cases	Use Cases, Use Case Actors, and Use Case Events	

Table 19. Governed Work Products within Metabase System Modules.

5.1 Governed Work Products

The work products corresponding to the identified meta entities are depicted in high level diagrams in Figures 7 through 27. A third normal form set of database tables, for the work products are presented at the end of this chapter as Figures 29 through 47.

Each work product is cross referenced to its detailed figure, that is, Figures 29 through 47. The corresponding processes that represent the governance-based audits and evaluations to determine integrity and correctness of the work products are provided in Chapter 6, Governance Processes. These processes are accomplished by the persons identified within the Metabase System functional module, Governance.

5.2 Enterprise Architecture Governed Work Products

The governed work products identified within this section include:

- Missions
- Organizations
- Functions
- Position
- Information Needs
- Resource Life Cycles
- Database Domains
- Database Objects
- Documents
- Forms
- Requirements

Governed within the Governance Module of the Metabase System but not explicitly addressed in this section are

- Mission-Organizations
- Mission-Organization-Functions
- Persons
- Information Need Characteristics
- Database Object Primitive Data Transformations

- Database Object Information Systems
- Database Object States
- Resources

5.2.1 Business Missions

The Metabase System module, Mission-Organization-Function-Position, has its data model depicted in Figure 29. It sets out the essential missions that define the very existence of the enterprise, and that are the ultimate goals and objectives that measure enterprise accomplishment from within different business functions and organizations.

Sets out the organizations are accomplishing what aspects of missions with what databases, business information systems and through which functions?

Sets out the procedures are performed by groups in their achievement the various missions of the enterprise from within different enterprise organizations?

Missions, defined in Figure 29, should contain at least the following:

1. Mission administrative information
   a. Identification information
      i. Organization authors
      ii. Person authors
   b. Configuration management information
      i. Status (development, test, production)
      ii. Version (xx,yy.zz)

2. Mission object class tables
   a. Mission

3. Mission inter-object relationships
   a. Mission contains Mission

4. Mission related objects
   a. Mission is referenced by Mission-Organization

5.2.2 Business Organizations

The Metabase System module, Mission-Organization-Function-Position, has its data model depicted in Figure 29. This module also sets out the organizations that are accomplishing aspects of missions with what databases, business information systems and through which functions?

Sets out the procedures are performed by groups in their achievement the various missions of the enterprise from within different enterprise organizations?

[Business] Organizations, defined in Figure 29, should contain at least the following:

1. Business Organization administrative information
   a. Identification information
      i. Organization authors
      ii. Person authors
   b. Configuration management information
      i. Status (development, test, production)
      ii. Version (xx,yy.zz)

2. Business Organization object class tables
   a. Business Organization

3. Business Organization inter-object relationships
   a. Business organization contains business organization

4. Business Organization related objects
   a. Business Organization is referenced by Mission-Organization

5.2.3 Business Functions

The Metabase System module, Mission-Organization-Function-Position, has its data model depicted in Figure 29. This module also sets out the business functions performed by persons by one or more mission-organizations.

[Business] Functions, defined in Figure 29, should contain at least the following:

1. Business Function administrative information
    a. Identification information
        i. Organization authors
        ii. Person authors
    b. Configuration management information
        i. Status (development, test, production)
        ii. Version (xx,yy.zz)

2. Business Function object class tables
    a. Business Function

3. Business Function inter-object relationships
    a. Business Function contains business function

4. Business Function related objects
    a. Business Function is referenced by Mission-Organization-Function

5.2.4 Position

The Metabase System module, Mission-Organization-Function-Position, has its data model depicted in Figure 29. This module also sets out the positions performed by persons within certain management levels that are set within one or more mission-organizations.

Positions, defined in Figure 29, should contain at least the following:

1. Position administrative information
    a. Identification information
        i. Organization authors
        ii. Person authors
    b. Configuration management information
        i. Status (development, test, production)
        ii. Version (xx,yy.zz)

2. Position object class tables
    a. Position
    b. Management Levels
    c. Person

   d. Position Person
   e. Mission Organization Function Position

3. Position inter-object relationships
   a. Management Level contains Position
   b. Position contains Mission Organization Function Position
   c. Position contains Position Person
   d. Person contains Position Person

4. Position related objects
   a. Mission-Organization-Function Position is referenced by Mission Organization Function

5.2.5 Information Needs

The Metabase System module, Information Needs Analysis, has its data model depicted in Figure 30. It sets out the information (a.k.a., query results or reports)that is needed by various organizations in their functional accomplishment of missions and what databases and business information systems provide this information.

Information Needs, defined in Figure 30 should contain at least the following:

1. Information Needs administrative information
   a. Identification information
      i. Organization authors
      ii. Person authors
   b. Configuration management information
      i. Status (development, test, production)
      ii. Version (xx,yy.zz)
2. Information object class tables
   a. Information Needs Types
   b. Information Needs
   c. Ranking
   d. Characteristic Type
   e. Characteristic
   f. Information Need Characteristic Assignment

g. Mission-Organization-Functional Ranked Information Need Assignment

3. Information Needs inter-object relationships
   a. Information Need Type contains Information Need
   b. Information Need contains Mission-Organization-Functional Ranked Information Need Assignment
   c. Information Need contains Information Need Characteristic Assignment
   d. Characteristic Type contains Characteristic
   e. Characteristic contains Information Need Characteristic Assignment
   f. Ranking contains Information Need Characteristic Assignment

4. Information Needs related objects
   a. Mission-Organization-Functional Ranked Information Need Assignment is referenced by Mission-Organization-Function

5.2.6 Resource Life Cycle Analysis

The Metabase System module, Resource Life Cycle Analysis, has its data model depicted in Figure 31. It organizes the resources of the enterprise, their life cycles, the interrelationships among the resources, and is the bridge between the information needed for missions-organization-functions, and the Information Technology databases and business information systems that provide data and processes.

Resource Life Cycles, defined in Figure 31 plans should contain at least the following:

1. Resource administrative information
   a. Identification information
      i. Organization authors
      ii. Person authors
   b. Configuration management information
      i. Status (development, test, production)
      ii. Version (xx,yy.zz)

2. Resource Life Cycle Analysis class tables

   a. Resource Type
   b. Resource
   c. Resource Life Cycle Node Structure
   d. Resource Life Cycle Node Structure Type
   e. Resource Life Cycle Node Database Object Assignment
   f. Resource Life Cycle Node Business Information System Assignment
   g. Resource Life Cycle Node Information Needs Assignment

3. Project plan inter-object relationships
   a. Resource references Resource Type
   b. Resource Life Cycle Node references Resource
   c. Resource Life Cycle Node Database Object Assignment references Resource Life Cycle Node
   d. Resource Life Cycle Node Database Object Assignment references database object Resource Life Cycle Node Business Information System Assignment references Resource Life Cycle Node Resource Life Cycle Node Business Information System Assignment references Business Information System Resource Life Cycle Node Information Needs Assignment references Resource Life Cycle Node
   e. Resource Life Cycle Node Information Needs Assignment references Resource Life Cycle Node Information Need

4. Project Plan related objects
   a. Project plan references project plan
   b. Project plan references Enterprise Identifier
   c. Project plan references Transaction Data Staging Area Data Model

5.2.7 Database Domains

A database domain is a hierarchically organized set of noun-intensive descriptions associated with a mission leaf. Analyzed database domains lead to the identification of database object classes, enterprise data elements, and property classes. Property classes, in turn, often become database tables.

Database Domains, defined in Figure 29 should contain at least the following:

1. Database domain administrative information

   a. Identification information
      i. Organization authors
      ii. Person authors
   b. Configuration management information
      i. Status (development, test, production)
      ii. Version (xx,yy.zz)
2. Database domain object class tables
   a. Database domain
3. Database domain inter-object relationships
   a. Database domain contains database domain
4. Database domain related objects
   a. Database domain references mission
   b. Database-domain database-object references database domain

5.2.8 Database Objects

The Metabase System module, Database Objects, has its data model depicted in Figure 32. It defines Database Object Classes in terms of the Implemented Database Model tables that comprise the database object's data structure. The module also defines the states the database object proceeds through. In accomplishing a database object state transformation, database object information systems are executed. These systems are actually defined in terms of row-centric processes from the database object tables defined within the database object class.

The reason why Database Object Classes are defined at the Implemented Database Model level and not the Operational Database Model level is because DBMSs, such as Oracle, Sybase, DB2, and SQL-Server 2005 all implement database object classes differently at the physical, that is, Operational Database Model level.

Regardless of the physical implementation, database object classes are the common "specification unit" for business information system designers and implementors, hence a need for a coherent means for their specification and maintenance.

Database Objects, defined in Figure 32, should contain at least the following:

1. Database objects administrative information

   a. Identification information
      i. Organization authors
      ii. Person authors
   b. Configuration management information
      i. Status (development, test, production)
      ii. Version (xx,yy.zz)
2. Database object object class tables
   a. Database object tables
   b. Database object information systems
   c. Database object states
   d. Database object information system states
   e. Database object table processes
3. Database object inter-object relationships
   a. Database object contains database object tables
   b. Database object contains business information systems
   c. Database object contains states
   d. Database object state contains database object information system states
   e. Database object information system contains database object information system states
4. Database object related objects
   a. Database object table references table
   b. Database object table process references data integrity rule
   c. Database object references database domain

5.2.9 Documents

Documents, depicted in Figure 33, are those materials that provide some specification and/or description of one or more aspects of enterprise work products. Documents are able to be interrelated into hierarchies or networks. Each document is able to be subdivided into a hierarchy of sections. Within each section there can be document cells. The document cells can be mapped to View Columns, Mission-Organization-Functions, and project management deliverables.

5.2.10 Forms

Forms, depicted in Figure 33, represent well-defined documents onto which data values are to be entered individually or in groups. Forms are able to be interrelated into hierarchies or networks. Each form is able to be subdivided into a hierarchy of sections. Within each section there can be form cells. The form cells can be mapped to View Columns, and Mission-Organization-Functions.

5.2.11 Requirements

Requirements, as depicted in Figure 34, represent the identification, name and description of a documented need of a particular product or service that should be or be performed. Requirements can be categorized and can be interrelated through Requirement Structures. The specification of a requirement consists of necessary Mission-Organization-Functions, Resource Life Cycle Nodes, Data Integrity Rules, Use Cases, Business Events, Business Information Systems, DBMS Columns, User Acceptance Test Steps via Structures, and Database Objects. Requirements, identified in Figure 34, should contain at least the following:

1. Requirements administrative information
   a. Identification information
      i. Organization authors
      ii. Person authors
   b. Configuration management information
      i. Status (development, test, production)
      ii. Version (xx,yy.zz)

2. Requirements tables
   a. Requirement Category
   b. Requirement
   c. Requirement Structure
   d. Requirement Structure Type
   e. Mission Organization Function and Requirement Structure
   f. Resource Life Cycle Node and Requirement Structure
   g. Data Integrity Rule Structure and Requirement Structure

h. Use Case and Requirement Structure
i. Database Object and Requirement Structure
j. Implemented Data Model Schema and Requirement Structure
k. Operational Data Model DBMS Schema and Requirement Structure
l. Business Event and Requirement Structure
m. Business Information System and Requirement Structure
n. DBMS Column and Requirement Structure
o. User Acceptance Test Step Structure and Requirement Structure
p. Data Element and Requirement Structure
q. Specified Data Model Subject Requirement Structure
r. Document and Requirement Structure

3. Requirement inter-object relationships
    a. Requirement contains Requirement Structure
    b. Requirement Category contains Requirement
    c. Requirement Structure Type contains Requirement Structure

4. Requirement related objects
    a. Requirement Structure Related to Mission Organization Function
    b. Requirement Structure Related to Resource Life Cycle Node and
    c. Requirement Structure Related to Data Integrity Rule
    d. Requirement Structure Related to Use Case
    e. Requirement Structure Related to Database Object
    f. Requirement Structure Related to Implemented Data Model Schema
    g. Requirement Structure Related to Operational Data Model DBMS Schema
    h. Requirement Structure Related to Business Event
    i. Requirement Structure Related to Business Information System
    j. Requirement Structure Related to DBMS Column
    k. Requirement Structure Related to User Acceptance Test Step Structure
    l. Requirement Structure Related to Data Element
    m. Requirement Structure Related to Specified Data Model Subject
    n. Requirement Structure Related to Document

5.3 Business Information System Governed Work Products

The governed work products identified within this section include:

- Business Information Systems
- Business Events
- Business Cycles
- Business Calendars
- User Acceptance Tests
- Use Cases
- Reports

5.3.1 Business Information Systems

The Metabase System module, Business Information Systems, has its data model depicted in Figure 35. It identifies business information systems, where are they, how are they related to mission, organization, function, and databases, and how are they interrelated to each other including their calendar and business event execution schedules.

This module also addresses the impact on these business information systems when policy (a.k.a., data) is required or changed.

Finally, the Business Information Systems module creates Business Events that are the triggers between the Business Information System and the Database Management System such that a view is executed, which, in turn, causes database data to be created, updated, deleted, or retrieved.

Shared data is not "accomplished" through interoperable databases. Rather it is accomplished through business information systems that capture, transform, store, and employ business data in interoperable formats and processes.

Business Information Systems, defined in Figure 35 should contain at least the following:

1. Business Information Systems administrative information
   a. Identification information
      i. Organization authors
      ii. Person authors

   b. Configuration management information
      i. Status (development, test, production)
      ii. Version (xx,yy.zz)

2. Business Information System object class tables
   a. Programming language
   b. Level
   c. Construction method
   d. Status
   e. Application type
   f. Environment type
   g. Predominant user class
   h. DBMS Environment

3. Business Information System inter-object relationships
   a. Business information system references business information system

4. Business Information System related objects
   a. Business information system references Programming language
   b. Business information system references Level
   c. Business information system references Construction method
   d. Business information system references Status
   e. Business information system references Application type
   f. Business information system references Environment type
   g. Business information system references Predominant user class
   h. Business information system references DBMS Environment
   i. Business information system references Database object information system
   j. Business information system referenced by Business Event
   k. Business information system referenced by Business Information System View
   l. Business information system referenced by resource life cycle business information system
   m. Business information system referenced by business information system database object information system assignment
   n. Business information system referenced by business information system

5.3.2 Business Event

The Metabase System module, Business Events, has its data model depicted in Figure 36. It includes the specification of business events that, in turn, enable a business-event-based invocation of identified business information systems.

Business Events, defined in Figure 36 should contain at least the following:

1. Business Event administrative information
   a. Identification information
      i. Organization authors
      ii. Person authors
   b. Configuration management information
      i. Status (development, test, production)
      ii. Version (xx,yy.zz)

2. Business Event object class tables
   a. Business Event

3. Business Event inter-object relationships
   a. None

4. Business Event related objects
   a. Business Event references Business Event Cycle
   b. Business Event references Calendar Cycle
   c. Business Event is referenced by Business Information System
   d. Business Event references Mission-Organization-Function

5.3.3 Business Cycle

The Metabase System module, Business Information Systems, has its data model depicted in Figure 36. It includes the specification of business cycles that, in turn, enable a business-cycle-based invocation of identified business information systems.

Business Cycle, defined in Figure 36 should contain at least the following:

1. Business Cycle administrative information
   a. Identification information
      i. Organization authors
      ii. Person authors
   b. Configuration management information
      i. Status (development, test, production)
      ii. Version (xx,yy.zz)

2. Business Cycle object class tables
   a. Business Cycle Structure
   b. Business Cycle
   c. Business Cycle Structure Type

3. Business Cycle inter-object relationships
   a. Business Cycle Structure references Business Cycle Structure Type
   b. Business Cycle Structure [active] references Business Cycle
   c. Business Cycle Structure [passive] references Business Cycle.

4. Business Cycle related objects
   Business Event references Business Event Cycle

5.3.4 Business Calendar

The Metabase System module, Business Information Systems, has its data model depicted in Figure 36. It includes the specification of business calendars that, in turn, enable a calendar-based invocation of identified business information systems.

Business Calender, defined in Figure 36 should contain at least the following:

1. Business Calender administrative information
   a. Identification information
      i. Organization authors
      ii. Person authors
   b. Configuration management information
      i. Status (development, test, production)
      ii. Version (xx,yy.zz)

2. Business Calender object class tables
    a. Business Calender Structure
    b. Business Calender
    c. Business Calender Structure Type.

3. Business Calender inter-object relationships
    a. Business Calender Structure references Business Calendar Structure Type
    b. Business Calender Structure [active] references Business Calendar
    c. Business Calender Structure [passive] references Business Calendar.

4. Business Calender related objects
    Business Event references Business Event Calender

5.3.5 User Acceptance Test

The Metabase System module, User Acceptance Test, has its data model depicted in Figure 37. It includes the specification of business calendars that, in turn, enable a calendar-based invocation of identified business information systems. User Acceptance Test, defined in Figure 37 should contain at least the following:

1. User Acceptance Test administrative information
    a. Identification information
        i. Organization authors
        ii. Person authors
    b. Configuration management information
        i. Status (development, test, production)
        ii. Version (xx,yy.zz)

2. User Acceptance Test object class tables
    a. Business Calender Structure
    b. Business Calender
    c. Business Calender Structure Type.

3. User Acceptance Test inter-object relationships

   a. Business Calender Structure references Business Calendar Structure Type
   b. Business Calender Structure [active] references Business Calendar
   c. Business Calender Structure [passive] references Business Calendar.

4. User Acceptance Test related objects
   Business Event references Business Event Calender

5.3.6 Use Cases

The Metabase System module, Use Cases, has its data model depicted in Figure 38. It includes the specification of business calendars that, in turn, enable a calendar-based invocation of identified business information systems.

Use Cases, defined in Figure 38 should contain at least the following:

1. Use Cases administrative information
   a. Identification information
      i. Organization authors
      ii. Person authors
   b. Configuration management information
      i. Status (development, test, production)
      ii. Version (xx,yy.zz)

2. Use Cases object class tables
   a. Business Calender Structure
   b. Business Calender
   c. Business Calender Structure Type.

3. Use Cases inter-object relationships
   a. Business Calender Structure references Business Calendar Structure Type
   b. Business Calender Structure [active] references Business Calendar
   c. Business Calender Structure [passive] references Business Calendar.

4. Use Cases related objects
   Business Event references Business Event Calender

5. Use Case Actors
   a. Use Case Actor Roles
   b. Use Case Event Actors

6. Use Case Events
   a. Use Case Event hierarchies
   b. Use Case Event Facts
   c. Use Case Event Business Information Systems
   d. Use Case Event Mission Organization Functions

7. Use Case Pre-, Post-, and Special Conditions
   a. Use Case Fact assignments
   b. Use Case Fact Column assignments

5.3.7 Reports

The Metabase System module, Reports, has its data model depicted in Figure 39. It includes the specification of business calendars that, in turn, enable a calendar-based invocation of identified business information systems.

Reports, defined in Figure 39 should contain at least the following:

1. Reports administrative information
   a. Identification information
      i. Organization authors
      ii. Person authors
   b. Configuration management information
      i. Status (development, test, production)
      ii. Version (xx,yy.zz)

Reports object class tables
   c. Business Calender Structure
   d. Business Calender
   e. Business Calender Structure Type.

2. Reports inter-object relationships
   a. Business Calender Structure references Business Calendar Structure Type

b. Business Calender Structure [active] references Business Calendar
c. Business Calender Structure [passive] references Business Calendar.

3. Reports related objects
   Business Event references Business Event Calender

5.3.8 External File Interface

An external file is a data set that is to be interfaced with one or more business information systems for use to create records in a database or that may be interfaced directly to a database through a DBMS utility.

External File Interface, defined should contain at least the following:

1. View information
   a. Specification of the Business Information System view that is to interface with the Operational Database Model DBMS tables for each External File data segment.
   b. The identification and encoding of the rules that govern the creation of DBMS tables, DBMS Columns, and as appropriate all Operational Database keys.
   c. Identification of all the data integrity rules that govern the transformation of externally created and formatted data into the database data.

5.4 Data Integrity Rules

Simply put, a data integrity rule is a rule that, when executed, either restores integrity or tests whether integrity remains. Data Integrity Rules, defined in Figure 40, are drawn from the following:

- Data Elements,
- Specified Data Models,
- Implemented Data Models,
- Operational Data Models
- View Data Models
- Business Information Systems

Data integrity rules, should contain at least the following:

1. Data integrity rule administrative information
   a. Identification information
      i. Organization authors
      ii. Person authors
   b. Configuration management information
      i. Status (development, test, production)
      ii. Version (xx,yy.zz)

2. Data integrity rule object class tables
   a. Data integrity rule
   b. Data integrity rule pseudo code
      i. Data integrity rule contained items
         (1) Data integrity rule object class
         (2) Data integrity rule object
         (3) Data integrity rule object value
            (a) alphabetic value
            (b) numeric value
      ii. Data integrity rule inter-contained item operator
   c. On success action
   d. On failure action

3. Data integrity rule inter-object relationships
   a. Data integrity rule references data integrity rule

4. Data integrity Rule related objects
   a. Attribute references data integrity rule contained item
   b. Entity references data integrity rule
   c. Column references data integrity rule contained item
   d. Table references data integrity rule
   e. DBMS column references data integrity rule contained item
   f. DBMS table references data integrity rule
   g. View column references data integrity rule contained item
   h. View references data integrity rule
   i. [ISO 11179] data element references data integrity rule contained item
   j. Data element concept references data integrity rule contained item

k. Compound data element references data integrity rule contained item
l. Derived data element references data integrity rule contained item
m. Database object table process references data integrity rule
n. Data integrity rule references Enterprise Identifier

5.5 Data Architecture Governed Objects

A data architecture reference model, at the center of Figure 6, is in the area of data engineering and serves as a framework for understanding the scope and interrelationships among clearly definable sets of data that represents the persistent memory of the enterprise. Data is executed policy. Quality policy enables quality data. Conversely, bad, confused, or conflicting policy prevents quality enterprise data. Accomplished, a data architecture reference model enhances clear communication among deployed data instances across the enterprise.

The governed work products identified within this section include:

- Data Elements
- Specified Data Models (Subjects)
- Implemented Database Models (Schemas)
- Operational Database Models (DBMS Schemas)
- View Database Models

Governed within the Governance Module of the Metabase System but not explicitly addressed in this section are:

- Concepts
- Conceptual Value Domains
- Data Element Concepts
- Data Types
- Meta Category Value Types
- Value Domains
- Database Architectures
- Databases
- DBMS

5.5.1 Data Element Model

The Metabase System module, Data Elements, has its data model depicted in Figure 41. It defines the enterprise-level business fact templates which are employed to provide the meaning, data types, value domains and other types of data-centric rules to whichever context-dependent facts employ these defined data elements.

Thus, a data element may provide the semantics for screen fields, entity attributes, database table columns, view columns, XML Element Tags, and XML Attributes, electronic structured message fields and the like.

The purpose of the Metabase Module, Data Elements is to allow the comprehensive definition of these enterprise-level business fact templates. The data element module conforms to the ISO Standard, 11179 for data element metadata.

Because the Whitemarsh Data Element model conforms to ISO 11179 (Version 2, Part 3), it supports the definition of semantic taxonomies, classification schemes, data element concepts, value domains and their interrelationships, concepts, and conceptual value domains. Collectively these complex ISO Standards-based data structures enable the most critical foundation stone of governance, business fact semantic standardization.

Data elements are a critical component in any effort to achieve shared data across databases within and between organizations.

[ISO 11179] Data Elements, defined in Figure 41, should contain at least the following:

1. [ISO 11179] data element administrative information
   a. Identification information
      i. Organization authors
      ii. Person authors
   b. Configuration management information
      i. Status (development, test, production)
      ii. Version (xx,yy.zz)

2. [ISO 11179] Data element object class tables
   a. Concepts
   b. Concept structure
   c. Concept structure type
   d. Conceptual value domains

e. Conceptual value domain structure
f. Conceptual value domain structure type
g. Data element concepts
h. Data element concept structure
i. Data element concept structure type
j. Value domains
k. Value domain structure
l. Value domain structure type
m. Value domain values
n. Value domain value structure
o. Value domain value structure type
p. Data types
q. Compound data elements
r. Derived data elements
s. Data element classifications

3. [ISO 11179] Data Element inter-object relationships
    a. Concepts
        i. Concept contains concept structures
        ii. Concept is contained in concept structures
        iii. Concept structure type contains concept structures
    b. Conceptual value domains
        i. Conceptual value domain contains conceptual value domain structures
        ii. Conceptual value domain is contained in conceptual value domain structures
        iii. Concept value domain structure type contains concept value domain structures
    c. Data element concepts
        i. Data element concept contains data element concept structures
        ii. Data element concept is contained in data element concept structures
        iii. Data element concept structure type contains Data element concept structures
    d. Data element classifications
        i. Data element classification contains data element classification structures
        ii. Data element classification is contained in data element

classification structures
    iii. Data element classification type contains data element classification structures
  e. Value domains
    i. Value domain contains value domain structures
    ii. Value domain is contained in value domain structures
    iii. Value domain structure type contains value domain structures
  f. Value domain values
    i. Value domain value contains value domain value structures
    ii. Value domain value is contained in value domain value structures
    iii. Value domain value structure type contains value domain value structures
  g. Compound data elements
    i. Compound data element contains compound data element structure
    ii. Compound data element is contained in compound data element structure
    iii. Compound data element structure type contains compound data element structures
  h. Data element concept references conceptual value domain structure
  i. Data element concept references concept structure
  j. Data element references data element concept structure
  k. Data element references value domain structure
  l. Compound data element contains data element
  m. Derived data element contains data element
  n. Value domain references conceptual value domain structure
  o. Value domain value references value domain structure

4. [ISO 11179] data element model related objects
  a. Concept references Enterprise Identifier
  b. Conceptual value domain references Enterprise Identifier
  c. Value domain references Enterprise Identifier
  d. Data element concept references Enterprise Identifier
  e. [ISO 11179] data element references Enterprise Identifier

5.5.2 Business Domains

Business Domains represent terms and descriptions that describe aspects of the enterprise that while relevant to Data Elements are also relevant to many other work products. Business Domains, identified in Figure 41, should contain at least the following:

1. Business Domain administrative information
   a. Identification information
      i. Organization authors
      ii. Person authors
   b. Configuration management information
      i. Status (development, test, production)
      ii. Version (xx,yy.zz)

2. Business Domain object class tables
   a. Business Domain

3. Business Domain inter-object relationships
   a. Business Domain contains Business Domain

4. Business Domain related objects
   a. Business Domain is referenced by <meta-entity attribute: description>

5.5.3 Specified Data Models

The Metabase System module, Specified Data Model, has its data model depicted in Figure 42. It essentially defines concept data models of abstract concepts. Specified Data Model enables the specification, maintenance and employment of standardized data structures that can be deployed within one or more database data models.

The triple for the Specified Data Model is Subject, Entity, and Attribute. Collections of entities are related. A specific collection of entities might become the standard data structure of an Invoice, Payment, Order, Shipment, or for if for a person, their Full Name, Address, Educational achievement, or performance evaluation. Every attribute is related to a "parent" enterprise-level data element.

When database schemas are created, they deploy uses of these specified data structures. This greatly enhances data semantics standardization and maintenance. This also instantly enables interrelationships between tables and columns of the database schemas because of their common Specified Data Model "parents."

Specified data models are the second critical element the specification, implementation and maintenance of data-based interoperability across the enterprise.

Without the Data Element model and the Implemented Database Model enterprise-wide governance is very hard work and is exceptionably difficult to maintain.

Specified data models, defined in Figure 42, should contain at least the following:

1. Specified data model administrative information
   a. Identification information
      i. Organization authors
      ii. Person authors
   b. Configuration management information
      i. Status (development, test, production)
      ii. Version (xx,yy.zz)

2. Specified model object class tables
   a. Subject
   b. Entities
   c. Attributes
   d. Relationships
      i. Primary Key
         (1) Primary key attributes
      ii. Candidate Key
         (1) Candidate key attributes
      iii. Foreign Key
         (1) Foreign key attributes

3. Specified model inter-object relationships
   a. Subject contains subjects
   b. Subject contains entity
   c. Entity contains entity subtypes

d. Entity contains attributes
e. Attribute contains attributes
f. Entity contains primary key
g. Entity contains foreign key
h. Entity contains candidate key
i. Primary key contains foreign key
j. Primary key contains primary key attributes
k. Attribute contains primary key attributes
l. Foreign key contains foreign key attributes
m. Attribute contains foreign key attributes
n. Candidate key contains candidate key attributes
o. Attribute contains candidate key attributes

4. Specified model related objects
   a. Attribute references [ISO 11179] data element
   b. Attribute references value domain structure
   c. Subject references Enterprise Identifier

5.5.4 Implemented Database Model

The Metabase System module, Implemented Database Model, has its data model depicted in Figure 43. The purpose of the Implemented Database Model is to enable the creation of DBMS (Database management system) independent data models. Implemented data models inherit the semantics of the Specified Data Model, and, in turn, provide inheritable semantics to one or more Operational (DBMS dependent) data models.

The Metabase System module, the Implemented Data Model, is essentially an implemented database model of a database. Implemented data models are Schema-based models. That is, they consist of a schema, tables, columns within the tables, and relationships among the tables. All columns of database tables should relate to attributes, which, in turn, should relate to the enterprise data elements.

It is almost always the case that the tables and columns of the Implemented Database Model to be sourced from many different Specified Data Models. For example, a Marketing database includes organizations, products, people, locations, sales, invoices, and the like. Each of these comes from a different Specified Data Model.

It is also often the case that multiple columns in a given table are sourced from the same attributes from a Specified Data Model entity. For example, in one table there might be the Salesman's name, the Customer Support person's name, and the Legal contact person's name. All of these are derived from the single Specified Data Model's set of attributes for a Person.

Because of the inheritance quality, which is from Specified to Implemented, Where-defined and Where-used reports are simple.

Implemented data models are also a critical component in effecting shared data across different physically constructed databases within the same overall domain.

Implemented Data Models, defined in Figure 43, should contain at least the following:

1. Implemented Database Model administrative information
   a. Identification information
      i. Organization authors
      ii. Person authors
   b. Configuration management information
      i. Status (development, test, production)
      ii. Version (xx,yy.zz)

2. Implemented Database Model tables
   a. Schema
   b. Tables
   c. Columns
   d. Relationships
      i. Primary Key
         (1) Primary key columns
      ii. Candidate Key
         (1) Candidate key columns
      iii. Foreign Key
         (1) Foreign key columns

3. Implemented Database Model inter-object relationships
   a. Schema contains table
   b. Table contains table subtypes
   c. Table contains columns
   d. Column contains columns

e. Table contains primary key
f. Table contains foreign key
g. Table contains candidate key
h. Primary key contains foreign key
i. Primary key contains primary key columns
j. Column contains primary key columns
k. Foreign key contains foreign key columns
l. Column contains foreign key columns
m. Candidate key contains candidate key columns
n. Column contains candidate key columns

4. Implemented Database Model related objects
   a. Column references [ISO 11179] data element
   b. Column references value domain structure
   c. Column references SQL data type
   d. Column references attribute
   e. Schema references Enterprise Identifier

5.5.5 Operational Datbasea Model

The Metabase System module, Operational Database Model, has its data model depicted in Figure 44. is focused on physical database models that are bound to the requirements and needs of a particular DBMS. The Operational Database Model is to be exported as SQL DDL, compiled by a DBMS, and is to support one or more Business Information Systems. The triple for the Operational Database Model is DBMS Schema, DBMS Table, and DBMS Column. DBMS Tables are interrelated by relationships.

At first glance it is a common belief that an Operational Database Model's tables are from a single Implemented Database Model. That is of course not correct with data warehouse data models. The data specifications for these models comes from multiple Implemented Data Models.

The Operational Database Model are the data-centric schematics through which interoperable data flows. This data is stored, accessed, and updated through these models. These models are managed by the Database Management System (DBMS) which, in turn, is accessed by Business Information Systems.

It must be said that without the higher level data models, that is,

Implemented, Specified, and Data Elements, any level of governance is very difficult, bordering on accidental, and is very difficult to engineer and maintain.

Operational Database Models, defined in Figure 44, should contain at least the following:

1. Operational Database Model administrative information
   a. Identification information
      i. Organization authors
      ii. Person authors
   b. Configuration management information
      i. Status (development, test, production)
      ii. Version (xx,yy.zz)

2. Operational database model object class tables
   a. DBMS Schema
   b. DBMS Tables
   c. DBMS Columns
   d. Relationships
      i. Primary Key
         (1) Primary key DBMS Columns
      ii. Candidate Key
         (1) Candidate key DBMS Columns
      iii. Foreign Key
         (1) Foreign key DBMS Columns
      iv. Secondary Key
         (1) Secondary key DBMS Columns

3. Operational database model inter-object relationships
   a. DBMS Schema contains DBMS Table
   b. DBMS Table contains DBMS Table subtypes
   c. DBMS Table contains DBMS Columns
   d. DBMS Column contains DBMS Columns
   e. DBMS Table contains primary key
   f. DBMS Table contains foreign key
   g. DBMS Table contains candidate key
   h. Primary key contains foreign key
   i. Primary key contains primary key DBMS Columns

   j. DBMS Column contains primary key DBMS Columns
   k. Foreign key contains foreign key DBMS Columns
   l. DBMS Column contains foreign key DBMS Columns
   m. Candidate key contains candidate key DBMS Columns
   n. DBMS Column contains candidate key DBMS Columns
   o. Secondary key contains secondary key DBMS Columns
   p. DBMS Column contains secondary key DBMS Columns

4. Operational Database Model related objects
   a. DBMS Column references value domain structure
   b. DBMS Schema references database
   c. DBMS Column references data type
   d. DBMS Column references column
   e. DBMS Schema references Enterprise Identifier

5.5.6 View Data Model

The Metabase System module, View, has its data model depicted in Figure 45. It enables the creation of View specifications, and the mapping of one "input" view-columns to one or more other "output" view columns from different views, and also the specification of processes that generate compound and derived values based on view columns that arrive from DBMS columns. View data models, defined in Figure 45, should contain at least the following:

1. View data model administrative information
   a. Identification information
      i. Organization authors
      ii. Person authors
   b. Configuration management information
      i. Status (development, test, production)
      ii. Version (xx,yy.zz)

2. View object class tables
   a. View
   b. View column
   c. View column structure

   d. View column structure type
   e. View column structure process
   f. View column DBMS column

3. View inter-object relationships
   a. View contains view columns
   b. View column contains view column structure
   c. View column structure type contains view column structure
   d. View column structure process contains view column structure
   e. View column contains view column DBMS column

4. View related objects
   a. View columns
   b. View column DBMS column references DBMS column
   c. View column references [ISO 11179] derived data element
   d. View column references [ISO 11179] compound data element
   e. View references business information system

5.6 Project Management

The Metabase System module, Project management, has its data model depicted in Figure 46. It enables projects to be defined, monitored, accomplished, and maintained on an enterprise wide-basis. This is critical for a Governance Program as almost nothing is in isolation. The work products identified within this section include:

1. Deliverable Template
2. Project Template
3. Skill
4. Task Template
5. Work Environment Factor

Project Management, defined in Figure 46, plans should contain at least the following:

1. Project Plan administrative information
   a. Identification information

        i. Organization authors
        ii. Person authors
    b. Configuration management information
        i. Status (development, test, production)
        ii. Version (xx,yy.zz)

2. Project object class tables
    a. Project Plan tasks
        i. Task
        ii. Predecessors
        iii. Critical dates
        iv. Unit effort
        v. Deliverable unit quantity
    b. Project Plan milestones
    c. Project Plan employed resource information
    d. Project Plan deliverables
    e. Project Plan success factors

3. Project plan inter-object relationships
    a. Task references deliverable
    b. Task references previous tasks
    c. Milestone references feeder tasks
    d. Task references previous milestone

4. Project Plan related objects
    a. Project plan references project plan
    b. Project plan references Enterprise Identifier
    c. Project plan references Transaction Data Staging Area Data Model

5.7 Governance

Governance plans, defined in Figure 47, should contain at least the following:

- Mission Organization Function Position Person
- Selected Work products from within:
    - Enterprise Data Architecture
    - Business Information Systems

- Data Integrity Rules
- Data Architecture
- Project Management

Governance, defined in Figure 47, plans should contain at least the following:

1. Governance administrative information
   a. Identification information
      i. Organization authors
      ii. Person authors
   b. Configuration management information
      i. Status (development, test, production)
      ii. Version (xx,yy.zz)

2. Governance Mission-Organization-Function-Position-Person governance intersection tables for specific Work Products.

3. The ability to capture the "bottom line" results of an assessment (e.g., Red, Yellow, or Green), who accomplished the assessment, when it was done and over time a history of all the assessments on a given work product.

The list of work products from the Metabase System's database map to the work product categories cited above are specifically listed in Chapter 6. Prototypical assessment processes for these identified work products are contained in Appendix 1.

5.8 U.S. Department of Defense Architecture Framework Deliverables

The U.S. Department of Defense expended considerable resources over the past years developing its Department of Defense Architecture Framework (DoDAF). This life cycle is a successor to another that was created during the 1970s and 1980s. The DoDAF is a general purpose framework, and has been used for multiple classes of architectures. Included for example are: weapon systems, force deployments, all manners and classes of hardware and software, and for information technology systems.

This collection of architecture products is generalized. A specialization of these generalized DoDAF architecture work products is in the area of IT Systems engineering architecture. Table 20 presents that specialization. The first column identifies the overall class of a set of products. The second column is the short name for the framework product. The third column is the name of the product. The fourth column is an overall description of the product. The fifth column identifies the Governance work products from Chapter 5 that needed for governance. This table then represents a governance specialization of the DoD's Architecture Framework.

U.S. Department of Defense DoD Architecture Frame Framework (Version 2.2, February 2010)				
View	**Frame-work Product**	**Frame Product Name**	**General Description**	**Metabase System Database Objects**
All Views	AV-1	Overview and Summary Information	Describes a Project's Visions, Goals, Objectives, Plans, Activities, Events, Conditions, Measures, Effects (Outcomes), and produced objects.	Mission, Database Domains
	AV-2	Integrated Dictionary	An architectural data repository with definitions of all terms used throughout the architectural data and presentations.	Business Terms, Data Element Model
Capa-bility View Point	CV-1	Vision	The overall vision for transformational endeavors, which provides a strategic context for the capabilities described and a high level scope	Missions, Organizations and Functions along with Mission-Organizations and Mission-Organization Functions.
	CV-2	Capability Taxonomy	A hierarchies of capabilities which specify all the capabilities that are referenced throughout one or more	Missions, Organizations and Functions along with Mission-Organizations and Mission-Organization Functions.

U.S. Department of Defense DoD Architecture Frame Framework (Version 2.2, February 2010)				
View	**Frame-work Product**	**Frame Product Name**	**General Description**	**Metabase System Database Objects**
			Architectural Descriptions.	
	CV-3	Capability Phasing	The planned achievement of capability at different points in time or during specific periods of time. The CV-3 shows the capability phasing in terms of the activities, conditions, desired effects, rules complied with, resource consumption and production, and measures, without regard to the performer and location solutions	Reports on the intersection between Business Information Systems and Business Events along with their Business Calendar Cycles and Business Cycles.
	CV-4	Capability Dependen-cies	The dependencies between planned capabilities and the definition of logical groupings of capabilities.	Reports from the intersection of Mission-Organization-Function, Information Needs Analysis, Resource Life Cycle Nodes and Business Information Systems
	CV-5	Capability to Organiza-tional Mapping	The fulfillment of capability requirements shows the planned capability deployment and interconnection for a particular Capability Phase. The CV-5 shows the planned	Missions, Organizations and Functions along with Mission-Organizations and Mission-Organization Functions and the Business Information Systems.

U.S. Department of Defense DoD Architecture Frame Framework (Version 2.2, February 2010)				
View	**Frame-work Product**	**Frame Product Name**	**General Description**	**Metabase System Database Objects**
			solution for the phase in terms of performers and locations and their associated concepts.	
	CV-6	Capability to Organizational Activities Mapping	A mapping between the capabilities required and the operational activities that those capabilities support.	Missions, Organizations and Functions along with Mission-Organizations and Mission-Organization Functions and the Business Information Systems.
	CV-7	Capability to Services Mapping	Mapping A mapping between the capabilities and the services that these capabilities enable.	View Data Model as it interfaces with Internet-based services
Data and Information Viewpoint	DIV-1	Conceptual Data Model	The required high-level data concepts and their relationships.	Data Element Model and Specified Data Model
	DIV-2	Logical data model	The documentation of the data requirements and structural business process (activity) rules.	Implemented Database Model
	Div-3	Physical data model	The physical implementation format of the Implemented database model entities, e.g., message formats, file structures, physical schema.	Operational Database Model

U.S. Department of Defense DoD Architecture Frame Framework (Version 2.2, February 2010)				
View	**Frame-work Product**	**Frame Product Name**	**General Description**	**Metabase System Database Objects**
Oper-ational View-point	OV-1	High-Level Operational Concept Graphic	High-level graphical/textual description of operational concept	Mission, Database Domains, Functions, and Organizations
	OV-2	Operational Node Connectivity Description	Description A description of the Resource Flows exchanged between operational activities.	Business Event, Business Calendar, Business Cycle, Business Information Systems, Organization, and Function
	OV-3	Operational Information Exchange Matrix	A description of the resources exchanged and the relevant attributes of the exchanges.	Transaction Data Staging Area Data Model via operational database model, with Business Information Systems, Business Event, Business Calendar, and Business Cycle
	OV-4	Organiza-tional Relationships Chart	Organizational, role, or other relationships among organizations	Organization, Function, and Business Event
	OV-5a	Operational Decompos-ition Tree	The capabilities and activities (operational activities) organized in a hierarchal structure.	Business Function, Business Events, Operational database model, and View Data Model
	OV-5b	Operational Activity Model	The context of capabilities and activities (operational activities) and their relationships among activities, inputs, and outputs; Additional data can show cost, performers or other	Missions, Organizations and Functions along with Mission-Organizations and Mission-Organization Functions mapped to Business Information Systems.

U.S. Department of Defense DoD Architecture Frame Framework (Version 2.2, February 2010)				
View	**Frame-work Product**	**Frame Product Name**	**General Description**	**Metabase System Database Objects**
			pertinent information.	
	OV-6a	Operational Rules Model	One of three models used to describe activity (operational activity). It identifies business rules that constrain operations.	Business Functions, Business Events, Operational database model, Views, Data Integrity Rules, Business Information Systems, and Database Objects.
	OV-6b	State Transition Description	One of three models used to describe operational activity (activity). It identifies business process (activity) responses to events (usually, very short activities).	Projects (To Be and As-is) That Identify Business Functions, Business Events, Operational database model, Views, Data Integrity Rules, Business Information Systems, and Database Objects.
	OV-6c	Event-Trace Description	One of three models used to describe activity (operational activity). It traces actions in a scenario or sequence of events.	Mappings Regarding Business Functions, Business Events, Operational database model, Views, Data Integrity Rules, Business Information Systems, and Database Objects.
	PV-1	Project Portfolio Relationships	It describes the dependency relationships between the organizations and projects and the organizational structures needed to manage a portfolio of projects.	Intersection between Project Management Projects and Business-Organization-Functions.

U.S. Department of Defense DoD Architecture Frame Framework (Version 2.2, February 2010)				
View	**Frame-work Product**	**Frame Product Name**	**General Description**	**Metabase System Database Objects**
	PV-2	Project Time lines	A time line perspective on programs or projects, with the key milestones and interdependencies.	Report from Project Management module
	PV-2	Project to Capability Mapping	A mapping of programs and projects to capabilities to show how the specific projects and program elements help to achieve a capability.	Intersection between Mission-Organization-Function, Business Information Systems with their Business Events, and Resource Life Cycle Analysis Nodes all based on the Project Deliverable sequences from Project Management module.
Service Model	SvcV-1	Services Context Description	The identification of services, service items, and their interconnections.	View Models intersection with Business Information System.
	SvcV-2	Services Resource Flow Description	A description of Resource Flows exchanged between services.	View Models intersection with Business Information System.
	SvcV-3a	Systems Services Matrix	The relationships among or between systems and services in a given Architectural Description.	View Models intersection with Business Information System.

U.S. Department of Defense DoD Architecture Frame Framework (Version 2.2, February 2010)				
View	**Frame-work Product**	**Frame Product Name**	**General Description**	**Metabase System Database Objects**
	SvcV-3b	Service Services Matrix	The relationships among services in a given Architectural Description. It can be designed to show relationships of interest, (e.g., service-type interfaces, planned vs. existing interfaces).	View Models intersection with Business Information System.
	SvcV-4	Services Functionality Description	The functions performed by services and the service data flows among service functions (activities).	Intersection between Mission-Organization-Function and View Models intersection with Business Information System.
	SvcV-5	Operational Activity to Services Traceability Matrix	A mapping of services (activities) back to operational activities (activities).	Intersection between Mission-Organization-Function and View Models intersection with Business Information System.
	SvcV-6	Services Resource Flow	It provides details of service Resource Flow elements being exchanged between services and the attributes of that exchange.	Intersection between Mission-Organization-Function and View Models intersection with Business Information System.
	SvcV-7	Services Measures Matrix	The measures (metrics) of Services Model elements for the appropriate time frame(s).	Intersection between Mission-Organization-Function and View Models intersection with Business Information System.

U.S. Department of Defense DoD Architecture Frame Framework (Version 2.2, February 2010)				
View	**Frame-work Product**	**Frame Product Name**	**General Description**	**Metabase System Database Objects**
	SvcV-8	Services Evolution Description	The planned incremental steps toward migrating a suite of services to a more efficient suite or toward evolving current services to a future implementation.	Intersection between Mission-Organization-Function and View Models intersection with Business Information System subsetted from Project Deliverables from Project Management module.
	SvcV-9	Services Technology & Skills	The emerging technologies, software/hardware products, and skills that are expected to be available in a given set of time frames and that will affect future service development.	Project Deliverables from Project Management module.
	SvcV-10a	Services Rules Model	One of three models used to describe service functionality. It identifies constraints that are imposed on systems functionality due to some aspect of system design or implementation.	Intersection between Mission-Organization-Function and View Models intersection with Business Information System along with Data Integrity Rules.
	SvcV-10b	Services State Transition Description	One of three models used to describe service functionality. It identifies responses of services to events.	Business Information Systems along with Business Events, Business Event Cycles, and Calendar Cycles intersected with selected Resource Life Cycle Nodes.

U.S. Department of Defense DoD Architecture Frame Framework (Version 2.2, February 2010)				
View	**Frame-work Product**	**Frame Product Name**	**General Description**	**Metabase System Database Objects**
	SvcV-10c	Services Event-Trace	One of three models used to describe service functionality. It identifies service-specific refinements of critical sequences of events described in the Operational Viewpoint.	Intersection between Mission-Organization-Function and View Models intersection with Business Information System.
Standards Viewpoint	StdV-1	Standards Profile	The listing of standards that apply to solution elements.	N/A
	StdV-2	Standards Forecast	The description of emerging standards and potential impact on current solution elements, within a set of time frames.	N/A
Systems	SV-1	Systems Interface Description	The identification of systems, system items, and their interconnections.	Business Information Systems, Views, and Inter-view Mappings
	SV-2	Systems Resource Flow	A description of Resource Flows exchanged between systems.	Not directly applicable to governance communities of interest.

U.S. Department of Defense DoD Architecture Frame Framework (Version 2.2, February 2010)				
View	**Frame-work Product**	**Frame Product Name**	**General Description**	**Metabase System Database Objects**
	SV-3	Systems to Systems Matrix	The relationships among systems in a given Architectural Description. It can be designed to show relationships of interest, (e.g., system-type interfaces, planned vs. existing interfaces).	Business Information Systems, View Models, and Operational database models
	SV-4	Systems Functionality Description	Description The functions (activities) performed by systems and the system data flows among system functions (activities).	Business Information Systems, Database Objects Model, and Implemented database model
	SV-5a	Operational Activity to System Function Traceability Matrix	Traceability Matrix A mapping of system functions (activities) back to operational activities (activities).	Business Information Systems, Business Events, Business Functions, and Optionally to Organizations and Missions
	SV-5b	Operational Activity to Systems Traceability Matrix	A mapping of systems back to capabilities or operational activities (activities).	Intersection between Mission-Organization-Function and View Models intersection with Business Information Systems.
	SV-6	Systems Resource Flow Matrix	Provides details of system resource flow elements being exchanged between systems and the attributes of that exchange.	Business Information Systems, Views, and Inter-view Mappings

U.S. Department of Defense DoD Architecture Frame Framework (Version 2.2, February 2010)				
View	**Frame-work Product**	**Frame Product Name**	**General Description**	**Metabase System Database Objects**
	SV-7	Systems Measures Matrix	The measures (metrics) of Systems Model elements for the appropriate time frame(s).	Not directly applicable to governance communities of interest.
	SV-8	Systems Evolution Description	The planned incremental steps toward migrating a suite of systems to a more efficient suite, or toward evolving a current system to a future implementation.	Projects Relative to the "To Be" and "As-is" That Identify Business Functions, Business Events, Operational database model, Views, Data Integrity Rules, Business Information Systems, and Database Objects.
	SV-9	Systems Technology & Skills Forecast	The emerging technologies, software/hardware products, and skills that are expected to be available in a given set of time frames and that will affect future system development.	Not directly applicable to governance communities of interest.
	SV-10a	Systems Rules Model	One of three models used to describe system functionality. It identifies constraints that are imposed on systems functionality due to some aspect of system design or implementation.	Business Information System, Database Objects, Data Integrity Rules and Implemented database model.

U.S. Department of Defense DoD Architecture Frame Framework (Version 2.2, February 2010)				
View	**Frame-work Product**	**Frame Product Name**	**General Description**	**Metabase System Database Objects**
	SV-10b	Systems State Transition Description	One of three models used to describe system functionality. It identifies responses of systems to events.	Business Events and Database Objects
	SV-10c	Systems Event Trace Description	One of three models used to describe system functionality. It identifies system-specific refinements of critical sequences of events described in the Operational Viewpoint.	Mappings among Business Events and Database Objects
	SV-11	Physical Schema	Physical implementation of the Implemented database model entities, e.g., message formats, file structures, physical schema	Operational database model and View Data Model

Table 20. U.S. Department of Defense Generalized Architecture Framework and Metabase System Database Objects.

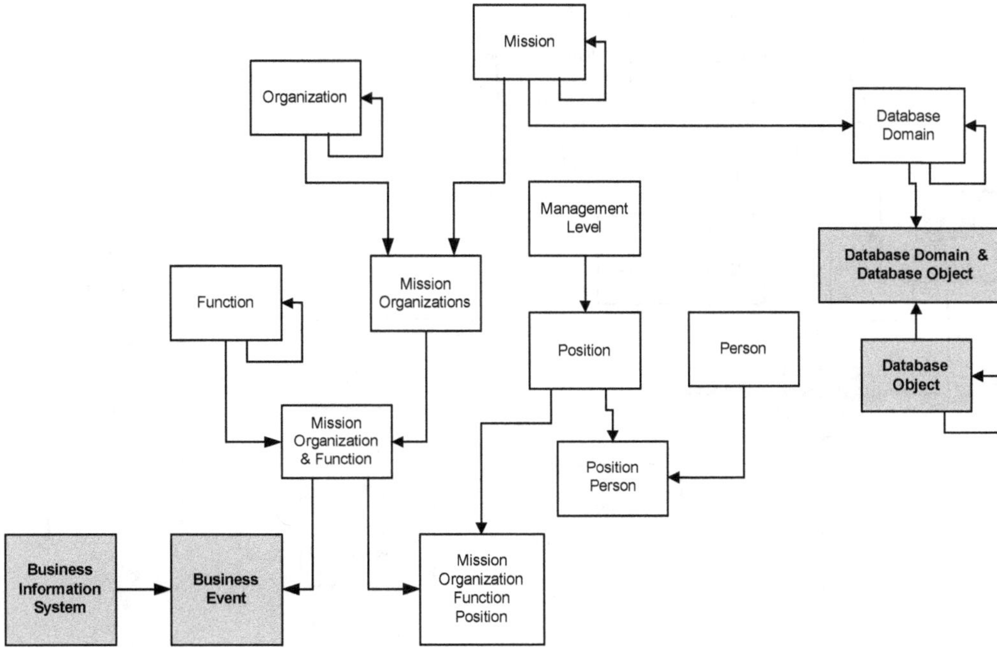

Figure 29. Mission Organization Function Position.

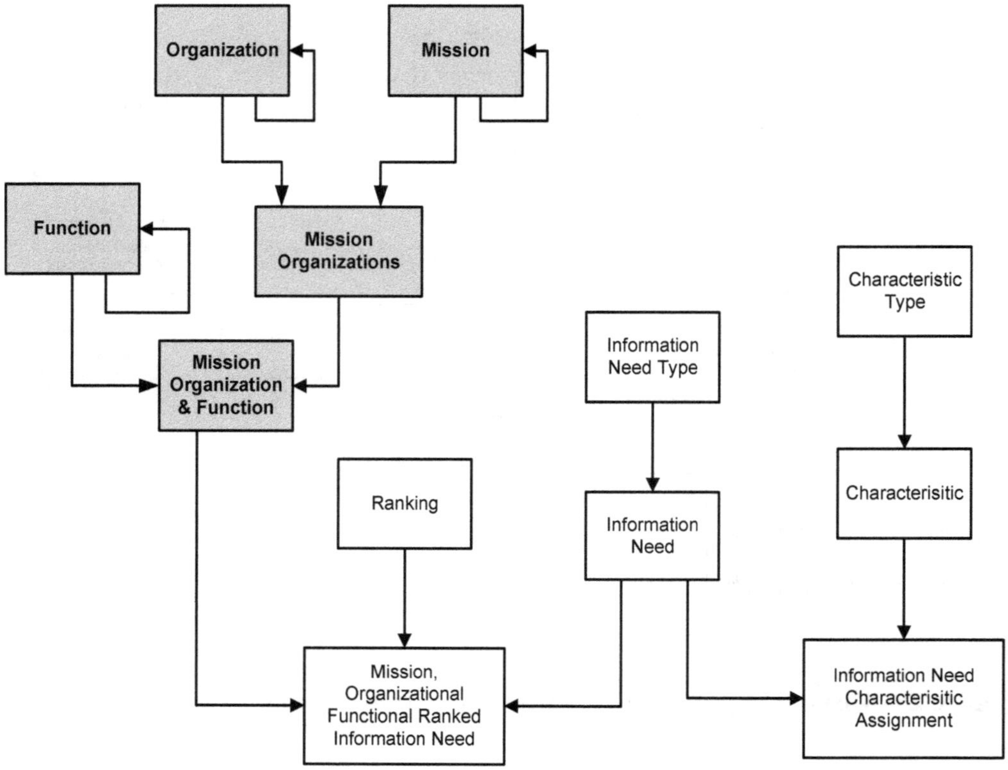

Figure 30. Information Needs Analysis.

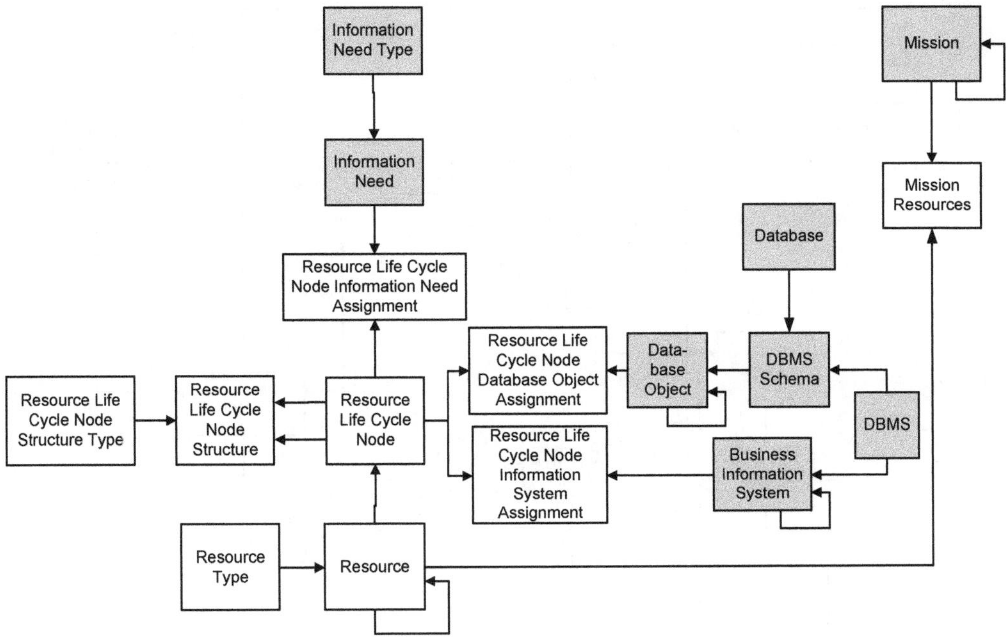

Figure 31. Resource Life Cycle Analysis.

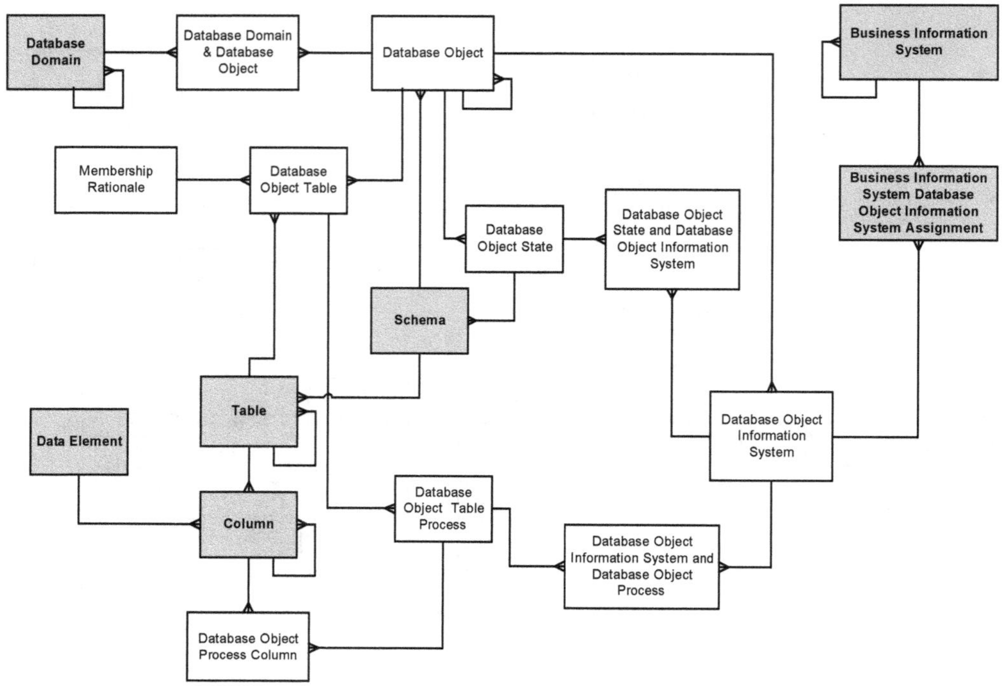

Figure 32. Database Objects.

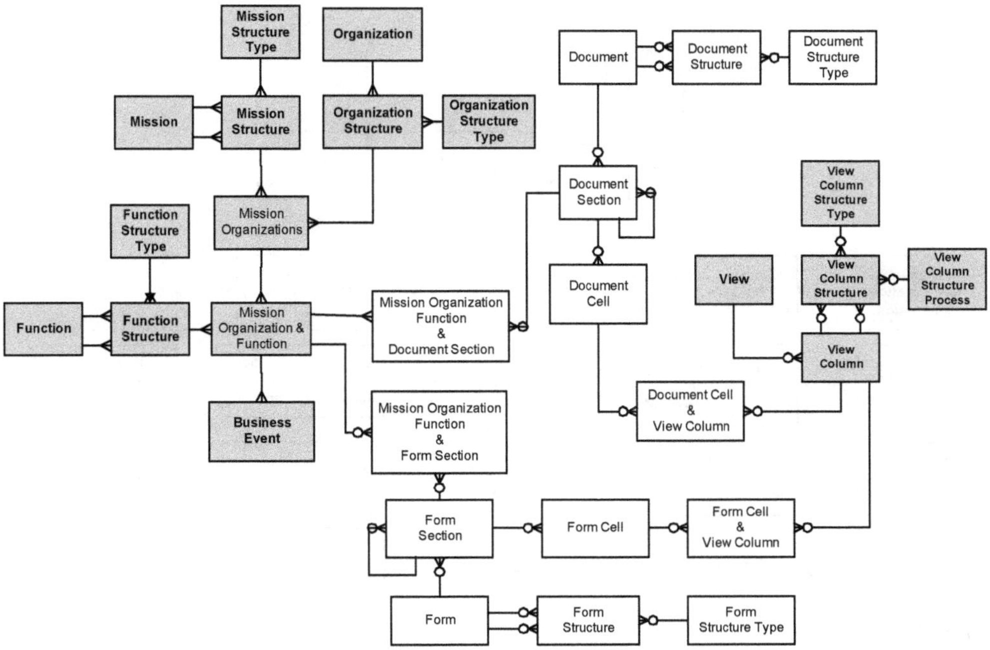

Figure 33. Documents and Forms.

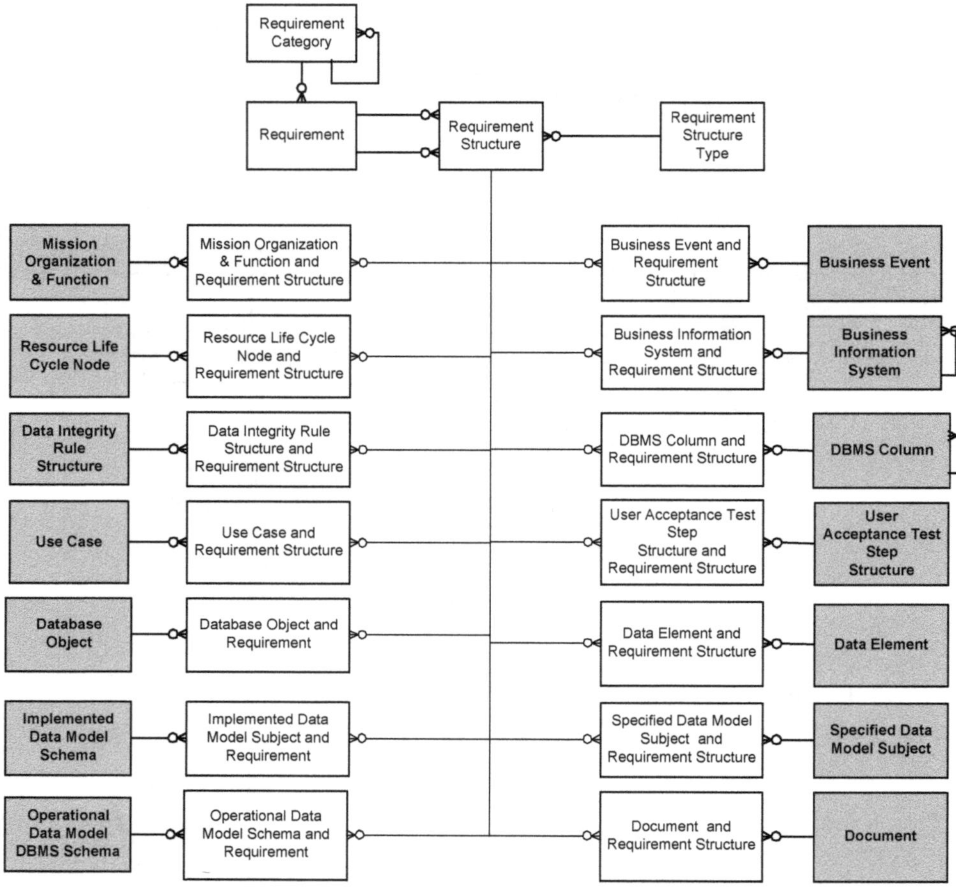

Figure 34. Requirements.

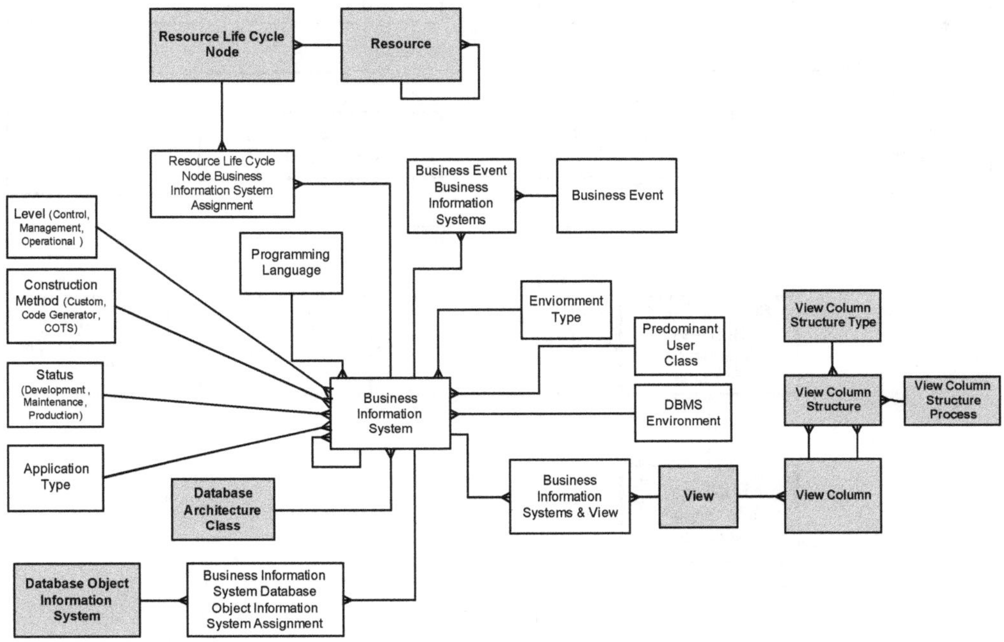

Figure 35. Business Information Systems.

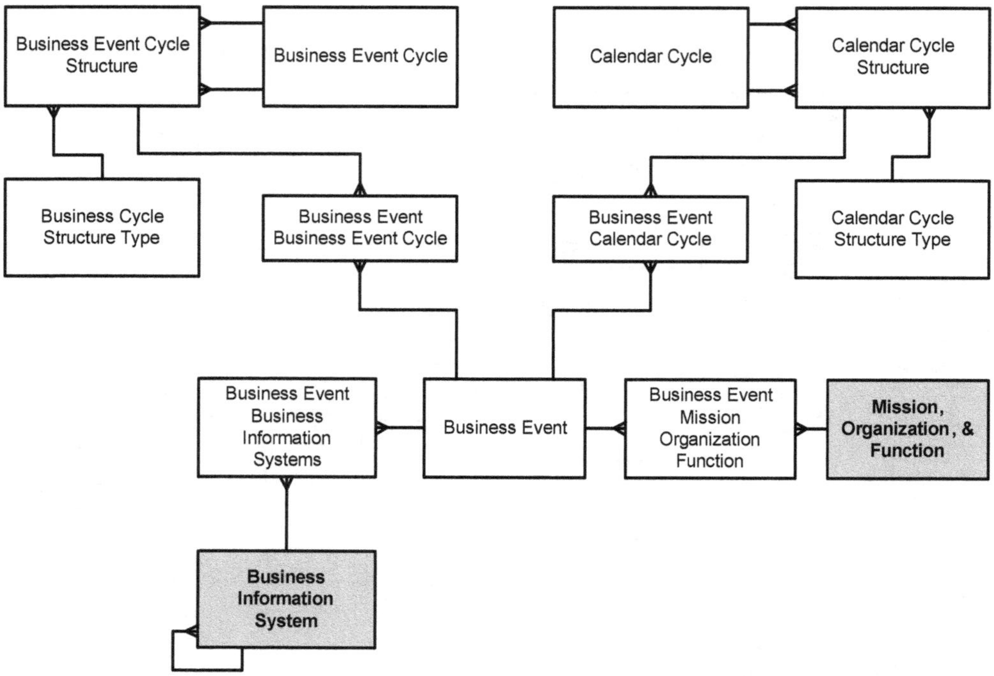

Figure 36. Business Events.

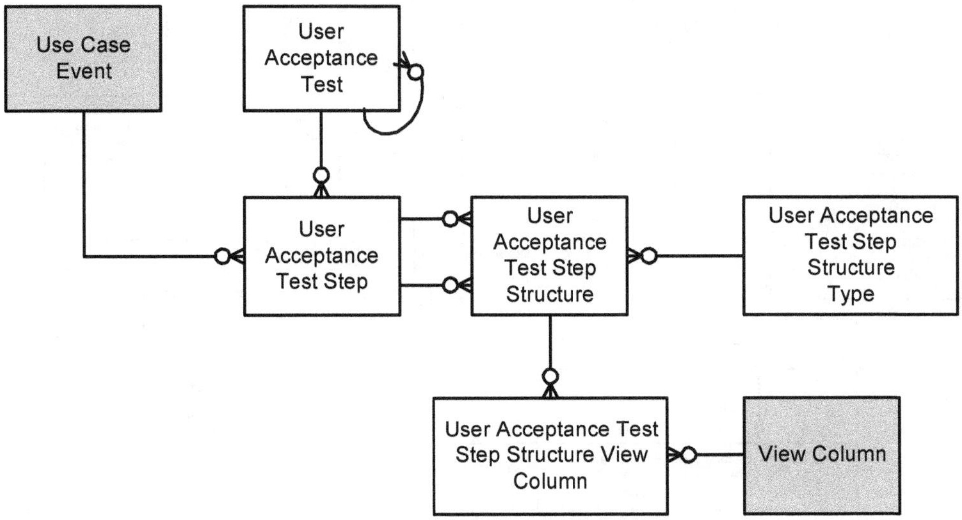

Figure 37. User Acceptance Tests.

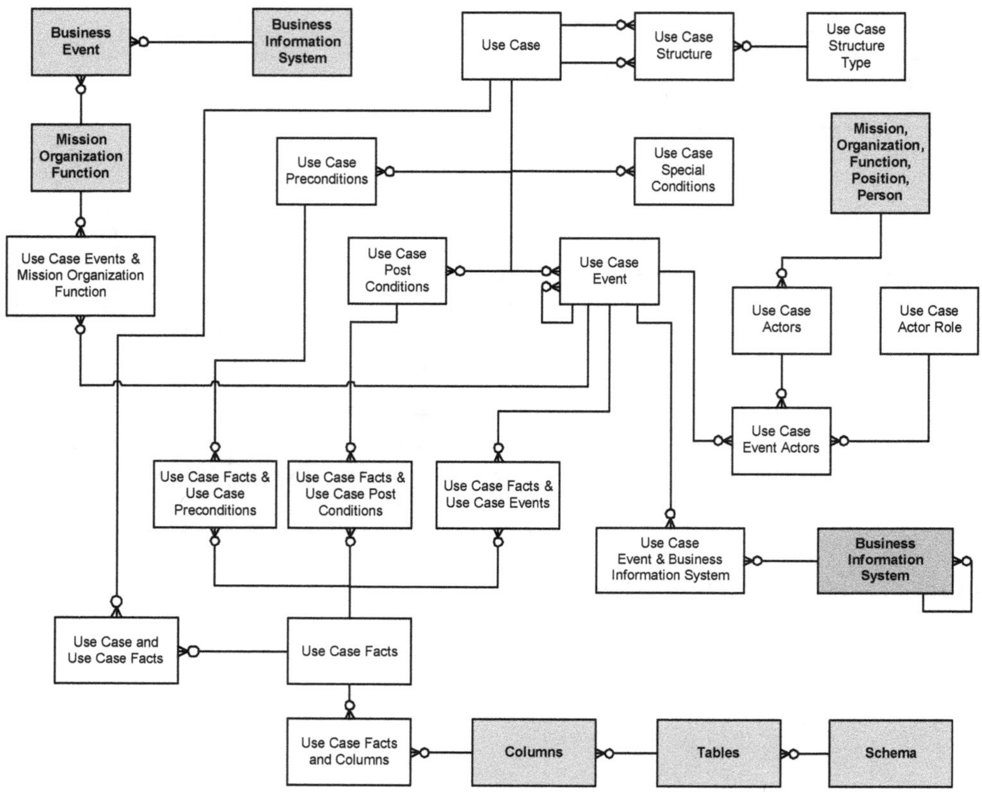

Figure 38. Use Cases.

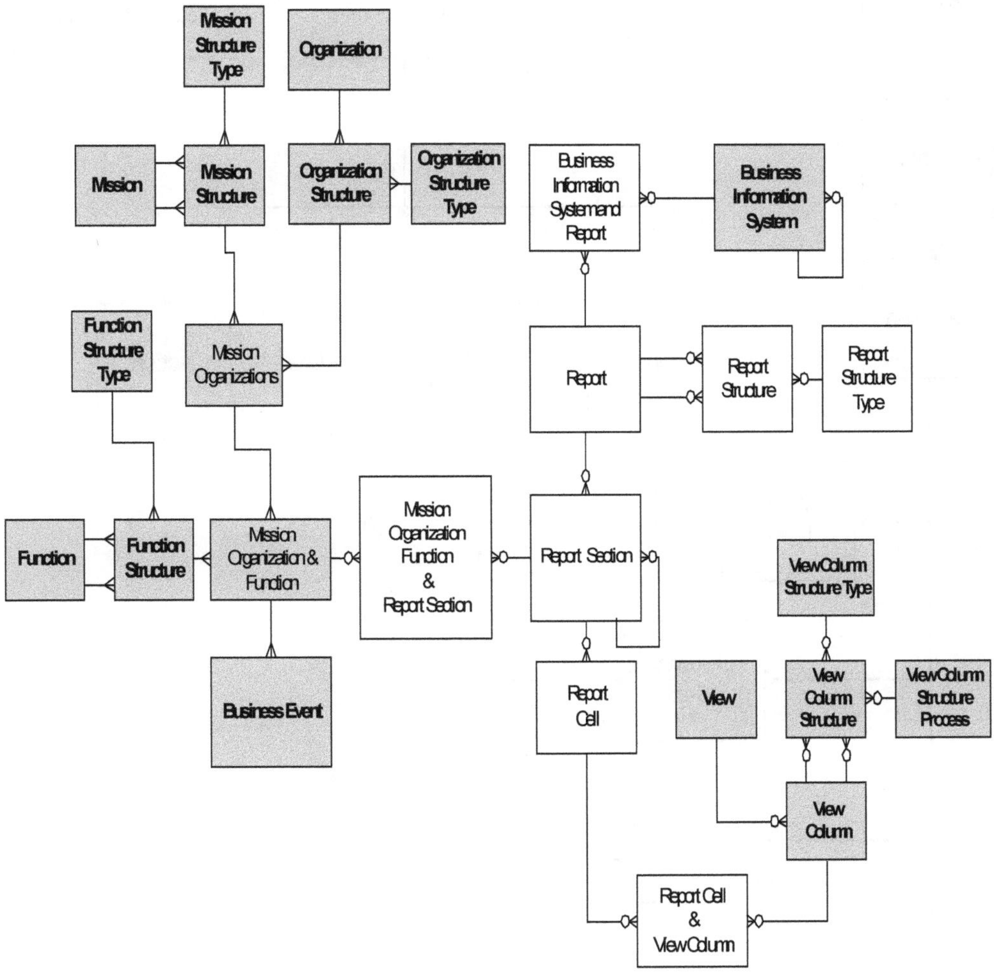

Figure 39. Reports.

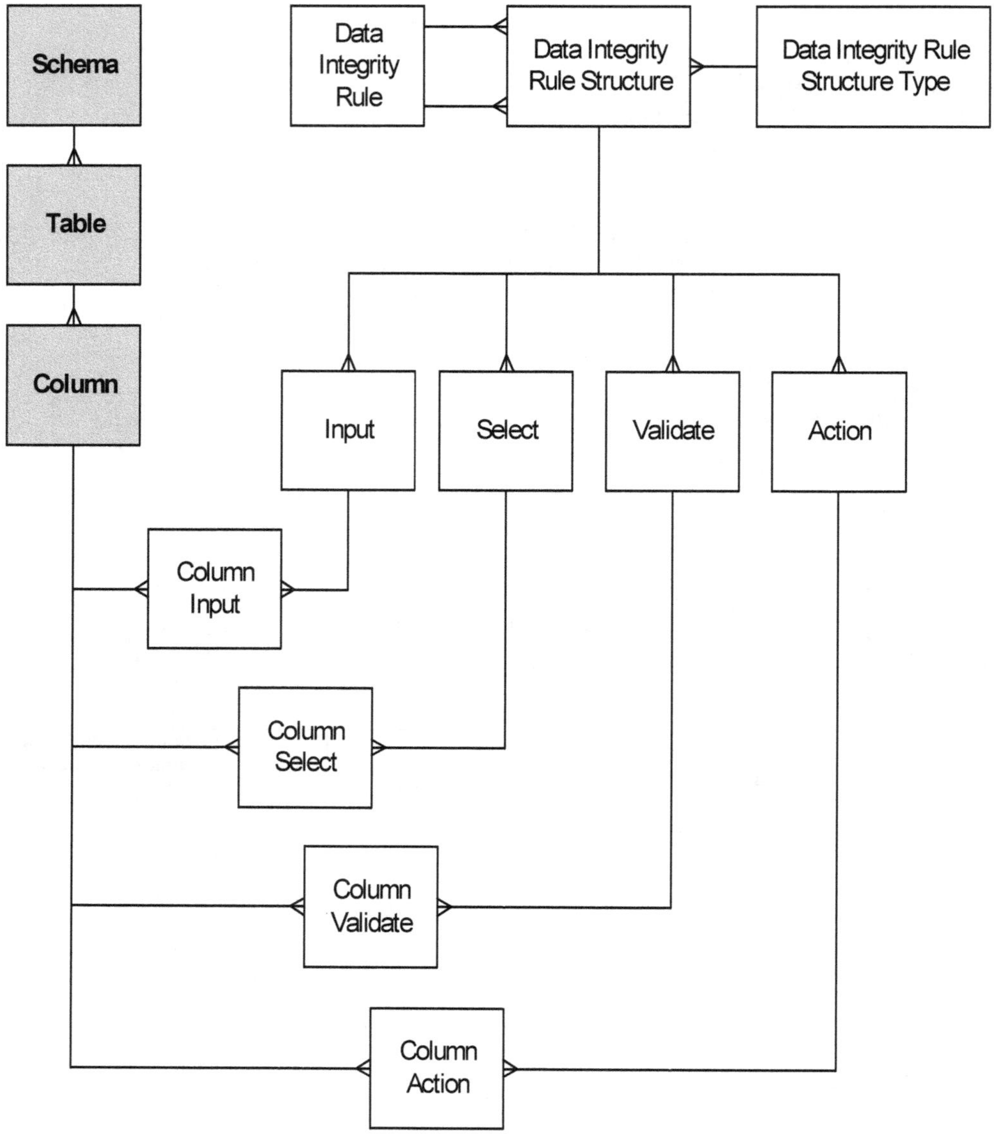

Figure 40. Data Integrity Rules

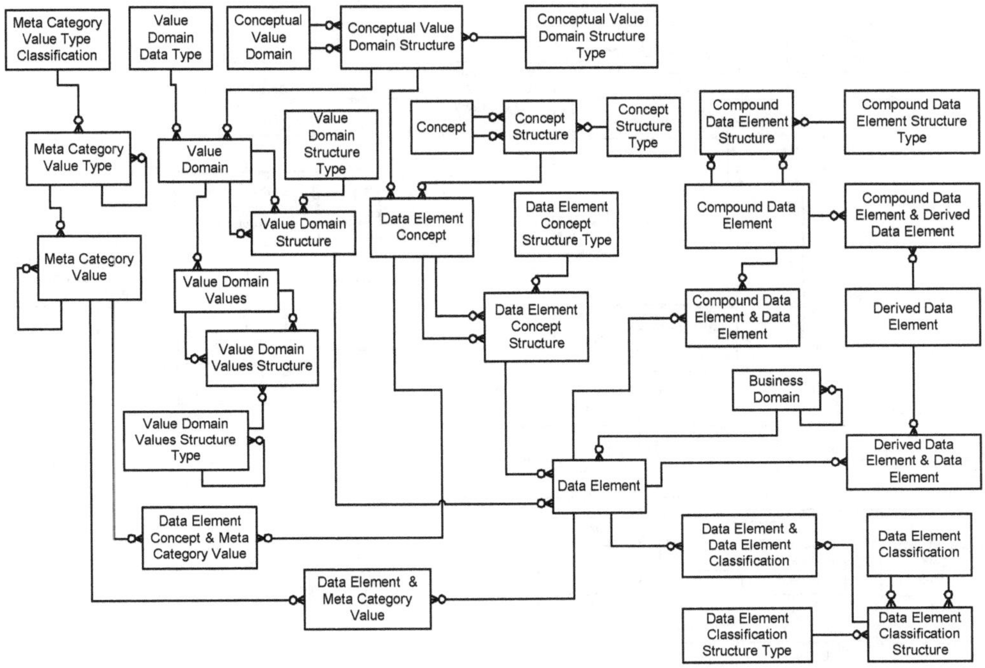

Figure 41. Data Element Model.

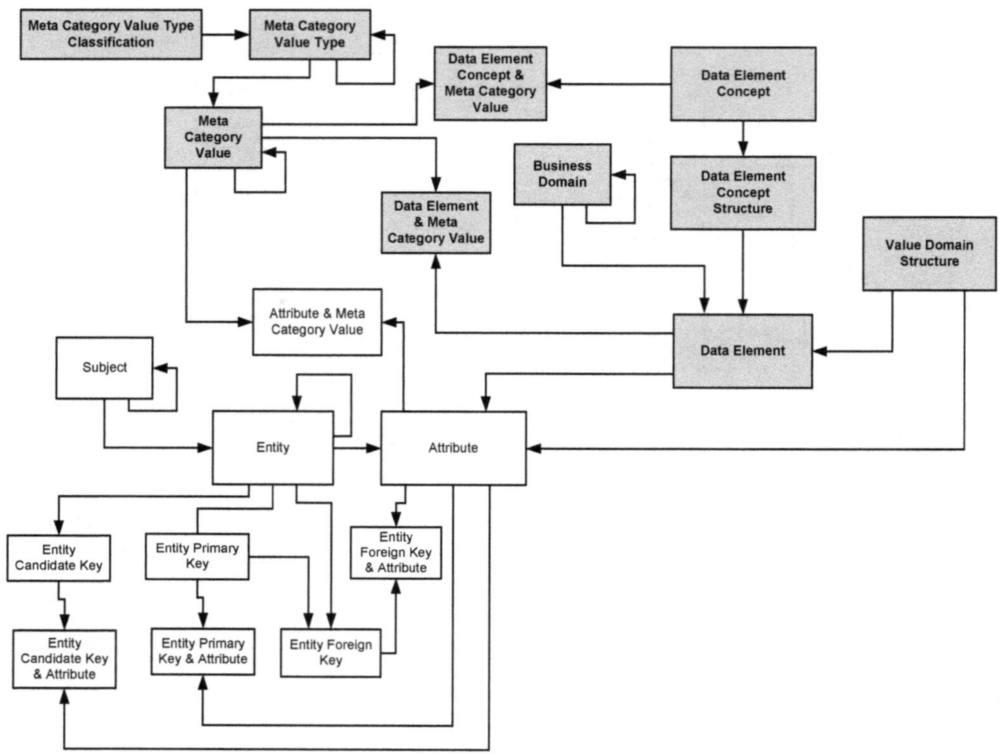

Figure 42. Specified Data Model.

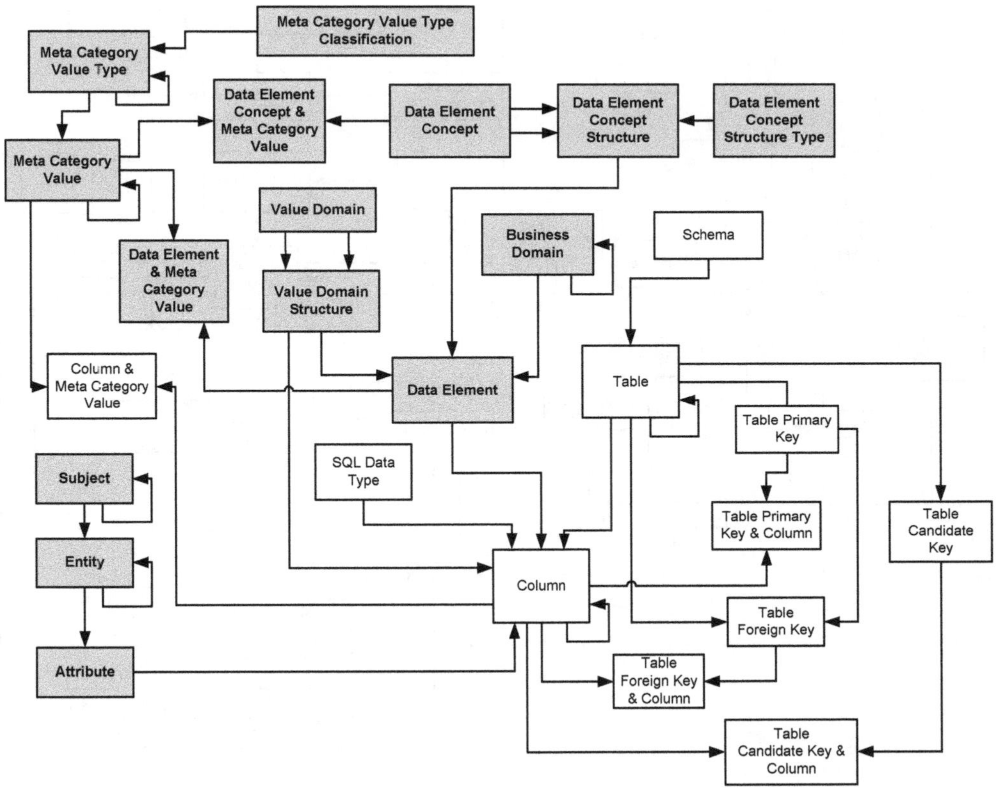

Figure 43. Implemented Database Model.

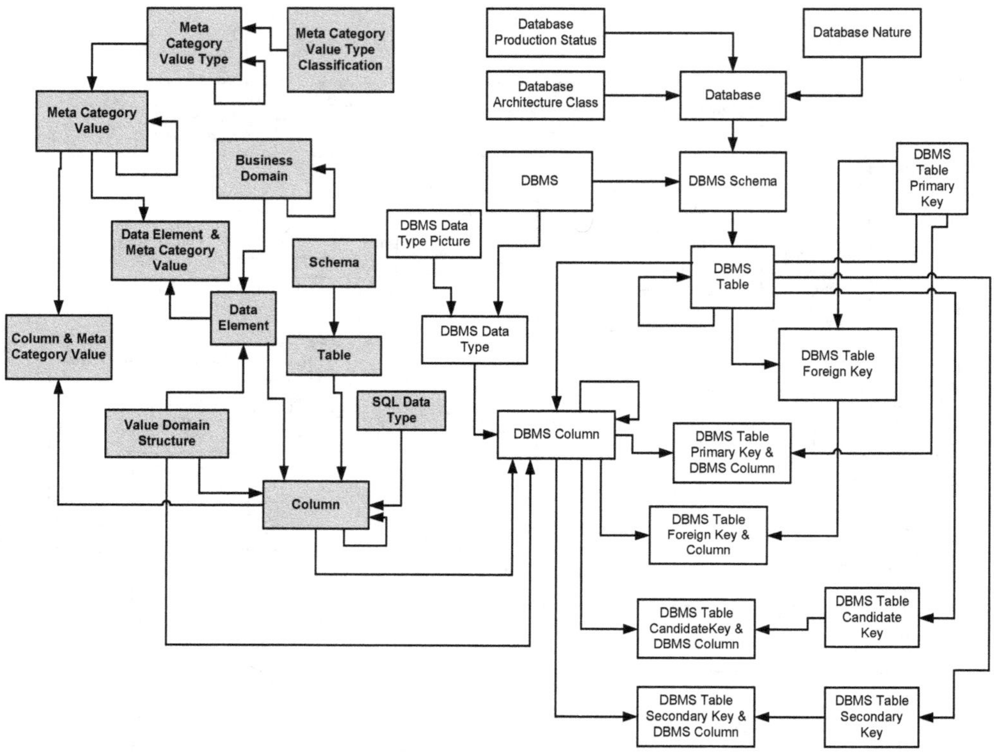

Figure 44. Operational Database Model.

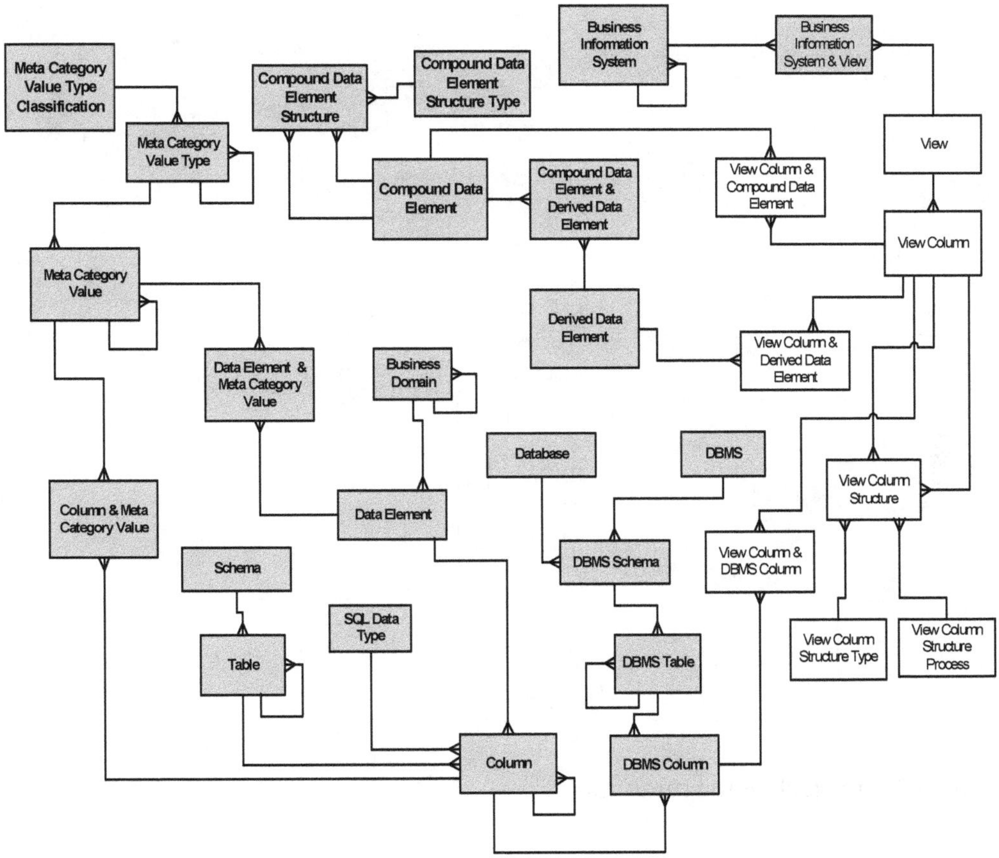

Figure 45. View Data Model.

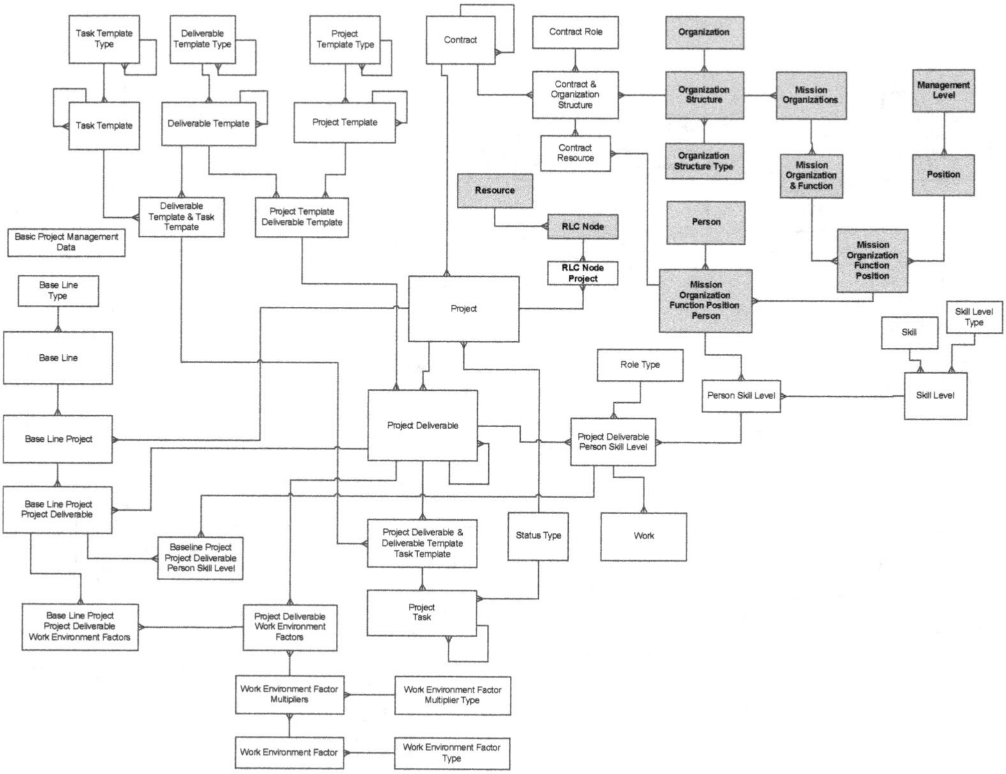

Figure 46. Project Management.

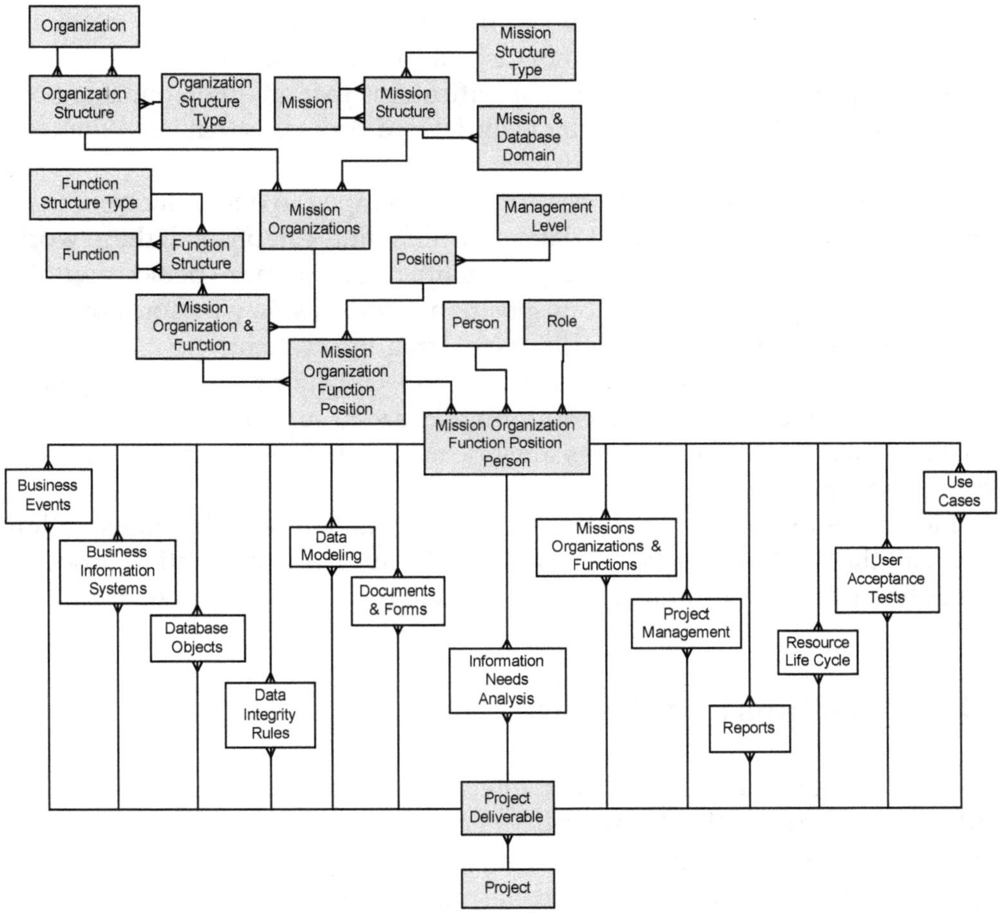

Figure 47. Governance

5.8 Work Product Governance Summary

Work products are the "what" that is collected in support of shared missions. Work products specifications are not just simple database table specifications. Each work product is a collection of specifications that are interconnected by relationships, and are controlled by well-defined processes that keep the work products in a state of high-integrity.

Every work product should be ultimately mapped to one or more missions. Further, once a shared data environment is established, these work product instances should be the responsibility of one or more persons within their mission-organization-function-position context as they perform their governance functions through business information systems.

Work products are essentially the policy specifications surrounding the shared word product. If shared environments are to support audits, or to reflect history, these requirements must be manifest in the specifications of the work products.

Figures 29 through 47 are third-normal form data model diagrams within which all the work products can be found. The audit and evaluation processes through which work products are assessed are found in Chapter 6.

5.9 Questions and Exercises

1. Every collection of metadata must interrelate seamlessly, horizontally, vertically, and by depth. Horizontally means that work products have the same work product parent. Vertically means that work products of different types related in a parent-child or "uncle" relationship. By depth, it means that the work products that exist from different projects, or databases, across time are interrelated. Do you agree with this three dimensional characterization?

What benefits accrue by the integration non-redundancy, and inheritance? Does such a strategy enable team work and a greater quantity of consistency across a wider domain? If yes, why? If not, why not? Provide examples from within your own organization.

2. How much time, effort, and energy would be saved if your enterprise metadata were organized according to the work products contained in this strategy?

3. If your organization does not have integrated metadata across all your projects, what is that costing the enterprise in terms of increased resolution time, increased construction of bridge data structures, semantic conflicts, mismatched precision, granularity, and timeliness? Could these problems have been avoided if there was integrated, non-redundant, and semantically harmonious metadata from which to build you databases and business information systems? If yes, why? If not, why not? Provide examples from within your own organization.

4. Do you fundamentally agree with the engineering of work products as specified at the start of Chapter 5? That is, isn't each work product a collection of tables, row-based processes, Metabase System functional module based processes that create and update them, that ultimately form collections of the work products?

5. When engineering, the complete set of work products for a Metabase, isn't it really the same overall process as engineering and designing any other database? If yes, then why? If no, what's really different? Provide examples from within your own organization.

6. As background, a careful examination of Figures 29 thorough 47 show three classes of work products: simple hierarchies, recursions, and networks. Simple hierarchies are depicted by a crow's-foot between to two meta-objects. Figure 35, for example, has a simple relationship between Programming Language and Business Information System.

Recursions are depicted by a crow's-foot from and to the same meta-object. Figure 35 also shows a recursive relationship between Business Information System and itself. Network meta-objects are depicted by two crow's-foot lines from one meta-object to another.

Finally, Figure 36 shows a network relationship between Business Even Cycle and Business Event Cycle Structure.

These three meta-object classes have all been proven critical through intense analysis of the metadata needed for enterprise architectures, data models, and process models. All are required. None are optional. An examination of the complete set of Figures 29 through 47 show about a dozen networks and about 18 recursions.

Now, shouldn't the metadata end-user be responsible for deeply knowing the complexity of these data structures, or should the supporting Metabase System be responsible for dealing with all the complexity, navigation, integrity and non-redundancy? If you agree, what benefits accrue from the Metabase System knowing and handling these complexities versus the end user having to know and handle these complexities? If you disagree, how would the complete set of end-users know what is required, how it should be interrelated, integrated, and made non-redundant? Provide examples from within your own organization of the benefits and costs for both sides.

7. If you didn't use a database centric information system for collecting, storing, and interrelating metadata, what do you use? How is it faster, easier and more able to interrelate, be non-redundant, and current than a Metabase System? If it isn't, how much does that affect your ability to have enterprise-wide governance?

8. Do you keep metadata for all these work products? If not, do you keep that metadata in different forms? What is the cost in terms of time, effort, and energy of having metadata in different forms? What could be saved if all your metadata was in a single metadata repository (i.e., a Metabase System database) and the metadata was integrated, interrelated, non-redundant and timely? Provide examples from within your own organization.

9. While the DoDAF framework in Section 5.8 is different from the Knowledge Worker Framework, it seems to require very similar work products as does the Knowledge Worker Framework. Isn't it more important to know what the framework requires than possibly the style and organization of the Framework? Does your organization have multiple or different frameworks? If yes, how different are they in terms of requiring what ensures success? Provide examples of similarity and differences from your business.

6

Governance Process Management

In the broadest sense, the Metabase System, which essentially is a metadata management system, is an application that captures, stores, reports and updates metadata through a business information system. Most likely metadata management system has as its "data management engine" a database management system (DBMS). Similar to all other management business information systems, there is a database design (See Chapter 5), which are the "targets" of governance, and then, a process design, which are the methods for accomplishing governance assessments.

This chapter centers on the execution of the processes at the heart of determining the integrity and correctness of the various work products that are actually stored in the Metabase System databases as a consequence of the various Metabase System functional modules. Contained in this chapter are the functional specifications of the various governance processes that accomplish enterprise governance. The sections are:

- Enterprise Architecture Governance
- Business Information Systems Governance
- Data Architecture Governance
- Project Management Governance

Each section has an overall general description, a set of subsections, and, then for each subsection, a table of the processes that need to exist to accomplish the governance. These processes are described generically so that they can be used to evaluate the integrity and correctness of the work products that the Community of Interest assesses. How and when and what sequence governance processes should be accomplished is implied within the Whitemarsh database project methodologies.

6.1 Enterprise Architecture Governance

Enterprise architecture work products consist of the following classes:

- Missions
- Organizations
- Functions
- Position
- Information Needs
- Resource Life Cycles
- Database Domains
- Database Objects
- Requirements

Collectively these metadata components define the enterprise's architecture. It is within these metadata-based work product collections that all databases and business information systems exist. It is critical that these metadata classes are very carefully governed. The time and effort it takes to create these metadata-based work product collections is quite small compared to the resources required for the creation and implementation of the databases and business information systems represented by the metadata contained in these metadata work product collections. The value however is not only very great, but if done wrong or incompletely, the possibility of identifying the correct databases and business information systems is tremendously lessened. In an analysis of 13 multi-hundred million dollar IT debacles that were analyzed by the United States Congress's Office of Accountability, it was shown that 95% of the errors that occur are outside the proper tasks of IT. That is, they occur almost totally with the proper collection and specification of enterprise architecture metadata.

6.1.1 Missions, Organizations, and Functions

The mission models, depicted in Figure 29 are the boundaries of the scope of the enterprise. It is within mission models that database domains that lead to database designs are created. Missions are also the scope boundaries for all enterprise organizations and functions.

As a database project commences, an organization model, depicted in

Figure 29 is built and then allocated to the various missions. This permits the easy identification of those components of the enterprise that are involved in any effort. Once organizations are created, they are allocated to missions such that every mission is addressed and every organization is responsible for one or more missions. Unallocated missions and/or missions that are allocated to every organization should be investigated.

As a database project continues, it is important to know just what functions, depicted in Figure 29, are accomplished by any organization within the scope of a mission. In the context of this book, all functions are manual processes. The hierarchical function models are created and interrelated with the various mission-organizations that perform them. Because functions are human activities, there may be multiples sets of functions that are generally equivalent but differ in style of knowledge worker processes. The differences are not critical because the relationship between a business information system and a business function is through the intermediary, business event.

Missions, Organizations, and Functions can exist both in hierarchical and network forms. The actual Mission, Organization, and Function actual instances are specified independent of their interrelationships. The relationships are present in the "structure" tables. Assessed as well are the relationships between Missions and Organizations, Mission-Organizations and Functions, Mission-Organization-Functions and other work products such as Business Events, Document Sections, and the like. Assess as well are both Positions and Persons are these are related to the various Mission-Organization-Functions as a way to know who is responsible for creating and updating a Mission-Organization-Function work product or who assessed a work product.

The assessment processes are listed in Table 21. The assessments are contained in Appendix 1. They are listed there in alphabetical order except for the data architecture processes that are listed in "logical" order.

Assessment Process Id	Assessment Process Name
42.	Assess Missions-Organizations-Functions Positions Persons
42.1.	Assess Mission
42.2.	Assess Mission Structure

Assessment Process Id	Assessment Process Name
42.3.	Assess Organization
42.4.	Assess Organization Structure
42.5.	Assess Function
42.6.	Assess Function Structure
42.7.	Assess Mission-Organization
42.8.	Assess Mission-Organization-Function
42.9.	Assess Mission-Organization-Function Business Event
42.10.	Assess Mission-Organization-Function Document Section
42.11.	Assess Mission-Organization-Function Form Section
42.12.	Assess Mission-Organization-Function Information Need
42.13.	Assess Mission-Organization-Function Position
42.14.	Assess Mission-Organization-Function Project Deliverable
42.15.	Assess Mission-Organization-Function Report Section
42.16.	Assess Mission-Organization-Function Requirement
42.17.	Assess Mission-Organization-Function Use Case Event
42.18.	Assess Position
42.19.	Assess Person
42.20.	Assess Database Domain

Table 21. Mission-Organization-Function Related Assessments.

6.1.2 Positions and Persons

The position, person and management levels, depicted in Figure 29, enable organizations to identify positions by management levels and the assignment of those to particular mission-organization-function combinations. This process also allows the inclusion of specific individuals and the association of those individuals to positions.

The assessment processes for this area are listed in Table 21.

6.1.3 Information Needs Analysis

The purpose of Information Needs Analysis, depicted in Figure 30, is to answer the questions:

- Who needs what and in what organizational context?
- What function purpose does the information serve?
- What resource life cycle node does the information pertain to?
- What are the critical characteristics of the information?
- Through which databases and information needs is this information provided?

The information needs analysis permits recording of the characteristics of the information needs of the enterprise. Each information need can be described and the various characteristics and characteristic types can be allocated to each information need. Once information needs are characterized, they can be allocated to the various mission-organization-functions and then ranked. This permits enterprises to know the characteristics of what information is needed by whom within the different organizations in the performance enterprise missions.

Information needs' analysis is essential for comprehensive database design. It is the necessary first step before beginning good database domain specification and Entity Relationship diagram building.

The assessment processes are listed in Table 22. The assessments are contained in Appendix 1. They are listed there in alphabetical order except for the data architecture processes that are listed in "logical" order.

Assessment Process Id	Assessment Process Name
41.	Assess Information Needs
41.1.	Assess Characteristic
41.2.	Assess Information Need
41.3.	Assess Information Need Resource Life Cycle Node
41.4.	Assess Information Need Mission-Organization-Function

Table 22. Information Needs Related Assessments.

6.1.4 Resource Life Cycle Analysis

Resources and Life Cycles, depicted in Figure 31, metadata enable the identification of the various resources within the enterprise that collectively represent either the infrastructure or an external product set of the enterprise. Infrastructure resources include for example, staff, facilities, contracts, finance, and the like. External products include manufactured products, services to customers, and the like. Each resource is then defined in terms of its life cycle. Resource life cycle nodes from different life cycles are interrelated to show enterprise-based interdependencies. Databases and Business information systems, and information needs are then interrelated to each life cycle node. Collectively the fully attributed resource life cycles enable the enterprise to view its complete operation in terms of its essential resources that define its very existence.

The assessment processes are listed in Table 23. The assessments are contained in Appendix 1. They are listed there in alphabetical order except for the data architecture processes that are listed in "logical" order.

Assessment Process Id	Assessment Process Name
46.	Assess Resource Life Cycles
46.1.	Assess Resource

Assessment Process Id	Assessment Process Name
46.2.	Assess Resource Life Cycle Node
46.3.	Assess Resource Life Cycle Node Structure
46.4.	Assess Resource Life Cycle Node Business Information System
46.5.	Assess Resource Life Cycle Node Database Object

Table 23. Resource Life Cycle Related Assessments.

6.1.5 Database Object Class

Database object classes, depicted in Figure 32, are the encapsulated data structures, processes, and constraints necessary to transform a set of data from one value state to the next. Database object classes are essential to the integrity of databases. In this book, and throughout all Whitemarsh literature, the data structure of a database object class consists of an identified set of database tables within a single schema. A database table can be in only one database object class unless that database table is to represent the intersection between two or more database object classes. In such a case, only one of the database object classes can have cascade-delete behavior over that inter-database-object-table. The other database object classes can only have "set null" delete behavior.

In modern SQL DBMSs, there is no explicit notion of a database object class through explicit SQL syntax. Consequently, database object classes, while clearly and explicitly defined in the Implemented Data Model, have to be operationally realized in the Operational Database Model through existing SQL:2003 and earlier syntax. This can largely be done through the use of persistent SQL views that map to a collection of columns across a set of tables. While this is certainly far from ideal, it is the best that ANSI standard SQL has to offer.

The value state integrity of database objects within database object classes is governed by columns and table constraints. The value states are transformed through stored procedures within assertions and triggers. It is important to define database object classes within the domain of the DBMS to ensure that all external language agents such as 4GLs, query languages, and 3GLs are forced to proceed through these DBMS defined and encapsulated database object classes.

The assessment processes are listed in Table 24. The assessments are contained in Appendix 1. They are listed there in alphabetical order except for the data architecture processes that are listed in "logical" order.

Assessment Process Id	Assessment Process Name
33.	Assess Database Objects
33.1.	Assess Database Object
33.2.	Assess Database Object Table
33.3.	Assess Database Object Primitive Data Transformation
33.4.	Assess Database Object State
33.5.	Assess Database Object Information System
33.6.	Assess Database Object Requirement
33.7.	Assess Database Object Data Integrity Rule
33.8.	Assess Database Object Database Domain
33.9.	Assess Database Object Resource Life Cycle
33.10.	Assess Database Object Information System Business Information System

Table 24. Database Object Class Related Assessments.

6.1.6 Database Domain Models

Database Domains, depicted in Figure 29, are "noun-intensive" descriptions of the data inferred by the lowest level of a mission structures. Each database domain is thus restricted in scope to that mission leaf. Additionally, each database domain is represented by a simple entity-relationship diagram.

When all the relevant database domains are completed, these entity-relationship diagrams are combined to ensure that the entities that are named the same are in fact the same and represent the same level of granularity. Similarity, all entities that are the same should have the same name and definition.

The assessment processes for this area are listed in Table 21.

6.1.7 Documents & Forms

Documents are those materials that provide some specification and/or description about one or more aspects of one or more enterprise work products. Documents are able to be interrelated into hierarchies or networks.

Additionally each document is able to be subdivided into a hierarchy of sections, and within each section there can be document cells. In turn, these document cells can be mapped to View Columns, Mission-Organization-Functions, and project management deliverables.

Forms are represent well-defined forms into which data values can be entered individually or in groups. Forms are able to be interrelated into hierarchies or networks.

As with Documents, each form is able to be subdivided into a hierarchy of sections, and within each section there can be form cells. The form cells, in turn, the cells can be mapped to View Columns, and Mission-Organization-Functions.

The assessment processes for both Documents and Forms are listed in Table 25. The assessments are contained in Appendix 1. They are listed there in alphabetical order except for the data architecture processes that are listed in "logical" order.

Assessment Process Id	Assessment Process Name
40.	Assess Documents and Forms
40.1.	Assess Document Model
40.2.	Assess Document
40.3.	Assess Document Structure

Assessment Process Id	Assessment Process Name
40.4.	Assess Document Section
40.5.	Assess Document Section Cell
40.6.	Assess Document Section Cell View Column
40.7.	Assess Form Model
40.8.	Assess Form
40.9.	Assess Form Structure
40.10.	Assess Form Section
40.11.	Assess Form Section Cell
40.12.	Assess Form Section Cell View Column

Table 25. Documents & Forms Related Assessments.

6.1.8 Requirements

Requirements represent one or more conditions or capabilities needed solve a problem or achieve an objective. Requirements must be met or possessed by a solution or solution component to satisfy a contract, standard, specification, or other formally imposed documents. The characteristics of a quality set of requirements:

- **Unitary**. Addresses one and only one thing.
- **Complete**. It is fully stated in one place with no missing information.
- **Consistent**. Is not in conflict with any other requirement and is fully consistent with all authority documentation.
- **Traceable**. Meets all or part of a business' needs as stated and is authoritatively documented.

- **Current**. Has not been obsoleted by the passage of time.
- **Unambiguous**. Expresses objective facts, not subjective opinions, and is subject to one and only one interpretation.
- **Ranked**. Indication that the requirement is mandatory or optional, and for each, a level of importance.
- **Verifiable**. Accomplishment can be through thorough inspection, demonstration, or testing.

Requirements are able to be specified and interrelated into a hierarchy or a network. Requirements are then able to be associated with other work products such as Mission-Organization-Functions, Resource Life Cycles, Data Integrity Rules, and the like.

The assessment processes are listed in Table 26. The assessments are contained in Appendix 1. They are listed there in alphabetical order except for the data architecture processes that are listed in "logical" order.

Assessment Process Id	Assessment Process Name
45.	Assess Requirements
45.1.	Assess Requirement
45.2.	Assess Requirement Category
45.3.	Assess Requirement Structure
45.5.	Assess Requirement Structure Business Information System
45.6.	Assess Requirement Structure Data Element
45.7.	Assess Requirement Structure Database Object
45.8.	Assess Requirement Structure Data Integrity Rule
45.9.	Assess Requirement Structure DBMS Column
45.10.	Assess Requirement Structure Document

Assessment Process Id	Assessment Process Name
45.11.	Assess Requirement Structure Implemented Database Schema
45.12.	Assess Requirement Structure Mission-Organization-Function
45.13.	Assess Requirement Structure Operational Database DBMS Schema
45.14.	Assess Requirement Structure Resource Life Cycle Node
45.15.	Assess Requirement Structure Specified Data Model Subject
45.16.	Assess Requirement Structure Use Case
45.17.	Assess Requirement Structure User Acceptance Test

Table 26. Requirements Related Assessments.

6.2 Business Information Systems Architecture Governance

Business Information Systems, depicted in Figure 35, Metadata enables the identification and interrelationship of various business information systems and their components to the business information system views that reference the databases upon which the business information systems act, and the business events that act as the triggers for the systems. Through these relationships the various business events along with their business cycles and calendars can be listed to then know of processing loads for each business information system.

The governed work products identified within this section include:

- Business Information Systems
- Business Events
- Business Even Cycle
- Business Calendar
- User Acceptance Test

- Use Cases
- Reports
- External File Interface

6.2.1 Business Information Systems

A Business Information System, depicted in Figure 35, is a computer-based information system. It is known by its characteristics, its operation cycles (business event and calendar), subordinate business information systems, employed databases, views, and associated resource life cycle nodes.

The assessment processes are listed in Table 27. The assessments are contained in Appendix 1. They are listed there in alphabetical order except for the data architecture processes that are listed in "logical" order.

Assessment Process Id	Assessment Process Name
32.	Assess Business Information Systems
32.1.	Assess Business Information System
32.2.	Assess Business Information System Context
32.3.	Assess Business Information System Business Event
32.4.	Assess Business Information System View
32.5.	Assess Business Information System Database Object
32.6.	Assess Business Information System Mission-Organization-Function
32.7.	Assess Business Information System Data Integrity Rule
32.8.	Assess Business Information System Resource Life Cycle Node
32.9.	Assess Business Information System User Acceptance Test
32.10.	Assess Business Information System Use Case
32.11.	Assess Business Information System Requirement

Assessment Process Id	Assessment Process Name

Table 27. Business Information System Related Assessments.

6.2.2 Business Events

Business Events metadata, depicted in Figure 36, enables the identification and interrelationship of the various business events that occur within the accomplishment of functions and then for each business event the various collections of business information systems that are executed in support of that particular business event.

Business event calendars and business cycle components enable the creation and interrelationship of the various business calendars and business cycles that govern the accomplishment of business information systems.

The assessment processes are listed in Table 28. The assessments are contained in Appendix 1. They are listed there in alphabetical order except for the data architecture processes that are listed in "logical" order.

Assessment Process Id	Assessment Process Name
31.	Assess Business Event
31.1.	Assess Business Events
31.2.	Assess Business Event Cycle
31.3.	Assess Business Event Cycle Structure
31.4.	Assess Calendar Cycle
31.5.	Assess Calendar Cycle Structure
31.6.	Assess Business Event Business Event Cycle
31.7.	Assess Business Event Calendar Cycle
31.8.	Assess Business Event Cycle
31.9.	Assess Business Event Mission-Organization-Function

Assessment Process Id	Assessment Process Name

Table 28. Business Event Related Assessments.

6.2.3 Business Cycles

A Business Cycle is a cycle during which business activities occur such as sales, manufacturing, reporting, distribution, and inventory may occur. A business cycle may be simple or complex. If complex, the business cycle can be represented through business cycle structures either through a hierarchy or network of other business cycles.

Business Event Cycles are linked to Business Events so that the timing of business event triggering can be known.

The assessment processes for this area are listed in Table 27.

6.2.4 Business Calendars

A Business Calendar Cycle is a set of recurring calendar-based dates of interest to the enterprise. Examples are quarterly, biweekly, monthly, daily, and the like. A business calendar cycle may be simple or complex. If complex, the calendar cycle can be represented through calendar cycle structures either through a hierarchy or network of other calendar cycles.

Business Calender cycles are linked to Business Events so that the timing of business event triggering can be known.

The assessment processes for this area are listed in Table 27.

6.2.5 User Acceptance Tests

The assessment processes are listed in Table 29. The assessments are contained in Appendix 1. They are listed there in alphabetical order except for the data architecture processes that are listed in "logical" order.

Assessment Process Id	Assessment Process Name
47.	Assess User Acceptance Tests
47.1.	Assess User Acceptance Test
47.2.	Assess User Acceptance Test Step
47.3.	Assess User Acceptance Test Structure
47.4.	Assess User Acceptance Test Column
47.5.	Assess User Acceptance Test Column View Column
47.6.	Assess User Acceptance Test Use Case
47.7.	Assess User Acceptance Test Mission-Organization-Function

Table 29. User Acceptance Test Related Assessments.

6.2.6 Use Cases

Use Cases are business process scenarios required to accomplish the necessary work of the enterprise. Use Cases are able to be interrelated with other Use Cases in hierarchies or networks. Use cases are able to be related to one or more Use Case Events that, in turn, can be hierarchical.

Use Cases can be allocated pre-, post-, and special-conditions that can be used as prerequisites or end result tests. Use Cases not only involve processes that must be performed, but also allocated with Use Case Facts that, in turn, are mapped to View Columns.

Use Case Events can be associated with specific Use Case Actors who are Persons within a Position who are performing a Function from within an Organization in the accomplishment of an Enterprise Mission. Additionally, Use Case Events can be directly associated with Mission-Organization-Functions and identified Business Information Systems.

The assessment processes are listed in Table 30. The assessments are contained in Appendix 1. They are listed there in alphabetical order except for the data architecture processes that are listed in "logical" order.

Assessment Process Id	Assessment Process Name
48.	Assess Use Cases
48.1.	Assess Use Case
48.2.	Assess Use Case Structure
48.3.	Assess Use Case Actor
48.4.	Assess Use Case Event
48.5.	Assess Use Case Event Actor
48.6.	Assess Use Case Pre Test
48.7.	Assess Use Case Post Test
48.8.	Assess Use Case Special Test
48.9.	Assess Use Case Fact
48.10.	Assess Use Case Fact View Column
48.11	Assess Use Case Fact Use Case Pre Test
48.12	Assess Use Case Fact Use Case Post Test
48.13	Assess Use Case Fact Use Case Event
48.14	Assess Use Case Events Business Information System
48.15	Assess Use Case Events Mission-Organization-Function

Table 30. Use Case Related Assessments.

6.2.7 Reports

Reports represent the specifications of data access, calculation, and formatting of end-user viewable result sets generated by business information systems, DBMS ad hoc query language, or package report writers.

Reports can interrelated by means of hierarchies or networks.

Additionally, Reports can be subdivided into Report Sections which in turn can be hierarchically organized. Each Report Section can have one or more Report Cells that, in turn are related to one or more View Columns.

Reports are able to be associated with Business Information Systems and Mission-Organization-Functions.

The assessment processes are listed in Table 31. The assessments are contained in Appendix 1. They are listed there in alphabetical order except for the data architecture processes that are listed in "logical" order.

Assessment Process Id	Assessment Process Name
44.	Assess Reports
44.1.	Assess Report
44.2.	Assess Report Structure
44.3.	Assess Report Business Information System
44.4.	Assess Report Mission Organization Function
44.5.	Assess Report Section
44.6.	Assess Report Section Cell
44.7.	Assess Report Section Cell View Column

Table 31. Reports Related Assessments.

6.2.8 External File Interfaces

An external file is a data set that is to be interfaced with one or more business information systems for use to create records in a database or that may be interfaced directly to a database through a DBMS utility.

The assessment processes are listed in Table 32. The assessments are contained in Appendix 1. They are listed there in alphabetical order except for the data architecture processes that are listed in "logical" order.

Assessment Process Id	Assessment Process Name
49.	Assess External Data Interfaces
49.1.	Assess External Data Interface

Table 32. External File Interface Related Assessments.

6.3 Data Integrity Rule Governance

The purpose of Data Integrity Rules, also sometimes called Data integrity rules is to represent and then enforce through implied and/or explicitly defined processes data constraints throughout the metadata management environment. Data Integrity Rules answer the questions:

- What relationships exist across the set of metadata and/or specifications implied by that metadata that are enforced in one-to-one, one-to-many, and many-to-many relationships?
- What metadata values are restricted across the set of metadata and/or specifications implied by that metadata and what are the domains of these values?
- What metadata values across the set of metadata and/or specifications implied by that metadata are contextually or hierarchically restricted across assignments of these metadata values?
- What metadata values across the set of complete metadata and/or specifications implied by that metadata are combined through processes?

The data integrity rules are not shown on any diagram because they are pervasive across all the models. The governed work products that are almost certainly to be affected by one or data integrity rules are:

- Data Elements,
- Specified Data Models,
- Implemented Data Models,

- Operational Data Models
- View Data Models
- Business Information Systems

The assessment processes are listed in Table 33. The assessments are contained in Appendix 1. They are listed there in alphabetical order except for the data architecture processes that are listed in "logical" order.

Assessment Process Id	Assessment Process Name
34.	Assess Data Integrity Rules
34.1.	Assess Data Integrity Rule
34.2.	Assess Data Integrity Rule Structure
34.3.	Assess Data Integrity Rule Binding

Table 33. Data Integrity Rule Related Assessments.

6.4 Data Architecture Governance

A data architecture reference model, at the center of Figure 6, is a data-based framework for understanding the scope and interrelationships among clearly definable sets of data that represent the persistent memory of the enterprise. Accomplished, a data architecture reference model enhances clear communication among deployed data instances across the enterprise.

The governed work products identified within this section include:

- Data Elements
- Specified Data Models (Subjects)
- Implemented Database Models (Schemas)
- Operational Database Models (DBMS Schemas)
- View Database Models

6.4.1 Data Elements

The data element and semantics, depicted in Figure 41, components are engineered to capture data element specifications. That is, context independent business fact semantic templates. Fully supporting data elements are semantic hierarchies, conceptual value domains, value domains, data element classifications, data element concepts, compound data elements, and derived data elements.

Data Elements represent the inheritable semantics for attributes of entities, and columns of tables. A data element is a context independent (i.e., entity and/or table independent) business fact semantic template. It is well-accepted practice that the quantity of data elements is a small fraction of the quantity of attributes and/or columns.

For example, if an enterprise has 100 databases and each has 200 tables, and each table has 10 columns then there are 200,000 columns. In this example, if, as is commonly true, a data element's semantics is reused 50 or more times over all the database tables then there are only 4,000 data elements.

Supporting data elements are multiple higher levels of data element metadata including concepts, conceptual value domains, data element concepts, value domains and sets of value domain values. The value sets can be directly allocated to DBMS schema columns as constraints. Often, they might form the rows of data within the reference data database.

The data element model also contains compound and derived data elements. A compound data element is a special data element that contains multiple data elements that ultimately represent a value might be for example, a Telephone Number with the contained data elements of Country Code, Area Code, Exchange, Number, and possibly extension. A derived data element is another specialized data element where its value is calculated or derived through some process. An example is age. The value, in years, would be ("Today" minus Birthdate)/365.5, or Total Department Salary where the value is calculated by summing the values from all employee salaries.

Within the scope of data elements, the following contained subcomponents are:

- Meta Category Values
- Concept
- Conceptual Value Domains

- Data Element Concepts
- Value Domain Models
- Data Element Classification Models

Meta Category Models. Meta Category models, depicted in Figure 41, support the creation of the semantics of data items, that is, data element concepts, data elements, attributes, and columns are both inherited and assigned. For example, a data element concept inherits its semantics from Concepts and Conceptual Value Domain; a data element inherits its semantics from a data element concept, its business domain and a value domain; and attributes inherit their semantics from their host entities and data elements.

In addition to this method of semantic inheritance, meta category values, for example geography, and precision serve to additionally modify the semantics of data element concepts, data elements, attributes or columns. Meta category values are either prefix semantics or suffix semantics. Prefix meta category values appear prior to the data item's common business name. Suffix meta category values appear at after the data item's common business name. The order of appearance is not arbitrary or able to be change by an end-user. The order is specified by the metadata administrator within the table and meta category type. If the geographic meta category value type's sequence number is 2 and the temporal meta category value type's is 3, then regardless of the sequence of tagging, geographic meta category values will always be prefixed into the data item's constructed name before those for the temporal meta category value type.

Once the meta category values are assigned, for example, to the data element concept, or the data element, etc., the process automatically constructs the data item's name.

Concepts. Concepts, depicted in Figure 41, represent the sets of ideas, abstractions, or even things in the real world that are identified with explicit boundaries and meaning and whose properties and behavior follow the same rules. Concepts are used as a basis for specifying the concepts of data elements, that is, data element concepts.

Conceptual Value Domains. Conceptual Value Domains, depicted in Figure 41, are collections of meanings that apply to both value domains and also data element concepts. A data element concept can have only one conceptual value domain. A conceptual value domain may be composed of other conceptual value domains or may be a member (component) of a larger conceptual value domain. Conceptual value domains may also be interrelated in a bill-of-materials network fashion to fully support the underlying concepts of data element domains and value domains.

Conceptual value domains also encompass value domains. If, for example, the conceptual value domain relates to the notion of countries, then the corresponding value domain for countries would relate to the enumerated set of countries that might be specified in ISO standard 3166, Codes for the representation of names of countries.

Data Element Concepts. Data element concepts, depicted in Figure 41, represent the joining of concepts and conceptual value domains. Data element concepts are a key component for the development of data elements. The components of the meta entities that comprise data element concepts focus on semantics rather than on any internal or external physical representation.

Data element concepts also allow for a full bill-of-materials structure supporting both network and hierarchical data element concepts in support of data element specifications.

Value Domains. Value Domains, depicted in Figure 41, are to provide specific descriptions about the allowed values associated with one or more value domains. Value domains that are assignable to a data element must be in the same conceptual domain family as is the data element's data element concept. Value domains assigned to an attribute of an entity within the specified data model, or column within a table of the Implemented Database Model or a DBMS column within a DBMS table of the Operational Database Model must all be hierarchically related.

Data Element Classifications. Data element classifications, depicted in Figure 41, are used to manage classification schemes and the classification scheme items that are in the classification schemes. A classification scheme may be a taxonomy, a network, an ontology, or any other system for systematizing where the categories are mutually exclusive. The classification may also be just a list of controlled vocabulary of property words (or terms). The list might be taken from the "leaf level" of taxonomy.

The classification scheme allows for a full bill-of-materials structure supporting both network and hierarchical classification schemes in support of an administered item. Administered items relate to one or more data elements.

The assessment processes are listed in Table 34. The assessments are contained in Appendix 1. They are listed there in alphabetical order except for the data architecture processes that are listed in "logical" order.

Assessment Process Id	Assessment Process Name
35.	Assess Data Elements
35.1.	Assess Concept
35.2.	Assess Concept Structure
35.3.	Assess Conceptual Value Domain
35.4.	Assess Conceptual Value Domain Structure
35.5.	Assess Data Element Concept
35.6.	Assess Data Element Concept Structure
35.7.	Assess Data Element
35.8.	Assess Value Domain
35.9.	Assess Value Domain Structure
35.10.	Assess Meta Category Value
35.11.	Assess Meta Category Value Type
35.12.	Assess Meta Category Value Type Class
35.13.	Assess Derived Data Element
35.14.	Assess Compound Data Element
35.15	Assess Compound Data Element Structure
35.16.	Assess Business Domains
35.17.	Assess Data Types

Assessment Process Id	Assessment Process Name

Table 34. Data Element Related Assessments.

6.4.2 Business Domains

The purpose of Business Domains is to act as a dictionary and/or glossary across the three classes of architecture: enterprise, business information systems, and data. Business Terms answer the questions:

- What business domains, that is, words, specific terms, or whole phrases are important to the enterprise?
- How are business domains related one to the other?
- Where are business domains found in each of the architectures?

The business domains are not shown on any diagram because they are pervasive across all the models.

The assessment processes for this area are listed in Table 34.

6.4.3 Specified Data Models

Specified Data Models, depicted in Figure 42, are collections of entities, attributes and relationships that can be used as data model templates for implemented databases. Each entity within a specified model should be the data specification of a well-defined policy within the enterprise. A collection of entities within a particular subject should conform to a larger and more complex policy.

An implemented database is bounded by schema and is intended to be implemented by a particular DBMS that arises from an operational database that collects, stores, and maintains actual business data. In contrast, the specified database's entities are bounded only by the subject within which it is defined. In the construction of an Implemented Data Model, one or more entities may contribute attributes to form the column of the Implemented Data Model's tables.

Specified Data Models enable the creation of standard data structures that when employed in an Implemented Database Model ensure completeness, rigor, and the data standardization essential for data sharing. The semantics of attributes of a Specified Data Model entity are derived from ISO 11179 data elements. Specified Data Models can be created inductively through the promotion of a single Implemented Database Model to the Specified Data Model level. Then, data modeling activities would occur to break apart the Specified Data Model into individual subjects and collections of entities within those subjects. Entities can be interrelated across subject areas to represent Specified Data Model factoring.

The Implemented Database Model should represent a completely third normal form database if its database architecture class is original data capture, reference data, or subject area databases. If the database architecture class is an Transaction Data Staging Area Data Model or a data warehouse, the design may not be in third normal form. Regardless, the goal of this effort is to discover entity collections within narrow subject areas. These are most often related to a functionally cohesive community of interest. This goal stands in stark contrast to the goal of the Implemented Database Model that is, that it is the union of all subject matter related Operational Data Models. It is likely that enterprise-wide data models of concepts exist at the Specified Data Model level while the multiple cross-functional data models exist at the Implemented and Operational Database Model levels.

Because Specified Data Models are models of concepts not databases, there will likely be many more Specified Data Models than Implemented Data Models. That is because an Implemented Database Model may consist of some tables that are in a one-to-one relationship with a Specified Data Model entity. Or multiple implemented model tables may represent a single entity where the attributes are essentially the same only named differently. Examples include customer address, employee address, shipping address, or billing address. Finally, a given Implemented Database Model tables may contain attributes from an entity multiple times. For example in the customer entity there may be a person name attribute set for the customer key contact, billing contact, shipping contact, etc. This is not only acceptable but desired as the goal of the Specified Data Model effort is to create narrowly focused subject of highly third-normal form entity collections.

The collection of all entities across all the subjects represent the complete data requirements for the enterprise. Each set of subject area entities acts as a data model template for one or more Implemented Data Models. This enables (and requires) all the columns in all the tables of all Implemented Data

Models to be mapped to Specified Data Model attributes.

The assessment processes are listed in Table 35. The assessments are contained in Appendix 1. They are listed there in alphabetical order except for the data architecture processes that are listed in "logical" order.

Assessment Process Id	Assessment Process Name
36.	Assess Specified Data Model
36.1.	Assess Subject
36.2.	Assess Entity
36.3.	Assess Attribute
36.4.	Assess Primary Key
36.5.	Assess Candidate Key
36.6.	Assess Foreign Key

Table 35. Specified Data Model Related Assessments.

6.4.4 Implemented Database Models

An Implemented Database Model, depicted in Figure 43, is a collection of tables, columns, and relationships bounded by a schema. Implemented Database Models are built as a precursor to the design of DBMS-bound database that operates to maintain data integrity and value transformations. It is common to build an implemented database within the scope of a reasonably large mission hierarchy such as human resources, finance, facilities, customers, sales management, distribution, or inventory.

Implemented database table columns should all be derived from attributes of entities from one or more Specified Data Models. Implemented Data Models also act as the "parent" of one or more Operational Data Models. Implemented Data Models can be created inductively through Operational Database Model imports that exist within a certain scope, and then, through the promotion of a single Operational Data Model, to the Implemented

Database Model level. Then, data modeling activities would occur to expand the scope of the Implemented Database Model to be that of the union of all the Operational Data Models.

The assessment processes are listed in Table 36. The assessments are contained in Appendix 1. They are listed there in alphabetical order except for the data architecture processes that are listed in "logical" order.

Assessment Process Id	Assessment Process Name
37.	Assess Implemented Database Model
37.1.	Assess Schema
37.2.	Assess Table
37.3.	Assess Column
37.4.	Assess Primary Key
37.5.	Assess Candidate Key
37.6.	Assess Foreign Key
37.7.	Assess SQL Data Type

Table 36. Implemented Data Model Related Assessments.

6.4.5 Operational Database Models

The Operational Database Model, depicted in Figure 44, is the representation of an implemented database that may have been subsetted and/or transformed to serve the particular needs of a DBMS, or performance requirement.

Operational databases are mapped back to their "parent" implemented models through a column (Implemented Data Model) to DBMS column (Operational Data Model) mapping. Operational Data Models are "hosts" to the various SQL views that in turn act as intermediaries to the business information systems that access the databases. There may be multiple transformations of a particular implemented database, and each exists and is mapped back to its "parent" implemented database.

Operational databases commonly conform to particular database architecture classes such as original data collection, Transaction Data Staging Area Data Model, data warehouses, data marts, and reference data databases.

The process of discovering operational databases involves identifying and cataloguing all the existing database schemas within running business information systems. Database schemas should be used in preference to entity-relationship (ER) modeler data models as they seldom match the actual running database schemas. For the same reason, COBOL based file structures, or where enforced, COPYLIBS, are employed for non-database file structures.

The assessment processes are listed in Table 37. The assessments are contained in Appendix 1. They are listed there in alphabetical order except for the data architecture processes that are listed in "logical" order.

Assessment Process Id	Assessment Process Name
38.	Assess Operational Database Model
38.1.	Assess DBMS Schema
38.2.	Assess DBMS Table
38.3.	Assess DBMS Column
38.4.	Assess Primary Key
38.5.	Assess Candidate Key
38.6.	Assess Secondary Key
38.7.	Assess Foreign Key
38.8.	Assess Database Architecture
38.9.	Assess Database
38.10.	Assess DBMS
38.11.	Assess DBMS Data Type

Table 37. Operational Data Model Related Assessments.

6.4.6 View Data Models

The view data model, depicted in Figure 45, is designed to capture specifications of models of data that represent the interface between a DBMS's database schema as expressed in the Operational Data Model, and the Business Information Systems' need for data.

The assessment processes are listed in Table 38. The assessments are contained in Appendix 1. They are listed there in alphabetical order except for the data architecture processes that are listed in "logical" order.

Assessment Process Id	Assessment Process Name
39.	Assess View Data Model
39.1.	Assess View
39.2.	Assess View Column
39.3.	Assess View Column DBMS Column
39.4.	Assess View Column Compound Column
39.5.	Assess View Column Derived Column
39.6.	Assess View Process

Table 38. View Data Model Related Assessments.

6.5 Project Management Governance

The purpose of a Governance Project, depicted in Figure 46, is to accomplish some identified significant activity within the scope of accomplishing governance across the enterprise. Governance Projects answer the questions:

- What activities are currently underway in the accomplishment of some significant aspect of achieving an interoperable data environment?
- What are the work plans, deliverables, organizations, time lines, costs, and

current states of governance projects?

- What are the interrelationships among governance projects in regards to processes being performed, products built, and staff or organizations employed or affected?
- What governance products are going to be completed on what time line and how will these completed products affect other products in other projects?

The work products identified within this section include:

- Project Template Types and Project Templates
- Deliverable Template Types and Deliverable Templates
- Project Template Deliverable Template pairs
- Task Template Types and Task Templates
- Deliverable Templates Task Template Pairs
- Projects
- Project Resource Life Cycle pairs
- Project Deliverables
- Project Tasks
- Skills, Skill Level Types, and Skill Levels
- Work Environment Factors
- Work

The assessment processes are listed in Table 39. The assessments are contained in Appendix 1. They are listed there in alphabetical order except for the data architecture processes that are listed in "logical" order.

Assessment Process Id	Assessment Process Name
43.	Assess Project Management
43.1.	Assess Project Template Type
43.2	Assess Project Template

Assessment Process Id	Assessment Process Name
43.3	Assess Deliverable Template Type
43.4	Assess Deliverable Template
43.5.	Assess Project Template Deliverable Template
43.6	Assess Task Template Type
43.7	Assess Task Template
43.8.	Assess Deliverable Template Task Template
43.9.	Assess Skill
43.10.	Assess Skill Level Type
43.11.	Assess Skill Level
43.12	Assess Work Environment Factor Type
43.13.	Assess Work Environment Factor
43.14.	Assess Work Environment Factor Multiplier Type
43.15	Assess Work Environment Factor Multiplier
43.16	Assess Project Deliverable Work Environment Factor Multiplier
43.17	Assess Project
43.18	Assess Resource Life Cycle Node Project
43.19.	Assess Project Deliverable
43.20.	Assess Project Template Deliverable Template Deliverable Template Task Template
43.21	Assess Person Skill Level
43.22	Assess Project Deliverable Person Skill Level

Assessment Process Id	Assessment Process Name
43.23.	Assess Work

Table 39. Project Management Related Assessments.

6.6 Governance Process Summary

This chapter serves several purposes. First it sets out the overall architectural context of the business information systems, that is, Enterprise Architecture, Business Information Systems Architecture, and Data Architecture. Within each of these, this chapter sets out the various metadata-base business information systems that need to exist to capture the metadata sufficient for governed environments. And, within each of these business information systems, this chapter sets out the database object table processes that need to exist to accomplish the work of the metadata-based business information systems.

Second, this chapter sets down two strategies for capturing metadata: Reverse, and Forward Engineering. Reverse engineering is far and away the most common as almost all enterprises have large collections of un-integrated databases and business information systems. Once the reverse engineering is accomplished, then Forward Engineering can occur in support of manufacturing databases and business information systems. Once the change over occurs, what used to take years and months will now take months and weeks.

Experience has shown that the payoff from these efforts is almost immediate and sometimes occurs within the first project.

6.7 Questions and Exercises

1. Metabase systems not only have databases that contain metadata, they also have very sophisticated business information systems to enter, interrelate, and manage the metadata. Section 6.1 lists the major metadata information systems that must be supported. Do you agree, given the complex data structures contained in Figures 29 through 47 that the metadata information

systems must be as sophisticated and complex? If yes, then how would having simple data entry and update screens suffice? What would the knowledge requirement be on the novice end-user to properly enter, interrelated, integrate, and make all the enterprise metadata non-redundant? Provide examples from within your own organization.

2. After a careful review of all the different Metadata-Management Information Systems that are described at a high level in Sections 6.2 through 6.6, provide examples from within your own organization.

3. Given the meta data models in Figures 29 through 47, are the high level descriptions of each of the metadata-management information systems sufficient to provide an understanding of the required processes that must occur? Provide examples from within your own organization.

4. Suppose a Metadata-Management Information Systems were restricted to just a simple "list-and-form" format, would that be sufficient to accomplish all the complex processes identified in the various process-description tables? What would be the effect on time, effort and resources if the end-users were responsible for knowing and accomplishing all the processes as opposed to the Metadata-Management Information Systems accomplishing these processes? How is your organization accomplishing these processes? How time-consuming are they to perform? How do you keep all the metadata interrelated, integrated, and non-redundant? Provide examples from within your own organization.

5. Many of the required metadata objects are complex networks. See for example in Figure 41, and all the processes set out in Section 6.4.1, Data Elements. These metadata models, one for metadata objects and the other metadata model for Metabase System processes deal with seven network data structures. These network structures are recognized by the two lines that connect two different meta objects. Now, to update such a required metadata object, the end-user must know, within context the context of the existing network, 1) how to identify and display the network structure, 2) how to ensure that a circular reference is not being installed, and 3) that a duplicate reference is not being installed.

Note also in Figure 41 that several of the networks structures are related to each other. That means that the network constructed data is set within the context of other network structures. Suppose the Metabase System only has simple lists and forms. In such a case the end user would be 100% responsible for knowing about and determining the correct processing and linkages.

Should the Metabase System handle all that, or should the end-user be required to understand all the intricacies of network processing and accomplish that correctly? Compare and contrast the time, effort and energy required to teach network structures to end users, and manually auditing their work verus having the Metabase System handle all this effort for you.

Compare and contrast the relative level of sophistication required on the end user of a manual approach versus a Metabase System approach? Which way does your organization handle these requirements now? What's the cost of metadata management if these real metadata object structure requirements are just ignored? Provide examples from within your own organization.

7

Governance Events

There are five classes of events within the governance program. These are:

- General events.
- Subgroup establishment events.
- Officer appointment events.
- Governance Program events.
- Community of Interest events.

7.1 General Events

7.1.1 Meeting Calender Establishment

Subgroups within the Governance Program create a meeting calendar of all meetings and publish it to all committees within the Governance Program. Meeting calendars will project out at least one year. Meeting schedules of technical committees within Communities of Interest are subject to review by the Community of Interest. Similarly, meeting schedules of Communities of Interest are subject to review by the Governance Projects committee. And finally, all Governance Program contained committee meetings are subject to review by the Governance Program Committee.

7.1.2 Meetings

All meeting agendas, and thus all minutes should have a similar format which is suggested to be:

Doc. No.: <document number>
Date: <document last update date>
Project: <specific project> or "N/A"
Ref. Doc: <reference to main document> or "NA"
Status: <draft | final>
Reply to: <subgroup secretary name>
: <subgroup secretary organization name>
: <subgroup secretary address line 1>
: <subgroup secretary city, state zip>
: <subgroup secretary telephone number>
: Internet: <subgroup secretary email address>

SUBGROUP: <Subgroup Official Name>
SUBJECT: <Title of this document> Note: usually Minutes of Meeting ###
Date: <Start date of the meeting>
Location: <Actual location of the meeting> or Electronic

The <English words for the meeting number> meeting of <Subgroup Official Name> was called to order by <Chair Name> | <designated chair name> at <Time and Time zone> on <start date of meeting>

AGENDA

1 Preliminary and Administrative Matters
1.1 Attendance and Membership Status
1.1.1 Introduce participants
1.1.1.1 <Standing Document Number>:Participants List
1.1.2 Membership status
1.1.2.1 <Standing Document Number>: Attendance Rules
1.1.2.2 Membership Jeopardy notices (<Document Number> - Author)
1.2 Agenda
1.2.1 Document distribution
1.2.1.1 Agenda for Meeting <Meeting Number> <Meeting Date> (<Document Number> - Author)
1.2.2 Agenda revision and approval
1.3 Review of the INCITS Antitrust Guidelines
1.3.1 <Document Number> - Author
1.4 Minutes
1.4.1 Approval of minutes

1.4.1.1 Minutes for Meeting <Meeting Number> <Meeting Date> (<Document Number> - Author)
1.4.2 Action item review
1.5 Liaison Reports
1.5.1 Domestic Liaison
1.5.1.1 <document within this category that is to be presented and/or requires subgroup action> (<Document Number> - Author)
1.5.2 International liaison
1.5.3 Other liaison
1.5.3.1 <Standing Document Number>: Liaisons List
1.6 Administration
1.6.1 Treasurer's report
1.6.1.1 Treasurer's Report (<Document Number> - Author)
1.6.2 Future meetings
1.6.2.1 <Standing Document Number>: Meeting Schedule
1.6.3 Other administrative matters
1.6.3.1 <Standing Document Number>: Standing Documents

2 Unfinished Business from Previous Meetings

3 <First Main Governance Assessment Title> <Governance Assessment Project Identifier>

3.1 <Maintenance project for existing Governance Assessment within overall main project> [<Project Identifier>]
3.1.1 <document within this category that is to be presented and/or requires subgroup action> (<Document Number> - Author)

3.2 <First subproject within main project for development of new Governance Assessment version> [<Project Identifier>]
3.2.1 <First formal document within Governance Assessment for Framework [<Project Identifier><.><Document Sequence Number>]
3.2.1.1 <document within this category that is to be presented and/or requires subgroup action> (<Document Number> - Author)
3.2.2 <Second formal document within Governance Assessment for Framework [<Project Identifier><.><Document Sequence Number>]
3.2.2.1 <document within this category that is to be presented and/or requires subgroup action> (<Document Number> - Author)

4 <Second Governance Assessment Title><Governance Assessment Project Identifier>

5 Other Projects

6 New Business

7 Late Papers

8 Adjourn

9 Action Items

10 Carry Forward Papers

11 Meeting Document Log

<Document Number> <Agenda number> <Document Title> (<Author>)

7.2 Subgroup Establishment

Within the governance program the key subgroups are:

- Governance Program Committee
- Subsidiary Boards
- Communities of Interest
- Community of Interest Technical Committees

The subgroups are described in Chapter 9 of this book. To stand up the Governance Program committee the following needs to be adopted or revised from the materials set out in Table 40

Materials Necessary for Subgroup Establishment	
Chapter	**Description**
Chapter 4, Mission of Governance	The set of work products that address the enterprise itself. Every work product across the framework is able to be described in terms of what aspect of the enterprise's mission it accomplishes or supports. Simply put, all work products are essential, not accidental attributes of the enterprise's mission
Chapter 5, Governance Work Products	The set of work products that represent the identification, architecture and specification of the work products that are necessary for the fulfillment of the enterprise's mission.
Chapter 6, Governance Process Management	The processes, which, in the case of a Governance Program, the audit and evaluation processes to be used by members of the various Governance Programs to determine the integrity and correctness of the work products set out in Chapter 5.
Chapter 7, Governance Events	The set of work products that act as the triggering mechanism for the business information system column's work products. The activation of the triggers is set out through the various business functions performed by persons within the enterprise.
Chapter 8, Governance Functions	The set of work products that identify and specify the human activities performed by persons within the context of their enterprise organizations.
Chapter 9, Governance Organizations	The enterprise's bureaucratic structures within which enterprise work is identified, planned, and managed.
Chapter 13, Rules	The bureaucratic regulations through which all the Governance organizations operate.

Table 40 Materials Needed to be Reviewed for Subgroup Establishment.

Once these materials are created for the Governance Program Committee and are approved by the parent organization, the committee can set about standing up the contained subsidiary boards. That is, the Finance, Procedures, Governance Assessments Policy and Governance Assessments Development boards. Each subsidiary board would also have these same seven items adopted or modified from this book.

The Governance Assessments Development Board of the Governance Program identifies the Governance Assessments that need to be created. Once the Governance Assessments are identified, and a project proposal (see Section 11.1) is created then the various Communities of Interest can start. The first task of every Community of Interest is to either adopt or adapt the seven materials that would be appropriate for that Community of Interest. A second task of the Community of Interest would be to establish their Technical Committees by creating for each an appropriate set of the seven materials.

Throughout the life of every subgroup that is established these seven materials can be modified to fit the needs of the subgroup, subject, of course to the oversight of the subgroup's parent subgroup.

7.3 Officer Appointment

Three officers make or break any subgroup. These are:

- Chair
- Editor
- Secretary

All three offices must be faceless. That is, the officer must not have any particular agenda save moving the scope and program of work forward. If an officer is appointed that has a set of personal goals such as peer recognition, professional advancement, business development, or such, then the first organization to suffer will be the subgroup. Members of the subgroup will almost instantly recognize that there are ulterior motives behind actions of the officer. This will cause "games" to be played. Work will suffer both in terms of quantity and quality. The value of these three offices cannot be overestimated.

Because the offices of Chair and Editor are so important, an analysis was made of the top five reasons that make a great chair and the five reasons why a chair will likely cause the work of the committee to fail. The top five characteristics of a great chair of a community of interest are:

- Impartial - treats all participants equally (no personal agenda or ax to grind).

- Single focus on carrying out work of group (e.g., producing the Governance Assessment).

- Ability to keep participants on track and working constructively toward group objective.

- Pleasant/welcoming demeanor conducive to leading collegial cooperative effort.

- Knowledgeable about the subgroup's procedures and Robert's (and/or other applicable) Rules.

The 5 or so worst characteristics of a Chair of a Community of Interest are:

- Bias toward one person, group or agenda.

- Lack of understanding of and focus on the subgroup's objective.

- Weak leadership not resulting in convergence on the group's objective.

- Attempt to mandate (in drill sergeant fashion) work by reluctant subgroup of volunteers.

- Ignorance of subgroup's procedures and relevant rules.

Similarly, the top five characteristics of a great editor of a community of interest are:

- Ability to build trust, ensuring that all participants feel comfortable that their proposals will be properly handled.

- Commitment to do the work in a timely fashion, in spite of conflicts.

- Well-organized, with attention to detail; ability to do the work in face of incomplete or inadequate proposals.

- Good-natured and self-effacing -- ability to accept criticism and continue to the job.

- Technical competence in field of discourse of the community.

The 5 or so worst characteristics of an Editor of a Community of Interest are:

- Exaggerated sense of self-important ("I know better, so I'll do it the 'right' way, regardless of community decisions").

- Inattention to intent of decisions, inability (or unwillingness) to ask for clarification when needed.

- Rigidity, low tolerance for ambiguity, significantly impatient.

- Inability to distinguish own roles (allow partisan opinions to affect editorial work).

- Absence of commitment to deliver work on communities schedule.

The events associated with an officer appointment are:

- Officer vacancy announcement
- Officer candidate review
- Officer appointment
- Officer training
- Officer performance review
- Officer recall

An officer vacancy announcement should go to all organizations that are currently participating in the affected subgroup. If there are no acceptable candidates within the subgroup, the vacancy announcement should go to other subgroups within the Governance Program. Only thereafter should an officer vacancy notice go to outside organizations. Those applying for a vacancy should communicate that desire to the immediate parent subgroup and/or one subgroup higher and the names of the candidates should be held confidential.

Officer candidate review is critical to determine the best candidate for the office. For the chair, editor and secretary, these offices are the most critical because they ultimately determine the quality and velocity of the Governance Assessments being produced. Officer candidate review should be accomplished by the immediate parent subgroup and/or one subgroup higher so that there can be a fair evaluation of all candidates. All evaluations should be held confidential.

Officer appointments from among the candidates should merely be announced. No grades should be given and no evaluation materials should be released. This is especially important since it is likely that all the candidates are already members of the subgroup.

Officer training is very important since over time, and regardless of the officer, the committee documents and products of a given class should have the same format and level of quality. Chair training is especially important because a well organized and operating committees is essential to the timely production and/or maintenance of a Governance Assessment.

Every year the performance of officers should be reviewed by the immediate parent subgroup and/or one subgroup higher to ensure that productivity of all subgroups are maintained at a high level and at a high quality.

If officers are not able to perform on par with the rest of the officers of that class across the other subgroups then that officer should be evaluated and remedied if at all possible. If remediation is not possible then the officer should be encouraged to resign. Failing that, the officer should be removed by recommendation of the immediate parent subgroup and confirmed by one subgroup higher.

7.4 Governance Program Events

The key events for the Governance Program committee are:

- Governance Program Management Plan Development
- Governance Program Integrated Schedule Development

The overall governance program management plan includes the overall architecture and operations strategy for an entire governance program. This book is largely that document. It defines scope, mission, functions, roles, offices and the like. The Governance Program project committee should review this book and propose changes to it to the Governance Program committee to ensure that the material fits the needs of all the governance projects.

The Governance Program Integrated Schedule is a document that results from the input from all the different Communities of Interest for all the different Governance Assessments that are under development. This schedule also includes Governance Assessments review activities, officer training, and the various meetings and product development schedules of all the subsidiary Governance Program committee boards.

7.5 Community of Interest Events

Communities of Interest events are generally centered around the milestones that should be reached to mark the progress of developing a Governance Assessment. These mile stones are:

- Milestone 1 - Approval of the Project Proposal
- Milestone 2 - Project Approval Notification
- Milestone 3 - Technical Development
- Milestone 4 - Initial Review
- Milestone 5 - Management Review
- Milestone 6 - Governance Program Committee Approval
- Milestone 7 - Community of Interest Approval
- Milestone 8 - Publication.

7.5.1 Milestone 1 -Approval of the Project Proposal

A Project Proposal may be developed by any individual or organization whether or not affiliated with the Governance Program. Project proposals should be developed in accordance with the format of the Governance Program Project Proposal Guide.

No technical work may be done in developing or revising a Governance Assessment without an authorizing Project Proposal. Each Governance Assessment requires its own authorizing Project Proposal.

If the Project Proposal originates within a Community of Interest, voting on the submission of the Project Proposal is conducted by the Community of Interest; the vote must be included with submission of the Project Proposal.

The Project Proposal must meet the two-week rule for the meeting at which action is expected. If the Project Proposal is approved, work on the project may begin immediately on the project.

Within fourteen calendar-days, the Chair of the originating Community of Interest will forward to the Governance Program Committee the following information:

- The approved Project Proposal.
- The next Community of Interest meeting information.
- Any other supplemental information the Community of Interest may wish to provide (i.e., draft press release) for registration of the Community of Interest project number and web announcement.

Upon receipt of the information package from the Chair of the originating Community of Interest, the Governance Program Committee chair will electronically notify the Governance Program Committee members of the approved Project Proposal.

Any Governance Program Committee member may request an appeal of the approved Project Proposal within seven calendar-days.

If there is no appeal of the approved Project Proposal, a project number is assigned and announced by the Governance Program Committee.

If an appeal is made of the approved Project Proposal, the Chair of the originating Community of Interest is notified and Governance Program Committee voting is conducted.

If the Project Proposal is not approved, the Governance Program Committee so notifies the proposer.

7.5.2 Milestone 2 - Project Approval Notification

If the project is approved, the Governance Program Committee announces the assignment of the project. The project number assigned by the Governance Program Committee is entered into the Community of Interest Projects database.

The Governance Program Committee will issue a press release announcing the establishment of the project and solicit technical contributions and membership.

7.5.3 Milestone 3 - Technical Development

The Community of Interest will prepare a detailed work plan for completion of the project. The Community of Interest will review and/or revise the work plan as part of its annual report presented to Governance Assessments Development Board.

Contributions may include collections of basic data, suggested drafts of text, candidate Governance Assessments, etc. Contributions from any source will be accepted and considered. Use of trademarks, copyrighted, or patented material will be in accordance with the Governance Program approved policy.

7.5.4 Milestone 4 - Initial Review

When the Community of Interest determines that the development process has reached the step where the initial 45-day review is warranted, the vote to initiate the initial review will be conducted. For a draft Governance Assessment that has reached Committee Draft stage, the initial review is initiated by the Community of Interest upon receipt of the Committee Draft ballot.

The Community of Interest Chair will forward the draft to any close liaisons, and will simultaneously forward to the Governance Program Committee a submittal package that includes, but is not limited to:

- The draft Governance Assessment.
- The expository remarks, i.e., the background or history of the project development.
- A copy of the authorizing Project Proposal.
- The tally of the ballot by the Community of Interest developing the draft Governance Assessment.
- The name, address and telephone number of the project editor.

Liaisons identified in the project proposal are expected to review the draft in accordance with the voting requirements. Liaisons must inform the

Governance Program Committee and the Chair of the Community of Interest developing the draft Governance Assessment by correspondence prior to the close of the initial review period if the draft Governance Assessment appears to raise questions or conflicts with the work of the liaison Committee. Lack of comment will be considered as an indication that no problems were identified.

The Governance Program Committee will initiate several simultaneous activities for draft Governance Assessments:

- Assignment of a Governance Assessments number to the draft Governance Assessment because the draft has now reached the status of draft Governance Assessment.
- An announcement in the Governance Assessment progress report of a 45-day review through the submittal of a draft Governance Assessment's review package.
- A compliance review. The Governance Program Committee will conduct a review of the draft Governance Assessment for compliance with its authorizing Project Proposal.

When the Governance Program Committee review indicates that the draft Governance Assessment is in compliance with the scope and program of work of the authorizing Project Proposal, the Community of Interest is so notified. When the compliance review indicates that the proposed draft Governance Assessment is not in compliance, the Governance Program Committee will so advise the Community of Interest. The Governance Program Committee concerns must be resolved prior to the initiation of the second review. The Governance Program Committee is notified of the review result via:

- A call for information on potentially pertinent patents will be made to the Governance Program members and the Community of Interest simultaneously. The call will also encourage disclosure, where possible, of the existence of pending U.S. patent applications relating to the Governance Assessment under development, and of any relevant unexpired foreign patents.
- Notification to the Community of Interest of the responses received by the Governance Program Committee resulting from previous calls for patents.

- Issuance of a press release describing the draft Governance Assessment, and announcing the availability of the document for a 45-day technical review and comment period.

- The Community of Interest preliminary edit of the draft Governance Assessment.

All comments received during the initial review are distributed to the Community of Interest developing the Governance Assessment. A formal response must be developed for each comment and approved by the Community of Interest. The Governance Assessment submitted for review will contain a notice that any comments should to be sent to the Governance Program Committee with a copy to the Community of Interest. The Governance Program Committee will register every review comment.

Each comment will be sent immediately to the originating Community of Interest for consideration and to the Governance Program Committee for information. Formal responses generated for each comment is subject to approval by a Community of Interest vote. Responses to registered comments will include the provision that the commenter has twenty working days from the postmark to reply and indicate if the comment(s) has not been satisfactorily resolved. If no response from the commented is received, the comment will be considered as satisfactorily resolved.

The response may be either a modification to the draft Governance Assessment, or a statement of the rationale for not making a change. Serious effort should be made to accommodate the comment by correspondence or discussion with the author.

Editorial recommendations from the Community of Interest will be considered and incorporated if practicable.

7.5.5 Milestone 5 - Management Review

For a Governance Assessment that has reached draft Governance Assessment stage, Milestone 5 consists of the second review that is initiated by the Community of Interest upon receipt of the draft Governance Assessment ballot.

For other projects, the second review may begin after the Community of

Interest approval ballot and the Governance Program Committee review.

After consideration of all comments and resolution of as many comments as possible, the Community of Interest approves the text as suitable for adoption as a Governance Assessment. The Community of Interest approval vote will be conducted.

The Community of Interest forwards the proposed final text of the Governance Assessment to the Governance Program Committee. The submittal package includes, but is not limited to:

- The draft Governance Assessment.
- The expository remarks, i.e., the background or history of the project development, the final tally of the ballot, and any unresolved comments by the Community of Interest developing the draft Governance Assessment.
- Any comments from other Communities of Interest reviewing the draft Governance Assessment.
- The response to Governance Program Committee concerns that were communicated to the Community of Interest with the results of the compliance review.
- All review comments and the Community of Interest response to each (identifying any unresolved comments).
- A record of attempts to resolve comments on negative votes during the Community of Interest vote to forward the document.
- The name, address and telephone number of the project editor.
- The list of Community of Interest participants.

The Governance Assessments Development Board will conduct a review of the submittal package to ensure that the Governance Program procedural requirements have been met. This review may be initiated at the commencement of the initial review. An indication that the Governance Program procedures have been violated will result in the submittal package being returned to the Community of Interest without action.

When the management review indicates a second or subsequent review is not warranted, the Governance Program Committee will provide the Community of Interest with the results of the review. If review comments are not received, the Governance Program Committee will initiate the Governance Program Committee Letter Ballot. If review comments are received, the management review will be extended to consider the Community of Interest disposition of those comments.

When the Governance Assessments Development Board management review indicates processing should continue, the Governance Program Committee will initiate several simultaneous activities:

- An announcement in the Governance Program's Governance Assessments Action publication of a 45-day review.

- A call for information on potentially pertinent patents will be made to the Governance Program Committee members and the Community of Interest simultaneously. The call will also encourage disclosure, where possible, of the existence of pending U.S. patent applications relating to the Governance Assessment under development, and of any relevant unexpired foreign patents.

- Notification to the Community of Interest of the responses received by the Governance Program resulting from previous calls for patents.

- Issuance of a press release describing the draft Governance Assessment, and announcing availability of the document for a 2-month technical review and comment period.

The draft Governance Assessment submitted for review will contain a notice that any comments should to be sent to the Governance Program Committee with a copy to the Community of Interest. The Governance Program Committee will register every review comment. Each comment will be sent immediately to the originating Community of Interest for consideration and to the Community of Interest for information. A formal response must be developed for each comment and approved by the Community of Interest.

Responses to registered comments will include the provision that the commenter has twenty working days from the postmark/email-date to reply and indicate if the comment(s) has not been satisfactorily resolved. If no response from the commented is received, the comment will be considered as satisfactorily resolved.

The response may be either a modification to the draft Governance Assessment, or a statement of the rationale for not making a change. Serious effort should be made to accommodate the comment by correspondence or discussion with the author.

In the case of changes that are editorial only, all comments are resolved, either by changes to the draft Governance Assessment or by communication with the commenter. The Community of Interest will advise the Governance Program Committee and provide all pertinent correspondence.

In the case of one or more substantive changes to the draft Governance Assessment in order to resolve the review comments, the Community of Interest votes. If the Community of Interest achieves the criteria for approval, the Community of Interest will send the comments, the replies to the comments, ballot results, the revised text, a summary of the changes and rationale to the Governance Program Committee.

The Governance Program Committee will advise the Community of Interest that a further review is required, and will take action to notify the purchasers of the latest draft Governance Assessment that another review is necessary. Subsequent reviews will begin no sooner than thirty days after the mailing of responses to review comments. Processing returns to the beginning of Milestone 5.

If there are no review comments during the second (or subsequent) review, the Community of Interest will forward the document to the Governance Program Committee for final approval.

7.5.6 Milestone 6 - Governance Program Committee Approval

If the Governance Program Committee letter ballot or meeting vote to submit the draft Governance Assessment passes with no negative votes or comments, the Governance Program Committee immediately submits the draft Governance Assessment to the Community of Interest along with all documentation required by the Community of Interest.

When there are negative votes or comments, the voting tally and all comments are sent to the Governance Program Committee and to the Community of Interest that developed the draft Governance Assessment. An effort to resolve all expressed objections will be made, and each objector will be advised in writing of the disposition of the objection and the reasons therefore. Any unresolved objections (including all documentation) and any substantive changes made in a proposed Governance Assessment will be reported to the Governance Program Committee in order to afford all members an opportunity to respond, reaffirm or change their vote.

If the letter ballot or meeting vote fails due to the number of negative votes, the record is referred to the Community of Interest that developed the draft Governance Assessment.

If the letter ballot or meeting vote fails due to insufficient affirmative votes and there are no negative ballots cast, the record is referred to the Governance Program Committee for reconsideration.

If the letter ballot or meeting vote is canceled due to review comments, the package is returned to the Community of Interest and processing continues at the beginning of Milestone 5.

7.5.7 Milestone 7 - Enterprise Approval

If the Governance Program operates within a corporation or business, or for example operates within the domain of the Chief Information Officer, an additional level of approval may be necessary. In that case, upon receipt of the transmittal of the draft Governance Assessment, the appropriate organization reviews the submittal and processes it according to the established procedures.

Upon notification of the corporate approval, the Governance Program Committee advises, by individual letter, those Governance Program Committee members that may have had unresolved negatives that they have fifteen days from the date of the notification letter from the Governance Program Committee to appeal the approval. Such an appeal would be filed with the appropriate organization within the business.

In case the business disapproves the Governance Assessment, it is sent back to the Governance Program Committee for further processing or disposition.

7.5.8 Milestone 8 - Publication

The originating Community of Interest may not convert to Maintenance status until the Governance Assessment has been published.

7.6 Governance Event Summary

This chapter sets out the classes of events that will commonly occur during within a governance program. Two classes stand out as more critical than the others: Office appointment, and Community of Interest.

Officer appointment is very crucial because it is the quality of the officers, especially Chair and Editor that determine the overall success of any governance program subgroup. Great care should be expended that these two individuals should have one and only one objective: The achievement of Governance Assessments.

Community of Interest events are also very important. These eight milestones have been chiseled into crispness over a period of 50+ years by the American National Standards Institute (ANSI) and the International Committee for Information Technology Standards (INCITS). It is almost not arguable that the most sophisticated and widely accepted IT standards have been created and are being maintained by these two organizations.

Every event is a milestone of some sort. Additionally, it may also signify the requirement for some support from the business information systems. For example, the business event, Milestone 1: Approval of the Project Proposal, presumes that the project proposal functions from Chapter 8 have been accomplished by some person occupying a position (Chapter 10) within an organization (Chapter 9). The project proposal should then be constructed according to the format specified in Chapter 11, and should then be entered in the metadata repository system (Chapter 6), and result in some project metadata (Chapter 5). Voting on the project proposal is governed by rules from Chapter 13.

Virtually everything in this book has a function, and is integrated in some way with something else. This integration is not an accident. It is a direct consequence of all those persons and organizations who are acknowledged at the front of this book.

7.7 Questions and Exercises

1. First and foremost, a Community of Interest is an organization that either operates well or chaotically. Highly organized COIs, that is, those with policies, procedures, milestones, deliverables, agendas, rules for voting, and the like run exceedingly well. The converse is also true. From your experience

in your organization, is this true? If yes, provide examples, and compare and contrast with organizations in your enterprise where the organizations are chaotic? What are the key differences? How much more beneficial in terms of time, effort, and resources is the efficient organization versus the chaotic one? Provide examples from within your own organization.

2. The Chapter lists five classes of business events. What is the effect of business events. What are the characteristics of good and bad business events in your organization? Provide examples from within your own organization.

3. Section 7.1 identifies general business events such as establishing calendars and holding meetings. From the prototypical agenda presented in Figure 36, does it seem like meetings are well organized and "move" as a consequence of projects and papers? If yes, what's been your experience with "meetings?" What has made good and bad meetings? When there are too many "bad" meetings, what's been the result in terms of attendance, meeting objectives, making deliverables, and the like? Provide examples from within your own organization.

4. Section 7.2 identifies the types of subgroups that need to exist in a Governance Community of Interest. Why are these subgroups needed? What role does each subgroup play? What would be the likely result if one or more of the subgroups are missing? Or badly executed? Review your own organization and compare and contrast organizational efforts when key subgroups are missing or badly executed. Provide examples from within your own organization.

5. Section 7.3 identifies the key officers that should exist in every Governance Community of Interest. Most subgroups have this set of offices. Review the list of good and bad characteristics of Chair and Editor within this section. Do you agree with these characteristics? If yes, why? If no, why?

6. Section 7.4 indicates that this very book is generally a program management plan for accomplishing governance in the enterprise. After reviewing the contents of the remaining chapters, do you think that is an acceptable assertion? If yes, why? If no, why not??

Review management plans of your organization and compare and contrast them with the overall content of this book in terms of scope, mission, functions, roles, offices, deliverables, and the like. If this book was adopted as-is, and then reviewed for modifications after six or so months, would that have a positive or negative impact on the schedule and ability to complete the work of a governance community of interest? Compare and contrast with other program management plans in your organization. Which approach would be faster, and more efficient? Provide examples from within your own organization.

7. Section 7.5 enumerates the key milestones for the creation of any Governance Assessments produced by a Governance Community of Interest. Which milestone will take the longest? Which is the most important?

Does your organization have a similar set of milestones for its work? If not, why not? How has not having recognized and completed milestones affected the velocity, quantity, and quality of work accomplished? Compare and contrast with milestones of your enterprise. How are they different or similar?

Suppose you just adopted the milestones set out here with no modification, how would that help or hurt? Could you get to "real work" faster? Provide examples from within you own organization where you spent four to six months developing all these materials. How did that affect the enthusiasm, workload, and overall budget that was allocated to develop a governance solutions?

8

Governance Functions

There are the following classes of functions within the Governance Program:

- General functions.
- Governance Program functions.
- Community of Interest functions.
- Officer Appointment functions.
- Service Fee Waver functions.
- Appeal procedures.
- Parliamentary functions.

8.1 General Business Functions

The general functions relate to the positions that exist in almost every Governance Program subgroup. That is,

- Chair
- Vice Chair
- Secretary
- Editor

8.1.1 Chair

The general duties of every subgroup chair include:

- Preside at meetings.

- Ensure that the Governance Program work is carried out in a prompt, efficient and an effective manner in accordance with the objectives, policies, and procedures of the Governance Program.

- Prepare and present Subgroup Annual Report to the Governance Assessments Development Board.
- Communities of Interest and Study Groups must prepare and present an annual report to the Governance Assessments Development Board.
- Disseminate in writing the 'Call for Volunteers' for officer positions for the Subgroup.
- Ensure that the Administrative Duties (shown under Vice Chair duties) are carried out.
- Provide or arrange for tutorials to membership on procedures.
- Forward to the appropriate subgroup parent timely and complete subgroup documentation.
- Send timely warning letters on endangered memberships.
- Attend required training sessions.
- Represent the body to other committees and organizations.
- Prepare and forward to the Governance Program Committee press releases and other publicity material about the Subgroup's program of work.

Appoint:

- ♦ Vice Chair.
- ♦ Secretary.
- ♦ Vocabulary Representative.
- ♦ Project Editor(s) for each project, as appropriate.

- ♦ Liaisons.
- ♦ Head of Delegation for each inter-organizational meeting.
- ♦ Other (e.g., ad hoc group Chairs).

- Ensure the Subgroup mailings are reviewed for information, possible action, and redistribution as appropriate.
- Ensure the orderly transfer of any Subgroup documents upon appointment of new officers.
- Schedule Subgroup meetings for a rolling full calendar year; ensure administrative meeting arrangements are addressed: and notify the Governance Program Committee to update the Meeting Schedule and Calendar.
- Ensure that any coordinating liaison responsibilities are carried out in a timely manner.

8.1.2 Vice Chair

The duties of the Vice-Chair are:

- In the absence of the Chair, perform the duties of the Chair.
- Act as Subgroup administrator with the following duties (unless redistributed, by agreement, among the membership).
- Register, control, and distribute documents, ensuring that the original or a reproducible copy of each is sent to the Governance Program Committee staff for the permanent file. A complete document register must be sent to the Governance Program Committee at the end of each calendar year.
- Prepare and distribute meeting notices and agendas in accordance with the Governance Program procedures and in consultation with the Chair.

- Prepare, distribute, tally, and report the results of letter ballots.
- Maintain mailing lists, record attendance and ballot responses, and notify the Chair of any individual requiring membership jeopardy notice.
- Prepare supporting documentation for submission of proposed Governance Assessments to the next higher Subgroup level.
- Prepare, for approval, status reports of work as required by the Subgroup.
- Ensure the timely distribution of mailings from the Subgroup pertinent to its work and administration.
- Review documents prior to distribution for legibility, clarity, accuracy, and appropriateness, and modify when appropriate.
- Notify the Governance Program Committee of changes in the Subgroup membership.
- Attend required training sessions.

8.1.3 Secretary

The duties of the secretary include:

- Record and transcribe meeting minutes in consultation with the Chair and Vice Chair.
- Provide minutes to the Vice Chair so that they can be distributed within four weeks of the meeting.

8.1.4 Editor

The duties of the editor are:

- Maintain documents and make timely changes as agreed by the Subgroup.
- Prepare documents according to the most recent edition of the Community of Interest style manual for preparation of proposed Governance Assessments.
- Submit an electronic version of the Governance Assessment according to the guidelines for submitting proposed Governance Assessments in an electronic format.
- Make arrangements for all artwork and engineering diagrams to be prepared and submitted electronically.
- Plan and schedule document preparation, taking into consideration lead times for document transmission, review and approval periods, meeting schedules and target dates established by the Governance Program and by Communities of Interest.
- Maintain an awareness of the development and approval process, including required lead times.
- Report the status of the document at each meeting.
- Attend required training sessions.

8.2 Governance Program

8.2.1 Overall

As such, the Governance Program Committee is required to:

- Serve as the consensus body of the Governance Program.

- Ensure the efficiency and ethical stature of the entire organization.
- Continually evolve the organization to ensure the highest quality of work and Governance Assessments development.
- Retain ultimate responsibility for all Governance Assessments developed and approved by the various Communities of Interest.
- Create and disband its immediate Subgroups and Communities of Interest.
- Elect the Chair and Vice-chair of the Governance Program Committee, the Chairs of the Governance Assessments Development Board and the Governance Assessments Policy Board. Elect the Chairs of the Communities of Interest and Governance Program Committee committees. Recall elected officials, as circumstances require.
- Oversee and coordinate the work of the Governance Assessments Development Board and the Governance Assessments Policy Board. Harmonize recommendations from all of the Governance Program Committee Subgroups.
- Approve and determine external distribution of nonstandard documents from the Governance Assessments Development Board, the Governance Assessments Policy Board and all the Communities of Interest.
- Approve and disseminate organizational collateral.
- Retain and recruit members.
- Approve and fund trade shows, symposiums and seminar opportunities.
- Maintain and approve procedures as necessary.
- Forecast services required for administrative support.
- Ensure a financially viable organization.
- Evaluate and approve recommendations for Governance Program

Committee operating expenses, revenues and special accounts. Approve the three-year rolling financial plan.

- Resolve administrative issues.
- Determine which matters can only be considered in Executive Sessions.

8.2.2 Governance Program Chair

The Governance Program Chair will carry out the following responsibilities:

- Chair meetings of the Governance Program Committee providing a neutral viewpoint to facilitate the achievement of the Governance Program.
- Coordinate with Governance Program Committee member organizations to ensure the effective meetings. This would include coordination related to meeting room requirements, production of minutes of the meeting, et al.
- The Vice Chairman will support the Chairman as required.

8.2.3 Finance Board

The Finance Board, for a rolling two year plan, shall:

- Review financial results (budget and actual) of the Governance Program Committee, all Boards, Communities of Interest.
- Make recommendations on the Governance Program Committee service fees.
- Recommend budgets for the Governance Program Committee.
- Make recommendations on the finance aspects of acquisition, retention and divestiture of the Communities of Interest assets.

- Make recommendations on and monitor financial aspects associated with new services and requirements.

8.2.4 Procedures Board

The Procedures Board shall:

- Draft and recommend to the Governance Program Committee the procedures for operation of the Communities of Interest; review Community of Interest operations to ensure that they comply with the Governance Program policies and procedures.
- Amend the procedures as necessary.
- Respond to requests for additions, changes, deletions, or new developments to the procedures.
- Review procedures changes originated outside of Procedures Board Committee prior to ballot by the Governance Program Committee.
- Circulate proposed changes, modifications, and enhancements to affected Subgroup(s) for preliminary review and comment.
- Render interpretations on procedural issues. Maintain a record of interpretations. Consider these for future incorporation into appropriate procedure documents.
- Review and submit to the Governance Program Committee for approval any internal operating procedures developed by Communities of Interest organizational entities to ensure compliance with this document.

8.2.5 Governance Assessments Policy Board

The Governance Assessments Policy Board initiates activities to accomplish the following:

- Identify and develop methods for rapid inter-organizational adoption of Governance Assessments.

- Find, facilitate and promote opportunities for inter-organizational collaborative standardization activities that enhance interests.

- Monitor and determine impact of relevant policies and make recommendations accordingly.

- Define and implement methods for the Communities of Interest to collaborate with other organizations on technology policy issues.

- Identify and determine how to form inter-organizational alliances, partnerships, joint projects, etc.

- Create a coexistence strategy with consortia and other Governance Assessments' organizations.

- Investigate expansion of scope.

8.2.6 Governance Assessments Development Board

The Governance Assessments Development Board is the most important of the Governance Program boards. The functions of this board include:

- Governance Assessments review.
- Managing the Governance Assessments process.
- General functions.
- Community of Interest Management.
- Community of Interest Discovery.

8.2.6.1 Governance Assessments Review

In carrying out its program of work, the Governance Assessments Development Board has the following major responsibilities for standardization within its scope:

- Review and approve proposed Governance Assessments.
- Develop and maintain the Governance Program Management Plan.
- Develop and maintain the Governance Program Integrated Schedule.
- Make recommendations to the Governance Program Committee regarding the appointment of officers in all Subgroups reporting to the Governance Assessments Development Board and any recalls of officers as needed.
- Maintain current approved Governance Assessments and respond to requests for standardization within its scope.
- Avoid conflicting Governance Assessments but not preclude development of families of Governance Assessments.
- Minimize duplication of Governance Assessments through the creation of appropriate liaison and coordination mechanisms among the Governance Assessments of the Governance Assessments Development Board and with other Governance Assessment's bodies having common interests.
- Provide the opportunity to participate in the standardization process for all those know to be or who indicate they are directly and materially affected by the Governance Assessments Development Board scope.
- Make recommendations to the Governance Program Committee regarding the creation and disbandment of management groups, Communities of Interest, and other subgroups as may be necessary to accomplish the Governance Assessments' work of the Governance Assessments Development Board and the Governance Program Committee.
- Maintain the Project Proposal Guide, and Community of Interest Annual Report Guide.
- Maintain a complete list of Communities of Interests, the projects assigned to each, and the Governance Assessments.
- Maintain the Governance Program database that lists the officers of each Community of Interest as well as the meeting schedules of the

Community of Interest and its Subgroups.

8.2.6.2 Managing the Governance Assessments Process

To manage the standardization process, the Governance Assessments Development Board shall:

- Perform defect management reviews.
- Perform management reviews (Milestone 5).
- Monitor 5 Year Recommendations for Maintenance.
- Develop and submit maintenance recommendations due for Governance Assessments assigned to the Community of Interest.
- Perform first level of response to, and resolve as appropriate, issues of Communities of Interest.
- After Governance Program approval, request for approval of new projects.
- Approval of project proposals for new areas of work, including evaluating the needs for systems of Governance Assessments within the scope of the Governance Program

8.2.6.3 General Functions

The Governance Assessments Development Board also has the following general functions:

- Coordinate the training of officers.
- Act as liaison with Communities of Interest.
- Perform the work of any Communities of Interest or other Subgroup when no appropriate Subgroup exists to perform the function or an existing Subgroup is not responsive.

- Analyze and evaluate promptly, including organizing and managing Study Groups as needed, all proposals to the Governance Program Committee for new or revised Governance Assessments development projects.

- Organize and manage the processes needed to study, over a short term, closely related topics and to prepare advisory reports for guidance to specific elements of the Governance Program, as needed.

- Monitor, manage, and validate the initiation and development of all the Governance Program Governance Assessments' projects in accordance with Governance Program Committee direction, assuring there is no overlap or duplication of work, and pro-actively managing project milestones.

- Prepare the charter, scope and program of work for Collaborative Subgroups.

- Manage liaison functions to other Governance Assessments' organizations projects as necessary to improve working relations and minimize overlap or redundant work

8.2.6.4 Community of Interest Management

The Governance Assessments Development Board also exercises the following functions in regard to the general management of the Communities of Interest:

- Effect co-ordination between the Governance Program Communities of Interest and ensure the effectiveness of the technical groups.

- Make implementation level decisions and perform risk mitigation as necessary.

- Develop and maintain the Governance Program communication and liaison plan.

- Develop and maintain the Governance Program vision and scope.
- Develop and maintain any other the Governance Program Documents as directed by the Governance Program Committee.
- Provide direction and guidance to the Governance Program representatives in the Governance Program.
- Establish and maintain the Governance Program web site.
- Develop and maintain the Governance Program work plan.
- Provide support for staffing of Governance Program management documents.
- Report Governance Program Community of Interest activities to the Governance Program Committee.
- Raise issues as necessary for resolution by the Governance Program Committee.
- Maintain a formal record of all Governance Program Projects Committee meetings.
- Develop and Maintain the Governance Program briefings.
- Execute other specific tasks as may be directed by the Governance Program Committee.

8.2.6.5 Community of Interest Discovery

A critical function of the Governance Assessments Development Board is the discovery of communities of interest within the enterprise. The following functions are performed to that end:

- Establish and manage Community of Interest Infrastructure

- Create Prototypical Concept of Operations
- Create Metabase System and Database Environment
- Create Methodology for Community of Interest Efforts
- Create Governance Project Assessment Specifications

- Identify the Enterprise Architecture Communities of Interest
  - Mission-Organization-Function COIs
  - Position COIs
  - Information Needs COIs
  - Resource Life Cycle Analysis COIs
  - Database Domain COIs
  - Database Object COIs
  - Business Terms COIs

- Identify the Business Information System Architecture Communities of Interest

  - Business Information Systems COIs
  - Business Event COIs
  - Business Cycle COIs
  - Business Calendar COIs
  - User Acceptance Test COIs
  - Use Case COIs
  - Reports COIs

- Identify Data Integrity Rule Communities of Interest
  - Data Architecture Governed Models
  - Data Element Models COIs
  - Specified Data Model COIs
  - Implemented Data Model COIs
  - Operational Data Model COIs
  - View Data Model COIs

- Identify Project Management Communities of Interest
  - Project Template COIs
  - Deliverable Template COIs
  - Task COIs
  - Skill COIs
  - Work Environment Factor COIs

- Establish Community of Interest Project Proposals for each Community of Interest

8.2.7 Study Groups

The steps involved in every Study Group project include:

- Developing the problem statement, or external statement of the requirement to be satisfied, or existing deficiency in support of identifying the need, or the identification of the deficiency or need to be addressed, or the need for improved performance.

- Performing the requisite analysis includes employing enterprise missions, functions, and organization to frame or focus the analysis. If possible, refine this analysis to the point of specifying the problem space to the appropriate level of detail. Develop an initial governance project planning problem statement. Identify the specific objectives that must be achieved to support mission performance. This is a statement of desired results, with specific, quantifiable, and measurable outcomes that contribute to achievement.

- Configuring Governance project plans that include work breakdown structures of task statements that support the achievement of the Governance project. The Governance project also includes the various goals and objectives that are to be achieved. Alternative approaches are created and evaluated through Proof of Principle Projects that validate the recommended alternative (risk reduction) or validate the specifications (for issuance to the developer).

- Managing the Governance projects that include the accomplishment of the actual project deliverables. Additionally, it includes monitoring and evaluating the proper use of a created Governance Assessment, that is, cycling back lessons learned reports, issue resolution reports, or refinement of performance metrics that were employed in the development effort. In the Governance project, the nature of the technical solution, evaluations via the functional (user) and technical environments are accomplished.

8.3 Community of Interest

The overall business functions of a Community of Interest are really just two, which are:

- Governance Assessment Development
- Governance Assessment Maintenance

In support of these two main functions, the Community of Interest will in general:

- Develop draft Governance Assessment.

- Submit to the Governance Assessments Development Board approved new projects within the Community of Interest's general area of interest.

- Participate technically on behalf of or advise the Governance Assessments Development Board on related inter-organizational Governance Assessments' activity

.

The program of work includes the following functional elements for each assigned project:

- Develop and update the work plan and schedule of target dates for completing the project.

- Collect data needed to develop a Governance Assessment.

- Develop the outline and table of contents of a Governance Assessment.
- Draft the Governance Assessment, appendices, and associated expository remarks.
- Vote until Community of Interest consensus is reached or it is apparent that a consensus cannot be reached.
- Prepare responses to review and Community of Interest letter ballot comments.
- Recommend defect management actions during a Governance Assessment's maintenance phase.
- Recommend revisions when experience with a Governance Assessment so indicates.
- Conduct the required review and recommendation for revision, reaffirmation, designation as an archival Governance Assessment, or withdrawal.

8.3.1 Governance Assessment Development

Within the development of any Governance Assessment there are four main functions that must be performed by the technical committees within the Community of Interest. These deal with:

- Enterprise Architecture Governance Assessments
- Business Information Systems Architecture Governance Assessments
- Data Integrity Rule Governance Assessments
- Data Architecture Governance Assessments
- Project Management Governance Assessments

8.3.1.1 Enterprise Architecture Governance Assessments

For these enterprise architecture components, the establishment of Governance Assessments for each of:

- Missions and descriptions for the Enterprise
- Organizations and descriptions for the Enterprise
- Functions that are universal across the Enterprise
- Mission-Organizations and descriptions of the interrelationships
- Mission-Organization-Functions and descriptions of the interrelationships
- Positions across the Enterprise
- [Information Need] Characteristics
- Enterprise Resources
- Resource Life Cycle Nodes and descriptions across the Resources
- Precedence Vectors between Resource Life Cycle Nodes
- Information Needs across the Enterprise
- Mission-Organization-Function relationships and descriptions with Information Needs
- Database domains based on leaves of Mission Model
- ER models for each Database Domain
- ER model for entire enterprise based on Database Domain ER models
- Database Object Classes from Entities from ER Models

- Relationship and descriptions between database object classes and Resource Life Cycle Nodes
- Property Classes from Entities from ER Models
- Data Elements from Entities from ER Models
- Business Terms and definitions as needed across all Enterprise Architecture Component descriptions
- Relationship between Mission-Organization-Functions and Positions
- Relationship between Persons and Mission-Organization-Function-Positions

8.3.1.2 Business Information Systems Architecture Governance Assessments

For these enterprise architecture components, the establishment of Governance Assessments for each of:

- Name and description of business information systems needed to satisfy a resource life cycle node state
- Business cycles that need to exist to satisfy the achievement of Resource Life Cycle Nodes within the enterprise
- Business calendars that need to exist to satisfy the achievement of Resource Life Cycle Nodes
- Business events within business cycles that need to exist to satisfy the achievement of Resource Life Cycle Nodes
- Business events within calendar cycles that need to exist to satisfy the achievement of Resource Life Cycle Nodes
- User acceptance tests necessary for the end-user acceptance of a

developed database and/or business information system

- Use cases necessary for the functional behavior of business information systems

8.3.1.3 Data Integrity Rule Governance Assessments

For these enterprise architecture components, the establishment of Governance Assessments for each of:

- Data integrity rule name and description
- Data integrity rule relationships to appropriate DBMS Columns
- Data integrity rule relationships to appropriate local variables
- Data integrity rule relationships to appropriate non-DBMS file structures
- Data integrity rule process logic for required tests
- Data integrity rule specified actions for success and for failure
- Data integrity rule binding to Data Architecture model component
- Data integrity rule binding to appropriate business information system component

8.3.1.4 Data Architecture Governance Assessments

The data architecture Governance Assessments embrace the following:

- Meta Category Values
- Data Elements
- Specified Data Models
- Implemented Database Models
- Operational Database Models
- View Data Models

8.3.1.4.1 Meta Category Value Governance Assessments

For these data architecture components, the establishment of Governance Assessments for each of:

- Establishment and description of meta category value type classes
- Establishment and description of meta category value type hierarchies within meta category value type classes
- Establishment and description of meta category value hierarchies within meta category value types

8.3.1.4.2 Data Element Governance Assessments

For these data architecture components, the establishment of Governance Assessments for each of:

- Data element specifications including concepts, conceptual value domains, data element concepts, value domains, and value domain values
- Relationships between data element concepts with concepts and conceptual value domains
- Relationships between meta category values and data element concepts
- Relationships between value domains and data element concepts
- Data elements
- Relationships between data elements and data element concepts
- Relationships between meta category values and data elements
- Assignment of value domains to data elements
- Derived data elements

- Compound data elements
- Relationships between data elements and derived data elements
- Relationships between data elements and compound data elements

8.3.1.4.3 Specified Data Model Governance Assessments

For these data architecture components, the establishment of Governance Assessments for each of:

- Specified data model specifications including subjects, entities, attributes, keys and relationships
- Relationships between entity attributes and data elements
- Assignment of meta category values to attributes
- Assignment of value domains to attributes

8.3.1.4.4 Implemented Database Model Governance Assessments

For these data architecture components, the establishment of Governance Assessments for each of:

- Implemented data model specifications including schemas, tables, columns, keys, and relationships
- Relationships between table columns and entity attributes
- Assignment of meta category values to columns
- Assignment of value domains to columns

8.3.1.4.5 Operational Database Model Governance Assessments

For these data architecture components, the establishment of Governance Assessments for each of:

- Operational data model specifications including DBMS schemas, DBMS tables, DBMS columns, DBMS keys, and relationships
- Relationships between DBMS table columns and table columns
- Assignment of value domains to DBMS columns

8.3.1.4.6 View Data Model Governance Assessments

For these data architecture components, the establishment of Governance Assessments for each of:

- View data model specifications including views, view columns, inter-view column relationships and processes
- View column relationships to derived data element
- View column relationships to compound data elements
- View column relationships to DBMS columns

8.3.1.5 Project Management Governance Assessments

For these enterprise architecture components, the establishment of Governance Assessments for each of:

- Project Templates
- Deliverable Templates
- Task Templates

- Skills
- Work Environment Factors
- Relationships between Projects and Deliverables
- Relationships between Deliverables and Tasks
- Relationship between Persons and Mission-Organization-Function-Persons
- Relationship between Project and Resource Life Cycle Node
- Relationship between Project Deliverable and Work Accomplishment record
- Relationship between Project Deliverable and Work Environment Factor

8.3.2 Maintenance of Governance Assessments

Upon the Community of Interest approval of Governance Assessment that document is automatically assigned to a maintenance project.

A maintenance project retains that status until experience indicates a need for revision, reaffirmation, or withdrawal, or has been converted to status as a stabilized Governance Assessment.

On the four-year anniversary of the Governance Assessment's approval a determination is made whether the Governance Assessment is to be revised, reaffirmed, or withdrawn.

During the maintenance phase, experience in using and implementing a Governance Assessment may cause questions to arise. These questions are processed under the procedures for defect management.

The Community of Interest responsible for the Governance Assessment will use the voting procedures to process the response to a report of an alleged defect.

8.3.2.1 Revision

Whenever it is determined that a revision of the Governance Assessment is needed, a project proposal for the revision will be developed by the Community of Interest in accordance with the provisions in the Community of Interest, Project Proposal Guide. After approval by the Community of Interest, the Project Proposal will be submitted to the Governance Program Committee. Processing continues at Milestone 1.

If a revision is planned or underway, but not completed by the four-year anniversary of either the approval or the last reaffirmation of the Governance Assessment, the Community of Interest must determine whether the Governance Assessment being revised will be reaffirmed or withdrawn while the revision is being developed, and make a recommendation to the Governance Assessments Development Board.

NOTE: If the revision process extends for four years beyond a previous reaffirmation, this process will be repeated. The effect of this is that the Community of Interest must forward to the Governance Assessments Development Board by the above mentioned four-year or nine-year anniversary, either a completed revision to the Governance Assessment, or a recommendation for reaffirmation or withdrawal.

8.3.2.2 Reaffirmation/Withdrawal

If it is determined that the Governance Assessment should be reaffirmed or withdrawn, the Community of Interest will forward a package that includes all of the following:

- A recommendation of reaffirmation or withdrawal.
- The final tally of the Community of Interest vote recommending reaffirmation or withdrawal with a copy of any unresolved negative votes, and the Community of Interest response to each.

The Community of Interest package is forwarded to the Governance Program Committee and the Governance Program Committee initiates the review of the Community of Interest recommendation.

- If comments are received as a result of the review, these comments are forwarded to the Community of Interest that made the recommendation and the Community of Interest will consider these comments at their next meeting, provide a response to each commenter, and forward final Community of Interest recommendation to the Governance Program Committee for final action. The final Community of Interest recommendation will contain a copy of each comment and the Community of Interest 's response to each, in addition to the information contained in the package.

- If there are no comments, the Governance Program Committee will initiate a Governance Program Committee letter ballot for approval of the Community of Interest recommendation. If there are any negative votes on the Governance Program Committee Letter Ballot, a 15-day reconsideration ballot will be issued. At the completion of the letter ballot process, if the Governance Program Committee letter ballot passes, the Governance Program Committee submits the recommendation to Board of Governance Assessments Review for a Governance Assessment.

If the Governance Program Committee letter ballot fails, for lack of affirmative votes, and there are no negative votes, final action is taken by the Governance Program Committee at its next meeting.

If the Governance Program Committee letter ballot fails based on the number of negatives, the recommendation is returned to the Community of Interest that originated it for further deliberation.

8.3.2.3 Amendments and Supplements

Amendments are separately processed documents that modify a Governance Assessment with technical changes or additions, or with changes in what it means to conform to the Governance Assessment. If it is determined that one or more amendments are needed prior to the revision of the Governance Assessment, such amendments, other than Defect Management, will be processed in the same manner as Governance Assessments, e.g., initiated with a project proposal.

8.3.2.4 Defect Management

These procedures are for the Governance Assessments falling under the following conditions:

- The rapid amendment of Governance Assessments for which proper use is dependent upon the rapid promulgation of errata or amendments as defects are detected.

- The rapid promulgation of commentary consisting of clarifying interpretations without technical amendment of the Governance Assessment.

The submission of the report of an alleged defect may result in one or more of the following:

- Erratum to a Governance Assessment.
- Amendment to a Governance Assessment.
- Interpretation of a Governance Assessment.
- Response to the submitter explaining why an erratum, amendment, or interpretations will not be issued.

Each of these, except the last is discussed in turn. For the Governance Assessment, the concepts in this section generally apply except where indicated.

8.3.2.4.1 Erratum

A Governance Assessment may be modified with corrigenda to:

- Correct a typographical error.
- Insert a missing word, sentence, paragraph, figure, example, table, or clause.
- Delete an extraneous word, sentence, paragraph, figure, example, table, or clause.

Any such modification of the Governance Assessment will not introduce technical changes or changes in what it means to conform to the Governance Assessment.

8.3.2.4.2 Amendment

Any modification of the Governance Assessment that introduces technical changes or changes in what it means to conform to the Governance Assessment will be treated as an amendment to the Governance Assessment.

8.3.2.4.3 Interpretation

An interpretation is a clarifying commentary on the Governance Assessment that does not introduce either a technical change or a change in what it means to conform to the Governance Assessment.

8.3.2.5 When the Community of Interest No Longer Exists

If the Community of Interest responsible for the Governance Assessment no longer exists, the Governance Program Committee is responsible for dealing with reaffirmation, revision, or withdrawal of the Governance Assessment. The Governance Program Committee will also process any defect management documents associated with the Governance Assessment.

If, by the four-year anniversary of the approval or last reaffirmation of a Governance Assessment, the Community of Interest responsible for the Governance Assessment has not forwarded a proposed revision to the Governance Assessment or a recommendation for reaffirmation or withdrawal of the Governance Assessment, the Governance Program Committee will take action during the fifth year to approve reaffirmation or withdrawal of the Governance Assessment.

8.3.2.6 Alleged Defect

8.3.2.6.1 Action by the Governance Program Committee

If the Governance Program Committee receives a report of an alleged defect, the Governance Program Committee will forward the report to the Community of Interest responsible for the Governance Assessment.

8.3.2.6.2 Action by Community of Interest

Upon receipt of a report of an alleged defect, the Community of Interest Chair or designee will:

- Enter the report in a permanent register of defect reports.
- Distribute the report to all Community of Interest members within two weeks of receipt.
- Send an acknowledgment of receipt to the submitter within thirty calendar days of receipt of the report.
- Place the report on the agenda for the next meeting of the Community of Interest, if the meeting is scheduled within two months of receipt of the alleged defect; in this case the submitter of the report will be invited to participate in discussion of the report.

If a meeting of the Community of Interest has not been or cannot be conveniently scheduled no later than two months after receipt of the report of the alleged defect by the Community of Interest Chair or designee, the Community of Interest Chair or designee, in consultation with the Governance Program Committee, will appoint a group of experts to expedite the preparation of a recommendation to the Community of Interest. In this case, the submitter of the request is not necessarily involved.

If the Community of Interest determines that an erratum, amendment, or interpretation will not be issued, the submitter of the report will be advised why no further action is expected to be taken.

8.4.2.6.3 Processing of Responses

The Community of Interest will forward a package to the Governance Program Committee that will include all of the following:

- A letter recommending the action to be taken.
- The final tally of the Community of Interest vote recommending the action

with a copy of any unresolved negative votes and the Community of Interest response to each.

The Community of Interest package is reviewed by the Governance Assessments Development Board, which recommends action to the Governance Program Committee as appropriate. If the Governance Program Committee agrees with the Community of Interest recommendation, processing continues as specified in the following sections.

8.4.2.6.3.1 Erratum

If the Community of Interest determines that the response will be processed as an erratum to the Governance Assessment, the Governance Program Committee will forward the report, response, and erratum for a Governance Program Committee Letter Ballot and concurrently to the Community of Interest for any required the Community of Interest review. The submitter of the report will be advised of this action by the Governance Program Committee. Processing will continue at Milestone 5.

8.4.2.6.3.3 Amendment

If the Community of Interest determines that the response will be processed as an amendment to the Governance Assessment, the Governance Program Committee will forward the report, response, and amendment for a concurrent Governance Program Committee Letter Ballot and the Community of Interest review. The submitter of the report will be advised of this action by the Governance Program Committee. Processing will continue at Milestone 5.

8.4.2.6.3.4 Interpretation

If the Community of Interest determines that the response will be processed as an interpretation of the Governance Assessment, the Governance Program Committee will forward the report, response, and interpretation for a Governance Program Committee Letter Ballot. If the Governance Program Committee Letter Ballot results in the approval of the interpretation, the submitter of the report will be advised of this action and the interpretation is published by the Governance Program Committee as the Community of Interest interpretation bulletin.

At the discretion of the Community of Interest, approved interpretations can be collected and published by the Governance Program Committee. Interpretations will be published within two years of their approval.

8.3.2.7 Stabilized Governance Assessments

Whenever it is determined that a Governance Assessment has ongoing validity and effectiveness, but is mature and unlikely to require maintenance of any sort, it can be designated as a stabilized Governance Assessment, that removes the requirement for periodic reaffirmation.

In order for a Governance Assessment to be declared a stabilized Governance Assessment, at least five years must have passed since the previous reaffirmation, without any modifications.

If it is determined that the Governance Assessment should be designated as a stabilized Governance Assessment, the Community of Interest will forward a package that includes all of the following:

- The rationale for the recommendation.
- The final tally of the Community of Interest vote recommending status as a stabilized Governance Assessment with a copy of any unresolved negative votes and the Community of Interest response to each.

The Community of Interest package is forwarded to the Governance Program Committee and the Governance Program Committee initiates the review of the Community of Interest recommendation.

- If comments are received as a result of the review, these comments are forwarded to the Community of Interest that made the recommendation and the Community of Interest will consider these comments at their next meeting, provide a response to each commenter, and forward final Community of Interest recommendation to the Governance Assessments Development Board for review and subsequently to the Governance Program Committee for final action. The final Community of Interest recommendation will contain a copy of each comment and the Community of Interest 's response to each, in addition to the information contained in paragraphs above.

- If there are no comments, the Governance Program Committee will initiate a Governance Program Committee Letter Ballot for approval of the Community of Interest recommendation. If there are any negative votes on the Governance Program Committee Letter Ballot, a 15-day reconsideration ballot will be issued. At the completion of the letter ballot process, if the Governance Program Committee Letter Ballot passed, the Governance Program Committee submits the recommendation to Board of Governance Assessments Review.

If the Governance Program Committee Letter Ballot failed, for lack of affirmative votes, and there were no negative votes, final action is taken by the Governance Program Committee at its next meeting.

If the Governance Program Committee Letter Ballot failed based on the number of negatives, the recommendation is returned to the Community of Interest that originated it for further deliberation.

The Governance Program Committee will maintain a list of stabilized Governance Assessments. Besides providing status of the Governance Assessments, this list will be used by the Governance Program Committee to:

- Report to the Community of Interest on reaffirmation of the Governance Assessments that the Governance Assessment is reaffirmed, without requiring a Community of Interest ballot or review.

- Report to Governance Program Committee on reaffirmation of ISO Governance Assessments for which a Community of Interest holds the Technical Advisory Group, that the Governance Assessment is reaffirmed, without requiring a Community of Interest ballot or review.

In either case, the Governance Program Committee will post the action on the Community of Interest web site and respond to the authority requesting the reaffirmation.

If a new work proposal is generated and adopted against a stabilized Governance Assessment, the Governance Assessment will revert to maintenance status.

8.3.2.8 Introductory Statements for the Response

An introductory statement will be included in the response to a report of an alleged defect in a Governance Assessment. Thereafter, the response will include one or more of the following responses depending on type:

- Erratum
- Amendment
- Interpretation

8.3.2.8.1 Erratum

An erratum is issued in response to questions that have been raised regarding certain specifications contained in the Governance Assessment. The erratum will identify the affected Governance Assessment, the Community of Interest preparing the erratum, the problem specifications, the approach to a solution, and the erratum solution itself. The erratum will be created as quickly as possible so as to avoid any unnecessary rework on the part of Governance Assessment adopters.

This erratum is to be considered as part of the Governance Assessment and must be used in conjunction with that Governance Assessment. Any subsequent revision, erratum, or amendment to the Governance Assessment may or may not reflect the contents of this erratum.

8.3.2.8.2 Amendment

An amendment is issued in response to questions that have been raised regarding certain specifications contained in the Governance Assessment. The amendment will identify the affected Governance Assessment, the Community of Interest preparing the amendment, the problem specifications, the approach to a solution, and the amendment solution itself. The amendment will be created as quickly as possible so as to avoid any unnecessary rework on the part of Governance Assessment adopters.

This amendment is to be considered as part of the Governance Assessment and must be used in conjunction with that Governance Assessment. The amendment may alter the meaning of the Governance

Assessment. Any subsequent revision, erratum, or amendment to the Governance Assessment may or may not reflect the contents of this amendment.

8.3.2.8.3 Interpretation

An interpretation is issued in response to questions that have been raised regarding certain specifications contained in the Governance Assessment. The interpretation will identify the affected Governance Assessment, the Community of Interest preparing the interpretation, the problem specifications, the approach to an understanding of the Governance Assessment. The interpretation will be created as quickly as possible so as to avoid any unnecessary rework on the part of Governance Assessment adopters.

This interpretation, while reflecting the technical opinion of the Committee responsible for maintaining the Governance Assessment, is intended solely as supplementary information to users of the Governance Assessment. The Governance Assessment is not altered by the issuance of this interpretation. Any subsequent revision, erratum, amendment, or interpretation to the Governance Assessment may or may not reflect the contents of this interpretation.

8.4 Officer Appointment

8.4.1 Election Procedures

At the time an elected officer position becomes vacant or within six months prior to an incumbent officer's term expiring, a thirty-day call for volunteers for candidates to fill the officer position will be issued to the Chair of the Subgroup with the vacancy. The Subgroup Chair will expeditiously forward this call to the Subgroup membership.

In order to be considered, candidates must apply within the time frame specified in the call for volunteers. The incumbent may also apply unless this would cause a violation of the term limitations for the office.

For the Governance Program Committee and Subsidiary Boards, a candidate for an officer position must be a principal representative of a voting member of the Governance Program Committee.

For all other subgroup, the candidate must be a principle or alternate representative of a voting member of the Subgroup.

In the event of two or more officer positions from a Subgroup being filled at the same time, the Governance Program Committee will stagger the Subgroup officers' appointment process for those offices (i.e., conclude one election before closing the call for another position) in order to allow candidates to apply for more than one vacancy.

When a new Subgroup is formed, the Governance Program Committee will appoint a convener and issue the call for volunteers for candidates to fill the officer positions. The call will be issued to the convener of the Subgroup who must expeditiously forward it to the Subgroup membership. Until a Chair has been elected, the convener will continue to assume the Chair responsibilities.

Each volunteer candidate, whether for appointment or reappointment, must submit to the Governance Program Committee the following documentation in support of their candidacy:

- A statement of experience, indicating the volunteer's expertise in the Subgroup's program of work, voluntary Governance Assessments' efforts, and leadership abilities .

- A statement of management support acknowledging the additional workload, financial resources, and duties required of an officer over and above that of a technical participant.

Statements of management support on behalf of officer candidates must be submitted from those organizations that are affected by the additional workload and financial resources required. Letters of management support should indicate a commitment for at least one year, although commitment for the full term of office is preferred.

The Governance Program Committee will review the documentation to determine if it satisfies all of the procedural requirements and review the membership records of the Subgroup involved to determine if the candidate(s) is a principal or an alternate in good standing in the Subgroup.

The Governance Program Committee is the officer appointment body for Chair positions in all Communities of Interest. When there is more than one qualified candidate applying for the position, the Governance Program Committee will provide the Chair of the Community of Interest, an advisory, thirty-day letter ballot with a request that it be distributed to the Community of Interest membership for completion. This letter ballot will contain the names of all qualified candidates with a request to indicate the candidate the member prefers fill the vacant position. The letter ballot will be returned to the Governance Program Committee by the individual Community of Interest members and the results of the letter ballot will be provided to the Governance Program Committee as information in the appointment process.

Letter ballots received by the Governance Program Committee after the close of the ballot period may not be processed depending upon the postmark. The results of Community of Interest letter ballots are confidential and are only advisory to the Governance Program Committee in the appointment process.

The Governance Program Committee will furnish the Governance Program Committee the documentation provided by the candidates and the summary of the results of the advisory Community of Interest letter ballot. The Governance Program Committee will take final appointment action in executive session. When Governance Program Committee appointment action is completed, the Governance Program Committee will advise the Community of Interest and the candidates. The individual appointed will assume the officer position upon completion of the term of the incumbent, or, if the officer position is vacant or the incumbent's term has expired, the individual appointed will assume the officer position immediately.

8.4.2 Terms of Elected Officers

Terms of elected officers normally end at their designated termination dates or by resignation of officer, termination of the body, termination of officer's membership, or by recall, whichever occurs first. In the event that the issuance of a call for candidates prior to the designated termination date is delayed, the term will be extended either until the election of a successor is completed, or the call is issued and closed with no response, whichever occurs first.

8.4.3 Officer Recall Procedures

When circumstances require, it is the responsibility of the Governance Program Committee to recall the Chair, elected Vice-chair of a Subgroup.

Recall is a very serious responsibility discharged with utmost regard to confidentiality and due process.

For all matters considered by the Governance Program Committee, the following procedures apply:

- Formal consideration of corrective action or recall begins with a written communication between a concerned party and the staff of the Governance Program Committee. The matter is discussed in an executive session at the next Governance Program Committee meeting at that time the Governance Program Committee decides whether sufficient grounds exist to investigate it.

- If it is decided to investigate the matter, the Governance Program Committee will notify in writing the officer involved. A Governance Program Committee member is designated to follow up on the original communication to the Governance Program Committee, discuss the matter with the officer involved, gather other information and opinions, as appropriate, and make a report in an executive session at the next Governance Program Committee meeting. At that time, the Governance Program Committee decides whether to take no further action, to continue its investigation or to recall the officer involved. In any case, the officer involved is notified in writing.

8.5 Service Fee Waiver Procedures

Any organization believing there is justification to obtain a full or partial waiver of the Governance Program Committee service fee may apply in writing to the Governance Program Committee. The requester should provide documentation that would enable the Governance Program Committee to make a recommendation for final action. Waiver requests will be handled in strict confidence. Results of the request are conveyed directly to the requester and are not reported to any other individual or group.

8.6 Appeals Procedures

8.6.1 Introduction

The provision for appeals is important for the protection of directly and materially affected interests and of the Governance Assessment's developers. An appeals mechanism is required as a part of due process by the Governance Program.

8.6.2 Right of Appeal

Directly and materially affected interests who believe they have been or will be adversely affected by a Governance Assessment or any action or inaction relative thereto within the Governance Program Committee 's jurisdiction have the right to appeal such actions or inactions of the Community of Interest subgroup or the Governance Program Committee in accordance with the following procedures.

The Community of Interest will not normally hear an appeal of an action or inaction by a Subgroup or its Governance Program Committee until the procedures provided by the Community of Interest have been completed as prescribed below. Such appeals will be directed to the Community of Interest in accordance with the procedures of the appropriate the Community of Interest entity (e.g., Board of Governance Assessments Review, Executive Governance Assessments Council, or Governance Assessments boards).

8.6.3 Criteria for Appeals Mechanism

It is the intention of the Governance Program Committee that the following general criteria are encompassed in these appeal's procedures:

- Appeals will be addressed promptly and a decision made expeditiously.
- The right of the involved parties to present their cases will not be denied.
- These procedures will provide for participation by all parties concerned without imposing an undue burden on them.

- Consideration of appeals will be fair and unbiased and will fully address the concerns expressed.

- Records of appeals will be kept and made available upon request. The Governance Program Committee may levy a nominal charge to cover the cost of reproduction, handling and distribution for requests received from other than the involved parties.

8.6.4 Appeals

The appellant will file a formal complaint with the Governance Program Committee within thirty calendar days after the date of notification of the action being appealed or at any time with respect to inaction. The complaint will state the nature of the objection(s) including any direct and material adverse effects, the section(s) of these procedures or the Governance Assessments that are at issue, actions or inactions that are at issue, and the specific remedial action(s) that would satisfy the appellant's concerns. Previous efforts to resolve the objection(s) and the outcome of each will be noted.

Within thirty calendar days after receipt of the complaint, the Governance Program Committee will respond by correspondence to the appellant, specifically addressing each allegation of fact in the complaint to the extent of the respondent's knowledge.

If the appellant and the Governance Program Committee are unable to resolve the complaint informally in a manner consistent with these procedures within fifteen calendar days, the Governance Program Committee will schedule a hearing with an appeal's panel on a date agreeable to all participants but within forty-five calendar days, giving at least ten calendar days notice. If there is not a mutually agreeable date, the Governance Program Committee will set the date and time for the appeal hearing. Should any party of interest not be present at the meeting, the decision of the appeal's panel will be based on the written submissions and any presentations made by the parties.

The appeal's panel will consist of three individuals who have not been directly involved in the matter in dispute. At least two members will be acceptable to the appellant and at least two will be acceptable to the

Governance Program Committee. The appeal's panel members will be selected as follows:

- The appellant selects one.

- The Governance Program Committee selects one.

In the event the appellant does not wish to select a panelist or a third panelist cannot be agreed upon, the Governance Program Committee will appoint these individuals to the panel in order to hold a hearing. The appeal's panel will convene at a mutually agreed site is selected.

The appellant has the burden of demonstrating adverse effects, improper actions or inaction, and the efficacy of the requested remedial action. The Governance Program Committee has the burden of demonstrating that the Community of Interest and the Governance Program Committee took all actions in compliance with these procedures and that the requested remedial action would be ineffective or detrimental. Each party may adduce other pertinent arguments, and members of the appeal's panel may address questions to individuals.

The appeal's panel will render its decision in writing within thirty calendar days, stating findings of fact and conclusions, with reasons therefore, based on a preponderance of the evidence. Consideration may be given to the following positions, among others, in formulating the decision:

- Finding for the appellant, remanding the action to the Governance Program Committee for remedy by the Community of Interest with a specific statement of the issues and facts in regard to that fair and equitable action was not taken.

- Finding for the Governance Program Committee with a specific statement of the facts that demonstrate fair and suitable treatment of the appellant and the appellant's objections.

- Finding that new, substantive evidence has been introduced, and remanding the entire action to the Governance Program Committee for appropriate reconsideration.

If, for whatever reason(s), the appellant chooses to forego the process detailed above, the Governance Program Committee will forward the appeal action to the Community of Interest. Included in the materials forwarded to the Community of Interest will be all documents pertaining to the Governance Program Committee 's attempts to resolve the matter at hand.

8.6.5 Further Appeal

If the appellant gives notice to the Governance Program Committee that further appeal is intended, a full record of the complaint, response, hearing, and decision will be submitted by the Governance Program Committee to the appropriate organization within the business.

8.7 Parliamentary Procedures

On questions of parliamentary procedure not covered in these procedures, Robert's Rules of Order.

8.8 Governance Functions Summary

Business functions are those activities performed by "humans." If they were just the functions that are inside the IT boundary, then there would be many processes missing from this book. All critical processes should be described in sufficient detail that different groups of persons would ultimately produce the same products according to the same Governance Assessments for quality and completeness.

Different collections of functions may produce the same overall results. That is perfectly acceptable. The architecture of the processes in Chapter 6 that build the products of Chapter 5, can fully support multiple collections of functions that are effectively equivalent.

Business functions also have a many-to-many relationship with business events. This is quite important because then business events can be generalized and used to serve multiple purposes.

The business functions that are more critical than others are those related to the governance program, community of interest, and officer appointments.

A key function of the governance program is how to discover the need for a community of interest. Critical too are the four key functions within communities of interest that support the construction of the four technology pillars of governance: Authoritative data sources, enterprise identifiers, information exchange models, and XML data exchanges.

Necessary as well within the set of functions are the processes for Governance Assessments maintenance including revision, affirmation, and withdrawal.

A very necessary component of any governance program are service fees. Governance Assessments are very costly to create and if fees are not imposed there will likely be no feeling of ownership or perceived value.

8.9 Questions and Exercises

1. The opening section of this chapter lists the set of functions that are to be performed by the various subgroups within a Governance Program and also within a given Community of Interest. After a quick review of the functions how are these functions accomplished in your organization? Same? Differently? Explain.

2. The duties of the offices of Chair, Vice Chair, Secretary, and Editor have been drawn from the experiences of other highly successful Communities of Interest. After reviewing these offices and their duties, are these the necessary set of duties? If these are all accomplished, and assuming due diligence by the office holder, will the office be carried out in an acceptable manner? Will Governance Assessments emerge? Is it clear from these offices and duties that accomplishment rather than personality is key?

3. Section 8.2 and its contained subsections sets out the functions that need to be accomplished by the Governance Program as a whole. Are these the right set of functions? Have the functions been described to indicate direction rather than strangle initiative and creativity? Are any key functions missing? If so, what are they?

4. Section 8.2.6 describes the functions of the Governance Assessments Development Board. How key is this board? What would happen if this Board were improperly staffed? Or, if the members of this Board had a specific "agenda" to pursue?

After reviewing the subsections, can you see that when the functions are followed Governance Assessments emerge? If so, why, If not, why?

Compare and contrast the functions of the Governance Assessments Development Board with a similar organization in your enterprise. Are they engineered the same? How different? Is one better structured than the other?

5. Section 8.2.6.4 and 8.2.6.5 directly relate to Communities of Interest. The first section identifies the functions of the management of Communities of Interest. The second section sets out the process of discovering new Communities of Interest and determining whether they are needed including creating all the necessary material to justify their existence.

How does your organization discover the need for Communities of Interest? Is the process adequate? What is missing? If something's missing, how will it hurt the proper discovery and engineering of COIs?

6. Section 8.3 and all its subsections detail rather extensively the functions of Communities of Interest. After a careful review of the process models contained in each of the 8.3.1 subsections, are these processes the necessary ones to then create a Governance Assessment? Compare and contrast how Governance Assessments are proposed to be created in this book versus your organization. Which is more comprehensive and complete? Which is likely to produce better results?

If the process models were adopted, as is, could the work of creating Governance Assessments move faster? Wouldn't all the effort of reinventing the processes that are already known to work be avoided? If so, then how much faster could the work start and how many arguments could be avoided on deciding all the different process model strategies and deliverables?

If the Metabase (which has a free version available from the Whitemarsh website) were employed, wouldn't that dramatically increase the quantity, quality, and velocity of meta-objects that could be stored as there wouldn't be an effort required for designing, implementing, and maintaining the business information system that supports meta-object definition, instantiation, and interrelationships?

It has been the clear recommendation of the U.S. Department of Defense that Governance Communities of Interest have a six-month golden window to produce or die. By die they mean, death by bureaucratic inertia. If this book and the Metabase are adopted, can't the Community of Interest immediately start instead of wasting that valuable six months? Once products start rolling out the door, wouldn't the experience then exist to know just what needs to be changed? Compare and contrast the process of being able to immediately start real and productive work with the process of taking the first six or so months figuring it out. What's the effect on the volume, velocity, quality, and quantity of deliverables? The cost of deliverables? The enthusiasm to keep working?

Provide examples from your own organization.

7. Section 8.3.2 is focused on the Maintenance of Governance Assessments. After a review of the contents of these sections, how critical is an orderly and careful process of Governance Assessments maintenance once these Governance Assessments have been accomplished and are employed in the myriad of business information systems that have adopted them? Compare and contrast this process in this book with what your organization as established. What's different?

If your organization has no formal process, wouldn't this one be much better than your current one?

8. Section 8.4 is focused on officer appointments. How important are officers? Can they make or break a Community of Interest? Which is worse, a timid one or a dictator? Are there any implied functions missing from the contained subsections in this area? Compare and contrast how "officers" are appointed in your Corporate Communities of Interest. Should they be elected or appointed? Is there a right approach?

9

Governance Organizations

9.1 Governance Program Organization Structure

The Governance organization is divided among two classes of organizations:

- Governance Program Committee
- Communities of Interest

In the event there is just one governance community of interest, then these two levels can be collapsed into just the single level community of interest. As more Communities of Interest arise then the additional levels should be created to ensure that there is consistency and consensus semantics across the communities.

9.2 Governance Program Committee

The overall architecture of the Governance Program is based on a top-down and bottom-up approach. Figure 48 shows the composition of the Governance Program Committee.

The Governance Program itself consists of policy, guidance, procedures, methodologies, courses, workshops, and a metadata repository software tool support which are engineered, tested, and administered. The roles, functions and duties of the main committee and the boards that report to the committee are provided in the sections that follow.

The top-down components, the Governance Program Committee provides guidance and facilitation. The Governance Program is accomplished through Communities of Interest throughout the enterprise to ensure both vertical and

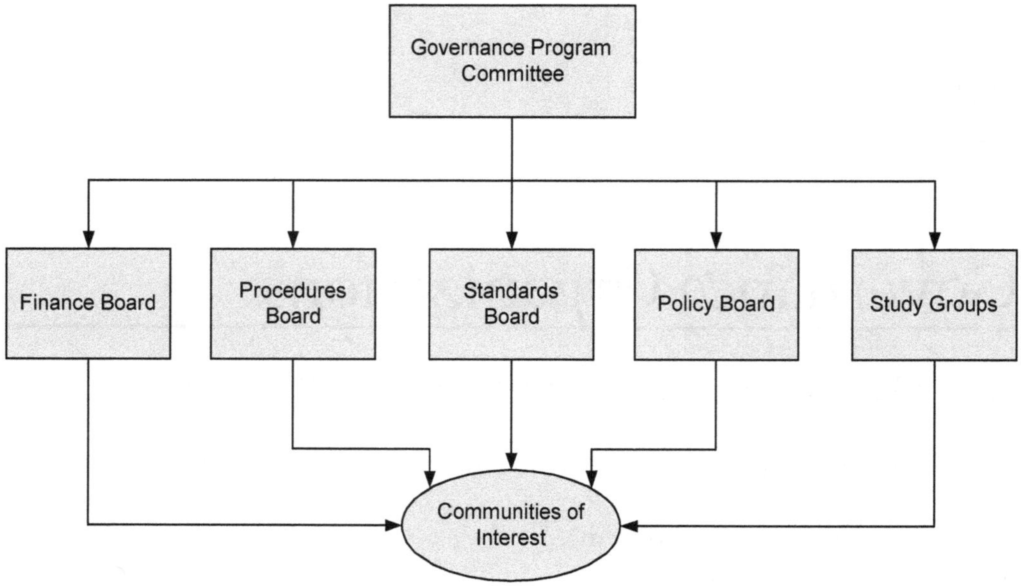

Figure 48. Governance Program Committee Subgroups.

horizontal semantics integration. The data represented through the Transaction Data Staging Area Data Models created by these committees are made trustworthy through authoritative data sources for all critical reference data. The data is guaranteed uniqueness through enterprise identifiers. Finally, data exchanges occur through highly managed XML definitions and exchanges.

The bottom-up components, the Communities of Interest, provide empowerment to the ultimate creators, owners and users of the governance's centerpiece, the Transaction Data Staging Area Data Model. The Transaction Data Staging Area Data Model and all other required metadata products reside within Communities of Interest and are manifest in a federated metadata environment. The Transaction Data Staging Area Data Model products across Communities of Interest are harmonized.

The governance of the Governance Program is through policy, guidance, and Communities of Interest data goals assessments. Supporting the guidance is a myriad of workshops, white papers, seminars, and software tool sets. These collectively assist staff as they develop, publish, integrate, and maintain all Governance Program work products within and across Communities of Interest.

The designation of a Chairman and Vice Chairman of the Governance Program Committee is by election of the Governance Program Committee members.

9.2.1 Governance Program Committee Membership

Membership on the Governance Program Committee is mandatory at all membership levels and gives the entity a right to vote on all matters before the Governance Program Committee. If the Governance Program is such that participants outside of an organization are of value, then other Business, Government and Governance Assessments Development Organizations level memberships may be allowed to request to be a member of the Governance Assessments Development Board and/or the Governance Assessments Policy Board at no additional charge. User Groups, Academics, Consortia members and Advisory level memberships may also be allowed to be members of the Governance Assessments Development Board and/or the Governance Assessments Policy Board for an additional fee.

9.2.2 Governance Program Committee Voting Rights

Only members in good standing can vote on Governance Program Committee matters. Similarly, only members in good standing can vote on subgroups.

9.2.3 Governance Program Committee Leadership

When multiple leadership positions are open, elections will be conducted in the following non-overlapping priority sequence.

- Governance Program Committee Chair
- Governance Assessments Development Board Chair
- Governance Assessments Policy Board Chair
- Governance Program Committee Vice-chair
- All Governance Program Committee committees.

This permits all interested parties to respond to a call for volunteers for the positions and minimizes the possibility of facing more than one term expiring at the same time. The Governance Program Committee Chair, Vice-chair and the Chairs of the Governance Assessments Development Board and Governance Assessments Policy Board are elected by the Governance Program Committee for a three-year term with a limit of two consecutive terms. A single person may not occupy two of the above positions.

9.2.4 Governance Program Committee Activity

The Governance Program Committee is the consensus body and has the ultimate responsibility for all Governance Assessments developed and approved by the Communities of Interest.

The Governance Program Committee accepts recommendations from the Governance Assessments Development Board and the Governance Assessments Policy Board, which are responsible for the day-to-day operations of the Governance Program. The Governance Program Committee has final approval authority for recommendations from the Governance Assessments Development Board, Governance Assessments Policy Board and the Governance Program Committee committees.

The Governance Assessments Development Board and Governance Assessments Policy Board only provide consensus recommendations. The formal vote on all such consensus recommendations is taken at the Governance Program Committee level; therefore, none of the voting requirements (criteria and approval) apply to the Governance Assessments Development Board and Governance Assessments Policy Board.

There are two Committees reporting directly to the Governance Program Committee that are responsible for developing operational positions with respect to the Community of Interest. These subcommittees make recommendations directly to the Governance Program Committee, which has final approval authority. Chairs for these Committees are elected by the Governance Program Committee for a three-year term and may serve for an unlimited number of terms.

The current Governance Program Committee chair, Governance Program Committee Vice-chair and the Governance Assessments Development Board and Governance Assessments Policy Board Chairs may not serve in these offices. These two subcommittees are:

- Finance Board
- Procedures Board

.

The Governance Program Committee also has two subsidiary Boards:

- Governance Assessments Development Board
- Governance Assessments Policy Board

.

Both Subsidiary Boards operate in an advisory capacity to the Governance Program Committee.

Membership on these subsidiary Boards has a prerequisite of being a Governance Program Committee member.

9.2.5 Finance Board

The Finance Board operates under the auspices of the Governance Program Committee.

The Finance Board is advisory to the Governance Program Committee and is responsible for making recommendations to the Governance Program Committee on all matters pertaining to the finances of the Governance Program.

The Finance Board consists of a Chair, Vice Chair, an Editor, and a Secretary. Additional members are those determined necessary by the Governance Program Committee.

9.2.6 Procedures Board

The Procedures Board operates under the auspices of the Governance Program Committee.

The Procedures Board Committee is advisory to the Governance Program Committee and is responsible for making recommendations to the Governance Program Committee on all matters pertaining to the Communities of Interest.

Each Board consists of a Chair, Vice Chair, an Editor, and a Secretary. Additional members are those determined necessary by the Governance Program Committee.

9.2.7 Governance Assessments Policy Board

The Governance Assessments Policy Board addresses all policy matters related to the Governance Assessments' work of the various Governance Committees. This Board makes recommendations, for Governance Program Committee approval, that affect Communities of Interest Governance Assessments. Such recommendations will always have a focus on policies to support improving the market relevance of the Community of Interest.

Each Governance Assessments Policy Board consists of a Chair, Vice Chair, an Editor, and a Secretary. Additional members are those determined necessary by the Governance Program Committee.

9.2.8 Governance Assessments Development Board

The general responsibilities of the Governance Assessments Development Board are:

- Identify, engineer, plan, and evaluate the accomplishment of Governance Assessments that are to be accomplished by Communities of Interest.
- Adopt and promote externally developed specifications.
- Enable collaboration with other Governance Assessments' organizations.
- Create and agree to methodology for new work identification.

The Governance Assessments Development Board program of work is segmented into "projects," each related to the development of a specific Governance Assessment. In addition, in the management of operations, the Governance Assessments Development Board manages the Governance Assessment standardization process within Communities of Interest.

Each Governance Projects Committee consists of a Chair, Vice Chair, an Editor, and a Secretary. Additional members are those determined necessary by the Governance Program Committee.

9.2.9 Study Groups

The Governance Program Committee, Governance Assessments Development Board or Governance Assessments Policy Board may establish Study Groups to investigate a general subarea of information processing technology, to assess trends and relationships, and to provide advisory study reports to its parent body. While study groups have a finite duration they are formally constituted. Once their final report is completed with respect their charter, the study group dissolves.

A Study Group may also be established to conduct a study of a proposal for a Governance Assessment's development project, or group of related projects, or for similar projects leading to a Governance Assessment. When the mission of a Study Group is to examine an assigned proposal(s) in light of the requirements delineated in the Project Proposal Guide, the Study Group will submit a report, upon completion, to its parent body recommending:

- Support for introduction of a project, or
- Objections against the Community of Interest initiating the proposed project, or
- When a consensus cannot be reached, the report includes both the supporting and dissenting recommendations.

The Governance Program Committee or the Governance Assessments Development Board may alternatively request the study of a project proposal by an existing Community of Interest, if related to the Community of Interest's assigned projects. Each Study Group is established for a specific study. Upon completion and acceptance of its report by the parent body, the group is disbanded.

Each Study Group consists of a Chair, Vice Chair, an Editor, and a Secretary. Additional members are those determined necessary by the Governance Program Committee.

9.2.9.1 Study Group Charter

The parent body prepares a scope and program of work as the charter for a Study Group. The charter may contain additional guidance or constraints, as appropriate. The program of work contains the expected time schedule for completion and submission of the Study Group report and recommendation for (or against) a proposed project. At its organizational meeting, the Study Group reviews its scope and program of work, and may then or later recommends modification(s) to its parent body.

9.2.9.2 Study Group Project

Study group project planning begins with a problem statement that is taken through a rigorous functional and technical analysis process, resulting in a feasible solution for the Governance requirements.

9.2.9.3 Study Group Report and Project Recommendation

The Study Group report should be submitted to the parent body with a transmittal letter including the following:

- Reference to the meeting at which the report was approved.
- The Study Group vote on the report.
- Brief history of the study, showing the date of first meeting, the number of meetings, the extent of general agreement or disagreement, a brief summary of major issues considered, and the rationale for not accepting significant possible alternatives.
- The final report or recommendation.
- Any minority view(s) or supplemental statements provided by members of the Study Group.
- Membership mailing list.

9.2.10 Ad Hoc Groups

An ad hoc group may be established by the Chair of any formal committee within the Governance Program for one or more specific tasks to be completed not later than the end of the second following meeting of the parent body. Ad hoc groups are thus very different from Study Groups which are formally constituted and last until their study area final report is completed.

Ad hoc groups may consist of one or more persons. Its function is to do a specific job and report back. Upon completion of its report, or at the second meeting of the parent body following the ad hoc group's establishment, the group is dissolved.

Since an ad hoc group is limited in duration and scope, its business may be conducted informally. The principal record-keeping effort should be the documentation of its report. However, when the ad hoc group meets between scheduled meetings of its parent group, then the requirements for meeting notices and agenda will be followed. Results of such meetings may be documented in minutes or the final report to the parent committee.

9.3 Communities of Interest

The technical work of the Governance Program is distributed among a number of Communities of Interest. Upon completion of all currently assigned tasks and acquiescence by the Governance Program Committee, they may:

- Assume inactive status until required to resume activity for the required five-year review of published Governance Assessments.
- Provide interpretations of their Governance Assessments.
- Undertake new project assignments.

All work of the Communities of Interest is subject to approval of the Governance Program Committee. Each Community of Interest consists of a Chair, Vice Chair, an Editor, and a Secretary. Additional members are the Chairs and Vice Chairs from each contained technical committee. Each Community of Interest may determine if additional members are appropriate considering that virtually all the work of a Community of Interest is to be accomplished by Community of Interest Technical Committees.

The technical scope of each Community of Interest comprises the scope of its assigned projects. A Community of Interest may also develop proposals for new Governance projects related to its existing work, following the requirements and guidance of the Project Proposal Guide.

9.3.1 Establishment/Disbandment

New Communities of Interests are established only upon approval of the Governance Program Committee. A Community of Interest 's status will be reviewed, and the Community of Interest may be disbanded upon a vote of the Governance Program Committee if:

- The voting membership of the Community of Interest is not sufficient to meet quorum requirements.
- After two calls for officer candidates, no candidate has been identified.
- The Community of Interest program of work has been eliminated.
- Any other conditions that preclude the effective functioning of the Community of Interest in accordance with the policies and procedures of the Governance Program.

If any projects of the Community of Interest are transferred to another Community of Interest, members in good standing who maintain an interest in the projects may apply for membership in the Community of Interest accepting the transferred projects. Voting privileges begin with the first meeting attended, providing that the member attends one of the next two meetings of the Community of Interest. The member will be credited with any fees paid for membership in the disbanded Community of Interest.

9.3.2 Maintenance Communities of Interest

When a Community of Interest has completed all of its Governance Assessments' development and Governance Assessments' revision projects, these projects become maintenance projects. The duties that continue are:

- Recommend defect management actions during the Governance Assessment's maintenance phase.
- Recommend revisions when experience with the Governance Assessment so indicates.
- Conduct the required review and recommendation for revision, reaffirmation, designation as an archival Governance Assessment, or withdrawal.

The Community of Interest may decide, however, that it can perform these specific duties in a less formal manner than that required of active Communities of Interest. To carry out its Governance Assessments' maintenance duties without remaining a fully active Community of Interest, the Community of Interest may elect to revert to the status of Maintenance Community of Interest.

A Maintenance Community of Interest is relieved from the following requirements levied on Communities of Interest engaged in Governance Assessments' development activities:

- Maintenance Communities of Interest do not need to hold at least one meeting a year.
- Members of Maintenance Communities of Interest do not have to pay service fees.
- No document distribution by the Governance Program Committee is provided unless it is specifically addressed to the Maintenance Community of Interest.

Technical Committees under the Community of Interest are automatically terminated when a Community of Interest changes its status to Maintenance

Community of Interest.

To attain the status of Maintenance Community of Interest, the Community of Interest must approve, by Community of Interest letter ballot, a recommendation to the Governance Assessments Development Board for a change in status. A Super Majority of those voting must agree to the change in status in order for the recommendation to be approved. The approved recommendation is forwarded to the Governance Program Committee by the Governance Assessments Development Board for final approval action.

The officers and membership of the Community of Interest of record in the Governance Program Committee at the time the letter ballot is taken are the officers and membership of the Maintenance Community of Interest. The officers' appointments are indefinite and they are not subject to the three-year election process required of other Communities of Interest.

When it becomes necessary for an officer of a Maintenance Community of Interest to resign, the Maintenance Community of Interest Chair will so notify the Governance Program Committee, a call for candidates for the officer position will be issued by the Governance Program Committee.

Members of Maintenance Communities of Interest may lose their membership by failure to respond to two out of three successive ballots, in which case the membership will be terminated if the next ballot is not returned. Applications for membership will be by correspondence to the respective Chair or to the Governance Program Committee for forwarding. Membership becomes effective after the return of one letter ballot. However, that member's vote will not be counted in that ballot.

The Chair will continue to provide an Annual Report for the Governance Assessments Development Board. This report does not need to be delivered in person.

Should circumstances dictate that a Maintenance Community of Interest change its status back to an active Community of Interest, a recommendation will be made to the Governance Assessments Development Board using the same voting procedure as indicated above. The Governance Program Committee will take final approval action on this Governance Assessments Development Board recommendation, or the Governance Program Committee may initiate the action itself.

When changing status from Maintenance Community of Interest to an active Community of Interest, the Community of Interest will be bound by all of the procedures required of an active Community of Interest. Upon change of status from Maintenance Community of Interest to an active Community of Interest, the rules relating to meetings and service fees will apply only after the approval of the change in status of the Community of Interest.

Membership of the maintenance Community of Interest becomes the membership of the reactivated Community of Interest. In addition, attendees at the first meeting following activation will also attain voting rights.

9.3.3 Community of Interest Projects

Community of Interest projects are mainly about the specification, development, and evolution of Governance Assessments. In general, every Governance Assessment includes subprojects that deal with:

- Metadata Infrastructure,
- Transaction Data Staging Area Data Models
- Evolution, Maintenance and Support.

9.3.4 Community of Interest Technical Committees

As depicted in Figure 49, each Community of Interest is broken into six technical committees which are:

- Operational Technical Committee
- System Engineering Technical Committee
- Data Modeling Technical Committee
- Test and Evaluation Technical Committee
- Configuration Control Technical Committee
- Eterprise Architecture Technical Committee.

9.3.4.1 Operations Technical Committee

The Operations Technical Committee is the technical committee performing the operational modeling discipline in the Community of Interest with support from the other technical committees.

The Operations Technical Committee consists of a Chair, Vice Chair, Secretary, and Editor. There are at least four additional members to assist in the accomplishment of the work that is set forth in the committee's work plans.

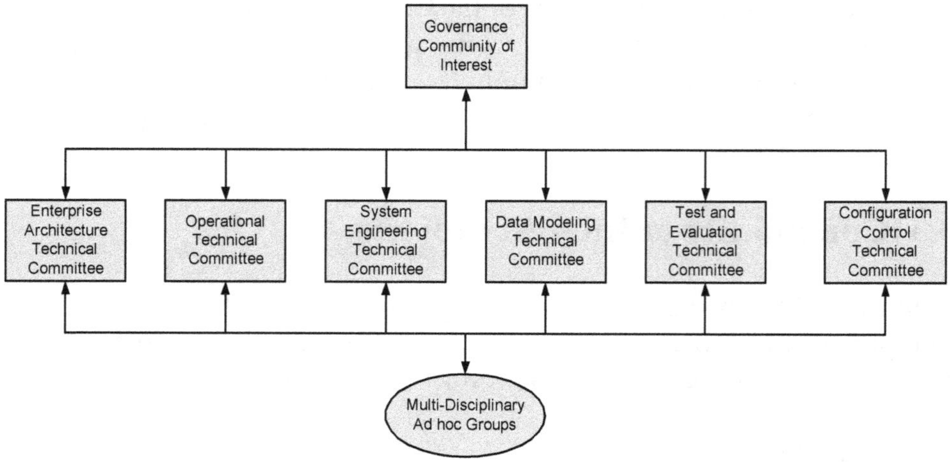

Figure 49. Community of Interest Technical Committees.

It is the responsibility of the Operations Technical Committee to make a report of its activities to the Community of Interest as appropriate.

9.3.4.2 Systems Engineering & Architecture Technical Committee

The System Engineering and Architecture Technical Committee is the technical committee performing the system modeling discipline in the Community of Interest with support from the other technical committees.

The System Engineering and Architecture Technical Committee consists of a Chair, Vice Chair, Secretary, and Editor. There are at least four additional members to assist in the accomplishment of the work that is set forth in the committee's work plans.

9.3.4.3 Data Modeling Technical Committee

The Data Modeling Technical Committee is the technical Committee defining the data architecture and a common data model for interoperability.

The Data Modeling Technical Committee consists of a Chair, Vice Chair, Secretary, and Editor. There are at least four additional members to assist in the accomplishment of the work that is set forth in the committee's work plans.

9.3.4.4 Test and Evaluation Technical Committee

Test and Engineering Technical Committee provides the overall framework for the Community of Interest testing and evaluation. In addition, it conducts all tests regarding a given Transaction Data Staging Area Data Model so as to certify its trustworthiness, reliability and performance sufficiency.

The Test and Evaluation Technical Committee consists of a Chair, Vice Chair, Secretary, and Editor. There are at least four additional members to assist in the accomplishment of the work that is set forth in the committee's work plans.

9.3.4.5 Configuration Control Technical Committee

The Configuration Control Technical Committee specifies a common set of procedures, methods and processes for controlling the Governance Assessment's configuration. The Configuration Control Technical Committee also provides configuration control advice to all other technical committees on an as required basis. It also makes a report of its activities to the Community of Interest as appropriate.

The Configuration Control Technical Committee consists of a Chair, Vice Chair, Secretary, and Editor. There are at least four additional members to assist in the accomplishment of the work that is set forth in the committee's work plans.

9.3.4.6 Multi-disciplinary Committee

Multi-disciplinary Committees are short lived and ad-hoc in nature. They exist to address problems that span technical committees, or that are specially commissioned by the Community of Interest. In that regard, the Community of Interest officers initiate Multi-disciplinary Committees, define their scope and program of work, identify the various Community of Interest technical committees that must supply members to participate in the Multi-disciplinary effort, and set out the initial work plan, deliverables, and schedule that should be met by the Multi-disciplinary Committee. Governance Multi-disciplinary Committees:

- Address specific subjects or groups of subjects usually requiring a multi-disciplinary approach.

- Bring results back to the tasking Communities of Interest for further action and directions while the group members report the results back to their parent communities of as appropriate to keep their peers up to date on current efforts and results.

- Integrate with other Community of Interest Technical Committees as necessary.

- Integrate with other governance Communities of Interest as necessary.

Each Multi-disciplinary Committee consists of a Chair, Vice Chair, Secretary, and Editor. Additional members from other technical committees assist in the accomplishment of the work that is set forth in the committee's work plans. Upon completion of its work, the Multi-disciplinary Committee dissolves.

9.4 Organization Summary

There are the traditional set of organizations within the governance program except for the technical committees. These special technical committees are depicted in Figure 49 and are described within Section 9.3.4. Special care should be paid to these technical organizations to ensure that they are sufficiently funded and staffed. These committees are the "work-horse" committees. Without them the whole governance program will fail.

9.5 Questions and Exercises

1. This chapter enumerates and describes the organizations contained in a Governance Program and also Communities of Interest. After a brief review of the various organizations listed and described in Sections 9.2 and 9.3, are

these the right organizations? If yes, why? If no, why not? Provide examples of similar organizations within your business.

2. After a careful review of the Governance Program committee organizations, do these organizations properly match the meta-objects and processes that have to be built from Chapters 5 and 6, and to these organizations match the Business Events and Functions from Chapters 7 and 8?

3. Why are rules for membership so important? What happens if one organization within your enterprise dominates a Community of Interest?

4. Why are voting rights so important? What happens when one organization is able to dominate the votes on Governance Assessments issues?

5. Why is it so important for the various organizations within a Community of Interest to be able to work together and through near unanimous decisions?

10

Governance Positions

Positions within a Governance Program are critical to its success. There is real work to be done, some of it is bureaucratic, some of it is planning and management, but most of it is the specification, implementation, and maintenance of the data models, process models, software specifications that comprise the entire governance environment. There are also all of the information technology aspects with the real implementation of the databases and database oriented business information systems that bring interoperable data environments alive and that enables them to be evolved and maintained.

This chapter concentrates exclusively on the positions that are necessary for the engineering, specification, and maintenance of the specifications of interoperable data environments rather than on the actual information technology aspects for implementation, operation, and evolution.

10.1 Membership Classes

Membership within the Governance Program is open to all members of an organization. There are, in general, three classes of membership: Full, Associate, and Observer. There are also liaison and ex officio memberships as well. In addition to classes of membership there are special memberships to the Governance Program Committee, its subcommittees, and subsidiary boards, to the Governance Program Projects committee, and finally to Communities of Interest.

10.1.1 Full Members

A Full Member is an organization that commits to support the collaborative development of succeeding versions of the Governance Program interoperability solution. Full Members undertake to be represented in Communities of Interest and must be prepared to expend the resources required to develop and sustain the Governance Program solution. A Full Member must be involved in and contribute actively to the decision-making process throughout the specification and development cycle. Full Members have voting and access rights at all meetings.

A full member may appoint no more than one principal representative to each subgroup. A full member may also appoint one or more principal member alternatives who can participate in any subgroup's activities. In all subgroup actions that require a vote, only full members can vote.

10.1.1.1 Requirements

Only an organization is eligible to become a Full Member. Before an organization becomes eligible for Full Membership, it must first be an Associate Member, it must agree to the program and scope of work of the overall Governance Program. The organization applying for full membership must have a governance interest, that is, one or more Business Information Systems either available, or in the planning or development stage that would be involved in one or more governance solutions, and inform the Governance Program Committee accordingly.

10.1.1.2 Application

The official request will be made by formal written proposal to any of the Governance Program Full Member organizations through the Governance Program Committee. This proposal must contain a statement indicating the organization's commitment to the Governance Program, and its agreement to conform to current baseline documents, architecture, configuration and employment concepts. The request must also acknowledge commitment to the Governance Program administrative requirements.

10.1.1.3 Acceptance

Acceptance as a Full Member to the Governance Program requires super majority agreement of all the Governance Program Full Members at a Governance Program Committee meeting.

10.1.2 Associate Members

Associate Members include organizations showing an interest in this program, which have been granted Associate Member status by the Governance Program Committee. Associate Members enjoy all the rights and privileges of a Full Member as agreed by the Governance Program Committee except Associate Members do not have any voting rights at meetings. Associate members need to attend all Governance Program Committee meetings and need to be represented in at least one Community of Interest at all the Community of Interest meetings.

10.1.2.1 Requirements

Organizations wishing to become Associate Members to the Governance Program must meet the following requirements:

- Be sponsored by a Governance Program Full Member.
- Be involved with a Business Information Systems either at an organizational or inter-organizational level.
- Agree to abide by the decisions of the Governance Program Committee.

10.1.2.2 Application

The official request will be made by formal written proposal that must be endorsed by a current the Governance Program Full Member. This Full Member becomes the sponsoring member and assumes the responsibility for forwarding the endorsed application to all other Full Members.

The application must include a statement on the status of involvement in a Business Information Systems in one or more governance solutions, the nature of interest in the Governance Program, and an agreement to abide by Governance Program Committee.

The Governance Program Committee as an empowered body will, at the next available opportunity, consider the application for membership as presented by the sponsoring member. On super majority agreement, the Governance Program Committee will issue direction to the host member to extend an invitation to the applicant to attend the next Governance Program Committee.

10.1.2.3 Associate Member Restrictions

Associate Members do not have any voting rights at meetings.

10.1.2.4 Associate Member Privileges

Associate Members will have full access to information within the Governance Program. Associate members should:

- Attend and participate in Governance Program Committee and one or more Community of Interest meetings.
- Be represented in at least one Technical Committee at all Community of Interest meetings.

At their discretion, they may engage in any of the following activities:

- Access all the Governance Program documentation.
- Participate in testing, including provision of staff, facilities and equipment.
- Host Governance Program meetings.
- Make proposals for the Governance Program agendas.

- Submit Change Proposals to the Governance Program specifications and program documents.
- Register concerns for discussion at the Governance Program Committee and Community of Interest levels.

10.1.3 Observers

Observers are not members, but are representatives from organizations with a cooperation and/or coordination relation to the Governance Program and may participate in an observer status in meetings of Communities of Interest. The coordination and/or cooperation relations are established through the Governance Program Committee. Privileges for observers are determined on a case-by-case basis, but observers will have no voting rights.

Observers can attend Community of Interest meetings only when invited by a Full Member. The invitation for attendance must receive a majority vote of all Full Members. After attending the first meeting, the observer must then apply for observer status through a written application, declaring their interest in the Governance Program to the Governance Program Committee Chairman.

10.1.4 Liaison Members

A Liaison member of a Community of Interest is someone who is a full member of different Community of Interest or a Community of Interest Technical Committee but desires to represent that different Community of Interest's position to the Community of Interest to which they are a liaison. Liaison members must be approved by the Governance Program Committee.

Liaison members may attend meetings, speak, and submit contributions. Liaison members receive meeting notices, draft agenda and minutes, and draft Governance Assessments, and Study Group reports being voted upon by letter ballot. Other documents are not required to be distributed to liaison members.

10.1.5 Ex Officio Members

Ex officio members of the Governance Program's Committee or any of its subgroups may attend meetings, speak, and submit contributions. Ex officio members may also present motions; such motions require no second. Ex officio members may receive, if they request, meeting notices, draft agenda and minutes, and draft Governance Assessments, and Study Group reports being voted upon by letter ballot. Other documents are not required to be distributed to ex officio members.

The Chairs of the Governance Program Committee, Governance Assessments Development Board, Governance Assessments Policy Board, and Communities of Interest are eligible to be ex officio members of the committee or board they formerly chaired.

10.2 Governance Program Committees

10.2.1 Governance Program Committee

Full Member status, that is, voting membership, in the Governance Program Committee is open to organizations directly and materially affected by the scope of the Community of Interest that are willing to participate regularly and that have paid the designated service fee.

A representative of a prospective voting member will initially attend a meeting without voting privileges and reaffirm interest in the work of the Community of Interest. Voting privileges become effective immediately with attendance at one of the next two successive meetings and upon receipt by the Governance Program Committee of applicable fees for the membership year. Failure to attend one of those two successive meetings constitutes withdrawal of the application for voting membership.

An organization with voting membership will appoint one and only one principal representative and may appoint one or more alternate representatives.

No representative will have more than one vote except in the case where two or more organizations appoint the same individual to represent them (as principal or alternate representative). An individual so designated may cast a separate vote for each organization represented. Each organization will confirm in writing to the Governance Program Committee that it is aware of the multiple role of the individual and will accept the results of the arrangement. Representation of more than one organization by the same individual will require the approval of the Governance Program Committee.

10.2.2 Governance Program Committee Subcommittees and Boards

Governance Program Committee contained subcommittees and boards develop recommendations for the Governance Program Committee to approve. Membership is achieved at the start of the first meeting at ended.

Voting membership is open to any organization with voting membership on the Governance Program Committee that is willing to participate regularly and has paid the appropriate service fee(s).

Voting rights are achieved when Governance Program Committee membership is achieved and all designated service fees have been paid.

10.2.3 Study Groups

Voting membership in Study Groups is open to all directly and materially affected parties that meet attendance and voting requirements and pay the designated service fee(s).

A representative of a prospective voting member will initially attend a meeting of the Study Group without voting privileges and reaffirm interest in the work of the Community of Interest or Study Group. Voting privileges become effective with attendance at one of the next two successive meetings and receipt by the Governance Program Committee of the applicable fees for the membership year. For a new Subgroup, all attendees at the formation meeting or second meeting will be considered voting members.

An organization with voting membership will appoint one and only one principal representative and may appoint one or more alternate

10.2.4 Ad Hoc Groups

There is no formal voting in Ad Hoc Groups.

10.3 Community of Interest Membership

Applications for membership to a Community of Interest will be by correspondence to the Governance Program Committee. Applicants will state their organization's reasons for interest.

Applications for or notifications of membership will be in writing to the Governance Program Committee and the Committee Chair. A representative of a prospective voting member will initially attend a meeting of the Community of Interest without voting privileges and reaffirm interest in the work of the Community of Interest. Voting privileges become effective with attendance at one of the next two successive meetings and receipt by the Governance Program Committee of the applicable fees for the membership year. For a new Community of Interest, all attendees at the formation meeting or second meeting will be considered voting members.

10.4 Limitations on Organizational Memberships

All directly and materially affected parties will have the opportunity for fair and equitable participation in the Governance Program.

Governance Program Committee and its subgroups will not be dominated by any single interest category, individual or organization. Unless it is claimed in writing by a directly and materially affected party that a single interest category, individual or organization dominated the Governance Assessments development process, no test for dominance is required.

10.4.1 Single Federal, State, or Local Government Agency

When a Governance Program is wholly contained within a single Federal, State, or Local Government agency, there will be only one voting membership for separate government subdivisions within that agency, whether it is a Federal, State, or Local Government. A separate government subdivision is defined as an entity that reports to its parent executive, legislative, or judicial branch of government.

10.4.2 Multiple Federal, State, or Local Government Agencies

When a Governance Program extends across multiple Federal, State, or Local Government agencies, there will be only one voting membership for each separate government subdivisions or agencies, whether it is a Federal, State, or Local Government that is represented on the subgroup. A separate government subdivision or agency is defined as an entity that reports to its parent executive, legislative, or judicial branch of government.

However, in the case of the U.S. Department of Defense, it allowed a maximum of four votes from separate and unrelated entities such as the Department of Army, Department of Navy, Department of Air Force, Defense Logistics Agency, Defense Mapping Agency, etc. This exception is due to the unique nature of the DoD and is, therefore, not considered a precedent for any further exceptions.

10.4.3 Single Corporation or Company

When a Governance Program is wholly contained within a single Corporation or Company, there will be only one voting membership for each separate subdivision within that Corporation or Company. A separate subdivision is defined as an entity that reports to its parent executive.

10.4.4 Multiple Corporations or Companies

When a Governance Program spans multiple Corporations or Companies, there will be only one voting membership for each separate Corporation or Company. A separate Corporation or Company is defined as an entity that reports to its parent executive.

10.4.5 Mixed Governance Program Organizations

When a Governance Program subgroup spans Governments and Corporations or Companies, there will be one voting member for each separate government subdivisions or agencies, whether it is a Federal, State, or Local Government that is represented on the subgroup. A separate government subdivision or agency is defined as an entity that reports to its parent executive, legislative, or judicial branch of government.

However, in the case of the U.S. Department of Defense, it allowed a maximum of four votes from separate and unrelated entities such as the Department of Army, Department of Navy, Department of Air Force, Defense Logistics Agency, Defense Mapping Agency, etc. This exception is due to the unique nature of the DoD and is, therefore, not considered a precedent for any further exceptions.

Further, there will be only one voting membership for each separate Corporation or Company. A separate Corporation or Company is defined as an entity that reports to its parent executive.

Members from academic communities such as Universities or University related institutions or corporations will have only one voting membership for each separate educational institution. A separate educational institution is defined as an entity that has a controlling body, such as a Board of Regents.

Finally, if membership is requested by Governance Assessments Development Organizations, User Groups, or Consortia, then only one member from each such organization will be allowed. Because those members are voting the interests of the Governance Assessments Development Organizations, User Groups, or Consortia, the principal and alternate representatives may be employed by other organizations who have voting memberships.

10.5 Executive Sessions

For those matters considered by the Governance Program Committee which require consideration in Executive Session, participation in Executive Session is limited to the Committee membership plus anyone invited by the Committee.

10.6 Membership Status Review Process

Whenever a Full Member is of the opinion that a Member is not fulfilling their obligations toward the Governance Program, it may bring it to the attention of the Governance Program Committee and request a formal review of the efforts of the Member concerned. The Governance Program Committee review takes in consideration the arguments of the Member under review and may decide to give that Member an official warning.

After an official warning has been issued, the Governance Program Committee Chairman will request the Governance Program Committee Chairman for a Governance Program Committee review at a future Governance Program Committee meeting, leaving ample time for the Member under review to reinstate its commitment to the Governance Program.

The Governance Program Committee will hear the Member concerned and decide on possible implications for that member, if any.

In this review process the Governance Program Committee is the only management body that may apply consequences to a Member or that may grant a waiver to a Member regarding its responsibilities toward the Governance Program.

Whenever a Full Member is of the opinion that an Observer is not any more beneficial to the Governance Program, the same procedure is applied.

Members of the Governance Program Committee and subgroups will be terminated by the Governance Program Committee for failure to pay appropriate service fees within the time specified by the Governance Program Committee.

An organization that has had its voting membership terminated may reestablish it. If this membership is reestablished within the same billing period and the organization has paid its fee, no new service fee will be accessed.

Members of the Communities of Interest or Study Groups will be terminated under the following conditions:

- The principal and all alternate representative(s) will be warned in writing upon failure of the organization to:

    - ♦ Attend two out of three successive meetings, in that case the membership will be terminated if not represented at the next meeting; or

- ♦ Return two out of three successive non accelerated letter ballots if the next non accelerated letter ballot after the warning is not returned, An organization fails to perform an above action when none of the organization's representatives performs the action.

.

- Voting and advisory memberships will be canceled by the Governance Program Committee for failure to pay appropriate service fees within the time specified by the Governance Program Committee.

Communities of Interest or Study Groups may vote to continue the membership despite failure of the member to comply with the attendance and/ or ballot criteria.

An organization that has had its voting membership terminated may reestablish membership. If this membership is reestablished within the same billing period and the organization has paid its fee, no new service fee will be accessed.

10.7 Membership Withdrawal

A Full Member, an Associate Member or an Observer may withdraw at any time from the Governance Program upon written notification to the Governance Program Committee. Any Full Member or Associate Member that has withdrawn from participation in the Governance Program and requests reinstatement must re-apply in accordance with the Governance Program Membership procedures.

Members of the Governance Program Committee and Subgroups will be terminated by the Governance Program Committee for failure to pay appropriate service fees within the time specified by the Governance Program Committee.

An organization that has had its voting membership terminated may reestablish it. If this membership is reestablished within the same billing period and the organization has paid its fee, no new service fee will be accessed.

10.8 Community of Interest Officers

10.8.1 Chair

For each Subgroup, the Chair is responsible for presiding at meetings and ensuring that the program of work for that body is carried out in a prompt, efficient, and effective manner. Chairs are either elected or appointed.

Unless otherwise stated, appointed chairs have an indefinite term of office and elected chairs have a three-year term of office.

Chairs of the Governance Program Committee, the Governance Assessments Development Board and the Governance Assessments Policy Board are elected positions from the principal or alternate representatives of voting members on the Governance Program Committee. They may not serve for more than two consecutive terms nor may a member provide more than a single elected officer on these three boards.

Chairs of the four Governance Program Committee Boards are elected positions from the principal or alternate voting representatives of members on the Governance Program Committee. They may not serve for more than two consecutive terms.

Chairs of Study Groups, Communities of Interest are elected by the Governance Program Committee from their constituency on a recommendation from that constituency. There is no limitation on number of terms.

All other Chairs are appointed by the Chair of their parent bodies. Their term is indefinite except for ad hoc Chairs, who are limited to the duration of the ad hoc subgroup.

10.8.2 Vice Chair

For each Subgroup, the Vice-chair (if one exists) performs the duties of the Chair, in the absence of the Chair. Vice-chairs may vote and participate according to membership rules.

Except for the Governance Program Committee, the Vice-chair of those groups with a Vice-chair is considered the chief administrative officer and is responsible for the administrative duties.

The Vice-Chair of the Governance Program Committee is an elected position from the principal or alternate representatives of members on the

Governance Program Committee. If a member's representative is elected as Governance Program Committee Vice-Chair that member may not provide another elected officer on the Governance Program Committee, Governance Assessments Policy Board or Governance Assessments Development Board.

For all other subgroup, the Vice-chair is appointed by and serves at the pleasure of the Chair of the parent

10.8.3 Secretary

The Secretary is responsible for the recording and transcribing of meeting minutes. The Secretary may also be responsible for other administrative as required by the Chair of a Subgroup.

The Secretary of a Subgroup is appointed by the Chair of that Subgroup. The Governance Program Committee Secretary serves at the pleasure of the Chair of that Subgroup.

10.8.4 Editor

The Editor is responsible for maintaining the governance products, i.e., making timely and accurate changes as approved by the group. The Project Editor will report the status of each product at each meeting of the group.

Editors are appointed by and serve at the pleasure of their respective Chairs with no limitation on terms.

10.8.5 Other Positions

Chairs may appoint members to other positions (e.g., meeting coordinator, Committee librarian, etc.) with titles and responsibilities as required.

These other positions are appointed by and serve at the pleasure of their respective Chairs with no limitation on terms.

10.9 Position Summary

Positions within the governance program are mainly by organization versus by individual. That is because it is mainly organizations that have systems that are required to interoperate.

The various memberships are formally identified and described. Different membership classes have different responsibilities, duties, and authorities.

Described also are the methods of constructing governance programs that consist of organizations from different corporate structures.

10.10 Questions and Exercises

1. Why are "positions" so important?

2. Why should there be different classes of membership? Full, Associate, Observers, and Liaisons. Why should full memberships be restricted to only those organizations committed to fully implement a Governance Assessment?

3. Why are there additional Membership rules for Communities of Interest? Why should COI memberships be spread across multiple enterprise organizations?

4. Why are there special rules that apply specifically to the Officers of these Committees.

11

Governance Documents and Guidance

There are a number of documents that are created and comprise the everyday business of a Community of Interest. These include:

- Project Proposal Guide (Section 11.1)
- Annual Report (Section 11.2)
- Governance Assessments (Section 11.3)
- Change Proposals (Section 11.4)
- Standing Documents (Section 11.5)
  - Procedures
  - Guidelines for Proposals
  - Letter Ballots
  - Ballot Comments
  - Guidelines for hosting meetings

11.1 Community of Interest Project Proposal Guide

The Community of Interest Project Proposal Guide defines the information to be submitted by any person, organization, or group as a proposal to initiate a project to develop a new or revised the Governance Assessment.

The person, organization, group, or the Community of Interest Community of Interest initiating a Governance Assessment development project proposal is asked to provide, in as complete a manner as possible and practicable, the information indicated. If supplementary material is required for presenting the proposal to pursue the activity, this should also be supplied.

Proposals should be uploaded to the Governance Program server.

Alternatively, proposals should be emailed to:

DataInteroperabilityProgram@Organization.Com

Or finally, it should be mailed to the Governance Program address, which is:

The Governance Program
<Street Address 1>
<Street Address 2>
<City, State Zip>

During the review by the Governance Program Committee, and in developing its recommendation, the proposal will be examined to determine whether:

- A rational purpose and substantive goal exists.
- There is a need, an interest is evident, and the economic benefits are obtainable.
- The proposed Governance Assessment development is technically feasible.

In preparing the recommendation, the definition of the Governance Assessment development project in the original proposal may be augmented or modified. If the recommendation is that no Community of Interest activity be undertaken, the reasons for this negative decision will be appended. It must be kept in mind that Community of Interest recommendations are based on current judgment, and reconsideration of proposals may be appropriate in the event of changes in the conditions examined during the review.

The time and effort expended in the preparation of a well-researched and well-documented proposal will generally reduce the time and effort required to develop the recommendation for a Governance Assessment's development and the recommendation to start that process.

The information that should be included in the proposal for a Governance project is provided in Table 41.

Proposal for Project to Develop a New or Revised Governance Assessment		
Section	**Title**	**Description**
1.	**Source of the Proposed Project**	
1.1	Title	Provide a descriptive subject matter title.
		The date should be the date of submission of the proposal to the Governance Program Committee.
1.3	Proposer(s)	If the proposer is not an existing Community of Interest, identify the individual who will serve as the acting chairman until a new Community of Interest has been established.
2.	**Process Description for the Proposed Project**	
2.1	Project Type (Development or Revision)	Indicate "D" if DEVELOPMENT will be done within a Community of Interest and the expected result in the Governance Assessment. Indicate "R" if the project proposal describes a proposed REVISION to a Governance Assessment.
2.2	Definitions of Concepts and Special Terms	Provide definitions of key concepts and special terms (if any) needed in developing and understanding the Governance Assessment.
2.3	Expected Relationship with Approved Reference Models, Frameworks, Architectures, etc.	Identify relevant reference models, frameworks, architectures, etc., that are being used to conceptualize the relationships among the various information technologies and this project, and any known or anticipated areas of conformance or conflict.
2.4	Recommendation regarding a Community of Interest (Existing or New)	Indicate a preference for assignment of the proposed project to a particular existing Community of Interest, or propose creation of a new Community of Interest. Creation of a new Community of Interest must include the rationale. Include a description of available resources, that is, at least four organizations which are capable of the Community of Interest work effort and interested in the subject matter to assure that adequate resources exist to accomplish the proposed program of work. Indicate which are members of the Community of Interest.

Proposal for Project to Develop a New or Revised Governance Assessment		
Section	**Title**	**Description**
2.6	Anticipated Frequency and Duration of Meetings	Estimate of the anticipated frequency and duration of meetings.
2.6	Target Date for Initial Review (Milestone 4)	Estimate the target date for releasing the draft Governance Assessment for review (See Milestone 4).
2.7	Estimated Useful Life of Governance Assessment	Estimate the useful life of the Governance Assessment.
3.	**Business Case for Developing the Proposed Governance Assessment**	
3.1	Description	Describe the technical information that will be covered by the Governance Assessment.
3.2.	Existing Practice and the Need for a Governance Assessment	Identify why a Governance Assessment is needed, rather than another kind of solution. Describe existing practice in the area of a proposed Governance Assessment to aid in judging timeliness and appropriateness of the project. Address the expected stability of the proposed Governance Assessment with respect to both current technology and potential technological advances.
3.3.	Implementation Impacts of the Proposed Governance Assessment	Address the potential impacts of the proposed Governance Assessment. To the extent possible, address the following implementation considerations:
3.3.1	Development Costs	Provide an overall estimate of the technical development costs for this Governance Assessment. Include labor costs for technical editor(s), logistical costs for meetings, work between meetings, and any other significant costs.

Proposal for Project to Develop a New or Revised Governance Assessment		
Section	**Title**	**Description**
3.3.2	Impact on Existing or Potential Markets	Provide a cost/benefit statement (qualitative or quantitative) on the impact on users and suppliers, should this Governance Assessment be implemented.
3.3.3	Costs and Method for Conformity Assessment	What testing environment is appropriate for this technology (e.g., suppliers' declaration, accreditation of testing laboratories, certification bodies)? Will this Governance Assessment contain the necessary and sufficient testing information for assessing conformity to this Governance Assessment? If not, how will this information be developed, and what are the associated development costs?
3.3.4	Return on Investment	What is the estimated ROI for development of this Governance Assessment and the conformity assessment costs associated with it?
3.4	Legal Considerations	Address the following legal consecrations:
3.4.1	Patent Assertions	Identify assertions of patent rights in accordance with the relevant the Community of Interest. Is the proposer aware of any patent assertions that may be made? If so, describe. How will the possible extent of patent rights be determined and redetermined during the life of the development of the Governance Assessment?
3.4.2	Dissemination of the Governance Assessment	Identify how drafts of this Governance Assessment will be disseminated electronically. How will the final Governance Assessment be disseminated. Is the proposer aware of any intellectual property rights assertions that will hinder this distribution? If so, describe?
4.	**Related Governance Assessments Activities**	
4.1	Existing Governance Assessments	Identify existing Governance Assessments including but not limited to the particular Community of Interest that may affect or be affected by the proposed project.

Proposal for Project to Develop a New or Revised Governance Assessment		
Section	**Title**	**Description**
4.2	Related Governance Assessments Activity	Identify projects under development, including but not limited to the Community of Interest, that may affect or be affected by the proposed project. For each project identified, indicate if the liaison arrangements have been made with these activities.
4.3	Recommendations for Close Liaison	Recommend which Communities of Interest should be identified as close liaisons. Close liaisons require an exchange of information, but the work of one is not dependent upon the work of the other Communities of Interest
5.	**Units of Measurement used in the Governance Assessment**	**Indicate units of measurement used in the Governance Assessment.**

Table 41. Format for Governance Assessment's development project.

11.2 Subgroup Annual Report

11.2.1 Format/Period Covered

All Subgroups are required to produce an Annual Report. The Annual Report covers the period from the previous Report to the date the current Report is being prepared.

11.2.2 Report Schedule

The Annual Report must be provided electronically to the Subgroup's parent Subgroup in a format suitable for posting to the Governance Program web site. The Annual Report is due one month in advance of the Governance

Program Meeting at which the report is scheduled for discussion. Communities of Interest provide their annual report to the Governance Program

11.2.3 Validation of Governance Program Databases

Most of the material related to a subgroup's work activities should be maintained on a regular basis in the Governance Program Committee 's projects' database. Approximately one to two months prior to the scheduled presentation of the Annual Report, the subgroup should ensure that the Projects database accurately reflects the current status of the subgroup's work.

In addition, the Subgroup Chair will validate the Membership database no less often than annually and certify that the membership database is up-to-date when the annual report is presented.

11.2.4 Oral Presentation

The Annual Report must be presented orally by the subgroup's Chair (or designee) according to the subgroup's parent's reporting schedule. Chairs of maintenance Communities of Interest do not need to provide oral reports.

The scheduled oral presentation by a Community of Interest concentrates on projects that did not reach the projected Milestone during the year and on administrative and procedural issues of concern. Other aspects of the Annual Report may also be covered as agreed upon by a Community of Interest Chair.

11.2.5 Format and Required Contents

The information that should be contained in every subgroup annual report is presented in Table 42.

Section	Title	Description
1.0	Annual Report for:	Name of the Subgroup
2.0	Covering the Period from [ ] to [ ]	Start date and end date
3.0	Title of the Subgroup's main work effort	Name of the main work effort chartered to the subgroup
4.0	Links:	• Subgroup's web site (if applicable) • Executive summary • Link to Subgroup's area on the Governance Program Committee 's Projects Database • Significant accomplishments • Significant challenges • Expected challenges • Previous year's meetings • Next year's meetings • Liaison activities • Membership and Officers • Future Trends • Other administrative information
5.0	**Informal Description of Work**	
5.1	Executive Summary	The Executive Summary should address the overall status of the subgroup areas such as the current level of participation, general reasons for any delays in progressing Governance Assessments activities, and any overall administrative or procedural matters of note. This section should be written to provide the Governance Program committee an overview of the current situation within the subgroup.
5.2	Significant Accomplishments	This section should address significant accomplishments since the previous annual report. This should be free form and not exceed a page. It should include a list of significant publications during the past year. A significant

Section	Title	Description
		publication is one that, in the Chairman's judgment, contains information that could be useful to someone desiring descriptive background information not incorporated in the subgroup's work.
5.3	Significant Challenges	Significant challenges since previous annual report. What problems have been faced? Are the issues resolved? If not, what is the plan for resolving the issues? If approved milestones exist, status should be in terms of these milestones. Any delays should be explained and future plans highlighted.
5.4	Expected Challenges	Expected challenges in the next twelve months. Is controversy expected for approving a subgroup's work? Is there likely to be a huge mass of comments?
6.0	**Committee Activities**	
6.1	Previous Year	This should be a list that shows the dates and locations for each meeting held during the previous 12-month period, i.e., between reports. If the activity uses number designations for meetings they should be included.
6.2	Next Year	Same as above, except for the forthcoming year. Include full twelve months, if known.
7.0	**Membership and Officers**	
7.1	Officers:	The title, name and address of each person that held an office during the year. If an office was held by more than one person, list each and indicate dates in office. Include the date each officer last attended a training course held by the Governance Program Committee.
7.2	Membership:	Names, organization, and contact information (phone, fax and email address) of all members, associate members, and observers.
8.0	Future Trends and Related Technical	This section allows for comment on the market relevance of this area of the subgroup's work.

Section	Title	Description
	Activities	Areas that should be addressed are the number of organizations participating in the activity, new members attracted to this area of work, and survey data regarding the economic impact of this area of Governance Assessment standardization should be cited. The subgroup should prepare a brief analysis of technical trends leading to future work needs and how this may affect its program of work. In the interest of more proactive and strategic planning, insights on trends surrounding the Governance Assessment should be shared. In considering related technical activities, it is helpful if the report included a description of where this subgroup's work fits within the realm of Information Technology. To aid you in the response to this future trends section these kinds of questions should be considered: a. What is your vision of the technology for the subgroup? b. What are the emerging technologies or user requirements that might require some level of standardization? c. Where is the work growing and possibly linking (e.g., bindings, profiles) with or requiring close coordination with other the subgroup? The subgroup should report on its future standardization plans and briefly describe probable project proposals.
9.0	Requested changes to subgroup procedures.	The Chair will submit any internal procedures or changes to the Governance Assessments Development Board for approval through inclusion in the annual report.
10.0	Other Administrative Information	At a minimum, this needs to include a financial statement for any funds collection.

Section	Title	Description
		The report should also identify any administrative matters the subgroup feels should be brought to the attention of its parent subgroup. Examples might be: reports on letter ballots taken, voting patterns, document processing, or preparation issues. This section can also be used to provide the reporting of any procedural matters the subgroup feels should be brought to the attention of its parent subgroup. Examples might be: issues raised by the Community of Interest interaction with other Communities of Interest, or compliance with the Governance Assessments. This section can also be used to make a recommendation to the Governance Program as a result of the subgroup's experiences during the year. The subgroup will include a financial statement. This report will indicate - total receipts, receivables outstanding, total disbursements, debts outstanding and current balance of the fund. If the subgroup does not collect funds, a note to that effect should be included in the Annual Report.

Table 42. Subgroup annual report format.

11.3 Governance Assessments

Every Governance Assessment should consist of at least the information contained in the Table 43.

Governance Assessment Format		
Section	**Section Title**	**Description**
1.0	Governance Assessment Admin-istration Information	This section should contain the identifying Governance Assessment identifying number, name, title, version and effective date. There should also be Community of Interest title, and list of officers and full and associate members who contributed to the creation of the Governance Assessment. Included as well is the Governance Assessment's scope.
2.0	Normative References	This section contains references to other Governance Assessments that are used as a basis for some sections of this Governance Assessment.
3.0	Definitions, notations, and conventions	This section contains a complete set of definitions in the form of a glossary, any notations such as symbols that have special meaning within the Governance Assessment. Conventions would include for example, the form for informative notes and whether they are part of the Governance Assessment or not, the sequence and format of sections and subsections within the Governance Assessment. For example, function then format, then syntax rules, then access rules, then general rules, then leveling rules.
4.0	Concepts	This section contains a complete list of all the concepts and their detailed definition. The definitions should be detailed to the extent that there should be little or no ambiguity in the understanding of the concepts or how these concepts are applied within any of the technical components of the Governance Assessment.
5.0	Parts of the Governance Assessment	The names and descriptions of the various parts of the Governance Assessment that provide information such as the Enterprise Architecture, business information systems, and data model components comprise the total specification of the Governance Assessment.
6.0	Enterprise Architecture	The Enterprise Architecture part of the Governance Assessment should includes all relevant regarding the

Governance Assessment Format		
Section	**Section Title**	**Description**
		missions, organizations, functions, information needs analysis resource life cycles, and database objects. Included also are all the cross references among these enterprise architecture components.
7.0	Business Information Systems	The Business Information Systems part of the Governance Assessment includes all relevant metadata about the business information systems involved in the creation of a database based on the Governance Assessment's Transaction Data Staging Area Data Model. Included as well are all the business events, calendars, and business event calendars involved in acquisition, staging, transforming and loading data into any database that is to act as an Tranasaction Data Staging Area database. Included also are all the cross references among these business information system components and their relationship to the enterprise architecture components.
8.0	Data Architecture	The Data Architecture data includes all relevant metadata regarding the data element models, specified, implemented, operational, and view data models necessary to fully understand the Governance Assessment. The data element model metadata includes concepts, conceptual value domains, value domains, data element concepts, and data elements. Specified data model metadata includes all subjects, entities, attributes, and relationships of all data model templates employed in the development of the Transaction Data Staging Area Data Model. Similarly, the Implemented Database Model metadata includes all the schemas, tables, columns, and relationships involved in any database related to the development of the Transaction Data Staging Area Data Model. Also included from the Operational Data Models are the metadata included in the DBMS Schemas, DBMS Tables, DBMS Columns, and relationships involved in any business information system that is employed in the acquisition and staging of data for the information-exchanged-based databases. Finally included are all necessary Views that are the interconnection between database metadata and business information system metadata. Included also are all the cross references among these data model components and their relationship to the

Governance Assessment Format		
Section	Section Title	Description
		enterprise architecture and business information system components.

Table 43. Format for an annual Governance Assessment's report.

11.4 Change Proposals

Change proposals advance the program and scope of work of Communities of Interest subgroup more than do the work of any other subgroup within the Governance Program. After all, if there are no change proposals, why meet? There's no agenda. It is critical that a strawman base document exists if at all possible before a Community of Interest starts its activities. By base document, the following should be specified with respect to the Community of Interest:

- Missions
- Organizations
- Functions
- Business Information Systems
- Database Domains

These should all exist and hopefully be part of the Community of Interest's project proposal. It is on the basis of a collection of organizations wanting to have shared data across a mission with business information systems which are ready as sources for the shared data that forms the basis for the Community of Interest. Without these there is no "community." From the missions the database domains, which are high level specifications of the shared data, can be created. These metadata should all be collected and made available to those organizations willing to participate in the Community of Interest.

Once the Community of Interest is created and started, several meetings should occur to refine these base document materials. The mechanisms of refinement are change proposals. The general format of a change proposal should follow the guidelines established by the Community of Interest that is set out in one of its standing documents.

11.5 Standing Documents

Every Community of Interest should have a set of standing documents that contain commonly employed guidance and instructions. The list of standing documents that follow represents the key standing documents from a very successful IT Community of Interest. Four of these standing documents are further detailed in later sections of this chapter.

- Procedures (Section 11.5.1)
- Guidelines for Submission of Proposals (Section 11.5.2)
- Letter Ballots (Section 11.5.3)
- Ballot Comments (Section 11.5.4)
- Guidelines for Hosting Meetings (Section 11.5.5)

An enumeration and description of the key standing documents are provided in Table 44

Community of Interest Standing Documents		
Document Title	**Responsi-bility**	**Description**
Standing Documents List	Chair	This document contains the list of standing documents, the officer responsible for each, and a short description. Each document also contains its own introduction and description of contents. Standing documents are created and are placed on the next meeting's agenda for review and if appropriate approval. All standing documents are retained for historical purposes.
Documents Log	Secretary	This document contains a listing of documents that the committee has considered and taken action on during a calendar year.
Procedures	Vice Chair	This document contains the set of procedures under which the committee operates. These

Community of Interest Standing Documents		
Document Title	**Responsi-bility**	**Description**
		procedures cannot be in conflict nor more strict than the procedures set down by the Governance Program committee for Communities of Interest.
Projects and Governance Assessments	Chair	This document contains a list of all the current Governance Assessments under maintenance, revision, and/or development.
Projects Schedule	Editor	This document contains the current schedule for processing Governance Assessments. This document also identifies the current milestone for each Governance Assessment and the expected time anticipated to achieve the next milestone.
Participants List	Chair	This document lists the current membership of the committee including members, associate members, and observers. Provide with each member's listing is contact information.
Meetings Schedule	Chair	This document contains the meeting schedule for the community of interest and all its technical committees. The schedule should be extend out at least one year.
Guidelines for Submission of Proposals	Editor	This document contains guidelines for the submission of technical proposals. These guidelines may contain mandatory checklists that ensure that a proposal that changes a Governance Assessment has been carefully crafted to ensure that it changes the Governance Assessment in a way that does not introduce "bugs."
Directions for Posting and Downloading Papers	Editor	This document contains the instructions for uploading and downloading papers to and from the Governance Assessments server via FTP.
Template for Submission	Editor	This document contains the template for

Community of Interest Standing Documents		
Document Title	**Responsi-bility**	**Description**
of Letter Ballot Comments		constructing comments about a Governance Assessment during a formal letter ballot process. The resulting document is then able to be consolidated into a single document used by the editor to present a committee's position on a Governance Assessment.
Guidelines for Hosting Meetings	Vice Chair	This document contains the set of guidelines that a host should follow for obtaining suitable space, table sizes, electrical outlets, and meeting refreshments for attendees.
Attendance	Vice Chair	This document contains the attendance log for the committee so that a member's standing with respect to attendance can be determined.

Table 44. Community of Interest Standing Documents.

11.5.1 Procedures

A key standing document is the one containing the procedures of the Community of Interest. These procedures are supplemental to those overall procedures that govern the operation and behavior of all subgroups within the Governance Program. Each subgroup may need to have its own set of additional procedures because its mission and mode of operations are slightly different.

The procedures that follow are those for a Community of Interest, which is the main "action committee" of any Governance Program. These procedures were adapted from the ANSI INCITS DM32.2 Technical Committee on Database's procedures. Each Community of Interest should review and adapt these procedures to meet their own needs.

11.5.1.1 Meetings

Meetings of the Community of Interest will be conducted in accordance with the latest edition of Robert's Rules of Order, with the following two exceptions.

First, Robert's Rules will not apply when strict adherence would conflict with Community of Interest procedures, with the objectives of Community of Interest as set forth in its Scope and Program of Work, or with any governing Governance Program rules.

Second, at the discretion of the Chair, discussion may be conducted informally, especially on technical matters, unless any member objects. Members are given the opportunity to make a presentation of their Change Proposal or Working Paper at the appropriate point in the agenda. After the member concludes the presentation, the Chair will solicit questions from the committee, and the presenter of the paper will have the opportunity to respond to those questions. Debate is not allowed during the question period.

At some point, a member may request that the Change Proposal be "moved," or the Chair may solicit the membership to "move" the Change Proposal. Once the Change Proposal has been moved, the Chair will solicit a "second." Once moved and seconded, the Change Proposal may be debated (questions are still allowed). The person seconding a motion will not represent the same organization as the person who made that motion.

A Change Proposal may be amended by the presenter prior to it being moved and seconded. Once moved and seconded, the proposal "belongs to the body" and cannot be withdrawn or modified without general consent or a motion. An amendment can be amended; however, an amendment to an amendment cannot be amended. A member will not address a motion and "call the question" (request a vote) in the same turn.

11.5.1.2 Documents and Distribution

11.5.1.2.1 Change Proposals

Proposals to modify a prospective Governance Assessment will be made in the form of Change Proposals that specify deletions, additions, or changes to the current Base Document for the prospective Governance Assessment. Change Proposals are the mechanism by which progress is made in advancing the current Base Document towards becoming a Governance Assessment document.

The Editor has the right to refuse to process a Change Proposal if the instructions regarding the changes to the current Base Document are incomplete or unclear, or if the Change Proposal is not written against the current Base Document. In particular, the Editor may refuse to process a Change Proposal that fails to cite the number and title of the document being changed, the proper Clause and/or Subclause numbers and titles affected, or the Rule numbers and partial text of Rules that are changed. In such cases, the Editor will bring the Change Proposal back the Community of Interest for revision.

Members are referred to the Standing Document, Guidelines for Submission of Proposals. For Change Proposals written for the purpose of defect management (such as an erratum or an amendment to a Governance Assessment, or an interpretation of a Governance Assessment), there may be additional requirements. Generic requirements relating to Change Proposals written against Defect Documents are summarized below:

- If a Change Proposal affects parts of a Governance Assessment that have already been changed in a Defect Document, then those parts of the Change Proposal are required to be written against the appropriate parts of the Defect Document. Those parts of the Change Proposal that do not touch areas that have been changed in the Defect Document should be written against the Governance Assessment.

- Change Proposals are required to include a brief Rationale section for inclusion in the Defect Document.

- If a Change Proposal is written against the Defect Document, it may be necessary to alter the Rationale section in the Defect Document.

11.5.1.2.2 Working Papers

A Working Paper is a technical document, other than a Change Proposal, that is distributed for consideration by the committee. Generally, a member will solicit informal feedback from the committee regarding the advisability and desirability of the content of the Working Paper. Working Papers do not cause any changes to the current Base Document. Members should keep in mind that feedback (including straw votes) obtained on a Working Paper may not necessarily correspond to the vote that may take when the Working Paper is followed up by a Change Proposal.

11.5.1.2.3 Electronic Distribution

The Chair will designate a document server site and an electronic mailing list (reflector) server. All documents will be posted to this server, preferably in PDF format, although other common usage formats are also acceptable. Electronically posting a document also requires sending an email message to the reflector, notifying Community of Interest members of the posting. Members are responsible for obtaining copies of the electronic documents. If, for some reason, the Chair has not designated an official server, electronic posting will not be a valid document distribution method.

11.5.1.2.4 Documents Eligible for Disposition

Documents to be considered at a meeting will be properly numbered and made available to members (i.e., electronically posted) at least two weeks before the meeting. Specifically, change proposals and working papers must be available on the same day of the week on which the meeting will commence two weeks prior to the meeting week; e.g., on the 2nd Monday before a meeting starting on Monday, the 2nd Tuesday before a meeting starting on Tuesday, etc.

Documents distributed after the two-week deadline defined above may be considered only if there is no objection from any voting member. Such an objection can be made at any time before the document is considered at the meeting, but must be made prior to the start of debate on the paper. That is, a member may object any time prior to or during presentation of and questions about a late paper, but the member cannot object after a motion is on the floor and debate has started. The Chair will ask if there are any objections before entertaining a motion to act on a late paper.

11.5.2 Guidelines for Proposals

Proposals to be accepted into any part and any version of the Governance Assessment should be written in such a way that allows readers to quickly understand the proposals (in the context of the Governance Assessment, of course) and that allows the Editor to readily apply the proposals in a manner that satisfies the intent of the proposal author and of the approving body.

In addition, all proposals for changes to any and every part and any and every version of the Governance Assessment should be subjected to scrutiny for completeness and lack of ambiguity. In short, all proposals must be formulated to reassure the reader that all relevant material has been considered and addressed.

There are a number of guidelines for writing proposals that are maximally friendly both to proposal readers and to the Editor. There is also a checklist of criteria that must be satisfied by every change proposal's author so that the editor can know what should be done with the proposal's content should the proposal be approved by the committee.

11.5.2.1 Text Changes

The main form of the "data" that comprises Governance Assessments are the records that reside in the metadata repository's Governance Assessment tables and to the actual metadata records of the assessed work products. Changes to any text should be specified such that the editor can quickly and easily find the text that is to be changed and then via a "cut and past" strategy change the actual text in the repository presentation layer window. It is additionally critical that the impact of any such changes be fully explained in the change proposal.

11.5.2.2 Transaction Data Staging Area Data Model Changes

In the case of metadata for one or more components within an Transaction Data Staging Area Data Model, the change proposals must include not only the addition, deletion, or modification of any data model component but also any changes that would be required to any related data model component.

Since the Transaction Data Staging Area Data Model is the heart of Information Exchange Governance Assessments, then any changes that impact business information systems that would provide data to an Transaction Data Staging Area Data Model must also be thoroughly analyzed to ensure that complete database integrity continues. This extends also to business events and their associated business event calenders

11.5.2.3 Change Proposal Format

11.5.2.3.1 Title Section

This section of the change proposal should contain the change proposal's administrative information. That is, the change proposal document number, its date, the submitting organization, the author and coauthors if any. This section should provide a clear title and abstract of the change proposal so that any informed reader can quickly know the purpose of the proposal and the sections of the Governance Assessment that are to be affected by the change.

11.5.2.3.2 Discussion Section

It is helpful to the reader if the discussion part makes quite clear why the proposal is being made. It also helps if any approaches that were considered and rejected are also mentioned, together with the reasons for their rejection.

Proposal writers should strive to describe all changes and their implications in the discussion part. Readers should not have to proceed through the detailed changes to understand the consequences of the change.

11.5.2.3.3 Proposed Changes

The following are critical to the understanding of the proposed changes.

- Every separate item of the proposal should be numbered.
- When referring to a specific section of the Governance Assessment, or to a metadata item within the repository that is to be changed, always specify

both section number and exact sequence of steps that the editor will have to take to quickly and accurately locate the component that is to be changed.

- When inserting, deleting, or replacing text in the Governance Assessment, specify the precise set of steps that the reader and editor will have to perform to then add, delete, or replace the text.

- Where only a few words of existing text are to be changed, it is clearer both to the reviewer and to the Editor to flag differences in some way, e.g., by striking out deleted text and underlining new text or setting new text in boldface. Whatever convention is used should be explained. The use of color to distinguish between existing text, new text, and deleted text is also encouraged; it is quite helpful to proposal readers and to the Editor, especially when proposals are read and used in PDF (as opposed to a printed) form.

11.5.2.4 Use of Notes

Change proposals often must draw the proposal reader's attention to some detail or explanation. This is best done by means of a note starting off with "Note to proposal reader:".

Similarly, change proposal sometimes need to call the Editor's attention to some detail, such as the need to assign a value to a value-domain-values set. This is best done by means of a note starting off with "Note to the Editor."

However, there is also the need for change proposals to insert notes into the text of the document that they modify, so that the reader of the resulting Governance Assessment has access to the note text. This is best done by specifying something like "NOTE nnn: text of the note."

11.5.2.5 Quality Proposal Checklist

Every proposed change to a component of the Governance Assessment should be assessed against all possible related components. This is best done by examining the complete repository meta model and determining all related components to those that are being changed. The checklist that should be in the proposal therefore should list all these related components, and via the repository report writer print out the before change state and the after change state of the repository so that the proposal reader can assess that the change is acceptable. Any effect on any related component needs to be fully explained and justified.

11.5.3 Letter Ballots

Letter ballots beyond those called for in a Community of Interest for some important business item are almost always employed to cause a focus on those areas of a Governance Assessment that need work before proceeding to the next stage of a Governance Assessment. The stages are commonly committee draft, final committee draft, draft Governance Assessment, and Governance Assessment. Each letter ballot is designed to force members of a Community of Interest to formally identify what parts, sections, and specific aspects of a Governance Assessment need additional work. The table that follows provides the general form for a letter ballot. If there are multiple parts of a Governance Assessment that are being voted, then there would be additional columns to the right of the second column. The header would then identify which part the vote applies to. Table 45 presents the overall structure and content for a letter ballot.

Suggested Format for a Letter Ballot	
Vote: I vote as follows: (check one only)	**<Identification Information of Governance Assessment>**
Approve the draft as presented	
Approve the draft with comments given in the attached document	
Disapprove the draft for reasons given in the attached document.	
Abstain from voting on the draft for reasons given in the attached document	

Name:____ Organization:____ Full Member Primary (___) or Alternate (___) Date:_____ / ______ / ______

Table 45. Letter Ballot Format.

11.5.4 Ballot Comments

Table 46 provides the general format for recording comments regarding the Governance Assessment that requires work. The table after that contains definitions for each of the columns.

Seq Number	Com-ment Id	See Also	Severity	Ref-erence	Descrip-tion	Addres s-ed By
<number>	<for-matted string>	<for-matted string>	One of four choices	<for-matted string>	Text descrip-tion and if available, a solution	<for-matted string>

Table 46. Ballot Comment Columns.

The definitions for the columns of the information that should be contained in a letter ballot response is provided in Table 47.

Ballot Comment Column Definitions	
Sequence Number	This is a permanent sequence number once a consolidated comment from all Community of Interest full members has been created. This number is created by the editor once all ballot comments have been received.

Ballot Comment Column Definitions	
Comment Id	This is completed by each Community of Interest member organization submitting a comment. The format of the values in this column should be abc-P##-seq# or nbc-T##-seq#, where: abc is an abbreviation assigned to the submitting organization, P## is the part number of the Governance Assessment if it is a multi-part Governance Assessment. Else it is 00. Seq# is the sequence number that the Community of Interest member organization has assigned to the comment.
See Also	This enables a submitting organization to reference other comments.
Severity	This is a four value severity assigned to the comment. The codes are: Major Technical, Minor Technical, Major Editorial, Minor Editorial. In general a Major classification represents something that must be changed before the Governance Assessment can proceed to the next stage. A Minor classification represents something that should be changed. The initial classification is at the discretion of the submitted. The final classification is voted by the entire Community of Interest.
Reference	This identifies the specific document to which the comment applies and to the location in the document to which it applies.
Description	This contains two sections. The first, starting immediately at the beginning of the column, should be a textual description of the comment being submitted. This text may be in any form, with WYSIWYG aspects if required to get the message of the comment to the reader, and with multiple paragraphs if so required. It should be followed by a line with the word "Solution" After that line, the submitted may choose to insert additional text specifying the solution to their comment; alternatively, the text "None supplied with comment" may be inserted.
Addressed By	This should normally be left blank. However, if the submitted description has solution with their comment, they should put the string "See Comment" or "See comment" into the Addressed By column. If the submitter has provided a separately numbered paper containing a proposal that addresses the comment, they are encouraged to put that paper's number into the Addressed By column.

Table 47. Ballot Comment Column Definitions.

11.5.5 Guidelines for Hosting Meetings

The following are guidelines for hosting a Community of Interest meeting. Generally it involves:

- Finding a Hotel
- Financial Arrangements
- Contractual Arrangements
- Other Considerations
- Meeting Room and Hotel Facilities
- Food service
- Meeting Announcement
- At the Meeting

11.5.5.1 Finding Hotels

One of the easiest ways to locate hotels suitable for our meeting is to contact the Visitor's Bureau, the Convention Bureau, or the equivalent in the city in which the meeting is planned. This office will take the necessary information (dates, meeting size, etc.) and can pass along that information to the hotels. The hotels themselves will then send proposals directly to you.

11.5.5.2 Financial Arrangements

One goal in negotiating hotel accommodations is to minimize the cost of sleeping rooms in order to allow all participants to stay in the hotel where the meeting is held. Ask about the availability of rooms at government per-diem rates. When the room rate is much higher than the corporate rates at co-located hotels, members have been known to stay at those hotels. Make sure the hotel knows that this will occur. If possible, call hotels to find out what their corporate rates are.

Many hotels will offer you a "free" meeting room and adjust the price of the sleeping rooms upward accordingly. Community of Interest members would rather pay a higher meeting fee than a higher sleeping room rate. Indicate that hotel proposals must separate the cost of meeting rooms and the cost of sleeping room. Ask the hotel for the attendance level above or below which fees for the meeting rooms would be affected (upward or downward), if applicable. E.g., booking 75 sleeping room nights for a three-day meeting might qualify for a reduced meeting room price, or booking less than 60 meeting room nights for a three-day meeting might result in a higher per day meeting room price. Just ensure that as host you understand any such relationships/dependencies between the cost of sleeping rooms and meeting rooms.

11.5.5.3 Contractual Arrangements

The following are the key points from the guidelines of the ANSI INCITS H2 Technical Committee on Database that are used by H2 members when making contractual arrangements of a Committee of Interest meeting at a commercial hotel.

- The Community of Interest will not enter into legal commitments; i.e., the Community of Interest will not sign a hotel contract. Therefore the meeting host should be prepared to either sign the contract individually or as a representative of their organization, or convince the hotel that no contract signature is necessary (which usually is not acceptable to hotels).

- Most hotels will offer a contract with various penalty clauses. Don't sign such a contract unless you or your employer is prepared to honor it. You may be asked to provide the hotel with an advance deposit for the meeting space, if so, the Community of Interest can agree to a reasonable deposit (typically $500) at time of contract signing.
- Some hotels will accept a credit card to serve as guarantee for the deposit - the Community of Interest does not have credit card, but some member hosts have used their own credit card for this - but such is the decision of the individual host and the hotel they are working with.

- If the hotel doesn't want to do business on terms that are mutually agreeable to them and the Community of Interest, then consider another hotel or even another city.

- In most cases, you can strike the penalty clauses or at least negotiate them downward, and the hotel will agree.

- Many hotels will request a signing of a "letter of intent." Many hosts have signed these. To reassure the hotel representatives, you can point to the fact that this committee has been meeting six times a year for twenty years and has always met its financial obligations.

- You may occasionally be asked for previous hotel names to serve as references - if so, contact the Community of Interest chair and references will be furnished. Indicate for example that the Committee of Interest, to date, has never cancelled a meeting. When adjustments had to be made, e.g., change the date, the committee has always provided more than two months notice. Inform the hotels that we will pay them by cash and check at the end of the meeting.

- Some hotels have difficulty differentiating the organizational reason for the meeting, that is, the specific name of the Community of Interest, from the corporate hosting organization such as NCR, Oracle, IBM, etc. These names are typically used by hotel reservations staff when making sleeping room reservations to ensure affiliation with the correct hotel group function, and that you get quoted the correct sleeping room prices and options. Thus, you should consider listing the meeting both under the Community of Interest name and your corporate organization name.

11.5.5.4 Other Considerations

Some hotels will want you to coordinate in some way the sleeping room arrangements. You might volunteer to send reservation cards with the meeting announcement, brochures, etc., but ensure that the hotel understands and that the contract states all arrangements for sleeping rooms (e.g., guarantees for late arrival, etc.) are solely between the individual attendee and the hotel.

We may finish our meeting before the scheduled adjournment date. Some members may wish to leave before the meeting is over. There should be no commitment to pay for sleeping rooms that are vacated early. It's also desirable to be able to cancel the meeting room and avoid payment for any final, unused days (but this is not required). However, the Community of Interest will not pay for food service that we cancel with sufficient notice (e.g., > twelve hours notice).

11.5.5.5 Meeting Room and Hotel Facilities

The meeting should be held at the hotel where members are sleeping. The Community of Interest does not meet at a host company's facility. The committee has been averaging about 25 people. As a guideline, a minimum room size of approximately 50′ x 30′ is typically sufficient for the Community of Interest meeting of 25 persons. Such rooms can usually be configured to comfortably seat up to 28-30 persons.

Tables in the larger meeting room should be arranged in an "open rectangle" or similar fashion. There must be 3 to 4 linear feet per person. The tables should also be 30 to 36 inches deep. In addition, one or two extra tables should be set up at a side in the meeting room for papers and documents brought to the meeting. A diagram might be helpful to hotels to give them an idea of our needs.

The meeting room should be reserved for 8 a.m. to 8 p.m. except on the last day, when it should be reserved until 5 p.m. Rooms should be accessible overnight. Keeping the room overnight is known as a "24 hour hold."

No ashtrays, podium, projectors, or microphone should be provided in the meeting room. Lighting in the meeting rooms should be ample for business work, reading, writing, using the laptop computers. The lighting suitable for an evening social function is insufficient for a technical working meeting. Trash cans should be available in the meeting rooms.

The hotel must be made aware that we cannot hold a meeting while, for example, a sales meeting with microphones, applause, loud music, etc., is being held in an adjacent meeting room. It has been learned the hard way that an adjacent meeting with even only a microphone is sufficient to interfere with committee work. The hotel must ensure that no such meetings will be scheduled in the rooms adjacent to ours.

The meeting room should have extension cords and power strips as almost all members bring laptop computers. The committee requires power strips for approximately 20-25 laptops, spaced at intervals around the inside of the table arrangement. Check on the hotel charges for use of such power strips, some hotels have such priced these quite expensively, while others will provide these reasonably or even without additional charge.

Touch-tone phone facilities should be available in both the meeting room area and in the individual sleeping rooms. The sleeping rooms should be equipped with modular jacks for computer laptops and modem use.

Meeting rooms are more pleasant with windows and/or direct outdoor access. The hotel should provide copy services and fax services at a reasonable charge. Note that fax charges may include separate charges for incoming and outgoing fax transmissions. The hotel should be asked to indicate its charges for these services beforehand. As we have found out, they can be either reasonable or exorbitant. As host, you should attempt to locate in advance off-site copy and fax services, which tend to be much less expensive.

115.5.6 Food Service

The Food Service should include:

- Water service.

- Continental Breakfast. Generous portion continental breakfast including coffee, tea, decaffeinated coffee, decaffeinated tea, juice, soft drinks (regular and diet), and rolls. It has been suggested that a variety of rolls, both sweet (e.g., Danish), and not so sweet (e.g., croissants or muffins) be included. Bagels and cream cheese usually go over very well. A fruit plate is also Governance Assessment. The breakfast service should be set up by 8:00am each meeting day.
- Throughout the meeting day the hotel food service staff will check with the meeting host for any additional needed items, or leave a phone number to call when special service is needed.

- At approximately 10:00 a.m. and 1:30 p.m., coffee, tea, decaffeinated coffee, and soft drinks should be checked for restocking. A smaller restocking check should be made around 3:00 - 3:30pm. No late afternoon service should be scheduled on the last day unless it is known that the meeting will last long enough on that day to make such service desirable. If it is consistent with hotel policy, "continual replenishment" rather than "specific time" service is preferred.

- Afternoon food service is optional, but popular with members. This can include cookies or other light dessert type items (brownies), and should be arranged for 2:00- 2:30 PM setup.

11.5.5.7 Meeting Announcement

You should send out a meeting announcement as soon as possible after the preceding meeting. According to our rules, e-mail no later than four weeks prior to the meeting - and preferably six weeks in advance to give members the best opportunity at lowest airfares, etc. The earlier, the better. The meeting announcement is to be emailed to the Community of Interest email distribution list. The announcement should include:

- Meeting dates.

- Hotel information including name, location, phone number, and the rates you've arranged, including government rates; i.e., sufficient information to make reservations.

- Complete hotel information - name, address, phone, fax, website if available.

- Information on transportation from the airport(s), and additional information such as availability and price of limousines, public transportation, and parking fees at the hotel.

- You might also wish to include information about the area; e.g., maps, tourist sites, list of restaurants, and so on. A call to the local Chamber of Commerce or Visitor's Bureau will usually get you all the copies you need.

11.5.5.8 At the Meeting

As soon as possible, introduce yourself to the hotel's catering, meeting, banquet (whatever) staff. Let them know that you will be their point of contact. Check the meeting rooms as soon as possible upon your arrival to ensure they will meet the Community of Interest meeting requirements. In addition, be prepared to spend some time with the hotel staff straightening out any problems that might occur (Murphy's law). One of Murphy's laws is that you can never find what you need in Robert's Rules. Similarly, one of Robert's rules is that Murphy's Laws are always out of order.

11.6 Motions for Inter-Community of Interest Meetings

Whenever a Community of Interest participates in an inter-Community of Interest meeting there commonly are only delegates from each participating Community of Interest. Those delegates should be instructed as to the types and kinds of authority they have on behalf of their "home" Community of Interest. Each Community of Interest appoints delegates to the meetings. Delegate instructions are given during a Community of Interest meeting shortly before the multi-Community of Interest meeting. There are two such motions that are provided here as template for delegate instructions.

- Delegate behavior on non-"Home" Community of Interest motions and proposals when not instructed and not unanimous.

  Motion (mover, seconder, Vote: tally) that the delegates to the <meeting name> abstain on all motions and change proposals for which they have not been given explicit direction by a "home" Community of Interest decision, unless the delegates to the meeting agree unanimously to vote "Yes" or "No" on the motion or change proposal under consideration.

- Delegate behavior regarding "Home" Community of Interest proposals not previously approved by the "home" Community of Interest.

  Motion (mover, seconder, Vote: tally) that the delegates to the <meeting name> will not make visible to any person or persons other that "home" Community of Interest participants any paper (change proposal, discussion paper, position paper, etc.), unless the delegates to the meeting agree unanimously that the paper is acceptable to make visible.

11.7 Document Summary

Documents within a governance program are very important. It is through formally constituted documents that subgroups are determined, established, brought into existence, and of course, operate.

All Governance Assessments are started as a consequence of a Governance Assessment's proposal document. If this document is not properly created, then the Governance Assessment's effort just does not even start. Along the way, and at the end of the Governance Assessment's process, the Governance Assessment itself must be able to be generated as a properly formatted document that is exact, unambiguous, and "votable."

All through the life of a Governance Assessment, the progress of the committee occurs because of change proposals. These documents are not only essential to the operation of the committee, the impact or consequence of change proposals can be in the 10s of millions of dollars.

Decisions by committees are made by ballots. Hence there is a document format for ballots, and another document format for ballot comments. Ballots are focusing mechanisms, and ballot comments are the specifications of the focus. Entire meetings are devoted to reviewing and determining the proper set of words in each ballot comment. That is because the technical work that then has to follow to resolve the ballot comment can only be based on those words.

Other classes of documents include subgroup annual reports, meeting minutes, agendas, document registries, and standing documents that provide the current status of various subgroup topics.

There is even a document that suggests the appropriate way to find a location for a meeting. At any meeting, if it lasts for a whole week, and has 25 persons in attendance can have a cost of about $150,000. The staff costs of those attending the meeting can be upwards of $100,000. Travel and hotel costs for the staff can easily be another $40,000. And finally, the costs for the hotel's meeting room and refreshments can be another $5,000. That's a grand total of about $150,000 per meeting. Consequently, meeting locations and arrangements should be carefully accomplished.

11.8 Questions and Exercises

1. This chapter enumerates and describes a collection of documents that are necessary for successful Governance Communities of Interest. After a brief review, how are these documents critical to the creation of your Governance Committees and/or the creation of a Governance Assessment?

2. Section 11.1 sets out a four-page table that identifies and describes the required entries for a Governance Assessment. Is this the required information for starting a Governance Assessment?

3. Section 11.2 sets out a multi-page table that identifies and describes the required entries for the various groups in the overall Governance Program. Is this information sufficient to provide all members of all subgroups the information they need to ensure there are not conflicting or overlapping Governance Assessments?

4. Section 11.3 sets out the overall format and content description of a Governance Assessment. Since these Governance Assessments can be hundreds to several thousand pages long, it is critical to understand whether the categories of information are the necessary and sufficient set.

After carefully review these sections, if they are provided in the Governance Assessments document, is there sufficient information to design, build and maintain databases and supporting business information systems that represent uses of the Governance Assessment? If not, why?

Compare and contrast the information required in this format with that required to build a database and supporting business information systems in your organization. Is one more sufficient than the other?

5. Sections 11.4 and 11.5 identify and describe the various document formats that should be Governance Assessment fare for the moving the program and scope of work of the Governance Communities of Interest forward. How do these documents call for the critical work to be done? Provide examples from your organizations.

6. Section 11.5.2.3 contains the overall structure, format and description of Governance Assessment change proposals. After a careful review of this format, can you see that if specified that you could build interoperable

systems and databases from this information? If yes, why? If no, why not?

7. Section 11.5.3 outlines what should be in a Letter Ballot on any Governance Assessment. If this information is provided are there clear directions on what and how to report a vote?

8. Section 11.5.4 outlines what should be in Ballot Comments associated with any Letter Ballot. If this information is provided are there clear directions on what to do to repair and/or change the Governance Assessment?

9. Section 11.5.5 outlines an overall process for getting hotels, meeting rooms, and the like. If all these items are accomplished wouldn't there be a good meeting? How much time has your organization spent on arranging meetings only to find that key things have been forgotten? How do these Sections on meetings help? Compare and contrast your organization's way of engineering and executing meetings? Provide examples from within your organization.

12

Governance Projects

Governance Program projects fall into these categories:

- General projects.
- Governance Program projects.
- Community of Interest Projects.

12.1 General Projects

There are five types of Governance Program projects that are general in nature. These are:

- Annual report projects.
- Special event projects.
- Administrative procedure projects.
- Membership procedure projects.
- Governance Assessments' development projects.

Annual Report projects engineer the content and procedures for Governance Program subgroup preparation of annual reports.

Special Events projects define the contents and procedures necessary for the creation and presentation of the business plans associated with special events.

Administrative Procedures projects examine the processes that every subgroup performs on a regular basis for meeting planing and scheduling, the conduct of meetings, the development of minutes, and the content and format of Governance Assessments for the Transaction Data Staging Area Data Models.

Membership Procedures projects determine the rules and processes for identifying individuals and organizations to participate in all the Governance Program subgroups.

Governance Assessments' development projects determine the detailed processes that are to be performed to create Transaction Data Staging Area Data Models and all the supporting products necessary to fully define Governance Assessments.

12.2 Governance Program Projects

Governance Program projects that are to be accomplished in support of some aspect of the overall program. Thus, there are projects related to the program's architecture, governance, and components. Each project has a firm goal, specific objectives, a work plan, metrics, deliverables, and a schedule that must be accomplished. All deliverables must fit within the overall set of all deliverables from all the other Governance Program projects

- Component Architecture projects, which are specifically targeted at the engineering, design, deployment, and long-term evolution and maintenance of the components within the Governance Program. Components of the Governance Program include its overall process, specific Governance Assessments, metrics, project management, the technical components of Governance Programs within and across all Communities of Interest. Each component architecture project would be scoped, its work plan developed, resource loaded and staffed, and managed during its accomplishment.

- Concept of Operations projects address either the Governance Program in general, or specific components of the Governance Program architecture. Thus, there would be concepts of operations documents addressing process, Governance Assessments, metrics, project management, and Governance Program technical components. Each project would be scoped, its work plan developed, resource loaded and staffed, and managed during its accomplishment.

- Governance Program planning environment projects are generally in three areas: work product management, the ongoing evolution of the environment's functionality, and extensions to the Governance Program planning.

- Training and awareness projects are those that cause the creation of various presentations, workshops, courses, and support services such as hot-line, on-line tutorials, and the like.

A key type of Governance Program project is one accomplished by the Governance Assessments Development Board. These projects identify and implement strategies that achieve objectives of governance across the enterprise, and attain interoperability capabilities. First and foremost these projects are the development of action plans.

The Governance Assessments Development Board's projects do not actually effect the creation and/or evolution of Governance Assessment work products. Rather, their projects are to identify, plan, and manage Governance Assessments accomplishment.

Governance Program planning projects begin with a problem statement that is taken through a rigorous functional and technical analysis process, resulting in a feasible solution for implementation at the appropriate level, ranging from specific, pair-wise, database-to-database exchanges up to enterprise level data sharing in a "virtual, distributed single database" environment. Data management planning projects result in the identification of specific projects.

12.3 Community of Interest Projects

The projects associated with Communities of Interest are:

- Enterprise Architectures ,
- Business Information Systems
- Data Integrity Rules
- Data Architectures
- Project Management

12.3.1 Enterprise Architectures

Enterprise architecture projects are those that cause the creation of the necessary and sufficient metadata to support contextually accurate Governance Program projects. Included are the creation and evolution of:

- Business Missions
- Business Organizations
- Business Functions
- Position
- Information Needs
- Resource Life Cycle Analysis
- Database Domains
- Database Objects
- Documents & Forms
- Requirements

12.3.2 Business Information Systems

Business Information System projects are those that cause the creation of the necessary and sufficient metadata to support contextually accurate Governance Program projects. Included are the creation and evolution of:

- Business Information Systems
- Business Events
- Business Cycle
- Business Calendar
- User Acceptance Test
- Use Cases
- Reports
- External File Interface

12.3.3 Data Integrity Rules

Data Integrity Rule projects are those that cause the creation of the necessary and sufficient metadata to support contextually accurate Governance Program projects. Included are the creation and evolution of:

- Data Integrity Rule Specification
- Data Integrity Rule Binding

12.3.4 Data Architectures

Business Information System projects are those that cause the creation of the necessary and sufficient metadata to support contextually accurate Governance Program projects. Included are the creation and evolution of:

- Database Architectures
  - Reference Data
  - Original Data Capture
  - Transaction Data Staging Area
  - Operational Data Store
  - Data Warehouses
- Data Element Model Metadata
- Specified Data Metadata Model
- Implemented Database Metadata Model
- Operational Database Model Metadata
- View Model Metadata

12.3.5 Project Management

Business Information System projects are those that cause the creation of the necessary and sufficient metadata to support contextually accurate Governance Program projects. Included are the creation and evolution of:

- Projects
- Project Deliverables
- Project Tasks

- Project Templates
- Deliverable Templates
- Task Templates
- Skills
- Work Environment Factors

12.4 Projects Summary

Projects are not explicitly identified in the Knowledge Worker Framework depicted in Figure 1. Rather, projects exist implicitly as collections of performed functions by groups of individuals within organizations that set out to achieve some aspect of a mission. That is, to build a Governance Assessment, create a metadata infrastructure environment, and the like.

Every project ultimately consists of a work plan, a budget, a set of deliverables, and is set within an organizational construct. In this book, while the project classes are identified in this chapter, the functions, organizations, positions, processes, and product specifications for every project are defined in Chapter 6 .

To charter a project, it's class must be identified, and its description and rationale set out. Once approved, then the project's work plan would be developed from tasks in appropriate Governance Assessment section from Chapter 6. The organizations that are to participate will have been identified in the same chapter.

Project products will be identified from within the Chapter 6. Once all this is assembled, then an estimate can be made of the resources needed to carry out the project. All the project's "metadata" is recorded in an appropriate area of the Metabase's Project Management inferred from within Figure 46.

The task and deliverable template entities, along with the actual task and deliverable entities exist so as to preserve the actual project's history. As the project is accomplished, the products that are built are identified and the resources that are expended are recorded in other entities found on Figure 46.

If possible, all project metadata should be integrated with other governance program metadata so that there can be consolidated reporting. Additionally, as projects are accomplished, some of the resulting metadata products could well impact the resource estimates of other projects. By having all the project metadata integrated, those impacts can easily be employed to re-estimate other projects.

12 5 Questions and Exercises

1. Meetings are not what make progress. Rather, projects and within projects, change proposals make progress. From the list in Section 12.1, are these project classes the sufficient set to then cause progress and to operate in an orderly way? If yes, why? If no, why not?

2. After reviewing the sets of Governance Program projects in Section 12.2, are there any that are missing? What is the likely achievement from each project class? How can there be an assurance that the results will cause integration of all the Governance Projects?

3. What is the likely effect in terms of time, effort, and resources by requiring that all the Governance Assessments be developed more or less the same why?

4. What is the likely effect in terms of time, effort, and resources if the work products of the various Governance Assessments projects are stored in a Metabase that is integrated, interrelated, and non-redundant across all the work products of all the Governance Assessments projects?

5. What would be the effects in terms of time, effort, and resources if all the projects are accomplished using the Metabase in a stove-pipe fashion?

6. What would be the effects in terms of time, effort, and resources on all the projects with respect to integration, interrelationships and non-redundancy if they are accomplished without a Metabase and without a metadata management tool?

7. Section 12.3 lists the types of Community of Interest projects. The subsections of 12.3 describe each type and subtype of the projects. Are there any project classes missing? Is so, what is the likely effect on the development of Governance Assessments?

13

Governance Rules

The rules contained in this chapter relate generally to all Governance Program subgroups except when specifically stated. All actions by any Governance Program subgroup are governed by Robert's Rules of Order except where specifically noted. The rules relate to:

- Meetings
- Voting
- File Retention
- Officer Training
- Fees
- Reports and Review
- Finance Management
- Membership in Good Standing

• 13.1 Meetings

Rules for meetings relate to:

- Schedule
- Notice and Draft Agenda
- Document for Action
- Quorum
- Minutes

13.1.1 Schedule of Meetings

The Governance Program subgroups meet regularly. The schedule is governed as follows:

- The Governance Program Committee normally meets four times per year.
- The Governance Assessments Development Board and Governance Assessments Policy Board normally meet at the same venue as the Governance Program Committee.
- All Communities of Interest and Study Groups will meet at least once a year.
- Maintenance Committees will meet as required.
- The Governance Program Committee committees will meet as required.

All meetings are held at the call of the Chair and within the frequencies indicated. Each agenda should include a standing item for review and confirmation of the date and location of the next meeting(s). Periodically, the schedule should be extended to a nine- to eighteen-month period ahead, with "tentative" indications when appropriate.

A duly called meeting is one for which the meeting notice and draft agenda are issued at least 4 weeks of the start date of the meeting.

When a quorum is not met at such a duly called meeting or fewer than the number of voting members required to approve an action, the members who are present may propose actions for submission to the entire membership for letter ballot or action at the next meeting. They may conduct all business not requiring voting action. For Communities of Interest, Study Groups and Technical Groups, a duly called meeting will count in determining the members' attendance record.

13.1.2 Meeting Notice and Draft Agenda

The meeting notice and draft agenda will be distributed no closer than four weeks before the meeting.

13.1.3 Documents for Action (Two-Week Rule)

Documents should be distributed at least two weeks prior to the meeting. Recommendations that come from the Governance Assessments Development Board and Governance Assessments Policy Board to the Governance Program Committee and vice-versa are exempted from the two-week rule.

Any documents sent later may be considered, but final action may only be taken in the absence of an objection by any voting member present or by suspension of this rule by vote of the Governance Program Committee; otherwise, they must be acted upon by letter ballot or deferred until the next meeting.

Documents may be revised during the meeting and still be considered to have met the two-week rule if the original document met this requirement. Note that this provision is intended to provide a means for discussing the document and advancing the progress of the work, and is not intended to permit the introduction of new or orthogonal material.

Project Proposals not posted to the Draft agenda two weeks prior to the meeting must be acted upon by letter ballot or deferred until the next meeting.

13.1.4 Quorum

Quorum for all subgroups is defined accordingly:

- For the Governance Program Committee and the Subsidiary Boards, quorum is a majority of the voting membership.
- For Study Groups there is no minimum attendance required for a quorum.
- For Communities of Interest and contained subgroups, a quorum is one-third of the voting membership with at least four members present.

13.1.5 Minutes

All subgroups, except ad hoc groups, are required to produce minutes of their meetings. Minutes will be distributed within four weeks after the adjournment of the meeting. When prepared by someone other than a member of the Governance Program Committee staff, the draft minutes will be reviewed by Governance Program Committee staff prior to distribution to the Committee.

The required contents of minutes are as follows:

- Date(s), location(s), Chair, Secretary, hour of opening and adjournment.
- Summary of significant actions taken.
- List of all attendees.
- Approved agenda (or approved changes to draft agenda).
- Approval of previous meeting minutes.
- Each motion seconded and not withdrawn, identifying the maker of the motion, the fact of and the maker of a second, and the voting results.
- Future meeting schedule.
- List of action items assigned to members.

Individual remarks or detailed transcripts need not to be recorded; however, any specific statement should be recorded when requested by the Chair or a member. Records of discussions and actions taken pertaining to any topic for which attendance is restricted will not be included in the minutes, except to record that a position was developed.

13.2 Voting

Voting can only occur by subgroup members in good standing. There will be only one voting membership per organization. An alternate representative may vote only if the principal representative fails to vote. In all subgroup actions that require a vote, only full members can vote.

Voting by proxy will not be permitted. A written vote on an issue to be acted upon at the meeting may be submitted by correspondence by an absent voting member provided it is received by the Chair prior to the point when the issue is brought to a vote.

13.2.1 Voting Practice

13.2.1.1 Types of Voting Positions

Three types of voting positions are allowed:

- Affirmative
- Negative
- Abstention

13.2.1.2 Method of Voting and Criteria for Approval

Five voting methods are permitted. These are:

- Letter ballot
- Roll call vote
- Show of hands
- Voice vote
- Unanimous consent

With the exception of letter ballots, all of the above votes are taken at a meeting. The method of meeting votes is at the discretion of the Chair unless otherwise specified in this document. However, a roll call vote may be requested by any voting member on any action that this document permits be handled by a meeting vote. For a roll call vote, the voting position of each member will be recorded in the minutes.

Letter ballot votes are authorized by any of the following methods:

- Majority vote of those present at a meeting.
- The Chair.
- The Governance Program Committee.
- This document.
- Written request to the Chair from five or more voting members of the Subgroup.

13.2.1.2.1 Letter Ballots

Affirmative votes may include comments. Negative votes must include reasons for the negative and, if possible, recommend specific modifications necessary to change the negative position to an affirmative position. Abstention votes will include the reason for not taking a position.

For purposes of determining a member's voting record, negative and abstention votes cast without reasons will be counted as non-responses and may place the member in jeopardy for failure to vote.

The voting period for letter ballots is usually thirty days. The duration period for all letter ballots commences on the date of issue of the letter ballot. An extension may be granted by the Governance Program Committee when warranted and when the extension does not cause undue problems, such as failure to submit an inter-organizational vote on time.

13.2.1.2.2 Letter Ballot Reconsideration Procedure

A copy of the letter ballot notification will be sent to the Principal and all Alternate representatives of every Voting Member.

If the letter ballot resulted in any negative votes, the comments that accompanied the votes will be circulated to the Governance Program Committee membership along with the letter ballot voting tally. All Governance Program Committee members who returned a ballot on the issue have ten days to reconsider their vote and change it, if applicable, based on the new information provided in the comments accompanying the votes. The Governance Program Committee will prescribe the form to be used to change a vote.

13.2.1.3 Default Ballots

Default ballots are used when lack of objection presumes approval. A default ballot fails in the presence of any objections. The voting period for default ballots is thirty days unless otherwise specified on the ballot.

13.2.1.4 Accelerated Letter Ballots

The Governance Program Committee may approve an accelerated letter ballot with a voting period of less than thirty days. An accelerated ballot may not be issued for final approval of a draft Governance Assessment. Failure to vote on an accelerated letter ballot will not affect membership privileges where voting is a requirement for membership.

13.2.1.5 Report of Final Letter Ballot Results

The final result of voting on letter ballots will be reported to the membership of the Committee that conducted the ballot immediately upon completion of the letter ballot action. Although negative votes without comments are not counted in determining whether the ballot passed, these votes will be recorded in the report of results. During the balloting period, all votes will be a matter of confidence between the Chair and whoever is tallying the votes.

The report of voting on personnel ballots will only state that the candidate has (or has not) received the required approval.

No tallies will be given, no reconsideration ballots will be conducted, no negatives will be distributed, and no members will be placed in jeopardy for failure to respond where voting is a requirement for membership.

13.2.2 Definition of Criteria for Approval

The following definitions apply to subgroups.

13.2.2.1 Majority

For meeting votes, a majority is defined as approval by more than half of the members voting; abstentions are excluded when determining whether a majority has been satisfied. For letter ballot votes, a majority is defined as approval by more than half of the members eligible to vote, excluding abstentions.

13.2.2.2 Super Majority Voting Rule

The super-majority voting rule is defined as:

- Approval by at least two-thirds of those voting YES or NO, and
- Approval by a majority of the voting membership. That is, the threshold is not affected by the number of members present at the meeting for a meeting vote.

13.3 File Retention

The Governance Program Committee and all contained subcommittees and boards share a document register. All other subgroups maintain their own document registers. Owners of Document Registers must register, control, and distribute documents. The original, full-size reproducible copy, or electronic copy of each membership list, minutes, or document will be submitted to the Governance Program Committee for file retention.

At least annually, a copy of each Subgroup's document register must also be sent to the Governance Program Committee for file retention.

Records concerning new, revised or reaffirmed Governance Assessments will be retained for one complete Governance Assessment's cycle, or until the Governance Assessment is revised. Records concerning withdrawn Governance Assessments will be retained for at least five years from the date of withdrawal.

13.4 Training

13.4.1 Officer Training

Training of Governance Program Committee chairs, elected Vice-chairs, and project editors is mandatory within one year of appointment. Officers of Maintenance Communities of Interest who have already received this training need not be trained again. Under certain circumstances, training may be waived for experienced officers. Requests for such a waiver should be sent to the Governance Program Committee for consideration. The Governance

Program Committee, in consultation with the Governance Program Committee, may choose to waive the training requirement after consideration of conditions including the following:

- The officer has attended training at least once.
- The officer has served at least one term and demonstrates an exceptional knowledge of, and compliance with, the procedures; e.g., by conducting training sessions, etc.
- The Governance Program Committee records confirm compliance with the administrative requirements within this document (e.g., membership updates, complete Community of Interest archives, etc.).
- There have not been significant changes in the relevant procedures, or the officer has demonstrated a thorough knowledge of the significant changes.

The Governance Program Committee will develop the training materials, and schedule and provide the training sessions. Prospective officers and other interested parties are also encouraged to attend these sessions.

13.4.2 Community of Interest Training

Each newly formed Community of Interest will establish time on its first agenda prior to conducting any technical business for presentation of an overview on the Community of Interest and its procedures. A representative from the Governance Program Committee will provide this presentation.

Additionally, all Communities of Interest are encouraged to arrange periodically (e.g., every two years) for training by a representative from the Governance Program Committee. Arrangements for this training should be made in conjunction with scheduled Community of Interest meetings.

13.5 Fees

13.5.1 Service Fees

Service fees are those fees necessary for the good order and operation of the entire Governance Program.

The Governance Program Committee service fees are not refundable. Members of Maintenance Communities of Interest are exempted from paying service fees.

The Governance Program Committee will determine the required service fees that will be required to operate the entire Governance Program. These services fees will be allocated to the various subgroups of the Governance Program as the Governance Program Committee deems appropriate. Timely payment (90 days from invoiced service-fees) will be required to continue membership in any Governance Program subgroup.

13.5.2 Subgroup Fees

13.5.2.1 General Rules

If a Subgroup finds it necessary to collect funds to pay for services to progress the work of the Subgroup, the Subgroup members will agree in advance to the collection of such a fee. Fee amounts will be subject to Subgroup approval. Any changes to set fees also will be approved by the Subgroup. All such fees are required to be approved by the Governance Program Committee.

13.5.2.2 Reporting Requirements

A financial report will be made a standing agenda item of the Subgroup and be included in the meeting's minutes if any Subgroup fees are assessed to the membership of the Subgroup. The financial report will include a statement of funds received, disbursed, outstanding debits and receivables, and the current balance. Each report will have an attachment that itemizes each individual collection and disbursement for the service(s) rendered and lists the individual(s) or organization(s) providing the agreed to service(s).

As a part of its annual report, the Subgroup will include a financial statement providing a summary of the total receivables, total disbursements, and the current balance for the reporting period.

13.5.3 Document Distribution Subscription Fees

Subgroups may make their documents available to their members through the Document Distribution Program that entails the assessment of subscription fees. In order to participate in the program, the Subgroup Chair will follow the policy established by the Governance Program Committee.

13.6 Reports and Review

13.6.1 Annual Reports

In order to maintain the management continuity of the entire Governance Program, and to keep the Governance Assessments Development Board informed on matters pertaining to the overall organization, membership, management, and policy, Subgroup Chairs will submit an annual report. This Annual Report Guide will be delivered to the Governance Assessments Development Board for review on a time schedule developed by the Governance Assessments Development Board.

13.7 Finance Management

13.7.1 Approved Uses of Subgroup Funds

Several of the subgroups may find it necessary to collect funds to pay for services to progress work. This section sets forth the policy for subgroups to establish, collect, disburse, maintain and account for such funds. Funds collected under this policy are restricted to the following use(s):

- Meeting room rental.
- Meeting refreshments.

- Current meeting document reproduction.
- Per meeting rental of audio-visual, computer and/or office equipment rental.
- Contracting for professional meeting planner.
- Bonding fees for Subgroup Chair and Treasurer.
- Purchase of durable goods (e.g., projectors, LANs, peripherals, etc.).

All purchased items must be approved by the Governance Program Committee in advance of purchase.

13.7.2 Establishment of the Subgroup Fee

A subgroup will only establish a subgroup fee by issuing a letter ballot that explains the need for and use of a fee, along with the initial fee to be charged. The letter ballot establishing the fund will also document the subgroup procedures for collecting, disbursing and administering these funds. The letter ballot will pass by a super-majority vote for the subgroup fee to be established.

13.7.3 Participation

Because subgroup fees can only be instituted to support meeting-related expenses, fees should be determined based on the number of persons participating. If a member has not paid all authorized subgroup fees for all principal and alternate members desiring to participate in a meeting, the member will be considered to have failed to attend the meeting. The member's voting privileges would be subject to the rules for membership in good standing. The subgroup may grant exceptions by subgroup super-majority vote. If the subgroup fee is established for the purchase of durable goods, the fee will be paid by all voting members. The total purchase amount should be divided equally among all voting members.

13.7.4 Changes to the Fee

Changes to the fee amount will be approved by a majority vote of the Subgroup at least thirty calendar days in advance of the assessment of any revised fee.

13.7.5 Subgroup Fund Administration

13.7.5.1 Treasurer Appointment

Any subgroup establishing a subgroup fee will have a Chair-appointed Treasurer. The Chair shall not serve as the Treasurer.

13.7.5.2 Reporting Requirements

13.7.5.2.1 Subgroup Reporting

The Treasurer will prepare a report following each meeting to be distributed with the minutes of that meeting. This report also will be a standing agenda item of the subgroup. This report should include:

- Names of individual Subgroup members (and any other applicable parties) who have or have not paid their assessed fees.
- All disbursements made, including the name of the individual(s) and/or organization(s) receiving payments.
- Debts outstanding.
- Receivables outstanding.
- The current balance of the Fund.

13.7.5.2.2 Annual Report

As part of its Annual Report, the subgroup will include a financial statement containing the following items:

- Total receipts.
- Receivables outstanding.
- Total disbursements.
- Debts outstanding.
- Current balance of the Fund.

The Annual Report will also include a copy of the procedures for administering the fund.

13.7.5.3 Account Management

- Bank accounts will be established for accrued funds that exceed $500.00. Note: If funds are collected for a one-time purchase of durable goods, this is not considered an accrual of funds and establishing a bank account is not necessary.

- Accrued funds will not exceed $25,000.00.

- Bank accounts will have the Treasurer and an elected officer as signatory authority. Only one signature may be required for banking purposes.

- Bank accounts being established will use the Governance Program Committee tax ID number for the account.

- Subgroups that are not required to establish a bank account will institute procedures for handling any surplus funds remaining at the end of a meeting.

13.7.5.4 Treasurer Duties

The Treasurer will be responsible for the following:

- Collection, disbursement and accounting of the Subgroup funds.

- Where appropriate, establish and maintain an account at a full service bank that is federally insured by the FDIC.

- Maintain a file of all receipts, bank statements, invoices, interest and other pertinent documents. The period of retention for this file will be five years. The file will be made available for inspection by any member of the subgroup, the subgroup's parent's officers, or the Chair of the Governance Program Committee upon request.

- Durable goods purchased on behalf of the subgroup, including maintaining an inventory of durable goods and reporting it to the Governance Program Committee.

13.7.5.5 Bonding

Any persons with signature authority over a subgroup bank account will be bonded in the amount of $25,000.00 each. Subgroups not using bank accounts may also have their Treasurer bonded. Bonding will be obtained through the Governance Program Committee prior to the collection of any funds. Bonding fees will be reimbursed from the subgroup funds.

13.7.6 Dissolution of the Subgroup Fund

A fund will be dissolved in one of two ways:

- By a subgroup Letter Ballot receiving super-majority approval; or

- Disbandment of the subgroup.

In either case, a final financial statement will be distributed to the subgroup members and the Governance Program Committee. Any remaining balance in the fund will be signed over to the Governance Program Committee by the subgroup Chair and/or Treasurer for deposit into the Governance Program equity account. If any durable goods are held by the subgroup, the Treasurer will turn them over to the Governance Program Committee. If the subgroup dissolved the fund but did not disband, it may request to retain the durable goods; otherwise, the Governance Program Committee may retain the durable goods, offer the goods to other Governance Program subgroups, or may dispose of the goods as it sees fit. Any proceeds will be deposited in the Governance Program equity account.

13.7.7 The Community of Interest Equity Account

The Governance Program equity account serves as a financial fund into which excess revenues (derived primarily from Governance Program Committee Dues and Fees) over expenses could be deposited. Periodic review of the account is done through reports by the Governance Program Committee. The funds held in this account are to be used for such purposes as meeting expenses when such expenses exceed revenues in any given fiscal year(s), not anticipated within the current fiscal year budget. Use of the Equity Account funds will require prior approval by the Governance Program Committee. No set figure is required to be maintained within the Equity Account. However, if the account exceeds six months of the Governance Program Committee operating expenses or the account is depleted to a balance below two month's operating expenses, the equity account should be reexamined by the Governance Program Committee in light of the current Service Fees.

13.7.8 Special Events

In order for the Governance Program subgroup to evaluate and grant its sponsorship of a subgroup special activity/event, a business plan that contains the information set forth in Table 48 must be provided.

Item	Business Plan Component	Example Response
1	Sponsoring the Subgroup	Database Study Group
2	Additionally involved Subgroups	Other Subgroups having an interest in object-oriented systems standards. The Chairs of the H2, Database, and X3T3, ODP, have indicated that their Communities of Interest are planning to participate.
3	Title of the activity/event	Objects in Data Management
4	Activity/Event date	January 14-15, <calendar year>
5	Activity/Event location	Grand Hotel, Anaheim, CA
6	Type of activity/event (e.g., symposium, conference, publication, database)	Conference
7	Description and purpose of the activity/event	The conference will bring together representatives of subgroups, other Governance Assessments groups and developers of object-oriented database management systems. Through formal presentations of input papers, general discussion sessions and ad hoc groups, the participants will compare the directions of the various Governance Assessments bodies relative to technological advances. Areas of potential divergence will be investigated and recommended actions will be identified.
8	Type and number of participants anticipated	Approximately 100 standards developers, implementors and users of object-oriented database systems.
9	Expected benefits to participants	The conference will provide the opportunity for individuals to present their contributions on object-oriented database technology and standardization, provide a forum for exchange of information and generally raise the participants awareness of current and planned standardization activities.
10	Expected benefits to the Community of Interest in sponsoring this activity/event	In addition to the benefit of having the Community of Interest's name associated with this conference, the conference will bring together various Community of Interest representatives (both from the Community of Interest and other groups) to

Item	Business Plan Component	Example Response
		share plans, etc.
11	What benefits/opportunities missed if the Community of Interest does not sponsor/authorize this activity/event	As the conference is intended to investigate areas of potential conflict among Governance Assessments developing groups, this information, which could help avoid future problems in the Governance Assessments approval process, would not otherwise be available.
12	Who will oversee the planning of the activity/event	The XYZ Corporation has volunteered to oversee the planning, which includes making hotel arrangements, providing a conference coordinator prior to and during the conference, handling registration, processing input papers and publishing the proceedings of the conference. A letter from XYZ Corporation indicating their sponsorship of this event is attached.
13	One-time or anticipated recurring event? (Note: A separate business plan and approval will be required for each occurrence)	This is a one-time event. Future conferences may be planned on related or other topics based on the success of this conference. It is understood that separate business plans and approval will be required for any future events.
14.	Financial and Staffing Considerations	The cost of meeting rooms, refreshments and copying at the meeting are the anticipated expenses. XYZ Corporation has agreed to cover other associated costs, e.g. conference coordinator, publication of proceedings, etc.
14.1	What expenses are anticipated for this activity/event	The cost of meeting rooms, refreshments and copying at the meeting are the anticipated expenses. XYZ Corporation has agreed to cover other associated costs, e.g., conference coordinator, publication of proceedings, etc.
14.2	Will this be a profit, loss or break-even event	The event is intended to be break-even; however, subsequent sales of the proceedings could generate a profit.
14.3	Who will fund the costs for this activity/event: (i.e., How much of the costs will be borne by the participants	The meeting expenses are intended to be covered by a registration fee. The meeting expenses will be negotiated so that they can be covered by a registration fee of not more than $100. The exact fee

Item	Business Plan Component	Example Response
	and how did you calculate this number? Do you request Governance Program Committee funding? Do you have other funding?)	will be determined at the hotel registration cut-off date approximately two months prior to the event.
14.4	Is the Governance Program Committee time and personnel necessary for the activity/event	No. However, arrangements will need to be made for the on-going sale of the proceedings after the conference.
14.5	If "YES", provide rationale for staff involvement (include estimate of staff time and travel expense)	Not applicable
14.6	Are there any provisions to cancel activity/event due to lack of interest	At the time of the hotel registration cut-off date, a final decision will be made on holding the conference. The hotel will be made aware of this during arrangement negotiations.
14.7	If proceedings are published, what is the publication plan? (i.e., Who will print them? Who will sell them? Who will hold the copyright?)	XYZ Corporation will print the proceedings. It is anticipated that the Governance Program will hold the copyright and handle the sale and distribution of the proceedings through a currently utilized (or new) service bureau. The Governance Program Committee should determine the best means for handling the sales and distribution.

Table 48. Subgroup Event Business Plan Components.

13.8 Membership in Good Standing

A member of a subgroup is in good standing if and only if they are current on their service fees, their subgroup's fees, attendance rules, and letter ballot voting.

Members are warned if any fee is unpaid beyond 30 days of invoice tender. A member's standing is in jeopardy if the fee is unpaid between 60 and 90 days. A member is terminated from voting privileges if a fee is unpaid after 90 days.

Members are warned if they miss two out of three successive meetings. If they miss the next meeting then their voting privileges are terminated.

Members are warned if they fail to return two out of three letter ballots. If they miss the next letter ballot then their voting privileges are terminated.

13.9 Rules Summary

Rules are bought out only when there is no other choice. At least that is the intention of the rules contained in this chapter. Because the impact of the cost of a Governance Assessment is so significant, then the actions of a committee regarding Governance Assessment's development must be above reproach. All meetings, change proposals, voting, the application of changes to a Governance Assessment must all be very carefully governed so that in the event of a dispute it can be quickly resolved not only to the satisfaction of the majority but also to the organization that has brought the dispute forward.

13.10 Questions and Exercises

1. Rules, rules, rules. Everybody's got to have rules. Why? What is the likely effect of creating and managing a Governance Program without rules? What will be the effect on the organizations, projects, products, and achievements?

2. The opening section of this Chapter has 8 classes of rules. How would these classes of rules address issues that arise in any Governance Community of Interest setting?

3. Section 13.1 enumerates five different sets of rules for meetings. If these rules are followed, what are the chances for orderly meetings? If good, why? If not good, why not?

4. Carefully review the meeting rules and compare and contrast the set of rules with characteristics of good and bad meetings that occur in your enterprise. What are the similarities and differences? How do the differences affect good order and progress?

5. Given a meeting of 25 staff over three days, and a burdened rate of $100 per

hour per staff member, meetings cost about $60,000 each not counting preparation time, travel, per-diem, meeting facility expenses and the like. What is there to show from meetings that are poorly run versus expertly run as opposed to meetings that are run like well-oiled machines with agendas, papers, crisp decision making and the like?

6. Carefully review the rules for voting in Section 13.2. Are they adequate? Do they cover all the necessary situations? How many situations have you encountered when there were disputes over when something was settled or not? Would the rules in these sections have dealt with these situations?

7. Review Section 13.2.2.1. Does that cover the rules necessary for a decision? Contrast that with a Super Majority decision in Section 13.2.2.2. When should one method of decision be used over the other? Should the Super Majority decision rule be for every committee action? Which ones? What is the criteria for determining which?

8. The world is run by the Golden Rule. He who has the gold, rules. Carefully review Section 13.5, and 13.7. How do the rules contained in these sections relate to the other Finance sections, that is, Sections 8.2.3 and 9.2.5 support each other. How can a Governance Program operate efficiently or effectively without adequate finances and finance management.

9. Section 13.7.8 sets out the description and plan for Special Events. Is the information required for the plan adequate? What is missing and what would be the effect of the missing information on the planning and execution of the special event?

Appendix
Assessment Processes

31. Business Event Assessment[11]

31.1. Assess Business Event
31.1.1. Assess Business Events
31.1.1. Assess Identify artifacts that bear on Business Event documents.
31.1.1.1. Identify the appropriate set of Business Event documents.
31.1.1.1.1. Review Business Event documents.
31.1.1.1.2. Review scope and business problem related documentation.
31.1.1.1.3. Identify the Business Events that are defined and captured.
31.1.1.1.4. Identify the Business Events related work products.
31.1.1.2. For each Business Event related work product:
31.1.1.2.1. Identify the relevant components, that is, Business Event Cycles, Business Event Calendar Cycles, Business Information Systems.
31.1.1.2.2. Identify the description for each interrelated Business Event component.
31.1.2. Perform the Assessment.
31.1.2.1. Assess each Business Event.
31.1.2.1.1. Assess the accuracy, quality and completeness of each Business Event with respect to the business requirements.
31.1.2.1.2. Assess whether Business Events are able to be inferred from business requirements, and if not whether business requirements or Business Events need to be enhanced.
31.1.2.2. Assess whether the Business Events are properly identified and are appropriately engineered to address a Business Event project.
31.1.2.2.1. Assess whether all the Business Events have been delivered in terms of components, instances, and stored metadata work products.
31.1.2.2.2. Assess whether all the Business Events have been properly detailed as to content, description, methodology, evaluation, presentation, and delivery work steps.
31.1.2.2.3. Assess whether all the Business Events have been properly allocated sufficient unit effort estimates.
31.1.2.2.4. Assess whether all the Business Events have been properly allocated sufficient quantity of units that have to be developed.
31.1.2.2.5. Assess whether all the Business Events have been properly allocated work environment factors to determine an accurate estimate of required resources.

---

[11]. The number starts with 31 because these data are to be stored in the Metabase System module, Enterprise Project Management, and "31" is the appropriate starting number.

31.1.2.2.6. Assess whether all the Business Events have been properly allocated work accomplishment and recording functions necessary to support earned value reporting.
31.1.2.2.7. Assess whether all the Business Events have been properly allocated metadata recording effort to ensure that all interrelationships are properly recorded into the Metabase System database.
31.1.2.3. Assign the risk level associated with each Business Event not properly constructed.
31.1.3. Determine the findings and create draft assessment report.
31.1.4. Present the findings and revise draft assessment report.
31.1.5. Create final assessment report and deliver to the auditing organization.

31.2. Assess Business Event Cycle.
31.2.1. Identify artifacts that bear on the assessment.
31.2.1.1. Identify the appropriate set of Business Event Cycles documents.
31.2.1.1.1. Review Business Event Cycle documents.
31.2.1.1.2. Review scope and business problem related documentation.
31.2.1.1.3. Identify the Business Event Cycles that are defined and captured.
31.2.1.1.4. Identify the Business Event Cycles related work products.
31.2.1.2. For each Business Event Cycle related work product assessment:.
31.2.1.2.1. Identify the relevant components, that is, business events and Business Event Calendar Cycles.
31.2.1.2.2. Identify the description for each interrelated Business Event Cycle component.
31.2.2. Perform the assessment.
31.2.2.1. Assess each Business Event Cycle.
31.2.2.1.1. Assess the accuracy, quality and completeness of each Business Event Cycle with respect to the business requirements.
31.2.2.1.2. Assess whether Business Event Cycles are able to be inferred from business requirements, and if not whether business requirements or Business Event Cycles need to be enhanced.
31.2.2.2. Assess whether the Business Event Cycles are properly identified and are appropriately engineered to address a Business Event Cycle project.
31.2.2.2.1. Assess whether all the Business Event Cycles have been delivered in terms of components, instances, and stored metadata work products.
31.2.2.2.2. Assess whether all the Business Event Cycles have been properly detailed as to content, description, methodology, evaluation, presentation, and delivery work steps.
31.2.2.2.3. Assess whether all the Business Event Cycles have been properly allocated sufficient unit effort estimates.
31.2.2.2.4. Assess whether all the Business Event Cycles have been properly allocated sufficient quantity of units that have to be developed.

31.2.2.2.5. Assess whether all the Business Event Cycles have been properly allocated work environment factors to determine an accurate estimate of required resources.
31.2.2.2.6. Assess whether all the Business Event Cycles have been properly allocated work accomplishment and recording functions necessary to support earned value reporting.
31.2.2.2.7. Assess whether all the Business Event Cycles have been properly allocated metadata recording effort to ensure that all interrelationships are properly recorded into the Metabase System database.
31.2.2.3. Assign the risk level associated with each Business Event Cycle not properly constructed.
31.2.3. Determine the findings and create draft assessment report.
31.2.4. Present the findings and revise draft assessment report.
31.2.5. Create final assessment report and deliver to the auditing organization.

31.3. Assess Business Event Cycle Structure
31.3.1. Identify artifacts that bear on the assessment.
31.3.1.1. Identify the appropriate set of Business Event Cycle Structures.
31.3.1.1.1. Review Business Event Cycle Structure documents.
31.3.1.1.2. Review scope and business problem related documentation.
31.3.1.1.3. Identify the Business Event Cycle Structures that are defined and captured.
31.3.1.1.4. Identify the Business Event Cycle Structures related work products.
31.3.1.2. For each Business Event Cycle Structure related work product assessment:
31.3.1.2.1. Identify the relevant component.
31.3.1.2.2. Identify the description for each interrelated Business Event Cycle Structure component.
31.3.2. Perform the assessment.
31.3.2.1. Assess each Business Event Cycle Structure.
31.3.2.1.1. Assess the accuracy, quality and completeness of each Business Event Cycle Structure with respect to the business requirements.
31.3.2.1.2. Assess whether Business Event Cycle Structures are able to be inferred from business requirements, and if not whether business requirements or Business Event Cycle Structures need to be enhanced.
31.3.2.1.3. Assess whether each Business Event Cycle Structure hierarchy/network is properly specified, and that all Business Event Cycle Structure names and descriptions are well defined, non-overlapping, and have been formally approved.
31.3.2.2. Assess whether the Business Event Cycle Structures are properly identified and are appropriately engineered to address a Business Event Cycle Structure project.

31.3.2.2.1. Assess whether all the Business Event Cycles Structures have been delivered in terms of components, instances, and stored metadata work products.
31.3.2.2.2. Assess whether all the Business Event Cycles Structures have been properly detailed as to content, description, methodology, evaluation, presentation, and delivery work steps.
31.3.2.2.3. Assess whether all the Business Event Cycles Structures have been properly allocated sufficient unit effort estimates.
31.3.2.2.4. Assess whether all the Business Event Cycles Structures have been properly allocated sufficient quantity of units that have to be developed.
31.3.2.2.5. Assess whether all the Business Event Cycles Structures have been properly allocated work environment factors to determine an accurate estimate of required resources.
31.3.2.2.6. Assess whether all the Business Event Cycles Structures have been properly allocated work accomplishment and recording functions necessary to support earned value Business Event Cycles.
31.3.2.2.7. Assess whether all the Business Event Cycles Structures have been properly allocated metadata recording effort to ensure that all interrelationships are properly recorded into the Metabase System database.
31.3.2.3. Assign the risk level associated with each Business Event Cycle Structure not properly constructed.
31.3.3. Determine the findings and create draft assessment Business Event Cycle.
31.3.4. Present the findings and revise draft assessment Business Event Cycle.
31.3.5. Create final assessment report Business Event Cycle and deliver to the auditing organization.

31.4. Assess Calendar Cycle.
31.4.1. Identify artifacts that bear on the assessment.
31.4.1.1. Identify the appropriate set of Calendar Cycle documents.
31.4.1.1.1. Review Calendar Cycle documents.
31.4.1.1.2. Review scope and business problem related documentation.
31.4.1.1.3. Identify the Calendar Cycles that are defined and captured.
31.4.1.1.4. Identify the Calendar Cycle related work products.
31.4.1.2. For each Calendar Cycles related work product assessment:
31.4.1.2.1. Identify the relevant components, that is, Business Events and Business Event cycles.
31.4.1.2.2. Identify the description for each interrelated Calendar Cycle component.
31.4.2. Perform the assessment.
31.4.2.1. Assess each Calendar Cycle.
31.4.2.1.1. Assess the accuracy, quality and completeness of each Calendar Cycle with respect to the business requirements.

31.4.2.1.2. Assess whether Calendar Cycles are able to be inferred from business requirements, and if not whether business requirements or Calendar Cycles need to be enhanced.

31.4.2.2. Assess whether each Calendar Cycle is addressed by one or more WBS as may be appropriate.

31.4.2.2.1. Assess whether all the Calendar Cycles have been delivered in terms of components, instances, and stored metadata work products.

31.4.2.2.2. Assess whether all the Calendar Cycles have been properly detailed as to content, description, methodology, evaluation, presentation, and delivery work steps.

31.4.2.2.3. Assess whether all the Calendar Cycles have been properly allocated sufficient unit effort estimates.

31.4.2.2.4. Assess whether all the Calendar Cycles have been properly allocated sufficient quantity of units that have to be developed.

31.4.2.2.5. Assess whether all the Calendar Cycles have been properly allocated work environment factors to determine an accurate estimate of required resources.

31.4.2.2.6. Assess whether all the Calendar Cycles have been properly allocated work accomplishment and recording functions necessary to support earned value reporting.

31.4.2.2.7. Assess whether all the Calendar Cycles have been properly allocated metadata recording effort to ensure that all interrelationships are properly recorded into the Metabase System database.

31.4.2.3. Assign the risk level associated with each Calendar Cycle not properly constructed.

31.4.3. Determine the findings and create draft assessment report.

31.4.4. Present the findings and revise draft assessment report.

31.4.5. Create final assessment report and deliver to the auditing organization.

31.5. Assess Calendar Cycle Structure

31.5.1. Identify artifacts that bear on the assessment.

31.5.1.1. Identify the appropriate set of Calendar Cycle Structures.

31.5.1.1.1. Review Calendar Cycle Structure documents.

31.5.1.1.2. Review scope and business problem related documentation

31.5.1.1.3. Identify the Calendar Cycle Structures that are defined and captured.

31.5.1.1.4. Identify the Calendar Cycle Structures related work products.

31.5.1.2. For each Calendar Cycle Structure related work product assessment:

31.5.1.2.1. Identify the relevant component.

31.5.1.2.2. Identify the description for each interrelated Calendar Cycle Structure component.

31.5.2. Perform the assessment.

31.5.2.1. Assess each Calendar Cycle Structure.

31.5.2.1.1. Assess the accuracy, quality and completeness of each Calendar Cycle Structure with respect to the business requirements.
31.5.2.1.2. Assess whether Calendar Cycle Structures are able to be inferred from business requirements, and if not whether business requirements or Calendar Cycle Structures need to be enhanced.
31.5.2.1.3. Assess whether each Calendar Cycle Structure hierarchy/network is properly specified, and that all Calendar Cycle Structures names and descriptions are well defined, non-overlapping, and have been formally approved.
31.5.2.2. Assess whether the Calendar Cycle Structures are properly identified and are appropriately engineered to address a Calendar Cycle Structure project.
31.5.2.2.1. Assess whether all the Calendar Cycle Structures have been delivered in terms of components, instances, and stored metadata work products.
31.5.2.2.2. Assess whether all the Calendar Cycle Structures have been properly detailed as to content, description, methodology, evaluation, presentation, and delivery work steps.
31.5.2.2.3. Assess whether all the Calendar Cycle Structures have been properly allocated sufficient unit effort estimates.
31.5.2.2.4. Assess whether all the Calendar Cycle Structures have been properly allocated sufficient quantity of units that have to be developed.
31.5.2.2.5. Assess whether all the Calendar Cycle Structures have been properly allocated work environment factors to determine an accurate estimate of required resources.
31.5.2.2.6. Assess whether all the Calendar Cycle Structures have been properly allocated work accomplishment and recording functions necessary to support earned value reporting.
31.5.2.2.7. Assess whether all the Calendar Cycle Structures have been properly allocated metadata recording effort to ensure that all interrelationships are properly recorded into the Metabase System database.
31.5.2.3. Assign the risk level associated with each Calendar Cycle Structure not properly constructed.
31.5.3. Determine the findings and create draft assessment report.
31.5.4. Present the findings and revise draft assessment report.
31.5.5. Create final assessment report and deliver to the auditing organization.

31.6. Assess Business Event Business Event Cycle.
31.6.1. Identify artifacts that bear on the assessment.
31.6.1.1. Identify the appropriate set of Business Event Cycle documents.
31.6.1.1.1. Review Business Event Cycle documents.
31.6.1.1.2. Review scope and business problem related documentation.
31.6.1.1.3. Identify the Business Event Cycles that are defined and captured.

31.6.1.1.4. Identify the Business Event Cycle related work products.
31.6.1.2. For each Business Event Cycle related work product assessment:
31.6.1.2.1. Identify the relevant components, that is, Business Events and Business Information Systems.
31.6.1.2.2. Identify the description for each Business Event Cycle.
31.6.2. Perform the assessment.
31.6.2.1. Assess each Business Event Cycle.
31.6.2.1.1. Assess the accuracy, quality and completeness of each Business Event Cycle with respect to the business requirements.
31.6.2.1.2. Assess whether Business Event Cycle are able to be inferred from business requirements, and if not whether business requirements or Business Event Cycle need to be enhanced.
31.6.2.1.3. Assess whether each Business Event Cycle pair properly associates one or more Business Events with one or more Business Information Systems.
31.6.2.1.4. Assess whether each Business Event Cycle pair is properly named and described.
31.6.2.2. Assess whether the Business Event Cycles are properly identified and are appropriately engineered to address a Business Event Cycle project.
31.6.2.2.1. Assess whether all the Business Event Cycle have been delivered in terms of components, instances, and stored metadata work products.
31.6.2.2.2. Assess whether all the Business Event Cycle have been properly detailed as to content, description, methodology, evaluation, presentation, and delivery work steps.
31.6.2.2.3. Assess whether all the Business Event Cycle have been properly allocated sufficient unit effort estimates.
31.6.2.2.4. Assess whether all the Business Event Cycle have been properly allocated sufficient quantity of units that have to be developed.
31.6.2.2.5. Assess whether all the Business Event Cycle have been properly allocated work environment factors to determine an accurate estimate of required resources.
31.6.2.2.6. Assess whether all the Business Event Cycle have been properly allocated work accomplishment and recording functions necessary to support earned value reporting.
31.6.2.2.7. Assess whether all the Business Event Cycle have been properly allocated metadata recording effort to ensure that all interrelationships are properly recorded into the Metabase System database.
31.6.2.3. Assign the risk level associated with each Business Event Cycle not properly constructed.
31.6.3. Determine the findings and create draft assessment report.
31.6.4. Present the findings and revise draft assessment report.
31.6.5. Create final assessment report and deliver to the auditing organization.

31.7. Assess Business Event Calendar Cycle.
31.7.1. Identify artifacts that bear on the assessment.
31.7.1.1. Identify the appropriate set of Calendar Cycle documents.
31.7.1.1.1. Review Business Event Calendar Cycle documents.
31.7.1.1.2. Review scope and business problem related documentation.
31.7.1.1.3. Identify the Business Event Calendar Cycle that are defined and captured.
31.7.1.1.4. Identify the Business Event Calendar Cycle related work products.
31.7.1.2. For each Business Event Calendar Cycle related work product assessment:
31.7.1.2.1. Identify the relevant components, that is, Business Events and Business Information Systems.
31.7.1.2.2. Identify the description for each Business Event Calendar Cycle.
31.7.2. Perform the assessment.
31.7.2.1. Assess each Business Event Calendar Cycle.
31.7.2.1.1. Assess the accuracy, quality and completeness of each Business Event Calendar Cycle with respect to the business requirements.
31.7.2.1.2. Assess whether Business Event Calendar Cycle are able to be inferred from business requirements, and if not whether business requirements or Business Event Calendar Cycle need to be enhanced.
31.7.2.1.3. Assess whether each Calendar Cycle pair properly associates one or more Business Events with one or more Calendar Cycles.
31.7.2.1.4. Assess whether each Business Event Calendar Cycle pair is properly named and described.
31.7.2.2. Assess whether the Business Event Calendar Cycles are properly identified and are appropriately engineered to address a Business Event Calendar Cycle project.
31.7.2.2.1. Assess whether all the Business Event Calendar Cycles have been delivered in terms of components, instances, and stored metadata work products.
31.7.2.2.2. Assess whether all the Business Event Calendar Cycles have been properly detailed as to content, description, methodology, evaluation, presentation, and delivery work steps.
31.7.2.2.3. Assess whether all the Business Event Calendar Cycles have been properly allocated sufficient unit effort estimates.
31.7.2.2.4. Assess whether all the Business Event Calendar Cycles have been properly allocated sufficient quantity of units that have to be developed.
31.7.2.2.5. Assess whether all the Business Event Calendar Cycles have been properly allocated work environment factors to determine an accurate estimate of required resources.
31.7.2.2.6. Assess whether all the Business Event Calendar Cycles have been properly allocated work accomplishment and recording functions necessary to support earned value reporting.
31.7.2.2.7. Assess whether all the Business Event Calendar Cycles have been

properly allocated metadata recording effort to ensure that all interrelationships are properly recorded into the Metabase System database.

31.7.2.3. Assign the risk level associated with each Business Event Calendar Cycle not properly constructed.

31.7.3. Determine the findings and create draft assessment report.

31.7.4. Present the findings and revise draft assessment report.

31.7.5. Create final assessment report and deliver to the auditing organization.

31.8. Assess Business Event Cycle.

31.8.1. Identify artifacts that bear on the assessment.

31.8.1.1. Identify the appropriate set of Business Event Cycle documents.

31.8.1.1.1. Review Business Event Cycle documents.

31.8.1.1.2. Review scope and business problem related documentation.

31.8.1.1.3. Identify the Business Event Cycles that are defined and captured.

31.8.1.1.4. Identify the Business Event Cycle related work products.

31.8.1.2. For each Business Event Cycle related work product assessment:

31.8.1.2.1. Identify the relevant components, that is, Business Events and Business Information Systems.

31.8.1.2.2. Identify the description for each Business Event Cycle.

31.8.2. Perform the assessment.

31.8.2.1. Assess each Business Event Cycle.

31.8.2.1.1. Assess the accuracy, quality and completeness of each Business Event Cycle with respect to the business requirements.

31.8.2.1.2. Assess whether Business Event Cycles are able to be inferred from business requirements, and if not whether business requirements or Business Event Cycle need to be enhanced.

31.8.2.1.3. Assess whether each Business Event Cycle pair properly associates one or more Business Events with one or more Business Information Systems.

31.8.2.1.4. Assess whether each Business Event Cycle pair is properly named and described.

31.8.2.2. Assess whether the Business Event Cycles are properly identified and are appropriately engineered to address a Business Event Cycle project.

31.8.2.2.1. Assess whether all the Business Event Cycles have been delivered in terms of components, instances, and stored metadata work products.

31.8.2.2.2. Assess whether all the Business Event Cycles have been properly detailed as to content, description, methodology, evaluation, presentation, and delivery work steps.

31.8.2.2.3. Assess whether all the Business Event Cycles have been properly allocated sufficient unit effort estimates.

31.8.2.2.4. Assess whether all the Business Event Cycles have been properly allocated sufficient quantity of units that have to be developed.

31.8.2.2.5. Assess whether all the Business Event Cycles have been properly allocated work environment factors to determine an accurate estimate of required resources.
31.8.2.2.6. Assess whether all the Business Event Cycles have been properly allocated work accomplishment and recording functions necessary to support earned value reporting.
31.8.2.2.7. Assess whether all the Business Event Cycles have been properly allocated metadata recording effort to ensure that all interrelationships are properly recorded into the Metabase System database.
31.8.2.3. Assign the risk level associated with each Business Event Cycle not properly constructed.
31.8.3. Determine the findings and create draft assessment report.
31.8.4. Present the findings and revise draft assessment report.
31.8.5. Create final assessment report and deliver to the auditing organization.

31.9. Assess Business Event Mission-Organization-Function.
31.9.1. Identify artifacts that bear on the assessment.
31.9.1.1. Identify the appropriate set of Business Event Mission-Organization-Function documents.
31.9.1.1.1. Review Business Event Mission-Organization-Function documents.
31.9.1.1.2. Review scope and business problem related documentation.
31.9.1.1.3. Identify the Business Event Mission-Organization-Functions that are defined and captured.
31.9.1.1.4. Identify the Business Event Mission-Organization-Function related work products.
31.9.1.2. For each Business Event Mission-Organization-Function related work product assessment:
31.9.1.2.1. Identify the relevant components, that is, Business Events and Mission-Organization- Functions.
31.9.1.2.2. Identify the description for each Business Event Mission-Organization-Function.
31.9.2. Perform the assessment.
31.9.2.1. Assess each Business Event Mission-Organization-Function.
31.9.2.1.1. Assess the accuracy, quality and completeness of each Business Event Mission- Organization-Function with respect to the business requirements.
31.9.2.1.2. Assess whether Business Event Mission-Organization-Functions are able to be inferred from business requirements, and if not whether business requirements or Business Event Mission-Organization-Functions need to be enhanced.
31.9.2.1.3. Assess whether each Business Event Mission-Organization-Function pair properly associates one or more Mission-Organization-Functions with one

or more Business Events.

31.9.2.1.4. Assess whether each Business Event Mission-Organization-Function pair is properly named and described.

31.9.2.2. Assess whether the Business Event Mission-Organization-Functions are properly identified and are appropriately engineered to address a Business Event Mission- Organization-Function project.

31.9.2.2.1. Assess whether all the Business Event Mission-Organization-Functions have been delivered in terms of components, instances, and stored metadata work products.

31.9.2.2.2. Assess whether all the Business Event Mission-Organization-Functions have been properly detailed as to content, description, methodology, evaluation, presentation, and delivery work steps.

31.9.2.2.3. Assess whether all the Business Event Mission-Organization-Functions have been properly allocated sufficient unit effort estimates.

31.9.2.2.4. Assess whether all the Business Event Mission-Organization-Functions have been properly allocated sufficient quantity of units that have to be developed.

31.9.2.2.5. Assess whether all the Business Event Mission-Organization-Functions have been properly allocated work environment factors to determine an accurate estimate of required resources.

31.9.2.2.6. Assess whether all the Business Event Mission-Organization-Functions have been properly allocated work accomplishment and recording functions necessary to support earned value reporting.

31.9.2.2.7. Assess whether all the Business Event Mission-Organization-Functions have been properly allocated metadata recording effort to ensure that all interrelationships are properly recorded into the Metabase System database.

31.9.2.3. Assign the risk level associated with each Business Event Mission-Organization-Function not properly constructed.

31.9.3. Determine the findings and create draft assessment report.

31.9.4. Present the findings and revise draft assessment report.

31.9.5. Create final assessment report and deliver to the auditing organization.

32. Business Information System Assessment

32.1. Assess Business Information System.
32.1.1. Identify artifacts that bear on the assessment.
32.1.1.1. Identify the appropriate set of Business Information Systems documents.
32.1.1.1.1. Review Business Information System documents.
32.1.1.1.2. Review scope and business problem related documentation.
32.1.1.1.3. Identify the Business Information Systems that are defined and captured.
32.1.1.1.4. Identify the Business Information Systems related work products.
32.1.1.2. For each Business Information Systems assessment:
32.1.1.2.1. Identify the relevant components, that is, Business Requirements, Data Integrity Rules, Database Objects, Resource Life Cycles, Use Cases, and User Acceptance Tests.
32.1.1.2.2. Identify the description for each interrelated Business Information System component.
32.1.2. Perform the assessment.
32.1.2.1. Assess each Business Information System.
32.1.2.1.1. Assess the accuracy, quality and completeness of each Business Information System with respect to the business requirements.
32.1.2.1.2. Assess whether Business Information Systems are able to be inferred from business requirements, and if not whether business requirements or Business Information Systems need to be enhanced.
32.1.2.1.3. Assess whether each Business Information System hierarchy is properly specified, and that all Business Information System names and descriptions are well defined, non-overlapping, and have been formally approved.
32.1.2.2. Assess whether the Business Information System is properly identified and are appropriately engineered to address a Business Information System project.
32.1.2.2.1. Assess whether all the Business Information Systems have been delivered in terms of components, instances, and stored metadata work products.
32.1.2.2.2. Assess whether all the Business Information Systems have been properly detailed as to content, description, methodology, evaluation, presentation, and delivery work steps.
32.1.2.2.3. Assess whether all the Business Information Systems have been properly allocated sufficient unit effort estimates.
32.1.2.2.4. Assess whether all the Business Information Systems have been properly allocated sufficient quantity of units that have to be developed.
32.1.2.2.5. Assess whether all the Business Information Systems have been properly allocated work environment factors to determine an accurate estimate of required resources.
32.1.2.2.6. Assess whether all the Business Information Systems have been properly

allocated work accomplishment and recording functions necessary to support earned value reporting.

32.1.2.2.7. Assess whether all the Business Information Systems have been properly allocated metadata recording effort to ensure that all interrelationships are properly recorded into the Metabase System database.

32.1.2.3. Assign the risk level associated with each Business Information System not properly constructed.

32.1.3. Determine the findings and create draft assessment report.

32.1.4. Present the findings and revise draft assessment report.

32.1.5. Create final assessment report and deliver to the auditing organization.

32.2. Assess Business Information System Context.

32.2.1. Identify artifacts that bear on the assessment.

32.2.1.1. Identify the appropriate set of Business Information System documents.

32.2.1.1.1. Review Business Information System documents.

32.2.1.1.2. Review scope and business problem related documentation.

32.2.1.1.3. Identify the Business Information System contexts that are defined and captured.

32.2.1.1.4. Identify the Business Information System context related work products.

32.2.1.2. For each Business Information System context related work product assessment:

32.2.1.2.1. Identify the relevant context components, that is, Level, Construction Method, Status, Application Type, Programming Language, Environment Type, Predominant User Class, and DBMS Environment.

32.2.1.2.2. Identify and Review the definition of the Business Information Systems context component.

32.2.2. Perform the assessment.

32.2.2.1. Assess each Business Information System context.

32.2.2.1.1. Assess the accuracy, quality and completeness of each Business Information System context with respect to the business requirements.

32.2.2.1.2. Assess whether Business Information System contexts are able to be inferred from business requirements, and if not whether business requirements or Business Information System contexts need to be enhanced.

32.2.2.2. Assess whether the Business Information System contexts are appropriately engineered to address a Business Information System context project.

32.2.2.2.1. Assess whether all the Business Information System contexts have been delivered in terms of components, instances, and stored metadata work products.

32.2.2.2.2. Assess whether all the Business Information System contexts have been properly detailed as to content, description, methodology, evaluation,

presentation, and delivery work steps.

32.2.2.2.3. Assess whether all the Business Information System contexts have been properly allocated sufficient unit effort estimates.

32.2.2.2.4. Assess whether all the Business Information System contexts have been properly allocated sufficient quantity of units that have to be developed.

32.2.2.2.5. Assess whether all the Business Information System contexts have been properly allocated work environment factors to determine an accurate estimate of required resources.

32.2.2.2.6. Assess whether all the Business Information System contexts have been properly allocated work accomplishment and recording functions necessary to support earned value reporting.

32.2.2.2.7. Assess whether all the Business Information System contexts have been properly allocated metadata recording effort to ensure that all interrelationships are properly recorded into the Metabase System database.

32.2.2.3. Assign the risk level associated with each Business Information System context not properly constructed.

32.2.3. Determine the findings and create draft assessment report.

32.2.4. Present the findings and revise draft assessment report.

32.2.5. Create final assessment report and deliver to the auditing organization.

32.3. Assess Business Information System Business Event.

32.3.1. Identify artifacts that bear on the assessment.

32.3.1.1. Identify the appropriate set of Business Information System Businesses Events documents.

32.3.1.1.1. Review Business Information System Businesses Events documents.

32.3.1.1.2. Review scope and business problem related documentation.

32.3.1.1.3. Identify the Business Information System Business Events that are defined and captured.

32.3.1.1.4. Identify the Business Information System Events related work products.

32.3.1.2. For each Business Information System Events related work product assessment:

32.3.1.2.1. Identify the relevant components, that is, Business Event, and Business Information System Business Event.

32.3.1.2.2. Identify the description for each interrelated Business Information System Business Event component.

32.3.2. Perform the assessment.

32.3.2.1. Assess each Business Information System Business Event.

32.3.2.1.1. Assess the accuracy, quality and completeness of each Business Information System Business Event with respect to the business requirements.

32.3.2.1.2. Assess whether Business Information System Business Events are able to be inferred from business requirements, and if not whether business requirements or Business Information System Businesses Events need to be enhanced.

32.3.2.1.3. Assess whether each Business Information System Business Event pair properly associates one or more Business Information Systems with one or more Business Events.

32.3.2.1.4. Assess whether each Business Information System Businesses Event pair is properly named and described.

32.3.2.2. Assess whether the Business Information System Business Event is properly identified and are appropriately engineered to address a Business Information System Business Event project.

32.3.2.2.2. Assess whether all the Business Information System Business Events have been delivered in terms of components, instances, and stored metadata work products.

32.3.2.2.2. Assess whether all the Business Information System Business Events have been properly detailed as to content, description, methodology, evaluation, presentation, and delivery work steps.

32.3.2.2.3. Assess whether all the Business Information System Business Events have been properly allocated sufficient unit effort estimates.

32.3.2.2.4. Assess whether all the Business Information System Business Events have been properly allocated sufficient quantity of units that have to be developed.

32.3.2.2.5. Assess whether all the Business Information System Business Events have been properly allocated work environment factors to determine an accurate estimate of required resources.

32.3.2.2.6. Assess whether all the Business Information System Business Events have been properly allocated work accomplishment and recording functions necessary to support earned value reporting.

32.3.2.2.7. Assess whether all the Business Information System Business Events have been properly allocated metadata recording effort to ensure that all interrelationships are properly recorded into the Metabase System database.

32.3.2.3. Assign the risk level associated with each Business Information System Businesses Event not properly constructed.

32.3.3. Determine the findings and create draft assessment report.

32.3.4. Present the findings and revise draft assessment report.

32.3.5. Create final assessment report and deliver to the auditing organization.

32.4. Assess Business Information System View.

32.4.1. Identify artifacts that bear on the assessment.

32.4.1.1. Identify the appropriate set of Business Information System View documents.

32.4.1.1.1. Review Business Information System View documents.

32.4.1.1.2. Review scope and business problem related documentation.
32.4.1.1.3. Identify the Business Information System Views that are defined and captured.
32.4.1.1.4. Identify the Business Information System View related work products.
32.4.1.2. For each Business Information System View related work product assessment:
32.4.1.2.1. Identify the relevant components, that is, Views, View Columns, and View Processes.
32.4.1.2.2. Identify the description for each interrelated Business Information System component.
32.4.2. Perform the assessment.
32.4.2.1. Assess each Business Information System View.
32.4.2.1.1. Assess the accuracy, quality and completeness of each Business Information System View with respect to the business requirements.
32.4.2.1.2. Assess whether Business Information System Views are able to be inferred from business requirements, and if not whether business requirements or Business Information System Views need to be enhanced.
32.4.2.1.3. Assess whether each Business Information System View pair properly associates one or more Business Information Systems with one or more Views.
32.4.2.1.4. Assess whether each Business Information System View pair is properly named and described.
32.4.2.2. Assess whether the Business Information System Views are properly identified and are appropriately engineered to address a Business Information System View project.
32.4.2.2.1. Assess whether all the Business Information System Views have been delivered in terms of components, instances, and stored metadata work products.
32.4.2.2.2. Assess whether all the Business Information System Views have been properly detailed as to content, description, methodology, evaluation, presentation, and delivery work steps.
32.4.2.2.3. Assess whether all the Business Information System Views have been properly allocated sufficient unit effort estimates.
32.4.2.2.4. Assess whether all the Business Information System Views have been properly allocated sufficient quantity of units that have to be developed.
32.4.2.2.5. Assess whether all the Business Information System Views have been properly allocated work environment factors to determine an accurate estimate of required resources.
32.4.2.2.6. Assess whether all the Business Information System Views have been properly allocated work accomplishment and recording functions necessary to support earned value reporting.
32.4.2.2.7. Assess whether all the Business Information System Views have been

properly allocated metadata recording effort to ensure that all interrelationships are properly recorded into the Metabase System database.

32.4.2.3. Assign the risk level associated with each Business Information System View not properly constructed.

32.4.3. Determine the findings and create draft assessment report.

32.4.4. Present the findings and revise draft assessment report.

32.4.5. Create final assessment report and deliver to the auditing organization.

32.5. Assess Business Information System Database Object.

32.5.1. Identify artifacts that bear on the assessment.

32.5.1.1. Identify the appropriate set of Business Information System Database Object documents.

32.5.1.1.1. Review Business Information System Database Object documents.

32.5.1.1.2. Review scope and business problem related documentation.

32.5.1.1.3. Identify the Business Information System Database Objects that are defined and captured.

32.5.1.1.4. Identify the Business Information System Database Object related work products.

32.5.1.2. For each Business Information System Database Object related work product assessment:

32.5.1.2.1. Identify the relevant components, that is, Business Information System, Database Objects.

32.5.1.2.2. Identify the description for each interrelated Business Information System component.

32.5.2. Perform the assessment.

32.5.2.1. Assess each Business Information System Database Object.

32.5.2.1.1. Assess the accuracy, quality and completeness of each Business Information System Database Object with respect to the business requirements.

32.5.2.1.2. Assess whether Business Information System Database Object are able to be inferred from business requirements, and if not whether business requirements or Business Information System Database Object need to be enhanced.

32.5.2.1.3. Assess whether each Business Information System Database Object pair properly associates one or more Business Information Systems with one or more Database Objects.

32.5.2.1.4. Assess whether each Business Information System Database Object pair is properly named and described.

32.5.2.2. Assess whether the Business Information System Database Object is properly identified and are appropriately engineered to address a Business Information System Database Object project.

32.5.2.2.1. Assess whether all the Business Information System Database Objects have been delivered in terms of components, instances, and stored metadata work products.

32.5.2.2.2. Assess whether all the Business Information System Database Objects have been properly detailed as to content, description, methodology, evaluation, presentation, and delivery work steps.

32.5.2.2.3. Assess whether all the Business Information System Database Objects have been properly allocated sufficient unit effort estimates.

32.5.2.2.4. Assess whether all the Business Information System Database Objects have been properly allocated sufficient quantity of units that have to be developed.

32.5.2.2.5. Assess whether all the Business Information System Database Objects have been properly allocated work environment factors to determine an accurate estimate of required resources.

32.5.2.2.6. Assess whether all the Business Information System Database Objects have been properly allocated work accomplishment and recording functions necessary to support earned value reporting.

32.5.2.2.7. Assess whether all the Business Information System Database Objects have been properly allocated metadata recording effort to ensure that all interrelationships are properly recorded into the Metabase System database.

32.5.2.4. Assign the risk level associated with each Business Information System Database Object not properly constructed.

32.5.3. Determine the findings and create draft assessment report.

32.5.4. Present the findings and revise draft assessment report.

32.5.5. Create final assessment report and deliver to the auditing organization.

32.6. Assess Business Information System Mission-Organization-Function.

32.6.1. Identify artifacts that bear on the assessment.

32.6.1.1. Identify the appropriate set of Business Information System Mission-Organization-Function documents.

32.6.1.1.1. Review Business Information System Mission-Organization-Function documents.

32.6.1.1.2. Review scope and business problem related documentation.

32.6.1.1.3. Identify the Business Information System Mission-Organization-Functions that are defined and captured.

32.6.1.1.4. Identify the Business Information Systems Mission-Organization-Functions related work products.

32.6.1.2. For each Business Information Systems Mission-Organization-Functions related work product assessment:

32.6.1.2.1. Identify the relevant components, that is, Business Information Systems, and Mission-Organization-Functions.

32.6.1.2.2. Identify the description for each interrelated Business Information System component.

32.6.2. Perform the assessment.

32.6.2.1. Assess each Business Information System Mission-Organization-Function.

32.6.2.1.1. Assess the accuracy, quality and completeness of each Business Information System Mission-Organization-Function with respect to the business requirements.

32.6.2.1.2. Assess whether Business Information System Mission-Organization-Functions are able to be inferred from business requirements, and if not whether business requirements or Business Information System Mission-Organization-Function need to be enhanced.

32.6.2.1.3. Assess whether each Business Information System Mission-Organization-Function pair properly associates one or more Business Information Systems with one or more Mission-Organization-Functions.

32.6.2.1.4. Assess whether each Business Information System Mission-Organization-Function pair is properly named and described.

32.6.2.2. Assess whether the Business Information Systems Mission-Organization-Functions are properly identified and are appropriately engineered to address a Business Information Systems Mission-Organization-Function project.

32.6.2.2.1 Assess whether all the Business Information Systems Mission-Organization-Functions have been delivered in terms of components, instances, and stored metadata work products.

32.6.2.2.2. Assess whether all the Business Information Systems Mission-Organization-Functions have been properly detailed as to content, description, methodology, evaluation, presentation, and delivery work steps.

32.6.2.2.3. Assess whether all the Business Information Systems Mission-Organization-Functions have been properly allocated sufficient unit effort estimates.

32.6.2.2.4. Assess whether all the Business Information Systems Mission-Organization-Functions have been properly allocated sufficient quantity of units that have to be developed.

32.6.2.2.5. Assess whether all the Business Information Systems Mission-Organization-Functions have been properly allocated work environment factors to determine an accurate estimate of required resources.

32.6.2.2.6. Assess whether all the Business Information Systems Mission-Organization-Functions have been properly allocated work accomplishment and recording functions necessary to support earned value reporting.

32.6.2.2.7. Assess whether all the Business Information Systems Mission-Organization-Functions have been properly allocated metadata recording effort to ensure that all interrelationships are properly recorded into the Metabase System database.

32.6.2.3. Assign the risk level associated with each Business Information Systems Mission-Organization-Function not properly constructed.

32.6.3. Determine the findings and create draft assessment report.

32.6.4. Present the findings and revise draft assessment report.

32.6.5. Create final assessment report and deliver to the auditing organization.

32.7. Assess Business Information System Data Integrity Rule.

32.7.1. Identify artifacts that bear on the assessment.

32.7.1.1. Identify the appropriate set of Business Information System Data Integrity Rule documents.

32.7.1.1.1. Review Business Information System Data Integrity Rule documents.

32.7.1.1.2. Review scope and business problem related documentation.

32.7.1.1.3. Identify the Business Information System Data Integrity Rules that are defined and captured.

32.7.1.1.4. Identify the Business Information System Data Integrity Rule related work products.

32.7.1.2. For each Business Information System Data Integrity Rule assessment:

32.7.1.2.1. Identify the relevant components, that is, Business Requirements, Data Integrity Rules, Database Objects, Resource Life Cycles, Use Cases, and User Acceptance Tests.

32.7.1.2.2. Identify the description for each interrelated Business Information System Data Integrity Rule component.

32.7.2. Perform the assessment.

32.7.2.1. Assess each Business Information System Data Integrity Rule.

32.7.2.1.1. Assess the accuracy, quality and completeness of each Business Information System Data Integrity Rule with respect to the business requirements.

32.7.2.1.2. Assess whether Business Information System Data Integrity Rules are able to be inferred from business requirements, and if not whether business requirements or Business Information System Data Integrity Rule need to be enhanced.

32.7.2.1.3. Assess whether each Business Information System Data Integrity Rule pair properly associates one or more Business Information Systems with one or more Data Integrity Rules.

32.7.2.1.4. Assess whether each Business Information System Data Integrity Rule pair is properly named and described.

32.7.2.2. Assess whether the Business Information System Data Integrity Rule is properly identified and are appropriately engineered to address a Business Information System Data Integrity Rule project.

32.7.2.2.1. Assess whether all the Business Information System Data Integrity Rules have been delivered in terms of components, instances, and stored metadata work products.

32.7.2.2.2. Assess whether all the Business Information System Data Integrity Rules have been properly detailed as to content, description, methodology, evaluation, presentation, and delivery work steps.

32.7.2.2.3. Assess whether all the Business Information System Data Integrity Rules have been properly allocated sufficient unit effort estimates.

32.7.2.2.4. Assess whether all the Business Information System Data Integrity Rules have been properly allocated sufficient quantity of units that have to be developed.

32.7.2.2.5. Assess whether all the Business Information System Data Integrity Rules have been properly allocated work environment factors to determine an accurate estimate of required resources.

32.7.2.2.6. Assess whether all the Business Information System Data Integrity Rules have been properly allocated work accomplishment and recording functions necessary to support earned value reporting.

32.7.2.2.7. Assess whether all the Business Information System Data Integrity Rules have been properly allocated metadata recording effort to ensure that all interrelationships are properly recorded into the Metabase System database.

32.7.2.5. Assign the risk level associated with each Business Information System Data Integrity Rule not properly constructed.

32.7.3. Determine the findings and create draft assessment report.

32.7.4. Present the findings and revise draft assessment report.

32.7.5. Create final assessment report and deliver to the auditing organization.

32.8. Assess Business Information System Resource Life Cycle Node.

32.8.1. Identify artifacts that bear on the assessment.

32.8.1.1. Identify the appropriate set of Business Information System Resource Life Cycle Node documents.

32.8.1.1.1. Review Business Information System Resource Life Cycle Node documents.

32.8.1.1.2. Review scope and business problem related documentation.

32.8.1.1.3. Identify the Business Information System Resource Life Cycle Nodes that are defined and captured.

32.8.1.1.4. Identify the Business Information System Resource Life Cycle Node related work products.

32.8.1.2. For each Business Information System Resource Life Cycle Node assessment:

32.8.1.2.1. Identify the relevant components, that is, Business Requirements, Data Integrity Rules, Database Objects, Resource Life Cycles, Use Cases, and User Acceptance Tests.

32.8.1.2.2. Identify the description for each interrelated Business Information System Resource Life Cycle Node component.

32.8.2. Perform the assessment.

32.8.2.1. Assess each Business Information System Resource Life Cycle Node.

32.8.2.1.1. Assess the accuracy, quality and completeness of each Business Information System Resource Life Cycle Node with respect to the business requirements.

32.8.2.1.2. Assess whether Business Information System Resource Life Cycle Nodes are able to be inferred from business requirements, and if not whether business requirements or Business Information System Resource Life Cycle Nodes need to be enhanced.

32.8.2.1.3. Assess whether each Business Information System Resource Life Cycle Node pair properly associates one or more Business Information Systems with one or more Resource Life Cycle Nodes.

32.8.2.1.4. Assess whether each Business Information System Resource Life Cycle Node pair is properly named and described.

32.8.2.2. Assess whether the Business Information System Resource Life Cycle Nodes are properly identified and are appropriately engineered to address a Business Information System Resource Life Cycle Node project.

32.8.2.2.1. Assess whether all the Business Information System Resource Life Cycle Nodes have been delivered in terms of components, instances, and stored metadata work products.

32.8.2.2.2. Assess whether all the Business Information System Resource Life Cycle Nodes have been properly detailed as to content, description, methodology, evaluation, presentation, and delivery work steps.

32.8.2.2.3. Assess whether all the Business Information System Resource Life Cycle Nodes have been properly allocated sufficient unit effort estimates.

32.8.2.2.4. Assess whether all the Business Information System Resource Life Cycle Nodes have been properly allocated sufficient quantity of units that have to be developed.

32.8.2.2.5. Assess whether all the Business Information System Resource Life Cycle Nodes have been properly allocated work environment factors to determine an accurate estimate of required resources.

32.8.2.2.6. Assess whether all the Business Information System Resource Life Cycle Nodes have been properly allocated work accomplishment and recording functions necessary to support earned value reporting.

32.8.2.2.7. Assess whether all the Business Information System Resource Life Cycle Nodes have been properly allocated metadata recording effort to ensure that all interrelationships are properly recorded into the Metabase System database.

32.8.2.3. Assign the risk level associated with each Business Information System Resource Life Cycle Node not properly constructed.

32.8.3. Determine the findings and create draft assessment report.
32.8.4. Present the findings and revise draft assessment report.
32.8.5. Create final assessment report and deliver to the auditing organization.

32.9. Assess Business Information System User Acceptance Test.
32.9.1. Identify artifacts that bear on the assessment.
32.9.1.1. Identify the appropriate set of Business Information System User Acceptance Test documents.
32.9.1.1.1. Review Business Information System User Acceptance Test documents.
32.9.1.1.2. Review scope and business problem related documentation.
32.9.1.1.3. Identify the Business Information System User Acceptance Tests that are defined and captured.
32.9.1.1.4. Identify the Business Information System User Acceptance Test related work products.
32.9.1.2. For each Business Information System User Acceptance Test assessment:
32.9.1.2.1. Identify the relevant components, that is, Business Requirements, Data Integrity Rules, Database Objects, Resource Life Cycles, Use Cases, and User Acceptance Tests.
32.9.1.2.2. Identify the description for each interrelated Business Information System component.
32.9.2. Perform the assessment.
32.9.2.1. Assess each Business Information System User Acceptance Test.
32.9.2.1.1. Assess the accuracy, quality and completeness of each Business Information System User Acceptance Test with respect to the business requirements.
32.9.2.1.2. Assess whether Business Information System User Acceptance Tests are able to be inferred from business requirements, and if not whether business requirements or Business Information System User Acceptance Tests need to be enhanced.
32.9.2.1.3. Assess whether each Business Information System User Acceptance Test pair properly associates one or more Business Information Systems with one or more User Acceptance Tests.
32.9.2.1.4. Assess whether each Business Information System User Acceptance Test pair is properly named and described.
32.9.2.4. Assess whether the Business Information System User Acceptance Tests are properly identified and are appropriately engineered to address a Business Information System User Acceptance Test project.
32.9.2.4.1. Assess whether all the Business Information System User Acceptance Tests have been delivered in terms of components, instances, and stored metadata work products.
32.9.2.4.2. Assess whether all the Business Information System User Acceptance Tests have been properly detailed as to content, description,

methodology, evaluation, presentation, and delivery work steps.

32.9.2.4.3. Assess whether all the Business Information System User Acceptance Tests have been properly allocated sufficient unit effort estimates.

32.9.2.4.4. Assess whether all the Business Information System User Acceptance Tests have been properly allocated sufficient quantity of units that have to be developed.

32.9.2.4.5. Assess whether all the Business Information System User Acceptance Tests have been properly allocated work environment factors to determine an accurate estimate of required resources.

32.9.2.4.6. Assess whether all the Business Information System User Acceptance Tests have been properly allocated work accomplishment and recording functions necessary to support earned value reporting.

32.9.2.4.7. Assess whether all the Business Information System User Acceptance Tests have been properly allocated metadata recording effort to ensure that all interrelationships are properly recorded into the Metabase System database.

32.9.2.5. Assign the risk level associated with each Business Information System User Acceptance Test not properly constructed.

32.9.3. Determine the findings and create draft assessment report.

32.9.4. Present the findings and revise draft assessment report.

32.9.5. Create final assessment report and deliver to the auditing organization.

32.10. Assess Business Information System Use Case.

32.10.1. Identify artifacts that bear on the assessment.

32.10.1.1. Identify the appropriate set of Business Information System Use Case documents.

32.10.1.1.1. Review Business Information System Use Case documents.

32.10.1.1.2. Review scope and business problem related documentation.

32.10.1.1.3. Identify the Business Information System Use Cases that are defined and captured.

32.10.1.1.4. Identify the Business Information System Use Cases related work products.

32.10.1.2. For each Business Information System Use Case assessment:

32.10.1.2.1. Identify the relevant components, that is, Business Requirements, Data Integrity Rules, Database Objects, Resource Life Cycles, Use Cases, and User Acceptance Tests.

32.10.1.2.2. Identify the description for each interrelated Business Information System Use Case component.

32.10.2. Perform the assessment.

32.10.2.1. Assess each Business Information System Use Case.

32.10.2.1.1. Assess the accuracy, quality and completeness of each Business Information System Use Case with respect to the business requirements.

32.10.2.1.2. Assess whether Business Information System Use Cases are able to be inferred from business requirements, and if not whether business requirements or Business Information System Use Cases need to be enhanced.

32.10.2.1.3. Assess whether each Business Information System Use Case pair properly associates one or more Business Information Systems with one or more Use Cases.

32.10.2.1.4. Assess whether each Business Information System Use Case pair is properly named and described.

32.10.2.2. Assess whether the Business Information System Use Case is properly identified and are appropriately engineered to address a Business Information System Use Case project.

32.10.2.2.1. Assess whether all the Business Information System Use Cases have been delivered in terms of components, instances, and stored metadata work products.

32.10.2.2.2. Assess whether all the Business Information System Use Cases have been properly detailed as to content, description, methodology, evaluation, presentation, and delivery work steps.

32.10.2.2.3. Assess whether all the Business Information System Use Cases have been properly allocated sufficient unit effort estimates.

32.10.2.2.4. Assess whether all the Business Information System Use Cases have been properly allocated sufficient quantity of units that have to be developed.

32.10.2.2.5. Assess whether all the Business Information System Use Cases have been properly allocated work environment factors to determine an accurate estimate of required resources.

32.10.2.2.6. Assess whether all the Business Information System Use Cases have been properly allocated work accomplishment and recording functions necessary to support earned value reporting.

32.10.2.2.7. Assess whether all the Business Information System Use Cases have been properly allocated metadata recording effort to ensure that all interrelationships are properly recorded into the Metabase System database.

32.10.2.3. Assign the risk level associated with each Business Information System Use Case not properly constructed.

32.10.3. Determine the findings and create draft assessment report.

32.10.4. Present the findings and revise draft assessment report.

32.10.5. Create final assessment report and deliver to the auditing organization.

32.11. Assess Business Information System Requirement.

32.11.1. Identify artifacts that bear on the assessment.

32.11.1.1. Identify the appropriate set of Business Information System Requirement documents.

32.11.1.1.1. Review Business Information System Requirement documents.
32.11.1.1.2. Review scope and business problem related documentation.
32.11.1.1.3. Identify the Business Information System Requirements that are defined and captured.
32.11.1.1.4. Identify the Business Information System Requirements related work products.
32.11.1.2. For each Business Information System Requirement assessment:
32.11.1.2.1. Identify the relevant components, that is, Business Requirements, Data Integrity Rules, Database Objects, Resource Life Cycles, Use Cases, and User Acceptance Tests.
32.11.1.2.2. Identify the description for each interrelated Business Information System Requirement component.
32.11.2. Perform the assessment.
32.11.2.1. Assess each Business Information System Requirement.
32.11.2.1.1. Assess the accuracy, quality and completeness of each Business Information System Requirement with respect to the business requirements.
32.11.2.1.2. Assess whether Business Information System Requirements are able to be inferred from business requirements, and if not whether business requirements or Business Information System Requirements need to be enhanced.
32.11.2.1.3. Assess whether each Business Information System Requirement pair properly associates one or more Business Information Systems with one or more Requirements.
32.11.2.1.4. Assess whether each Business Information System Requirement pair is properly named and described.
32.11.2.2. Assess whether the Business Information System Requirement is properly identified and are appropriately engineered to address a Business Information System Requirement project.
32.11.2.2.1. Assess whether all the Business Information System Requirements have been delivered in terms of components, instances, and stored metadata work products.
32.11.2.2.2. Assess whether all the Business Information System Requirements have been properly detailed as to content, description, methodology, evaluation, presentation, and delivery work steps.
32.11.2.2.3. Assess whether all the Business Information System Requirements have been properly allocated sufficient unit effort estimates.
32.11.2.2.4. Assess whether all the Business Information System Requirements have been properly allocated sufficient quantity of units that have to be developed.
32.11.2.2.5. Assess whether all the Business Information System Requirements have been properly allocated work environment factors to determine an

accurate estimate of required resources.

32.11.2.2.6. Assess whether all the Business Information System Requirements have been properly allocated work accomplishment and recording functions necessary to support earned value reporting.

32.11.2.2.7. Assess whether all the Business Information System Requirements have been properly allocated metadata recording effort to ensure that all interrelationships are properly recorded into the Metabase System database.

32.11.2.3. Assign the risk level associated with each Business Information System Requirement not properly constructed.

32.11.3. Determine the findings and create draft assessment report.

32.11.4. Present the findings and revise draft assessment report.

32.11.5. Create final assessment report and deliver to the auditing organization.

33. Database Objects

33.1. Assess Database Object.
33.1.1. Identify artifacts that bear on the assessment.
33.1.1.1. Identify the appropriate set of Database Object documents.
33.1.1.1.1. Review Database Object documents.
33.1.1.1.2. Review scope and business problem related documentation.
33.1.1.1.3. Identify the Database Objects that are defined and captured.
33.1.1.1.4. Identify the Database Object related work products.
33.1.1.2. For each Database Object related work product assessment:
33.1.1.2.1. Identify the Database Object relevant components, that is, Database Object, Database Object Primitive Data Transformations, Database Object State, and Database Object Information System.
33.1.1.2.2. Identify the description for each interrelated Database Object component.
33.1.2. Perform the assessment.
33.1.2.1. Assess each Database Object.
33.1.2.1.1. Assess the accuracy, quality and completeness of each Database Object with respect to the business requirements.
33.1.2.1.2. Assess whether Database Objects are able to be inferred from business requirements, and if not whether business requirements or Database Objects need to be enhanced.
33.1.2.1.3. Assess whether each Database Object hierarchy is properly specified, and that all Database Object names and descriptions are well defined, non-overlapping, and have been formally approved.
33.1.2.2. Assess whether the appropriate Database Object database tables are properly identified and allocated to the appropriate Database Object.
33.1.2.3. Assess whether all the Implemented Database Tables have been properly allocated to Database Objects.
33.1.2.4. Assess whether the Database Objects are properly identified and are appropriately engineered to address a Database Object project.
33.1.2.4.1. Assess whether all the Database Objects have been delivered in terms of components, instances, and stored metadata work products.
33.1.2.4.2. Assess whether all the Database Objects have been properly detailed as to content, description, methodology, evaluation, presentation, and delivery work steps.
33.1.2.4.3. Assess whether all the Database Objects have been properly allocated sufficient unit effort estimates.
33.1.2.4.4. Assess whether all the Database Objects have been properly allocated sufficient quantity of units that have to be developed.
33.1.2.4.5. Assess whether all the Database Objects have been properly allocated work environment factors to determine an accurate estimate of required resources.

33.1.2.4.6. Assess whether all the Database Objects have been properly allocated work accomplishment and recording functions necessary to support earned value reporting.
33.1.2.4.7. Assess whether all the Database Objects have been properly allocated metadata recording effort to ensure that all interrelationships are properly recorded into the Metabase System database.
33.1.2.5. Assign the risk level associated with each Database Object not properly constructed.
33.1.3. Determine the findings and create draft assessment report.
33.1.4. Present the findings and revise draft assessment report.
33.1.5. Create final assessment report and deliver to the auditing organization.

33.2. Assess Database Object Table.
33.2.1. Identify artifacts that bear on the assessment.
33.2.1.1. Identify the appropriate set of Database Object Table documents.
33.2.1.1.1. Review Database Object Table documents.
33.2.1.1.2. Review scope and business problem related documentation.
33.2.1.1.3. Identify the Database Object Table that are defined and captured.
33.2.1.1.4. Identify the Database Object Table related work products.
33.2.1.2. For each Database Object Table related work product assessment:
33.2.1.2.1. Identify the Database Object Table relevant components, that is, Database Object, Database Object Primitive Data Transformations, Database Object State, and Database Object Information System.
33.2.1.2.2. Identify the description for each interrelated Database Object Table component.
33.2.2. Perform the assessment.
33.2.2.1. Assess each Database Object Table.
33.2.2.1.1. Assess the accuracy, quality and completeness of each Database Object Table with respect to the business requirements.
33.2.2.1.2. Assess whether Database Object Table are able to be inferred from business requirements, and if not whether business requirements or Database Object Table need to be enhanced.
33.2.2.2. Assess whether the appropriate Database Object Table database tables are properly identified and allocated to the appropriate Database Object.
33.2.2.3. Assess whether all the Implemented Database Tables have been properly allocated to Database Object Tables.
33.2.2.4. Assess whether the Database Object Tables are properly identified and are appropriately engineered to address a Database Object Table project.
33.2.2.4.1. Assess whether all the Database Object Table have been delivered in terms of components, instances, and stored metadata work products.
33.2.2.4.2. Assess whether all the Database Object Tables have been properly detailed as to content, description, methodology, evaluation, presentation,

and delivery work steps.

33.2.2.4.3. Assess whether all the Database Object Tables have been properly allocated sufficient unit effort estimates.

33.2.2.4.4. Assess whether all the Database Object Tables have been properly allocated sufficient quantity of units that have to be developed.

33.2.2.4.5. Assess whether all the Database Object Tables have been properly allocated work environment factors to determine an accurate estimate of required resources.

33.2.2.4.6. Assess whether all the Database Object Tables have been properly allocated work accomplishment and recording functions necessary to support earned value reporting.

33.2.2.4.7. Assess whether all the Database Object Tables have been properly allocated metadata recording effort to ensure that all interrelationships are properly recorded into the Metabase System database.

33.2.2.5. Assign the risk level associated with each Database Object Table not properly constructed.

33.2.3. Determine the findings and create draft assessment report.

33.2.4. Present the findings and revise draft assessment report.

33.2.5. Create final assessment report and deliver to the auditing organization.

33.3. Assess Database Object Primitive Data Transformation.

33.3.1. Identify artifacts that bear on the assessment.

33.3.1.1. Identify the appropriate set of Database Object Primitive Data Transformation documents.

33.3.1.1.1. Review Database Object Primitive Data Transformation documents.

33.3.1.1.2. Review scope and business problem related documentation.

33.3.1.1.3. Identify the Database Object Primitive Data Transformations that are defined and captured.

33.3.1.1.4. Identify the Database Object Primitive Data Transformations related work products.

33.3.1.2. For each Database Object Primitive Data Transformations related work product assessment:

33.3.1.2.1. Identify the relevant components, that is, Database Objects, and Database Object Data Structures.

33.3.1.2.2. Identify the description for each interrelated Database Object Primitive Data Transformations component.

33.3.2. Perform the assessment.

33.3.2.1. Assess each Database Object Primitive Data Transformation.

33.3.2.1.1. Assess the accuracy, quality and completeness of each Database Object Primitive Data Transformation with respect to the business requirements.

33.3.2.1.2. Assess whether Database Object Primitive Data Transformation are able to be inferred from business requirements, and if not whether business requirements or Database Object Primitive Data Transformation need to be enhanced.

33.3.2.2. Assess whether all the Database Object Primitive Data Transformations properly add, delete, or modify all Table Columns allocated to the database object Table.

33.3.2.3. Assess whether Database Object Primitive Data Transformations, upon failure return the database object Table row to its original state.

33.3.2.4. Assess whether the Database Object Primitive Data Transformations are properly identified and are appropriately engineered to address a Database Object Primitive Data Transformation project.

33.3.2.4.1. Assess whether all the Database Object Primitive Data Transformations have been delivered in terms of components, instances, and stored metadata work products.

33.3.2.4.2. Assess whether all the Database Object Primitive Data Transformations have been properly detailed as to content, description, methodology, evaluation, presentation, and delivery work steps.

33.3.2.4.3. Assess whether all the Database Object Primitive Data Transformations have been properly allocated sufficient unit effort estimates.

33.3.2.4.4. Assess whether all the Database Object Primitive Data Transformations have been properly allocated sufficient quantity of units that have to be developed.

33.3.2.4.5. Assess whether all the Database Object Primitive Data Transformations have been properly allocated work environment factors to determine an accurate estimate of required resources.

33.3.2.4.6. Assess whether all the Database Object Primitive Data Transformations have been properly allocated work accomplishment and recording functions necessary to support earned value reporting.

33.3.2.4.7. Assess whether all the Database Object Primitive Data Transformations have been properly allocated metadata recording effort to ensure that all interrelationships are properly recorded into the Metabase System database.

33.3.2.5. Assign the risk level associated with each Database Object Primitive Data Transformation not properly constructed.

33.3.3. Determine the findings and create draft assessment report.

33.3.4. Present the findings and revise draft assessment report.

33.3.5. Create final assessment report and deliver to the auditing organization.

33.4. Assess Database Object State.

33.4.1. Identify artifacts that bear on the assessment.

33.4.1.1. Identify the appropriate set of Database Object State documents.

33.4.1.1.1. Review Database Object State documents.

33.4.1.1.2. Review scope and business problem related documentation.

33.4.1.1.3. Identify the Database Object States that are defined and captured.

33.4.1.1.4. Identify the Database Object State related work products.

33.4.1.2. For each Database Object State related work product assessment:

33.4.1.2.1. Identify the relevant components, that is, Database Object State, Database Object State Primitive Data Transformation, and Database Object State Information System.

33.4.1.2.2. Identify the description for each interrelated Database Object State component.

33.4.2. Perform the assessment.

33.4.2.1. Assess each Database Object State.

33.4.2.1.1. Assess the accuracy, quality and completeness of each Database Object State with respect to the business requirements.

33.4.2.1.2. Assess whether Database Object State are able to be inferred from business requirements, and if not whether business requirements or Database Object State need to be enhanced.

33.4.2.2. Assess whether all the Database Object Data Structure Tables have been properly allocated to Database Object State states.

33.4.2.3. Assess whether all the Database Object State Structure Table states proceed from the null state to a series of valued-states in a proper sequence and finally return to a null state.

33.4.2.4. Assess whether all the Database Object State information systems are properly engineered to transform Database Object State Tables from one valid state to the next.

33.4.2.5. Assess whether the Database Object States are properly identified and are appropriately engineered to address a Database Object State project.

33.4.2.5.1. Assess whether all the Database Object States have been delivered in terms of components, instances, and stored metadata work products.

33.4.2.5.2. Assess whether all the Database Object States have been properly detailed as to content, description, methodology, evaluation, presentation, and delivery work steps.

33.4.2.5.3. Assess whether all the Database Object States have been properly allocated sufficient unit effort estimates.

33.4.2.5.4. Assess whether all the Database Object States have been properly allocated sufficient quantity of units that have to be developed.

33.4.2.5.5. Assess whether all the Database Object States have been properly allocated work environment factors to determine an accurate estimate of required resources.

33.4.2.5.6. Assess whether all the Database Object States have been properly allocated work accomplishment and recording functions necessary to support earned value reporting.

33.4.2.5.7. Assess whether all the Database Object States have been properly allocated metadata recording effort to ensure that all interrelationships

are properly recorded into the Metabase System database.
33.4.2.6. Assign the risk level associated with each Database Object State not properly constructed.
33.4.3. Determine the findings and create draft assessment report.
33.4.4. Present the findings and revise draft assessment report.
33.4.5. Create final assessment report and deliver to the auditing organization.

33.5. Assess Database Object Information System.
33.5.1. Identify artifacts that bear on the assessment.
33.5.1.1. Identify the appropriate set of Database Object Information System documents.
33.5.1.1.1. Review Database Object Information System documents.
33.5.1.1.2. Review scope and business problem related documentation.
33.5.1.1.3. Identify the Database Object Information Systems that are defined and captured.
33.5.1.1.4. Identify the Database Object Information Systems related work products.
33.5.1.2. For each Database Object Information Systems related work product assessment:
33.5.1.2.1. Identify the relevant components, that is, Database Objects, Database Object Data Structures, Database Object Primitive Data Transformations, and Database Object States.
33.5.1.2.2. Identify the description for each Database Object Information System component.
33.5.2. Perform the assessment.
33.5.2.1. Assess each Database Object Information System.
33.5.2.1.1. Assess the accuracy, quality and completeness of each Database Object Information System with respect to the business requirements.
33.5.2.1.2. Assess whether Database Object Information System are able to be inferred from business requirements, and if not whether business requirements or Database Object Information System need to be enhanced.
33.5.2.2. Assess whether each Database Object is addressed by one or more Database Object Information Systems as may be appropriate.
33.5.2.2.1. Assess whether Database Object data structures are properly employed by the Database Object Information Systems.
33.5.2.2.2. Assess whether Database Object Primitive Data Transformations are properly programmed processes of Database Object Information Systems.
33.5.2.2.3. Assess whether database object states are properly engineered to be achieved in Database Object Information Systems that are retained if the Database Object Information System is successful or are returned to a previous state if the Database Object Information System fails.
33.5.2.2.4. Assess whether Database Object Information Systems are properly

accomplished within the Business Information Systems to which they are allocated.

33.5.2.3. Assess whether the Database Object Information Systems are properly identified and are appropriately engineered to address a Database Object Information System project.

33.5.2.3.1. Assess whether all the Database Object Information Systems have been delivered in terms of components, instances, and stored metadata work products.

33.5.2.3.2. Assess whether all the Database Object Information Systems have been properly detailed as to content, description, methodology, evaluation, presentation, and delivery work steps.

33.5.2.3.3. Assess whether all the Database Object Information Systems have been properly allocated sufficient unit effort estimates.

33.5.2.3.4. Assess whether all the Database Object Information Systems have been properly allocated sufficient quantity of units that have to be developed.

33.5.2.3.5. Assess whether all the Database Object Information Systems have been properly allocated work environment factors to determine an accurate estimate of required resources.

33.5.2.3.6. Assess whether all the Database Object Information Systems have been properly allocated work accomplishment and recording functions necessary to support earned value reporting.

33.5.2.3.7. Assess whether all the Database Object Information Systems have been properly allocated metadata recording effort to ensure that all interrelationships are properly recorded into the Metabase System database.

33.5.2.4. Assign the risk level associated with each Database Object Information System not properly constructed.

33.5.3. Determine the findings and create draft assessment report.

33.5.4. Present the findings and revise draft assessment report.

33.5.5. Create final assessment report and deliver to the auditing organization.

33.6. Assess Database Object Requirement.

33.6.1. Identify artifacts that bear on the assessment.

33.6.1.1. Identify the appropriate set of Database Object Requirement documents.

33.6.1.1.1. Review Database Object Requirement documents.

33.6.1.1.2. Review scope and business problem related documentation.

33.6.1.1.3. Identify the Database Object Requirements that are defined and captured.

33.6.1.1.4. Identify the Database Object Requirements related work products.

33.6.1.2. For each Database Object Requirements related work product assessment:

33.6.1.2.1. Identify the relevant components, that is, Database Objects, Database Object Data Structures, Database Object Primitive Data Transformations, Database Object States, and Requirements.

33.6.1.2.2. Identify the description for each Database Object Requirements component.

33.6.2. Perform the assessment.

33.6.2.1. Assess each Database Object Requirement.

33.6.2.1.1. Assess the accuracy, quality and completeness of each Database Object Requirement with respect to the business requirements.

33.6.2.1.2. Assess whether Database Object Requirement are able to be inferred from business requirements, and if not whether business requirements or Database Object Requirement need to be enhanced.

33.6.2.2. Assess whether the Database Object Requirements are properly identified and are appropriately engineered to address a Database Object Requirement project.

33.6.2.2.1. Assess whether all the Database Object Requirements have been delivered in terms of components, instances, and stored metadata work products.

33.6.2.2.2. Assess whether all the Database Object Requirements have been properly detailed as to content, description, methodology, evaluation, presentation, and delivery work steps.

33.6.2.2.3. Assess whether all the Database Object Requirements have been properly allocated sufficient unit effort estimates.

33.6.2.2.4. Assess whether all the Database Object Requirements have been properly allocated sufficient quantity of units that have to be developed.

33.6.2.2.5. Assess whether all the Database Object Requirements have been properly allocated work environment factors to determine an accurate estimate of required resources.

33.6.2.2.6. Assess whether all the Database Object Requirements have been properly allocated work accomplishment and recording functions necessary to support earned value reporting.

33.6.2.2.7. Assess whether all the Database Object Requirements have been properly allocated metadata recording effort to ensure that all interrelationships are properly recorded into the Metabase System database.

33.6.2.3. Assign the risk level associated with each Database Object Requirement not properly constructed.

33.6.3. Determine the findings and create draft assessment report.

33.6.4. Present the findings and revise draft assessment report.

33.6.5. Create final assessment report and deliver to the auditing organization.

33.7. Assess Database Object Data Integrity Rule.

33.7.1. Identify artifacts that bear on the assessment.

33.7.1.1. Identify the appropriate set of Database Object Data Integrity Rule documents.

33.7.1.1.1. Review Database Object Data Integrity Rule documents.

33.7.1.1.2. Review scope and business problem related documentation.

33.7.1.1.3. Identify the Database Object Data Integrity Rules that are defined and captured.
33.7.1.1.4. Identify the Database Object Data Integrity Rules related work products.
33.7.1.2. For each Database Object Data Integrity Rules related work product assessment:
33.7.1.2.1. Identify the relevant components, that is, Database Objects, Database Object Data Structures, Database Object Primitive Data Transformations, and Database Object States.
33.7.1.2.2. Identify the description for each Database Object Data Integrity Rules component.
33.7.2. Perform the assessment.
33.7.2.1. Assess each Database Object Data Integrity Rule.
33.7.2.1.1. Assess the accuracy, quality and completeness of each Database Object Data Integrity Rule with respect to the business requirements.
33.7.2.1.2. Assess whether Database Object Data Integrity Rule are able to be inferred from business requirements, and if not whether business requirements or Database Object Data Integrity Rule need to be enhanced.
33.7.2.2. Assess whether each Database Object Data Structure instance is addressed by one or more Data Integrity Rules as may be appropriate.
33.7.2.2.1. Assess whether Database Object Data Structure Data Integrity Rules are properly configured to be achieved through SQL DDL data integrity clauses.
33.7.2.2.2. Assess whether Database Object Data Structure Data Integrity Rules are properly configured to be achieved through SQL stored procedures or Business Information System contained procedures.
33.7.2.2.3. Assess whether database object states Data Integrity Rules are properly configured to be properly sequenced and able to be achieved through Database Object Information Systems.
33.7.2.2.4. Assess whether Database Object Information Systems Data Integrity Rules are properly configured to be achieved through Business Information System contained processes.
33.7.2.3. Assess whether the Database Object Data Integrity Rules are properly identified and are appropriately engineered to address a Database Object Information System project.
33.7.2.3.1. Assess whether all the Database Object Data Integrity Rules have been delivered in terms of components, instances, and stored metadata work products.
33.7.2.3.2. Assess whether all the Database Object Data Integrity Rules have been properly detailed as to content, description, methodology, evaluation, presentation, and delivery work steps.
33.7.2.3.3. Assess whether all the Database Object Data Integrity Rules have been properly allocated sufficient unit effort estimates.

33.7.2.3.4. Assess whether all the Database Object Data Integrity Rules have been properly allocated sufficient quantity of units that have to be developed.
33.7.2.3.5. Assess whether all the Database Object Data Integrity Rules have been properly allocated work environment factors to determine an accurate estimate of required resources.
33.7.2.3.6. Assess whether all the Database Object Data Integrity Rules have been properly allocated work accomplishment and recording functions necessary to support earned value reporting.
33.7.2.3.7. Assess whether all the Database Object Data Integrity Rules have been properly allocated metadata recording effort to ensure that all interrelationships are properly recorded into the Metabase System database.
33.7.2.3. Assign the risk level associated with each Database Object Data Integrity Rule not properly constructed.
33.7.3. Determine the findings and create draft assessment report.
33.7.4. Present the findings and revise draft assessment report.
33.7.5. Create final assessment report and deliver to the auditing organization.

33.8. Assess Database Object Database Domain.
33.8.1. Identify artifacts that bear on the assessment.
33.8.1.1. Identify the appropriate set of Database Object Database Domain documents.
33.8.1.1.1. Review Database Object Database Domain documents.
33.8.1.1.2. Review scope and business problem related documentation.
33.8.1.1.3. Identify the Database Object Database Domains that are defined and captured.
33.8.1.1.4. Identify the Database Object Database Domains related work products.
33.8.1.2. For each Database Object Database Domains related work product assessment:
33.8.1.2.1. Identify the relevant components, that is, Database Objects, Database Object Data Structures, Database Object Primitive Data Transformations, and Database Object States.
33.8.1.2.2. Identify the description for each Database Object Information System component.
33.8.2. Perform the assessment.
33.8.2.1. Assess each Database Object Database Domain.
33.8.2.1.1. Assess the accuracy, quality and completeness of each Database Object Database Domain with respect to the business requirements.
33.8.2.1.2. Assess whether Database Object Database Domain are able to be inferred from business requirements, and if not whether business requirements or Database Object Database Domain need to be enhanced.
33.8.2.2. Assess whether each Database Object Database Domain is addressed by

one or more mission organization functions as may be appropriate.

33.8.2.2.1. Assess whether each Database Object Database Domain is able to be identified through a database domain description with a mission.

33.8.2.2.2. For database objects that are not discoverable from database domains within mission organization functions enhance the database domain statements and if necessary the mission organization function statements.

33.8.2.3. Assess whether the Database Object Database Domains are properly identified and are appropriately engineered to address a Database Object Information System project.

33.8.2.3.1. Assess whether all the Database Object Database Domains have been delivered in terms of components, instances, and stored metadata work products.

33.8.2.3.2. Assess whether all the Database Object Database Domains have been properly detailed as to content, description, methodology, evaluation, presentation, and delivery work steps.

33.8.2.3.3. Assess whether all the Database Object Database Domains have been properly allocated sufficient unit effort estimates.

33.8.2.3.4. Assess whether all the Database Object Database Domains have been properly allocated sufficient quantity of units that have to be developed.

33.8.2.3.5. Assess whether all the Database Object Database Domains have been properly allocated work environment factors to determine an accurate estimate of required resources.

33.8.2.3.6. Assess whether all the Database Object Database Domains have been properly allocated work accomplishment and recording functions necessary to support earned value reporting.

33.8.2.3.7. Assess whether all the Database Object Database Domains have been properly allocated metadata recording effort to ensure that all interrelationships are properly recorded into the Metabase System database.

33.8.2.4. Assign the risk level associated with each Database Object Database Domain not properly constructed.

33.8.3. Determine the findings and create draft assessment report.

33.8.4. Present the findings and revise draft assessment report.

33.8.5. Create final assessment report and deliver to the auditing organization.

33.9. Assess Database Object Resource Life Cycle.

33.9.1. Identify artifacts that bear on the assessment.

33.9.1.1. Identify the appropriate set of Database Object Resource Life Cycle documents.

33.9.1.1.1. Review Database Object Resource Life Cycle documents.

33.9.1.1.2. Review scope and business problem related documentation.

33.9.1.1.3. Identify the Database Object Resource Life Cycles that are defined and captured.

33.9.1.1.4. Identify the Database Object Resource Life Cycles related work products.

33.9.1.2. For each Database Object Resource Life Cycles related work product assessment:

33.9.1.2.1. Identify the relevant components, that is, Database Objects, Database Object Data Structures, Database Object Primitive Data Transformations, and Database Object States.

33.9.1.2.2. Identify the description for each Database Object Resource Life Cycle component.

33.9.2. Perform the assessment.

33.9.2.1. Assess each Database Object Resource Life Cycle.

33.9.2.1.1. Assess the accuracy, quality and completeness of each Database Object Resource Life Cycle with respect to the business requirements.

33.9.2.1.2. Assess whether Database Object Resource Life Cycles are able to be inferred from business requirements, and if not whether business requirements or Database Object Resource Life Cycles need to be enhanced.

33.9.2.1.3. Assess whether each Database Object Resource Life Cycles pair properly associates one or more Database Objects with one or more Resource Life Cycles.

33.9.2.1.4. Assess whether each Database Object Resource Life Cycle pair is properly named and described.

33.9.2.2. Assess whether the Database Object Resource Life Cycles are properly identified and are appropriately engineered to address a Database Object Information System project.

33.9.2.2.1. Assess whether all the Database Object Resource Life Cycles have been delivered in terms of components, instances, and stored metadata work products.

33.9.2.2.2. Assess whether all the Database Object Resource Life Cycles have been properly detailed as to content, description, methodology, evaluation, presentation, and delivery work steps.

33.9.2.2.3. Assess whether all the Database Object Resource Life Cycles have been properly allocated sufficient unit effort estimates.

33.9.2.2.4. Assess whether all the Database Object Resource Life Cycles have been properly allocated sufficient quantity of units that have to be developed.

33.9.2.2.5. Assess whether all the Database Object Resource Life Cycles have been properly allocated work environment factors to determine an accurate estimate of required resources.

33.9.2.2.6. Assess whether all the Database Object Resource Life Cycles have been properly allocated work accomplishment and recording functions necessary to support earned value reporting.

33.9.2.2.7. Assess whether all the Database Object Resource Life Cycles have been

properly allocated metadata recording effort to ensure that all interrelationships are properly recorded into the Metabase System database.

33.9.2.3. Assign the risk level associated with each Database Object Resource Life Cycle not properly constructed.

33.9.3. Determine the findings and create draft assessment report.

33.9.4. Present the findings and revise draft assessment report.

33.9.5. Create final assessment report and deliver to the auditing organization.

33.10. Assess Database Object Information System Business Information System.

33.10.1. Identify artifacts that bear on the assessment.

33.10.1.1. Identify the appropriate set of Database Object Information System Business Information System documents.

33.10.1.1.1. Review Database Object Information System Business Information System documents.

33.10.1.1.2. Review scope and business problem related documentation.

33.10.1.1.3. Identify the Database Object Information System Business Information Systems that are defined and captured.

33.10.1.1.4. Identify the Database Object Information System Business Information Systems related work products.

33.10.1.2. For each Database Object Information System Business Information System related work product assessment:

33.10.1.2.1. Identify the relevant components, that is, Database Objects, Database Object Data Structures, Database Object Primitive Data Transformations, and Database Object States.

33.10.1.2.2. Identify the description for each Database Object Information System Business Information System component.

33.10.2. Perform the assessment.

33.10.2.1. Assess each Database Object Information System Business Information System.

33.10.2.1.1. Assess the accuracy, quality and completeness of each Database Object Information System Business Information Systems with respect to the business requirements.

33.10.2.1.2. Assess whether Database Object Information System Business Information Systems are able to be inferred from business requirements, and if not whether business requirements or Database Object Information System Business Information Systems need to be enhanced.

33.10.2.1.3. Assess whether each Database Object Information System Business Information Systems pair properly associates one or more Database Object Information Systems with one or more Business Information Systems.

33.10.2.1.4. Assess whether each Database Object Information System Business

Information Systems pair is properly named and described.

33.10.2.2. Assess whether the Database Object Information System Business Information System are properly identified and are appropriately engineered to address a Database Object Information System Business Information System project.

33.10.2.2.1. Assess whether all the Database Object Information System Business Information System have been delivered in terms of components, instances, and stored metadata work products.

33.10.2.2.2. Assess whether all the Database Object Information System Business Information System have been properly detailed as to content, description, methodology, evaluation, presentation, and delivery work steps.

33.10.2.2.3. Assess whether all the Database Object Information System Business Information System have been properly allocated sufficient unit effort estimates.

33.10.2.2.4. Assess whether all the Database Object Information System Business Information System have been properly allocated sufficient quantity of units that have to be developed.

33.10.2.2.5. Assess whether all the Database Object Information System Business Information System have been properly allocated work environment factors to determine an accurate estimate of required resources.

33.10.2.2.6. Assess whether all the Database Object Information System Business Information System have been properly allocated work accomplishment and recording functions necessary to support earned value reporting.

33.10.2.2.7. Assess whether all the Database Object Information System Business Information System have been properly allocated metadata recording effort to ensure that all interrelationships are properly recorded into the Metabase System database.

33.10.2.3. Assign the risk level associated with each Database Object Information System Business Information System not properly constructed.

33.10.3. Determine the findings and create draft assessment report.

33.10.4. Present the findings and revise draft assessment report.

33.10.5. Create final assessment report and deliver to the auditing organization.

34. Data Integrity Rules

34.1. Assess Data Integrity Rule.
34.1.1. Identify artifacts that bear on the assessment.
34.1.1.1. Identify the appropriate set of Data Integrity Rule documents.
34.1.1.1.1. Review Data Integrity Rule documents.
34.1.1.1.2. Review scope and business problem related documentation.
34.1.1.1.3. Identify the Data Integrity Rules that are defined and captured.
34.1.1.1.4. Identify the Data Integrity Rules related work products.
34.1.1.2. For each Data Integrity Rule related work product assessment:
34.1.1.2.1. Identify the relevant components, that is, Implemented Data Model Tables and Implemented Data Model Table Columns.
34.1.1.2.2. Identify the description for each interrelated Data Integrity Rule component.
34.1.2. Perform the assessment.
34.1.2.1. Assess each Data Integrity Rule.
34.1.2.1.1. Assess the accuracy, quality and completeness of each Data Integrity Rule with respect to the business requirements.
34.1.2.1.2. Assess whether Data Integrity Rule are able to be inferred from business requirements, and if not whether business requirements or Data Integrity Rule need to be enhanced.
34.1.2.2. Assess the adequacy of each Implemented Database Tables and Columns with respect to the Data Integrity Rule.
34.1.2.2.1. Assess whether all the implied Implemented Database Model components, that is, Column, and Assigned Value Domain from the Data Integrity Rule have been addressed in one or more aspects of the Implemented Database Model.
34.1.2.2.2. Assess Implemented Database Model components, that is, Column, and Assigned Value Domain with respect to the specific Data Integrity Rule is sufficiently specified.
34.1.2.2.3. Assess whether every Column and Assigned Value Domain is called for by one or more business requirement.
34.1.2.3. Assess whether each Data Integrity Rule is addressed by one or more use case is addressed by one or more Value Domains and management as may be appropriate.
34.1.2.3.1. Assess whether the Data Integrity Rules is sufficiently detailed to reflect the actions, conditions, and logic of use cases as specified.
34.1.2.4. Assess whether each Data Integrity Rule is addressed by one or more User Acceptance Tests as may be appropriate.
34.1.2.4.1. Assess whether the User Acceptance Test allocated Data Integrity Rules are of sufficient detail to enable a pass/fail result.
34.1.2.4.2. Assess whether each Data Integrity Rule is addressed by one or more

User Acceptance Test is addressed by one or more Value Domains and management as may be appropriate.

34.1.2.4.3. Assess whether the allocated User Acceptance Test Data Integrity Rules do not result in conflicts that need to be resolved.

34.1.2.5. Assess whether each Data Integrity Rule is addressed by one or more Value Domain management as may be appropriate.

34.1.2.5.1. Assess whether the Data Integrity Rules is sufficiently detailed to address the Value Domains as specified.

34.1.2.5.2. Assess whether the allocated Value Domain Data Integrity Rules do not result in conflicts that need to be resolved.

34.1.2.6. Assess whether the Data Integrity Rules are properly identified and are appropriately engineered to address a Data Integrity Rule project.

34.1.2.6.1. Assess whether all the Data Integrity Rules have been delivered in terms of components, instances, and stored metadata work products.

34.1.2.6.2. Assess whether all the Data Integrity Rules have been properly detailed as to content, description, methodology, evaluation, presentation, and delivery work steps.

34.1.2.6.3. Assess whether all the Data Integrity Rules have been properly allocated sufficient unit effort estimates.

34.1.2.6.4. Assess whether all the Data Integrity Rules have been properly allocated sufficient quantity of units that have to be developed.

34.1.2.6.5. Assess whether all the Data Integrity Rules have been properly allocated work environment factors to determine an accurate estimate of required resources.

34.1.2.6.6. Assess whether all the Data Integrity Rules have been properly allocated work accomplishment and recording functions necessary to support earned value reporting.

34.1.2.6.7. Assess whether all the Data Integrity Rules have been properly allocated metadata recording effort to ensure that all interrelationships are properly recorded into the Metabase System database.

34.1.2.7. Assign the risk level associated with each Data Integrity Rule not properly constructed.

34.1.3. Determine the findings and create draft assessment report.

34.1.4. Present the findings and revise draft assessment report.

34.1.5. Create final assessment report and deliver to the auditing organization.

34.2. Assess Data Integrity Rule Structure

34.2.1. Identify artifacts that bear on the assessment.

34.2.1.1. Identify the appropriate set of Data Integrity Rule Structures documents.

34.2.1.1.1. Review Data Integrity Rule Structure documents.

34.2.1.1.2. Review scope and business problem related documentation.

34.2.1.1.3. Identify the Data Integrity Rule Structures that are defined and captured.

34.2.1.1.4. Identify the Data Integrity Rule Structures related work products.
34.2.1.2. For each Data Integrity Rule Structure related work product assessment:
34.2.1.2.1. Identify the relevant component.
34.2.1.2.2. Identify the description for each interrelated Data Integrity Rule Structure component.
34.2.2. Perform the assessment.
34.2.2.1. Assess each Data Integrity Rule Structure.
34.2.2.1.1. Assess the accuracy, quality and completeness of each Data Integrity Rule Structure with respect to the business requirements.
34.2.2.1.2. Assess whether Data Integrity Rule Structures are able to be inferred from business requirements, and if not whether business requirements or Data Integrity Rule Structures need to be enhanced.
34.2.2.1.3. Assess whether each Data Integrity Rule Structure hierarchy/network is properly specified, and that all Data Integrity Rule Structure names and descriptions are well defined, non-overlapping, and have been formally approved.
34.2.2.2. Assess whether the Data Integrity Rule Structures are properly identified and are appropriately engineered to address a Data Integrity Rule Structure project.
34.2.2.2.1. Assess whether all the Data Integrity Rule Structures have been delivered in terms of components, instances, and stored metadata work products.
34.2.2.2.2. Assess whether all the Data Integrity Rule Structures have been properly detailed as to content, description, methodology, evaluation, presentation, and delivery work steps.
34.2.2.2.3. Assess whether all the Data Integrity Rule Structures have been properly allocated sufficient unit effort estimates.
34.2.2.2.4. Assess whether all the Data Integrity Rule Structures have been properly allocated sufficient quantity of units that have to be developed.
34.2.2.2.5. Assess whether all the Data Integrity Rule Structures have been properly allocated work environment factors to determine an accurate estimate of required resources.
34.2.2.2.6. Assess whether all the Data Integrity Rule Structures have been properly allocated work accomplishment and recording functions necessary to support earned value Business Event Cycle.
34.2.2.2.7. Assess whether all the Data Integrity Rule Structures have been properly allocated metadata recording effort to ensure that all interrelationships are properly recorded into the Metabase System database.
34.2.2.3. Assign the risk level associated with each Data Integrity Rule Structure not properly constructed.
34.2.3. Determine the findings and create draft assessment report.
34.2.4. Present the findings and revise draft assessment report.
34.2.5. Create final assessment report and deliver to the auditing organization.

34.3. Assess Data Integrity Rule Binding.
34.3.1. Identify artifacts that bear on the assessment.
34.3.1.1. Identify the appropriate set of Data Integrity Rule Binding documents.
34.3.1.1.1. Review Data Integrity Rule Binding documents.
34.3.1.1.2. Review scope and business problem related documentation.
34.3.1.1.3. Identify the Data Integrity Rule Bindings that are defined and captured.
34.3.1.1.4. Identify the Data Integrity Rule Binding related work products.
34.3.1.2. For each Data Integrity Rule Binding related work product assessment:
34.3.1.2.1. Identify the relevant components, that is, Data Integrity Rule Specification, Views, View Columns, View Column Value Domains, DBMS Tables, DBMS Table Columns, DBMS Column Value Domains, Business Information Systems, External Data Interface Requirements, and User Acceptance Tests.
34.3.1.2.2. Identify the description for each interrelated Data Integrity Rule Binding component.
34.3.2. Perform the assessment.
34.3.2.1. Assess each Data Integrity Rule Binding.
34.3.2.1.1. Assess the accuracy, quality and completeness of each Data Integrity Rule Binding with respect to the business requirements.
34.3.2.1.2. Assess whether Data Integrity Rule Binding are able to be inferred from business requirements, and if not whether business requirements or Data Integrity Rule Binding need to be enhanced.
34.3.2.2. Assess the adequacy of each Data Element model with respect to the Data Integrity Rule Binding.
34.3.2.2.1. Assess whether all the implied Data Element model components, that is, Value Domains, and Data Elements from the Data Integrity Rule Binding have been addressed in one or more aspects of the Data Element model.
34.3.2.2.2. Assess Data Element model components, that is, Value Domains, and Data Elements with respect to the specific Data Integrity Rule are sufficiently specified.
34.3.2.2.3. Assess whether every Value Domain and Data Element is called for by one or more business requirement.
34.3.2.2.4. Assess whether the Data Element Data Integrity Rule Binding conflicts with one or more other bindings.
34.3.2.3. Assess the adequacy of each Implemented Database Model with respect to the Data Integrity Rule.
34.3.2.3.1. Assess whether all the implied Implemented Database Model components, that is, Column, and Assigned Value Domain from the Data Integrity Rule Binding have been addressed in one or more aspects of the Implemented Database Model.
34.3.2.3.2. Assess Implemented Database Model components, that is, Column, and Assigned Value Domain with respect to the specific Data Integrity Rule

Binding is sufficiently specified.

34.3.2.3.3. Assess whether every Column and Assigned Value Domain is called for by one or more business requirement.

34.3.2.3.4. Assess whether the Implemented Database Table Data Integrity Rule Binding conflicts with one or more other bindings.

34.3.2.3.4. Assess whether the Implemented Database Table Column Data Integrity Rule Binding conflicts with one or more other bindings.

34.3.2.4. Assess the adequacy of each Operational Database Model with respect to the business requirement.

34.3.2.4.1. Assess whether all the implied Operational Database Model components, that is, DBMS Columns and Assigned Value Domains from the Data Integrity Rule Binding have been addressed in one or more aspects of the Operational Database Model.

34.3.2.4.2. Assess Operational Database Model components, that is, DBMS Column, and Assigned Value Domain with respect to the specific Data Integrity Rule Binding are sufficiently specified.

34.3.2.4.3. Assess whether the Data Integrity Rule Binding use of DBMS Columns are appropriate with respect to data type, allowed operation, and if appropriate SQL functions.

34.3.2.4.4. Assess whether Data Integrity Rule Binding stored procedure implementations are correctly engineered and result in unambiguous messages provided the end user or up through the application system calling sequence.

34.3.2.4.5. Assess whether every DBMS Column and Assigned Value Domain is called for by one or more business requirement.

34.3.2.4.6. Assess whether the Operational Database DBMS Table Data Integrity Rule Binding conflicts with one or more any other bindings.

34.3.2.4.7. Assess whether the Operational Database DBMS Table Column Data Integrity Rule Binding conflicts with one or any more other bindings.

34.3.2.5. Assess the adequacy of each View Data Model with respect to the business requirement.

34.3.2.5.1. Assess whether all the implied View Data Model components, that is, View and View Columns from the Data Integrity Rule Binding have been addressed in one or more aspects of the XML data model.

34.3.2.5.2. Assess View Data Model components, that is, View and View Columns with respect to the specific Data Integrity Rule Binding are sufficiently specified.

34.3.2.5.3. Assess whether the Data Integrity Rule use of View Columns are appropriate with respect to allowed functionality of Views.

34.3.2.5.4. Assess whether Data Integrity Rule Binding stored procedure implementations are correctly engineered and result in unambiguous messages provided the end user or up through the application system calling sequence.

34.3.2.5.5. Assess whether every View and View Column is called for by one or more business requirement.

34.3.2.5.6. Assess whether the View Data Model View Data Integrity Rule Binding conflicts with one or more any other bindings.

34.3.2.5.7. Assess whether the View Data Model View Column Data Integrity Rule Binding conflicts with one or more any other bindings.

34.3.2.6. Assess the adequacy of each XML data model with respect to the business requirement.

34.3.2.6.1. Assess whether all the implied XML data model components, that is, XML schema, XML elements and supporting XML structures from the Data Integrity Rule Binding have been addressed in one or more aspects of the XML data model.

34.3.2.6.2. Assess XML data model components, that is, XML schema, XML elements and supporting XML structures with respect to the specific Data Integrity Rule Binding are sufficiently specified.

34.3.2.6.3. Assess whether every XML schema, XML elements and supporting XML structures is called for by one or more business requirement.

34.3.2.6.4. Assess whether the XML Data Model XML Element Data Integrity Rule Binding conflicts with one or more other bindings.

34.3.2.7. Assess, as applicable, whether each Data Integrity Rule Binding is addressed by one or more Business Information Systems as may be appropriate.

34.3.2.7.1. Assess whether there is sufficient logic within the Business Information System to adequately execute the Data Integrity Rule Binding in a pass/fail manner.

34.3.2.7.2. Assess whether the allocated Business Information System Data Integrity Rules do no adequately result in conflicts that need to be resolved.

34.3.2.7.3. Assess whether the XML Data Model XML Element Data Integrity Rule Binding conflicts with one or more other bindings.

34.3.2.8. Assess, as applicable, whether each Data Integrity Rule Binding is addressed by one or more database object is addressed by one or more Business Information Systems as may be appropriate.

34.3.2.8.1. Assess whether each Data Integrity Rule Binding is properly addressed by one or more database object data structures.

34.3.2.8.2. Assess whether each Data Integrity Rule Binding is properly addressed by one or more database object Primitive Data Transformations.

34.3.2.8.3. Assess whether each Data Integrity Rule Binding is properly addressed by one or more database object states.

34.3.2.8.4. Assess whether each Data Integrity Rule Binding is properly addressed by one or more database object Business Information Systems.

34.3.2.8.5. Assess whether the allocated database object Data Integrity Rule Bindings do not result in conflicts that need to be resolved.

34.3.2.9. Assess, as applicable, whether each Data Integrity Rule Binding is addressed by one or more External Data Interface Requirements as may be appropriate.

34.3.2.9.1. Assess whether the Data Integrity Rule Binding can be adequately supported by the specifications of the External Data Interface data Columns.

34.3.2.9.2. Assess whether the Data Integrity Rule Binding can be adequately supported by the specifications of the External Data Interface data Column data types.

34.3.2.9.3. Assess whether the Data Integrity Rule Binding can be adequately supported by the specifications of the External Data Interface data Column Value Domains.

34.3.2.9.4. Assess whether the Data Integrity Rule Binding can be adequately supported by the specifications of the External Data Interface data Column precision, scale, and granularity.

34.3.2.10. Assess whether each Data Integrity Rule Binding is addressed by one or more use case is addressed by one or more Value Domains and management as may be appropriate.

34.3.2.10.1. Assess whether the Data Integrity Rule Binding is sufficiently detailed to reflect the actions, conditions, and logic of use cases as specified.

34.3.2.11. Assess whether each Data Integrity Rule Binding is addressed by one or more User Acceptance Tests as may be appropriate.

34.3.2.11.1. Assess whether the User Acceptance Test allocated Data Integrity Rule Bindings are of sufficient detail to enable a pass/fail result.

34.3.2.11.2. Assess whether each Data Integrity Rule Binding is addressed by one or more User Acceptance Test is addressed by one or more Value Domains and management as may be appropriate.

34.3.2.11.3. Assess whether the allocated User Acceptance Test Data Integrity Rule Bindings do not result in conflicts that need to be resolved.

34.3.2.12. Assess whether each Data Integrity Rule Binding is addressed by one or more Value Domain management as may be appropriate.

34.3.2.12.1. Assess whether the Data Integrity Rule Binding is sufficiently detailed to address the Value Domains as specified.

34.3.2.12.2. Assess whether the allocated Value Domain Data Integrity Rules Binding do not result in conflicts that need to be resolved.

34.3.2.13. Assess whether the Data Integrity Rule Bindings are properly identified and are appropriately engineered to address a Data Integrity Rule Binding project.

34.3.2.13.1. Assess whether all the Data Integrity Rule Bindings have been delivered in terms of components, instances, and stored metadata work products.

34.3.2.13.2. Assess whether all the Data Integrity Rule Bindings have been properly

detailed as to content, description, methodology, evaluation, presentation, and delivery work steps.

34.3.2.13.3. Assess whether all the Data Integrity Rule Bindings have been properly allocated sufficient unit effort estimates.

34.3.2.13.4. Assess whether all the Data Integrity Rule Bindings have been properly allocated sufficient quantity of units that have to be developed.

34.3.2.13.5. Assess whether all the Data Integrity Rule Bindings have been properly allocated work environment factors to determine an accurate estimate of required resources.

34.3.2.13.6. Assess whether all the Data Integrity Rule Bindings have been properly allocated work accomplishment and recording functions necessary to support earned value reporting.

34.3.2.13.7. Assess whether all the Data Integrity Rule Bindings have been properly allocated metadata recording effort to ensure that all interrelationships are properly recorded into the Metabase System database.

34.3.2.14. Assign the risk level associated with each Data Integrity Rule Binding not properly constructed.

34.3.3. Determine the findings and create draft assessment report.

34.3.4. Present the findings and revise draft assessment report.

34.3.5. Create final assessment report and deliver to the auditing organization.

35. Data Elements

35.1. Assess Concept.
35.1.1. Identify artifacts that bear on the assessment.
35.1.1.1. Identify the appropriate set of Concept documents.
35.1.1.1.1. Review Concept documents.
35.1.1.1.2. Review scope and business problem related documentation.
35.1.1.1.3. Identify the Concepts that are defined and captured.
35.1.1.1.4. Identify the work products appropriate to the evaluation of Concept models.
35.1.1.2. For each Concept:
35.1.1.2.1. Identify components, that is, Concept, Data Element Concept, and Data Element.
35.1.1.2.2. Identify the definitions for each Concept component.
35.1.2. Perform the assessment.
35.1.2.1. Assess each Concept.
35.1.2.1.1. Assess the accuracy, quality and completeness of each Concept with respect to the business requirements.
35.1.2.1.2. Assess whether Concept are able to be inferred from business requirements, and if not whether business requirements or Concept need to be enhanced.
35.1.2.2. Assess Concept work products.
35.1.2.2.1. Assess that all Concepts are identified and are properly constructed.
35.1.2.2.2. Assess that all Concepts are directly related to enterprise data representations.
35.1.2.2.3. Assess that all contained Concepts are properly related subordinate Concepts.
35.1.2.3. Assess whether the Concepts are properly identified and are appropriately engineered to address a Concept project.
35.1.2.3.1. Assess whether all the Concepts have been delivered in terms of components, instances, and stored metadata work products.
35.1.2.3.2. Assess whether all the Concepts have been properly detailed as to content, description, methodology, evaluation, presentation, and delivery work steps.
35.1.2.3.3. Assess whether all the Concepts have been properly allocated sufficient unit effort estimates.
35.1.2.3.4. Assess whether all the Concepts have been properly allocated sufficient quantity of units that have to be developed.
35.1.2.3.5. Assess whether all the Concepts have been properly allocated work environment factors to determine an accurate estimate of required resources.
35.1.2.3.6. Assess whether all the Concepts have been properly allocated work

accomplishment and recording functions necessary to support earned value reporting.

35.1.2.3.7. Assess whether all the Concepts have been properly allocated metadata recording effort to ensure that all interrelationships are properly recorded into the Metabase System database.

35.1.2.4. Assign the risk level associated with each Concept not properly constructed.

35.1.3. Determine the findings and create draft assessment report.

35.1.4. Present the findings and revise draft assessment report.

35.1.5. Create final assessment report and deliver to the auditing organization.

35.2. Assess Concept Structure

35.2.1. Identify artifacts that bear on the assessment.

35.2.1.1. Identify the appropriate set of Concept Structures.

35.2.1.1.1. Review Concept Structure documents.

35.2.1.1.2. Review scope and business problem related documentation.

35.2.1.1.3. Identify the Concept Structures that are defined and captured.

35.2.1.1.4. Identify the Concept Structures related work products.

35.2.1.2. For each Concept Structure related work product assessment:

35.2.1.2.1. Identify the relevant component.

35.2.1.2.2. Identify the description for each interrelated Concept Structure component.

35.2.2. Perform the assessment.

35.2.2.1. Assess each Concept Structure.

35.2.2.1.1. Assess the accuracy, quality and completeness of each Concept Structure with respect to the business requirements.

35.2.2.1.2. Assess whether Concept Structures are able to be inferred from business requirements, and if not whether business requirements or Concept Structures need to be enhanced.

35.2.2.1.3. Assess whether each Concept Structures hierarchy/network is properly specified, and that all Concept Structures names and descriptions are well defined, non-overlapping, and have been formally approved.

35.2.2.2. Assess whether the Concept Structures are properly identified and are appropriately engineered to address a Concept Structure project.

35.2.2.2.1. Assess whether all the Concept Structures have been delivered in terms of components, instances, and stored metadata work products.

35.2.2.2.2. Assess whether all the Concept Structures have been properly detailed as to content, description, methodology, evaluation, presentation, and delivery work steps.

35.2.2.2.3. Assess whether all the Concept Structures have been properly allocated sufficient unit effort estimates.

35.2.2.2.4. Assess whether all the Concept Structures have been properly allocated sufficient quantity of units that have to be developed.

35.2.2.2.5. Assess whether all the Concept Structures have been properly allocated work environment factors to determine an accurate estimate of required resources.

35.2.2.2.6. Assess whether all the Concept Structures have been properly allocated work accomplishment and recording functions necessary to support earned value Business Event Cycle.

35.2.2.2.7. Assess whether all the Concept Structures have been properly allocated metadata recording effort to ensure that all interrelationships are properly recorded into the Metabase System database.

35.2.2.3. Assign the risk level associated with each Concept Structure not properly constructed.

35.2.3. Determine the findings and create draft assessment report.

35.2.4. Present the findings and revise draft assessment report.

35.2.5. Create final assessment report Concept Structures and deliver to the auditing organization.

35.3. Assess Conceptual Value Domain.

35.3.1. Identify artifacts that bear on the assessment.

35.3.1.1. Identify the appropriate set of Conceptual Value Domains.

35.3.1.1.1. Review Conceptual Value Domain documents.

35.3.1.1.2. Review scope and business problem related documentation.

35.3.1.1.3. Identify the Conceptual Value Domains that are defined and captured.

35.3.1.1.4. Identify the work products appropriate to the evaluation of Conceptual Value Domains.

35.3.1.2. For each Conceptual Value Domain:

35.3.1.2.1. Identify components, that is, Conceptual Value Domain Structures, Conceptual Value Domain Structure Types, Data Element Concept, and Data Element.

35.3.1.2.2. Identify the definitions for each Conceptual Value Domain component.

35.3.2. Perform the assessment.

35.3.2.1. Assess each Conceptual Value Domain.

35.3.2.1.1. Assess the accuracy, quality and completeness of each Conceptual Value Domain with respect to the business requirements.

35.3.2.1.2. Assess whether Conceptual Value Domain are able to be inferred from business requirements, and if not whether business requirements or Conceptual Value Domain need to be enhanced.

35.3.2.2. Assess whether the Conceptual Value Domains are properly identified and are appropriately engineered to address a Concept project.

35.3.2.2.1. Assess whether all the Conceptual Value Domains s have been delivered in terms of components, instances, and stored metadata work products.

35.3.2.2.2. Assess whether all the Conceptual Value Domains have been properly

detailed as to content, description, methodology, evaluation, presentation, and delivery work steps.

35.3.2.2.3. Assess whether all the Conceptual Value Domains have been properly allocated sufficient unit effort estimates.

35.3.2.2.4. Assess whether all the Conceptual Value Domains have been properly allocated sufficient quantity of units that have to be developed.

35.3.2.2.5. Assess whether all the Conceptual Value Domains have been properly allocated work environment factors to determine an accurate estimate of required resources.

35.3.2.2.6. Assess whether all the Conceptual Value Domains have been properly allocated work accomplishment and recording functions necessary to support earned value reporting.

35.3.2.2.7. Assess whether all the Conceptual Value Domains have been properly allocated metadata recording effort to ensure that all interrelationships are properly recorded into the Metabase System database.

35.3.2.4. Assign the risk level associated with each Conceptual Value Domain not properly constructed.

35.3.3. Determine the findings and create draft assessment report.

35.3.4. Present the findings and revise draft assessment report.

35.3.5. Create final assessment report and deliver to the auditing organization.

35.4. Assess Conceptual Value Domain Structure

35.4.1. Identify artifacts that bear on the assessment.

35.4.1.1. Identify the appropriate set of Conceptual Value Domain Structures.

35.4.1.1.1. Review Conceptual Value Domain Structure documents.

35.4.1.1.2. Review scope and business problem related documentation.

35.4.1.1.3. Identify the Conceptual Value Domain Structures that are defined and captured.

35.4.1.1.4. Identify the Conceptual Value Domain Structures related work products.

35.4.1.2. For each Conceptual Value Domain Structure related work product assessment:

35.4.1.2.1. Identify the relevant component.

35.4.1.2.2. Identify the description for each interrelated Conceptual Value Domain Structure component.

35.4.2. Perform the assessment.

35.4.2.1. Assess each Conceptual Value Domain Structure.

35.4.2.1.1. Assess the accuracy, quality and completeness of each Conceptual Value Domain Structure with respect to the business requirements.

35.4.2.1.2. Assess whether Conceptual Value Domain Structures are able to be inferred from business requirements, and if not whether business requirements or Conceptual Value Domain Structures need to be enhanced.

35.4.2.1.3. Assess whether each Conceptual Value Domain Structure hierarchy/network is properly specified, and that all Conceptual Value Domain Structure names and descriptions are well defined, non-overlapping, and have been formally approved.
35.4.2.2. Assess whether the Conceptual Value Domain Structures are properly identified and are appropriately engineered to address a Conceptual Value Domain Structure project.
35.4.2.2.1. Assess whether all the Conceptual Value Domain Structures have been delivered in terms of components, instances, and stored metadata work products.
35.4.2.2.2. Assess whether all the Conceptual Value Domain Structures have been properly detailed as to content, description, methodology, evaluation, presentation, and delivery work steps.
35.4.2.2.3. Assess whether all the Conceptual Value Domain Structures have been properly allocated sufficient unit effort estimates.
35.4.2.2.4. Assess whether all the Conceptual Value Domain Structures have been properly allocated sufficient quantity of units that have to be developed.
35.4.2.2.5. Assess whether all the Conceptual Value Domain Structures have been properly allocated work environment factors to determine an accurate estimate of required resources.
35.4.2.2.6. Assess whether all the Conceptual Value Domain Structures have been properly allocated work accomplishment and recording functions necessary to support earned value Business Event Cycle.
35.4.2.2.7. Assess whether all the Conceptual Value Domain Structures have been properly allocated metadata recording effort to ensure that all interrelationships are properly recorded into the Metabase System database.
35.4.2.3. Assign the risk level associated with each Conceptual Value Domain Structure not properly constructed.
35.4.3. Determine the findings and create draft assessment report
35.4.4. Present the findings and revise draft assessment report
35.4.5. Create final assessment report and deliver to the auditing organization.

35.5. Assess Data Element Concept.
35.5.1. Identify artifacts that bear on the assessment.
35.5.1.1. Identify the appropriate set of Data Element Concept documents.
35.5.1.1.1. Review Data Element Concept documents.
35.5.1.1.2. Review scope and business problem related documentation.
35.5.1.1.3. Identify the Data Element Concept that are defined and captured.
35.5.1.1.4. Identify the work products appropriate to the evaluation of Data Element Concept models.
35.5.1.2. For each Data Element Concept:

35.5.1.2.1. Identify components, that is, Data Element Concept, Data Element Data Element Concept, and Data Element.

35.5.1.2.2. Identify the definitions for each Data Element Concept component.

35.5.2. Perform the assessment.

35.5.2.1. Assess each Data Element Concept.

35.5.2.1.1. Assess the accuracy, quality and completeness of each Data Element Concept with respect to the business requirements.

35.5.2.1.2. Assess whether Data Element Concept are able to be inferred from business requirements, and if not whether business requirements or Data Element Concept need to be enhanced.

35.5.2.2. Assess Data Element Concept work products.

35.5.2.2.1. Assess that all Data Element Concepts are identified and are properly constructed.

35.5.2.2.2. Assess that all Data Element Concepts are directly related to enterprise data representations.

35.5.2.2.3. Assess that all contained Data Element Concepts are properly related subordinate Data Element Concepts.

35.5.2.2.4. Assess that all Data Element Concepts are properly related to appropriate Concept Structures.

35.5.2.2.5. Assess that all Data Element Concepts are properly related to appropriate Conceptual Value Domains.

35.5.2.3. Assess whether the Data Element Concepts are properly identified and are appropriately engineered to address a Data Element Concept project.

35.5.2.3.1. Assess whether all the Data Element Concepts have been delivered in terms of components, instances, and stored metadata work products.

35.5.2.3.2. Assess whether all the Data Element Concepts have been properly detailed as to content, description, methodology, evaluation, presentation, and delivery work steps.

35.5.2.3.3. Assess whether all the Data Element Concepts have been properly allocated sufficient unit effort estimates.

35.5.2.3.4. Assess whether all the Data Element Concepts have been properly allocated sufficient quantity of units that have to be developed.

35.5.2.3.5. Assess whether all the Data Element Concepts have been properly allocated work environment factors to determine an accurate estimate of required resources.

35.5.2.3.6. Assess whether all the Data Element Concepts have been properly allocated work accomplishment and recording functions necessary to support earned value reporting.

35.5.2.3.7. Assess whether all the Data Element Concepts have been properly allocated metadata recording effort to ensure that all interrelationships are properly recorded into the Metabase System database.

35.5.2.4. Assign the risk level associated with each Data Element Concept not properly constructed.

35.5.3. Determine the findings and create draft assessment report.

35.5.4. Present the findings and revise draft assessment report.

35.5.5. Create final assessment report and deliver to the auditing organization.

35.6. Assess Data Element Concept Structure

35.6.1. Identify artifacts that bear on the assessment.

35.6.1.1. Identify the appropriate set of Data Element Concept Structure documents.

35.6.1.1.1. Review Data Element Concept Structure documents.

35.6.1.1.2. Review scope and business problem related documentation.

35.6.1.1.3. Identify the Data Element Concept Structures that are defined and captured.

35.6.1.1.4. Identify the Data Element Concept Structures related work products.

35.6.1.2. For each Data Element Concept Structures related work product assessment:

35.6.1.2.1. Identify the relevant component.

35.6.1.2.2. Identify the description for each interrelated Data Element Concept Structure component.

35.6.2. Perform the assessment.

35.6.2.1. Assess each Data Element Concept Structure.

35.6.2.1.1. Assess the accuracy, quality and completeness of each Data Element Concept Structure with respect to the business requirements.

35.6.2.1.2. Assess whether Data Element Concept Structures are able to be inferred from business requirements, and if not whether business requirements or Data Element Concept Structures need to be enhanced.

35.6.2.1.3. Assess whether each Data Element Concept Structure hierarchy/network is properly specified, and that all Data Element Concept Structure names and descriptions are well defined, non-overlapping, and have been formally approved.

35.6.2.2. Assess whether the Data Element Concept Structures are properly identified and are appropriately engineered to address a Data Element Concept Structure project.

35.6.2.2.1. Assess whether all the Data Element Concept Structures have been delivered in terms of components, instances, and stored metadata work products.

35.6.2.2.2. Assess whether all the Data Element Concept Structures have been properly detailed as to content, description, methodology, evaluation, presentation, and delivery work steps.

35.6.2.2.3. Assess whether all the Data Element Concept Structures have been properly allocated sufficient unit effort estimates.

35.6.2.2.4. Assess whether all the Data Element Concept Structures have been properly allocated sufficient quantity of units that have to be developed.

35.6.2.2.5. Assess whether all the Data Element Concept Structures have been properly allocated work environment factors to determine an accurate estimate of required resources.

35.6.2.2.6. Assess whether all the Data Element Concept Structures have been properly allocated work accomplishment and recording functions necessary to support earned value Business Event Cycle.

35.6.2.2.7. Assess whether all the Data Element Concept Structures have been properly allocated metadata recording effort to ensure that all interrelationships are properly recorded into the Metabase System database.

35.6.2.3. Assign the risk level associated with each Data Element Concept Structure not properly constructed.

35.6.3. Determine the findings and create draft assessment report.

35.6.4. Present the findings and revise draft assessment report.

35.6.5. Create final assessment report and deliver to the auditing organization.

35.7. Assess Data Element.

35.7.1. Identify artifacts that bear on the assessment.

35.7.1.1. Identify the appropriate set of Data Element documents.

35.7.1.1.1. Review Data Element documents.

35.7.1.1.2. Review scope and business problem related documentation.

35.7.1.1.3. Identify the Data Elements that are defined and captured.

35.7.1.1.4. Identify the work products appropriate to the evaluation of Data Element models.

35.7.1.2. For each Data Element:

35.7.1.2.1. Identify components, that is, Concept, Conceptual Value Domain, Value Domain, Data Element Concept, Data Element Classification, and Data Element.

35.7.2. Perform the assessment.

35.7.2.1. Assess each Data Element.

35.7.2.1.1. Assess the accuracy, quality and completeness of each Data Element with respect to the business requirements.

35.7.2.1.2. Assess whether Data Element are able to be inferred from business requirements, and if not whether business requirements or Data Element need to be enhanced.

35.7.2.1.3. Assess the completeness and accuracy of Data Elements common business names, long definitions and local definitions against requirements.

35.7.2.3. Assess Data Element Value Domain Assignments.

35.7.2.3.1. Assess whether the set of Value Domains for every Data Element are defined unambiguously, clearly, distinctly, and not-overlapping.

35.7.2.3.2. Assess whether every Data Element that is to have a restricted Value Domain is identified and is correctly addressed by the appropriate set of properly configured Value Domain management metadata.

35.7.2.3.3. Assess Data Element Meta Category Value Assignments.

35.7.2.3.3.1. Assess whether the set of Meta Category Values for every Data Element are defined unambiguously, clearly, distinctly, and not-overlapping.

35.7.2.3.3.2. Assess whether every Data Element that is to have a restricted Value Domain is identified and is correctly addressed by the appropriate set of properly configured Value Domain management metadata.

35.7.2.4. Assess whether the Data Elements are properly identified and are appropriately engineered to address a Data Element project.

35.7.2.4.1. Assess whether all the Data Elements have been delivered in terms of components, instances, and stored metadata work products.

35.7.2.4.2. Assess whether all the Data Elements have been properly detailed as to content, description, methodology, evaluation, presentation, and delivery work steps.

35.7.2.4.3. Assess whether all the Data Elements have been properly allocated sufficient unit effort estimates.

35.7.2.4.4. Assess whether all the Data Elements have been properly allocated sufficient quantity of units that have to be developed.

35.7.2.4.5. Assess whether all the Data Elements have been properly allocated work environment factors to determine an accurate estimate of required resources.

35.7.2.4.6. Assess whether all the Data Elements have been properly allocated work accomplishment and recording functions necessary to support earned value reporting.

35.7.2.4.7. Assess whether all the Data Elements have been properly allocated metadata recording effort to ensure that all interrelationships are properly recorded into the Metabase System database.

35.7.2.5. Assign the risk level associated with each Data Element not properly constructed.

35.7.3. Determine the findings and create draft assessment report.

35.7.4. Present the findings and revise draft assessment report.

35.7.5. Create final assessment report and deliver to the auditing organization.

35.8. Assess Value Domain.

35.8.1. Identify artifacts that bear on the assessment.

35.8.1.1. Identify the appropriate set of Value Domain models.

35.8.1.1.1. Review Value Domain documents.

35.8.1.1.2. Review scope and business problem related documentation.

35.8.1.1.3. Identify the Value Domain that are defined and captured.

35.8.1.1.4. Identify the Value Domain work products appropriate to the evaluation of Value Domain models.

35.8.1.2. For each Value Domain:

35.8.1.2.1. Identify components, that is, Conceptual Value Domain, Value Domain Values, Data Element Value Domain, Attribute Value Domain, Column Value Domain, and DBMS Column Value Domain.

35.8.1.2.2. Identify the definitions for each Value Domain model component.

35.8.2. Perform the assessment.

35.8.2.1. Assess each Value Domain.

35.8.2.1.1. Assess the accuracy, quality and completeness of each Value Domain with respect to the business requirements.

35.8.2.1.2. Assess whether Value Domain are able to be inferred from business requirements, and if not whether business requirements or Value Domain need to be enhanced.

35.8.2.1.3. Assess whether each Value Domain is properly specified and that all Value Domain values allowed are well defined, non-overlapping, and have been formally approved for use in the databases and enforced.

35.8.2.2. Assess Data Element Value Domain Assignments.

35.8.2.2.1. Assess whether the set of Value Domains for every Data Element are defined unambiguously, clearly, distinctly, and not-overlapping.

35.8.2.2.2. Assess whether every Data Element that is to have a restricted Value Domain is identified and is correctly addressed by the appropriate set of properly configured Value Domain management metadata.

35.8.2.3. Assess Specified Data Model Entity Attribute Value Domain.

35.8.2.3.1. Assess whether the set of Value Domains for every Specified Data Model Entity Attribute are defined unambiguously, clearly, distinctly, and not-overlapping.

35.8.2.3.2. Assess whether every Specified Data Model Entity Attribute that is to have a restricted Value Domain is identified and is correctly addressed by the appropriate set of properly configured Value Domain management metadata.

35.8.2.3.3. Assess whether a Value Domain that is assigned to an Attribute is a subset of a Value Domain that is assigned to a Data Element.

35.8.2.4. Assess Implemented Database Table Column Value Domain.

35.8.2.4.1. Assess whether the set of Value Domains for every Implemented Data Model Table Column are defined unambiguously, clearly, distinctly, and not-overlapping.

35.8.2.4.2. Assess whether every Implemented Database Table Column that is to have a restricted Value Domain is identified and is correctly addressed by the appropriate set of properly configured Value Domain management metadata.

35.8.2.4.3. Assess whether a Value Domain that is assigned to an Implemented Database Table Column is a subset of a Value Domain that is assigned to an Attribute.

35.8.2.5. Assess Operational Database DBMS Table Column Value Domain.

35.8.2.5.1. Assess whether the set of Value Domains for every Operational Database DBMS Table Column are defined unambiguously, clearly, distinctly, and not-overlapping.

35.8.2.5.2. Assess whether every Operational Database DBMS Table Column that is to have a restricted Value Domain is identified and is correctly addressed by the appropriate set of properly configured Value Domain management metadata.

35.8.2.5.3. Assess whether a Value Domain that is assigned to an Operational Database DBMS Table Column is a subset of a Value Domain that is assigned to an Implemented Database Model DBMS Table Column.

35.8.2.6. Assess whether the Value Domains are properly identified and are appropriately engineered to address a Value Domain project.

35.8.2.6.1. Assess whether all the Value Domains have been delivered in terms of components, instances, and stored metadata work products.

35.8.2.6.2. Assess whether all the Value Domains have been properly detailed as to content, description, methodology, evaluation, presentation, and delivery work steps.

35.8.2.6.3. Assess whether all the Value Domains have been properly allocated sufficient unit effort estimates.

35.8.2.6.4. Assess whether all the Value Domains have been properly allocated sufficient quantity of units that have to be developed.

35.8.2.6.5. Assess whether all the Value Domains have been properly allocated work environment factors to determine an accurate estimate of required resources.

35.8.2.6.6. Assess whether all the Value Domains have been properly allocated work accomplishment and recording functions necessary to support earned value reporting.

35.8.2.6.7. Assess whether all the Value Domains have been properly allocated metadata recording effort to ensure that all interrelationships are properly recorded into the Metabase System database.

35.8.2.7. Assign the risk level associated with each Value Domain not properly constructed.

35.8.3. Determine the findings and create draft assessment report.

35.8.4. Present the findings and revise draft assessment report.

35.8.5. Create final assessment report and deliver to the auditing organization.

35.9. Assess Value Domain Structure

35.9.1. Identify artifacts that bear on the assessment.

35.9.1.1. Identify the appropriate set of Value Domain Structure documents.

35.9.1.1.1. Review Value Domain Structure documents.

35.9.1.1.2. Review scope and business problem related documentation.
35.9.1.1.3. Identify the Value Domain Structures that are defined and captured.
35.9.1.1.4. Identify the Value Domain Structures related work products.
35.9.1.2. For each Value Domain Structure related work product assessment:
35.9.1.2.1. Identify the relevant component.
35.9.1.2.2. Identify the description for each interrelated Value Domain Structure component.
35.9.2. Perform the assessment.
35.9.2.1. Assess each Value Domain Structure.
35.9.2.1.1. Assess the accuracy, quality and completeness of each Value Domain Structure with respect to the business requirements.
35.9.2.1.2. Assess whether Value Domain Structures are able to be inferred from business requirements, and if not whether business requirements or Value Domain Structures need to be enhanced.
35.9.2.1.3. Assess whether each Value Domain Structure hierarchy/network is properly specified, and that all Value Domain Structure names and descriptions are well defined, non-overlapping, and have been formally approved.
35.9.2.2. Assess whether the Value Domain Structures are properly identified and are appropriately engineered to address a Value Domain Structure project.
35.9.2.2.1. Assess whether all the Value Domain Structures have been delivered in terms of components, instances, and stored metadata work products.
35.9.2.2.2. Assess whether all the Value Domain Structures have been properly detailed as to content, description, methodology, evaluation, presentation, and delivery work steps.
35.9.2.2.3. Assess whether all the Value Domain Structures have been properly allocated sufficient unit effort estimates.
35.9.2.2.4. Assess whether all the Value Domain Structures have been properly allocated sufficient quantity of units that have to be developed.
35.9.2.2.5. Assess whether all the Value Domain Structures have been properly allocated work environment factors to determine an accurate estimate of required resources.
35.9.2.2.6. Assess whether all the Value Domain Structures have been properly allocated work accomplishment and recording functions necessary to support earned value Business Event Cycle.
35.9.2.2.7. Assess whether all the Value Domain Structures have been properly allocated metadata recording effort to ensure that all interrelationships are properly recorded into the Metabase System database.
35.9.2.3. Assign the risk level associated with each Value Domain Structure not properly constructed.
35.9.3. Determine the findings and create draft assessment report.

35.9.4. Present the findings and revise draft assessment report.
35.9.5. Create final assessment report and deliver to the auditing organization.

35.10. Assess Meta Category Value.
35.10.1. Identify artifacts that bear on the assessment.
35.10.1.1. Identify the appropriate set of Meta Category Value documents.
35.10.1.1.1. Review Meta Category Value documents.
35.10.1.1.2. Review scope and business problem related documentation.
35.10.1.1.3. Identify the Meta Category Value that are defined and captured.
35.10.1.1.4. Identify the work products appropriate to the evaluation of Meta Category Value models.
35.10.1.2. For each Meta Category Value :
35.10.1.2.1. Identify components, that is, Meta Category Value Type Class, Meta Category Value Type, and Meta Category Values, Data Element Meta Category Values, Attribute Meta Category Values, and Column Meta Category Values.
35.10.1.2.2. Identify the definitions for each Meta Category Value component.
35.10.2. Perform the assessment.
35.10.2.1. Assess each Meta Category Value.
35.10.2.1.1. Assess the accuracy, quality and completeness of each Meta Category Value with respect to the business requirements.
35.10.2.1.2. Assess whether Meta Category Values are able to be inferred from business requirements, and if not whether business requirements or Meta Category Value need to be enhanced.
35.10.2.1.3. Assess whether each Meta Category Value hierarchy is properly specified, and that all Meta Category Value names and descriptions are well defined, non-overlapping, and have been formally approved.
35.10.2.2. Assess Meta Category Value Type Classes.
35.10.2.2.1. Assess whether the first of the two Meta Category Type Class values is properly specified and clearly means that the assigned Meta Category Values will go before the common business name employed in name construction.
35.10.2.2.2. Assess whether second of the two Meta Category Type Class values is properly specified and clearly means that the assigned Meta Category Values will go after the common business name employed in name construction.
35.10.2.3. Assess Meta Category Value Types.
35.10.2.3.1. Assess whether each Meta Category Value Type hierarchies/networks are properly specified and that all Meta Category Type Values on a given level are proper peers while Meta Category Value Type Values on a lower level are well defined, non-overlapping, and have been formally approved for use in the databases and enforced.

35.10.2.3.2. Assess whether each Meta Category Value Type hierarchy is clearly assigned to appear either before or after the common business name employed in name construction.

35.10.2.3.3. Assess whether each Meta Category Value Type hierarchy sequence number is clearly assigned and is understood to mean that a given selected set of Meta Category Values appears in either a left-right before the common business name or in a left-right after order represented by the sequence number.

35.10.2.4. Assess Meta Category Values.

35.10.2.4.1. Assess whether each Meta Category Value hierarchies/networks are properly specified and that all Meta Category Values on a given level are proper peers while Meta Category Values on a lower level are well defined, non-overlapping, and have been formally approved for use in the databases and enforced.

35.10.2.4.2. Assess whether each Meta Category Value hierarchy is clearly assigned to a Meta Category Value Type.

35.10.2.5. Assess Data Element Meta Category Value Assignments.

35.10.2.5.1. Assess whether the set of Meta Category Values for every Data Element are defined unambiguously, clearly, distinctly, and not-overlapping.

35.10.2.5.2. Assess whether every Data Element that is to have a restricted Value Domain is identified and is correctly addressed by the appropriate set of properly configured Value Domain management metadata.

35.10.2.6. Assess Specified Data Model Entity Attribute Meta Category Value Assignments.

35.10.2.6.1. Assess whether the set of Meta Category Values for every Specified Data Model Entity Attribute are defined unambiguously, clearly, distinctly, and not-overlapping.

35.10.2.3.2. Assess whether every Specified Data Model Entity Attribute that is to have a restricted Meta Category Values is identified and is correctly addressed by the appropriate set of properly configured Meta Category Values management metadata.

35.10.2.6.3. Assess whether a Meta Category Values that is assigned to an Attribute is a subset of a Meta Category Values assigned to a Data Element.

35.10.2.7. Assess Implemented Database Table Column Meta Category Value Assignments.

35.10.2.7.1. Assess whether the set of Meta Category Values for every Implemented Data Model Table Column are defined unambiguously, clearly, distinctly, and not-overlapping.

35.10.2.7.2. Assess whether every Implemented Database Table Column that is to have a restricted Meta Category Values is identified and is correctly addressed by the appropriate set of properly configured Meta Category Values management metadata.

35.10.2.7.3. Assess whether a Meta Category Values that is assigned to an Implemented Database Table Column is a subset of a Meta Category Values assigned to an Attribute.

35.10.2.9. Assess whether the Meta Category Values are properly identified and are appropriately engineered to address a Meta Category Value project.

35.10.2.9.1. Assess whether all the Meta Category Values have been delivered in terms of components, instances, and stored metadata work products.

35.10.2.9.2. Assess whether all the Meta Category Values have been properly detailed as to content, description, methodology, evaluation, presentation, and delivery work steps.

35.10.2.9.3. Assess whether all the Meta Category Values have been properly allocated sufficient unit effort estimates.

35.10.2.9.4. Assess whether all the Meta Category Values have been properly allocated sufficient quantity of units that have to be developed.

35.10.2.9.5. Assess whether all the Meta Category Values have been properly allocated work environment factors to determine an accurate estimate of required resources.

35.10.2.9.6. Assess whether all the Meta Category Values have been properly allocated work accomplishment and recording functions necessary to support earned value reporting.

35.10.2.9.7. Assess whether all the Meta Category Values have been properly allocated metadata recording effort to ensure that all interrelationships are properly recorded into the Metabase System database.

35.10.2.10. Assign the risk level associated with each Meta Category Value not properly constructed.

35.10.3. Determine the findings and create draft assessment report.

35.10.4. Present the findings and revise draft assessment report.

35.10.5. Create final assessment report and deliver to the auditing organization.

35.11. Assess Meta Category Value Type.

35.11.1. Identify artifacts that bear on the assessment.

35.11.1.1. Identify the appropriate set of Meta Category Value Type documents.

35.11.1.1.1. Review Meta Category Value Type documents.

35.11.1.1.2. Review scope and business problem related documentation.

35.11.1.1.3. Identify the Meta Category Value Type that are defined and captured.

35.11.1.1.4. Identify the work products appropriate to the evaluation of Meta Category Value Types.

35.11.1.2. For each Meta Category Value Type :

35.11.1.2.1. Identify components, that is, Meta Category Value Type Class, Meta Category Value Type, and Meta Category Value Types, Data Element Meta Category Value Types, Attribute Meta Category Value Types, and Column Meta Category Value Types.

35.11.1.2.2. Identify the definitions for each Meta Category Value Type component.

35.11.2. Perform the assessment.

35.11.2.1. Assess each Meta Category Value Type.

35.11.2.1.1. Assess the accuracy, quality and completeness of each Meta Category Value Type with respect to the business requirements.

35.11.2.1.2. Assess whether Meta Category Value Types are able to be inferred from business requirements, and if not whether business requirements or Meta Category Value Type need to be enhanced.

35.11.2.1.3. Assess whether each Meta Category Value Type hierarchy is properly specified, and that all Meta Category Value Type names and descriptions are well defined, non-overlapping, and have been formally approved.

35.11.2.3.4. Assess whether each Meta Category Value Type hierarchy is clearly assigned to appear either before or after the common business name employed in name construction.

35.11.2.3.5. Assess whether each Meta Category Value Type hierarchy sequence number is clearly assigned and is understood to mean that a given selected set of Meta Category Value Types appears in either a left-right before the common business name or in a left-right after order represented by the sequence number.

35.11.2.4. Assess whether the Meta Category Value Types are properly identified and are appropriately engineered to address a Meta Category Value Type project.

35.11.2.4.1. Assess whether all the Meta Category Value Types have been delivered in terms of components, instances, and stored metadata work products.

35.11.2.4.2. Assess whether all the Meta Category Value Types have been properly detailed as to content, description, methodology, evaluation, presentation, and delivery work steps.

35.11.2.4.3. Assess whether all the Meta Category Value Types have been properly allocated sufficient unit effort estimates.

35.11.2.4.4. Assess whether all the Meta Category Value Types have been properly allocated sufficient quantity of units that have to be developed.

35.11.2.4.5. Assess whether all the Meta Category Value Types have been properly allocated work environment factors to determine an accurate estimate of required resources.

35.11.2.4.6. Assess whether all the Meta Category Value Types have been properly allocated work accomplishment and recording functions necessary to support earned value reporting.

35.11.2.4.7. Assess whether all the Meta Category Value Types have been properly allocated metadata recording effort to ensure that all interrelationships are properly recorded into the Metabase System database.

35.11.2.5. Assign the risk level associated with each Meta Category Value Type not properly constructed.

35.11.3. Determine the findings and create draft assessment report.
35.11.4. Present the findings and revise draft assessment report.
35.11.5. Create final assessment report and deliver to the auditing organization.

35.12. Assess Meta Category Value Type Class Type.
35.12.1. Identify artifacts that bear on the assessment.
35.12.1.1. Identify the appropriate set of Meta Category Value Type Class documents.
35.12.1.1.1. Review Meta Category Value Type Class documents.
35.12.1.1.2. Review scope and business problem related documentation.
35.12.1.1.3. Identify the Meta Category Value Type Class that are defined and captured.
35.12.1.1.4. Identify the work products appropriate to the evaluation of Meta Category Value Type Classes.
35.12.1.2. For each Meta Category Value Type Class :
35.12.1.2.1. Identify components, that is, Meta Category Value Type,
35.12.1.2.2. Identify the definitions for each Meta Category Value Type Class component.
35.12.2. Perform the assessment.
35.12.2.1. Assess each Meta Category Value Type Class.
35.12.2.1.1. Assess the accuracy, quality and completeness of each Meta Category Value Type Class with respect to the business requirements.
35.12.2.1.2. Assess whether Meta Category Value Type Classes are able to be inferred from business requirements, and if not whether business requirements or Meta Category Value Type Class need to be enhanced.
35.12.2.1.3. Assess whether each Meta Category Value Type Class hierarchy is properly specified, and that all Meta Category Value Type Class names and descriptions are well defined, non-overlapping, and have been formally approved.
35.12.2.3.4 Assess whether each Meta Category Value Type Class hierarchy sequence number is clearly assigned and is understood to mean that a given selected set of Meta Category Value Type and Meta Category Values appears in either a left-right before the common business name or in a left-right after order represented by the sequence number.
35.12.2.4. Assess whether the Meta Category Value Type Classes are properly identified and are appropriately engineered to address a Meta Category Value Type Class project.
35.12.2.4.1. Assess whether all the Meta Category Value Type Classes have been delivered in terms of components, instances, and stored metadata work products.
35.12.2.4.2. Assess whether all the Meta Category Value Type Classes have been properly detailed as to content, description, methodology, evaluation,

presentation, and delivery work steps.
35.12.2.4.3. Assess whether all the Meta Category Value Type Classes have been properly allocated sufficient unit effort estimates.
35.12.2.4.4. Assess whether all the Meta Category Value Type Classes have been properly allocated sufficient quantity of units that have to be developed.
35.12.2.4.5. Assess whether all the Meta Category Value Type Classes have been properly allocated work environment factors to determine an accurate estimate of required resources.
35.12.2.4.6. Assess whether all the Meta Category Value Type Classes have been properly allocated work accomplishment and recording functions necessary to support earned value reporting.
35.12.2.4.7. Assess whether all the Meta Category Value Type Classes have been properly allocated metadata recording effort to ensure that all interrelationships are properly recorded into the Metabase System database.
35.12.2.5. Assign the risk level associated with each Meta Category Value Type Class not properly constructed.
35.12.3. Determine the findings and create draft assessment report.
35.12.4. Present the findings and revise draft assessment report.
35.12.5. Create final assessment report and deliver to the auditing organization.

35.13. Assess Derived Data Element.
35.13.1. Identify artifacts that bear on the assessment.
35.13.1.1. Identify the appropriate set of Derived Data Element documents.
35.13.1.1.1. Review Derived Data Element documents.
35.13.1.1.2. Review scope and business problem related documentation.
35.13.1.1.3. Identify the Derived Data Elements that are defined and captured.
35.13.1.1.4. Identify the work products appropriate to the evaluation of Derived Data Element models.
35.13.1.2. For each Derived Data Element:
35.13.1.2.1. Identify components, that is, Compound Data Elements, Derived Data Elements, Data Elements and View Columns.
35.13.1.2.2. Identify the definitions for each Derived Data Element component.
35.13.2. Perform the assessment.
35.13.2.1. Assess each Derived Data Element.
35.13.2.1.1. Assess the accuracy, quality and completeness of each Derived Data Element with respect to the business requirements.
35.13.2.1.2. Assess whether Derived Data Elements are able to be inferred from business requirements, and if not whether business requirements or Derived Data Elements need to be enhanced.
35.13.2.1.3. Assess the completeness and accuracy of Derived Data Elements common business names, long definitions and local definitions against

requirements.

35.13.2.1.4. Assess that all Data Elements, which are the proper sources of contextual Derived Data Elements are identified and are properly constructed.

35.13.2.1.5. Assess the process through which the Derived Data Element value is constructed.

35.13.2.2. Assess the adequacy of each View Data Model with respect to the Derived Data Elements.

35.13.2.2.1. Assess whether each Derived Data Element View Column is properly mapped to a DBMS Column.

35.13.2.3. Assess whether the Derived Data Elements are properly identified and are appropriately engineered to address a Derived Data Element project.

35.13.2.3.1. Assess whether all the Derived Data Elements have been delivered in terms of components, instances, and stored metadata work products.

35.13.2.3.2. Assess whether all the Derived Data Elements have been properly detailed as to content, description, methodology, evaluation, presentation, and delivery work steps.

35.13.2.3.3. Assess whether all the Derived Data Elements have been properly allocated sufficient unit effort estimates.

35.13.2.3.4. Assess whether all the Derived Data Element have been properly allocated sufficient quantity of units that have to be developed.

35.13.2.3.5. Assess whether all the Derived Data Elements have been properly allocated work environment factors to determine an accurate estimate of required resources.

35.13.2.3.6. Assess whether all the Derived Data Elements have been properly allocated work accomplishment and recording functions necessary to support earned value reporting.

35.13.2.3.7. Assess whether all the Derived Data Elements have been properly allocated metadata recording effort to ensure that all interrelationships are properly recorded into the Metabase System database.

35.13.2.4. Assign the risk level associated with each Derived Data Element not properly constructed.

35.13.3. Determine the findings and create draft assessment report.

35.13.4. Present the findings and revise draft assessment report.

35.13.5. Create final assessment report and deliver to the auditing organization.

35.14. Assess Compound Data Element.

35.14.1. Identify artifacts that bear on the assessment.

35.14.1.1. Identify the appropriate set of Compound Data Element documents.

35.14.1.1.1. Review Compound Data Element documents.

35.14.1.1.2. Review scope and business problem related documentation.

35.14.1.1.3. Identify the Compound Data Elements that are defined and captured.

35.14.1.1.4. Identify the work products appropriate to the evaluation of Compound

Data Element models.

35.14.1.2. For each Compound Data Element:

35.14.1.2.1. Identify components, that is, Derived Data Elements, Compound Data Elements, Data Elements and View Columns.

35.14.1.2.2. Identify the definitions for each Compound Data Element model component.

35.14.2. Perform the assessment.

35.14.2.1. Assess each Compound Data Element.

35.14.2.1.1. Assess the accuracy, quality and completeness of each Compound Data Element with respect to the business requirements.

35.14.2.1.2. Assess whether Compound Data Elements are able to be inferred from business requirements, and if not whether business requirements or Compound Data Elements need to be enhanced.

35.14.2.1.3. Assess the completeness and accuracy of Compound Data Elements common business names, long definitions and local definitions against requirements.

35.14.2.1.4. Assess that all Data Elements, which are the proper sources of components of Compound Data Elements are identified and are properly constructed.

35.14.2.1.5. Assess the process through which the Compound Data Element value is constructed through the joining of Data Elements assigned to the Compound Data Element.

35.14.2.2. Assess the adequacy of each View Data Model with respect to the Compound Data Elements.

35.14.2.2.1. Assess whether each Compound Data Element View Column is properly mapped to a DBMS Column.

35.14.2.3. Assess whether the Compound Data Elements are properly identified and are appropriately engineered to address a Compound Data Element project.

35.14.2.3.1. Assess whether all the Compound Data Elements have been delivered in terms of components, instances, and stored metadata work products.

35.14.2.3.2. Assess whether all the Compound Data Elements have been properly detailed as to content, description, methodology, evaluation, presentation, and delivery work steps.

35.14.2.3.3. Assess whether all the Compound Data Elements have been properly allocated sufficient unit effort estimates.

35.14.2.3.4. Assess whether all the Compound Data Element have been properly allocated sufficient quantity of units that have to be developed.

35.14.2.3.5. Assess whether all the Compound Data Elements have been properly allocated work environment factors to determine an accurate estimate of required resources.

35.14.2.3.6. Assess whether all the Compound Data Elements have been properly

allocated work accomplishment and recording functions necessary to support earned value reporting.

35.14.2.3.7. Assess whether all the Compound Data Element have been properly allocated metadata recording effort to ensure that all interrelationships are properly recorded into the Metabase System database.

35.14.2.4. Assign the risk level associated with each Compound Data Element not properly constructed.

35.14.3. Determine the findings and create draft assessment report.

35.14.4. Present the findings and revise draft assessment report.

35.14.5. Create final assessment report and deliver to the auditing organization.

35.15 Assess Compound Data Element Structure

35.15.1. Identify artifacts that bear on the assessment.

35.15.1.1. Identify the appropriate set of Compound Data Element Structure documents.

35.15.1.1.1. Review Compound Data Element Structure documents.

35.15.1.1.2. Review scope and business problem related documentation.

35.15.1.1.3. Identify the Compound Data Element Structures that are defined and captured.

35.15.1.1.4. Identify the Compound Data Element Structures related work products.

35.15.1.2. For each Compound Data Element Structures related work product assessment:

35.15.1.2.1. Identify the relevant component.

35.15.1.2.2. Identify the description for each interrelated Compound Data Element Structure component.

35.15.2. Perform the assessment.

35.15.2.1. Assess each Compound Data Element Structure.

35.15.2.1.1. Assess the accuracy, quality and completeness of each Compound Data Element Structure with respect to the business requirements.

35.15.2.1.2. Assess whether Compound Data Element Structures are able to be inferred from business requirements, and if not whether business requirements or Compound Data Element Structures need to be enhanced.

35.15.2.1.3. Assess whether each Compound Data Element Structure hierarchy/network is properly specified, and that all Compound Data Element Structure names and descriptions are well defined, non-overlapping, and have been formally approved.

35.15.2.2. Assess whether the Compound Data Element Structures are properly identified and are appropriately engineered to address a Compound Data Element Structure project.

35.15.2.2.1. Assess whether all the Compound Data Element Structures have been delivered in terms of components, instances, and stored metadata work

products.

35.15.2.2.2. Assess whether all the Compound Data Element Structures have been properly detailed as to content, description, methodology, evaluation, presentation, and delivery work steps.

35.15.2.2.3. Assess whether all the Compound Data Element Structures have been properly allocated sufficient unit effort estimates.

35.15.2.2.4. Assess whether all the Compound Data Element Structures have been properly allocated sufficient quantity of units that have to be developed.

35.15.2.2.5. Assess whether all the Compound Data Element Structures have been properly allocated work environment factors to determine an accurate estimate of required resources.

35.15.2.2.6. Assess whether all the Compound Data Element Structures have been properly allocated work accomplishment and recording functions necessary to support earned value Business Event Cycle.

35.15.2.2.7. Assess whether all the Compound Data Element Structures have been properly allocated metadata recording effort to ensure that all interrelationships are properly recorded into the Metabase System database.

35.15.2.3. Assign the risk level associated with each Compound Data Element Structure not properly constructed.

35.15.3. Determine the findings and create draft assessment report.

35.15.4. Present the findings and revise draft assessment report.

35.15.5. Create final assessment report and deliver to the auditing organization.

35.16. Assess Business Domains.

35.16.1. Identify artifacts that bear on the assessment.

35.16.1.1. Identify the appropriate set of Business Domain documents.

35.16.1.1.1. Review Business Domain documents.

35.16.1.1.2. Review scope and business problem related documentation.

35.16.1.1.3. Identify the Business Domains that are defined and captured.

35.16.1.1.4. Identify the work products appropriate to the evaluation of Business Domain models.

35.16.1.2. For each Business Domain:

35.16.1.2.1. Identify components, that is, Data Elements.

35.16.1.2.2. Identify the definitions for each Business Domain model component.

35.16.2. Perform the assessment.

35.16.2.1. Assess each Business Domain.

35.16.2.1.1. Assess the accuracy, quality and completeness of each Business Domain with respect to the business requirements.

35.16.2.1.2. Assess whether Business Domains are able to be inferred from business requirements, and if not whether business requirements or Business Domains need to be enhanced.

35.16.2.1.3. Assess that all Business Domains are identified and are properly constructed.
35.16.2.1.4. Assess whether each Business Domain hierarchy is properly specified and that all Business Domain Values on a given level are proper peers while Business Domain Values on a lower level are well defined, non-overlapping, and have been formally approved for use in the databases and enforced.
35.16.2.1.5. Assess that all Data Elements, which are referred to by a Business Domain are identified and are properly constructed.
35.16.2.1.6. Assess that all Business Domains have a properly constructed generated short name and a common business name.
35.16.2.2. Assess whether the Business Domains are properly identified and are appropriately engineered to address a Business Domain project.
35.16.2.2.1. Assess whether all the Business Domains have been delivered in terms of components, instances, and stored metadata work products.
35.16.2.2.2. Assess whether all the Business Domains have been properly detailed as to content, description, methodology, evaluation, presentation, and delivery work steps.
35.16.2.2.3. Assess whether all the Business Domains have been properly allocated sufficient unit effort estimates.
35.16.2.2.4. Assess whether all the Business Domains have been properly allocated sufficient quantity of units that have to be developed.
35.16.2.2.5. Assess whether all the Business Domains have been properly allocated work environment factors to determine an accurate estimate of required resources.
35.16.2.2.6. Assess whether all the Business Domains have been properly allocated work accomplishment and recording functions necessary to support earned value reporting.
35.16.2.2.7. Assess whether all the Business Domains have been properly allocated metadata recording effort to ensure that all interrelationships are properly recorded into the Metabase System database.
35.16.2.3. Assign the risk level associated with each Business Domain not properly constructed.
35.16.3. Determine the findings and create draft assessment report.
35.16.4. Present the findings and revise draft assessment report.
35.16.5. Create final assessment report and deliver to the auditing organization.

35.17. Assess Data Types.
35.17.1. Identify artifacts that bear on the assessment.
35.17.1.1. Identify the appropriate set of Data Type documents.
35.17.1.1.1. Review Data Type documents.
35.17.1.1.2. Review scope and business problem related documentation.

35.17.1.1.3. Identify the Data Types that are defined and captured.
35.17.1.1.4. Identify the work products appropriate to the need for Data Types.
35.17.1.2. For each Data Type:
35.17.1.2.1. Identify components, that is, Data Element.
35.17.1.2.2. Identify the definitions for each Data Type model.
35.17.2. Perform the assessment.
35.17.2.1. Assess each Data Type.
35.17.2.1.1. Assess the accuracy, quality and completeness of each Data Type with respect to the business requirements.
35.17.2.1.2. Assess whether Data Type are able to be inferred from business requirements, and if not whether business requirements or Data Type need to be enhanced.
35.17.2.2. Assess that all Data Types are identified and are properly constructed.
35.17.2.3. Assess the adequacy of each Implemented Database Table Column required SQL Data Types with respect to Data Types.
35.17.2.4. Assess whether a SQL Data Type assigned to an Column is a subset of a Data Type assigned to its parent Data Element.
35.17.2.5. Assess whether the Data Types are properly identified and are appropriately engineered to address a Data Type project.
35.17.2.5.1. Assess whether all the Data Types have been delivered in terms of components, instances, and stored metadata work products.
35.17.2.5.2. Assess whether all the Data Types have been properly detailed as to content, description, methodology, evaluation, presentation, and delivery work steps.
35.17.2.5.3. Assess whether all the Data Types have been properly allocated sufficient unit effort estimates.
35.17.2.5.4. Assess whether all the Data Types have been properly allocated sufficient quantity of units that have to be developed.
35.17.2.5.5. Assess whether all the Data Types have been properly allocated work environment factors to determine an accurate estimate of required resources.
35.17.2.5.6. Assess whether all the Data Types have been properly allocated work accomplishment and recording functions necessary to support earned value reporting.
35.17.2.5.7. Assess whether all the Data Types have been properly allocated metadata recording effort to ensure that all interrelationships are properly recorded into the Metabase System database.
35.17.2.6. Assign the risk level associated with each Data Type not properly constructed.
35.17.3. Determine the findings and create draft assessment report.
35.17.4. Present the findings and revise draft assessment report.
35.17.5. Create final assessment report and deliver to the auditing organization.

36. Specified Data Model

36.1. Assess Subject.
36.1.1. Identify artifacts that bear on the assessment.
36.1.1.1. Identify the appropriate set of Subject documents.
36.1.1.1.1. Review Subject documents.
36.1.1.1.2. Review scope and business problem related documentation.
36.1.1.1.3. Identify the data-based Subjects that are defined and captured.
36.1.1.1.4. Identify the work products appropriate to the evaluation of Subjects.
36.1.1.2. For each Subjects:
36.1.1.2.1. Identify components, that is, Subjects.
36.1.1.2.2. Identify the definitions for each Subject component.
36.1.2. Perform the assessment.
36.1.2.1. Assess each Subject.
36.1.2.1.1. Assess the accuracy, quality and completeness of each Subject with respect to the business requirements.
36.1.2.1.2. Assess whether Subject are able to be inferred from business requirements, and if not whether business requirements or Subject need to be enhanced.
36.1.2.1.3. Assess whether each Subject hierarchy is properly specified, and that all Subject names and descriptions are well defined, non-overlapping, and have been formally approved.
36.1.2.2. Assess whether the Subjects are properly identified and are appropriately engineered to address a Subject project.
36.1.2.2.1. Assess whether all the Subjects have been delivered in terms of components, instances, and stored metadata work products.
36.1.2.2.2. Assess whether all the Subjects have been properly detailed as to content, description, methodology, evaluation, presentation, and delivery work steps.
36.1.2.2.3. Assess whether all the Subjects have been properly allocated sufficient unit effort estimates.
36.1.2.2.4. Assess whether all the Subjects have been properly allocated sufficient quantity of units that have to be developed.
36.1.2.2.5. Assess whether all the Subjects have been properly allocated work environment factors to determine an accurate estimate of required resources.
36.1.2.2.6. Assess whether all the Subjects have been properly allocated work accomplishment and recording functions necessary to support earned value reporting.
36.1.2.2.7. Assess whether all the Subjects have been properly allocated metadata recording effort to ensure that all interrelationships are properly recorded into the Metabase System database.

36.1.2.3. Assign the risk level associated with each Subject not properly constructed.
36.1.3. Determine the findings and create draft assessment report.
36.1.4. Present the findings and revise draft assessment report.
36.1.5. Create final assessment report and deliver to the auditing organization.

36.2. Assess Entity.
36.2.1. Identify artifacts that bear on the assessment.
36.2.1.1. Identify the appropriate set of Entity documents.
36.2.1.1.1. Review Entity documents.
36.2.1.1.2. Review scope and business problem related documentation.
36.2.1.1.3. Identify the Entities that are defined and captured.
36.2.1.1.4. Identify the work products appropriate to the evaluation of Entities.
36.2.1.2. For each Entity:
36.2.1.2.1. Identify components, that is, Subjects, Entities, Attributes and relationships.
36.2.1.2.2. Identify the definitions for each Entity component.
36.2.2. Perform the assessment.
36.2.2.1. Assess each Entity.
36.2.2.1.1. Assess the accuracy, quality and completeness of each Entity with respect to the business requirements.
36.2.2.1.2. Assess whether Entity are able to be inferred from business requirements, and if not whether business requirements or Entity need to be enhanced.
36.2.2.1.3. Assess whether each Entity hierarchy is properly specified, and that all Entity names and descriptions are well defined, non-overlapping, and have been formally approved.
36.2.2.2. Assess whether the Entities are properly identified and are appropriately engineered to address a Entity project.
36.2.2.2.1. Assess whether all the Entities have been delivered in terms of components, instances, and stored metadata work products.
36.2.2.2.2. Assess whether all the Entities have been properly detailed as to content, description, methodology, evaluation, presentation, and delivery work steps.
36.2.2.2.3. Assess whether all the Entities have been properly allocated sufficient unit effort estimates.
36.2.2.2.4. Assess whether all the Entities have been properly allocated sufficient quantity of units that have to be developed.
36.2.2.2.5. Assess whether all the Entities have been properly allocated work environment factors to determine an accurate estimate of required resources.
36.2.2.2.6. Assess whether all the Entities have been properly allocated work accomplishment and recording functions necessary to support earned

value reporting.

36.2.2.2.7. Assess whether all the Entities have been properly allocated metadata recording effort to ensure that all interrelationships are properly recorded into the Metabase System database.

36.2.2.3. Assign the risk level associated with each Entity not properly constructed.

36.2.3. Determine the findings and create draft assessment report.

36.2.4. Present the findings and revise draft assessment report.

36.2.5. Create final assessment report and deliver to the auditing organization.

36.3. Assess Attribute.

36.3.1. Identify artifacts that bear on the assessment.

36.3.1.1. Identify the appropriate set of Attribute documents.

36.3.1.1.1. Review Attribute documents.

36.3.1.1.2. Review scope and business problem related documentation.

36.3.1.1.3. Identify the data-based Attributes that are defined and captured.

36.3.1.1.4. Identify the work products appropriate to the evaluation of Attributes.

36.3.1.2. For each Attributes:

36.3.1.2.1. Identify components, that is, Subjects, Entities, Attributes, Value Domains, and Meta Category Values.

36.3.1.2.2. Identify the definitions for each Attribute.

36.3.2. Perform the assessment.

36.3.2.1. Assess each Attribute.

36.3.2.1.1. Assess the accuracy, quality and completeness of each Attribute with respect to the business requirements.

36.3.2.1.2. Assess whether Attribute are able to be inferred from business requirements, and if not whether business requirements or Attribute need to be enhanced.

36.3.2.1.3. Assess the adequacy of each Attributes with respect to the Business Requirements.

36.3.2.1.4. Assess the completeness and accuracy of Attributes common business names, long definitions and local definitions against requirements.

36.3.2.1.5. Assess whether all implied business requirement Attributes are reflected in an appropriate Entity.

36.3.2.1.6. Ensure that there are Attributes addressing Information Technology infrastructure necessary facts to support Entities for history and auditing.

36.3.2.1.7. Assess the appropriateness of each Attribute assigned Value Domain.

36.3.2.1.7.1. Assess whether the set of Value Domains for every Attribute is defined unambiguously, clearly, distinctly, and not-overlapping.

36.3.2.1.7.2. Assess whether every Attribute that is to have a restricted Value Domain is identified and is correctly addressed by the appropriate set of properly configured Value Domain management metadata.

36.3.2.1.7.3. Assess that every Attribute Value Domain does not semantically conflict with a Data Element Value Domain.

36.3.2.1.8. Assess the appropriateness of each Attributes assigned Meta Category Value.

36.3.2.1.8.1. Assess whether the set of Meta Category Value assigned to Attributes are defined unambiguously, clearly, distinctly, and not-overlapping.

36.3.2.1.8.2. Assess whether every Attributes that is to have a restricted Meta Category Value is identified and is correctly addressed by the appropriate set of properly configured Meta Category Values management metadata.

36.3.2.1.8.3. Assess that every Attributes Meta Category Value does not semantically conflict with a Data Element Meta Category Value.

36.3.2.2. Assess whether the Attributes are properly identified and are appropriately engineered to address a Attribute project.

36.3.2.2.1. Assess whether all the Attributes have been delivered in terms of components, instances, and stored metadata work products.

36.3.2.2.2. Assess whether all the Attributes have been properly detailed as to content, description, methodology, evaluation, presentation, and delivery work steps.

36.3.2.2.3. Assess whether all the Attributes have been properly allocated sufficient unit effort estimates.

36.3.2.2.4. Assess whether all the Attributes have been properly allocated sufficient quantity of units that have to be developed.

36.3.2.2.5. Assess whether all the Attributes have been properly allocated work environment factors to determine an accurate estimate of required resources.

36.3.2.2.6. Assess whether all the Attributes have been properly allocated work accomplishment and recording functions necessary to support earned value reporting.

36.3.2.2.7. Assess whether all the Attributes have been properly allocated metadata recording effort to ensure that all interrelationships are properly recorded into the Metabase System database.

36.3.2.3. Assign the risk level associated with each Attribute not properly constructed.

36.3.3. Determine the findings and create draft assessment report.

36.3.4. Present the findings and revise draft assessment report.

36.3.5. Create final assessment report and deliver to the auditing organization.

36.4. Assess Primary Key.

36.4.1. Identify artifacts that bear on the assessment.

36.4.1.1. Identify the appropriate set of Primary Key documents.

36.4.1.1.1. Review Primary Key documents.

36.4.1.1.2. Review scope and business problem related documentation.

36.4.1.1.3. Identify the data-based Primary Key that are defined and captured.

36.4.1.1.4. Identify the work products appropriate to the evaluation of Primary Key.
36.4.1.2. For each Primary Key:
36.4.1.2.1. Identify components, that is, Entities, and Attributes.
36.4.1.2.2. Identify the definitions for each Primary Key.
36.4.2. Perform the assessment.
36.4.2.1. Assess each Primary Key.
36.4.2.1.1. Assess the accuracy, quality and completeness of each Primary Key with respect to the business requirements.
36.4.2.1.2. Assess whether Primary Key are able to be inferred from business requirements, and if not whether business requirements or Primary Key need to be enhanced.
36.4.2.1.3. Assess the adequacy of each Primary Key with respect to the Business Requirements.
36.4.2.1.4. Assess whether all implied business requirement Primary Key are reflected in an appropriate.
36.4.2.1.5. Assess whether all Primary Key are reflected in business Requirements.
36.4.2.1.6. Assess the appropriateness of each Primary Key assigned Attributes.
36.4.2.1.6.1. Assess the correctness of the assignment and sequence of the Attributes to the Primary Key for the selection of a single row.
36.4.2.2. Assess whether the Primary Key is properly identified and are appropriately engineered to address a Primary Key project.
36.4.2.2.1. Assess whether all the Primary Keys have been delivered in terms of components, instances, and stored metadata work products.
36.4.2.2.2. Assess whether all the Primary Keys have been properly detailed as to content, description, methodology, evaluation, presentation, and delivery work steps.
36.4.2.2.3. Assess whether all the Primary Keys have been properly allocated sufficient unit effort estimates.
36.4.2.2.4. Assess whether all the Primary Keys have been properly allocated sufficient quantity of units that have to be developed.
36.4.2.2.5. Assess whether all the Primary Keys have been properly allocated work environment factors to determine an accurate estimate of required resources.
36.4.2.2.6. Assess whether all the Primary Keys have been properly allocated work accomplishment and recording functions necessary to support earned value reporting.
36.4.2.2.7. Assess whether all the Primary Keys have been properly allocated metadata recording effort to ensure that all interrelationships are properly recorded into the Metabase System database.
36.4.2.3. Assign the risk level associated with each Primary Key not properly constructed.
36.4.3. Determine the findings and create draft assessment report.

36.4.4. Present the findings and revise draft assessment report.
36.4.5. Create final assessment report and deliver to the auditing organization.

36.5. Assess Candidate Key.
36.5.1. Identify artifacts that bear on the assessment.
36.5.1.1. Identify the appropriate set of Candidate Key documents.
36.5.1.1.1. Review Candidate Key documents.
36.5.1.1.2. Review scope and business problem related documentation.
36.5.1.1.3. Identify the data-based Candidate Key that are defined and captured.
36.5.1.1.4. Identify the work products appropriate to the evaluation of Candidate Key.
36.5.1.2. For each Candidate Key:
36.5.1.2.1. Identify components, that is, Entities, and Attributes.
36.5.1.2.2. Identify the definitions for each Candidate Key.
36.5.2. Perform the assessment.
36.5.2.1.1. Assess the accuracy, quality and completeness of each Candidate Key with respect to the business requirements.
36.5.2.1.2. Assess whether Candidate Key are able to be inferred from business requirements, and if not whether business requirements or Candidate Key need to be enhanced.
36.5.2.1. Assess each Candidate Key.
36.5.2.1.1. Assess the adequacy of each Candidate Key with respect to the Business Requirements.
36.5.2.1.2. Assess whether all implied business requirement Candidate Key are reflected in an appropriate.
36.5.2.1.3. Assess whether all Candidate Key are reflected in business Requirements.
36.5.2.1.4. Assess the appropriateness of each Candidate Key assigned Attributes.
36.5.2.1.4.1. Assess the correctness of the assignment and sequence of the Attributes to the Candidate Key for the selection of a single row.
36.5.2.2. Assess whether the Candidate Key is properly identified and are appropriately engineered to address a Candidate Key project.
36.5.2.2.1. Assess whether all the Candidate Keys have been delivered in terms of components, instances, and stored metadata work products.
36.5.2.2.2. Assess whether all the Candidate Keys have been properly detailed as to content, description, methodology, evaluation, presentation, and delivery work steps.
36.5.2.2.3. Assess whether all the Candidate Keys have been properly allocated sufficient unit effort estimates.
36.5.2.2.4. Assess whether all the Candidate Keys have been properly allocated sufficient quantity of units that have to be developed.
36.5.2.2.5. Assess whether all the Candidate Keys have been properly allocated work environment factors to determine an accurate estimate of required

resources.

36.5.2.2.6. Assess whether all the Candidate Keys have been properly allocated work accomplishment and recording functions necessary to support earned value reporting.

36.5.2.2.7. Assess whether all the Candidate Keys have been properly allocated metadata recording effort to ensure that all interrelationships are properly recorded into the Metabase System database.

36.5.2.3. Assign the risk level associated with each Candidate Key not properly constructed.

36.5.3. Determine the findings and create draft assessment report.

36.5.4. Present the findings and revise draft assessment report.

36.5.5. Create final assessment report and deliver to the auditing organization.

36.6. Assess Foreign Key.

36.6.1. Identify artifacts that bear on the assessment.

36.6.1.1. Identify the appropriate set of Foreign Key documents.

36.6.1.1.1. Review Foreign Key documents.

36.6.1.1.2. Review scope and business problem related documentation.

36.6.1.1.3. Identify the data-based Foreign Key that are defined and captured.

36.6.1.1.4. Identify the work products appropriate to the evaluation of Foreign Key.

36.6.1.2. For each Foreign Key:

36.6.1.2.1. Identify components, that is, Entities, and Attributes.

36.6.1.2.2. Identify the definitions for each Foreign Key.

36.6.2. Perform the assessment.

36.6.2.1. Assess each Foreign Key.

36.6.2.1.1. Assess the accuracy, quality and completeness of each Foreign Key with respect to the business requirements.

36.6.2.1.2. Assess whether Foreign Key are able to be inferred from business requirements, and if not whether business requirements or Foreign Key need to be enhanced.

36.6.2.1.3. Select the source for the Foreign Key.

36.6.2.1.4. Select the target for the Foreign Key.

36.6.2.1.5. Construct the Foreign Key name.

36.6.2.2. Assess the adequacy of each Foreign Key with respect to the Business Requirements.

36.6.2.2. Assess whether all implied business requirement Foreign Key are reflected in an appropriate.

36.6.2.3. Assess whether all Foreign Key are reflected in business Requirements.

36.6.2.4. Assess the appropriateness of each Foreign Key assigned Attributes.

36.6.2.5.1. Assess the correctness of the assignment and sequence of the Attributes to the Foreign Key corresponding to the Primary Key of the.

36.6.2.6. Assess whether the Foreign Key is properly identified and are appropriately engineered to address a Foreign Key project.

36.6.2.6.1. Assess whether all the Foreign Keys have been delivered in terms of components, instances, and stored metadata work products.

36.6.2.6.2. Assess whether all the Foreign Keys have been properly detailed as to content, description, methodology, evaluation, presentation, and delivery work steps.

36.6.2.6.3. Assess whether all the Foreign Keys have been properly allocated sufficient unit effort estimates.

36.6.2.6.4. Assess whether all the Foreign Keys have been properly allocated sufficient quantity of units that have to be developed.

36.6.2.6.5. Assess whether all the Foreign Keys have been properly allocated work environment factors to determine an accurate estimate of required resources.

36.6.2.6.6. Assess whether all the Foreign Keys have been properly allocated work accomplishment and recording functions necessary to support earned value reporting.

36.6.2.6.7. Assess whether all the Foreign Keys have been properly allocated metadata recording effort to ensure that all interrelationships are properly recorded into the Metabase System database.

36.6.2.7. Assign the risk level associated with each Foreign Key not properly constructed.

36.6.3. Determine the findings and create draft assessment report.

36.6.4. Present the findings and revise draft assessment report.

36.6.5. Create final assessment report and deliver to the auditing organization.

37. Implemented Data Model

37.1. Assess Schema.
37.1.1. Identify artifacts that bear on the assessment.
37.1.1.1. Identify the appropriate set of Schema documents.
37.1.1.1.1. Review Schema documents.
37.1.1.1.2. Review scope and business problem related documentation.
37.1.1.1.3. Identify the data-based Schemas that are defined and captured.
37.1.1.1.4. Identify the work products appropriate to the evaluation of Schemas.
37.1.1.2. For each Implemented Schema:
37.1.1.2.1. Identify components, that is, Schemas.
37.1.1.2.2. Identify the definitions for each Schema component.
37.1.2. Perform the assessment.
37.1.2.1. Assess each Schema.
37.1.2.1.1. Assess the accuracy, quality and completeness of each Schema with respect to the business requirements.
37.1.2.1.2. Assess whether Schemas are able to be inferred from business requirements, and if not whether business requirements or Schemas need to be enhanced.
37.1.2.1.1. Assess the adequacy of each Schema with respect to the Business Requirements.
37.1.2.1.2. Assess whether all implied business requirement are reflected in an appropriate Schema.
37.1.2.1.3. Assess whether all Schemas are reflected in business Requirements.
37.1.2.2. Assess whether the Schemas are properly identified and are appropriately engineered to address a Schema project.
37.1.2.2.1. Assess whether all the Schemas have been delivered in terms of components, instances, and stored metadata work products.
37.1.2.2.2. Assess whether all the Schemas have been properly detailed as to content, description, methodology, evaluation, presentation, and delivery work steps.
37.1.2.2.3. Assess whether all the Schemas have been properly allocated sufficient unit effort estimates.
37.1.2.2.4. Assess whether all the Schemas have been properly allocated sufficient quantity of units that have to be developed.
37.1.2.2.5. Assess whether all the Schemas have been properly allocated work environment factors to determine an accurate estimate of required resources.
37.1.2.2.6. Assess whether all the Schemas have been properly allocated work accomplishment and recording functions necessary to support earned value reporting.
37.1.2.2.7. Assess whether all the Schemas have been properly allocated metadata

recording effort to ensure that all interrelationships are properly recorded into the Metabase System database.

37.1.2.3. Assign the risk level associated with each Schema not properly constructed.

37.1.3. Determine the findings and create draft assessment report.

37.1.4. Present the findings and revise draft assessment report.

37.1.5. Create final assessment report and deliver to the auditing organization.

37.2. Assess Table.

37.2.1. Identify artifacts that bear on the assessment.

37.2.1.1. Identify the appropriate set of Table documents.

37.2.1.1.1. Review Table documents.

37.2.1.1.2. Review scope and business problem related documentation.

37.2.1.1.3. Identify the Tables that are defined and captured.

37.2.1.1.4. Identify the work products appropriate to the evaluation of Tables.

37.2.1.2. For each Table:

37.2.1.2.1. Identify components, that is, Schemas, Tables, Columns and relationships.

37.2.1.2.2. Identify the definitions for each Table component.

37.2.2. Perform the assessment.

37.2.2.1. Assess each Table.

37.2.2.1.1. Assess the accuracy, quality and completeness of each Table with respect to the business requirements.

37.2.2.1.2. Assess whether Tables are able to be inferred from business requirements, and if not whether business requirements or Tables need to be enhanced.

37.2.2.1.3. Assess whether each Table hierarchy is properly specified, and that all Table names and descriptions are well defined, non-overlapping, and have been formally approved.

37.2.2.2. Assess whether the Tables are properly identified and are appropriately engineered to address a Table project.

37.2.2.2.1. Assess whether all the Tables have been delivered in terms of components, instances, and stored metadata work products.

37.2.2.2.2. Assess whether all the Tables have been properly detailed as to content, description, methodology, evaluation, presentation, and delivery work steps.

37.2.2.2.3. Assess whether all the Tables have been properly allocated sufficient unit effort estimates.

37.2.2.2.4. Assess whether all the Tables have been properly allocated sufficient quantity of units that have to be developed.

37.2.2.2.5. Assess whether all the Tables have been properly allocated work environment factors to determine an accurate estimate of required resources.

37.2.2.2.6. Assess whether all the Tables have been properly allocated work accomplishment and recording functions necessary to support earned value reporting.

37.2.2.2.7. Assess whether all the Tables have been properly allocated metadata recording effort to ensure that all interrelationships are properly recorded into the Metabase System database.

37.2.2.3. Assign the risk level associated with each Table not properly constructed.

37.2.3. Determine the findings and create draft assessment report.

37.2.4. Present the findings and revise draft assessment report.

37.2.5. Create final assessment report and deliver to the auditing organization.

37.3. Assess Column.

37.3.1. Identify artifacts that bear on the assessment.

37.3.1.1. Identify the appropriate set of Column documents.

37.3.1.1.1. Review Column documents.

37.3.1.1.2. Review scope and business problem related documentation.

37.3.1.1.3. Identify the data-based Columns that are defined and captured.

37.3.1.1.4. Identify the work products appropriate to the evaluation of Columns.

37.3.1.2. For each Columns:

37.3.1.2.1. Identify components, that is, Subjects, DBMS Tables, Columns, Value Domains, and Meta Category Values.

37.3.1.2.2. Identify the definitions for each Column.

37.3.2. Perform the assessment.

37.3.2.1. Assess each Column.

37.3.2.1.1. Assess the accuracy, quality and completeness of each Column with respect to the business requirements.

37.3.2.1.2. Assess whether Columns are able to be inferred from business requirements, and if not whether business requirements or Columns need to be enhanced.

37.3.2.1.3 Assess whether each Column hierarchy is properly specified, and that all Column names and descriptions are well defined, non-overlapping, and have been formally approved.

37.3.2.1.4. Assess the completeness and accuracy of Columns common business names, long definitions and local definitions against requirements.

37.3.2.1.5 Ensure that there are Columns addressing Information Technology infrastructure facts in Tables for history and auditing.

37.3.2.1.6. Assess the appropriateness of each Column assigned Value Domain.

37.3.2.1.6.1. Assess whether the set of Value Domains for every Column is defined unambiguously, clearly, distinctly, and not-overlapping.

37.3.2.1.6.2. Assess whether every Column that is to have a restricted Value Domain is identified and is correctly addressed by the appropriate set of properly configured Value Domain management metadata.

37.3.2.1.6.3. Assess that every Column Value Domain does not semantically conflict with a Data Element Value Domain.

37.3.2.1.6.4. Assess that every Column Value Domain does not semantically conflict with a Specified Data Model Attribute Value Domain.

37.3.2.1.7. Assess the appropriateness of each Columns assigned Meta Category Value.

37.3.2.1.7.1. Assess whether the set of Meta Category Value assigned to Columns are defined unambiguously, clearly, distinctly, and not-overlapping.

37.3.2.1.7.2. Assess whether every Columns that is to have a restricted Meta Category Value is identified and is correctly addressed by the appropriate set of properly configured Meta Category Values management metadata.

37.3.2.1.7.3. Assess that every Columns Meta Category Value does not semantically conflict a Data Element Meta Category Value.

37.3.2.1.7.4. Assess that every Columns Meta Category Value does not semantically conflict a Specified Data Model Attribute Meta Category Value.

37.3.2.2. Assess whether the Columns are properly identified and are appropriately engineered to address a Column project.

37.3.2.2.1. Assess whether all the Columns have been delivered in terms of components, instances, and stored metadata work products.

37.3.2.2.2. Assess whether all the Columns have been properly detailed as to content, description, methodology, evaluation, presentation, and delivery work steps.

37.3.2.2.3. Assess whether all the Columns have been properly allocated sufficient unit effort estimates.

37.3.2.2.4. Assess whether all the Columns have been properly allocated sufficient quantity of units that have to be developed.

37.3.2.2.5. Assess whether all the Columns have been properly allocated work environment factors to determine an accurate estimate of required resources.

37.3.2.2.6. Assess whether all the Columns have been properly allocated work accomplishment and recording functions necessary to support earned value reporting.

37.3.2.2.7. Assess whether all the Columns have been properly allocated metadata recording effort to ensure that all interrelationships are properly recorded into the Metabase System database.

37.3.2.3. Assign the risk level associated with each Column not properly constructed.

37.3.3. Determine the findings and create draft assessment report.

37.3.4. Present the findings and revise draft assessment report.

37.3.5. Create final assessment report and deliver to the auditing organization.

37.4. Assess Primary Key.

37.4.1. Identify artifacts that bear on the assessment.

37.4.1.1. Identify the appropriate set of Primary Key documents.
37.4.1.1.1. Review Primary Key documents.
37.4.1.1.2. Review scope and business problem related documentation.
37.4.1.1.3. Identify the data-based Primary Key that are defined and captured.
37.4.1.1.4. Identify the work products appropriate to the evaluation of Primary Key.
37.4.1.2. For each Primary Key:
37.4.1.2.1. Identify components, that is, DBMS Tables, and Columns.
37.4.1.2.2. Identify the definitions for each Primary Key.
37.4.2. Perform the assessment.
37.4.2.1. Assess each Primary Key.
37.4.2.1.1. Assess the accuracy, quality and completeness of each Primary Key with respect to the business requirements.
37.4.2.1.2. Assess whether Primary Keys are able to be inferred from business requirements, and if not whether business requirements or Primary Keys need to be enhanced.
37.4.2.1.3. Assess the adequacy of each Primary Key with respect to the Business Requirements.
37.4.2.1.4. Assess whether all implied business requirement Primary Key are reflected in an appropriate.
37.4.2.1.5. Assess whether all Primary Key are reflected in business Requirements.
37.4.2.1.6. Assess the appropriateness of each Primary Key assigned Columns.
37.4.2.1.6.1. Assess the correctness of the assignment and sequence of the Columns to the Primary Key for the selection of a single row.
37.4.2.2. Assess whether the Primary Key is properly identified and are appropriately engineered to address a Primary Key project.
37.4.2.2.1. Assess whether all the Primary Keys have been delivered in terms of components, instances, and stored metadata work products.
37.4.2.2.2. Assess whether all the Primary Keys have been properly detailed as to content, description, methodology, evaluation, presentation, and delivery work steps.
37.4.2.2.3. Assess whether all the Primary Keys have been properly allocated sufficient unit effort estimates.
37.4.2.2.4. Assess whether all the Primary Keys have been properly allocated sufficient quantity of units that have to be developed.
37.4.2.2.5. Assess whether all the Primary Keys have been properly allocated work environment factors to determine an accurate estimate of required resources.
37.4.2.2.6. Assess whether all the Primary Keys have been properly allocated work accomplishment and recording functions necessary to support earned value reporting.
37.4.2.2.7. Assess whether all the Primary Keys have been properly allocated metadata recording effort to ensure that all interrelationships are properly

recorded into the Metabase System database.

37.4.2.3. Assign the risk level associated with each Primary Key not properly constructed.

37.4.3. Determine the findings and create draft assessment report.

37.4.4. Present the findings and revise draft assessment report.

37.4.5. Create final assessment report and deliver to the auditing organization.

37.5. Assess Candidate Key.

37.5.1. Identify artifacts that bear on the assessment.

37.5.1.1. Identify the appropriate set of Candidate Key documents.

37.5.1.1.1. Review Candidate Key documents.

37.5.1.1.2. Review scope and business problem related documentation.

37.5.1.1.3. Identify the data-based Candidate Key that are defined and captured.

37.5.1.1.4. Identify the work products appropriate to the evaluation of Candidate Key.

37.5.1.2. For each Candidate Key:

37.5.1.2.1. Identify components, that is, DBMS Tables, and Columns.

37.5.1.2.2. Identify the definitions for each Candidate Key.

37.5.2. Perform the assessment.

37.5.2.1. Assess each Candidate Key.

37.5.2.1.1. Assess the accuracy, quality and completeness of each Candidate Key with respect to the business requirements.

37.5.2.1.2. Assess whether Candidate Keys are able to be inferred from business requirements, and if not whether business requirements or Candidate Keys need to be enhanced.

37.5.2.1.3. Assess the adequacy of each Candidate Key with respect to the Business Requirements.

37.5.2.1.4. Assess whether all implied business requirement Candidate Key are reflected in an appropriate.

37.5.2.1.5. Assess whether all Candidate Key are reflected in business Requirements.

37.5.2.1.6. Assess the appropriateness of each Candidate Key assigned Columns.

37.5.2.1.6.1. Assess the correctness of the assignment and sequence of the Columns to the Candidate Key for the selection of a single row.

37.5.2.2. Assess whether the Candidate Key is properly identified and are appropriately engineered to address a Candidate Key project.

37.5.2.2.1. Assess whether all the Candidate Keys have been delivered in terms of components, instances, and stored metadata work products.

37.5.2.2.2. Assess whether all the Candidate Keys have been properly detailed as to content, description, methodology, evaluation, presentation, and delivery work steps.

37.5.2.2.3. Assess whether all the Candidate Keys have been properly allocated sufficient unit effort estimates.

37.5.2.2.4. Assess whether all the Candidate Keys have been properly allocated sufficient quantity of units that have to be developed.
37.5.2.2.5. Assess whether all the Candidate Keys have been properly allocated work environment factors to determine an accurate estimate of required resources.
37.5.2.2.6. Assess whether all the Candidate Keys have been properly allocated work accomplishment and recording functions necessary to support earned value reporting.
37.5.2.2.7. Assess whether all the Candidate Keys have been properly allocated metadata recording effort to ensure that all interrelationships are properly recorded into the Metabase System database.
37.5.2.3. Assign the risk level associated with each Candidate Key not properly constructed.
37.5.3. Determine the findings and create draft assessment report.
37.5.4. Present the findings and revise draft assessment report.
37.5.5. Create final assessment report and deliver to the auditing organization.

37.6. Assess Foreign Key.
37.6.1. Identify artifacts that bear on the assessment.
37.6.1.1. Identify the appropriate set of Foreign Key documents.
37.6.1.1.1. Review Foreign Key documents.
37.6.1.1.2. Review scope and business problem related documentation.
37.6.1.1.3. Identify the data-based Foreign Key that are defined and captured.
37.6.1.1.4. Identify the work products appropriate to the evaluation of Foreign Key.
37.6.1.2. For each Specified Database Model Table Foreign Key:
37.6.1.2.1. Identify components, that is, DBMS Tables, and Columns.
37.6.1.2.2. Identify the definitions for each Specified Database Model Table Foreign Key.
37.6.2. Perform the assessment.
37.6.2.1. Assess each Foreign Key.
37.6.2.1.1. Assess the accuracy, quality and completeness of each Foreign Key with respect to the business requirements.
37.6.2.1.2. Assess whether Foreign Keys are able to be inferred from business requirements, and if not whether business requirements or Foreign Keys need to be enhanced.
37.6.2.1.3. Select the source for the Foreign Key.
37.6.2.1.4. Select the target for the Foreign Key.
37.6.2.1.5. Construct the Foreign Key name.
37.6.2.1.6. Assess whether all Foreign Keys are reflected in business Requirements.
37.6.2.1.7. Assess the appropriateness of each Foreign Key assigned Columns.
37.6.2.1.7.1. Assess the correctness of the assignment and sequence of the Columns to the Foreign Key corresponding to the Primary Key of the.

37.6.2.2. Assess whether the Foreign Key is properly identified and are appropriately engineered to address a Foreign Key project.

37.6.2.2.1. Assess whether all the Foreign Key have been delivered in terms of components, instances, and stored metadata work products.

37.6.2.2.2. Assess whether all the Foreign Key have been properly detailed as to content, description, methodology, evaluation, presentation, and delivery work steps.

37.6.2.2.3. Assess whether all the Foreign Key have been properly allocated sufficient unit effort estimates.

37.6.2.2.4. Assess whether all the Foreign Key have been properly allocated sufficient quantity of units that have to be developed.

37.6.2.2.5. Assess whether all the Foreign Key have been properly allocated work environment factors to determine an accurate estimate of required resources.

37.6.2.2.6. Assess whether all the Foreign Key have been properly allocated work accomplishment and recording functions necessary to support earned value reporting.

37.6.2.2.7. Assess whether all the Foreign Key have been properly allocated metadata recording effort to ensure that all interrelationships are properly recorded into the Metabase System database.

37.6.2.3. Assign the risk level associated with each Foreign Key not properly constructed.

37.6.3. Determine the findings and create draft assessment report.

37.6.4. Present the findings and revise draft assessment report.

37.6.5. Create final assessment report and deliver to the auditing organization.

37.7. Assess SQL Data Type.

37.7.1. Identify artifacts that bear on the assessment.

37.7.1.1. Identify the appropriate set of SQL Data Type documents.

37.7.1.1.1. Review SQL Data Type documents.

37.7.1.1.2. Review scope and business problem related documentation.

37.7.1.1.3. Identify the SQL Data Types that are defined and captured.

37.7.1.1.4. Identify the work products appropriate to the need for SQL Data Types.

37.7.1.2. For each SQL Data Type:

37.7.1.2.1. Identify components, that is, Column.

37.7.1.2.2. Identify the definitions for each SQL Data Type.

37.7.2. Perform the assessment.

37.7.2.1.1. Assess the accuracy, quality and completeness of each SQL Data Type with respect to the business requirements.

37.7.2.1.2. Assess whether SQL Data Types are able to be inferred from business requirements, and if not whether business requirements or SQL Data Types need to be enhanced.

37.7.2.1.3. Assess that all SQL Data Types are identified and are properly constructed.

37.7.2.1.4. Assess the adequacy of each Column required data types with respect to SQL Data Types.

37.7.2.2. Assess whether a SQL Data Type assigned to an Column is a subset of a Data Type assigned to its parent Data Element.

37.7.2.3. Assess whether the SQL Data Types are properly identified and are appropriately engineered to address a SQL Data Type project.

37.7.2.3.1. Assess whether all the SQL Data Types have been delivered in terms of components, instances, and stored metadata work products.

37.7.2.3.2. Assess whether all the SQL Data Types have been properly detailed as to content, description, methodology, evaluation, presentation, and delivery work steps.

37.7.2.3.3. Assess whether all the SQL Data Types have been properly allocated sufficient unit effort estimates.

37.7.2.3.4. Assess whether all the SQL Data Types have been properly allocated sufficient quantity of units that have to be developed.

37.7.2.3.5. Assess whether all the SQL Data Types have been properly allocated work environment factors to determine an accurate estimate of required resources.

37.7.2.3.6. Assess whether all the SQL Data Types have been properly allocated work accomplishment and recording functions necessary to support earned value reporting.

37.7.2.3.7. Assess whether all the SQL Data Types have been properly allocated metadata recording effort to ensure that all interrelationships are properly recorded into the Metabase System database.

37.7.2.4. Assign the risk level associated with each SQL Data Type not properly constructed.

37.7.3. Determine the findings and create draft assessment report.

37.7.4. Present the findings and revise draft assessment report.

37.7.5. Create final assessment report and deliver to the auditing organization.

38. Operational Data Model

38.1. Assess DBMS Schema.
38.1.1. Identify artifacts that bear on the assessment.
38.1.1.1. Identify the appropriate set of DBMS Schema documents.
38.1.1.1.1. Review DBMS Schemas documents.
38.1.1.1.2. Review scope and business problem related documentation.
38.1.1.1.3. Identify the data-based DBMS Schemas that are defined and captured.
38.1.1.1.4. Identify the work products appropriate to the evaluation of DBMS Schemas.
38.1.1.2. For each DBMS Schemas:
38.1.1.2.1. Identify components, that is, DBMS Schemas.
38.1.1.2.2. Identify the definitions for each DBMS Schema component.
38.1.2. Perform the assessment.
38.1.2.1. Assess each DBMS Schema.
38.1.2.1.1. Assess the accuracy, quality and completeness of each DBMS Schema with respect to the business requirements.
38.1.2.1.2. Assess whether DBMS Schemas are able to be inferred from business requirements, and if not whether business requirements or DBMS Schema need to be enhanced.
38.1.2.1.3. Assess the adequacy of each DBMS Schema with respect to the Business Requirements.
38.1.2.2. Assess whether the DBMS Schemas are properly identified and are appropriately engineered to address a DBMS Schema project.
38.1.2.2.1. Assess whether all the DBMS Schemas have been delivered in terms of components, instances, and stored metadata work products.
38.1.2.2.2. Assess whether all the DBMS Schemas have been properly detailed as to content, description, methodology, evaluation, presentation, and delivery work steps.
38.1.2.2.3. Assess whether all the DBMS Schemas have been properly allocated sufficient unit effort estimates.
38.1.2.2.4. Assess whether all the DBMS Schemas have been properly allocated sufficient quantity of units that have to be developed.
38.1.2.2.5. Assess whether all the DBMS Schemas have been properly allocated work environment factors to determine an accurate estimate of required resources.
38.1.2.2.6. Assess whether all the DBMS Schemas have been properly allocated work accomplishment and recording functions necessary to support earned value reporting.
38.1.2.2.7. Assess whether all the DBMS Schemas have been properly allocated metadata recording effort to ensure that all interrelationships are properly recorded into the Metabase System database.

38.1.2.3. Assign the risk level associated with each DBMS Schema not properly constructed.
38.1.3. Determine the findings and create draft assessment report.
38.1.4. Present the findings and revise draft assessment report.
38.1.5. Create final assessment report and deliver to the auditing organization.

38.2. Assess DBMS Table.
38.2.1. Identify artifacts that bear on the assessment.
38.2.1.1. Identify the appropriate set of DBMS Table documents.
38.2.1.1.1. Review DBMS Table documents.
38.2.1.1.2. Review scope and business problem related documentation.
38.2.1.1.3. Identify the data-based DBMS Tables that are defined and captured.
38.2.1.1.4. Identify the work products appropriate to the evaluation of DBMS Tables.
38.2.1.2. For each DBMS Table:
38.2.1.2.1. Identify components, that is, DBMS Schema, DBMS Tables, DBMS Columns and relationships.
38.2.1.1.2. Assess the completeness and accuracy of DBMS Tables common business names, long definitions and local definitions against requirements.
38.2.1.2.3. Identify the definitions for each DBMS Table component.
38.2.2. Perform the assessment.
38.2.2.1. Assess each DBMS Table.
38.2.2.1.1. Assess the accuracy, quality and completeness of each DBMS Table with respect to the business requirements.
38.2.2.1.2. Assess whether DBMS Table are able to be inferred from business requirements, and if not whether business requirements or DBMS Table need to be enhanced.
38.2.2.1.3. Assess whether each DBMS Table hierarchy is properly specified, and that all DBMS Table names and descriptions are well defined, non-overlapping, and have been formally approved.
38.2.2.2. Assess whether the DBMS Tables are properly identified and are appropriately engineered to address a DBMS Table project.
38.2.2.2.1. Assess whether all the DBMS Tables have been delivered in terms of components, instances, and stored metadata work products.
38.2.2.2.2. Assess whether all the DBMS Tables have been properly detailed as to content, description, methodology, evaluation, presentation, and delivery work steps.
38.2.2.2.3. Assess whether all the DBMS Tables have been properly allocated sufficient unit effort estimates.
38.2.2.2.4. Assess whether all the DBMS Tables have been properly allocated sufficient quantity of units that have to be developed.
38.2.2.2.5. Assess whether all the DBMS Tables have been properly allocated work environment factors to determine an accurate estimate of required

resources.

38.2.2.2.6. Assess whether all the DBMS Tables have been properly allocated work accomplishment and recording functions necessary to support earned value reporting.

38.2.2.2.7. Assess whether all the DBMS Tables have been properly allocated metadata recording effort to ensure that all interrelationships are properly recorded into the Metabase System database.

38.2.2.3. Assign the risk level associated with each DBMS Table not properly constructed.

38.2.3. Determine the findings and create draft assessment report.

38.2.4. Present the findings and revise draft assessment report.

38.2.5. Create final assessment report and deliver to the auditing organization.

38.3. Assess DBMS Column.

38.3.1. Identify artifacts that bear on the assessment.

38.3.1.1. Identify the appropriate set of DBMS Column documents.

38.3.1.1.1. Review DBMS Column documents.

38.3.1.1.2. Review scope and business problem related documentation.

38.3.1.1.3. Identify the data-based DBMS Columns that are defined and captured.

38.3.1.1.4. Identify the work products appropriate to the evaluation of DBMS Columns.

38.3.1.2. For each DBMS Columns:

38.3.1.2.1. Identify components, that is, DBMS Schemas, Tables, DBMS Columns, Value Domains, and Meta Category Values.

38.3.1.2.2. Identify the definitions for each DBMS Column.

38.3.2. Perform the assessment.

38.3.2.1. Assess each DBMS Column.

38.3.2.1.1. Assess the accuracy, quality and completeness of each DBMS Column with respect to the business requirements.

38.3.2.1.2. Assess whether DBMS Columns are able to be inferred from business requirements, and if not whether business requirements or DBMS Columns need to be enhanced.

38.3.2.1.3. Assess whether each DBMS Column hierarchy is properly specified, and that all DBMS Column names and descriptions are well defined, non-overlapping, and have been formally approved.

38.3.2.1.4. Assess the completeness and accuracy of DBMS Columns common business names, long definitions and local definitions against requirements.

38.3.2.1.6. Ensure that there are DBMS Columns addressing Information Technology infrastructure necessary facts to support history and auditing.

38.3.2.1.5. Assess the appropriateness of each DBMS Column assigned Value Domain.

38.3.2.1.5.1. Assess whether the set of Value Domains for every DBMS Column is defined unambiguously, clearly, distinctly, and not-overlapping.
38.3.2.1.5.2. Assess whether every DBMS Column that is to have a restricted Value Domain is identified and is correctly addressed by the appropriate set of properly configured Value Domain management metadata.
38.3.2.1.5.3. Assess that every DBMS Column Value Domain does not semantically conflict with a Data Element Value Domain.
38.3.2.2. Assess whether the DBMS Columns are properly identified and are appropriately engineered to address a DBMS Column project.
38.3.2.2.1. Assess whether all the DBMS Columns have been delivered in terms of components, instances, and stored metadata work products.
38.3.2.2.2. Assess whether all the DBMS Columns have been properly detailed as to content, description, methodology, evaluation, presentation, and delivery work steps.
38.3.2.2.3. Assess whether all the DBMS Columns have been properly allocated sufficient unit effort estimates.
38.3.2.2.4. Assess whether all the DBMS Columns have been properly allocated sufficient quantity of units that have to be developed.
38.3.2.2.5. Assess whether all the DBMS Columns have been properly allocated work environment factors to determine an accurate estimate of required resources.
38.3.2.2.6. Assess whether all the DBMS Columns have been properly allocated work accomplishment and recording functions necessary to support earned value reporting.
38.3.2.2.7. Assess whether all the DBMS Columns have been properly allocated metadata recording effort to ensure that all interrelationships are properly recorded into the Metabase System database.
38.3.2.3. Assign the risk level associated with each DBMS Column not properly constructed.
38.3.3. Determine the findings and create draft assessment report.
38.3.4. Present the findings and revise draft assessment report.
38.3.5. Create final assessment report and deliver to the auditing organization.

38.4. Assess Primary Key.
38.4.1. Identify artifacts that bear on the assessment.
38.4.1.1. Identify the appropriate set of Primary Key documents.
38.4.1.1.1. Review Primary Key documents.
38.4.1.1.2. Review scope and business problem related documentation.
38.4.1.1.3. Identify the data-based Primary Key that are defined and captured.
38.4.1.1.4. Identify the work products appropriate to the evaluation of Primary Key.
38.4.1.2. For each Primary Key:
38.4.1.2.1. Identify components, that is, DBMS Tables, and DBMS Columns.

38.4.1.2.2. Identify the definitions for each Primary Key.
38.4.2. Perform the assessment.
38.4.2.1. Assess each Primary Key.
38.4.2.1.1. Assess the accuracy, quality and completeness of each Primary Key with respect to the business requirements.
38.4.2.1.2. Assess whether Primary Keys are able to be inferred from business requirements, and if not whether business requirements or Primary Keys need to be enhanced.
38.4.2.1.3. Assess the appropriateness of each Primary Key assigned DBMS Columns.
38.4.2.1.3.1. Assess the correctness of the assignment and sequence of the DBMS Columns to the Primary Key for the selection of a single row.
38.4.2.2. Assess whether the Primary Key is properly identified and are appropriately engineered to address a Primary Key project.
38.4.2.2.1. Assess whether all the Primary Keys have been delivered in terms of components, instances, and stored metadata work products.
38.4.2.2.2. Assess whether all the Primary Keys have been properly detailed as to content, description, methodology, evaluation, presentation, and delivery work steps.
38.4.2.2.3. Assess whether all the Primary Keys have been properly allocated sufficient unit effort estimates.
38.4.2.2.4. Assess whether all the Primary Keys have been properly allocated sufficient quantity of units that have to be developed.
38.4.2.2.5. Assess whether all the Primary Keys have been properly allocated work environment factors to determine an accurate estimate of required resources.
38.4.2.2.6. Assess whether all the Primary Keys have been properly allocated work accomplishment and recording functions necessary to support earned value reporting.
38.4.2.2.7. Assess whether all the Primary Keys have been properly allocated metadata recording effort to ensure that all interrelationships are properly recorded into the Metabase System database.
38.4.2.3. Assign the risk level associated with each Primary Key not properly constructed.
38.4.3. Determine the findings and create draft assessment report.
38.4.4. Present the findings and revise draft assessment report.
38.4.5. Create final assessment report and deliver to the auditing organization.

38.5. Assess Candidate Key.
38.5.1. Identify artifacts that bear on the assessment.
38.5.1.1. Identify the appropriate set of Candidate Key documents.
38.5.1.1.1. Review Candidate Key documents.

38.5.1.1.2. Review scope and business problem related documentation.
38.5.1.1.3. Identify the data-based Candidate Key that are defined and captured.
38.5.1.1.4. Identify the work products appropriate to the evaluation of Candidate Key.
38.5.1.2. For each Candidate Key:
38.5.1.2.1. Identify components, that is, DBMS Tables, and DBMS Columns.
38.5.1.2.2. Identify the definitions for each Candidate Key.
38.5.2. Perform the assessment.
38.5.2.1. Assess each Candidate Key.
38.5.2.1.1. Assess the accuracy, quality and completeness of each Candidate Key with respect to the business requirements.
38.5.2.1.2. Assess whether Candidate Keys are able to be inferred from business requirements, and if not whether business requirements or Candidate Keys need to be enhanced.
38.5.2.1.3. Assess the appropriateness of each Candidate Key assigned DBMS Columns.
38.5.2.1.3.1. Assess the correctness of the assignment and sequence of the DBMS Columns to the Candidate Key for the selection of a single row.
38.5.2.2. Assess whether the Candidate Key is properly identified and are appropriately engineered to address a Candidate Key project.
38.5.2.2.1. Assess whether all the Candidate Keys have been delivered in terms of components, instances, and stored metadata work products.
38.5.2.2.2. Assess whether all the Candidate Keys have been properly detailed as to content, description, methodology, evaluation, presentation, and delivery work steps.
38.5.2.2.3. Assess whether all the Candidate Keys have been properly allocated sufficient unit effort estimates.
38.5.2.2.4. Assess whether all the Candidate Keys have been properly allocated sufficient quantity of units that have to be developed.
38.5.2.2.5. Assess whether all the Candidate Keys have been properly allocated work environment factors to determine an accurate estimate of required resources.
38.5.2.2.6. Assess whether all the Candidate Keys have been properly allocated work accomplishment and recording functions necessary to support earned value reporting.
38.5.2.2.7. Assess whether all the Candidate Keys have been properly allocated metadata recording effort to ensure that all interrelationships are properly recorded into the Metabase System database.
38.5.2.3. Assign the risk level associated with each Candidate Key not properly constructed.
38.5.3. Determine the findings and create draft assessment report.
38.5.4. Present the findings and revise draft assessment report.

38.5.5. Create final assessment report and deliver to the auditing organization.

38.6. Assess Secondary Key.
38.6.1. Identify artifacts that bear on the assessment.
38.6.1.1. Identify the appropriate set of Secondary Key documents.
38.6.1.1.1. Review Secondary Key documents.
38.6.1.1.2. Review scope and business problem related documentation.
38.6.1.1.3. Identify the data-based Secondary Key that are defined and captured.
38.6.1.1.4. Identify the work products appropriate to the evaluation of Secondary Key.
38.6.1.2. For each Secondary Key:
38.6.1.2.1. Identify components, that is, DBMS Tables, and DBMS Columns.
38.6.1.2.2. Identify the definitions for each Secondary Key.
38.6.2. Perform the assessment.
38.6.2.1. Assess each Secondary Key.
38.6.2.1.1. Assess the accuracy, quality and completeness of each Secondary Key with respect to the business requirements.
38.6.2.1.2. Assess whether Secondary Keys are able to be inferred from business requirements, and if not whether business requirements or Secondary Keys need to be enhanced.
38.6.2.1.3. Assess the appropriateness of each Secondary Key assigned DBMS Columns.
38.6.2.1.3.1. Assess the correctness of the assignment and sequence of the DBMS Columns to the Secondary Key for the selection of rows.
38.6.2.2. Assess whether the Secondary Key is properly identified and are appropriately engineered to address a Secondary Key project.
38.6.2.2.1. Assess whether all the Secondary Keys have been delivered in terms of components, instances, and stored metadata work products.
38.6.2.2.2. Assess whether all the Secondary Keys have been properly detailed as to content, description, methodology, evaluation, presentation, and delivery work steps.
38.6.2.2.3. Assess whether all the Secondary Keys have been properly allocated sufficient unit effort estimates.
38.6.2.2.4. Assess whether all the Secondary Keys have been properly allocated sufficient quantity of units that have to be developed.
38.6.2.2.5. Assess whether all the Secondary Keys have been properly allocated work environment factors to determine an accurate estimate of required resources.
38.6.2.2.6. Assess whether all the Secondary Keys have been properly allocated work accomplishment and recording functions necessary to support earned value reporting.
38.6.2.2.7. Assess whether all the Secondary Keys have been properly allocated

metadata recording effort to ensure that all interrelationships are properly recorded into the Metabase System database.

38.6.2.3. Assign the risk level associated with each Secondary Key not properly constructed.

38.6.3. Determine the findings and create draft assessment report.

38.6.4. Present the findings and revise draft assessment report.

38.6.5. Create final assessment report and deliver to the auditing organization.

38.7. Assess Foreign Key.

38.7.1. Identify artifacts that bear on the assessment.

38.7.1.1. Identify the appropriate set of Foreign Key documents.

38.7.1.1.1. Review Foreign Key documents.

38.7.1.1.2. Review scope and business problem related documentation.

38.7.1.1.3. Identify the data-based Foreign Key that are defined and captured.

38.7.1.1.4. Identify the work products appropriate to the evaluation of Foreign Key.

38.7.1.2. For each Table Foreign Key:

38.7.1.2.1. Identify components, that is, DBMS Tables, and DBMS Columns.

38.7.1.2.2. Identify the definitions for each Foreign Key.

38.7.2. Perform the assessment.

38.7.2.1. Assess each Foreign Key.

38.7.2.1.1. Assess the accuracy, quality and completeness of each Foreign Key with respect to the business requirements.

38.7.2.1.2. Assess whether Foreign Keys are able to be inferred from business requirements, and if not whether business requirements or Foreign Keys need to be enhanced.

38.7.2.1.3. Select the DBMS Table source for the Foreign Key.

38.7.2.1.4. Select the DBMS Table target for the Foreign Key.

38.7.2.1.5. Construct the Foreign Key name.

38.7.2.1.6. Assess the appropriateness of each Foreign Key assigned DBMS Columns.

38.7.2.1.6.1. Assess the correctness of the assignment and sequence of the DBMS Columns to the Foreign Key corresponding to the Primary Key of the DBMS Table source.

38.7.2.6. Assess whether the Foreign Key is properly identified and are appropriately engineered to address a Foreign Key project.

38.7.2.6.1. Assess whether all the Foreign Keys have been delivered in terms of components, instances, and stored metadata work products.

38.7.2.6.2. Assess whether all the Foreign Keys have been properly detailed as to content, description, methodology, evaluation, presentation, and delivery work steps.

38.7.2.6.3. Assess whether all the Foreign Keys have been properly allocated sufficient unit effort estimates.

38.7.2.6.4. Assess whether all the Foreign Keys have been properly allocated sufficient quantity of units that have to be developed.

38.7.2.6.5. Assess whether all the Foreign Keys have been properly allocated work environment factors to determine an accurate estimate of required resources.

38.7.2.6.6. Assess whether all the Foreign Keys have been properly allocated work accomplishment and recording functions necessary to support earned value reporting.

38.7.2.6.7. Assess whether all the Foreign Keys have been properly allocated metadata recording effort to ensure that all interrelationships are properly recorded into the Metabase System database.

38.7.2.7. Assign the risk level associated with each Foreign Key not properly constructed.

38.7.3. Determine the findings and create draft assessment report.

38.7.4. Present the findings and revise draft assessment report.

38.7.5. Create final assessment report and deliver to the auditing organization.

38.8. Assess Database Architecture.

38.8.1. Identify artifacts that bear on the assessment.

38.8.1.1. Identify the appropriate set of Database Architecture documents.

38.8.1.1.1. Review Database Architecture documents.

38.8.1.1.2. Review scope and business problem related documentation.

38.8.1.1.3. Identify the Database Architectures that are defined and captured.

38.8.1.1.4. Identify the work products appropriate to the evaluation of Database Architectures.

38.8.1.2. For each Database Architecture:

38.8.1.2.1. Identify components, that is, Database Architectures, and DBMS schemas.

38.8.1.2.2. Identify the definitions for each Database Architecture component.

38.8.2. Perform the assessment.

38.8.2.1. Assess each Database Architecture.

38.8.2.1.1. Assess the accuracy, quality and completeness of each Database Architecture with respect to the business requirements.

38.8.2.1.2. Assess whether Database Architectures are able to be inferred from business requirements, and if not whether business requirements or Database Architectures need to be enhanced.

38.8.2.1.1. Assess the adequacy of each Database Architectures.

38.8.2.1.2. Assess the completeness and accuracy of Database Architectures name and definitions against requirements.

38.8.2.2. Assess whether the Database Architectures are properly identified and are appropriately engineered to address a Database Architecture project.

38.8.2.2.1. Assess whether all the Database Architectures have been delivered in terms of components, instances, and stored metadata work products.

38.8.2.2.2. Assess whether all the Database Architectures have been properly

detailed as to content, description, methodology, evaluation, presentation, and delivery work steps.

38.8.2.2.3. Assess whether all the Database Architectures have been properly allocated sufficient unit effort estimates.

38.8.2.2.4. Assess whether all the Database Architectures have been properly allocated sufficient quantity of units that have to be developed.

38.8.2.2.5. Assess whether all the Database Architectures have been properly allocated work environment factors to determine an accurate estimate of required resources.

38.8.2.2.6. Assess whether all the Database Architectures have been properly allocated work accomplishment and recording functions necessary to support earned value reporting.

38.8.2.2.7. Assess whether all the Database Architectures have been properly allocated metadata recording effort to ensure that all interrelationships are properly recorded into the Metabase System database.

38.8.2.3. Assign the risk level associated with each Database Architecture not properly constructed.

38.8.3. Determine the findings and create draft assessment report.

38.8.4. Present the findings and revise draft assessment report.

38.8.5. Create final assessment report and deliver to the auditing organization.

38.9. Assess Database.

38.9.1. Identify artifacts that bear on the assessment.

38.9.1.1. Identify the appropriate set of Database documents.

38.9.1.1.1. Review Database documents.

38.9.1.1.2. Review scope and business problem related documentation.

38.9.1.1.3. Identify the Databases that are defined and captured.

38.9.1.1.4. Identify the work products appropriate to the evaluation of Databases.

38.9.1.2. For each Databases:

38.9.1.2.1. Identify components, that is, Databases, and DBMS schemas.

38.9.1.2.2. Identify the definitions for each Database component.

38.9.2. Perform the assessment.

38.9.2.1. Assess each Database.

38.9.2.1.1. Assess the accuracy, quality and completeness of each Database with respect to the business requirements.

38.9.2.1.2. Assess whether Databases are able to be inferred from business requirements, and if not whether business requirements or Databases need to be enhanced.

38.9.2.1.3. Assess the adequacy of each Databases.

38.9.2.1.4. Assess the completeness and accuracy of Databases name, and long definitions against requirements.

38.9.2.2. Assess whether the Databases are properly identified and are appropriately engineered to address a Database project.

38.9.2.2.1. Assess whether all the Databases have been delivered in terms of components, instances, and stored metadata work products.

38.9.2.2.2. Assess whether all the Databases have been properly detailed as to content, description, methodology, evaluation, presentation, and delivery work steps.

38.9.2.2.3. Assess whether all the Databases have been properly allocated sufficient unit effort estimates.

38.9.2.2.4. Assess whether all the Databases have been properly allocated sufficient quantity of units that have to be developed.

38.9.2.2.5. Assess whether all the Databases have been properly allocated work environment factors to determine an accurate estimate of required resources.

38.9.2.2.6. Assess whether all the Databases have been properly allocated work accomplishment and recording functions necessary to support earned value reporting.

38.9.2.2.7. Assess whether all the Databases have been properly allocated metadata recording effort to ensure that all interrelationships are properly recorded into the Metabase System database.

38.9.2.3. Assign the risk level associated with each Database not properly constructed.

38.9.3. Determine the findings and create draft assessment report.

38.9.4. Present the findings and revise draft assessment report.

38.9.5. Create final assessment report and deliver to the auditing organization.

38.10. Assess DBMS.

38.10.1. Identify artifacts that bear on the assessment.

38.10.1.1. Identify the appropriate set of DBMS.

38.10.1.1.1. Review DBMS documents.

38.10.1.1.2. Review scope and business problem related documentation.

38.10.1.1.3. Identify the DBMS that are defined and captured.

38.10.1.1.4. Identify the work products appropriate to the evaluation of DBMS.

38.10.1.2. For each DBMS:

38.10.1.2.1. Identify components, that is, DBMS schemas, DBMS Database,.

38.10.1.2.2. Identify the definitions for each DBMS component.

38.10.2. Perform the assessment.

38.10.2.1. Assess each DBMS.

38.10.2.1.1. Assess the accuracy, quality and completeness of each DBMS with respect to the business requirements.

38.10.2.1.2. Assess whether DBMSs are able to be inferred from business requirements, and if not whether business requirements or DBMSs need to be enhanced.

38.10.2.1.3. Assess the adequacy of each DBMS with respect to the Business Information Systems.

38.10.2.1.3.1. Assess whether the Business Information Systems environment on which the DBMS is to be operated has the most efficient and effective architecture and deployment strategy for the performance needs of the physical model.

38.10.2.3. Assess the completeness and accuracy of DBMS common business names, long definitions and local definitions against requirements.

38.10.2.4. Assess against requirements the completeness, accuracy, performance and appropriateness of the DBMS in regards to capabilities for DBMS Logical Database, that is, Data Structure, and Relationships and Operations.

38.10.2.5. Assess against requirements the completeness, accuracy, performance and appropriateness of the DBMS in regards to capabilities for DBMS Physical Database, that is, Storage Structure (Dictionary, Indexes, Relationships, Data, and Data Storage Definition Language), Access Strategy, Data Loading, Data Update, Database Maintenance.

38.10.2.6. Assess against requirements the completeness, accuracy, performance and appropriateness of the DBMS in regards to capabilities for DBMS Interrogation, that is, Views, Screen Development, System Control, Host Language Interface, Natural Language, Procedure-Oriented Language, Report Writers, and Query-Update Languages.

38.10.2.7. Assess against requirements the completeness, accuracy, performance and appropriateness of the DBMS in regards to capabilities for DBMS System Control, that is, Audit Trails, Message Processing, Backup & Recovery, Reorganization, Concurrent Operations, Multiple-Database Processing, Security & Privacy, Installation & Maintenance, and Application Optimization.

38.10.2.8. Assess that all Operational Database DBMS Schemas are identified and are able to be properly constructed by the DBMS.

38.10.2.9. Assess that all Operational Database DBMS Tables within the schemas are identified and are able to be properly constructed by the DBMS.

38.10.2.10. Assess that all Operational Database DBMS Table super and subtypes are identified and are able to be properly constructed by the DBMS.

38.10.2.11. Assess that all DBMS Columns are identified and are able to be properly constructed by the DBMS.

38.10.2.12. Assess that all DBMS Columns are able to be properly constructed by the DBMS and can contain the appropriate integrity constraints that are supported by assertions and triggers.

38.10.2.13. Assess that all DBMS stored procedures are able to be properly constructed by the DBMS and can be properly identified, designed, coded and tested to meet integrity Requirements.

38.10.2.14. Assess the DBMS generation of SQL DDL Scripts.

38.10.2.14.1. Ensure that the SQL scripts for reference data match the Value Domain Requirements.

38.10.2.14.2. Ensure that the SQL scripts for security roles match the security Requirements as it relates to the use cases, named user roles, organizations, and extent of permission to read, write, update, and select data.

38.10.2.14.3. Ensure that the SQL scripts for primary key sequence value specifications match the primary key Requirements.

38.10.2.14.4. Ensure that the SQL scripts for Tables, Columns and appropriate key specifications match the DBMS Table Requirements.

38.10.2.14.5. Ensure that the SQL scripts for triggers and other stored procedures match the data integrity constraints.

38.10.2.15. Assess whether all the needed SQL features and capabilities are able to be performed with SQL 1992:Internediate Syntax so as to maximize portability of databases and programs across DBMSs.

38.10.2.16. Assess whether the DBMS are properly identified and are appropriately engineered to address a DBMS project.

38.10.2.16.1. Assess whether all the DBMS have been delivered in terms of components, instances, and stored metadata work products.

38.10.2.16.2. Assess whether all the DBMSs have been properly detailed as to content, description, methodology, evaluation, presentation, and delivery work steps.

38.10.2.14.3. Assess whether all the DBMSs have been properly allocated sufficient unit effort estimates.

38.10.2.16.4. Assess whether all the DBMSs have been properly allocated sufficient quantity of units that have to be developed.

38.10.2.16.5. Assess whether all the DBMSs have been properly allocated work environment factors to determine an accurate estimate of required resources.

38.10.2.16.6. Assess whether all the DBMSs have been properly allocated work accomplishment and recording functions necessary to support earned value reporting.

38.10.2.16.7. Assess whether all the DBMSs have been properly allocated metadata recording effort to ensure that all interrelationships are properly recorded into the Metabase System database.

38.10.2.17. Assign the risk level associated with each DBMS not properly constructed.

38.10.3. Determine the findings and create draft assessment report.

38.10.4. Present the findings and revise draft assessment report.

38.10.5. Create final assessment report and deliver to the auditing organization.

38.11. Assess DBMS Data Type.

38.11.1. Identify artifacts that bear on the assessment.

38.11.1.1. Identify the appropriate set of DBMS Data Type documents.

38.11.1.1.1. Review DBMS Data Type documents.

38.11.1.1.2. Review scope and business problem related documentation.

38.11.1.1.3. Identify the DBMS Data Types that are defined and captured.

38.11.1.1.4. Identify the work products appropriate to the need for DBMS Data Types.

38.11.1.2. For each DBMS Data Type:

38.11.1.2.1. Identify components, that is, DBMS.

38.11.1.2.2. Identify the definitions for each DBMS Data Type.

38.11.2. Perform the assessment.

38.11.2.1. Assess each DBMS Data Type.

38.11.2.1.1. Assess the accuracy, quality and completeness of each DBMS Data Type with respect to the business requirements.

38.11.2.1.2. Assess whether DBMS Data Types are able to be inferred from business requirements, and if not whether business requirements or DBMS Data Types need to be enhanced.

38.11.2.2. Assess that all DBMS Data Types are identified and are properly constructed.

38.11.2.3. Assess the adequacy of each DBMS Column required data types with respect to SQL Data Types.

38.11.2.4. Assess whether a DBMS Data Type assigned to a DBMS Column is a subset of a SQL Data Type assigned to its parent Table Column.

38.11.2.5. Assess whether the DBMS Data Types are properly identified and are appropriately engineered to address a Data Type project.

38.11.2.5.1. Assess whether all the DBMS Data Types have been delivered in terms of components, instances, and stored metadata work products.

38.11.2.5.2. Assess whether all the DBMS Data Types have been properly detailed as to content, description, methodology, evaluation, presentation, and delivery work steps.

38.11.2.5.3. Assess whether all the DBMS Data Types have been properly allocated sufficient unit effort estimates.

38.11.2.5.4. Assess whether all the DBMS Data Types have been properly allocated sufficient quantity of units that have to be developed.

38.11.2.5.5. Assess whether all the DBMS Data Types have been properly allocated work environment factors to determine an accurate estimate of required resources.

38.11.2.5.6. Assess whether all the DBMS Data Types have been properly allocated work accomplishment and recording functions necessary to support earned value reporting.

38.11.2.5.7. Assess whether all the DBMS Data Types have been properly allocated metadata recording effort to ensure that all interrelationships are properly

recorded into the Metabase System database.

38.11.2.6. Assign the risk level associated with each DBMS Data Type not properly constructed.

38.11.3. Determine the findings and create draft assessment report.

38.11.4. Present the findings and revise draft assessment report.

38.11.5. Create final assessment report and deliver to the auditing organization.

39. View Data Model

39.1. Assess View.
39.1.1. Identify artifacts that bear on the assessment.
39.1.1.1. Identify the appropriate set of Views documents.
39.1.1.1.1. Review View documents.
39.1.1.1.2. Review scope and business problem related documentation.
39.1.1.1.3. Identify the Views that are defined and captured.
39.1.1.1.4. Identify the work products appropriate to the evaluation of Views.
39.1.1.2. For each View:
39.1.1.2.1. Identify components, that is, Business Information Systems, DBMS schemas, DBMS Tables, DBMS Columns, and DBMS relationships.
39.1.1.2.2. Identify the definitions for each View component.
39.1.2. Perform the assessment.
39.1.2.1. Assess each View.
39.1.2.1.1. Assess the accuracy, quality and completeness of each View with respect to the business requirements.
39.1.2.1.2. Assess whether Views are able to be inferred from business requirements, and if not whether business requirements or Views need to be enhanced.
39.1.2.1.3. Assess the adequacy of each View with respect to the Business Information Systems.
39.1.2.1.3.1. Assess whether the Business Information Systems environment on which the View is to be based has the most efficient and effective architecture and deployment strategy for the performance needs of the Operational Database Model.
39.1.2.1.4. Assess the completeness and accuracy of View names, and definitions against requirements.
39.1.2.1.5. Assess the adequacy of each View with respect to the Data Integrity Rules.
39.1.2.1.5.1. Assess whether all implied Data Integrity are reflected in an appropriate View.
39.1.2.1.5.2. Assess whether all View components are reflected in Data Integrity Rules.
39.1.2.1.6. Assess the adequacy of each View that is to be populated by with respect to the External Data Interface Requirements.
39.1.2.1.6.1. Assess whether every View that is to be populated by external data is addressed by at least one External Data Interface requirement.
39.1.2.1.6.2. Assess whether every View that is to be populated by external data is designed appropriately so that it can respond to the External Data Interface requirement.
39.1.2.1.7. Assess the adequacy of each View with respect to the External Quality Standards.
39.1.2.1.7.1. Assess whether the facilities defined within every View is properly drawn

from an DBMS facility that is at most ISO ANSI Standard for entry level SQL:1992.

39.1.2.1.7.2. Assess whether every View that may be appropriate within the collection of Operational Database Models is properly defined through the use of Operational Database Modeling standards.

39.1.2.1.8. Assess the SQL DDL Scripts.

39.1.2.1.8.1. Ensure that the SQL scripts for reference data match the Value Domain Requirements.

39.1.2.1.8.2. Ensure that the SQL scripts for security roles match the security Requirements as it relates to the use cases, named user roles, organizations, and extent of permission to read, write, update, and select data.

39.1.2.1.8.3. Ensure that the SQL scripts for primary key sequence value specifications match the primary key Requirements.

39.1.2.1.8.4. Ensure that the SQL scripts for Tables, Columns and appropriate key specifications match the DBMS Table Requirements.

39.1.2.1.8.5. Ensure that the SQL scripts for triggers and other stored procedures match the data integrity constraints.

39.1.2.2. Assess whether the View Models are properly identified and are appropriately engineered to address a View Model project.

39.1.2.2.1. Assess whether all the View Models have been delivered in terms of components, instances, and stored metadata work products.

39.1.2.2.2. Assess whether all the View Models have been properly detailed as to content, description, methodology, evaluation, presentation, and delivery work steps.

39.1.2.2.3. Assess whether all the View Models have been properly allocated sufficient unit effort estimates.

39.1.2.2.4. Assess whether all the View Models have been properly allocated sufficient quantity of units that have to be developed.

39.1.2.2.5. Assess whether all the View Models have been properly allocated work environment factors to determine an accurate estimate of required resources.

39.1.2.2.6. Assess whether all the View Models have been properly allocated work accomplishment and recording functions necessary to support earned value reporting.

39.1.2.2.7. Assess whether all the View Models have been properly allocated metadata recording effort to ensure that all interrelationships are properly recorded into the Metabase System database.

39.1.2.3. Assign the risk level associated with each View Model not properly constructed.

39.1.3. Determine the findings and create draft assessment report.

39.1.4. Present the findings and revise draft assessment report.

39.1.5. Create final assessment report and deliver to the auditing organization.

39.2. Assess View Column.
39.2.1. Identify artifacts that bear on the assessment.
39.2.1.1. Identify the appropriate set of View Column documents.
39.2.1.1.1. Review View Column documents.
39.2.1.1.2. Review scope and business problem related documentation.
39.2.1.1.3. Identify the View Columns that are defined and captured.
39.2.1.1.4. Identify the work products appropriate to the evaluation of View Columns.
39.2.1.2. For each View Columns:
39.2.1.2.1. Identify components, that is, Business Information Systems, Views, DBMS schemas, DBMS Tables, DBMS Columns, and DBMS relationships.
39.2.1.2.2. Identify the definitions for each View Columns.
39.2.2. Perform the assessment.
39.2.2.1. Assess each View Column.
39.2.2.1.1. Assess the accuracy, quality and completeness of each View Column with respect to the business requirements.
39.2.2.1.2. Assess whether View Columns are able to be inferred from business requirements, and if not whether business requirements or View Columns need to be enhanced.
39.2.2.1.3. Assess the adequacy of each View Columns with respect to the Business Information Systems.
39.2.2.1.3.1. Assess whether the Business Information Systems environment on which the View Columns are to be based has the most efficient and effective architecture and deployment strategy for the performance needs of the operational database model.
39.2.2.1.4. Assess the adequacy of each View Columns with respect to the Data Integrity Rules.
39.2.2.1.4.1. Assess whether all implied Data Integrity Rules implied View Columns components are reflected in an appropriate View Columns.
39.2.2.1.4.2. Assess whether all View Columns components are reflected in Data Integrity Rules.
39.2.2.1.5. Assess the adequacy of each View Column that is to be populated by with respect to the External Data Interface Requirements.
39.2.2.1.5.1. Assess whether every View Column that is to be populated by external data is addressed by at least one External Data Interface requirement.
39.2.2.1.5.2. Assess whether every View Column that is to be populated by external data is designed appropriately so that it can respond to the External Data Interface requirement.
39.2.2.1.6. Assess the adequacy of each View Column with respect to the External Quality Standards.

39.2.2.1.6.1. Assess whether the facilities defined within every View Column is properly drawn from an DBMS facility that is at most ISO ANSI Standard for entry level SQL:1992.

39.2.2.1.6.2. Assess whether every View Column DBMS Columns that may be appropriate within the collection of DBMS Columns.

39.2.2.2. Assess View Columns work products.

39.2.2.2.1. Assess the completeness of each View Columns work product.

39.2.2.2.1.1. Assess that all View Columns are identified and are properly constructed.

39.2.2.2.1.2. Assess that all View Columns are identified and are properly constructed.

39.2.2.2.1.3. Assess that all View Columns contain the appropriate integrity constraints that are supported by assertions and triggers.

39.2.2.2.1.4. Assess that all View Columns stored procedures are properly identified, designed, coded and tested to meet integrity Requirements.

39.2.2.2.1.5. Assess that all View Columns are mapped to DBMS Columns.

39.2.2.2.1.6. Assess that appropriate DBMS Columns are properly constrained by Value Domain assignments to DBMS Columns.

39.2.2.3. Assess whether the View Columns are properly identified and are appropriately engineered to address a View Column project.

39.2.2.3.1. Assess whether all the View Columns have been delivered in terms of components, instances, and stored metadata work products.

39.2.2.3.2. Assess whether all the View Columns have been properly detailed as to content, description, methodology, evaluation, presentation, and delivery work steps.

39.2.2.3.3. Assess whether all the View Columns have been properly allocated sufficient unit effort estimates.

39.2.2.3.4. Assess whether all the View Columns have been properly allocated sufficient quantity of units that have to be developed.

39.2.2.3.5. Assess whether all the View Columns have been properly allocated work environment factors to determine an accurate estimate of required resources.

39.2.2.3.6. Assess whether all the View Columns have been properly allocated work accomplishment and recording functions necessary to support earned value reporting.

39.2.2.3.7. Assess whether all the View Columns have been properly allocated metadata recording effort to ensure that all interrelationships are properly recorded into the Metabase System database.

39.2.2.4. Assign the risk level associated with each View Column not properly constructed.

39.2.3. Determine the findings and create draft assessment report.

39.2.4. Present the findings and revise draft assessment report.

39.2.5. Create final assessment report and deliver to the auditing organization.

39.3. Assess View Column DBMS Column.
39.3.1. Identify artifacts that bear on the assessment.
39.3.1.1. Identify the appropriate set of View Column DBMS Column documents.
39.3.1.1.1. Review View Column DBMS Column documents.
39.3.1.1.2. Review scope and business problem related documentation.
39.3.1.1.3. Identify the View Column DBMS Columns that are defined and captured.
39.3.1.1.4. Identify the work products appropriate to the evaluation of View Column DBMS Columns.
39.3.1.2. For each View Column DBMS Columns:
39.3.1.2.1. Identify components, that is, Business Information Systems, Views, View Columns, DBMS schemas, DBMS Tables, DBMS Columns, and DBMS relationships.
39.3.1.2.2. Identify the definitions for each View Column DBMS Columns component.
39.3.2. Perform the assessment.
39.3.2.1. Assess each View Column DBMS Column.
39.3.2.1.1. Assess the accuracy, quality and completeness of each View Column DBMS Columns with respect to the business requirements.
39.3.2.1.2. Assess whether View Column DBMS Columns are able to be inferred from business requirements, and if not whether business requirements or View Column DBMS Columns need to be enhanced.
39.3.2.1.3. Assess whether each View Column DBMS Columns pair properly associates one or more View Columns with one or more DBMS Columns.
39.3.2.1.4. Assess whether each View Column DBMS Column pair is properly named and described.
39.3.2.2. Assess View Column DBMS Column work products.
39.3.2.2.1. Assess the completeness of each work product.
39.3.2.2.1.1. Assess that all View Column DBMS Columns are identified and are properly constructed.
39.3.2.2.1.5. Assess that all View Column DBMS Columns contain the appropriate integrity constraints that are supported by assertions and triggers.
39.3.2.2.1.6. Assess that all stored procedures are properly identified, designed, coded and tested to meet integrity Requirements.
39.3.2.2.1.7. Assess that all DBMS Columns are mapped to View Columns.
39.3.2.3. Assess whether the View Column DBMS Columns are properly identified and are appropriately engineered to address a View Column DBMS Column project.
39.3.2.3.1. Assess whether all the View Column DBMS Columns have been delivered in terms of components, instances, and stored metadata work products.
39.3.2.3.2. Assess whether all the View Column DBMS Columns have been properly detailed as to content, description, methodology, evaluation, presentation,

and delivery work steps.

39.3.2.3.3. Assess whether all the View Column DBMS Columns have been properly allocated sufficient unit effort estimates.

39.3.2.3.4. Assess whether all the View Column DBMS Columns have been properly allocated sufficient quantity of units that have to be developed.

39.3.2.3.5. Assess whether all the View Column DBMS Columns have been properly allocated work environment factors to determine an accurate estimate of required resources.

39.3.2.3.6. Assess whether all the View Column DBMS Columns have been properly allocated work accomplishment and recording functions necessary to support earned value reporting.

39.3.2.3.7. Assess whether all the View Column DBMS Columns have been properly allocated metadata recording effort to ensure that all interrelationships are properly recorded into the Metabase System database.

39.3.2.4. Assign the risk level associated with each View Column DBMS Column not properly constructed.

39.3.3. Determine the findings and create draft assessment report.

39.3.4. Present the findings and revise draft assessment report.

39.3.5. Create final assessment report and deliver to the auditing organization.

39.4. Assess View Column Compound Column.

39.4.1. Identify artifacts that bear on the assessment.

39.4.1.1. Identify the appropriate set of View Column Compound Column documents.

39.4.1.1.1. Review View Column Compound Column documents.

39.4.1.1.2. Review scope and business problem related documentation.

39.4.1.1.3. Identify the View Column Compound Columns that are defined and captured.

39.4.1.1.4. Identify the work products appropriate to the evaluation of View Column Compound Columns.

39.4.1.2. For each View Column Compound Column:

39.4.1.2.1. Identify components, that is, Business Information Systems, Views, View Columns, DBMS schemas, DBMS Tables, DBMS Columns, and DBMS relationships.

39.4.1.2.2. Identify the definitions for each View Column Compound Column component.

39.4.2. Perform the assessment.

39.4.2.1. Assess each View Column Compound Column.

39.4.2.1.1. Assess the accuracy, quality and completeness of each View Column Compound Column with respect to the business requirements.

39.4.2.1.2. Assess whether View Column Compound Columns are able to be inferred from business requirements, and if not whether business requirements or View Column Compound Columns need to be enhanced.

39.4.2.1.3. Assess whether each View Column Compound Column pair properly associates one or more View Columns with one or more Compound Columns.

39.4.2.1.4. Assess whether each View Column Compound Column pair is properly named and described.

39.4.2.2. Assess whether the View Column Compound Columns are properly identified and are appropriately engineered to address a View Column Compound Column project.

39.4.2.2.1. Assess whether all the View Column Compound Columns have been delivered in terms of components, instances, and stored metadata work products.

39.4.2.2.2. Assess whether all the View Column Compound Columns have been properly detailed as to content, description, methodology, evaluation, presentation, and delivery work steps.

39.4.2.2.3. Assess whether all the View Column Compound Columns have been properly allocated sufficient unit effort estimates.

39.4.2.2.4. Assess whether all the View Column Compound Columns have been properly allocated sufficient quantity of units that have to be developed.

39.4.2.2.5. Assess whether all the View Column Compound Columns have been properly allocated work environment factors to determine an accurate estimate of required resources.

39.4.2.2.6. Assess whether all the View Column Compound Columns have been properly allocated work accomplishment and recording functions necessary to support earned value reporting.

39.4.2.2.7. Assess whether all the View Column Compound Columns have been properly allocated metadata recording effort to ensure that all interrelationships are properly recorded into the Metabase System database.

39.4.2.3. Assign the risk level associated with each View Column Compound Column not properly constructed.

39.4.3. Determine the findings and create draft assessment report.

39.4.4. Present the findings and revise draft assessment report.

39.4.5. Create final assessment report and deliver to the auditing organization.

39.5. Assess View Column Derived Column.

39.5.1. Identify artifacts that bear on the assessment.

39.5.1.1. Identify the appropriate set of View Column Derived Column documents.

39.5.1.1.1. Review View Column Derived Column documents.

39.5.1.1.2. Review scope and business problem related documentation.

39.5.1.1.3. Identify the View Column Derived Columns that are defined and captured.

39.5.1.1.4. Identify the work products appropriate to the evaluation of View Column Derived Columns.
39.5.1.2. For each View Column Derived Column:
39.5.1.2.1. Identify components, that is, Business Information Systems, Views, View Columns, DBMS schemas, DBMS Tables, DBMS Columns, and DBMS relationships.
39.5.1.2.2. Identify the definitions for each View Column Derived Column component.
39.5.2. Perform the assessment.
39.5.2.1. Assess each View Column Derived Column.
39.5.2.1.1. Assess the accuracy, quality and completeness of each View Column Derived Column with respect to the business requirements.
39.5.2.1.2. Assess whether View Column Derived Column are able to be inferred from business requirements, and if not whether business requirements or View Column Derived Column need to be enhanced.
39.5.2.1.3. Assess whether each View Column Derived Column pair properly associates one or more View Columns with one or more Derived Columns.
39.5.2.1.4. Assess whether each View Column Derived Column pair is properly named and described.
39.5.2.2. Assess View Column Derived Column work products.
39.5.2.2.1. Assess the completeness of each work product.
39.5.2.2.1.1. Assess that all View Column Derived Columns are identified and are properly constructed.
39.5.2.3. Assess whether the View Column Derived Columns are properly identified and are appropriately engineered to address a View Column Derived Column project.
39.5.2.3.1. Assess whether all the View Column Derived Columns have been delivered in terms of components, instances, and stored metadata work products.
39.5.2.3.2. Assess whether all the View Column Derived Columns have been properly detailed as to content, description, methodology, evaluation, presentation, and delivery work steps.
39.5.2.3.3. Assess whether all the View Column Derived Columns have been properly allocated sufficient unit effort estimates.
39.5.2.3.4. Assess whether all the View Column Derived Columns have been properly allocated sufficient quantity of units that have to be developed.
39.5.2.3.5. Assess whether all the View Column Derived Columns have been properly allocated work environment factors to determine an accurate estimate of required resources.
39.5.2.3.6. Assess whether all the View Column Derived Columns have been properly allocated work accomplishment and recording functions

necessary to support earned value reporting.

39.5.2.3.7. Assess whether all the View Column Derived Columns have been properly allocated metadata recording effort to ensure that all interrelationships are properly recorded into the Metabase System database.

39.5.2.4. Assign the risk level associated with each View Column Derived Column not properly constructed.

39.5.3. Determine the findings and create draft assessment report.

39.5.4. Present the findings and revise draft assessment report.

39.5.5. Create final assessment report and deliver to the auditing organization.

39.6. Assess View Process.

39.6.1. Identify artifacts that bear on the assessment.

39.6.1.1. Identify the appropriate set of View Process documents.

39.6.1.1.1. Review View Process documents.

39.6.1.1.2. Review scope and business problem related documentation.

39.6.1.1.3. Identify the View Processes that are defined and captured.

39.6.1.1.4. Identify the work products appropriate to the evaluation of View Processes.

39.6.1.2. For each View Processes:

39.6.1.2.1. Identify components, that is, DBMS schemas, DBMS Tables, DBMS Columns, and DBMS relationships.

39.6.1.2.2. Identify the definitions for each View Processes component.

39.6.2. Perform the assessment.

39.6.2.1. Assess each View Process.

39.6.2.1.1. Assess the accuracy, quality and completeness of each View Process with respect to the business requirements.

39.6.2.1.2. Assess whether View Processes are able to be inferred from business requirements, and if not whether business requirements or View Processes need to be enhanced.

39.6.2.1.3. Assess whether each View Process hierarchy is properly specified, and that all View Process names and descriptions are well defined, non-overlapping, and have been formally approved.

39.6.2.1.3. Assess the adequacy of each View Process with respect to the Business Information Systems.

39.6.2.1.3.1. Assess whether the Business Information Systems environment on which the View Process is to be located has the most efficient and effective architecture and deployment strategy for the performance needs of the physical model.

39.6.2.1.4. Assess the adequacy of each View Process with respect to the Data Integrity Rules.

39.6.2.1.4.1. Assess whether all implied Data Integrity Rules implied View Process components are reflected in an appropriate View Process.

39.6.2.1.4.2. Assess whether all View Process components are reflected in Data Integrity Rules.

39.6.2.1.5. Assess the adequacy of each View Process with respect to the Use Cases.

39.6.2.1.5.1. Assess whether there is a sufficient set of use cases to account for all the View Processes.

39.6.2.1.5.2. Assess whether every View Process is addressed by at least one use case.

39.6.2.1.5.3. Assess whether the use cases are sufficiently detailed to fully address all the View Processes needed for Business Information Systems.

39.6.2.1.6. Assess the adequacy of each View Process with respect to the User Acceptance Tests.

39.6.2.1.6.1. Assess whether the tests adequately test Inserts, Deletes, and Modifies for every View.

39.6.2.1.6.4. Assess whether every Value Domain management action correctly executes and provide end-user violation messages that are clear, unambiguous, and helpful to the end user.

39.6.2.1.6.5. Assess whether every inappropriate and/or out-of-bounds value for every View Process database Column is appropriately trapped.

39.6.2.2. Assess View Process work products.

39.6.2.3. Assess whether the View Processes are properly identified and are appropriately engineered to address a View Process project.

39.6.2.3.1. Assess whether all the View Processes have been delivered in terms of components, instances, and stored metadata work products.

39.6.2.3.2. Assess whether all the View Processes have been properly detailed as to content, description, methodology, evaluation, presentation, and delivery work steps.

39.6.2.3.3. Assess whether all the View Processes have been properly allocated sufficient unit effort estimates.

39.6.2.3.4. Assess whether all the View Processes have been properly allocated sufficient quantity of units that have to be developed.

39.6.2.3.5. Assess whether all the View Processes have been properly allocated work environment factors to determine an accurate estimate of required resources.

39.6.2.3.6. Assess whether all the View Processes have been properly allocated work accomplishment and recording functions necessary to support earned value reporting.

39.6.2.3.7. Assess whether all the View Processes have been properly allocated metadata recording effort to ensure that all interrelationships are properly recorded into the Metabase System database.

39.6.2.4. Assign the risk level associated with each View Process not properly constructed.

39.6.3. Determine the findings and create draft assessment report.

39.6.4. Present the findings and revise draft assessment report.
39.6.5. Create final assessment report and deliver to the auditing organization.

40. Documents and Forms

40.1. Assess Document Model.
40.1.1. Identify artifacts that bear on the assessment.
40.1.1.1. Identify the appropriate set of Document Model documents.
40.1.1.1.1. Review Document Model documents.
40.1.1.1.2. Review scope and business problem related documentation.
40.1.1.1.3. Identify the Document Models that are defined and captured.
40.1.1.1.4. Identify the work products appropriate to the evaluation of Document Models.
40.1.1.2. For each Document Model:
40.1.1.2.1. Identify components, that is, Document, Document Structure, Document Structure Type, Document Section, and Document Cell.
40.1.1.2.2. Identify the definitions for each Document Model component.
40.1.2. Perform the assessment.
40.1.2.1. Assess each Document Model.
40.1.2.1.1. Assess the accuracy, quality and completeness of each Document Model with respect to the business requirements.
40.1.2.1.2. Assess whether Document Models are able to be inferred from business requirements, and if not whether business requirements or Document Models need to be enhanced.
40.1.2.1.3. Assess Document Model components, that is, Document, Document Structure, Document Structure Type, Document Section, and Document Cell with respect to the specific business requirement are sufficiently specified.
40.1.2.2. Assess whether the Document Models are properly identified and are appropriately engineered to address a Document Model project.
40.1.2.2.1. Assess whether all the Document Models have been delivered in terms of components, instances, and stored metadata work products.
40.1.2.2.2. Assess whether all the Document Models have been properly detailed as to content, description, methodology, evaluation, presentation, and delivery work steps.
40.1.2.2.3. Assess whether all the Document Models have been properly allocated sufficient unit effort estimates.
40.1.2.2.4. Assess whether all the Document Models have been properly allocated sufficient quantity of units that have to be developed.
40.1.2.2.5. Assess whether all the Document Models have been properly allocated work environment factors to determine an accurate estimate of required resources.
40.1.2.2.6. Assess whether all the Document Models have been properly allocated work accomplishment and recording functions necessary to support earned value reporting.

40.1.2.2.7. Assess whether all the Document Models have been properly allocated metadata recording effort to ensure that all interrelationships are properly recorded into the Metabase System database.
40.1.2.3. Assign the risk level associated with each Document Model not properly constructed.
40.1.3. Determine the findings and create draft assessment report.
40.1.4. Present the findings and revise draft assessment report.
40.1.5. Create final assessment report and deliver to the auditing organization.

40.2. Assess Document.
40.2.1. Identify artifacts that bear on the assessment.
40.2.1.1. Identify the appropriate set of Document documents.
40.2.1.1.1. Review Document documents.
40.2.1.1.2. Review scope and business problem related documentation.
40.2.1.1.3. Identify the Documents that are defined and captured.
40.2.1.1.4. Identify the work products appropriate to the evaluation of Documents.
40.2.1.2. For each Document:
40.2.1.2.1. Identify components, that is, Document Structure, Document Structure Type, Document Section, and Document Cell.
40.2.1.2.2. Identify the definitions for each Document component.
40.2.2. Perform the assessment.
40.2.2.1. Assess each Document.
40.2.2.1.1. Assess the accuracy, quality and completeness of each Document with respect to the business requirements.
40.2.2.1.2. Assess whether Documents are able to be inferred from business requirements, and if not whether business requirements or Documents need to be enhanced.
40.2.2.1.3. Assess Document components, that is, Document Structure, Document Structure Type, Document Section, and Document Cell with respect to the specific business requirement are sufficiently specified.
40.2.2.2. Assess whether the Documents are properly identified and are appropriately engineered to address a Document project.
40.2.2.2.1. Assess whether all the Documents have been delivered in terms of components, instances, and stored metadata work products.
40.2.2.2.2. Assess whether all the Documents have been properly detailed as to content, description, methodology, evaluation, presentation, and delivery work steps.
40.2.2.2.3. Assess whether all the Documents have been properly allocated sufficient unit effort estimates.
40.2.2.2.4. Assess whether all the Documents have been properly allocated sufficient quantity of units that have to be developed.
40.2.2.2.5. Assess whether all the Documents have been properly allocated work

environment factors to determine an accurate estimate of required resources.

40.2.2.2.6. Assess whether all the Documents have been properly allocated work accomplishment and recording functions necessary to support earned value reporting.

40.2.2.2.7. Assess whether all the Documents have been properly allocated metadata recording effort to ensure that all interrelationships are properly recorded into the Metabase System database.

40.2.2.3. Assign the risk level associated with each Document not properly constructed.

40.2.3. Determine the findings and create draft assessment report.

40.2.4. Present the findings and revise draft assessment report.

40.2.5. Create final assessment report and deliver to the auditing organization.

40.3. Assess Document Structure.

40.3.1. Identify artifacts that bear on the assessment.

40.3.1.1. Identify the appropriate set of Document Structure documents.

40.3.1.1.1. Review Document Structure documents.

40.3.1.1.2. Review scope and business problem related documentation.

40.3.1.1.3. Identify the Document Structures that are defined and captured.

40.3.1.1.4. Identify the Document Structures related work products.

40.3.1.2. For each Document Structures related work product assessment:

40.3.1.2.1. Identify the relevant components, that is, Documents, Document Structure Type, Document Section, and Document Cell

40.3.1.2.2. Identify the description for each interrelated Document Structure component.

40.3.2. Perform the assessment.

40.3.2.1. Assess each Document Structure.

40.3.2.1.1. Assess the accuracy, quality and completeness of each Document Structure with respect to the business requirements.

40.3.2.1.2. Assess whether Document Structures are able to be inferred from business requirements, and if not whether business requirements or Document Structures need to be enhanced.

40.3.2.1.3. Assess whether each Document Structure hierarchy/network is properly specified, and that all Document Structure names and descriptions are well defined, non-overlapping, and have been formally approved.

40.3.2.2. Assess whether the Document Structures are properly identified and are appropriately engineered to address a Document Structure project.

40.3.2.2.1. Assess whether all the Document Structures have been delivered in terms of components, instances, and stored metadata work products.

40.3.2.2.2. Assess whether all the Document Structures have been properly detailed as to content, description, methodology, evaluation, presentation, and

delivery work steps.

40.3.2.2.3. Assess whether all the Document Structures have been properly allocated sufficient unit effort estimates.

40.3.2.2.4. Assess whether all the Document Structures have been properly allocated sufficient quantity of units that have to be developed.

40.3.2.2.5. Assess whether all the Document Structures have been properly allocated work environment factors to determine an accurate estimate of required resources.

40.3.2.2.6. Assess whether all the Document Structures have been properly allocated work accomplishment and recording functions necessary to support earned value Business Event Cycle.

40.3.2.2.7. Assess whether all the Document Structures have been properly allocated metadata recording effort to ensure that all interrelationships are properly recorded into the Metabase System database.

40.3.2.3. Assign the risk level associated with each Document Structure not properly constructed.

40.3.3. Determine the findings and create draft assessment report.

40.3.4. Present the findings and revise draft assessment report.

40.3.5. Create final assessment report and deliver to the auditing organization.

40.4. Assess Document Section.

40.4.1. Identify artifacts that bear on the assessment.

40.4.1.1. Identify the appropriate set of Document Section documents.

40.4.1.1.1. Review Document Sections document.

40.4.1.1.2. Review scope and business problem related Document Sections.

40.4.1.1.3. Identify the business requirements that are defined and captured.

40.4.1.1.4. Identify the business requirements related work products.

40.4.1.2. For each business requirement related work product assessment:

40.4.1.2.1. Identify the relevant components, that is, Document, Document Structure, Document Structure Type, and Document Cell.

40.4.1.2.2. Identify the description for each interrelated business Document Section component.

40.4.2. Perform the assessment.

40.4.2.1. Assess each Document Section.

40.4.2.1.1. Assess the accuracy, quality and completeness of each Document Section with respect to the business requirements.

40.4.2.1.2. Assess whether Document Sections are able to be inferred from business requirements, and if not whether business requirements or Document Sections need to be enhanced.

40.4.2.2. Assess whether the Document Sections are properly identified and are appropriately engineered to address a Document Section project.

40.4.2.2.1. Assess whether all the Document Sections have been delivered in terms of components, instances, and stored metadata work products.

40.4.2.2.2. Assess whether all the Document Sections have been properly detailed as to content, description, methodology, evaluation, presentation, and delivery work steps.

40.4.2.2.3. Assess whether all the Document Sections have been properly allocated sufficient unit effort estimates.

40.4.2.2.4. Assess whether all the Document Sections have been properly allocated sufficient quantity of units that have to be developed.

40.4.2.2.5. Assess whether all the Document Sections have been properly allocated work environment factors to determine an accurate estimate of required resources.

40.4.2.2.6. Assess whether all the Document Sections have been properly allocated work accomplishment and recording functions necessary to support earned value reporting.

40.4.2.2.7. Assess whether all the Document Sections have been properly allocated metadata recording effort to ensure that all interrelationships are properly recorded into the Metabase System database.

40.4.2.3. Assign the risk level associated with each Document Section not properly constructed.

40.4.3. Determine the findings and create draft assessment report.

40.4.4. Present the findings and revise draft assessment report.

40.4.5. Create final assessment report and deliver to the auditing organization.

40.5. Assess Document Section Cell.

40.5.1. Identify artifacts that bear on the assessment.

40.5.1.1. Identify the appropriate set of Document Section Cell documents.

40.5.1.1.1. Review Document Section Cell documents.

40.5.1.1.2. Review scope and business problem related Document Section Cells.

40.5.1.1.3. Identify the business requirements that are defined and captured.

40.5.1.1.4. Identify the business requirements related work products.

40.5.1.2. For each business requirement related work product assessment:

40.5.1.2.1. Identify the relevant components, that is, Document, Document Structure, Document Structure Type, and Document Section.

40.5.1.2.2. Identify the description for each interrelated business Document Section Cell component.

40.5.2. Perform the assessment.

40.5.2.1. Assess each Document Section Cell.

40.5.2.1.1. Assess the accuracy, quality and completeness of each Document Section Cell with respect to the business requirements.

40.5.2.1.2. Assess whether Document Section Cells are able to be inferred from business requirements, and if not whether business requirements or Document Section Cells need to be enhanced.

40.5.2.2. Assess whether the Document Section Cells are properly identified and are appropriately engineered to address a Document Section Cell project.

40.5.2.2.1. Assess whether all the Document Section Cells have been delivered in terms of components, instances, and stored metadata work products.

40.5.2.2.2. Assess whether all the Document Section Cells have been properly detailed as to content, description, methodology, evaluation, presentation, and delivery work steps.

40.5.2.2.3. Assess whether all the Document Section Cells have been properly allocated sufficient unit effort estimates.

40.5.2.2.4. Assess whether all the Document Section Cells have been properly allocated sufficient quantity of units that have to be developed.

40.5.2.2.5. Assess whether all the Document Section Cells have been properly allocated work environment factors to determine an accurate estimate of required resources.

40.5.2.2.6. Assess whether all the Document Section Cells have been properly allocated work accomplishment and recording functions necessary to support earned value reporting.

40.5.2.2.7. Assess whether all the Document Section Cells have been properly allocated metadata recording effort to ensure that all interrelationships are properly recorded into the Metabase System database.

40.5.2.3. Assign the risk level associated with each Document Section Cell not properly constructed.

40.5.3. Determine the findings and create draft assessment report.

40.5.4. Present the findings and revise draft assessment report.

40.5.5. Create final assessment report and deliver to the auditing organization.

40.6. Assess Document Section Cell View Column.

40.6.1. Identify artifacts that bear on the assessment.

40.6.1.1. Identify the appropriate set of Document Section Cell View Column documents.

40.6.1.1.1. Review Document Section Cell View Column documents.

40.6.1.1.2. Review scope and business problem related Document Section Cell View Columns.

40.6.1.1.3. Identify the business requirements that are defined and captured.

40.6.1.1.4. Identify the business requirements related work products.

40.6.1.2. For each business requirement related work product assessment:

40.6.1.2.1. Identify the relevant components, that is, Views, View Columns, DBMS Columns, Document, Document Structure, Document Structure Type, and Document Section, Document Cells.

40.6.1.2.2. Identify the description for each interrelated business Document Section Cell View Column component.

40.6.2. Perform the assessment.

40.6.2.1. Assess each Document Section Cell View Column.

40.6.2.1.1. Assess the accuracy, quality and completeness of each Document Section Cell View Column with respect to the business requirements.

40.6.2.1.2. Assess whether Document Section Cell View Columns are able to be inferred from business requirements, and if not whether business requirements or Document Section Cell View Columns need to be enhanced.

40.6.2.1.3. Assess whether each Document Section Cell View Column pair properly associates one or more Document Section Cells with one or more View Columns.

40.6.2.1.4. Assess whether each Document Section Cell View Column pair is properly named and described.

40.6.2.2. Assess whether the Document Section Cell View Columns are properly identified and are appropriately engineered to address a Document Section Cell View Column project.

40.6.2.2.1. Assess whether all the Document Section Cell View Columns have been delivered in terms of components, instances, and stored metadata work products.

40.6.2.2.2. Assess whether all the Document Section Cell View Columns have been properly detailed as to content, description, methodology, evaluation, presentation, and delivery work steps.

40.6.2.2.3. Assess whether all the Document Section Cell View Columns have been properly allocated sufficient unit effort estimates.

40.6.2.2.4. Assess whether all the Document Section Cell View Columns have been properly allocated sufficient quantity of units that have to be developed.

40.6.2.2.5. Assess whether all the Document Section Cell View Columns have been properly allocated work environment factors to determine an accurate estimate of required resources.

40.6.2.2.6. Assess whether all the Document Section Cell View Columns have been properly allocated work accomplishment and recording functions necessary to support earned value reporting.

40.6.2.2.7. Assess whether all the Document Section Cell View Columns have been properly allocated metadata recording effort to ensure that all interrelationships are properly recorded into the Metabase System database.

40.6.2.3. Assign the risk level associated with each Document Section Cell View Column not properly constructed.

40.6.3. Determine the findings and create draft assessment report.

40.6.4. Present the findings and revise draft assessment report.

40.6.5. Create final assessment report and deliver to the auditing organization.

40.7. Assess Form Model.

40.7.1. Identify artifacts that bear on the assessment.

40.7.1.1. Identify the appropriate set of Form Model documents.

40.7.1.1.1. Review Form Model Forms.

40.7.1.1.2. Review scope and business problem related Formation.

40.7.1.1.3. Identify the Form Models that are defined and captured.

40.7.1.1.4. Identify the work products appropriate to the evaluation of Form Models.

40.7.1.2. For each Form Model:

40.7.1.2.1. Identify components, that is, Form, Form Structure, Form Structure Type, Form Section, and Form Cell.

40.7.1.2.2. Identify the definitions for each Form Model component.

40.7.2. Perform the assessment.

40.7.2.1. Assess each Form Model.

40.7.2.1.1. Assess the accuracy, quality and completeness of each Form Model with respect to the business requirements.

40.7.2.1.2. Assess whether Form Models are able to be inferred from business requirements, and if not whether business requirements or Form Models need to be enhanced.

40.7.2.1.3. Assess Form Model components, that is, Form, Form Structure, Form Structure Type, Form Section, and Form Cell with respect to the specific business requirement are sufficiently specified.

40.7.2.2. Assess whether the Form Models are properly identified and are appropriately engineered to address a Form Model project.

40.7.2.2.1. Assess whether all the Form Models have been delivered in terms of components, instances, and stored metadata work products.

40.7.2.2.2. Assess whether all the Form Models have been properly detailed as to content, description, methodology, evaluation, presentation, and delivery work steps.

40.7.2.2.3. Assess whether all the Form Models have been properly allocated sufficient unit effort estimates.

40.7.2.2.4. Assess whether all the Form Models have been properly allocated sufficient quantity of units that have to be developed.

40.7.2.2.5. Assess whether all the Form Models have been properly allocated work environment factors to determine an accurate estimate of required resources.

40.7.2.2.6. Assess whether all the Form Models have been properly allocated work accomplishment and recording functions necessary to support earned value reporting.

40.7.2.2.7. Assess whether all the Form Models have been properly allocated metadata recording effort to ensure that all interrelationships are properly recorded into the Metabase System database.

40.7.2.3. Assign the risk level associated with each Form Model not properly constructed.

40.7.3. Determine the findings and create draft assessment report.
40.7.4. Present the findings and revise draft assessment report.
40.7.5. Create final assessment report and deliver to the auditing organization.

40.8. Assess Form.
40.8.1. Identify artifacts that bear on the assessment.
40.8.1.1. Identify the appropriate set of Form documents.
40.8.1.1.1. Review Form Forms.
40.8.1.1.2. Review scope and business problem related Formation.
40.8.1.1.3. Identify the Forms that are defined and captured.
40.8.1.1.4. Identify the work products appropriate to the evaluation of Forms.
40.8.1.2. For each Form:
40.8.1.2.1. Identify components, that is, Form Structure, Form Structure Type, Form Section, and Form Cell.
40.8.1.2.2. Identify the definitions for each Form component.
40.8.2. Perform the assessment.
40.8.2.1. Assess each Form.
40.8.2.1.1. Assess the accuracy, quality and completeness of each Form with respect to the business requirements.
40.8.2.1.2. Assess whether Forms are able to be inferred from business requirements, and if not whether business requirements or Forms need to be enhanced.
40.8.2.1.3. Assess Form components, that is, Form Structure, Form Structure Type, Form Section, and Form Cell with respect to the specific business requirement are sufficiently specified.
40.8.2.2. Assess whether the Forms are properly identified and are appropriately engineered to address a Form project.
40.8.2.2.1. Assess whether all the Forms have been delivered in terms of components, instances, and stored metadata work products.
40.8.2.2.2. Assess whether all the Forms have been properly detailed as to content, description, methodology, evaluation, presentation, and delivery work steps.
40.8.2.2.3. Assess whether all the Forms have been properly allocated sufficient unit effort estimates.
40.8.2.2.4. Assess whether all the Forms have been properly allocated sufficient quantity of units that have to be developed.
40.8.2.2.5. Assess whether all the Forms have been properly allocated work environment factors to determine an accurate estimate of required resources.
40.8.2.2.6. Assess whether all the Forms have been properly allocated work accomplishment and recording functions necessary to support earned value reporting.
40.8.2.2.7. Assess whether all the Forms have been properly allocated metadata

recording effort to ensure that all interrelationships are properly recorded into the Metabase System database.

40.8.2.3. Assign the risk level associated with each Form not properly constructed.

40.8.3. Determine the findings and create draft assessment report.

40.8.4. Present the findings and revise draft assessment report.

40.8.5. Create final assessment report and deliver to the auditing organization.

40.9. Assess Form Structure.

40.9.1. Identify artifacts that bear on the assessment.

40.9.1.1. Identify the appropriate set of Form Structure documents.

40.9.1.1.1. Review Form Structure documents.

40.9.1.1.2. Review scope and business problem related Formation.

40.9.1.1.3. Identify the Form Structures that are defined and captured.

40.9.1.1.4. Identify the Form Structures related work products.

40.9.1.2. For each Form Structures related work product assessment:

40.9.1.2.1. Identify the relevant components, that is, Forms, Form Structure Type, Form Section, and Form Cell

40.9.1.2.2. Identify the description for each interrelated Form Structure component.

40.9.2. Perform the assessment.

40.9.2.1. Assess each Form Structure.

40.9.2.1.1. Assess the accuracy, quality and completeness of each Form Structure with respect to the business requirements.

40.9.2.1.2. Assess whether Form Structures are able to be inferred from business requirements, and if not whether business requirements or Form Structures need to be enhanced.

40.9.2.1.3. Assess whether each Form Structure hierarchy/network is properly specified, and that all Form Structure names and descriptions are well defined, non-overlapping, and have been formally approved.

40.9.2.2. Assess whether the Form Structures are properly identified and are appropriately engineered to address a Form Structure project.

40.9.2.2.1. Assess whether all the Form Structures have been delivered in terms of components, instances, and stored metadata work products.

40.9.2.2.2. Assess whether all the Form Structures have been properly detailed as to content, description, methodology, evaluation, presentation, and delivery work steps.

40.9.2.2.3. Assess whether all the Form Structures have been properly allocated sufficient unit effort estimates.

40.9.2.2.4. Assess whether all the Form Structures have been properly allocated sufficient quantity of units that have to be developed.

40.9.2.2.5. Assess whether all the Form Structures have been properly allocated work environment factors to determine an accurate estimate of required resources.

40.9.2.2.6. Assess whether all the Form Structures have been properly allocated work accomplishment and recording functions necessary to support earned value Business Event Cycle.
40.9.2.2.7. Assess whether all the Form Structures have been properly allocated metadata recording effort to ensure that all interrelationships are properly recorded into the Metabase System database.
40.9.2.3. Assign the risk level associated with each Form Structure not properly constructed.
40.9.3. Determine the findings and create draft assessment report.
40.9.4. Present the findings and revise draft assessment report.
40.9.5. Create final assessment report and deliver to the auditing organization.

40.10. Assess Form Section.
40.10.1. Identify artifacts that bear on the assessment.
40.10.1.1. Identify the appropriate set of Form Section documents.
40.10.1.1.1. Review Form Sections documents.
40.10.1.1.2. Review scope and business problem related Form Sections.
40.10.1.1.3. Identify the business requirements that are defined and captured.
40.10.1.1.4. Identify the business requirements related work products.
40.10.1.2. For each business requirement related work product assessment:
40.10.1.2.1. Identify the relevant components, that is, Form, Form Structure, Form Structure Type, and Form Cell.
40.10.1.2.2. Identify the description for each interrelated business Form Section component.
40.10.2. Perform the assessment.
40.10.2.1. Assess each Form Section.
40.10.2.1.1. Assess the accuracy, quality and completeness of each Form Section with respect to the business requirements.
40.10.2.1.2. Assess whether Form Sections are able to be inferred from business requirements, and if not whether business requirements or Form Sections need to be enhanced.
40.10.2.2. Assess whether the Form Sections are properly identified and are appropriately engineered to address a Form Section project.
40.10.2.2.1. Assess whether all the Form Sections have been delivered in terms of components, instances, and stored metadata work products.
40.10.2.2.2. Assess whether all the Form Sections have been properly detailed as to content, description, methodology, evaluation, presentation, and delivery work steps.
40.10.2.2.3. Assess whether all the Form Sections have been properly allocated sufficient unit effort estimates.
40.10.2.2.4. Assess whether all the Form Sections have been properly allocated sufficient quantity of units that have to be developed.

40.10.2.2.5. Assess whether all the Form Sections have been properly allocated work environment factors to determine an accurate estimate of required resources.

40.10.2.2.6. Assess whether all the Form Sections have been properly allocated work accomplishment and recording functions necessary to support earned value reporting.

40.10.2.2.7. Assess whether all the Form Sections have been properly allocated metadata recording effort to ensure that all interrelationships are properly recorded into the Metabase System database.

40.10.2.3. Assign the risk level associated with each Form Section not properly constructed.

40.10.3. Determine the findings and create draft assessment report.

40.10.4. Present the findings and revise draft assessment report.

40.10.5. Create final assessment report and deliver to the auditing organization.

40.11. Assess Form Section Cell.

40.11.1. Identify artifacts that bear on the assessment.

40.11.1.1. Identify the appropriate set of Form Section Cell documents.

40.11.1.1.1. Review Form Section Cell documents.

40.11.1.1.2. Review scope and business problem related Form Section Cells.

40.11.1.1.3. Identify the business requirements that are defined and captured.

40.11.1.1.4. Identify the business requirements related work products.

40.11.1.2. For each business requirement related work product assessment:

40.11.1.2.1. Identify the relevant components, that is, Form, Form Structure, Form Structure Type, and Form Section.

40.11.1.2.2. Identify the description for each interrelated business Form Section Cell component.

40.11.2. Perform the assessment.

40.11.2.1. Assess each Form Section Cell.

40.11.2.1.1. Assess the accuracy, quality and completeness of each Form Section Cell with respect to the business requirements.

40.11.2.1.2. Assess whether Form Section Cells are able to be inferred from business requirements, and if not whether business requirements or Form Section Cells need to be enhanced.

40.11.2.2. Assess whether the Form Section Cells are properly identified and are appropriately engineered to address a Form Section Cell project.

40.11.2.2.1. Assess whether all the Form Section Cells have been delivered in terms of components, instances, and stored metadata work products.

40.11.2.2.2. Assess whether all the Form Section Cells have been properly detailed as to content, description, methodology, evaluation, presentation, and delivery work steps.

40.11.2.2.3. Assess whether all the Form Section Cells have been properly allocated sufficient unit effort estimates.

40.11.2.2.4. Assess whether all the Form Section Cells have been properly allocated sufficient quantity of units that have to be developed.

40.11.2.2.5. Assess whether all the Form Section Cells have been properly allocated work environment factors to determine an accurate estimate of required resources.

40.11.2.2.6. Assess whether all the Form Section Cells have been properly allocated work accomplishment and recording functions necessary to support earned value reporting.

40.11.2.2.7. Assess whether all the Form Section Cells have been properly allocated metadata recording effort to ensure that all interrelationships are properly recorded into the Metabase System database.

40.11.2.3. Assign the risk level associated with each Form Section Cell not properly constructed.

40.11.3. Determine the findings and create draft assessment report.

40.11.4. Present the findings and revise draft assessment report.

40.11.5. Create final assessment report and deliver to the auditing organization.

40.12. Assess Form Section Cell View Column.

40.12.1. Identify artifacts that bear on the assessment.

40.12.1.1. Identify the appropriate set of Form Section Cell View Columns documents.

40.12.1.1.1. Review Form Section Cell View Columns documents.

40.12.1.1.2. Review scope and business problem related Form Section Cell View Columns.

40.12.1.1.3. Identify the business requirements that are defined and captured.

40.12.1.1.4. Identify the business requirements related work products.

40.12.1.2. For each business requirement related work product assessment:

40.12.1.2.1. Identify the relevant components, that is, Views, View Columns, DBMS Columns, Form, Form Structure, Form Structure Type, and Form Section, Form Cells.

40.12.1.2.2. Identify the description for each interrelated business Form Section Cell View Column component.

40.12.2. Perform the assessment.

40.12.2.1. Assess each Form Section Cell View Column.

40.12.2.1.1. Assess the accuracy, quality and completeness of each Form Section Cell View Column with respect to the business requirements.

40.12.2.1.2. Assess whether Form Section Cell View Columns are able to be inferred from business requirements, and if not whether business requirements or Form Section Cell View Columns need to be enhanced.

40.12.2.1.3. Assess whether each Form Section Cell View Column pair properly associates one or more Form Section Cells with one or more View

Columns.

40.12.2.1.4. Assess whether each Form Section Cell View Column pair is properly named and described.

40.12.2.2. Assess whether the Form Section Cell View Columns are properly identified and are appropriately engineered to address a Form Section Cell View Column project.

40.12.2.2.1. Assess whether all the Form Section Cell View Columns have been delivered in terms of components, instances, and stored metadata work products.

40.12.2.2.2. Assess whether all the Form Section Cell View Columns have been properly detailed as to content, description, methodology, evaluation, presentation, and delivery work steps.

40.12.2.2.3. Assess whether all the Form Section Cell View Columns have been properly allocated sufficient unit effort estimates.

40.12.2.2.4. Assess whether all the Form Section Cell View Columns have been properly allocated sufficient quantity of units that have to be developed.

40.12.2.2.5. Assess whether all the Form Section Cell View Columns have been properly allocated work environment factors to determine an accurate estimate of required resources.

40.12.2.2.6. Assess whether all the Form Section Cell View Columns have been properly allocated work accomplishment and recording functions necessary to support earned value reporting.

40.12.2.2.7. Assess whether all the Form Section Cell View Columns have been properly allocated metadata recording effort to ensure that all interrelationships are properly recorded into the Metabase System database.

40.12.2.3. Assign the risk level associated with each Form Section Cell View Column not properly constructed.

40.12.3. Determine the findings and create draft assessment report.

40.12.4. Present the findings and revise draft assessment report.

40.12.5. Create final assessment report and deliver to the auditing organization..

41. Information Needs

41.1. Assess Characteristic.
41.1.1. Identify artifacts that bear on the assessment.
41.1.1.1. Identify the appropriate set of Characteristic documents.
41.1.1.1.1. Review Characteristic documents.
41.1.1.1.2. Review scope and business problem related documentation.
41.1.1.1.3. Identify the Characteristic that are defined and captured.
41.1.1.1.4. Identify the Characteristic related work products.
41.1.1.2. For each Characteristic work product assessment:
41.1.1.2.1. Identify the relevant component.
41.1.1.2.2. Identify the description for each interrelated Characteristic component.
41.1.2. Perform the assessment.
41.1.2.1. Assess each Characteristic.
41.1.2.1.1. Assess the accuracy, quality and completeness of each Characteristic with respect to the business requirements.
41.1.2.1.2. Assess whether Characteristics are able to be inferred from business requirements, and if not whether business requirements or Characteristics need to be enhanced.
41.1.2.1. Assess whether each Characteristic is addressed to ensure complete coverage.
41.1.2.2. Assess whether the Characteristics are properly identified and are appropriately engineered to address a Characteristic project.
41.1.2.2.1. Assess whether all the Characteristics have been delivered in terms of components, instances, and stored metadata work products.
41.1.2.2.2. Assess whether all the Characteristics have been properly detailed as to content, description, methodology, evaluation, presentation, and delivery work steps.
41.1.2.2.3. Assess whether all the Characteristics have been properly allocated sufficient unit effort estimates.
41.1.2.2.4. Assess whether all the Characteristics have been properly allocated sufficient quantity of units that have to be developed.
41.1.2.2.5. Assess whether all the Characteristics have been properly allocated work environment factors to determine an accurate estimate of required resources.
41.1.2.2.6. Assess whether all the Characteristics have been properly allocated work accomplishment and recording functions necessary to support earned value reporting.
41.1.2.2.7. Assess whether all the Characteristics have been properly allocated metadata recording effort to ensure that all interrelationships are properly recorded into the Metabase System database.
41.1.2.3 Assign the risk level associated with each Characteristic not properly

constructed.

41.1.3. Determine the findings and create draft assessment report.
41.1.4. Present the findings and revise draft assessment report.
41.1.5. Create final assessment report and deliver to the auditing organization.

41.2. Assess Information Need.
41.2.1. Identify artifacts that bear on the assessment.
41.2.1.1. Identify the appropriate set of Information Needs documents.
41.2.1.1.1. Review Information Needs documents.
41.2.1.1.2. Review scope and business problem related documentation.
41.2.1.1.3. Identify the Information Needs that are defined and captured.
41.2.1.1.4. Identify the Information Needs related work products.
41.2.1.2. For each Information Needs related work product assessment:
41.2.1.2.1. Identify the relevant component.
41.2.1.2.2. Identify the description for each interrelated Information Need component.
41.2.2. Perform the assessment.
41.2.2.1. Assess each Information Need.
41.2.2.1.1. Assess the accuracy, quality and completeness of each Information Need with respect to the business requirements.
41.2.2.1.2. Assess whether Information Needs are able to be inferred from business requirements, and if not whether business requirements or Information Needs need to be enhanced.
41.2.2.2. Assess whether the Information Needs are properly identified and are appropriately engineered to address a Information Need project.
41.2.2.2.1. Assess whether all the Information Needs have been delivered in terms of components, instances, and stored metadata work products.
41.2.2.2.2. Assess whether all the Information Needs have been properly detailed as to content, description, methodology, evaluation, presentation, and delivery work steps.
41.2.2.2.3. Assess whether all the Information Needs have been properly allocated sufficient unit effort estimates.
41.2.2.2.4. Assess whether all the Information Needs have been properly allocated sufficient quantity of units that have to be developed.
41.2.2.2.5. Assess whether all the Information Needs have been properly allocated work environment factors to determine an accurate estimate of required resources.
41.2.2.2.6. Assess whether all the Information Needs have been properly allocated work accomplishment and recording functions necessary to support earned value reporting.
41.2.2.2.7. Assess whether all the Information Needs have been properly allocated metadata recording effort to ensure that all interrelationships are properly

recorded into the Metabase System database.

41.2.2.3. Assign the risk level associated with each Information Need not properly constructed.

41.2.3. Determine the findings and create draft assessment report.

41.2.4. Present the findings and revise draft assessment report.

41.2.5. Create final assessment report and deliver to the auditing organization.

41.3. Assess Information Need Resource Life Cycle Node.

41.3.1. Identify artifacts that bear on the assessment.

41.3.1.1. Identify the appropriate set of Information Need Resource Life Cycle Node documents.

41.3.1.1.1. Review Information Need Resource Life Cycle Node documents.

41.3.1.1.2. Review scope and business problem related documentation.

41.3.1.1.3. Identify the Information Need Resource Life Cycle Node that are defined and captured.

41.3.1.1.4. Identify the Information Need Resource Life Cycle Node related work products.

41.3.1.2. For each Information Need Resource Life Cycle Node related work product assessment:

41.3.1.2.1. Identify the relevant component.

41.3.1.2.2. Identify the description for each interrelated Information Need Resource Life Cycle Node component.

41.3.2. Perform the assessment.

41.3.2.1. Assess each Information Need Resource Life Cycle Node.

41.3.2.1.1. Assess the accuracy, quality and completeness of each Information Need Resource Life Cycle Node with respect to the business requirements.

41.3.2.1.2. Assess whether Information Need Resource Life Cycle Nodes are able to be inferred from business requirements, and if not whether business requirements or Information Need Resource Life Cycle Nodes need to be enhanced.

41.3.2.1.3. Assess whether each Information Need Resource Life Cycle Node pair properly associates one or more Information Needs with one or more Resource Life Cycle Nodes.

41.3.2.1.4. Assess whether each Information Needs Resource Life Cycle Node pair is properly named and described.

41.3.2.2. Assess whether the Information Need Resource Life Cycle Nodes are properly identified and are appropriately engineered to address a Information Need Resource Life Cycle Node project.

41.3.2.2.1. Assess whether all the Information Need Resource Life Cycle Nodes have been delivered in terms of components, instances, and stored metadata work products.

41.3.2.2.2. Assess whether all the Information Need Resource Life Cycle Nodes have been properly detailed as to content, description, methodology, evaluation, presentation, and delivery work steps.

41.3.2.2.3. Assess whether all the Information Need Resource Life Cycle Nodes have been properly allocated sufficient unit effort estimates.

41.3.2.2.4. Assess whether all the Information Need Resource Life Cycle Nodes have been properly allocated sufficient quantity of units that have to be developed.

41.3.2.2.5. Assess whether all the Information Need Resource Life Cycle Nodes have been properly allocated work environment factors to determine an accurate estimate of required resources.

41.3.2.2.6. Assess whether all the Information Need Resource Life Cycle Nodes have been properly allocated work accomplishment and recording functions necessary to support earned value reporting.

41.3.2.2.7. Assess whether all the Information Need Resource Life Cycle Nodes have been properly allocated metadata recording effort to ensure that all interrelationships are properly recorded into the Metabase System database.

41.3.2.3. Assign the risk level associated with each Information Need Resource Life Cycle Node not properly constructed.

41.3.3. Determine the findings and create draft assessment report.

41.3.4. Present the findings and revise draft assessment report.

41.3.5. Create final assessment report and deliver to the auditing organization.

41.4. Assess Information Need Mission-Organization-Function.

41.4.1. Identify artifacts that bear on the assessment.

41.4.1.1. Identify the appropriate set of Information Need Mission-Organization-Function documents.

41.4.1.1.1. Review Information Need Mission-Organization-Function documents.

41.4.1.1.2. Review scope and business problem related documentation.

41.4.1.1.3. Identify the Information Needs Mission-Organization-Function that are defined and captured.

41.4.1.1.4. Identify the Information Needs Mission-Organization-Function related work products.

41.4.1.2. For each Information Needs Mission-Organization-Function related work product assessment:

41.4.1.2.1. Identify the relevant component.

41.4.1.2.2. Identify the description for each interrelated Information Needs Mission-Organization-Function component.

41.4.2. Perform the assessment.

41.4.2.1. Assess each Information Needs Mission-Organization-Function.

41.4.2.1.1. Assess the accuracy, quality and completeness of each Information Needs Mission-Organization-Function with respect to the business requirements.

41.4.2.1.2. Assess whether Information Needs Mission-Organization-Functions are able to be inferred from business requirements, and if not whether business requirements or Information Needs Mission-Organization-Functions need to be enhanced.

41.4.2.1.3. Assess whether each Information Need Mission-Organization-Function pair properly associates one or more Information Needs with one or more Mission-Organization-Functions.

41.4.2.1.4. Assess whether each Information Needs Mission-Organization-Functions pair is properly named and described.

41.4.2.2. Assess whether the Information Need Mission-Organization-Functions are properly identified and are appropriately engineered to address a Information Need Mission-Organization-Function project.

41.4.2.2.1. Assess whether all the Information Need Mission-Organization-Functions have been delivered in terms of components, instances, and stored metadata work products.

41.4.2.2.2. Assess whether all the Information Need Mission-Organization-Functions have been properly detailed as to content, description, methodology, evaluation, presentation, and delivery work steps.

41.4.2.2.3. Assess whether all the Information Need Mission-Organization-Functions have been properly allocated sufficient unit effort estimates.

41.4.2.2.4. Assess whether all the Information Need Mission-Organization-Functions have been properly allocated sufficient quantity of units that have to be developed.

41.4.2.2.5. Assess whether all the Information Need Mission-Organization-Functions have been properly allocated work environment factors to determine an accurate estimate of required resources.

41.4.2.2.6. Assess whether all the Information Need Mission-Organization-Functions have been properly allocated work accomplishment and recording functions necessary to support earned value reporting.

41.4.2.2.7. Assess whether all the Information Need Mission-Organization-Functions have been properly allocated metadata recording effort to ensure that all interrelationships are properly recorded into the Metabase System database.

41.4.2.3. Assign the risk level associated with each Information Need Mission-Organization-Function not properly constructed.

41.4.3. Determine the findings and create draft assessment report.

41.4.4. Present the findings and revise draft assessment report.

41.4.5. Create final assessment report and deliver to the auditing organization.

42. Missions-Organizations-Functions Positions Persons

42.1. Assess Mission.
42.1.1. Identify artifacts that bear on the assessment.
42.1.1.1. Identify the appropriate set of Mission documents.
42.1.1.1.1. Review Mission documents.
42.1.1.1.2. Review scope and business problem related documentation.
42.1.1.1.3. Identify the Missions that are defined and captured.
42.1.1.1.4. Identify the Missions related work products.
42.1.1.2. For each Mission related work product assessment:
42.1.1.2.1. Identify the relevant component.
42.1.1.2.2. Identify the description for each interrelated Mission component.
42.1.2. Perform the assessment.
42.1.2.1. Assess each Mission.
42.1.2.1.1. Assess the accuracy, quality and completeness of each Mission with respect to the business requirements.
42.1.2.1.2. Assess whether Missions are able to be inferred from business requirements, and if not whether business requirements or Missions need to be enhanced.
42.1.2.2. Assess whether the Missions are properly identified and are appropriately engineered to address a Mission project.
42.1.2.2.1. Assess whether all the Missions have been delivered in terms of components, instances, and stored metadata work products.
42.1.2.2.2. Assess whether all the Missions have been properly detailed as to content, description, methodology, evaluation, presentation, and delivery work steps.
42.1.2.2.3. Assess whether all the Missions have been properly allocated sufficient unit effort estimates.
42.1.2.2.4. Assess whether all the Missions have been properly allocated sufficient quantity of units that have to be developed.
42.1.2.2.5. Assess whether all the Missions have been properly allocated work environment factors to determine an accurate estimate of required resources.
42.1.2.2.6. Assess whether all the Missions have been properly allocated work accomplishment and recording functions necessary to support earned value reporting.
42.1.2.2.7. Assess whether all the Missions have been properly allocated metadata recording effort to ensure that all interrelationships are properly recorded into the Metabase System database.
42.1.2.3. Assign the risk level associated with each Mission not properly constructed.
42.1.3. Determine the findings and create draft assessment report.

42.1.4. Present the findings and revise draft assessment report.
42.1.5. Create final assessment report and deliver to the auditing organization.

42.2. Assess Mission Structure.
42.2.1. Identify artifacts that bear on the assessment.
42.2.1.1. Identify the appropriate set of Mission Structure documents.
42.2.1.1.1. Review Mission Structure documents.
42.2.1.1.2. Review scope and business problem related documentation.
42.2.1.1.3. Identify the Missions Structure that are defined and captured.
42.2.1.1.4. Identify the Missions Structure related work products.
42.2.1.2. For each Missions related work product assessment:
42.2.1.2.1. Identify the relevant component.
42.2.1.2.2. Identify the description for each interrelated Mission Structure component.
42.2.2. Perform the assessment.
42.2.2.1. Assess each Mission Structure.
42.2.2.1.1. Assess the accuracy, quality and completeness of each Mission Structure with respect to the business requirements.
42.2.2.1.2. Assess whether Mission Structures are able to be inferred from business requirements, and if not whether business requirements or Mission Structures need to be enhanced.
42.2.2.1.3. Assess whether each Mission Structure hierarchy/network is properly specified, and that all Mission Structure names and descriptions are well defined, non-overlapping, and have been formally approved.
42.2.2.2. Assess whether the Mission Structures are properly identified and are appropriately engineered to address a Mission Structure project.
42.2.2.2.1. Assess whether all the Mission Structures have been delivered in terms of components, instances, and stored metadata work products.
42.2.2.2.2. Assess whether all the Mission Structures have been properly detailed as to content, description, methodology, evaluation, presentation, and delivery work steps.
42.2.2.2.3. Assess whether all the Mission Structures have been properly allocated sufficient unit effort estimates.
42.2.2.2.4. Assess whether all the Mission Structures have been properly allocated sufficient quantity of units that have to be developed.
42.2.2.2.5. Assess whether all the Mission Structures have been properly allocated work environment factors to determine an accurate estimate of required resources.
42.2.2.2.6. Assess whether all the Mission Structures have been properly allocated work accomplishment and recording functions necessary to support earned value reporting.
42.2.2.2.7. Assess whether all the Mission Structures have been properly allocated

metadata recording effort to ensure that all interrelationships are properly recorded into the Metabase System database.

42.2.2.3. Assign the risk level associated with each Mission Structure not properly constructed.

42.2.3. Determine the findings and create draft assessment report.

42.2.4. Present the findings and revise draft assessment report.

42.2.5. Create final assessment report and deliver to the auditing organization.

42.3. Assess Organization.

42.3.1. Identify artifacts that bear on the assessment.

42.3.1.1. Identify the appropriate set of Organization documents.

42.3.1.1.1. Review Organization documents.

42.3.1.1.2. Review scope and business problem related documentation.

42.3.1.1.3. Identify the Organizations that are defined and captured.

42.3.1.1.4. Identify the Organizations related work products.

42.3.1.2. For each Organization related work product assessment:

42.3.1.2.1. Identify the relevant component.

42.3.1.2.2. Identify the description for each interrelated Organization component.

42.3.2. Perform the assessment.

42.3.2.1. Assess each Organization.

42.3.2.1.1. Assess the accuracy, quality and completeness of each Organization with respect to the business requirements.

42.3.2.1.2. Assess whether Organizations are able to be inferred from business requirements, and if not whether business requirements or Organizations need to be enhanced.

42.3.2.2. Assess whether the Organizations are properly identified and are appropriately engineered to address a Organization project.

42.3.2.2.1. Assess whether all the Organizations have been delivered in terms of components, instances, and stored metadata work products.

42.3.2.2.2. Assess whether all the Organizations have been properly detailed as to content, description, methodology, evaluation, presentation, and delivery work steps.

42.3.2.2.3. Assess whether all the Organizations have been properly allocated sufficient unit effort estimates.

42.3.2.2.4. Assess whether all the Organizations have been properly allocated sufficient quantity of units that have to be developed.

42.3.2.2.5. Assess whether all the Organizations have been properly allocated work environment factors to determine an accurate estimate of required resources.

42.3.2.2.6. Assess whether all the Organizations have been properly allocated work accomplishment and recording functions necessary to support earned value reporting.

42.3.2.2.7. Assess whether all the Organizations have been properly allocated metadata recording effort to ensure that all interrelationships are properly recorded into the Metabase System database.
42.3.2.3. Assign the risk level associated with each Organization not properly constructed.
42.3.3. Determine the findings and create draft assessment report.
42.3.4. Present the findings and revise draft assessment report.
42.3.5. Create final assessment report and deliver to the auditing organization.

42.4. Assess Organization Structure.
42.4.1. Identify artifacts that bear on the assessment.
42.4.1.1. Identify the appropriate set of Organization Structure documents.
42.4.1.1.1. Review Organization Structure documents.
42.4.1.1.2. Review scope and business problem related documentation.
42.4.1.1.3. Identify the Organization Structure that are defined and captured.
42.4.1.1.4. Identify the Organization Structure related work products.
42.4.1.2. For each Organization Structure related work product assessment:
42.4.1.2.1. Identify the relevant component.
42.4.1.2.2. Identify the description for each interrelated Organization Structure component.
42.4.2. Perform the assessment.
42.4.2.1. Assess each Organization Structure.
42.4.2.1.1. Assess the accuracy, quality and completeness of each Organization Structure with respect to the business requirements.
42.4.2.1.2. Assess whether Organization Structures are able to be inferred from business requirements, and if not whether business requirements or Organization Structures need to be enhanced.
42.4.2.1.3. Assess whether each Organization Structure hierarchy/network is properly specified, and that all Organization Structure names and descriptions are well defined, non-overlapping, and have been formally approved.
42.4.2.2. Assess whether the Organization Structures are properly identified and are appropriately engineered to address a Organization Structure project.
42.4.2.2.1. Assess whether all the Organization Structures have been delivered in terms of components, instances, and stored metadata work products.
42.4.2.2.2. Assess whether all the Organization Structures have been properly detailed as to content, description, methodology, evaluation, presentation, and delivery work steps.
42.4.2.2.3. Assess whether all the Organization Structures have been properly allocated sufficient unit effort estimates.
42.4.2.2.4. Assess whether all the Organization Structures have been properly allocated sufficient quantity of units that have to be developed.

42.4.2.2.5. Assess whether all the Organization Structures have been properly allocated work environment factors to determine an accurate estimate of required resources.
42.4.2.2.6. Assess whether all the Organization Structures have been properly allocated work accomplishment and recording functions necessary to support earned value reporting.
42.4.2.2.7. Assess whether all the Organization Structures have been properly allocated metadata recording effort to ensure that all interrelationships are properly recorded into the Metabase System database.
42.4.2.3. Assign the risk level associated with each Organization Structure not properly constructed.
42.4.3. Determine the findings and create draft assessment report.
42.4.4. Present the findings and revise draft assessment report.
42.4.5. Create final assessment report and deliver to the auditing organization.

42.5. Assess Function.
42.5.1. Identify artifacts that bear on the assessment.
42.5.1.1. Identify the appropriate set of Function documents.
42.5.1.1.1. Review Function documents.
42.5.1.1.2. Review scope and business problem related documentation.
42.5.1.1.3. Identify the Functions that are defined and captured.
42.5.1.1.4. Identify the Functions related work products.
42.5.1.2. For each Functions related work product assessment:
42.5.1.2.1. Identify the relevant component.
42.5.1.2.2. Identify the description for each interrelated Function component.
42.5.2. Perform the assessment.
42.5.2.1. Assess each Function.
42.5.2.1.1. Assess the accuracy, quality and completeness of each Function with respect to the business requirements.
42.5.2.1.2. Assess whether Functions are able to be inferred from business requirements, and if not whether business requirements or Functions need to be enhanced.
42.5.2.2. Assess whether the Functions are properly identified and are appropriately engineered to address a Function project.
42.5.2.2.1. Assess whether all the Functions have been delivered in terms of components, instances, and stored metadata work products.
42.5.2.2.2. Assess whether all the Functions have been properly detailed as to content, description, methodology, evaluation, presentation, and delivery work steps.
42.5.2.2.3. Assess whether all the Functions have been properly allocated sufficient unit effort estimates.
42.5.2.2.4. Assess whether all the Functions have been properly allocated sufficient

quantity of units that have to be developed.

42.5.2.2.5. Assess whether all the Functions have been properly allocated work environment factors to determine an accurate estimate of required resources.

42.5.2.2.6. Assess whether all the Functions have been properly allocated work accomplishment and recording functions necessary to support earned value reporting.

42.5.2.2.7. Assess whether all the Functions have been properly allocated metadata recording effort to ensure that all interrelationships are properly recorded into the Metabase System database.

42.5.2.6. Assign the risk level associated with each Function not properly constructed.

42.5.3. Determine the findings and create draft assessment report.

42.5.4. Present the findings and revise draft assessment report.

42.5.5. Create final assessment report and deliver to the auditing Function.

42.6. Assess Function Structure.

42.6.1. Identify artifacts that bear on the assessment.

42.6.1.1. Identify the appropriate set of Function Structure documents.

42.6.1.1.1. Review Function Structure documents.

42.6.1.1.2. Review scope and business problem related documentation.

42.6.1.1.3. Identify the Function Structures that are defined and captured.

42.6.1.1.4. Identify the Function Structure related work products.

42.6.1.2. For each Function Structure related work product assessment:

42.6.1.2.1. Identify the relevant component.

42.6.1.2.2. Identify the description for each interrelated Function component.

42.6.2. Perform the assessment.

42.6.2.1. Assess each Function Structure.

42.6.2.1.1. Assess the accuracy, quality and completeness of each Function Structure with respect to the business requirements.

42.6.2.1.2. Assess whether Function Structures are able to be inferred from business requirements, and if not whether business requirements or Function Structures need to be enhanced.

42.6.2.1.3. Assess whether each Function Structure hierarchy/network is properly specified, and that all Function Structure names and descriptions are well defined, non-overlapping, and have been formally approved.

42.6.2.2. Assess whether the Function Structures are properly identified and are appropriately engineered to address a Function Structure project.

42.6.2.2.1. Assess whether all the Function Structures have been delivered in terms of components, instances, and stored metadata work products.

42.6.2.2.2. Assess whether all the Function Structures have been properly detailed as to content, description, methodology, evaluation, presentation, and

delivery work steps.

42.6.2.2.3. Assess whether all the Function Structures have been properly allocated sufficient unit effort estimates.

42.6.2.2.4. Assess whether all the Function Structures have been properly allocated sufficient quantity of units that have to be developed.

42.6.2.2.5. Assess whether all the Function Structures have been properly allocated work environment factors to determine an accurate estimate of required resources.

42.6.2.2.6. Assess whether all the Function Structures have been properly allocated work accomplishment and recording functions necessary to support earned value reporting.

42.6.2.2.7. Assess whether all the Function Structures have been properly allocated metadata recording effort to ensure that all interrelationships are properly recorded into the Metabase System database.

42.6.2.3. Assign the risk level associated with each Function Structure not properly constructed.

42.6.3. Determine the findings and create draft assessment report.

42.6.4. Present the findings and revise draft assessment report.

42.6.5. Create final assessment report and deliver to the auditing organization.

42.7. Assess Mission-Organization.

42.7.1. Identify artifacts that bear on the assessment.

42.7.1.1. Identify the appropriate set of Mission-Organization documents.

42.7.1.1.1. Review Mission-Organization documents.

42.7.1.1.2. Review scope and business problem related documentation.

42.7.1.1.3. Identify the Mission-Organizations that are defined and captured.

42.7.1.1.4. Identify the Mission-Organizations related work products.

42.7.1.2. For each Mission-Organizations related work product assessment:

42.7.1.2.1. Identify the relevant component.

42.7.1.2.2. Identify the description for each interrelated Mission-Organization component.

42.7.2. Perform the assessment.

42.7.2.1. Assess each Mission-Organization.

42.7.2.1.1. Assess the accuracy, quality and completeness of each Mission-Organization with respect to the business requirements.

42.7.2.1.2. Assess whether Mission-Organization are able to be inferred from business requirements, and if not whether business requirements or Mission-Organization need to be enhanced.

42.7.2.2. Assess whether the Mission-Organizations are properly identified and are appropriately engineered to address a Mission-Organization project.

42.7.2.2.1. Assess whether all the Mission-Organizations have been delivered in terms of components, instances, and stored metadata work products.

42.7.2.2.2. Assess whether all the Mission-Organizations have been properly detailed as to content, description, methodology, evaluation, presentation, and delivery work steps.

42.7.2.2.3. Assess whether all the Mission-Organizations have been properly allocated sufficient unit effort estimates.

42.7.2.2.4. Assess whether all the Mission-Organizations have been properly allocated sufficient quantity of units that have to be developed.

42.7.2.2.5. Assess whether all the Mission-Organizations have been properly allocated work environment factors to determine an accurate estimate of required resources.

42.7.2.2.6. Assess whether all the Mission-Organizations have been properly allocated work accomplishment and recording functions necessary to support earned value reporting.

42.7.2.2.7. Assess whether all the Mission-Organizations have been properly allocated metadata recording effort to ensure that all interrelationships are properly recorded into the Metabase System database.

42.7.2.3. Assign the risk level associated with each Mission-Organization not properly constructed.

42.7.3. Determine the findings and create draft assessment report.

42.7.4. Present the findings and revise draft assessment report.

42.7.5. Create final assessment report and deliver to the auditing organization.

42.8. Assess Mission-Organization-Function.

42.8.1. Identify artifacts that bear on the assessment.

42.8.1.1. Identify the appropriate set of Mission-Organization-Function documents.

42.8.1.1.1. Review Mission-Organization-Function documents.

42.8.1.1.2. Review scope and business problem related documentation.

42.8.1.1.3. Identify the Mission-Organization-Functions that are defined and captured.

42.8.1.1.4. Identify the Mission-Organization-Functions related work products.

42.8.1.2. For each Mission-Organization-Functions related work product assessment:

42.8.1.2.1. Identify the relevant component.

42.8.1.2.2. Identify the description for each interrelated Mission-Organization-Function component.

42.8.2. Perform the assessment.

42.8.2.1. Assess each Mission-Organization-Function.

42.8.2.1.1. Assess the accuracy, quality and completeness of each Mission-Organization-Function with respect to the business requirements.

42.8.2.1.2. Assess whether Mission-Organization-Functions are able to be inferred from business requirements, and if not whether business requirements or Mission-Organization-Functions need to be enhanced.

42.8.2.2. Assess whether the Mission-Organization-Functions are properly identified and are appropriately engineered to address a Mission-Organization-Function project.

42.8.2.2.1. Assess whether all the Mission-Organization-Functions have been delivered in terms of components, instances, and stored metadata work products.

42.8.2.2.2. Assess whether all the Mission-Organization-Functions have been properly detailed as to content, description, methodology, evaluation, presentation, and delivery work steps.

42.8.2.2.3. Assess whether all the Mission-Organization-Functions have been properly allocated sufficient unit effort estimates.

42.8.2.2.4. Assess whether all the Mission-Organization-Functions have been properly allocated sufficient quantity of units that have to be developed.

42.8.2.2.5. Assess whether all the Mission-Organization-Functions have been properly allocated work environment factors to determine an accurate estimate of required resources.

42.8.2.2.6. Assess whether all the Mission-Organization-Functions have been properly allocated work accomplishment and recording functions necessary to support earned value reporting.

42.8.2.2.7. Assess whether all the Mission-Organization-Functions have been properly allocated metadata recording effort to ensure that all interrelationships are properly recorded into the Metabase System database.

42.8.2.3. Assign the risk level associated with each Mission-Organization-Function not properly constructed.

42.8.3. Determine the findings and create draft assessment report.

42.8.4. Present the findings and revise draft assessment report.

42.8.5. Create final assessment report and deliver to the auditing organization.

42.9. Assess Mission-Organization-Function Business Event.

42.9.1. Identify artifacts that bear on the assessment.

42.9.1.1. Identify the appropriate set of Mission-Organization-Function Business Event documents.

42.9.1.1.1. Review Mission-Organization-Function Business Event documents.

42.9.1.1.2. Review scope and business problem related documentation.

42.9.1.1.3. Identify the Mission-Organization-Function Business Event that are defined and captured.

42.9.1.1.4. Identify the Mission-Organization-Function Business Event related work products.

42.9.1.2. For each Mission-Organization-Function Business Event related work product assessment:

42.9.1.2.1. Identify the relevant component.

42.9.1.2.2. Identify the description for each interrelated Mission-Organization-Function Business Event component.

42.9.2. Perform the assessment.

42.9.2.1. Assess each Mission-Organization-Function Business Event.

42.9.2.1.1. Assess the accuracy, quality and completeness of each Mission-Organization-Function Business Event with respect to the business requirements.

42.9.2.1.2. Assess whether Mission-Organization-Function Business Events are able to be inferred from business requirements, and if not whether business requirements or Mission-Organization-Function Business Events need to be enhanced.

42.9.2.1.3. Assess whether each Mission-Organization-Function Business Event pair properly associates a one or more Mission-Organization-Function with one or more Business Events.

42.9.2.1.4. Assess whether each Mission-Organization-Function Business Event pair is properly named and described.

42.9.2.2. Assess whether the Mission-Organization-Function Business Events are properly identified and are appropriately engineered to address a Report Business Information System project.

42.9.2.2.1. Assess whether all the Mission-Organization-Function Business Events have been delivered in terms of components, instances, and stored metadata work products.

42.9.2.2.2. Assess whether all the Mission-Organization-Function Business Events have been properly detailed as to content, description, methodology, evaluation, presentation, and delivery work steps.

42.9.2.2.3. Assess whether all the Mission-Organization-Function Business Evens have been properly allocated sufficient unit effort estimates.

42.9.2.2.4. Assess whether all the Mission-Organization-Function Business Events have been properly allocated sufficient quantity of units that have to be developed.

42.9.2.2.5. Assess whether all the Mission-Organization-Function Business Events have been properly allocated work environment factors to determine an accurate estimate of required resources.

42.9.2.2.6. Assess whether all the Mission-Organization-Function Business Events have been properly allocated work accomplishment and recording functions necessary to support earned value reporting.

42.9.2.2.7. Assess whether all the Mission-Organization-Function Business Events have been properly allocated metadata recording effort to ensure that all interrelationships are properly recorded into the Metabase System database.

42.9.2.5. Assign the risk level associated with each Mission-Organization-Function Business Event not properly constructed.

42.9.3. Determine the findings and create draft assessment report.
42.9.4. Present the findings and revise draft assessment report.
42.9.5. Create final assessment report and deliver to the auditing organization.

42.10. Assess Mission-Organization-Function Document Section.
42.10.1. Identify artifacts that bear on the assessment.
42.10.1.1. Identify the appropriate set of Mission-Organization-Function Document Section documents.
42.10.1.1.1. Review Mission-Organization-Function Document Section documents.
42.10.1.1.2. Review scope and business problem related documentation.
42.10.1.1.3. Identify the Mission-Organization-Function Document Section that are defined and captured.
42.10.1.1.4. Identify the Mission-Organization-Function Document Section related work products.
42.10.1.2. For each Mission-Organization-Function Document Section related work product assessment:
42.10.1.2.1. Identify the relevant component.
42.10.1.2.2. Identify the description for each interrelated Mission-Organization-Function Document Section component.
42.10.2. Perform the assessment.
42.10.2.1. Assess whether each Mission-Organization-Function Document Section is addressed properly reflected in the enterprise.
42.10.2.2. Assess whether each Mission-Organization-Function Document Section is addressed by one or more business Requirement Structures as may be appropriate.
42.10.2.2.1. Assess whether each Mission-Organization-Function Document Section can be allocated to one or more business Requirement Structures.
42.10.2.2.2. Assess whether business Requirement Structures are able to be inferred from Mission-Organization-Function Document Section, and if not whether business Requirement Structures or Mission-Organization-Function Document Section need to be enhanced.
42.10.2.2.3. Assess whether each Mission-Organization-Function Document Section pair properly associates a one or more Mission-Organization-Functions with one or more Document Sections.
42.10.2.2.4. Assess whether each Mission-Organization-Function Document Section pair is properly named and described.
42.10.2.3. Assess whether the Mission-Organization-Function Document Sections are properly identified and are appropriately engineered to address a Mission-Organization-Function Document Section project.
42.10.2.3.1. Assess whether all the Mission-Organization-Function Document Sections have been delivered in terms of components, instances, and stored metadata work products.

42.10.2.3.2. Assess whether all the Mission-Organization-Function Document Sections have been properly detailed as to content, description, methodology, evaluation, presentation, and delivery work steps.

42.10.2.3.3. Assess whether all the Mission-Organization-Function Document Sections have been properly allocated sufficient unit effort estimates.

42.10.2.3.4. Assess whether all the Mission-Organization-Function Document Sections have been properly allocated sufficient quantity of units that have to be developed.

42.10.2.3.5. Assess whether all the Mission-Organization-Function Document Sections have been properly allocated work environment factors to determine an accurate estimate of required resources.

42.10.2.3.6. Assess whether all the Mission-Organization-Function Document Sections have been properly allocated work accomplishment and recording functions necessary to support earned value reporting.

42.10.2.3.7. Assess whether all the Mission-Organization-Function Document Sections have been properly allocated metadata recording effort to ensure that all interrelationships are properly recorded into the Metabase System database.

42.10.2.4. Assign the risk level associated with each Mission-Organization-Function Document Section not properly constructed.

42.10.3. Determine the findings and create draft assessment report.

42.10.4. Present the findings and revise draft assessment report.

42.10.5. Create final assessment report and deliver to the auditing organization.

42.11. Assess Mission-Organization-Function Form Section.

42.11.1. Identify artifacts that bear on the assessment.

42.11.1.1. Identify the appropriate set of Mission-Organization-Function Form Section documents.

42.11.1.1.1. Review Mission-Organization-Function Form Section documents.

42.11.1.1.2. Review scope and business problem related documentation.

42.11.1.1.3. Identify the Mission-Organization-Function Form Section that are defined and captured.

42.11.1.1.4. Identify the Mission-Organization-Function Form Section related work products.

42.11.1.2. For each Mission-Organization-Function Form Section related work product assessment:

42.11.1.2.1. Identify the relevant component.

42.11.1.2.2. Identify the description for each interrelated Mission-Organization-Function Form Section component.

42.11.2. Perform the assessment.

42.11.2.1. Assess whether each Mission-Organization-Function Form Section is addressed properly reflected in the enterprise.

42.11.2.2. Assess whether each Mission-Organization-Function Form Section is addressed by one or more business Requirement Structures as may be appropriate.

42.11.2.2.1. Assess whether each Mission-Organization-Function Form Section can be allocated to one or more business Requirement Structures.

42.11.2.2.2. Assess whether business Requirement Structures are able to be inferred from Mission-Organization-Function Form Section, and if not, whether business Requirement Structures or Mission-Organization-Function Form Sections need to be enhanced.

42.11.2.2.3. Assess whether each Mission-Organization-Function Form Section pair properly associates a one or more Mission-Organization-Functions with one or more Form Sections.

42.11.2.2.4. Assess whether each Mission-Organization-Function Form Section pair is properly named and described.

42.11.2.3. Assess whether the Mission-Organization-Function Form Sections are properly identified and are appropriately engineered to address a Mission-Organization-Function Form Section project.

42.11.2.3.1. Assess whether all the Mission-Organization-Function Form Sections have been delivered in terms of components, instances, and stored metadata work products.

42.11.2.3.2. Assess whether all the Mission-Organization-Function Form Sections have been properly detailed as to content, description, methodology, evaluation, presentation, and delivery work steps.

42.11.2.3.3. Assess whether all the Mission-Organization-Function Form Sections have been properly allocated sufficient unit effort estimates.

42.11.2.3.4. Assess whether all the Mission-Organization-Function Form Sections have been properly allocated sufficient quantity of units that have to be developed.

42.11.2.3.5. Assess whether all the Mission-Organization-Function Form Sections have been properly allocated work environment factors to determine an accurate estimate of required resources.

42.11.2.3.6. Assess whether all the Mission-Organization-Function Form Sections have been properly allocated work accomplishment and recording functions necessary to support earned value reporting.

42.11.2.3.7. Assess whether all the Mission-Organization-Function Form Sections have been properly allocated metadata recording effort to ensure that all interrelationships are properly recorded into the Metabase System database.

42.11.2.4. Assign the risk level associated with each Mission-Organization-Function Form Section not properly constructed.

42.11.3. Determine the findings and create draft assessment report.

42.11.4. Present the findings and revise draft assessment report.

42.11.5. Create final assessment report and deliver to the auditing organization.

42.12. Assess Mission-Organization-Function Information Need.
42.12.1. Identify artifacts that bear on the assessment.
42.12.1.1. Identify the appropriate set of Mission-Organization-Function Information Need documents.
42.12.1.1.1. Review Mission-Organization-Function Information Need documents.
42.12.1.1.2. Review scope and business problem related documentation.
42.12.1.1.3. Identify the Mission-Organization-Function Information Need that are defined and captured.
42.12.1.1.4. Identify the Mission-Organization-Function Information Need related work products.
42.12.1.2. For each Mission-Organization-Function Information Need related work product assessment:
42.12.1.2.1. Identify the relevant component.
42.12.1.2.2. Identify the description for each interrelated Mission-Organization-Function Information Need component.
42.12.2. Perform the assessment.
42.12.2.1. Assess whether each Mission-Organization-Function Information Need is addressed properly reflected in the enterprise.
42.12.2.2. Assess whether each Mission-Organization-Function Information Need is addressed by one or more business Requirement Structures as may be appropriate.
42.12.2.2.1. Assess whether each Mission-Organization-Function Information Need can be allocated to one or more business Requirement Structures.
42.12.2.2.2. Assess whether business Requirement Structures are able to be inferred from Mission-Organization-Function Information Need, and if not whether business Requirement Structures or Mission-Organization-Function Information Needs need to be enhanced.
42.12.2.2.3. Assess whether each Mission-Organization-Function Information Need pair properly associates a one or more Reports Business Information Systems.
42.12.2.2.4. Assess whether each Mission-Organization-Function Information Need pair is properly named and described.
42.12.2.3. Assess whether the Mission-Organization-Function Information Needs are properly identified and are appropriately engineered to address a Report Business Information System project.
42.12.2.3.1. Assess whether all the Mission-Organization-Function Information Need have been delivered in terms of components, instances, and stored metadata work products.
42.12.2.3.2. Assess whether all the Mission-Organization-Function Information Need have been properly detailed as to content, description, methodology,

evaluation, presentation, and delivery work steps.

42.12.2.3.3. Assess whether all the Mission-Organization-Function Information Need have been properly allocated sufficient unit effort estimates.

42.12.2.3.4. Assess whether all the Mission-Organization-Function Information Need have been properly allocated sufficient quantity of units that have to be developed.

42.12.2.3.5. Assess whether all the Mission-Organization-Function Information Need have been properly allocated work environment factors to determine an accurate estimate of required resources.

42.12.2.3.6. Assess whether all the Mission-Organization-Function Information Need have been properly allocated work accomplishment and recording functions necessary to support earned value reporting.

42.12.2.3.7. Assess whether all the Mission-Organization-Function Information Need have been properly allocated metadata recording effort to ensure that all interrelationships are properly recorded into the Metabase System database.

42.12.2.4. Assign the risk level associated with each Mission-Organization-Function Information Need not properly constructed.

42.12.3. Determine the findings and create draft assessment report.

42.12.4. Present the findings and revise draft assessment report.

42.12.5. Create final assessment report and deliver to the auditing organization.

42.13. Assess Mission-Organization-Function Position.

42.13.1. Identify artifacts that bear on the assessment.

42.13.1.1. Identify the appropriate set of Mission-Organization-Function Position documents.

42.13.1.1.1. Review Mission-Organization-Function Position documents.

42.13.1.1.2. Review scope and business problem related documentation.

42.13.1.1.3. Identify the Mission-Organization-Function Position that are defined and captured.

42.13.1.1.4. Identify the Mission-Organization-Function Position related work products.

42.13.1.2. For each Mission-Organization-Function Position related work product assessment:

42.13.1.2.1. Identify the relevant component.

42.13.1.2.2. Identify the description for each interrelated Mission-Organization-Function Position component.

42.13.2. Perform the assessment.

42.13.2.1. Assess whether each Mission-Organization-Function Position is addressed properly reflected in the enterprise.

42.13.2.2. Assess whether each Mission-Organization-Function Position is addressed by one or more business Requirement Structures as may be appropriate.

42.13.2.2.1. Assess whether each Mission-Organization-Function Position can be allocated to one or more business Requirement Structures.

42.13.2.2.2. Assess whether business Requirement Structures are able to be inferred from Mission-Organization-Function Position, and if not, determine whether business Requirement Structures or Mission-Organization-Function Position need to be enhanced.

42.13.2.2.3. Assess whether each Mission-Organization-Function Position pair properly associates a one or more Reports with one or more Business Information Systems.

42.13.2.2.4. Assess whether each Mission-Organization-Function Position pair is properly named and described.

42.13.2.3. Assess whether the Mission-Organization-Function Positions are properly identified and are appropriately engineered to address a Report Business Information System project.

42.13.2.3.1. Assess whether all the Mission-Organization-Function Positions have been delivered in terms of components, instances, and stored metadata work products.

42.13.2.3.2. Assess whether all the Mission-Organization-Function Positions have been properly detailed as to content, description, methodology, evaluation, presentation, and delivery work steps.

42.13.2.3.3. Assess whether all the Mission-Organization-Function Positions have been properly allocated sufficient unit effort estimates.

42.13.2.3.4. Assess whether all the Mission-Organization-Function Positions have been properly allocated sufficient quantity of units that have to be developed.

42.13.2.3.5. Assess whether all the Mission-Organization-Function Positions have been properly allocated work environment factors to determine an accurate estimate of required resources.

42.13.2.3.6. Assess whether all the Mission-Organization-Function Positions have been properly allocated work accomplishment and recording functions necessary to support earned value reporting.

42.13.2.3.7. Assess whether all the Mission-Organization-Function Positions have been properly allocated metadata recording effort to ensure that all interrelationships are properly recorded into the Metabase System database.

42.13.2.4. Assign the risk level associated with each Mission-Organization-Function Position not properly constructed.

42.13.3. Determine the findings and create draft assessment report.

42.13.4. Present the findings and revise draft assessment report.

42.13.5. Create final assessment report and deliver to the auditing organization.

42.14. Assess Mission-Organization-Function Project Deliverable.
42.14.1. Identify artifacts that bear on the assessment.
42.14.1.1. Identify the appropriate set of Mission-Organization-Function Project Deliverable documents.
42.14.1.1.1. Review Mission-Organization-Function Project Deliverable documents.
42.14.1.1.2. Review scope and business problem related documentation.
42.14.1.1.3. Identify the Mission-Organization-Function Project Deliverable that are defined and captured.
42.14.1.1.4. Identify the Mission-Organization-Function Project Deliverable related work products.
42.14.1.2. For each Mission-Organization-Function Project Deliverable related work product assessment:
42.14.1.2.1. Identify the relevant component.
42.14.1.2.2. Identify the description for each interrelated Mission-Organization-Function Project Deliverable component.
42.14.2. Perform the assessment.
42.14.2.1. Assess whether each Mission-Organization-Function Project Deliverable is addressed properly reflected in the enterprise.
42.14.2.2. Assess whether each Mission-Organization-Function Project Deliverable is addressed by one or more business Requirement Structures as may be appropriate.
42.14.2.2.1. Assess whether each Mission-Organization-Function Project Deliverable can be allocated to one or more business Requirement Structures.
42.14.2.2.2. Assess whether business Requirement Structures are able to be inferred from Mission-Organization-Function Project Deliverable, and if not whether business Requirement Structures or Mission-Organization-Function Project Deliverable need to be enhanced.
42.14.2.2.3. Assess whether each Mission-Organization-Function Project Deliverable pair properly associates a one or more Reports with one or more Business Information Systems.
42.14.2.2.4. Assess whether each Mission-Organization-Function Project Deliverable pair is properly named and described.
42.14.2.3. Assess whether the Mission-Organization-Function Project Deliverables are properly identified and are appropriately engineered to address a Report Business Information System project.
42.14.2.3.1. Assess whether all the Mission-Organization-Function Project Deliverables have been delivered in terms of components, instances, and stored metadata work products.
42.14.2.3.2. Assess whether all the Mission-Organization-Function Project Deliverables have been properly detailed as to content, description, methodology, evaluation, presentation, and delivery work steps.
42.14.2.3.3. Assess whether all the Mission-Organization-Function Project

Deliverables have been properly allocated sufficient unit effort estimates.

42.14.2.3.4. Assess whether all the Mission-Organization-Function Project Deliverables have been properly allocated sufficient quantity of units that have to be developed.

42.14.2.3.5. Assess whether all the Mission-Organization-Function Project Deliverables have been properly allocated work environment factors to determine an accurate estimate of required resources.

42.14.2.3.6. Assess whether all the Mission-Organization-Function Project Deliverables have been properly allocated work accomplishment and recording functions necessary to support earned value reporting.

42.14.2.3.7. Assess whether all the Mission-Organization-Function Project Deliverables have been properly allocated metadata recording effort to ensure that all interrelationships are properly recorded into the Metabase System database.

42.14.2.4. Assign the risk level associated with each Mission-Organization-Function Project Deliverable not properly constructed.

42.14.3. Determine the findings and create draft assessment report.

42.14.4. Present the findings and revise draft assessment report.

42.14.5. Create final assessment report and deliver to the auditing organization.

42.15. Assess Mission-Organization-Function Report Section.

42.15.1. Identify artifacts that bear on the assessment.

42.15.1.1. Identify the appropriate set of Mission-Organization-Function Report Section documents.

42.15.1.1.1. Review Mission-Organization-Function Report Section documents.

42.15.1.1.2. Review scope and business problem related documentation.

42.15.1.1.3. Identify the Mission-Organization-Function Report Section that are defined and captured.

42.15.1.1.4. Identify the Mission-Organization-Function Report Section related work products.

42.15.1.2. For each Mission-Organization-Function Report Section related work product assessment:

42.15.1.2.1. Identify the relevant component.

42.15.1.2.2. Identify the description for each interrelated Mission-Organization-Function Report Section component.

42.15.2. Perform the assessment.

42.15.2.1. Assess whether each Mission-Organization-Function Report Section is addressed properly reflected in the enterprise.

42.15.2.2. Assess whether each Mission-Organization-Function Report Section is addressed by one or more business Requirement Structures as may be appropriate.

42.15.2.2.1. Assess whether each Mission-Organization-Function Report Section can be allocated to one or more business Requirement Structures.

42.15.2.2.2. Assess whether Requirement Structures are able to be inferred from Mission-Organization-Function Report Section, and if not, then whether business Requirement Structures or Mission-Organization-Function Report Section need to be enhanced.

42.15.2.2.3. Assess whether each Mission-Organization-Function Report Section pair properly associates a one or more Reports with one or more Business Information Systems.

42.15.2.2.4. Assess whether each Mission-Organization-Function Report Section pair is properly named and described.

42.15.2.3. Assess whether the Mission-Organization-Function Report Sections are properly identified and are appropriately engineered to address a Report Business Information System project.

42.15.2.3.1. Assess whether all the Mission-Organization-Function Report Sections have been delivered in terms of components, instances, and stored metadata work products.

42.15.2.3.2. Assess whether all the Mission-Organization-Function Report Sections have been properly detailed as to content, description, methodology, evaluation, presentation, and delivery work steps.

42.15.2.3.3. Assess whether all the Mission-Organization-Function Report Sections have been properly allocated sufficient unit effort estimates.

42.15.2.3.4. Assess whether all the Mission-Organization-Function Report Sections have been properly allocated sufficient quantity of units that have to be developed.

42.15.2.3.5. Assess whether all the Mission-Organization-Function Report Sections have been properly allocated work environment factors to determine an accurate estimate of required resources.

42.15.2.3.6. Assess whether all the Mission-Organization-Function Report Sections have been properly allocated work accomplishment and recording functions necessary to support earned value reporting.

42.15.2.3.7. Assess whether all the Mission-Organization-Function Report Sections have been properly allocated metadata recording effort to ensure that all interrelationships are properly recorded into the Metabase System database.

42.15.2.4. Assign the risk level associated with each Mission-Organization-Function Report Section not properly constructed.

42.15.3. Determine the findings and create draft assessment report.

42.15.4. Present the findings and revise draft assessment report.

42.15.5. Create final assessment report and deliver to the auditing organization.

42.16. Assess Mission-Organization-Function Requirement.

42.16.1. Identify artifacts that bear on the assessment.

42.16.1.1. Identify the appropriate set of Mission-Organization-Function Requirement documents.
42.16.1.1.1. Review Mission-Organization-Function Requirement documents.
42.16.1.1.2. Review scope and business problem related documentation.
42.16.1.1.3. Identify the Mission-Organization-Function Requirements that are defined and captured.
42.16.1.1.4. Identify the Mission-Organization-Function Requirements related work products.
42.16.1.2. For each Mission-Organization-Function Requirements related work product assessment:
42.16.1.2.1. Identify the relevant component.
42.16.1.2.2. Identify the description for each interrelated Mission-Organization-Function Requirements component.
42.16.2. Perform the assessment.
42.16.2.1. Assess each Mission-Organization-Function Requirement.
42.16.2.1.1. Assess the accuracy, quality and completeness of each Mission-Organization-Function Requirement with respect to the business requirements.
42.16.2.1.2. Assess whether Mission-Organization-Function Requirement s are able to be inferred from business requirements, and if not whether business requirements or Mission-Organization-Function Requirements need to be enhanced.
42.16.2.1.3. Assess whether each Mission-Organization-Function Requirement pair properly associates one or more Mission-Organization-Functions with one or more Requirements.
42.16.2.1.4. Assess whether each Mission-Organization-Function Requirement pair is properly named and described.
42.16.2.2. Assess whether the Mission-Organization-Function Requirements are properly identified and are appropriately engineered to address a Report Business Information System project.
42.16.2.2.1. Assess whether all the Mission-Organization-Function Requirements have been delivered in terms of components, instances, and stored metadata work products.
42.16.2.2.2. Assess whether all the Mission-Organization-Function Requirements have been properly detailed as to content, description, methodology, evaluation, presentation, and delivery work steps.
42.16.2.2.3. Assess whether all the Mission-Organization-Function Requirements have been properly allocated sufficient unit effort estimates.
42.16.2.2.4. Assess whether all the Mission-Organization-Function Requirements have been properly allocated sufficient quantity of units that have to be developed.
42.16.2.2.5. Assess whether all the Mission-Organization-Function Requirements have

been properly allocated work environment factors to determine an accurate estimate of required resources.

42.16.2.2.6. Assess whether all the Mission-Organization-Function Requirements have been properly allocated work accomplishment and recording functions necessary to support earned value reporting.

42.16.2.2.7. Assess whether all the Mission-Organization-Function Requirements have been properly allocated metadata recording effort to ensure that all interrelationships are properly recorded into the Metabase System database.

42.16.2.4. Assign the risk level associated with each Mission-Organization-Function Requirement not properly constructed.

42.16.3. Determine the findings and create draft assessment report.

42.16.4. Present the findings and revise draft assessment report.

42.16.5. Create final assessment report and deliver to the auditing organization.

42.17. Assess Mission-Organization-Function Use Case Event.

42.17.1. Identify artifacts that bear on the assessment.

42.17.1.1. Identify the appropriate set of Mission-Organization-Function Use Case Event documents.

42.17.1.1.1. Review Mission-Organization-Function Use Case Event documents.

42.17.1.1.2. Review scope and business problem related documentation.

42.17.1.1.3. Identify the Mission-Organization-Function Use Case Event that are defined and captured.

42.17.1.1.4. Identify the Mission-Organization-Function Use Case Event related work products.

42.17.1.2. For each Mission-Organization-Function Use Case Event related work product assessment:

42.17.1.2.1. Identify the relevant component.

42.17.1.2.2. Identify the description for each interrelated Mission-Organization-Function Use Case Event component.

42.17.2. Perform the assessment.

42.17.2.1. Assess each Mission-Organization-Function Use Case Event.

42.17.2.1.1. Assess the accuracy, quality and completeness of each Mission-Organization-Function Use Case Event with respect to the business requirements.

42.17.2.1.2. Assess whether Mission-Organization-Function Use Case Events are able to be inferred from business requirements, and if not whether business requirements or Mission-Organization-Function Use Case Events need to be enhanced.

42.17.2.1.3. Assess whether each Mission-Organization-Function Use Case Events pair properly associates one or more Mission-Organization-Functions with one or more Use Case Events.

42.17.2.1.4. Assess whether each Mission-Organization-Function Use Case Events pair is properly named and described.

42.17.2.3. Assess whether the Mission-Organization-Function Use Case Events are properly identified and are appropriately engineered to address a Report Business Information System project.

42.17.2.3.1. Assess whether all the Mission-Organization-Function Use Case Events have been delivered in terms of components, instances, and stored metadata work products.

42.17.2.3.2. Assess whether all the Mission-Organization-Function Use Case Events have been properly detailed as to content, description, methodology, evaluation, presentation, and delivery work steps.

42.17.2.3.3. Assess whether all the Mission-Organization-Function Use Case Events have been properly allocated sufficient unit effort estimates.

42.17.2.3.4. Assess whether all the Mission-Organization-Function Use Case Events have been properly allocated sufficient quantity of units that have to be developed.

42.17.2.3.5. Assess whether all the Mission-Organization-Function Use Case Events have been properly allocated work environment factors to determine an accurate estimate of required resources.

42.17.2.3.6. Assess whether all the Mission-Organization-Function Use Case Events have been properly allocated work accomplishment and recording functions necessary to support earned value reporting.

42.17.2.3.7. Assess whether all the Mission-Organization-Function Use Case Events have been properly allocated metadata recording effort to ensure that all interrelationships are properly recorded into the Metabase System database.

42.17.2.4. Assign the risk level associated with each Mission-Organization-Function Use Case Event not properly constructed.

42.17.3. Determine the findings and create draft assessment report.

42.17.4. Present the findings and revise draft assessment report.

42.17.5. Create final assessment report and deliver to the auditing organization.

42.18. Assess Position.

42.18.1. Identify artifacts that bear on the assessment.

42.18.1.1. Identify the appropriate set of Position documents.

42.18.1.1.1. Review Position documents.

42.18.1.1.2. Review scope and business problem related documentation.

42.18.1.1.3. Identify the Positions that are defined and captured.

42.18.1.1.4. Identify the Positions related work products.

42.18.1.2. For each Positions related work product assessment:

42.18.1.2.1. Identify the relevant component.

42.18.1.2.2. Identify the description for each interrelated Position component.

42.18.2. Perform the assessment.

42.18.2.1. Assess each Position.

42.18.2.1.1. Assess the accuracy, quality and completeness of each Position with respect to the business requirements.

42.18.2.1.2. Assess whether Position are able to be inferred from business requirements, and if not whether business requirements or Position need to be enhanced.

42.18.2.2. Assess whether the Positions are properly identified and are appropriately engineered to address a Position project.

42.18.2.2.1. Assess whether all the Positions have been delivered in terms of components, instances, and stored metadata work products.

42.18.2.2.2. Assess whether all the Positions have been properly detailed as to content, description, methodology, evaluation, presentation, and delivery work steps.

42.18.2.2.3. Assess whether all the Positions have been properly allocated sufficient unit effort estimates.

42.18.2.2.4. Assess whether all the Positions have been properly allocated sufficient quantity of units that have to be developed.

42.18.2.2.5. Assess whether all the Positions have been properly allocated work environment factors to determine an accurate estimate of required resources.

42.18.2.2.6. Assess whether all the Positions have been properly allocated work accomplishment and recording functions necessary to support earned value reporting.

42.18.2.2.7. Assess whether all the Positions have been properly allocated metadata recording effort to ensure that all interrelationships are properly recorded into the Metabase System database.

42.18.2.3. Assign the risk level associated with each Position not properly constructed.

42.18.3. Determine the findings and create draft assessment report.

42.18.4. Present the findings and revise draft assessment report.

42.18.5. Create final assessment report and deliver to the auditing organization.

42.19. Assess Person.

42.19.1. Identify artifacts that bear on the assessment.

42.19.1.1. Identify the appropriate set of Persons documents.

42.19.1.1.1. Review Person documents.

42.19.1.1.2. Review scope and business problem related documentation.

42.19.1.1.3. Identify the Persons that are defined and captured.

42.19.1.1.4. Identify the Persons related work products.

42.19.1.2. For each Persons related work product assessment:

42.19.1.2.1. Identify the relevant component.

42.19.1.2.2. Identify the description for each interrelated Person component.
42.19.2. Perform the assessment.
42.19.2.1. Assess each Person.
42.19.2.1.1. Assess the accuracy, quality and completeness of each Person with respect to the business requirements.
42.19.2.1.2. Assess whether Persons are able to be inferred from business requirements, and if not whether business requirements or Persons need to be enhanced.
42.19.2.2. Assess whether the Persons are properly identified and are appropriately engineered to address a Person project.
42.19.2.2.1. Assess whether all the Persons have been delivered in terms of components, instances, and stored metadata work products.
42.19.2.2.2. Assess whether all the Persons have been properly detailed as to content, description, methodology, evaluation, presentation, and delivery work steps.
42.19.2.2.3. Assess whether all the Persons have been properly allocated sufficient unit effort estimates.
42.19.2.2.4. Assess whether all the Persons have been properly allocated sufficient quantity of units that have to be developed.
42.19.2.2.5. Assess whether all the Persons have been properly allocated work environment factors to determine an accurate estimate of required resources.
42.19.2.2.6. Assess whether all the Persons have been properly allocated work accomplishment and recording functions necessary to support earned value reporting.
42.19.2.2.7. Assess whether all the Persons have been properly allocated metadata recording effort to ensure that all interrelationships are properly recorded into the Metabase System database.
42.19.2.3. Assign the risk level associated with each Person not properly constructed.
42.19.3. Determine the findings and create draft assessment report.
42.19.4. Present the findings and revise draft assessment report.
42.19.5. Create final assessment report and deliver to the auditing organization.

42.20. Assess Database Domain.
42.20.1. Identify artifacts that bear on the assessment.
42.20.1.1. Identify the appropriate set Database Domains documents.
42.20.1.1.1. Review Database Domains documents.
42.20.1.1.2. Review scope and business problem related documentation.
42.20.1.1.3. Identify the Database Domains that are defined and captured.
42.20.1.1.4. Identify the Database Domains related work products.
42.20.1.2. For each Database Domains related work product assessment:

42.20.1.2.1. Identify the relevant component.
42.20.1.2.2. Identify the description for each interrelated Database Domain component.
42.20.2. Perform the assessment.
42.20.2.1. Assess each Database Domain.
42.20.2.1.1. Assess the accuracy, quality and completeness of each Database Domain with respect to the business requirements.
42.20.2.1.2. Assess whether Database Domains are able to be inferred from business requirements, and if not whether business requirements or Database Domains need to be enhanced.
42.20.2.1.3. Assess whether each Database Domain hierarchy is properly specified, and that all Database Domain names and descriptions are well defined, non-overlapping, and have been formally approved.
42.20.2.2. Assess whether each noun-phrase in a Database Domain leaf is properly analyzed to be a Database Object, a Property Class, or a Data Element.
42.20.2.3. Assess whether the Database Domains are properly identified and are appropriately engineered to address a Database Domain project.
42.20.2.3.1. Assess whether all the Database Domains have been delivered in terms of components, instances, and stored metadata work products.
42.20.2.3.2. Assess whether all the Database Domains have been properly detailed as to content, description, methodology, evaluation, presentation, and delivery work steps.
42.20.2.3.3. Assess whether all the Database Domains have been properly allocated sufficient unit effort estimates.
42.20.2.3.4. Assess whether all the Database Domains have been properly allocated sufficient quantity of units that have to be developed.
42.20.2.3.5. Assess whether all the Database Domains have been properly allocated work environment factors to determine an accurate estimate of required resources.
42.20.2.3.6. Assess whether all Database Domains have been properly allocated work accomplishment and recording functions necessary to support earned value reporting.
42.20.2.3.7. Assess whether all the Database Domains have been properly allocated metadata recording effort to ensure that all interrelationships are properly recorded into the Metabase System database.
42.20.2.4. Assign the risk level associated with each Database Domain not properly constructed.
42.20.3. Determine the findings and create draft assessment report.
42.20.4. Present the findings and revise draft assessment report.
42.20.5. Create final assessment report and deliver to the auditing organization.

43. Project Management

43.1. Assess Project Template Type
43.1.1. Identify artifacts that bear on the assessment.
43.1.1.1. Identify the appropriate set of Project Template Type documents.
43.1.1.1.1. Review Project Template Type documents.
43.1.1.1.2. Review scope and business problem related documentation.
43.1.1.1.3. Identify the Project Template Types that are defined and captured.
43.1.1.1.4. Identify the Project Template Type related work products.
43.1.1.2. For each Project Template Type related work product assessment:
43.1.1.2.1. Identify the relevant component.
43.1.1.2.2. Identify the description for each interrelated Project Template Type component.
43.1.2. Perform the assessment.
43.1.2.1. Assess each Project Template Type.
43.1.2.1.1. Assess the accuracy, quality and completeness of each Project Template Type with respect to the business requirements.
43.1.2.1.2. Assess whether Project Template Type are able to be inferred from business requirements, and if not whether business requirements or Project Template Type need to be enhanced.
43.1.2.1.3. Assess whether each Project Template Type hierarchy is properly specified, and that all Project Template Type names and descriptions are well defined, non-overlapping, and have been formally approved.
43.1.2.4. Assess whether the Project Template Types are properly identified and are appropriately engineered to address a Project Template Type project.
43.1.2.4.1. Assess whether all the Project Template Types have been delivered in terms of components, instances, and stored metadata work products.
43.1.2.4.2. Assess whether all the Project Template Types have been properly detailed as to content, description, methodology, evaluation, presentation, and delivery work steps.
43.1.2.4.3. Assess whether all the Project Template Types have been properly allocated sufficient unit effort estimates.
43.1.2.4.4. Assess whether all the Project Template Types have been properly allocated sufficient quantity of units that have to be developed.
43.1.2.4.5. Assess whether all the Project Template Types have been properly allocated work environment factors to determine an accurate estimate of required resources.
43.1.2.4.6. Assess whether all the Project Template Types have been properly allocated work accomplishment and recording functions necessary to support earned value reporting.
43.1.2.4.7. Assess whether all the Project Template Types have been properly allocated metadata recording effort to ensure that all interrelationships

are properly recorded into the Metabase System database.

43.1.2.5. Assign the risk level associated with each Project Template Type not properly constructed.

43.1.3. Determine the findings and create draft assessment report.

43.1.4. Present the findings and revise draft assessment report.

43.1.5. Create final assessment report and deliver to the auditing organization.

43.2. Assess Project Template.

43.2..1. Identify artifacts that bear on the assessment.

43.2..1.1. Identify the appropriate set of Project Template documents.

43.2..1.1.1. Review Project Template documents.

43.2..1.1.2. Review scope and business problem related documentation.

43.2..1.1.3. Identify the Project Templates that are defined and captured.

43.2..1.1.4. Identify the Project Template Type and Project Template related work products.

43.2..1.2. For each Project Template Type and Project Template related work product assessment:

43.2..1.2.1. Identify the relevant component.

43.2..1.2.2. Identify the description for each interrelated Project Template component.

43.2..2. Perform the assessment.

43.2..2.1. Assess each Project Templates.

43.2..2.1.1. Assess the accuracy, quality and completeness of each Project Templates with respect to the business requirements.

43.2..2.1.2. Assess whether Project Templates are able to be inferred from business requirements, and if not whether business requirements or Project Templates need to be enhanced.

43.2..2.1.3. Assess whether each Project Template hierarchy is properly specified, and that all Project Template names and descriptions are well defined, non-overlapping, and have been formally approved.

43.2..2.2. Assess whether the Project Templates are properly identified and are appropriately engineered to address a Project Template Type project and Project Template project.

43.2..2.2.1. Assess whether all the Project Templates have been delivered in terms of components, instances, and stored metadata work products.

43.2..2.2.2. Assess whether all the Project Templates have been properly detailed as to content, description, methodology, evaluation, presentation, and delivery work steps.

43.2..2.2.3. Assess whether all the Project Templates have been properly allocated sufficient unit effort estimates.

43.2..2.2.4. Assess whether all the Project Templates have been properly allocated sufficient quantity of units that have to be developed.

43.2..2.2.5. Assess whether all the Project Templates have been properly allocated work environment factors to determine an accurate estimate of required resources.

43.2..2.2.6. Assess whether all the Project Templates have been properly allocated work accomplishment and recording functions necessary to support earned value reporting.

43.2..2.2.7. Assess whether all the Project Templates have been properly allocated metadata recording effort to ensure that all interrelationships are properly recorded into the Metabase System database.

43.2..2.3. Assign the risk level associated with each Project Template not properly constructed.

43.2..3. Determine the findings and create draft assessment report.

43.2..4. Present the findings and revise draft assessment report.

43.2..5. Create final assessment report and deliver to the auditing organization.

43.3 Assess Deliverable Template Type.

43.3.1. Identify artifacts that bear on the assessment.

43.3.1.1. Identify the appropriate set of Deliverable Template Type documents.

43.3.1.1.1. Review Deliverable Template Type documents.

43.3.1.1.2. Review scope and business problem related documentation

43.3.1.1.3. Identify the Deliverable Template Types that are defined and captured.

43.3.1.1.4. Identify the Deliverable Template Type related work products.

43.3.1.2. For each Deliverable Template Type related work product assessment:

43.3.1.2.1. Identify the relevant component.

43.3.1.2.2. Identify the description for each interrelated Deliverable Template Type component.

43.3.2. Perform the assessment.

43.3.2.1. Assess each Deliverable Template Type.

43.3.2.1.1. Assess the accuracy, quality and completeness of each Deliverable Template Type with respect to the business requirements.

43.3.2.1.2. Assess whether Deliverable Template Types are able to be inferred from business requirements, and if not whether business requirements or Deliverable Template Types need to be enhanced.

43.3.2.1.3. Assess whether each Deliverable Template Types hierarchy is properly specified, and that all Deliverable Template Type names and descriptions are well defined, non-overlapping, and have been formally approved.

43.3.2.2. Assess whether the Deliverable Template Types are properly identified and are appropriately engineered to address a Deliverable Template Type project and Deliverable Template project.

43.3.2.2.1. Assess whether all the Deliverable Template Types have been delivered in terms of components, instances, and stored metadata work products.

43.3.2.2.2. Assess whether all the Deliverable Template Types have been properly detailed as to content, description, methodology, evaluation, presentation,

and delivery work steps.

43.3.2.2.3. Assess whether all the Deliverable Template Types have been properly allocated sufficient unit effort estimates.

43.3.2.2.4. Assess whether all the Deliverable Template Types have been properly allocated sufficient quantity of units that have to be developed.

43.3.2.2.5. Assess whether all the Deliverable Template Types have been properly allocated work environment factors to determine an accurate estimate of required resources.

43.3.2.2.6. Assess whether all the Deliverable Template Types have been properly allocated work accomplishment and recording functions necessary to support earned value reporting.

43.3.2.2.7. Assess whether all the Deliverable Template Types have been properly allocated metadata recording effort to ensure that all interrelationships are properly recorded into the Metabase System database.

43.3.2.5. Assign the risk level associated with each Deliverable Template Type not properly constructed.

43.3.3. Determine the findings and create draft assessment report.

43.3.4. Present the findings and revise draft assessment report.

43.3.5. Create final assessment report and deliver to the auditing organization.

43.4 Assess Deliverable Template.

43.4.1. Identify artifacts that bear on the assessment.

43.4.1.1. Identify the appropriate set of Deliverable Template documents.

43.4.1.1.1. Review Deliverable Template documents.

43.4.1.1.2. Review scope and business problem related documentation.

43.4.1.1.3. Identify the Deliverable Templates that are defined and captured.

43.4.1.1.4. Identify the Deliverable Template related work products.

43.4.1.2. For each Deliverable Template Type and Deliverable Template related work product assessment:

43.4.1.2.1. Identify the relevant component.

43.4.1.2.2. Identify the description for each interrelated Deliverable Template component.

43.4.2. Perform the assessment.

43.4.2.1. Assess each Deliverable Template.

43.4.2.1.1. Assess the accuracy, quality and completeness of each Deliverable Template with respect to the business requirements.

43.4.2.1.2. Assess whether Deliverable Templates are able to be inferred from business requirements, and if not whether business requirements or Deliverable Templates need to be enhanced.

43.4.2.1.3. Assess whether each Deliverable Template hierarchy/network is properly specified, and that all Deliverable Template names and descriptions are well defined, non-overlapping, and have been formally approved.

43.4.2.2. Assess whether the Deliverable Templates are properly identified and are appropriately engineered to address a Deliverable Template Type project and Deliverable Template project.

43.4.2.2.1. Assess whether all the Deliverable Templates have been delivered in terms of components, instances, and stored metadata work products.

43.4.2.2.2. Assess whether all the Deliverable Templates have been properly detailed as to content, description, methodology, evaluation, presentation, and delivery work steps.

43.4.2.2.3. Assess whether all the Deliverable Templates have been properly allocated sufficient unit effort estimates.

43.4.2.2.4. Assess whether all the Deliverable Templates have been properly allocated sufficient quantity of units that have to be developed.

43.4.2.2.5. Assess whether all the Deliverable Templates have been properly allocated work environment factors to determine an accurate estimate of required resources.

43.4.2.2.6. Assess whether all the Deliverable Templates have been properly allocated work accomplishment and recording functions necessary to support earned value reporting.

43.4.2.2.7. Assess whether all the Deliverable Templates have been properly allocated metadata recording effort to ensure that all interrelationships are properly recorded into the Metabase System database.

43.4.2.3. Assign the risk level associated with each Deliverable Template not properly constructed.

43.4.3. Determine the findings and create draft assessment report.

43.4.4. Present the findings and revise draft assessment report.

43.4.5. Create final assessment report and deliver to the auditing organization.

43.5. Assess Project Template Deliverable Template.

43.5.1. Identify artifacts that bear on the assessment.

43.5.1.1. Identify the appropriate set of Project Template Deliverable Template documents.

43.5.1.1.1. Review Project Template Deliverable Template documents.

43.5.1.1.2. Review scope and business problem related documentation.

43.5.1.1.3. Identify the Project Template Deliverable Templates that are defined and captured.

43.5.1.1.4. Identify the Project Template Deliverable Templates related work products.

43.5.1.2. For each Project Template Deliverable Templates related work product assessment:

43.5.1.2.1. Identify the relevant component.

43.5.1.2.2. Identify the description for each interrelated Project Template Deliverable Template component.

43.5.2. Perform the assessment.
43.5.2.1. Assess each Project Template Deliverable Template.
43.5.2.1.1. Assess the accuracy, quality and completeness of each Project Template Deliverable Templates with respect to the business requirements.
43.5.2.1.2. Assess whether Project Template Deliverable Templates are able to be inferred from business requirements, and if not whether business requirements or X need to be enhanced.
43.5.2.1.3. Assess whether each Project Template Deliverable Template pair properly associates one or more Project Templates with one or more Deliverable Templates.
43.5.2.1.4. Assess whether each Project Template Deliverable Template pair is properly named and described.
43.5.2.2. Assess whether the Project Template Deliverable Templates are properly identified and are appropriately engineered to address a Project Template Deliverable Template project and Deliverable Template project.
43.5.2.2.1. Assess whether all the Project Template Deliverable Templates have been delivered in terms of components, instances, and stored metadata work products.
43.5.2.2.2. Assess whether all the Project Template Deliverable Templates have been properly detailed as to content, description, methodology, evaluation, presentation, and delivery work steps.
43.5.2.2.3. Assess whether all the Project Template Deliverable Templates have been properly allocated sufficient unit effort estimates.
43.5.2.2.4. Assess whether all the Project Template Deliverable Templates have been properly allocated sufficient quantity of units that have to be developed.
43.5.2.2.5. Assess whether all the Project Template Deliverable Templates have been properly allocated work environment factors to determine an accurate estimate of required resources.
43.5.2.2.6. Assess whether all the Project Template Deliverable Templates have been properly allocated work accomplishment and recording functions necessary to support earned value reporting.
43.5.2.2.7. Assess whether all the Project Template Deliverable Templates have been properly allocated metadata recording effort to ensure that all interrelationships are properly recorded into the Metabase System database.
43.5.2.3. Assign the risk level associated with each Project Template Deliverable Template not properly constructed.
43.5.3. Determine the findings and create draft assessment report.
43.5.4. Present the findings and revise draft assessment report.
43.5.5. Create final assessment report and deliver to the auditing organization.

43.6 Assess Task Template Type

43.6.1. Identify artifacts that bear on the assessment.
43.6.1.1. Identify the appropriate set of Task Template Type documents.
43.6.1.1.1. Review Task Template Type documents.
43.6.1.1.2. Review scope and business problem related documentation.
43.6.1.1.3. Identify the Task Template Types that are defined and captured.
43.6.1.1.4. Identify the Task Template Type related work products.
43.6.1.2. For each Task Template Type related work product assessment:
43.6.1.2.1. Identify the relevant component.
43.6.1.2.2. Identify the description for each interrelated Task Template Type component.
43.6.2. Perform the assessment.
43.6.2.1. Assess each Task Template Type.
43.6.2.1.1. Assess the accuracy, quality and completeness of each Task Template Type with respect to the business requirements.
43.6.2.1.2. Assess whether Task Template Type are able to be inferred from business requirements, and if not whether business requirements or Task Template Type need to be enhanced.
43.6.2.1.3. Assess whether each Task Template Type hierarchy/network is properly specified, and that all Task Template Type names and descriptions are well defined, non-overlapping, and have been formally approved.
43.6.2.2. Assess whether the Task Template Types are properly identified and are appropriately engineered to address a Task Template Type project and Task Template project.
43.6.2.2.1. Assess whether all the Task Template Types have been delivered in terms of components, instances, and stored metadata work products.
43.6.2.2.2. Assess whether all the Task Template Types have been properly detailed as to content, description, methodology, evaluation, presentation, and delivery work steps.
43.6.2.2.3. Assess whether all the Task Template Types have been properly allocated sufficient unit effort estimates.
43.6.2.2.4. Assess whether all the Task Template Types have been properly allocated sufficient quantity of units that have to be developed.
43.6.2.2.5. Assess whether all the Task Template Types have been properly allocated work environment factors to determine an accurate estimate of required resources.
43.6.2.2.6. Assess whether all the Task Template Types have been properly allocated work accomplishment and recording functions necessary to support earned value reporting.
43.6.2.2.7. Assess whether all the Task Template Types have been properly allocated metadata recording effort to ensure that all interrelationships are properly recorded into the Metabase System database.
43.6.2.3. Assign the risk level associated with each Task Template Type not

properly constructed.
43.6.3. Determine the findings and create draft assessment report.
43.6.4. Present the findings and revise draft assessment report.
43.6.5. Create final assessment report and deliver to the auditing organization.

43.7 Assess Task Template.
43.7.1. Identify artifacts that bear on the assessment.
43.7.1.1. Identify the appropriate set of Task Template Type documents.
43.7.1.1.1. Review Task Template Type documents.
43.7.1.1.2. Review scope and business problem related documentation.
43.7.1.1.3. Identify the Task Template that are defined and captured.
43.7.1.1.4. Identify the Task Template related work products.
43.7.1.2. For each Task Template related work product assessment:
43.7.1.2.1. Identify the relevant component.
43.7.1.2.2. Identify the description for each interrelated Task Template component.
43.7.2. Perform the assessment.
43.7.2.1. Assess each Task Template.
43.7.2.1.1. Assess the accuracy, quality and completeness of each Task Template with respect to the business requirements.
43.7.2.1.2. Assess whether Task Template are able to be inferred from business requirements, and if not whether business requirements or Task Template need to be enhanced.
43.7.2.1.3. Assess whether each Task Template hierarchy is properly specified, and that all Task Template names and descriptions are well defined, non-overlapping, and have been formally approved.
43.7.2.2. Assess whether the Task Template Types are properly identified and are appropriately engineered to address a Task Template Type project and Task Template project.
43.7.2.2.1. Assess whether all the Task Template Types have been delivered in terms of components, instances, and stored metadata work products.
43.7.2.2.2. Assess whether all the Task Template Types have been properly detailed as to content, description, methodology, evaluation, presentation, and delivery work steps.
43.7.2.2.3. Assess whether all the Task Template Types have been properly allocated sufficient unit effort estimates.
43.7.2.2.4. Assess whether all the Task Template Types have been properly allocated sufficient quantity of units that have to be developed.
43.7.2.2.5. Assess whether all the Task Template Types have been properly allocated work environment factors to determine an accurate estimate of required resources.
43.7.2.2.6. Assess whether all the Task Template Types have been properly allocated work accomplishment and recording functions necessary to support

earned value reporting.

43.7.2.2.7. Assess whether all the Task Template Types have been properly allocated metadata recording effort to ensure that all interrelationships are properly recorded into the Metabase System database.

43.7.2.3. Assign the risk level associated with each Task Template Type not properly constructed.

43.7.3. Determine the findings and create draft assessment report.

43.7.4. Present the findings and revise draft assessment report.

43.7.5. Create final assessment report and deliver to the auditing organization.

43.8. Assess Deliverable Template Task Template.

43.8.1. Identify artifacts that bear on the assessment.

43.8.1.1. Identify the appropriate set of Deliverable Template Task Template documents.

43.8.1.1.1. Review Deliverable Template Task Template documents.

43.8.1.1.2. Review scope and business problem related documentation.

43.8.1.1.3. Identify the Deliverable Template Task Templates that are defined and captured.

43.8.1.1.4. Identify the Deliverable Template Task Templates related work products.

43.8.1.2. For each Deliverable Template Task Templates related work product assessment:

43.8.1.2.1. Identify the relevant component.

43.8.1.2.2. Identify the description for each interrelated Deliverable Template Task Template component.

43.8.2. Perform the assessment.

43.8.2.1. Assess each Deliverable Template Task Template.

43.8.2.1.1. Assess the accuracy, quality and completeness of each Deliverable Template Task Templates with respect to the business requirements.

43.8.2.1.2. Assess whether Deliverable Template Task Templates are able to be inferred from business requirements, and if not whether business requirements or Deliverable Template Task Templates need to be enhanced.

43.8.2.1.3. Assess whether each Deliverable Template Task Template pair properly associates one or more Deliverable Templates with one or more Task Templates.

43.8.2.1.4. Assess whether each Deliverable Template Task Template pair is properly named and described.

43.8.2.2. Assess whether the Deliverable Template Task Templates are properly identified and are appropriately engineered to address a Project Template Deliverable Template project and Deliverable Template project.

43.8.2.2.1. Assess whether all the Deliverable Template Task Templates have been delivered in terms of components, instances, and stored metadata work

products.

43.8.2.2.2. Assess whether all the Deliverable Template Task Templates have been properly detailed as to content, description, methodology, evaluation, presentation, and delivery work steps.

43.8.2.2.3. Assess whether all the Deliverable Template Task Templates have been properly allocated sufficient unit effort estimates.

43.8.2.2.4. Assess whether all the Deliverable Template Task Templates have been properly allocated sufficient quantity of units that have to be developed.

43.8.2.2.5. Assess whether all the Deliverable Template Task Templates have been properly allocated work environment factors to determine an accurate estimate of required resources.

43.8.2.2.6. Assess whether all the Deliverable Template Task Templates have been properly allocated work accomplishment and recording functions necessary to support earned value reporting.

43.8.2.2.7. Assess whether all the Deliverable Template Task Templates have been properly allocated metadata recording effort to ensure that all interrelationships are properly recorded into the Metabase System database.

43.8.2.3. Assign the risk level associated with each Deliverable Template Task Template not properly constructed.

43.8.3. Determine the findings and create draft assessment report.

43.8.4. Present the findings and revise draft assessment report.

43.8.5. Create final assessment report and deliver to the auditing organization.

43.9. Assess Skill.

43.9.1. Identify artifacts that bear on the assessment.

43.9.1.1. Identify the appropriate set of Skill documents.

43.9.1.1.1. Review Skill documents.

43.9.1.1.2. Review scope and business problem related documentation.

43.9.1.1.3. Identify the Skills that are defined and captured.

43.9.1.1.4. Identify the Skills related work products.

43.9.1.2. For each Skills related work product assessment:

43.9.1.2.1. Identify the relevant component.

43.9.1.2.2. Identify the description for each interrelated Skill component.

43.9.2. Perform the assessment.

43.9.2.1. Assess each Skill.

43.9.2.1.1. Assess the accuracy, quality and completeness of each Skill with respect to the business requirements.

43.9.2.1.2. Assess whether Skills are able to be inferred from business requirements, and if not whether business requirements or Skills need to be enhanced.

43.9.2.2. Assess whether the Skills are properly identified and are appropriately engineered to address a Skill project.

43.9.2.2.1. Assess whether all the Skills have been delivered in terms of components, instances, and stored metadata work products.

43.9.2.2.2. Assess whether all the Skills have been properly detailed as to content, description, methodology, evaluation, presentation, and delivery work steps.

43.9.2.2.3. Assess whether all the Skills have been properly allocated sufficient unit effort estimates.

43.9.2.2.4. Assess whether all the Skills have been properly allocated sufficient quantity of units that have to be developed.

43.9.2.2.5. Assess whether all the Skills have been properly allocated work environment factors to determine an accurate estimate of required resources.

43.9.2.2.6. Assess whether all the Skills have been properly allocated work accomplishment and recording functions necessary to support earned value reporting.

43.9.2.2.7. Assess whether all the Skills have been properly allocated metadata recording effort to ensure that all interrelationships are properly recorded into the Metabase System database.

43.9.2.3. Assign the risk level associated with each Skill not properly constructed.

43.9.3. Determine the findings and create draft assessment report.

43.9.4. Present the findings and revise draft assessment report.

43.9.5. Create final assessment report and deliver to the auditing organization.

43.10. Assess Skill Level Type.

43.10.1. Identify artifacts that bear on the assessment.

43.10.1.1. Identify the appropriate set of Skill Level Type documents.

43.10.1.1.1. Review Skill Level Type documents.

43.10.1.1.2. Review scope and business problem related documentation.

43.10.1.1.3. Identify the Skill Level Types that are defined and captured.

43.10.1.1.4. Identify the Skill Level Types related work products.

43.10.1.2. For each Skill Level Types related work product assessment:

43.10.1.2.1. Identify the relevant component.

43.10.1.2.2. Identify the description for each interrelated Skill Level Type component.

43.10.2. Perform the assessment.

43.10.2.1. Assess each Skill Level Type.

43.10.2.1.1. Assess the accuracy, quality and completeness of each Skill Level Type with respect to the business requirements.

43.10.2.1.2. Assess whether Skill Level Types are able to be inferred from business requirements, and if not whether business requirements or Skill Level Types need to be enhanced.

43.10.2.2. Assess whether the Skill Level Types are properly identified and are appropriately engineered to address a Skill Level Type project.

43.10.2.2.1. Assess whether all the Skill Level Types have been delivered in terms of components, instances, and stored metadata work products.
43.10.2.2.2. Assess whether all the Skill Level Types have been properly detailed as to content, description, methodology, evaluation, presentation, and delivery work steps.
43.10.2.2.3. Assess whether all the Skill Level Types have been properly allocated sufficient unit effort estimates.
43.10.2.2.4. Assess whether all the Skill Level Types have been properly allocated sufficient quantity of units that have to be developed.
43.10.2.2.5. Assess whether all the Skill Level Types have been properly allocated work environment factors to determine an accurate estimate of required resources.
43.10.2.2.6. Assess whether all the Skill Level Types have been properly allocated work accomplishment and recording functions necessary to support earned value reporting.
43.10.2.2.7. Assess whether all the Skill Level Types have been properly allocated metadata recording effort to ensure that all interrelationships are properly recorded into the Metabase System database.
43.10.2.3. Assign the risk level associated with each Skill Level Type not properly constructed.
43.10.3. Determine the findings and create draft assessment report.
43.10.4. Present the findings and revise draft assessment report.
43.10.5. Create final assessment report and deliver to the auditing organization.

43.11. Assess Skill Level.
43.11.1. Identify artifacts that bear on the assessment.
43.11.1.1. Identify the appropriate set of Skill Level documents.
43.11.1.1.1. Review Skill Level documents.
43.11.1.1.2. Review scope and business problem related documentation.
43.11.1.1.3. Identify the Skill Levels that are defined and captured.
43.11.1.1.4. Identify the Skill Levels related work products.
43.11.1.2. For each Skill Levels related work product assessment:
43.11.1.2.1. Identify the relevant component.
43.11.1.2.2. Identify the description for each interrelated Skill Level component.
43.11.2. Perform the assessment.
43.11.2.1. Assess each Skill Level.
43.11.2.1.1. Assess the accuracy, quality and completeness of each Skill Level with respect to the business requirements.
43.11.2.1.2. Assess whether Skill Levels are able to be inferred from business requirements, and if not whether business requirements or Skill Levels need to be enhanced.
43.11.2.1.3. Assess whether each Skill Level pair properly associates one or more

Skills with one or more Skill Level Types.

43.11.2.1.4. Assess whether each Skill Level pair is properly named and described.

43.11.2.2. Assess whether the Skill Levels are properly identified and are appropriately engineered to address a Skill Level project.

43.11.2.2.1. Assess whether all the Skill Levels have been delivered in terms of components, instances, and stored metadata work products.

43.11.2.2.2. Assess whether all the Skill Levels have been properly detailed as to content, description, methodology, evaluation, presentation, and delivery work steps.

43.11.2.2.3. Assess whether all the Skill Levels have been properly allocated sufficient unit effort estimates.

43.11.2.2.4. Assess whether all the Skill Levels have been properly allocated sufficient quantity of units that have to be developed.

43.11.2.2.5. Assess whether all the Skill Levels have been properly allocated work environment factors to determine an accurate estimate of required resources.

43.11.2.2.6. Assess whether all the Skill Levels have been properly allocated work accomplishment and recording functions necessary to support earned value reporting.

43.11.2.2.7. Assess whether all the Skill Levels have been properly allocated metadata recording effort to ensure that all interrelationships are properly recorded into the Metabase System database.

43.11.2.3. Assign the risk level associated with each Skill Level not properly constructed.

43.11.3. Determine the findings and create draft assessment report.

43.11.4. Present the findings and revise draft assessment report.

43.11.5. Create final assessment report and deliver to the auditing organization.

43.12 Assess Work Environment Factor Type.

43.12.1. Identify artifacts that bear on the assessment.

43.12.1.1. Identify the appropriate set of Work Environment Factor Type documents.

43.12.1.1.1. Review Work Environment Factor Type documents.

43.12.1.1.2. Review scope and business problem related documentation.

43.12.1.1.3. Identify the Work Environment Factor Types that are defined and captured.

43.12.1.1.4. Identify the Work Environment Factor Types related work products.

43.12.1.2. For each Work Environment Factor Types related work product assessment:

43.12.1.2.1. Identify the relevant component.

43.12.1.2.2. Identify the description for each interrelated Work Environment Factor Type component.

43.12.2. Perform the assessment.
43.12.2.1. Assess each Work Environment Factor Type.
43.12.2.1.1. Assess the accuracy, quality and completeness of each Work Environment Factor Type with respect to the business requirements.
43.12.2.1.2. Assess whether Work Environment Factor Types are able to be inferred from business requirements, and if not whether business requirements or Work Environment Factor Types need to be enhanced.
43.12.2.2. Assess whether the Work Environment Factor Types are properly identified and are appropriately engineered to address a Work Environment Factor Type project.
43.12.2.2.1. Assess whether all the Work Environment Factor Types have been delivered in terms of components, instances, and stored metadata work products.
43.12.2.2.2. Assess whether all the Work Environment Factor Types have been properly detailed as to content, description, methodology, evaluation, presentation, and delivery work steps.
43.12.2.2.3. Assess whether all the Work Environment Factor Types have been properly allocated sufficient unit effort estimates.
43.12.2.2.4. Assess whether all the Work Environment Factor Types have been properly allocated sufficient quantity of units that have to be developed.
43.12.2.2.5. Assess whether all the Work Environment Factor Types have been properly allocated work environment factors to determine an accurate estimate of required resources.
43.12.2.2.6. Assess whether all the Work Environment Factor Types have been properly allocated work accomplishment and recording functions necessary to support earned value reporting.
43.12.2.2.7. Assess whether all the Work Environment Factor Types have been properly allocated metadata recording effort to ensure that all interrelationships are properly recorded into the Metabase System database.
43.12.2.3. Assign the risk level associated with each Work Environment Factor Type not properly constructed.
43.12.3. Determine the findings and create draft assessment report.
43.13.4. Present the findings and revise draft assessment report.
43.12.5. Create final assessment report and deliver to the auditing organization.

43.13. Assess Work Environment Factor.
43.13.1. Identify artifacts that bear on the assessment.
43.13.1.1. Identify the appropriate set of Work Environment Factor documents.
43.13.1.1.1. Review Work Environment Factor documents.
43.13.1.1.2. Review scope and business problem related documentation.
43.13.1.1.3. Identify the Work Environment Factors that are defined and captured.

43.13.1.1.4. Identify the Work Environment Factors related work products.
43.13.1.2. For each Work Environment Factors related work product assessment:
43.13.1.2.1. Identify the relevant component.
43.13.1.2.2. Identify the description for each interrelated Work Environment Factor component.
43.13.2. Perform the assessment.
43.13.2.1. Assess each Work Environment Factor.
43.13.2.1.1. Assess the accuracy, quality and completeness of each Work Environment Factor with respect to the business requirements.
43.13.2.1.2. Assess whether Work Environment Factors are able to be inferred from business requirements, and if not whether business requirements or Work Environment Factors need to be enhanced.
43.13.2.2. Assess whether the Work Environment Factors are properly identified and are appropriately engineered to address a Work Environment Factor project.
43.13.2.2.1. Assess whether all the Work Environment Factors have been delivered in terms of components, instances, and stored metadata work products.
43.13.2.2.2. Assess whether all the Work Environment Factors have been properly detailed as to content, description, methodology, evaluation, presentation, and delivery work steps.
43.13.2.2.3. Assess whether all the Work Environment Factors have been properly allocated sufficient unit effort estimates.
43.13.2.2.4. Assess whether all the Work Environment Factors have been properly allocated sufficient quantity of units that have to be developed.
43.13.2.2.5. Assess whether all the Work Environment Factors have been properly allocated work environment factors to determine an accurate estimate of required resources.
43.13.2.2.6. Assess whether all the Work Environment Factors have been properly allocated work accomplishment and recording functions necessary to support earned value reporting.
43.13.2.2.7. Assess whether all the Work Environment Factors have been properly allocated metadata recording effort to ensure that all interrelationships are properly recorded into the Metabase System database.
43.13.2.3. Assign the risk level associated with each Work Environment Factor not properly constructed.
43.13.3. Determine the findings and create draft assessment report.
43.13.4. Present the findings and revise draft assessment report.
43.13.5. Create final assessment report and deliver to the auditing organization.

43.14. Assess Work Environment Factor Multiplier Type.
43.14.1. Identify artifacts that bear on the assessment.
43.14.1.1. Identify the appropriate set of Work Environment Factor Multiplier Type

documents.

43.14.1.1.1. Review Work Environment Factor Multiplier Type documents.

43.14.1.1.2. Review scope and business problem related documentation.

43.14.1.1.3. Identify the Work Environment Factor Multiplier Types that are defined and captured.

43.14.1.1.4. Identify the Work Environment Factor Multiplier Types related work products.

43.14.1.2. For each Work Environment Factor Multiplier Types related work product assessment:

43.14.1.2.1. Identify the relevant component.

43.14.1.2.2. Identify the description for each interrelated Work Environment Factor Multiplier Type component.

43.14.2. Perform the assessment.

43.14.2.1. Assess each Work Environment Factor Multiplier Type.

43.14.2.1.1. Assess the accuracy, quality and completeness of each Work Environment Factor Multiplier Type with respect to the business requirements.

43.14.2.1.2. Assess whether Work Environment Factor Multiplier Types are able to be inferred from business requirements, and if not whether business requirements or Work Environment Factor Multiplier Types need to be enhanced.

43.14.2.2. Assess whether the Work Environment Factor Multiplier Types are properly identified and are appropriately engineered to address a Work Environment Factor Multiplier Type project.

43.14.2.2.1. Assess whether all the Work Environment Factor Multiplier Types have been delivered in terms of components, instances, and stored metadata work products.

43.14.2.2.2. Assess whether all the Work Environment Factor Multiplier Types have been properly detailed as to content, description, methodology, evaluation, presentation, and delivery work steps.

43.14.2.2.3. Assess whether all the Work Environment Factor Multiplier Types have been properly allocated sufficient unit effort estimates.

43.14.2.2.4. Assess whether all the Work Environment Factor Multiplier Types have been properly allocated sufficient quantity of units that have to be developed.

43.14.2.2.5. Assess whether all the Work Environment Factor Multiplier Types have been properly allocated work environment factors to determine an accurate estimate of required resources.

43.14.2.2.6. Assess whether all the Work Environment Factor Multiplier Types have been properly allocated work accomplishment and recording functions necessary to support earned value reporting.

43.14.2.2.7. Assess whether all the Work Environment Factor Multiplier Types have been properly allocated metadata recording effort to ensure that all interrelationships are properly recorded into the Metabase System database.

43.14.2.3. Assign the risk level associated with each Work Environment Factor Multiplier Type not properly constructed.

43.14.3. Determine the findings and create draft assessment report.

43.14.4. Present the findings and revise draft assessment report.

43.14.5. Create final assessment report and deliver to the auditing organization.

43.15 Assess Work Environment Factor Multiplier.

43.15.1. Identify artifacts that bear on the assessment.

43.15.1.1. Identify the appropriate set of Work Environment Factor Multiplier documents.

43.15.1.1.1. Review Work Environment Factor Multiplier documents.

43.15.1.1.2. Review scope and business problem related documentation.

43.15.1.1.3. Identify the Work Environment Factor Multipliers. that are defined and captured.

43.15.1.1.4. Identify the Work Environment Factor Multipliers. related work products.

43.15.1.2. For each Work Environment Factor Multipliers. related work product assessment:

43.15.1.2.1. Identify the relevant component.

43.15.1.2.2. Identify the description for each interrelated Work Environment Factor Multiplier component.

43.15.2. Perform the assessment.

43.15.2.1. Assess each Work Environment Factor Multiplier.

43.15.2.1.1. Assess the accuracy, quality and completeness of each Work Environment Factor Multiplier with respect to the business requirements.

43.15.2.1.2. Assess whether Work Environment Factor Multipliers are able to be inferred from business requirements, and if not whether business requirements or Work Environment Factor Multipliers need to be enhanced.

43.15.2.1.3. Assess whether each Work Environment Factor Multipliers pair properly associates one or more Work Environment Factors with one or more Work Environment Factor Multiplier Types.

43.15.2.1.4. Assess whether each Work Environment Factor Multipliers pair is properly named and described.

43.15.2.2. Assess whether the Work Environment Factor Multipliers are properly identified and are appropriately engineered to address a Work Environment Factor Multiplier project and Deliverable Template project.

43.15.2.2.1. Assess whether all the Work Environment Factor Multipliers have been delivered in terms of components, instances, and stored metadata work products.

43.15.2.2.2. Assess whether all the Work Environment Factor Multipliers have been properly detailed as to content, description, methodology, evaluation, presentation, and delivery work steps.

43.15.2.2.3. Assess whether all the Work Environment Factor Multipliers have been properly allocated sufficient unit effort estimates.

43.15.2.2.4. Assess whether all the Work Environment Factor Multipliers have been properly allocated sufficient quantity of units that have to be developed.

43.15.2.2.5. Assess whether all the Work Environment Factor Multipliers have been properly allocated work environment factors to determine an accurate estimate of required resources.

43.15.2.2.6. Assess whether all the Work Environment Factor Multipliers have been properly allocated work accomplishment and recording functions necessary to support earned value reporting.

43.15.2.2.7. Assess whether all the Work Environment Factor Multipliers have been properly allocated metadata recording effort to ensure that all interrelationships are properly recorded into the Metabase System database.

43.15.2.3. Assign the risk level associated with each Work Environment Factor Multiplier not properly constructed.

43.15.3. Determine the findings and create draft assessment report.

43.15.4. Present the findings and revise draft assessment report.

43.15.5. Create final assessment report and deliver to the auditing organization.

43.16 Assess Project Deliverable Work Environment Factor Multiplier.

43.16.1. Identify artifacts that bear on the assessment.

43.16.1.1. Identify the appropriate set of Project Deliverable Work Environment Factor Multiplier documents.

43.16.1.1.1. Review Project Deliverable Work Environment Factor Multiplier documents.

43.16.1.1.2. Review scope and business problem related documentation.

43.16.1.1.3. Identify the Project Deliverable Work Environment Factor Multipliers that are defined and captured.

43.16.1.1.4. Identify the Project Deliverable Work Environment Factor Multipliers related work products.

43.16.1.2. For each Project Deliverable Work Environment Factor Multipliers related work product assessment:

43.16.1.2.1. Identify the relevant component.

43.16.1.2.2. Identify the description for each interrelated Project Deliverable Work Environment Factor Multiplier component.

43.16.2. Perform the assessment.

43.16.2.1. Assess each Project Deliverable Work Environment Factor Multiplier.

43.16.2.1.1. Assess the accuracy, quality and completeness of each Project Deliverable Work Environment Factor Multipliers with respect to the business requirements.

43.16.2.1.2. Assess whether Project Deliverable Work Environment Factor Multipliers are able to be inferred from business requirements, and if not whether business requirements or Project Deliverable Work Environment Factor Multipliers need to be enhanced.

43.16.2.1.3. Assess whether each Project Deliverable Work Environment Factor Multipliers pair properly associates one or more Project Deliverables with one or more Work Environment Factor Multiplier.

43.16.2.1.4. Assess whether each Project Deliverable Work Environment Factor Multiplier pair is properly named and described.

43.16.2.2. Assess whether the Project Deliverable Work Environment Factor Multipliers are properly identified and are appropriately engineered to address a Project Deliverable Work Environment Factor Multiplier project.

43.16.2.2.1. Assess whether all the Project Deliverable Work Environment Factor Multipliers have been delivered in terms of components, instances, and stored metadata work products.

43.16.2.2.2. Assess whether all the Project Deliverable Work Environment Factor Multipliers have been properly detailed as to content, description, methodology, evaluation, presentation, and delivery work steps.

43.16.2.2.3. Assess whether all the Project Deliverable Work Environment Factor Multipliers have been properly allocated sufficient unit effort estimates.

43.16.2.2.4. Assess whether all the Project Deliverable Work Environment Factor Multipliers have been properly allocated sufficient quantity of units that have to be developed.

43.16.2.2.5. Assess whether all the Project Deliverable Work Environment Factor Multipliers have been properly allocated work environment factors to determine an accurate estimate of required resources.

43.16.2.2.6. Assess whether all the Project Deliverable Work Environment Factor Multipliers have been properly allocated work accomplishment and recording functions necessary to support earned value reporting.

43.16.2.2.7. Assess whether all the Project Deliverable Work Environment Factor Multipliers have been properly allocated metadata recording effort to ensure that all interrelationships are properly recorded into the Metabase System database.

43.16.2.3. Assign the risk level associated with each Project Deliverable Work Environment Factor Multiplier not properly constructed.

43.16.3. Determine the findings and create draft assessment report.

43.16.4. Present the findings and revise draft assessment report.

43.16.5. Create final assessment report and deliver to the auditing organization.

43.17 Assess Project.

43.17.1. Identify artifacts that bear on the assessment.
43.17.1.1. Identify the appropriate set of Project documents.
43.17.1.1.1. Review Project documents.
43.17.1.1.2. Review scope and business problem related documentation.
43.17.1.1.3. Identify the Projects that are defined and captured.
43.17.1.1.4. Identify the Projects related work products.
43.17.1.2. For each Projects related work product assessment:
43.17.1.2.1. Identify the relevant component.
43.17.1.2.2. Identify the description for each interrelated Project component.
43.17.2. Perform the assessment.
43.17.2.1. Assess each Project.
43.17.2.1.1. Assess the accuracy, quality and completeness of each Project with respect to the business requirements.
43.17.2.1.2. Assess whether Projects are able to be inferred from business requirements, and if not whether business requirements or Projects need to be enhanced.
43.17.2.2. Assess whether the Projects are properly identified and are appropriately engineered to address a "Project" project.
43.17.2.2.1. Assess whether all the Projects have been delivered in terms of components, instances, and stored metadata work products.
43.17.2.2.2. Assess whether all the Projects have been properly detailed as to content, description, methodology, evaluation, presentation, and delivery work steps.
43.17.2.2.3. Assess whether all the Projects have been properly allocated sufficient unit effort estimates.
43.17.2.2.4. Assess whether all the Projects have been properly allocated sufficient quantity of units that have to be developed.
43.17.2.2.5. Assess whether all the Projects have been properly allocated work environment factors to determine an accurate estimate of required resources.
43.17.2.2.6. Assess whether all the Projects have been properly allocated work accomplishment and recording functions necessary to support earned value reporting.
43.17.2.2.7. Assess whether all the Projects have been properly allocated metadata recording effort to ensure that all interrelationships are properly recorded into the Metabase System database.
43.17.2.3. Assign the risk level associated with each Project not properly constructed.
43.17.3. Determine the findings and create draft assessment report.
43.17.4. Present the findings and revise draft assessment report.
43.17.5. Create final assessment report and deliver to the auditing organization.

43.18 Assess Resource Life Cycle Node Project.
43.18.1. Identify artifacts that bear on the assessment.
43.18.1.1. Identify the appropriate set of Resource Life Cycle Node Project documents.
43.18.1.1.1. Review Resource Life Cycle Node Project documents.
43.18.1.1.2. Review scope and business problem related documentation.
43.18.1.1.3. Identify the Resource Life Cycle Node Projects that are defined and captured.
43.18.1.1.4. Identify the Resource Life Cycle Node Project related work products.
43.18.1.2. For each Resource Life Cycle Node Project related work product assessment:
43.18.1.2.1. Identify the relevant component.
43.18.1.2.2. Identify the description for each interrelated Resource Life Cycle Node Project component.
43.18.2. Perform the assessment.
43.18.2.1. Assess each Resource Life Cycle Node Project:
43.18.2.1.1. Assess the accuracy, quality and completeness of each Resource Life Cycle Node Project with respect to the business requirements.
43.18.2.1.2. Assess whether Resource Life Cycle Node Project are able to be inferred from business requirements, and if not whether business requirements or Resource Life Cycle Node Project need to be enhanced.
43.18.2.1.3. Assess whether each Resource Life Cycle Node Project pair properly associates one or more Project Deliverables with one or more Resource Life Cycle Nodes.
43.18.2.1.4. Assess whether each Resource Life Cycle Node Project pair is properly named and described.
43.18.2.2. Assess whether the Resource Life Cycle Node Project are properly identified and are appropriately engineered to address a Resource Life Cycle Node Project project.
43.18.2.2.1. Assess whether all the Resource Life Cycle Node Projects have been delivered in terms of components, instances, and stored metadata work products.
43.18.2.2.2. Assess whether all the Resource Life Cycle Node Projects have been properly detailed as to content, description, methodology, evaluation, presentation, and delivery work steps.
43.18.2.2.3. Assess whether all the Resource Life Cycle Node Projects have been properly allocated sufficient unit effort estimates.
43.18.2.2.4. Assess whether all the Resource Life Cycle Node Projects have been properly allocated sufficient quantity of units that have to be developed.
43.18.2.2.5. Assess whether all the Resource Life Cycle Node Projects have been properly allocated work environment factors to determine an accurate estimate of required resources.

43.18.2.2.6. Assess whether all the Resource Life Cycle Node Projects have been properly allocated work accomplishment and recording functions necessary to support earned value reporting.
43.18.2.2.7. Assess whether all the Resource Life Cycle Node Projects have been properly allocated metadata recording effort to ensure that all interrelationships are properly recorded into the Metabase System database.
43.18.2.3. Assign the risk level associated with each Resource Life Cycle Node Project not properly constructed.
43.18.3. Determine the findings and create draft assessment report.
43.18.4. Present the findings and revise draft assessment report.
43.18.5. Create final assessment report and deliver to the auditing organization.

43.19. Assess Project Deliverable.
43.19.1. Identify artifacts that bear on the assessment.
43.19.1.1. Identify the appropriate set of Project Deliverable documents.
43.19.1.1.1. Review Project Deliverable documents.
43.19.1.1.2. Review scope and business problem related documentation.
43.19.1.1.3. Identify the Project Deliverables that are defined and captured.
43.19.1.1.4. Identify the Project Deliverables related work products.
43.19.1.2. For each Project Deliverables related work product assessment:
43.19.1.2.1. Identify the relevant component.
43.19.1.2.2. Identify the description for each interrelated Project Deliverable component.
43.19.2. Perform the assessment.
43.19.2.1. Assess each Project Deliverable.
43.19.2.1.1. Assess the accuracy, quality and completeness of each Project Deliverable with respect to the business requirements.
43.19.2.1.2. Assess whether Project Deliverables are able to be inferred from business requirements, and if not whether business requirements or Project Deliverable need to be enhanced.
43.19.2.1.3. Assess whether each Project Deliverable hierarchy/network is properly specified, and that all Project Deliverable names and descriptions are well defined, non-overlapping, and have been formally approved.
43.19.2.1.4. Assess whether each Project Deliverable pair properly associates one or more Project Template Deliverable Templates with one or more Projects.
43.19.2.1.5. Assess whether each Project Deliverable pair is properly named and described.
43.19.2.2. Assess whether the Project Deliverables are properly identified and are appropriately engineered to address a Project Deliverable project.
43.19.2.2.1. Assess whether all the Project Deliverables have been delivered in terms of components, instances, and stored metadata work products.

43.19.2.2.2. Assess whether all the Project Deliverables have been properly detailed as to content, description, methodology, evaluation, presentation, and delivery work steps.
43.19.2.2.3. Assess whether all the Project Deliverables have been properly allocated sufficient unit effort estimates.
43.19.2.2.4. Assess whether all the Project Deliverables have been properly allocated sufficient quantity of units that have to be developed.
43.19.2.2.5. Assess whether all the Project Deliverables have been properly allocated work environment factors to determine an accurate estimate of required resources.
43.19.2.2.6. Assess whether all the Project Deliverables have been properly allocated work accomplishment and recording functions necessary to support earned value reporting.
43.19.2.2.7. Assess whether all the Project Deliverables have been properly allocated metadata recording effort to ensure that all interrelationships are properly recorded into the Metabase System database.
43.19.2.3. Assign the risk level associated with each Project Deliverable not properly constructed.
43.19.3. Determine the findings and create draft assessment report.
43.19.4. Present the findings and revise draft assessment report.
43.19.5. Create final assessment report and deliver to the auditing organization

43.20. Assess Project Template Deliverable Template Deliverable Template Task Template.
43.20.1. Identify artifacts that bear on the assessment.
43.20.1.1. Identify the appropriate set of Project Template Deliverable Template Deliverable Template Task Template.
43.20.1.1.1. Review Project Template Deliverable Template Deliverable Template Task Template documents.
43.20.1.1.2. Review scope and business problem related documentation.
43.20.1.1.3. Identify the Project Template Deliverable Template Deliverable Template Task Templates that are defined and captured.
43.20.1.1.4. Identify the Project Template Deliverable Template Deliverable Template Task Templates related work products.
43.20.1.2. For each Project Template Deliverable Template Deliverable Template Task Templates related work product assessment:
43.20.1.2.1. Identify the relevant component.
43.20.1.2.2. Identify the description for each interrelated Project Template Deliverable Template Deliverable Template Task Template component.
43.20.2. Perform the assessment.
43.20.2.1. Assess each Project Template Deliverable Template Deliverable Template Task Template.

43.20.2.1.1. Assess the accuracy, quality and completeness of each Project Template Deliverable Template Deliverable Template Task Template with respect to the business requirements.

43.20.2.1.2. Assess whether Project Template Deliverable Template Deliverable Template Task Templates are able to be inferred from business requirements, and if not whether business requirements or Project Template Deliverable Template Deliverable Template Task Templates need to be enhanced.

43.20.2.1.3. Assess whether each Project Template Deliverable Template Deliverable Template Task Templates pair properly associates one or more Project Template Deliverable Templates with one or more Deliverable Template Task Templates.

43.20.2.1.4. Assess whether each Project Template Deliverable Template Deliverable Template Task Templates pair is properly named and described.

43.20.2.2. Assess whether the Project Template Deliverable Template Deliverable Template Task Templates are properly identified and are appropriately engineered to address a Project Template Deliverable Template Deliverable Template Task Template project.

43.20.2.2.1. Assess whether all the Project Template Deliverable Template Deliverable Template Task Templates have been delivered in terms of components, instances, and stored metadata work products.

43.20.2.2.2. Assess whether all the Project Template Deliverable Template Deliverable Template Task Templates have been properly detailed as to content, description, methodology, evaluation, presentation, and delivery work steps.

43.20.2.2.3. Assess whether all the Project Template Deliverable Template Deliverable Template Task Templates have been properly allocated sufficient unit effort estimates.

43.20.2.2.4. Assess whether all the Project Template Deliverable Template Deliverable Template Task Templates have been properly allocated sufficient quantity of units that have to be developed.

43.20.2.2.5. Assess whether all the Project Template Deliverable Template Deliverable Template Task Templates have been properly allocated work environment factors to determine an accurate estimate of required resources.

43.20.2.2.6. Assess whether all the Project Template Deliverable Template Deliverable Template Task Templates have been properly allocated work accomplishment and recording functions necessary to support earned value reporting.

43.20.2.2.7. Assess whether all the Project Template Deliverable Template Deliverable Template Task Templates have been properly allocated metadata recording effort to ensure that all interrelationships are properly recorded into the Metabase System database.

43.20.2.3. Assign the risk level associated with each Project Template Deliverable Template Deliverable Template Task Template not properly constructed.

43.20.3. Determine the findings and create draft assessment report.

43.20.4. Present the findings and revise draft assessment report.

43.20.5. Create final assessment report and deliver to the auditing organization.

43.21 Assess Person Skill Level.

43.21.1. Identify artifacts that bear on the assessment.

43.21.1.1. Identify the appropriate set of Person Skill Level documents.

43.21.1.1.1. Review Person Skill Level documents.

43.21.1.1.2. Review scope and business problem related documentation.

43.21.1.1.3. Identify the Person Skill Levels that are defined and captured.

43.21.1.1.4. Identify the Person Skill Levels related work products.

43.21.1.2. For each Person Skill Levels related work product assessment:

43.21.1.2.1. Identify the relevant component.

43.21.1.2.2. Identify the description for each interrelated Person Skill Level component.

43.21.2. Perform the assessment.

43.21.2.1. Assess each Person Skill Level.

43.21.2.1.1. Assess the accuracy, quality and completeness of each Person Skill Level with respect to the business requirements.

43.21.2.1.2. Assess whether Person Skill Levels are able to be inferred from business requirements, and if not whether business requirements or Person Skill Levels need to be enhanced.

43.21.2.1.3. Assess whether each Person Skill Level hierarchy/network is properly specified, and that all X names and descriptions are well defined, non-overlapping, and have been formally approved.

43.21.2.1.3. Assess whether each Person Skill Level pair properly associates one or more Mission-Organization-Function Position Persons with one or more Skill Levels.

43.21.2.1.4. Assess whether each Person Skill Level pair is properly named and described.

43.21.2.2. Assess whether the Person Skill Levels are properly identified and are appropriately engineered to address a Person Skill Level project.

43.21.2.2.1. Assess whether all the Person Skill Levels have been delivered in terms of components, instances, and stored metadata work products.

43.21.2.2.2. Assess whether all the Person Skill Levels have been properly detailed as to content, description, methodology, evaluation, presentation, and delivery work steps.

43.21.2.2.3. Assess whether all the Person Skill Levels have been properly allocated sufficient unit effort estimates.

43.21.2.2.4. Assess whether all the Person Skill Levels have been properly allocated sufficient quantity of units that have to be developed.
43.21.2.2.5. Assess whether all the Person Skill Levels have been properly allocated work environment factors to determine an accurate estimate of required resources.
43.21.2.2.6. Assess whether all the Person Skill Levels have been properly allocated work accomplishment and recording functions necessary to support earned value reporting.
43.21.2.2.7. Assess whether all the Person Skill Levels have been properly allocated metadata recording effort to ensure that all interrelationships are properly recorded into the Metabase System database.
43.21.2.3. Assign the risk level associated with each Person Skill Level not properly constructed.
43.21.3. Determine the findings and create draft assessment report.
43.21.4. Present the findings and revise draft assessment report.
43.21.5. Create final assessment report and deliver to the auditing organization.

43.22 Assess Project Deliverable Person Skill Level.
43.22.1. Identify artifacts that bear on the assessment.
43.22.1.1. Identify the appropriate set of Project Deliverable Person Skill Level documents.
43.22.1.1.1. Review Project Deliverable Person Skill Level documents.
43.22.1.1.2. Review scope and business problem related documentation.
43.22.1.1.3. Identify the Project Deliverable Person Skill Levels that are defined and captured.
43.22.1.1.4. Identify the Project Deliverable Person Skill Levels related work products.
43.22.1.2. For each Project Deliverable Person Skill Levels related work product assessment:
43.22.1.2.1. Identify the relevant component.
43.22.1.2.2. Identify the description for each interrelated Project Deliverable Person Skill Level component.
43.22.2. Perform the assessment.
43.22.2.1. Assess each Project Deliverable Person Skill Level.
43.22.2.1.1. Assess the accuracy, quality and completeness of each Project Deliverable Person Skill Level with respect to the business requirements.
43.22.2.1.2. Assess whether Project Deliverable Person Skill Levels are able to be inferred from business requirements, and if not whether business requirements or Project Deliverable Person Skill Levels need to be enhanced.
43.22.2.1.3. Assess whether each Project Deliverable Person Skill Level pair properly associates one or more Project Deliverables with one or more Person Skill Levels that, in turn, are set within the context of a Role Type.

43.22.2.1.4. Assess whether each Project Deliverable Person Skill Level pair is properly named and described.

43.22.2.2. Assess whether the Project Deliverable Person Skill Levels are properly identified and are appropriately engineered to address a Project Deliverable Person Skill Level project.

43.22.2.2.1. Assess whether all the Project Deliverable Person Skill Levels have been delivered in terms of components, instances, and stored metadata work products.

43.22.2.2.2. Assess whether all the Project Deliverable Person Skill Levels have been properly detailed as to content, description, methodology, evaluation, presentation, and delivery work steps.

43.22.2.2.3. Assess whether all the Project Deliverable Person Skill Levels have been properly allocated sufficient unit effort estimates.

43.22.2.2.4. Assess whether all the Project Deliverable Person Skill Levels have been properly allocated sufficient quantity of units that have to be developed.

43.22.2.2.5. Assess whether all the Project Deliverable Person Skill Levels have been properly allocated work environment factors to determine an accurate estimate of required resources.

43.22.2.2.6. Assess whether all the Project Deliverable Person Skill Levels have been properly allocated work accomplishment and recording functions necessary to support earned value reporting.

43.22.2.2.7. Assess whether all the Project Deliverable Person Skill Levels have been properly allocated metadata recording effort to ensure that all interrelationships are properly recorded into the Metabase System database.

43.22.2.3. Assign the risk level associated with each Project Deliverable Person Skill Level not properly constructed.

43.22.3. Determine the findings and create draft assessment report.

43.22.4. Present the findings and revise draft assessment report.

43.22.5. Create final assessment report and deliver to the auditing organization.

43.23. Assess Work.

43.23.1. Identify artifacts that bear on the assessment.

43.23.1.1. Identify the appropriate set of Work documents.

43.23.1.1.1. Review Work documents.

43.23.1.1.2. Review scope and business problem related documentation.

43.23.1.1.3. Identify the Work records that are defined and captured.

43.23.1.1.4. Identify the Work records related work products.

43.23.1.2. For each Work records related work product assessment:

43.23.1.2.1. Identify the relevant component.

43.23.1.2.2. Identify the description for each interrelated Work record component.

43.23.2. Perform the assessment.

43.23.2.1. Assess each Work record.

43.23.2.1.1. Assess the accuracy, quality and completeness of each Work record with respect to the business requirements.

43.23.2.1.2. Assess whether Work record are able to be inferred from business requirements, and if not whether business requirements or Work records need to be enhanced.

43.23.2.3. Assess whether the Work records are properly identified and are appropriately engineered to address a Work project.

43.23.2.3.1. Assess whether all the Work records have been delivered in terms of components, instances, and stored metadata work record products.

43.23.2.3.2. Assess whether all the Work records have been properly detailed as to content, description, methodology, evaluation, presentation, and delivery work steps.

43.23.2.3.3. Assess whether all the Work records have been properly allocated sufficient unit effort estimates.

43.23.2.3.4. Assess whether all the Work records have been properly allocated sufficient quantity of units that have to be developed.

43.23.2.3.5. Assess whether all the Work records have been properly allocated work environment factors to determine an accurate estimate of required resources.

43.23.2.3.6. Assess whether all the Work records have been properly allocated work accomplishment and recording functions necessary to support earned value reporting.

43.23.2.3.7. Assess whether all the Work records have been properly allocated metadata recording effort to ensure that all interrelationships are properly recorded into the Metabase System database.

43.23.2.4. Assign the risk level associated with each Work record not properly constructed.

43.23.3. Determine the findings and create draft assessment report.

43.23.4. Present the findings and revise draft assessment report.

43.23.5. Create final assessment report and deliver to the auditing organization.

44.. Reports

44.1. Assess Report.
44.1.1. Identify artifacts that bear on the assessment.
44.1.1.1. Identify the appropriate set of Report documents.
44.1.1.1.1. Review Report documents.
44.1.1.1.2. Review scope and business problem related documentation.
44.1.1.1.3. Identify the Reports that are defined and captured.
44.1.1.1.4. Identify the Reports related work products.
44.1.1.2. For each Reports related work product assessment:
44.1.1.2.1. Identify the relevant component.
44.1.1.2.2. Identify the description for each interrelated Report component.
44.1.2. Perform the assessment.
44.1.2.1. Assess each Report.
44.1.2.1.1. Assess the accuracy, quality and completeness of each Report with respect to the business requirements.
44.1.2.1.2. Assess whether Reports are able to be inferred from business requirements, and if not whether business requirements or Reports need to be enhanced.
44.1.2.2. Assess whether the Reports are properly identified and are appropriately engineered to address a Report project.
44.1.2.2.1. Assess whether all the Reports have been delivered in terms of components, instances, and stored metadata work products.
44.1.2.2.2. Assess whether all the Reports have been properly detailed as to content, description, methodology, evaluation, presentation, and delivery work steps.
44.1.2.2.3. Assess whether all the Reports have been properly allocated sufficient unit effort estimates.
44.1.2.2.4. Assess whether all the Reports have been properly allocated sufficient quantity of units that have to be developed.
44.1.2.2.5. Assess whether all the Reports have been properly allocated work environment factors to determine an accurate estimate of required resources.
44.1.2.2.6. Assess whether all the Reports have been properly allocated work accomplishment and recording functions necessary to support earned value reporting.
44.1.2.2.7. Assess whether all the Reports have been properly allocated metadata recording effort to ensure that all interrelationships are properly recorded into the Metabase System database.
44.1.2.3. Assign the risk level associated with each Report not properly constructed.
44.1.3. Determine the findings and create draft assessment report.

44.1.4. Present the findings and revise draft assessment report.
44.1.5. Create final assessment report and deliver to the auditing organization.

44.2. Assess Report Structure.
44.2.1. Identify artifacts that bear on the assessment.
44.2.1.1. Identify the appropriate set of Report Structure documents.
44.2.1.1.1. Review Report Structure documents.
44.2.1.1.2. Review scope and business problem related documentation.
44.2.1.1.3. Identify the Reports that are defined and captured.
44.2.1.1.4. Identify the Reports related work products.
44.2.1.2. For each Reports related work product assessment:
44.2.1.2.1. Identify the relevant component.
44.2.1.2.2. Identify the description for each interrelated Report component.
44.2.2. Perform the assessment.
44.2.2.1. Assess each Report Structure.
44.2.2.1.1. Assess the accuracy, quality and completeness of each Report Structure with respect to the business requirements.
44.2.2.1.2. Assess whether Report Structures are able to be inferred from business requirements, and if not whether business requirements or Report Structures need to be enhanced.
44.2.2.1.3. Assess whether each Report Structure hierarchy/network is properly specified, and that all Report Structure names and descriptions are well defined, non-overlapping, and have been formally approved.
44.2.2.2. Assess whether the Report Structures are properly identified and are appropriately engineered to address a Report Structure project.
44.2.2.2.1. Assess whether all the Report Structures have been delivered in terms of components, instances, and stored metadata work products.
44.2.2.2.2. Assess whether all the Report Structures have been properly detailed as to content, description, methodology, evaluation, presentation, and delivery work steps.
44.2.2.2.3. Assess whether all the Report Structures have been properly allocated sufficient unit effort estimates.
44.2.2.2.4. Assess whether all the Report Structures have been properly allocated sufficient quantity of units that have to be developed.
44.2.2.2.5. Assess whether all the Report Structures have been properly allocated work environment factors to determine an accurate estimate of required resources.
44.2.2.2.6. Assess whether all the Report Structures have been properly allocated work accomplishment and recording functions necessary to support earned value reporting.
44.2.2.2.7. Assess whether all the Report Structures have been properly allocated metadata recording effort to ensure that all interrelationships are properly

recorded into the Metabase System database.

44.2.2.3. Assign the risk level associated with each Report Structure not properly constructed.

44.2.3. Determine the findings and create draft assessment report.

44.2.4. Present the findings and revise draft assessment report.

44.2.5. Create final assessment report and deliver to the auditing organization.

44.3. Assess Report Business Information System.

44.3.1. Identify artifacts that bear on the assessment.

44.3.1.1. Identify the appropriate set of Report Business Information System documents.

44.3.1.1.1. Review Report Business Information System documents.

44.3.1.1.2. Review scope and business problem related documentation.

44.3.1.1.3. Identify the Report Business Information Systems that are defined and captured.

44.3.1.1.4. Identify the Report Business Information Systems related work products.

44.3.1.2. For each Report Business Information Systems related work product assessment:

44.3.1.2.1. Identify the relevant component.

44.3.1.2.2. Identify the description for each interrelated Report Business Information System component.

44.3.2. Perform the assessment.

44.3.2.1. Assess each Report Business Information System.

44.3.2.1.1. Assess the accuracy, quality and completeness of each Report Business Information System with respect to the business requirements.

44.3.2.1.2. Assess whether Report Business Information Systems are able to be inferred from business requirements, and if not whether business requirements or Report Business Information System need to be enhanced.

44.3.2.1.3. Assess whether each Report Business Information System pair properly associates one or more Reports with one or more Business Information Systems.

44.3.2.1.4. Assess whether each Report Business Information System pair is properly named and described.

44.3.2.2. Assess whether the Report Business Information Systems are properly identified and are appropriately engineered to address a Report Business Information System project.

44.3.2.2.1. Assess whether all the Report Business Information Systems have been delivered in terms of components, instances, and stored metadata work products.

44.3.2.2.2. Assess whether all the Report Business Information Systems have been properly detailed as to content, description, methodology, evaluation,

presentation, and delivery work steps.

44.3.2.2.3. Assess whether all the Report Business Information Systems have been properly allocated sufficient unit effort estimates.

44.3.2.2.4. Assess whether all the Report Business Information Systems have been properly allocated sufficient quantity of units that have to be developed.

44.3.2.2.5. Assess whether all the Report Business Information Systems have been properly allocated work environment factors to determine an accurate estimate of required resources.

44.3.2.2.6. Assess whether all the Report Business Information Systems have been properly allocated work accomplishment and recording functions necessary to support earned value reporting.

44.3.2.2.7. Assess whether all the Report Business Information Systems have been properly allocated metadata recording effort to ensure that all interrelationships are properly recorded into the Metabase System database.

44.3.2.3. Assign the risk level associated with each Report Business Information System not properly constructed.

44.3.3. Determine the findings and create draft assessment report.

44.3.4. Present the findings and revise draft assessment report.

44.3.5. Create final assessment report and deliver to the auditing organization.

44.4. Assess Report Mission Organization Function.

44.41. Identify artifacts that bear on the assessment.

44.41.1. Identify the appropriate set of Report Mission-Organization-Function documents.

44.41.1.1. Review Report Mission-Organization-Function documents.

44.41.1.2. Review scope and business problem related documentation.

44.41.1.3. Identify the Report Mission-Organization-Functions that are defined and captured.

44.41.1.4. Identify the Report Mission-Organization-Functions related work products.

44.41.2. For each Report Mission-Organization-Functions related work product assessment:

44.41.2.1. Identify the relevant component.

44.41.2.2. Identify the description for each interrelated Report Mission-Organization-Function component.

44.42. Perform the assessment.

44.42.1. Assess each Report Mission-Organization-Function.

44.42.1.1. Assess the accuracy, quality and completeness of each Report Mission-Organization-Function with respect to the business requirements.

44.42.1.2. Assess whether Report Mission-Organization-Functions are able to be inferred from business requirements, and if not whether business requirements or Report Mission-Organization-Functions need to be enhanced.

44.42.1.3. Assess whether each Report Mission-Organization-Function pair properly associates one or more Reports with one or more Mission-Organization-Functions.

44.42.1.4. Assess whether each Report Mission-Organization-Function pair is properly named and described.

44.42.2. Assess whether the Report Mission-Organization-Functions are properly identified and are appropriately engineered to address a Report Mission-Organization-Function project.

44.42.2.1. Assess whether all the Report Mission-Organization-Functions have been delivered in terms of components, instances, and stored metadata work products.

44.42.2.2. Assess whether all the Report Mission-Organization-Functions have been properly detailed as to content, description, methodology, evaluation, presentation, and delivery work steps.

44.42.2.3. Assess whether all the Report Mission-Organization-Functions have been properly allocated sufficient unit effort estimates.

44.42.2.4. Assess whether all the Report Mission-Organization-Functions have been properly allocated sufficient quantity of units that have to be developed.

44.42.2.5. Assess whether all the Report Mission-Organization-Functions have been properly allocated work environment factors to determine an accurate estimate of required resources.

44.42.2.6. Assess whether all the Report Mission-Organization-Functions have been properly allocated work accomplishment and recording functions necessary to support earned value reporting.

44.42.2.7. Assess whether all the Report Mission-Organization-Functions have been properly allocated metadata recording effort to ensure that all interrelationships are properly recorded into the Metabase System database.

44.42.3. Assign the risk level associated with each Report Mission-Organization-Function not properly constructed.

44.43. Determine the findings and create draft assessment report.

44.44. Present the findings and revise draft assessment report.

44.45. Create final assessment report and deliver to the auditing organization.

44.5. Assess Report Section.

44.5.1. Identify artifacts that bear on the assessment.

44.5.1.1. Identify the appropriate set of Report Section documents.

44.5.1.1.1. Review Report Section documents.

44.5.1.1.2. Review scope and business problem related documentation.

44.5.1.1.3. Identify the Report Sections that are defined and captured.

44.5.1.1.4. Identify the Report Sections related work products.
44.5.1.2. For each Report Sections related work product assessment:
44.5.1.2.1. Identify the relevant component.
44.5.1.2.2. Identify the description for each interrelated Report Section component.
44.5.2. Perform the assessment.
44.5.2.1. Assess each Report Section.
44.5.2.1.1. Assess the accuracy, quality and completeness of each Report Section with respect to the business requirements.
44.5.2.1.2. Assess whether Report Sections are able to be inferred from business requirements, and if not whether business requirements or Report Sections need to be enhanced.
44.5.2.1.3. Assess whether each Report Section hierarchy is properly specified, and that all Report Section names and descriptions are well defined, non-overlapping, and have been formally approved.
44.5.2.1.4. Assess whether each Report Sections is properly associated with its parent Report.
44.5.2.1.5. Assess the Report Section name description, headers, footers, control breaks and all calculated Report Section components that defines the Report Section to ensure that the data produced accurately reflects the headings.
44.5.2.2. Assess whether the Report Sections are properly identified and are appropriately engineered to address a Report Section project.
44.5.2.2.1. Assess whether all the Report Sections have been delivered in terms of components, instances, and stored metadata work products.
44.5.2.2.2. Assess whether all the Report Sections have been properly detailed as to content, description, methodology, evaluation, presentation, and delivery work steps.
44.5.2.2.3. Assess whether all the Report Sections have been properly allocated sufficient unit effort estimates.
44.5.2.2.4. Assess whether all the Report Sections have been properly allocated sufficient quantity of units that have to be developed.
44.5.2.2.5. Assess whether all the Report Sections have been properly allocated work environment factors to determine an accurate estimate of required resources.
44.5.2.2.6. Assess whether all the Report Sections have been properly allocated work accomplishment and recording functions necessary to support earned value Report Sectioning.
44.5.2.2.7. Assess whether all the Report Sections have been properly allocated metadata recording effort to ensure that all interrelationships are properly recorded into the Metabase System database.
44.5.2.3. Assign the risk level associated with each Report Section not properly constructed.

44.5.3. Determine the findings and create draft assessment Report Section.
44.5.4. Present the findings and revise draft assessment Report Section.
44.5.5. Create final assessment report Section and deliver to the auditing organization.

44.6. Assess Report Section Cell.
1. Identify artifacts that bear on the assessment.
44.6.1.1. Identify the appropriate set of Report Section Cell documents.
44.6.1.1.1. Review Report Section Cell documents.
44.6.1.1.2. Review scope and business problem related documentation.
44.6.1.1.3. Identify the Report Section Cells that are defined and captured.
44.6.1.1.4. Identify the Report Section Cells related work products.
44.6.1.2. For each Report Section Cells related work product assessment:
44.6.1.2.1. Identify the relevant component.
44.6.1.2.2. Identify the description for each interrelated Report Section Cell component.
44.6.2. Perform the assessment.
44.6.2.1. Assess each Report Section Cell.
44.6.2.1.1. Assess the accuracy, quality and completeness of each Report Section Cell with respect to the business requirements.
44.6.2.1.2. Assess whether Report Section Cells are able to be inferred from business requirements, and if not whether business requirements or Report Section Cells need to be enhanced.
44.6.2.1.3. Assess that the Report Section Cell elements are utilizing the proper data types, editing value domain restrictions and validation checks.
44.6.2.1.4. Assess that the outward data conversions for Report Section Cell elements are correctly specified and are programmed correctly.
44.6.2.1.5. Assess the Report Section Cell name, description, headers, footers, control breaks and all calculated Report Section Cell elements that defines the Report Section Cell to ensure that the data produced accurately reflects the headings.
44.6.2.2. Assess whether the Report Section Cells are properly identified and are appropriately engineered to address a Report Section Cell project.
44.6.2.2.1. Assess whether all the Report Section Cells have been delivered in terms of components, instances, and stored metadata products.
44.6.2.2.2. Assess whether all the Report Section Cells have been properly detailed as to content, description, methodology, evaluation, and presentation.
44.6.2.2.3. Assess whether all the Report Section Cells have been properly allocated sufficient unit effort estimates.
44.6.2.2.4. Assess whether all the Report Section Cells have been properly allocated sufficient quantity of units that have to be developed.
44.6.2.2.5. Assess whether all the Report Section Cells have been properly allocated

work environment factors to determine an accurate estimate of required resources.

44.6.2.2.6. Assess whether all the Report Section Cells have been properly allocated work accomplishment and recording functions necessary to support earned value Report Section Cells.

44.6.2.2.7. Assess whether all the Report Section Cells have been properly allocated metadata recording effort to ensure that all interrelationships are properly recorded into the Metabase System database.

44.6.2.3. Assign the risk level associated with each Report Section Cell not properly constructed.

44.6.3. Determine the findings and create draft assessment Report Section Cell.

44.6.4. Present the findings and revise draft assessment Report Section Cell.

44.6.5. Create final assessment report Section Cell and deliver to the auditing organization.

44.7. Assess Report Section Cell View Column.

44.7.1. Identify artifacts that bear on the assessment.

44.7.1.1. Identify the appropriate set of Report Section Cell documents.

44.7.1.1.1. Review Report Section Cell documents.

44.7.1.1.2. Review scope and business problem related documentation.

44.7.1.1.3. Identify the Report Section Cell View Columns that are defined and captured.

44.7.1.1.4. Identify the Report Section Cell View Columns related work products.

44.7.1.2. For each Report Section Cell View Columns related work product assessment:

44.7.1.2.1. Identify the relevant component.

44.7.1.2.2. Identify the description for each interrelated Report Section Cell View Column component.

44.7.2. Perform the assessment.

44.7.2.1. Assess each Report Section Cell View Column.

44.7.2.1.1. Assess the accuracy, quality and completeness of each Report Section Cell View Column with respect to the business requirements.

44.7.2.1.2. Assess whether Report Section Cell View Column are able to be inferred from business requirements, and if not whether business requirements or Report Section Cell View Column need to be enhanced.

44.7.2.1.3. Assess whether each Report Section Cell View Column pair properly associates one or more Report Section Cells with one or more View Columns.

44.7.2.1.4. Assess whether each Report Section Cell View Column pair is properly named and described.

44.7.2.2. Assess whether the Report Section Cell View Columns are properly identified and are appropriately engineered to address a Report Section

Cell View Column project.

44.7.2.2.1. Assess whether all the Report Section Cell View Columns have been delivered in terms of components, instances, and stored metadata products.

44.7.2.2.2. Assess whether all the Report Section Cell View Columns have been properly detailed as to content, description, methodology, evaluation, and presentation.

44.7.2.2.3. Assess whether all the Report Section Cell View Columns have been properly allocated sufficient unit effort estimates.

44.7.2.2.4. Assess whether all the Report Section Cell View Columns have been properly allocated sufficient quantity of units that have to be developed.

44.7.2.2.5. Assess whether all the Report Section Cell View Columns have been properly allocated work environment factors to determine an accurate estimate of required resources.

44.7.2.2.6. Assess whether all the Report Section Cell View Columns have been properly allocated work accomplishment and recording functions necessary to support earned value Report Section Cell View Columns.

44.7.2.2.7. Assess whether all the Report Section Cell View Columns have been properly allocated metadata recording effort to ensure that all interrelationships are properly recorded into the Metabase System database.

44.7.2.3. Assign the risk level associated with each Report Section Cell View Column not properly constructed.

44.7.3. Determine the findings and create draft assessment Report Section Cell View Column.

44.7.4. Present the findings and revise draft assessment Report Section Cell View Column.

44.7.5. Create final assessment report Section Cell View Column and deliver to the auditing organization.

45. Requirements

45.1. Assess Requirement.
45.5.1. Identify artifacts that bear on the assessment.
45.5.1.1. Identify the appropriate set of Requirement documents.
45.5.1.1.1. Review Requirement documents.
45.5.1.1.2. Review scope and business problem related documentation.
45.5.1.1.3. Identify the Requirements that are defined and captured.
45.5.1.1.4. Identify the Requirements related work products.
45.5.1.2. For each Requirements related work product assessment:
45.5.1.2.1. Identify the relevant component.
45.5.1.2.2. Identify the description for each interrelated Requirement component.
45.5.2. Perform the assessment.
45.5.2.1. Assess each Requirement.
45.5.2.1.1. Assess the accuracy, quality and completeness of each Requirement with respect to the business requirements.
45.5.2.1.2. Assess whether Requirements are able to be inferred from business requirements, and if not whether business requirements or Requirements need to be enhanced.
45.5.2.2. Assess whether the Requirements are properly identified and are appropriately engineered to address a Requirement project.
45.5.2.2.1. Assess whether all the Requirements have been delivered in terms of components, instances, and stored metadata work products.
45.5.2.2.2. Assess whether all the Requirements have been properly detailed as to content, description, methodology, evaluation, presentation, and delivery work steps.
45.5.2.2.3. Assess whether all the Requirements have been properly allocated sufficient unit effort estimates.
45.5.2.2.4. Assess whether all the Requirements have been properly allocated sufficient quantity of units that have to be developed.
45.5.2.2.5. Assess whether all the Requirements have been properly allocated work environment factors to determine an accurate estimate of required resources.
45.5.2.3.6. Assess whether all the Requirements have been properly allocated work accomplishment and recording functions necessary to support earned value reporting.
45.5.2.2.7. Assess whether all the Requirements have been properly allocated metadata recording effort to ensure that all interrelationships are properly recorded into the Metabase System database.
45.5.2.3. Assign the risk level associated with each Requirement not properly constructed.
45.5.3. Determine the findings and create draft assessment report.

45.5.4. Present the findings and revise draft assessment report.
45.5.5. Create final assessment report and deliver to the auditing organization.

45.2. Assess Requirement Category
45.2.1. Identify artifacts that bear on the assessment.
45.2.1.1. Identify the appropriate set of Requirement Category documents.
45.2.1.1.1. Review Requirement Category documents.
45.2.1.1.2. Review scope and business problem related documentation.
45.2.1.1.3. Identify the Requirement Categories that are defined and captured.
45.2.1.1.4. Identify the Requirements Category related work products.
45.2.1.2. For each Requirements Category related work product assessment:
45.2.1.2.1. Identify the relevant component.
45.2.1.2.2. Identify the description for each interrelated Requirement Category component.
45.2.2. Perform the assessment.
45.2.2.1. Assess each Requirement Category.
45.2.2.1.1. Assess the accuracy, quality and completeness of each Requirement Category with respect to the business requirements.
45.2.2.1.2. Assess whether Requirement Categories are able to be inferred from business requirements, and if not whether business requirements or Requirement need to be enhanced.
45.2.2.1.3. Assess whether each Requirement Categories hierarchy is properly specified, and that all Requirement names and descriptions are well defined, non-overlapping, and have been formally approved.
45.2.2.2. Assess whether the Requirement Categories are properly identified and are appropriately engineered to address a Requirement Category project.
45.2.2.2.1. Assess whether all the Requirement Categories have been delivered in terms of components, instances, and stored metadata work products.
45.2.2.2.2. Assess whether all the Requirement Categories have been properly detailed as to content, description, methodology, evaluation, presentation, and delivery work steps.
45.2.2.3.3. Assess whether all the Requirement Categories have been properly allocated sufficient unit effort estimates.
45.2.2.2.4. Assess whether all the Requirement Categories have been properly allocated sufficient quantity of units that have to be developed.
45.2.2.3.5. Assess whether all the Requirement Categories have been properly allocated work environment factors to determine an accurate estimate of required resources.
45.2.2.2.6. Assess whether all the Requirement Categories have been properly allocated work accomplishment and recording functions necessary to support earned value reporting.
45.2.2.2.7. Assess whether all the Requirement Categories have been properly

allocated metadata recording effort to ensure that all interrelationships are properly recorded into the Metabase System database.

45.2.2.3. Assign the risk level associated with each Requirement Category not properly constructed.

45.2.3. Determine the findings and create draft assessment report.

45.2.4. Present the findings and revise draft assessment report.

45.2.5. Create final assessment report and deliver to the auditing organization.

45.3. Assess Requirement Structure.

45.3.1. Identify artifacts that bear on the assessment.

45.3.1.1. Identify the appropriate set of Requirement Structure documents.

45.3.1.1.1. Review Requirement Structure documents.

45.3.1.1.2. Review scope and business problem related documentation.

45.3.1.1.3. Identify the Requirement Structures that are defined and captured.

45.3.1.1.4. Identify the Requirement Structure related work products.

45.3.1.2. For each Requirements related work product assessment:

45.3.1.2.1. Identify the relevant component.

45.3.1.2.2. Identify the description for each interrelated Requirement Structure component.

45.3.2. Perform the assessment.

45.3.2.1. Assess each Requirement Structure.

45.3.2.1.1. Assess the accuracy, quality and completeness of each Requirement Structure with respect to the business requirements.

45.3.2.1.2. Assess whether Requirement Structures are able to be inferred from business requirements, and if not whether business requirements or Requirement Structures need to be enhanced.

45.3.2.1.3. Assess whether each Requirement Structures hierarchy/network is properly specified, and that all Requirement Structure names and descriptions are well defined, non-overlapping, and have been formally approved.

45.3.2.2. Assess whether the Requirement Structures are properly identified and are appropriately engineered to address a Requirement Structure project.

45.3.2.2.1. Assess whether all the Requirement Structures have been delivered in terms of components, instances, and stored metadata work products.

45.3.2.2.2. Assess whether all the Requirement Structures have been properly detailed as to content, description, methodology, evaluation, presentation, and delivery work steps.

45.3.2.2.3. Assess whether all the Requirement Structures have been properly allocated sufficient unit effort estimates.

45.3.2.2.4. Assess whether all the Requirement Structures have been properly allocated sufficient quantity of units that have to be developed.

45.3.2.2.5. Assess whether all the Requirement Structures have been properly allocated work environment factors to determine an accurate estimate of required resources.

45.3.2.2.6. Assess whether all the Requirement Structures have been properly allocated work accomplishment and recording functions necessary to support earned value reporting.

45.3.2.2.7. Assess whether all the Requirement Structures have been properly allocated metadata recording effort to ensure that all interrelationships are properly recorded into the Metabase System database.

45.3.2.3. Assign the risk level associated with each Requirement Structure not properly constructed.

45.3.3. Determine the findings and create draft assessment report.

45.3.4. Present the findings and revise draft assessment report.

45.3.5. Create final assessment report and deliver to the auditing organization.

45.4. Assess Requirement Structure Business Event.

45.4.1. Identify artifacts that bear on the assessment.

45.4.1.1. Identify the appropriate set of Requirement Structure Business Event documents.

45.4.1.1.1. Review Requirement Structure Business Event documents.

45.4.1.1.2. Review scope and business problem related documentation.

45.4.1.1.3. Identify the Requirement Structure Business Events that are defined and captured.

45.4.1.1.4. Identify the Requirement Structure Business Events related work products.

45.4.1.2. For each Requirement Structure Business Events related work product assessment:

45.4.1.2.1. Identify the relevant component.

45.4.1.2.2. Identify the description for each interrelated Requirement Structure Business Event component.

45.4.2. Perform the assessment.

45.4.2.1. Assess each Requirement Structure Business Event.

45.4.2.1.1. Assess the accuracy, quality and completeness of each Requirement Structure Business Event with respect to the business requirements.

45.4.2.1.2. Assess whether Requirement Structure Business Events are able to be inferred from business requirements, and if not whether business requirements or Requirement Structure Business Events need to be enhanced.

45.4.2.1.3. Assess whether each Requirement Structure Business Events pair properly associates one or more Requirement Structures with one or more Business Events.

45.4.2.1.4. Assess whether each Requirement Structure Business Event pair is properly named and described.

45.4.2.2. Assess whether the Requirement Structure Business Events are properly identified and are appropriately engineered to address a Requirement Structure Business Event project.

45.4.2.2.1. Assess whether all the Requirement Structure Business Events have been delivered in terms of components, instances, and stored metadata work products.

45.4.2.2.2. Assess whether all the Requirement Structure Business Events have been properly detailed as to content, description, methodology, evaluation, presentation, and delivery work steps.

45.4.2.2.3. Assess whether all the Requirement Structure Business Events have been properly allocated sufficient unit effort estimates.

45.4.2.3.4. Assess whether all the Requirement Structure Business Events have been properly allocated sufficient quantity of units that have to be developed.

45.4.2.2.5. Assess whether all the Requirement Structure Business Events have been properly allocated work environment factors to determine an accurate estimate of required resources.

45.4.2.2.6. Assess whether all the Requirement Structure Business Events have been properly allocated work accomplishment and recording functions necessary to support earned value reporting.

45.4.2.2.7. Assess whether all the Requirement Structure Business Events have been properly allocated metadata recording effort to ensure that all interrelationships are properly recorded into the Metabase System database.

45.4.2.3. Assign the risk level associated with each Requirement Structure Business Event not properly constructed.

45.4.3. Determine the findings and create draft assessment report.

45.4.4. Present the findings and revise draft assessment report.

45.4.5. Create final assessment report and deliver to the auditing organization.

45.5. Assess Requirement Structure Business Information System.

45.5.1. Identify artifacts that bear on the assessment.

45.5.1.1. Identify the appropriate set of Requirement Business Information System documents.

45.5.1.1.1. Review Requirement Business Information System documents.

45.5.1.1.2. Review scope and business problem related documentation.

45.5.1.1.3. Identify the Requirement Structure Business Information Systems that are defined and captured.

45.5.1.1.4. Identify the Requirement Structure Business Information Systems related work products.

45.5.1.2. For each Requirement Structure Business Information Systems related work product assessment:

45.5.1.2.1. Identify the relevant component.

45.5.1.2.2. Identify the description for each interrelated Requirement Structure Business Information System component.

45.5.2. Perform the assessment.

45.5.2.1. Assess each Requirement Structure Business Information System.

45.5.2.1.1. Assess the accuracy, quality and completeness of each Requirement Structure Business Information System with respect to the business requirements.

45.5.2.1.2. Assess whether Requirement Structure Business Information Systems are able to be inferred from business requirements, and if not whether business requirements or Requirement Structure Business Information Systems need to be enhanced.

45.5.2.1.3. Assess whether each Requirement Structure Business Information Systems pair properly associates one or more Requirement Structures with one or more Business Information Systems.

45.5.2.1.4. Assess whether each Requirement Structure Business Information System pair is properly named and described.

45.5.2.2. Assess whether the Requirement Business Information Systems are properly identified and are appropriately engineered to address a Requirement Business Information System project.

45.5.2.2.1. Assess whether all the Requirement Business Information Systems have been delivered in terms of components, instances, and stored metadata work products.

45.5.2.2.2. Assess whether all the Requirement Business Information Systems have been properly detailed as to content, description, methodology, evaluation, presentation, and delivery work steps.

45.5.2.2.3. Assess whether all the Requirement Business Information Systems have been properly allocated sufficient unit effort estimates.

45.5.2.2.4. Assess whether all the Requirement Business Information Systems have been properly allocated sufficient quantity of units that have to be developed.

45.5.2.2.5. Assess whether all the Requirement Business Information Systems have been properly allocated work environment factors to determine an accurate estimate of required resources.

45.5.2.2.6. Assess whether all the Requirement Business Information Systems have been properly allocated work accomplishment and recording functions necessary to support earned value reporting.

45.5.2.2.7. Assess whether all the Requirement Business Information Systems have been properly allocated metadata recording effort to ensure that all interrelationships are properly recorded into the Metabase System database.

45.5.2.3. Assign the risk level associated with each Requirement Business Information System not properly constructed.

45.5.3. Determine the findings and create draft assessment report.
45.5.4. Present the findings and revise draft assessment report.
45.5.5. Create final assessment report and deliver to the auditing organization.

45.6. Assess Requirement Structure Data Element.
45.6.1. Identify artifacts that bear on the assessment.
45.6.1.1. Identify the appropriate set of Requirement Structure Data Element documents.
45.6.1.1.1. Review Requirement Structure Data Element documents.
45.6.1.1.2. Review scope and business problem related documentation.
45.6.1.1.3. Identify the Requirement Structure Data Elements that are defined and captured.
45.6.1.1.4. Identify the Requirement Structure Data Elements related work products.
45.6.1.2. For each Requirement Structure Data Elements related work product assessment:
45.6.1.2.1. Identify the relevant component.
45.6.1.2.2. Identify the description for each interrelated Requirement Structure Data Element component.
45.6.2. Perform the assessment.
45.6.2.1. Assess each Requirement Structure Data Element.
45.6.2.1.1. Assess the accuracy, quality and completeness of each Requirement Structure Data Element with respect to the business requirements.
45.6.2.1.2. Assess whether Requirement Structure Data Elements are able to be inferred from business requirements, and if not whether business requirements or Requirement Structure Data Elements need to be enhanced.
45.6.2.1.3. Assess whether each Requirement Structure Data Elements pair properly associates one or more Requirement Structures with one or more Data Elements.
45.6.2.1.4. Assess whether each Requirement Structure Data Element pair is properly named and described.
45.6.2.3. Assess whether the Requirement Structure Data Elements are properly identified and are appropriately engineered to address a Requirement Structure Data Element project.
45.6.2.3.1. Assess whether all the Requirement Structure Data Elements have been delivered in terms of components, instances, and stored metadata work products.
45.6.2.3.2. Assess whether all the Requirement Structure Data Elements have been properly detailed as to content, description, methodology, evaluation, presentation, and delivery work steps.
45.6.2.3.3. Assess whether all the Requirement Structure Data Elements have been properly allocated sufficient unit effort estimates.

45.6.2.3.4. Assess whether all the Requirement Structure Data Elements have been properly allocated sufficient quantity of units that have to be developed.
45.6.2.3.5. Assess whether all the Requirement Structure Data Elements have been properly allocated work environment factors to determine an accurate estimate of required resources.
45.6.2.3.6. Assess whether all the Requirement Structure Data Elements have been properly allocated work accomplishment and recording functions necessary to support earned value reporting.
45.6.2.3.7. Assess whether all the Requirement Structure Data Elements have been properly allocated metadata recording effort to ensure that all interrelationships are properly recorded into the Metabase System database.
45.6.2.4. Assign the risk level associated with each Requirement Structure Data Element not properly constructed.
45.6.3. Determine the findings and create draft assessment report.
45.6.4. Present the findings and revise draft assessment report.
45.6.5. Create final assessment report and deliver to the auditing organization.

45.7. Assess Requirement Structure Database Object.
45.7.1. Identify artifacts that bear on the assessment.
45.7.1.1. Identify the appropriate set of Requirement Structure Database Object documents.
45.7.1.1.1. Review Requirement Structure Database Object documents.
45.7.1.1.2. Review scope and business problem related documentation.
45.7.1.1.3. Identify the Requirement Structure Database Objects that are defined and captured.
45.7.1.1.4. Identify the Requirement Structure Database Objects related work products.
45.7.1.2. For each Requirement Structure Database Objects related work product assessment:
45.7.1.2.1. Identify the relevant component.
45.7.1.2.2. Identify the description for each interrelated Requirement Structure Database Object component.
45.7.2. Perform the assessment.
45.7.2.1. Assess each Requirement Structure Database Object.
45.7.2.1.1. Assess the accuracy, quality and completeness of each Requirement Structure Database Object with respect to the business requirements.
45.7.2.1.2. Assess whether Requirement Structure Database Objects are able to be inferred from business requirements, and if not whether business requirements or Requirement Structure Database Objects need to be enhanced.
45.7.2.1.3. Assess whether each Requirement Structure Database Objects pair

properly associates one or more Requirement Structures with one or more Database Objects.

45.7.2.1.4. Assess whether each Requirement Structure Database Object pair is properly named and described.

45.7.2.3. Assess whether the Requirement Structure Database Objects are properly identified and are appropriately engineered to address a Requirement Structure Database Object project.

45.7.2.3.1. Assess whether all the Requirement Structure Database Objects have been delivered in terms of components, instances, and stored metadata work products.

45.7.2.3.2. Assess whether all the Requirement Structure Database Objects have been properly detailed as to content, description, methodology, evaluation, presentation, and delivery work steps.

45.7.2.3.3. Assess whether all the Requirement Structure Database Objects have been properly allocated sufficient unit effort estimates.

45.7.2.3.4. Assess whether all the Requirement Structure Database Objects have been properly allocated sufficient quantity of units that have to be developed.

45.7.2.3.5. Assess whether all the Requirement Structure Database Objects have been properly allocated work environment factors to determine an accurate estimate of required resources.

45.7.2.3.6. Assess whether all the Requirement Structure Database Objects have been properly allocated work accomplishment and recording functions necessary to support earned value reporting.

45.7.2.3.7. Assess whether all the Requirement Structure Database Objects have been properly allocated metadata recording effort to ensure that all interrelationships are properly recorded into the Metabase System database.

45.7.2.4. Assign the risk level associated with each Requirement Structure Database Object not properly constructed.

45.7.3. Determine the findings and create draft assessment report.

45.7.4. Present the findings and revise draft assessment report.

45.7.5. Create final assessment report and deliver to the auditing organization.

45.8. Assess Requirement Structure Data Integrity Rule.

45.8.1. Identify artifacts that bear on the assessment.

45.8.1.1. Identify the appropriate set of Requirement Structure Data Integrity Rule documents.

45.8.1.1.1. Review Requirement Structure Data Integrity Rule documents.

45.8.1.1.2. Review scope and business problem related documentation.

45.8.1.1.3. Identify the Requirement Structure Data Integrity Rules that are defined and captured.

45.8.1.1.4. Identify the Requirement Structure Data Integrity Rules related work

products.

45.8.1.2. For each Requirement Structure Data Integrity Rules related work product assessment:

45.8.1.2.1. Identify the relevant component.

45.8.1.2.2. Identify the description for each interrelated Requirement Structure Data Integrity Rule component.

45.8.2. Perform the assessment.

45.8.2.1. Assess each Requirement Structure Data Integrity Rule.

45.8.2.1.1. Assess the accuracy, quality and completeness of each Requirement Structure Data Integrity Rule with respect to the business requirements.

45.8.2.1.2. Assess whether Requirement Structure Data Integrity Rules are able to be inferred from business requirements, and if not whether business requirements or Requirement Structure Data Integrity Rules need to be enhanced.

45.8.2.1.3. Assess whether each Requirement Structure Data Integrity Rule pair properly associates one or more Requirement Structures with one or more Data Integrity Rules.

45.8.2.1.4. Assess whether each Requirement Structure Data Integrity Rule pair is properly named and described.

45.8.2.3. Assess whether the Requirement Structure Data Integrity Rules are properly identified and are appropriately engineered to address a Requirement Structure Data Integrity Rule project.

45.8.2.3.1. Assess whether all the Requirement Structure Data Integrity Rules have been delivered in terms of components, instances, and stored metadata work products.

45.8.2.3.2. Assess whether all the Requirement Structure Data Integrity Rules have been properly detailed as to content, description, methodology, evaluation, presentation, and delivery work steps.

45.8.2.3.3. Assess whether all the Requirement Structure Data Integrity Rules have been properly allocated sufficient unit effort estimates.

45.8.2.3.4. Assess whether all the Requirement Structure Data Integrity Rules have been properly allocated sufficient quantity of units that have to be developed.

45.8.2.3.5. Assess whether all the Requirement Structure Data Integrity Rules have been properly allocated work environment factors to determine an accurate estimate of required resources.

45.8.2.3.6. Assess whether all the Requirement Structure Data Integrity Rules have been properly allocated work accomplishment and recording functions necessary to support earned value reporting.

45.8.2.3.7. Assess whether all the Requirement Structure Data Integrity Rules have been properly allocated metadata recording effort to ensure that all interrelationships are properly recorded into the Metabase System database.

45.8.2.4. Assign the risk level associated with each Requirement Structure Data Integrity Rule not properly constructed.

45.8.3. Determine the findings and create draft assessment report.

45.8.4. Present the findings and revise draft assessment report.

45.8.5. Create final assessment report and deliver to the auditing organization.

45.9. Assess Requirement Structure DBMS Column.

45.8.1. Identify artifacts that bear on the assessment.

45.8.1.1. Identify the appropriate set of Requirement Structure DBMS Column documents.

45.8.1.1.1. Review Requirement Structure DBMS Column documents.

45.8.1.1.2. Review scope and business problem related documentation.

45.8.1.1.3. Identify the Requirement Structure DBMS Columns that are defined and captured.

45.8.1.1.4. Identify the Requirement Structure DBMS Columns related work products.

45.8.1.2. For each Requirement Structure DBMS Columns related work product assessment:

45.8.1.2.1. Identify the relevant component.

45.8.1.2.2. Identify the description for each interrelated Requirement Structure DBMS Column component.

45.8.2. Perform the assessment.

45.8.2.1. Assess each Requirement Structure DBMS Column.

45.8.2.1.1. Assess the accuracy, quality and completeness of each Requirement Structure DBMS Column with respect to the business requirements.

45.8.2.1.2. Assess whether Requirement Structure DBMS Columns are able to be inferred from business requirements, and if not whether business requirements or Requirement Structure DBMS Columns need to be enhanced.

45.8.2.1.3. Assess whether each Requirement Structure DBMS Column pair properly associates one or more Requirement Structures with one or more DBMS Columns.

45.8.2.1.4. Assess whether each Requirement Structure DBMS Column pair is properly named and described.

45.8.2.3. Assess whether the Requirement Structure DBMS Columns are properly identified and are appropriately engineered to address a Requirement Structure DBMS Column project.

45.8.2.3.1. Assess whether all the Requirement Structure DBMS Columns have been delivered in terms of components, instances, and stored metadata work products.

45.8.2.3.2. Assess whether all the Requirement Structure DBMS Columns have been properly detailed as to content, description, methodology, evaluation, presentation, and delivery work steps.

45.8.2.3.3. Assess whether all the Requirement Structure DBMS Columns have been properly allocated sufficient unit effort estimates.

45.8.2.3.4. Assess whether all the Requirement Structure DBMS Columns have been properly allocated sufficient quantity of units that have to be developed.

45.8.2.3.5. Assess whether all the Requirement Structure DBMS Columns have been properly allocated work environment factors to determine an accurate estimate of required resources.

45.8.2.3.6. Assess whether all the Requirement Structure DBMS Columns have been properly allocated work accomplishment and recording functions necessary to support earned value reporting.

45.8.2.3.7. Assess whether all the Requirement Structure DBMS Columns have been properly allocated metadata recording effort to ensure that all interrelationships are properly recorded into the Metabase System database.

45.8.2.4. Assign the risk level associated with each Requirement Structure DBMS Column not properly constructed.

45.8.3. Determine the findings and create draft assessment report.

45.8.4. Present the findings and revise draft assessment report.

45.8.5. Create final assessment report and deliver to the auditing organization.

45.10. Assess Requirement Structure Document.

45.10.1. Identify artifacts that bear on the assessment.

45.10.1.1. Identify the appropriate set of Requirement Structure Document documents.

45.10.1.1.1. Review Requirement Structure Document documents.

45.10.1.1.2. Review scope and business problem related documentation.

45.10.1.1.3. Identify the Requirement Structure Documents that are defined and captured.

45.10.1.1.4. Identify the Requirement Structure Documents related work products.

45.10.1.2. For each Requirement Structure Documents related work product assessment:

45.10.1.2.1. Identify the relevant component.

45.10.1.2.2. Identify the description for each interrelated Requirement Structure Document component.

45.10.2. Perform the assessment.

45.10.2.1. Assess each Requirement Structure Document.

45.10.2.1.1. Assess the accuracy, quality and completeness of each Requirement Structure Document with respect to the business requirements.

45.10.2.1.2. Assess whether Requirement Structure Documents are able to be inferred from business requirements, and if not whether business requirements or

Requirement Structure Documents need to be enhanced.

45.10.2.1.3. Assess whether each Requirement Structure Document pair properly associates one or more Requirement Structures with one or more Documents.

45.10.2.1.4. Assess whether each Requirement Structure Documents pair is properly named and described.

45.10.2.3. Assess whether the Requirement Structure Documents are properly identified and are appropriately engineered to address a Requirement Structure Document project.

45.10.2.3.1. Assess whether all the Requirement Structure Documents have been delivered in terms of components, instances, and stored metadata work products.

45.10.2.3.2. Assess whether all the Requirement Structure Documents have been properly detailed as to content, description, methodology, evaluation, presentation, and delivery work steps.

45.10.2.3.3. Assess whether all the Requirement Structure Documents have been properly allocated sufficient unit effort estimates.

45.10.2.3.4. Assess whether all the Requirement Structure Documents have been properly allocated sufficient quantity of units that have to be developed.

45.10.2.3.5. Assess whether all the Requirement Structure Documents have been properly allocated work environment factors to determine an accurate estimate of required resources.

45.10.2.3.6. Assess whether all the Requirement Structure Documents have been properly allocated work accomplishment and recording functions necessary to support earned value reporting.

45.10.2.3.7. Assess whether all the Requirement Structure Documents have been properly allocated metadata recording effort to ensure that all interrelationships are properly recorded into the Metabase System database.

45.10.2.4. Assign the risk level associated with each Requirement Structure Document not properly constructed.

45.10.3. Determine the findings and create draft assessment report.

45.10.4. Present the findings and revise draft assessment report.

45.10.5. Create final assessment report and deliver to the auditing organization.

45.11. Assess Requirement Structure Implemented Database Schema.

45.11.1. Identify artifacts that bear on the assessment.

45.11.1.1. Identify the appropriate set of Requirement Structure Implemented Database Schema documents.

45.11.1.1.1. Review Requirement Structure Implemented Database Schemas documents.

45.11.1.1.2. Review scope and business problem related documentation.

45.11.1.1.3. Identify the Requirement Structure Implemented Database Schemas that are defined and captured.
45.11.1.1.4. Identify the Requirement Structure Implemented Database Schemas related work products.
45.11.1.2. For each Requirement Structure Implemented Database Schemas related work product assessment:
45.11.1.2.1. Identify the relevant component.
45.11.1.2.2. Identify the description for each interrelated Requirement Structure Implemented Database Model Schema component.
45.11.2. Perform the assessment.
45.11.2.1. Assess each Requirement Structure Implemented Database Schema.
45.11.2.1.1. Assess the accuracy, quality and completeness of each Requirement Structure Implemented Database Schema with respect to the business requirements.
45.11.2.1.2. Assess whether Requirement Structure Implemented Database Schemas are able to be inferred from business requirements, and if not whether business requirements or Requirement Structure Implemented Database Schemas need to be enhanced.
45.11.2.1.3. Assess whether each Requirement Structure Implemented Database Schema pair properly associates one or more Requirement Structures with one or more Implemented Database Schemas.
45.11.2.1.4. Assess whether each Requirement Structure Implemented Database Schema pair is properly named and described.
45.11.2.3. Assess whether the Requirement Structure Implemented Database Model Schemas are properly identified and are appropriately engineered to address a Requirement Structure Implemented Database Model Schema project.
45.11.2.3.1. Assess whether all the Requirement Structure Implemented Database Model Schemas have been delivered in terms of components, instances, and stored metadata work products.
45.11.2.3.2. Assess whether all the Requirement Structure Implemented Database Model Schemas have been properly detailed as to content, description, methodology, evaluation, presentation, and delivery work steps.
45.11.2.3.3. Assess whether all the Requirement Structure Implemented Database Model Schemas have been properly allocated sufficient unit effort estimates.
45.11.2.3.4. Assess whether all the Requirement Structure Implemented Database Model Schemas have been properly allocated sufficient quantity of units that have to be developed.
45.11.2.3.5. Assess whether all the Requirement Structure Implemented Database Model Schemas have been properly allocated work environment factors to determine an accurate estimate of required resources.

45.11.2.3.6. Assess whether all the Requirement Structure Implemented Database Model Schemas have been properly allocated work accomplishment and recording functions necessary to support earned value reporting.
45.11.2.3.7. Assess whether all the Requirement Structure Implemented Database Model Schemas have been properly allocated metadata recording effort to ensure that all interrelationships are properly recorded into the Metabase System database.
45.11.2.4. Assign the risk level associated with each Requirement Structure Implemented Database Model Schema not properly constructed.
45.11.3. Determine the findings and create draft assessment report.
45.11.4. Present the findings and revise draft assessment report.
45.11.5. Create final assessment report and deliver to the auditing organization.

45.12. Assess Requirement Structure Mission-Organization-Function.
45.12.1. Identify artifacts that bear on the assessment.
45.12.1.1. Identify the appropriate set of Requirement Structure Mission-Organization-Function documents.
45.12.1.1.1. Review Requirement Structure Mission-Organization-Function documents.
45.12.1.1.2. Review scope and business problem related documentation.
45.12.1.1.3. Identify the Requirement Structure Mission-Organization-Functions that are defined and captured.
45.12.1.1.4. Identify the Requirement Structure Mission-Organization-Functions related work products.
45.12.1.2. For each Requirement Structure Mission-Organization-Functions related work product assessment:
45.12.1.2.1. Identify the relevant component.
45.12.1.2.2. Identify the description for each interrelated Requirement Structure Mission-Organization-Function component.
45.12.2. Perform the assessment.
45.12.2.1. Assess each Requirement Structure Mission-Organization-Function.
45.12.2.1.1. Assess the accuracy, quality and completeness of each Requirement Structure Mission-Organization-Function with respect to the business requirements.
45.12.2.1.2. Assess whether Requirement Structure Mission-Organization-Functions are able to be inferred from business requirements, and if not whether business requirements or Requirement Structure Mission-Organization-Functions need to be enhanced.
45.12.2.1.3. Assess whether each Requirement Structure Mission-Organization-Functions pair properly associates one or more Requirement Structures with one or more Mission-Organization-Functions.
45.12.2.1.4. Assess whether each Requirement Structure Mission-Organization-

Function pair is properly named and described.

45.12.2.3. Assess whether the Requirement Structure Mission-Organization-Functions are properly identified and are appropriately engineered to address a Requirement Structure Mission-Organization-Function project.

45.12.2.3.1. Assess whether all the Requirement Structure Mission-Organization-Functions have been delivered in terms of components, instances, and stored metadata work products.

45.12.2.3.2. Assess whether all the Requirement Structure Mission-Organization-Functions have been properly detailed as to content, description, methodology, evaluation, presentation, and delivery work steps.

45.12.2.3.3. Assess whether all the Requirement Structure Mission-Organization-Functions have been properly allocated sufficient unit effort estimates.

45.12.2.3.4. Assess whether all the Requirement Structure Mission-Organization-Functions have been properly allocated sufficient quantity of units that have to be developed.

45.12.2.3.5. Assess whether all the Requirement Structure Mission-Organization-Functions have been properly allocated work environment factors to determine an accurate estimate of required resources.

45.12.2.3.6. Assess whether all the Requirement Structure Mission-Organization-Functions have been properly allocated work accomplishment and recording functions necessary to support earned value reporting.

45.12.2.3.7. Assess whether all the Requirement Structure Mission-Organization-Functions have been properly allocated metadata recording effort to ensure that all interrelationships are properly recorded into the Metabase System database.

45.12.2.4. Assign the risk level associated with each Requirement Structure Mission-Organization-Function not properly constructed.

45.12.3. Determine the findings and create draft assessment report.

45.12.4. Present the findings and revise draft assessment report.

45.12.5. Create final assessment report and deliver to the auditing organization.

45.13. Assess Requirement Structure Operational Database DBMS Schema.

45.13.1. Identify artifacts that bear on the assessment.

45.13.1.1. Identify the appropriate set of Requirement Structure Operational Database DBMS Schema documents.

45.13.1.1.1. Review Requirement Structure Operational Database DBMS Schema documents.

45.13.1.1.2. Review scope and business problem related documentation.

45.13.1.1.3. Identify the Requirement Structure Operational Database DBMS Schemas that are defined and captured.

45.13.1.1.4. Identify the Requirement Structure Operational Database DBMS Schemas related work products.

45.13.1.2. For each Requirement Structure Operational Database DBMS Schemas related work product assessment:

45.13.1.2.1. Identify the relevant component.

45.13.1.2.2. Identify the description for each interrelated Requirement Structure Operational Database DBMS Schema component.

45.13.2. Perform the assessment.

45.13.2.1. Assess each Requirement Structure Operational Database DBMS Schema.

45.13.2.1.1. Assess the accuracy, quality and completeness of each Requirement Structure Operational Database DBMS Schema with respect to the business requirements.

45.13.2.1.2. Assess whether Requirement Structure Business Events are able to be inferred from business requirements, and if not whether business requirements or Requirement Structure Business Events need to be enhanced.

45.13.2.1.3. Assess whether each Requirement Structure Operational Database DBMS Schema pair properly associates one or more Requirement Structures with one or more Operational Database DBMS Schemas.

45.13.2.1.4. Assess whether each Requirement Structure Operational Database DBMS Schema pair is properly named and described.

45.13.2.3. Assess whether the Requirement Structure Operational Database Model DBMS Schemas are properly identified and are appropriately engineered to address a Requirement Structure Operational Database Model DBMS Schema project.

45.13.2.3.1. Assess whether all the Requirement Structure Operational Database Model DBMS Schemas have been delivered in terms of components, instances, and stored metadata work products.

45.13.2.3.2. Assess whether all the Requirement Structure Operational Database Model DBMS Schemas have been properly detailed as to content, description, methodology, evaluation, presentation, and delivery work steps.

45.13.2.3.3. Assess whether all the Requirement Structure Operational Database Model DBMS Schemas have been properly allocated sufficient unit effort estimates.

45.13.2.3.4. Assess whether all the Requirement Structure Operational Database Model DBMS Schemas have been properly allocated sufficient quantity of units that have to be developed.

45.13.2.3.5. Assess whether all the Requirement Structure Operational Database Model DBMS Schemas have been properly allocated work environment factors to determine an accurate estimate of required resources.

45.13.2.3.6. Assess whether all the Requirement Structure Operational Database Model DBMS Schemas have been properly allocated work accomplishment and recording functions necessary to support earned value reporting.

45.13.2.3.7. Assess whether all the Requirement Structure Operational Database Model DBMS Schemas have been properly allocated metadata recording effort to ensure that all interrelationships are properly recorded into the Metabase System database.

45.13.2.4. Assign the risk level associated with each Requirement Structure Operational Database Model DBMS Schema not properly constructed.

45.13.3. Determine the findings and create draft assessment report.

45.13.4. Present the findings and revise draft assessment report.

45.13.5. Create final assessment report and deliver to the auditing organization.

45.14. Assess Requirement Structure Resource Life Cycle Node.

45.14.1. Identify artifacts that bear on the assessment.

45.14.1.1. Identify the appropriate set of Requirement Structure Resource Life Cycle Node documents.

45.14.1.1.1. Review Requirement Structure Resource Life Cycle Node documents.

45.14.1.1.2. Review scope and business problem related documentation.

45.14.1.1.3. Identify the Requirement Structure Resource Life Cycle Nodes that are defined and captured.

45.14.1.1.4. Identify the Requirement Structure Resource Life Cycle Nodes related work products.

45.14.1.2. For each Requirement Structure Resource Life Cycle Nodes related work product assessment:

45.14.1.2.1. Identify the relevant component.

45.14.1.2.2. Identify the description for each interrelated Requirement Structure Resource Life Cycle Node component.

45.14.2. Perform the assessment.

45.14.2.1. Assess each Requirement Structure Resource Life Cycle Node.

45.14.2.1.1. Assess the accuracy, quality and completeness of each Requirement Structure Resource Life Cycle Nodes with respect to the business requirements.

45.14.2.1.2. Assess whether Requirement Structure Resource Life Cycle Nodes are able to be inferred from business requirements, and if not whether business requirements or Requirement Structure Resource Life Cycle Nodes need to be enhanced.

45.14.2.1.3. Assess whether each Requirement Structure Resource Life Cycle Node pair properly associates one or more Requirement Structures with one or more Resource Life Cycle Nodes.

45.14.2.1.4. Assess whether each Requirement Structure Resource Life Cycle Node pair is properly named and described.

45.14.2.3. Assess whether the Requirement Structure Resource Life Cycle Nodes are properly identified and are appropriately engineered to address a

Requirement Structure Resource Life Cycle Node project.

45.14.2.3.1. Assess whether all the Requirement Structure Resource Life Cycle Nodes have been delivered in terms of components, instances, and stored metadata work products.

45.14.2.3.2. Assess whether all the Requirement Structure Resource Life Cycle Nodes have been properly detailed as to content, description, methodology, evaluation, presentation, and delivery work steps.

45.14.2.3.3. Assess whether all the Requirement Structure Resource Life Cycle Nodes have been properly allocated sufficient unit effort estimates.

45.14.2.3.4. Assess whether all the Requirement Structure Resource Life Cycle Nodes have been properly allocated sufficient quantity of units that have to be developed.

45.14.2.3.5. Assess whether all the Requirement Structure Resource Life Cycle Nodes have been properly allocated work environment factors to determine an accurate estimate of required resources.

45.14.2.3.6. Assess whether all the Requirement Structure Resource Life Cycle Nodes have been properly allocated work accomplishment and recording functions necessary to support earned value reporting.

45.14.2.3.7. Assess whether all the Requirement Structure Resource Life Cycle Nodes have been properly allocated metadata recording effort to ensure that all interrelationships are properly recorded into the Metabase System database.

45.14.2.4. Assign the risk level associated with each Requirement Structure Resource Life Cycle Node not properly constructed.

45.14.3. Determine the findings and create draft assessment report.

45.14.4. Present the findings and revise draft assessment report.

45.14.5. Create final assessment report and deliver to the auditing organization.

45.15. Assess Requirement Structure Specified Data Model Subject.

45.15.1. Identify artifacts that bear on the assessment.

45.15.1.1. Identify the appropriate set of Requirement Structure Specified Data Model Subject documents.

45.15.1.1.1. Review Requirement Structure Specified Data Model Subject documents.

45.15.1.1.2. Review scope and business problem related documentation.

45.15.1.1.3. Identify the Requirement Structure Specified Data Model Subjects that are defined and captured.

45.15.1.1.4. Identify the Requirement Structure Specified Data Model Subjects related work products.

45.15.1.2. For each Requirement Structure Specified Data Model Subjects related work product assessment:

45.15.1.2.1. Identify the relevant component.

45.15.1.2.2. Identify the description for each interrelated Requirement Structure

Specified Data Model Subject component.

45.15.2. Perform the assessment.

45.15.2.1. Assess each Requirement Structure Specified Data Model Subject.

45.15.2.1.1. Assess the accuracy, quality and completeness of each Requirement Structure Specified Data Model Subject with respect to the business requirements.

45.15.2.1.2. Assess whether Requirement Structure Specified Data Model Subjects are able to be inferred from business requirements, and if not whether business requirements or Requirement Structure Specified Data Model Subjects need to be enhanced.

45.15.2.1.3. Assess whether each Requirement Structure Specified Data Model Subject pair properly associates one or more Requirement Structures with one or more Specified Data Model Subjects.

45.15.2.1.4. Assess whether each Requirement Structure Specified Data Model Subject pair is properly named and described.

45.15.2.3. Assess whether the Requirement Structure Specified Data Model Subjects are properly identified and are appropriately engineered to address a Requirement Structure Specified Data Model Subject project.

45.15.2.3.1. Assess whether all the Requirement Structure Specified Data Model Subjects have been delivered in terms of components, instances, and stored metadata work products.

45.15.2.3.2. Assess whether all the Requirement Structure Specified Data Model Subjects have been properly detailed as to content, description, methodology, evaluation, presentation, and delivery work steps.

45.15.2.3.3. Assess whether all the Requirement Structure Specified Data Model Subjects have been properly allocated sufficient unit effort estimates.

45.15.2.3.4. Assess whether all the Requirement Structure Specified Data Model Subjects have been properly allocated sufficient quantity of units that have to be developed.

45.15.2.3.5. Assess whether all the Requirement Structure Specified Data Model Subjects have been properly allocated work environment factors to determine an accurate estimate of required resources.

45.15.2.3.6. Assess whether all the Requirement Structure Specified Data Model Subjects have been properly allocated work accomplishment and recording functions necessary to support earned value reporting.

45.15.2.3.7. Assess whether all the Requirement Structure Specified Data Model Subjects have been properly allocated metadata recording effort to ensure that all interrelationships are properly recorded into the Metabase System database.

45.15.2.4. Assign the risk level associated with each Requirement Structure Specified Data Model Subject not properly constructed.

45.15.3. Determine the findings and create draft assessment report.

45.15.4. Present the findings and revise draft assessment report.
45.15.5. Create final assessment report and deliver to the auditing organization.

45.16. Assess Requirement Structure Use Case.
45.16.1. Identify artifacts that bear on the assessment.
45.16.1.1. Identify the appropriate set of Requirement Structure Use Case documents.
45.16.1.1.1. Review Requirement Structure Use Case documents.
45.16.1.1.2. Review scope and business problem related documentation.
45.16.1.1.3. Identify the Requirement Structure Use Cases that are defined and captured.
45.16.1.1.4. Identify the Requirement Structure Use Cases related work products.
45.16.1.2. For each Requirement Structure Use Cases related work product assessment:
45.16.1.2.1. Identify the relevant component.
45.16.1.2.2. Identify the description for each interrelated Requirement Structure Use Case component.
45.16.2. Perform the assessment.
45.16.2.1. Assess each Requirement Structure Use Case.
45.16.2.1.1. Assess the accuracy, quality and completeness of each Requirement Structure Use Case with respect to the business requirements.
45.16.2.1.2. Assess whether Requirement Structure Use Cases are able to be inferred from business requirements, and if not whether business requirements or Requirement Structure Use Cases need to be enhanced.
45.16.2.1.3. Assess whether each Requirement Structure Use Case pair properly associates one or more Requirement Structures with one or more Use Cases.
45.16.2.1.4. Assess whether each Requirement Structure Use Case pair is properly named and described.
45.16.2.3. Assess whether the Requirement Structure Use Cases are properly identified and are appropriately engineered to address a Requirement Structure Use Case project.
45.16.2.3.1. Assess whether all the Requirement Structure Use Cases have been delivered in terms of components, instances, and stored metadata work products.
45.16.2.3.2. Assess whether all the Requirement Structure Use Cases have been properly detailed as to content, description, methodology, evaluation, presentation, and delivery work steps.
45.16.2.3.3. Assess whether all the Requirement Structure Use Cases have been properly allocated sufficient unit effort estimates.
45.16.2.3.4. Assess whether all the Requirement Structure Use Cases have been properly allocated sufficient quantity of units that have to be developed.

45.16.2.3.5. Assess whether all the Requirement Structure Use Cases have been properly allocated work environment factors to determine an accurate estimate of required resources.
45.16.2.3.6. Assess whether all the Requirement Structure Use Cases have been properly allocated work accomplishment and recording functions necessary to support earned value reporting.
45.16.2.3.7. Assess whether all the Requirement Structure Use Cases have been properly allocated metadata recording effort to ensure that all interrelationships are properly recorded into the Metabase System database.
45.16.2.4. Assign the risk level associated with each Requirement Structure Use Case not properly constructed.
45.16.3. Determine the findings and create draft assessment report.
45.16.4. Present the findings and revise draft assessment report.
45.16.5. Create final assessment report and deliver to the auditing organization.

45.17. Assess Requirement Structure User Acceptance Test.
45.17.1. Identify artifacts that bear on the assessment.
45.17.1.1. Identify the appropriate set of Requirement Structure User Acceptance Test documents.
45.17.1.1.1. Review Requirement Structure User Acceptance Test documents.
45.17.1.1.2. Review scope and business problem related documentation.
45.17.1.1.3. Identify the Requirement Structure User Acceptance Tests that are defined and captured.
45.17.1.1.4. Identify the Requirement Structure User Acceptance Tests related work products.
45.17.1.2. For each Requirement Structure User Acceptance Tests related work product assessment:
45.17.1.2.1. Identify the relevant component.
45.17.1.2.2. Identify the description for each interrelated Requirement Structure User Acceptance Test component.
45.17.2. Perform the assessment.
45.17.2.1. Assess each Requirement Structure User Acceptance Test.
45.17.2.1.1. Assess the accuracy, quality and completeness of each Requirement Structure User Acceptance Test with respect to the business requirements.
45.17.2.1.2. Assess whether Requirement Structure User Acceptance Tests are able to be inferred from business requirements, and if not whether business requirements or Requirement Structure User Acceptance Tests need to be enhanced.
45.17.2.1.3. Assess whether each Requirement Structure User Acceptance Test pair properly associates one or more Requirement Structures with one or more User Acceptance Tests.

45.17.2.1.4. Assess whether each Requirement Structure User Acceptance Test pair is properly named and described.

45.17.2.3. Assess whether the Requirement Structure User Acceptance Tests are properly identified and are appropriately engineered to address a Requirement Structure User Acceptance Test project.

45.17.2.3.1. Assess whether all the Requirement Structure User Acceptance Tests have been delivered in terms of components, instances, and stored metadata work products.

45.17.2.3.2. Assess whether all the Requirement Structure User Acceptance Tests have been properly detailed as to content, description, methodology, evaluation, presentation, and delivery work steps.

45.17.2.3.3. Assess whether all the Requirement Structure User Acceptance Tests have been properly allocated sufficient unit effort estimates.

45.17.2.3.4. Assess whether all the Requirement Structure User Acceptance Tests have been properly allocated sufficient quantity of units that have to be developed.

45.17.2.3.5. Assess whether all the Requirement Structure User Acceptance Tests have been properly allocated work environment factors to determine an accurate estimate of required resources.

45.17.2.3.6. Assess whether all the Requirement Structure User Acceptance Tests have been properly allocated work accomplishment and recording functions necessary to support earned value reporting.

45.17.2.3.7. Assess whether all the Requirement Structure User Acceptance Tests have been properly allocated metadata recording effort to ensure that all interrelationships are properly recorded into the Metabase System database.

45.17.2.4. Assign the risk level associated with each Requirement Structure User Acceptance Test not properly constructed.

45.17.3. Determine the findings and create draft assessment report.

45.17.4. Present the findings and revise draft assessment report.

45.17.5. Create final assessment report and deliver to the auditing organization.

46. Resource Life Cycles

46.1. Assess Resource.
46.1.1. Identify artifacts that bear on the assessment.
46.1.1.1. Identify the appropriate set of Resource documents.
46.1.1.1.1. Review Resource documents.
46.1.1.1.2. Review scope and business problem related documentation.
46.1.1.1.3. Identify the Resources that are defined and captured.
46.1.1.1.4. Identify the Resource related work products.
46.1.1.2. For each Resource related work product assessment:
46.1.1.2.1. Identify the relevant component.
46.1.1.2.2. Identify the description for each interrelated Resource component.
46.1.2. Perform the assessment.
46.1.2.1. Assess each Resource.
46.1.2.1.1. Assess the accuracy, quality and completeness of each Resource with respect to the business requirements.
46.1.2.1.2. Assess whether Resources are able to be inferred from business requirements, and if not whether business requirements or Resources need to be enhanced.
46.1.2.1.3. Assess whether each Resource hierarchy/network is properly specified, and that all X names and descriptions are well defined, non-overlapping, and have been formally approved.
46.1.2.2. Assess whether the Resources are properly identified and are appropriately engineered to address a Resource project.
46.1.2.2.1. Assess whether all the Resources have been delivered in terms of components, instances, and stored metadata work products.
46.1.2.2.2. Assess whether all the Resources have been properly detailed as to content, description, methodology, evaluation, presentation, and delivery work steps.
46.1.2.2.3. Assess whether all the Resources have been properly allocated sufficient unit effort estimates.
46.1.2.2.4. Assess whether all the Resources have been properly allocated sufficient quantity of units that have to be developed.
46.1.2.2.5. Assess whether all the Resources have been properly allocated work environment factors to determine an accurate estimate of required resources.
46.1.2.2.6. Assess whether all the Resources have been properly allocated work accomplishment and recording functions necessary to support earned value reporting.
46.1.2.2.7. Assess whether all the Resources have been properly allocated metadata recording effort to ensure that all interrelationships are properly recorded into the Metabase System database.

46.1.2.3. Assign the risk level associated with each Resource not properly constructed.
46.1.3. Determine the findings and create draft assessment report.
46.1.4. Present the findings and revise draft assessment report.
46.1.5. Create final assessment report and deliver to the auditing organization.

46.2. Assess Resource Life Cycle Node.
46.2.1. Identify artifacts that bear on the assessment.
46.2.1.1. Identify the appropriate set of Resource Life Cycle Node documents.
46.2.1.1.1. Review Resource Life Cycle Node documents.
46.2.1.1.2. Review scope and business problem related documentation.
46.2.1.1.3. Identify the Resource Life Cycle Nodes that are defined and captured.
46.2.1.1.4. Identify the Resource Life Cycle Node related work products.
46.2.1.2. For each Resource Life Cycle Node related work product assessment:
46.2.2. Perform the assessment.
46.2.2.1. Assess each Resource Life Cycle Node.
46.2.2.1.1. Assess the accuracy, quality and completeness of each Resource Life Cycle Node with respect to the business requirements.
46.2.2.1.2. Assess whether Resource Life Cycle Nodes are able to be inferred from business requirements, and if not whether business requirements or Resource Life Cycle Nodes need to be enhanced.
46.2.2.2. Assess whether the Resource Life Cycle Nodes are properly identified and are appropriately engineered to address a Resource Life Cycle Node project.
46.2.2.2.1. Assess whether all the Resource Life Cycle Nodes have been delivered in terms of components, instances, and stored metadata work products.
46.2.2.2.2. Assess whether all the Resource Life Cycle Nodes have been properly detailed as to content, description, methodology, evaluation, presentation, and delivery work steps.
46.2.2.2.3. Assess whether all the Resource Life Cycle Nodes have been properly allocated sufficient unit effort estimates.
46.2.2.2.4. Assess whether all the Resource Life Cycle Nodes have been properly allocated sufficient quantity of units that have to be developed.
46.2.2.2.5. Assess whether all the Resource Life Cycle Nodes have been properly allocated work environment factors to determine an accurate estimate of required resources.
46.2.2.2.6. Assess whether all the Resource Life Cycle Nodes have been properly allocated work accomplishment and recording functions necessary to support earned value reporting.
46.2.2.2.7. Assess whether all the Resource Life Cycle Nodes have been properly allocated metadata recording effort to ensure that all interrelationships are properly recorded into the Metabase System database.

46.2.2.3. Assign the risk level associated with each Resource Life Cycle Nodes not properly constructed.
46.2.3. Determine the findings and create draft assessment report.
46.2.4. Present the findings and revise draft assessment report.
46.2.5. Create final assessment report and deliver to the auditing organization.

46.3. Assess Resource Life Cycle Node Structure.
46.3.1. Identify artifacts that bear on the assessment.
46.3.1.1. Identify the appropriate set of Resource Life Cycle Node Structure documents.
46.3.1.1.1. Review Resource Life Cycle Node Structure documents.
46.3.1.1.2. Review scope and business problem related documentation.
46.3.1.1.3. Identify the Resource Life Cycle Node Structures that are defined and captured.
46.3.1.1.4. Identify the Resource Life Cycle Node Structures related work products.
46.3.1.2. For each Resource Life Cycle Node Structures related work product assessment:
46.3.1.2.1. Identify the relevant component.
46.3.1.2.2. Identify the description for each interrelated Resource Life Cycle Node Structure component.
46.3.2. Perform the assessment.
46.3.2.1. Assess each Resource Life Cycle Node Structure.
46.3.2.1.1. Assess the accuracy, quality and completeness of each Resource Life Cycle Node Structure with respect to the business requirements.
46.3.2.1.2. Assess whether Resource Life Cycle Node Structures are able to be inferred from business requirements, and if not whether business requirements or Resource Life Cycle Node Structure need to be enhanced.
46.3.2.1.3. Assess whether each Resource Life Cycle Node Structure hierarchy/network is properly specified, and that all Resource Life Cycle Node Structure names and descriptions are well defined, non-overlapping, and have been formally approved.
46.3.2.2. Assess whether the Resource Life Cycle Node Structures are properly identified and are appropriately engineered to address a Resource Life Cycle Node Structure project.
46.3.2.2.1. Assess whether all the Resource Life Cycle Node Structures have been delivered in terms of components, instances, and stored metadata work products.
46.3.2.2.2. Assess whether all the Resource Life Cycle Node Structures have been properly detailed as to content, description, methodology, evaluation, presentation, and delivery work steps.
46.3.2.2.3. Assess whether all the Resource Life Cycle Node Structures have been properly allocated sufficient unit effort estimates.

46.3.2.2.4. Assess whether all the Resource Life Cycle Node Structures have been properly allocated sufficient quantity of units that have to be developed.

46.3.2.2.5. Assess whether all the Resource Life Cycle Node Structures have been properly allocated work environment factors to determine an accurate estimate of required resources.

46.3.2.2.6. Assess whether all the Resource Life Cycle Node Structures have been properly allocated work accomplishment and recording functions necessary to support earned value reporting.

46.3.2.2.7. Assess whether all the Resource Life Cycle Node Structures have been properly allocated metadata recording effort to ensure that all interrelationships are properly recorded into the Metabase System database.

46.3.2.3. Assign the risk level associated with each Resource Life Cycle Node Structure not properly constructed.

46.3.3. Determine the findings and create draft assessment report.

46.3.4. Present the findings and revise draft assessment report.

46.3.5. Create final assessment report and deliver to the auditing organization.

46.4. Assess Resource Life Cycle Node Business Information System.

46.4.1. Identify artifacts that bear on the assessment.

46.4.1.1. Identify the appropriate set of Resource Life Cycle Node Business Information System documents.

46.4.1.1.1. Review Resource Life Cycle Node Business Information System documents.

46.4.1.1.2. Review scope and business problem related documentation.

46.4.1.1.3. Identify the Resource Life Cycle Node Business Information System that are defined and captured.

46.4.1.1.4. Identify the Resource Life Cycle Node Business Information System related work products.

46.4.1.2. For each Resource Life Cycle Node Business Information System related work product assessment:

46.4.2. Perform the assessment.

46.4.2.1. Assess each Resource Life Cycle Node Business Information System.

46.4.2.1.1. Assess the accuracy, quality and completeness of each Resource Life Cycle Node Business Information System with respect to the business requirements.

46.4.2.1.2. Assess whether Resource Life Cycle Node Business Information Systems are able to be inferred from business requirements, and if not whether business requirements or Resource Life Cycle Node Business Information Systems need to be enhanced.

46.4.2.1.3. Assess whether each Resource Life Cycle Node Business Information System pair properly associates one or more Resource Life Cycle Nodes with one or more Business Information Systems.

46.4.2.1.4. Assess whether each Resource Life Cycle Node Business Information System pair is properly named and described.

46.4.2.2. Assess whether the Resource Life Cycle Node Business Information Systems are properly identified and are appropriately engineered to address a Resource Life Cycle Node Business Information System project.

46.4.2.2.1. Assess whether all the Resource Life Cycle Node Business Information Systems have been delivered in terms of components, instances, and stored metadata work products.

46.4.2.2.2. Assess whether all the Resource Life Cycle Node Business Information Systems have been properly detailed as to content, description, methodology, evaluation, presentation, and delivery work steps.

46.4.2.2.3. Assess whether all the Resource Life Cycle Node Business Information Systems have been properly allocated sufficient unit effort estimates.

46.4.2.2.4. Assess whether all the Resource Life Cycle Node Business Information Systems have been properly allocated sufficient quantity of units that have to be developed.

46.4.2.2.5. Assess whether all the Resource Life Cycle Node Business Information Systems have been properly allocated work environment factors to determine an accurate estimate of required resources.

46.4.2.2.6. Assess whether all the Resource Life Cycle Node Business Information Systems have been properly allocated work accomplishment and recording functions necessary to support earned value reporting.

46.4.2.2.7. Assess whether all the Resource Life Cycle Node Business Information Systems have been properly allocated metadata recording effort to ensure that all interrelationships are properly recorded into the Metabase System database.

46.4.2.3. Assign the risk level associated with each Resource Life Cycle Node Business Information System not properly constructed.

46.4.3. Determine the findings and create draft assessment report.

46.4.4. Present the findings and revise draft assessment report.

46.4.5. Create final assessment report and deliver to the auditing organization.

46.5. Assess Resource Life Cycle Node Database Object.

46.5.1. Identify artifacts that bear on the assessment.

46.5.1.1. Identify the appropriate set of Resource Life Cycle Node Database Objects documents.

46.5.1.1.1. Review Resource Life Cycle Node Database Objects documents.

46.5.1.1.2. Review scope and business problem related documentation.

46.5.1.1.3. Identify the Resource Life Cycle Node Database Objects that are defined and captured.

46.5.1.1.4. Identify the Resource Life Cycle Node Database Objects related work

products.

46.5.1.2. For each Resource Life Cycle Node Database Objects work product assessment:

46.5.2. Perform the assessment.

46.5.2.1. Assess each Resource Life Cycle Node Database Object.

46.5.2.1.1. Assess the accuracy, quality and completeness of each Resource Life Cycle Node Database Object with respect to the business requirements.

46.5.2.1.2. Assess whether Resource Life Cycle Node Database Objects are able to be inferred from business requirements, and if not whether business requirements or Resource Life Cycle Node Database Objects need to be enhanced.

46.5.2.1.3. Assess whether each Resource Life Cycle Node Database Object pair properly associates one or more Resource Life Cycle Nodes with one or more Database Objects.

46.5.2.1.4. Assess whether each Resource Life Cycle Node Database Object pair is properly named and described.

46.5.2.2. Assess whether the Resource Life Cycle Node Database Objects are properly identified and are appropriately engineered to address a Resource Life Cycle Node Database Object project.

46.5.2.2.1. Assess whether all the Resource Life Cycle Node Database Objects have been delivered in terms of components, instances, and stored metadata work products.

46.5.2.2.2. Assess whether all the Resource Life Cycle Node Database Objects have been properly detailed as to content, description, methodology, evaluation, presentation, and delivery work steps.

46.5.2.2.3. Assess whether all the Resource Life Cycle Node Database Objects have been properly allocated sufficient unit effort estimates.

46.5.2.2.4. Assess whether all the Resource Life Cycle Node Database Objects have been properly allocated sufficient quantity of units that have to be developed.

46.5.2.2.5. Assess whether all the Resource Life Cycle Node Database Objects have been properly allocated work environment factors to determine an accurate estimate of required resources.

46.5.2.2.6. Assess whether all the Resource Life Cycle Node Database Objects have been properly allocated work accomplishment and recording functions necessary to support earned value reporting.

46.5.2.2.7. Assess whether all the Resource Life Cycle Node Database Objects have been properly allocated metadata recording effort to ensure that all interrelationships are properly recorded into the Metabase System database.

46.5.2.3. Assign the risk level associated with each Resource Life Cycle Node Database Object not properly constructed.

46.5.3. Determine the findings and create draft assessment report.
46.5.4. Present the findings and revise draft assessment report.
46.5.5. Create final assessment report and deliver to the auditing organization.

47. User Acceptance Tests

47.1. Assess User Acceptance Test.
47.1.1. Identify artifacts that bear on the assessment.
47.1.1.1. Identify the appropriate set of User Acceptance Test documents.
47.1.1.1.1. Review User Acceptance Tests documents.
47.1.1.1.2. Review scope and business problem related documentation.
47.1.1.1.3. Identify the User Acceptance Tests that are defined and captured.
47.1.1.1.4. Identify the User Acceptance Tests related work products.
47.1.1.2. For each User Acceptance Tests related work product assessment:
47.1.1.2.1. Identify the relevant component.
47.1.1.2.2. Identify the description for each interrelated User Acceptance Test component.
47.1.2. Perform the assessment.
47.1.2.1. Assess each User Acceptance Test.
47.1.2.1.1. Assess the accuracy, quality and completeness of each User Acceptance Tests with respect to the business requirements.
47.1.2.1.2. Assess whether User Acceptance Tests are able to be inferred from business requirements, and if not whether business requirements or User Acceptance Tests need to be enhanced.
47.1.2.1.3. Assess whether each User Acceptance Test hierarchy is properly specified, and that all User Acceptance Test names and descriptions are well defined, non-overlapping, and have been formally approved.
47.1.2.1.4. Assess whether each User Acceptance Test pair is properly named and described.
47.1.2.2. Assess whether the User Acceptance Tests are properly identified and are appropriately engineered to address a User Acceptance Test project.
47.1.2.2.1. Assess whether all the User Acceptance Tests have been delivered in terms of components, instances, and stored metadata work products.
47.1.2.2.2. Assess whether all the User Acceptance Tests have been properly detailed as to content, description, methodology, evaluation, presentation, and delivery work steps.
47.1.2.2.3. Assess whether all the User Acceptance Tests have been properly allocated sufficient unit effort estimates.
47.1.2.2.4. Assess whether all the User Acceptance Tests have been properly allocated sufficient quantity of units that have to be developed.
47.1.2.2.5. Assess whether all the User Acceptance Tests have been properly allocated work environment factors to determine an accurate estimate of required User Acceptance Tests.
47.1.2.2.6. Assess whether all the User Acceptance Tests have been properly allocated work accomplishment and recording functions necessary to support earned value reporting.

47.1.2.2.7. Assess whether all the User Acceptance Tests have been properly allocated metadata recording effort to ensure that all interrelationships are properly recorded into the Metabase System database.
47.1.2.3. Assign the risk level associated with each User Acceptance Test not properly constructed.
47.1.3. Determine the findings and create draft assessment report.
47.1.4. Present the findings and revise draft assessment report.
47.1.5. Create final assessment report and deliver to the auditing organization.

47.2. Assess User Acceptance Test Step.
47.2.1. Identify artifacts that bear on the assessment.
47.2.1.1. Identify the appropriate set of User Acceptance Test Step documents.
47.2.1.1.1. Review User Acceptance Test Steps documents.
47.2.1.1.2. Review scope and business problem related documentation.
47.2.1.1.3. Identify the User Acceptance Test Steps that are defined and captured.
47.2.1.1.4. Identify the User Acceptance Test Steps related work products.
47.2.1.2. For each User Acceptance Test Steps related work product assessment:
47.2.1.2.1. Identify the relevant component.
47.2.1.2.2. Identify the description for each interrelated User Acceptance Test Step component.
47.2.2. Perform the assessment.
47.2.2.1. Assess each User Acceptance Test Step.
47.2.2.1.1. Assess the accuracy, quality and completeness of each User Acceptance Test Step with respect to the business requirements.
47.2.2.1.2. Assess whether User Acceptance Test Steps are able to be inferred from business requirements, and if not whether business requirements or User Acceptance Test Steps need to be enhanced.
47.2.2.3. Assess whether the User Acceptance Test Steps are properly identified and are appropriately engineered to address a User Acceptance Test Step project.
47.2.2.3.1. Assess whether all the User Acceptance Test Steps have been delivered in terms of components, instances, and stored metadata work products.
47.2.2.3.2. Assess whether all the User Acceptance Test Steps have been properly detailed as to content, description, methodology, evaluation, presentation, and delivery work steps.
47.2.2.3.3. Assess whether all the User Acceptance Test Steps have been properly allocated sufficient unit effort estimates.
47.2.2.3.4. Assess whether all the User Acceptance Test Steps have been properly allocated sufficient quantity of units that have to be developed.
47.2.2.3.5. Assess whether all the User Acceptance Test Steps have been properly allocated work environment factors to determine an accurate estimate of required User Acceptance Test Steps.

47.2.2.3.6. Assess whether all the User Acceptance Test Steps have been properly allocated work accomplishment and recording functions necessary to support earned value reporting.
47.2.2.3.7. Assess whether all the User Acceptance Test Steps have been properly allocated metadata recording effort to ensure that all interrelationships are properly recorded into the Metabase System database.
47.2.2.4. Assign the risk level associated with each User Acceptance Test Step not properly constructed.
47.2.3. Determine the findings and create draft assessment report.
47.2.4. Present the findings and revise draft assessment report.
47.2.5. Create final assessment report and deliver to the auditing organization.

47.3. Assess User Acceptance Test Structure.
47.3.1. Identify artifacts that bear on the assessment.
47.3.1.1. Identify the appropriate set of User Acceptance Test Structure documents.
47.3.1.1.1. Review User Acceptance Test Structure documents.
47.3.1.1.2. Review scope and business problem related documentation.
47.3.1.1.3. Identify the User Acceptance Test Structure that are defined and captured.
47.3.1.1.4. Identify the User Acceptance Test Structure related work products.
47.3.1.2. For each User Acceptance Test Structure related work product assessment:
47.3.1.2.1. Identify the relevant component.
47.3.1.2.2. Identify the description for each interrelated User Acceptance Test Structure component.
47.3.2. Perform the assessment.
47.3.2.1. Assess each User Acceptance Test Structure.
47.3.2.1.1. Assess the accuracy, quality and completeness of each User Acceptance Test Structure with respect to the business requirements.
47.3.2.1.2. Assess whether User Acceptance Test Structures are able to be inferred from business requirements, and if not whether business requirements or User Acceptance Test Structures need to be enhanced.
47.3.2.1.3. Assess whether each User Acceptance Test Structure hierarchy/network is properly specified, and that all User Acceptance Test Structure names and descriptions are well defined, non-overlapping, and have been formally approved.
47.3.2.2. Assess whether the User Acceptance Test Structure are properly identified and are appropriately engineered to address a User Acceptance Test Structure Life Cycle Node Structure project.
47.3.2.2.1. Assess whether all the User Acceptance Test Structure have been delivered in terms of components, instances, and stored metadata work products.

47.3.2.2.2. Assess whether all the User Acceptance Test Structure have been properly detailed as to content, description, methodology, evaluation, presentation, and delivery work steps.

47.3.2.2.3. Assess whether all the User Acceptance Test Structure have been properly allocated sufficient unit effort estimates.

47.3.2.2.4. Assess whether all the User Acceptance Test Structure have been properly allocated sufficient quantity of units that have to be developed.

47.3.2.2.5. Assess whether all the User Acceptance Test Structure have been properly allocated work environment factors to determine an accurate estimate of required User Acceptance Test Structure.

47.3.2.2.6. Assess whether all the User Acceptance Test Structure have been properly allocated work accomplishment and recording functions necessary to support earned value reporting.

47.3.2.2.7. Assess whether all the User Acceptance Test Structure have been properly allocated metadata recording effort to ensure that all interrelationships are properly recorded into the Metabase System database.

47.3.2.3. Assign the risk level associated with each User Acceptance Test Structure not properly constructed.

47.3.3. Determine the findings and create draft assessment report.

47.3.4. Present the findings and revise draft assessment report.

47.3.5. Create final assessment report and deliver to the auditing organization.

47.4. Assess User Acceptance Test Column.

47.4.1. Identify artifacts that bear on the assessment.

47.4.1.1. Identify the appropriate set of User Acceptance Test Column documents.

47.4.1.1.1. Review User Acceptance Test Columns documents.

47.4.1.1.2. Review scope and business problem related documentation.

47.4.1.1.3. Identify the User Acceptance Test Columns that are defined and captured.

47.4.1.1.4. Identify the User Acceptance Test Columns related work products.

47.4.1.2. For each User Acceptance Test Columns related work product assessment:

47.4.1.2.1. Identify the relevant component.

47.4.1.2.2. Identify the description for each interrelated User Acceptance Test Column component.

47.4.2. Perform the assessment.

47.4.2.1. Assess whether each User Acceptance Test Column is addressed properly reflected in the enterprise.

47.4.2.2. Assess whether each User Acceptance Test Column is addressed by one or more business requirements as may be appropriate.

47.4.2.2.1. Assess whether each User Acceptance Test Columns can be allocated to one or more business requirements.

47.4.2.2.2. Assess whether business requirements are able to be inferred from User Acceptance Test Columns, and if not, determine whether business requirements or User Acceptance Test Columns need to be enhanced.

47.4.2.3. Assess whether the User Acceptance Test Columns are properly identified and are appropriately engineered to address a User Acceptance Test Column project.

47.4.2.3.1. Assess whether all the User Acceptance Test Columns have been delivered in terms of components, instances, and stored metadata work products.

47.4.2.3.2. Assess whether all the User Acceptance Test Columns have been properly detailed as to content, description, methodology, evaluation, presentation, and delivery work steps.

47.4.2.3.3. Assess whether all the User Acceptance Test Columns have been properly allocated sufficient unit effort estimates.

47.4.2.3.4. Assess whether all the User Acceptance Test Columns have been properly allocated sufficient quantity of units that have to be developed.

47.4.2.3.5. Assess whether all the User Acceptance Test Columns have been properly allocated work environment factors to determine an accurate estimate of required User Acceptance Test Columns.

47.4.2.3.6. Assess whether all the User Acceptance Test Columns have been properly allocated work accomplishment and recording functions necessary to support earned value reporting.

47.4.2.3.7. Assess whether all the User Acceptance Test Columns have been properly allocated metadata recording effort to ensure that all interrelationships are properly recorded into the Metabase System database.

47.4.2.4. Assign the risk level associated with each User Acceptance Test Column not properly constructed.

47.4.3. Determine the findings and create draft assessment report.

47.4.4. Present the findings and revise draft assessment report.

47.4.5. Create final assessment report and deliver to the auditing organization.

47.5. Assess User Acceptance Test Column View Column.

47.5.1. Identify artifacts that bear on the assessment.

47.5.1.1. Identify the appropriate set of User Acceptance Test Column View Column documents.

47.5.1.1.1. Review User Acceptance Test Column View Column documents.

47.5.1.1.2. Review scope and business problem related documentation.

47.5.1.1.3. Identify the User Acceptance Test Column View Column that are defined and captured.

47.5.1.1.4. Identify the User Acceptance Test Column View Column related work products.

47.5.1.2. For each User Acceptance Test Column View Column work product assessment:

47.5.2. Perform the assessment.

47.5.2.1. Assess each User Acceptance Test Column View Column.

47.5.2.1.1. Assess the accuracy, quality and completeness of each User Acceptance Test Column View Column with respect to the business requirements.

47.5.2.1.2. Assess whether User Acceptance Test Column View Columns are able to be inferred from business requirements, and if not whether business requirements or User Acceptance Test Column View Columns need to be enhanced.

47.5.2.1.3. Assess whether each User Acceptance Test Column View Column pair properly associates one or more User Acceptance Test Columns with one or more View Columns.

47.5.2.1.4. Assess whether each User Acceptance Test Column View Column pair is properly named and described.

47.5.2.2. Assess whether the User Acceptance Test Column View Column are properly identified and are appropriately engineered to address a Resource Life Cycle Node Database Object project.

47.5.2.2.1. Assess whether all the User Acceptance Test Column View Column have been delivered in terms of components, instances, and stored metadata work products.

47.5.2.2.2. Assess whether all the User Acceptance Test Column View Column have been properly detailed as to content, description, methodology, evaluation, presentation, and delivery work steps.

47.5.2.2.3. Assess whether all the User Acceptance Test Column View Column have been properly allocated sufficient unit effort estimates.

47.5.2.2.4. Assess whether all the User Acceptance Test Column View Column have been properly allocated sufficient quantity of units that have to be developed.

47.5.2.7.5. Assess whether all the User Acceptance Test Column View Column have been properly allocated work environment factors to determine an accurate estimate of required resources.

47.5.2.2.6. Assess whether all the User Acceptance Test Column View Column have been properly allocated work accomplishment and recording functions necessary to support earned value reporting.

47.5.2.7.7. Assess whether all the User Acceptance Test Column View Column have been properly allocated metadata recording effort to ensure that all interrelationships are properly recorded into the Metabase System database.

47.5.2.3. Assign the risk level associated with each User Acceptance Test Column View Column not properly constructed.

47.5.3. Determine the findings and create draft assessment report.

47.5.4. Present the findings and revise draft assessment report.

47.5.5. Create final assessment report and deliver to the auditing organization.

47.6. Assess User Acceptance Test Use Case

47.6.1. Identify artifacts that bear on the assessment.

47.6.1.1. Identify the appropriate set of User Acceptance Test Use Case documents.

47.6.1.1.1. Review User Acceptance Test Use Case documents.

47.6.1.1.2. Review scope and business problem related documentation.

47.6.1.1.3. Identify the User Acceptance Test Use Case that are defined and captured.

47.6.1.1.4. Identify the User Acceptance Test Use Case related work products.

47.6.1.2. For each User Acceptance Test Use Case work product assessment:

47.6.2. Perform the assessment.

47.6.2.1. Assess each User Acceptance Test Use Case.

47.6.2.1.1. Assess the accuracy, quality and completeness of each User Acceptance Test Use Case with respect to the business requirements.

47.6.2.1.2. Assess whether User Acceptance Test Use Cases are able to be inferred from business requirements, and if not whether business requirements or User Acceptance Test Use Case need to be enhanced.

47.6.2.1.3. Assess whether each User Acceptance Test Use Case pair properly associates one or more User Acceptance Tests with one or more Use Cases.

47.6.2.1.4. Assess whether each User Acceptance Test Use Case pair is properly named and described.

47.6.2.2. Assess whether the User Acceptance Test Use Cases are properly identified and are appropriately engineered to address a User Acceptance Test Use Case project.

47.6.2.2.1. Assess whether all the User Acceptance Test Use Cases have been delivered in terms of components, instances, and stored metadata work products.

47.6.2.2.2. Assess whether all the User Acceptance Test Use Cases have been properly detailed as to content, description, methodology, evaluation, presentation, and delivery work steps.

47.6.2.2.3. Assess whether all the User Acceptance Test Use Cases have been properly allocated sufficient unit effort estimates.

47.6.2.2.4. Assess whether all the User Acceptance Test Use Cases have been properly allocated sufficient quantity of units that have to be developed.

47.6.2.2.5. Assess whether all the User Acceptance Test Use Cases have been properly allocated work environment factors to determine an accurate estimate of required resources.

47.6.2.2.6. Assess whether all the User Acceptance Test Use Cases have been properly allocated work accomplishment and recording functions necessary to support earned value reporting.

47.6.2.2.7. Assess whether all the User Acceptance Test Use Cases have been properly allocated metadata recording effort to ensure that all interrelationships are properly recorded into the Metabase System database.

47.6.2.3. Assign the risk level associated with each User Acceptance Test Use Case not properly constructed.

47.6.3. Determine the findings and create draft assessment report.

47.6.4. Present the findings and revise draft assessment report.

47.6.5. Create final assessment report and deliver to the auditing organization.

47.7 Assess User Acceptance Test Mission-Organization-Function.

47.7.1. Identify artifacts that bear on the assessment.

47.7.1.1. Identify the appropriate set of User Acceptance Test Mission-Organization-Function documents.

47.7.1.1.1. Review User Acceptance Test Mission-Organization-Function documents.

47.7.1.1.2. Review scope and business problem related documentation.

47.7.1.1.3. Identify the User Acceptance Test Mission-Organization-Function that are defined and captured.

47.7.1.1.4. Identify the User Acceptance Test Mission-Organization-Function related work products.

47.7.1.2. For each User Acceptance Test Mission-Organization-Function work product assessment:

47.7.2. Perform the assessment.

47.7.2.1. Assess each User Acceptance Test Mission-Organization-Function.

47.7.2.1.1. Assess the accuracy, quality and completeness of each User Acceptance Test Mission-Organization-Function with respect to the business requirements.

47.7.2.1.2. Assess whether User Acceptance Test Mission-Organization-Functions are able to be inferred from business requirements, and if not whether business requirements or User Acceptance Test Mission-Organization-Functions need to be enhanced.

47.7.2.1.3. Assess whether each User Acceptance Test Mission-Organization-Function pair properly associates one or more User Acceptance Tests with one or more Mission-Organization-Functions.

47.7.2.1.4. Assess whether each User Acceptance Test Mission-Organization-Function pair is properly named and described.

47.7.2.2. Assess whether the User Acceptance Test Mission-Organization-Function are properly identified and are appropriately engineered to address a User Acceptance Test Mission-Organization-Function project.

47.7.2.2.1. Assess whether all the User Acceptance Test Mission-Organization-Functions have been delivered in terms of components, instances, and stored metadata work products.

47.7.2.2.2. Assess whether all the User Acceptance Test Mission-Organization-Functions have been properly detailed as to content, description, methodology, evaluation, presentation, and delivery work steps.

47.7.2.2.3. Assess whether all the User Acceptance Test Mission-Organization-Functions have been properly allocated sufficient unit effort estimates.

47.7.2.2.4. Assess whether all the User Acceptance Test Mission-Organization-Functions have been properly allocated sufficient quantity of units that have to be developed.

47.7.2.2.5. Assess whether all the User Acceptance Test Mission-Organization-Functions have been properly allocated work environment factors to determine an accurate estimate of required resources.

47.7.2.2.6. Assess whether all the User Acceptance Test Mission-Organization-Functions have been properly allocated work accomplishment and recording functions necessary to support earned value reporting.

47.7.2.2.7. Assess whether all the User Acceptance Test Mission-Organization-Functions have been properly allocated metadata recording effort to ensure that all interrelationships are properly recorded into the Metabase System database.

47.7.2.3. Assign the risk level associated with each User Acceptance Test Mission-Organization-Function not properly constructed.

47.7.3. Determine the findings and create draft assessment report.

47.7.4. Present the findings and revise draft assessment report.

47.7.5. Create final assessment report and deliver to the auditing organization.

48 Use Cases

48.1. Assess Use Case.
48.1.1. Identify artifacts that bear on the assessment.
48.1.1.1. Identify the appropriate set of Use Case documents.
48.1.1.1.1. Review Use Cases documents.
48.1.1.1.2. Review scope and business problem related documentation.
48.1.1.1.3. Identify the Use Cases that are defined and captured.
48.1.1.1.4. Identify the Use Cases related work products.
48.1.1.2. For each Use Cases related work product assessment:
48.1.1.2.1. Identify the relevant component.
48.1.1.2.2. Identify the description for each interrelated Use Case component.
48.1.2. Perform the assessment.
48.1.2.1. Assess each Use Case.
48.1.2.1.1. Assess the accuracy, quality and completeness of each Use Case with respect to the business requirements.
48.1.2.1.2. Assess whether Use Cases are able to be inferred from business requirements, and if not whether business requirements or Use Cases need to be enhanced.
48.1.2.3. Assess whether the Use Cases are properly identified and are appropriately engineered to address a Use Case project.
48.1.2.3.1. Assess whether all the Use Cases have been delivered in terms of components, instances, and stored metadata work products.
48.1.2.3.2. Assess whether all the Use Cases have been properly detailed as to content, description, methodology, evaluation, presentation, and delivery work steps.
48.1.2.3.3. Assess whether all the Use Cases have been properly allocated sufficient unit effort estimates.
48.1.2.3.4. Assess whether all the Use Cases have been properly allocated sufficient quantity of units that have to be developed.
48.1.2.3.5. Assess whether all the Use Cases have been properly allocated work environment factors to determine an accurate estimate of required Use Cases.
48.1.2.3.6. Assess whether all the Use Cases have been properly allocated work accomplishment and recording functions necessary to support earned value reporting.
48.1.2.3.7. Assess whether all the Use Cases have been properly allocated metadata recording effort to ensure that all interrelationships are properly recorded into the Metabase System database.
48.1.2.4. Assign the risk level associated with each Use Case not properly constructed.
48.1.3. Determine the findings and create draft assessment report.

48.1.4. Present the findings and revise draft assessment report.
48.1.5. Create final assessment report and deliver to the auditing organization.

48.2. Assess Use Case Structure.
48.2.1. Identify artifacts that bear on the assessment.
48.2.1.1. Identify the appropriate set of Use Case Structure documents.
48.2.1.1.1. Review Use Case Structure documents.
48.2.1.1.2. Review scope and business problem related documentation.
48.2.1.1.3. Identify the Use Case Structures that are defined and captured.
48.2.1.1.4. Identify the Use Case Structures related work products.
48.2.1.2. For each Use Case Structures related work product assessment:
48.2.1.2.1. Identify the relevant component.
48.2.1.2.2. Identify the description for each interrelated Use Case Structure component.
48.2.2. Perform the assessment.
48.2.2.1. Assess each Use Case Structure.
48.2.2.1.1. Assess the accuracy, quality and completeness of each Use Case Structures with respect to the business requirements.
48.2.2.1.2. Assess whether Use Case Structures are able to be inferred from business requirements, and if not whether business requirements or Use Case Structures need to be enhanced.
48.2.2.1.3. Assess whether each Use Case Structures hierarchy/network is properly specified, and that all Use Case Structures names and descriptions are well defined, non-overlapping, and have been formally approved.
48.2.2.2. Assess whether the Use Case Structures are properly identified and are appropriately engineered to address a Use Case Structure project.
48.2.2.2.1. Assess whether all the Use Case Structures have been delivered in terms of components, instances, and stored metadata work products.
48.2.2.2.2. Assess whether all the Use Case Structures have been properly detailed as to content, description, methodology, evaluation, presentation, and delivery work steps.
48.2.2.2.3. Assess whether all the Use Case Structures have been properly allocated sufficient unit effort estimates.
48.2.2.2.4. Assess whether all the Use Case Structures have been properly allocated sufficient quantity of units that have to be developed.
48.2.2.2.5. Assess whether all the Use Case Structures have been properly allocated work environment factors to determine an accurate estimate of required resources.
48.2.2.2.6. Assess whether all the Use Case Structures have been properly allocated work accomplishment and recording functions necessary to support earned value reporting.
48.2.2.2.7. Assess whether all the Use Case Structures have been properly allocated

metadata recording effort to ensure that all interrelationships are properly recorded into the Metabase System database.

48.2.2.3. Assign the risk level associated with each Use Case Structure not properly constructed.

48.2.3. Determine the findings and create draft assessment report.

48.2.4. Present the findings and revise draft assessment report.

48.2.5. Create final assessment report and deliver to the auditing organization.

48.3. Assess Use Case Actor.

48.3.1. Identify artifacts that bear on the assessment.

48.3.1.1. Identify the appropriate set of Use Case Actor documents.

48.3.1.1.1. Review Use Case Actors documents.

48.3.1.1.2. Review scope and business problem related documentation.

48.3.1.1.3. Identify the Use Case Actors that are defined and captured.

48.3.1.1.4. Identify the Use Case Actors related work products.

48.3.1.2. For each Use Case Actors related work product assessment:

48.3.1.2.1. Identify the relevant component.

48.3.1.2.2. Identify the description for each interrelated Use Case Actor component.

48.3.2. Perform the assessment.

48.3.2.1. Assess each Use Case Actor.

48.3.2.1.1. Assess the accuracy, quality and completeness of each Use Case Actor with respect to the business requirements.

48.3.2.1.2. Assess whether Use Case Actors are able to be inferred from business requirements, and if not whether business requirements or Use Case Actors need to be enhanced.

48.3.2.2. Assess whether the Use Case Actors are properly identified and are appropriately engineered to address a Use Case Actor project.

48.3.2.2.1. Assess whether all the Use Case Actors have been delivered in terms of components, instances, and stored metadata work products.

48.3.2.2.2. Assess whether all the Use Case Actors have been properly detailed as to content, description, methodology, evaluation, presentation, and delivery work steps.

48.3.2.2.3. Assess whether all the Use Case Actors have been properly allocated sufficient unit effort estimates.

48.3.2.2.4. Assess whether all the Use Case Actors have been properly allocated sufficient quantity of units that have to be developed.

48.3.2.2.5. Assess whether all the Use Case Actors have been properly allocated work environment factors to determine an accurate estimate of required Use Case Actors.

48.3.2.2.6. Assess whether all the Use Case Actors have been properly allocated work accomplishment and recording functions necessary to support earned value reporting.

48.3.2.2.7. Assess whether all the Use Case Actors have been properly allocated metadata recording effort to ensure that all interrelationships are properly recorded into the Metabase System database.
48.3.2.3. Assign the risk level associated with each Use Case Actor not properly constructed.
48.3.3. Determine the findings and create draft assessment report.
48.3.4. Present the findings and revise draft assessment report.
48.3.5. Create final assessment report and deliver to the auditing organization.

48.4. Assess Use Case Event.
48.4.1. Identify artifacts that bear on the assessment.
48.4.1.1. Identify the appropriate set of Use Case Event documents.
48.4.1.1.1. Review Use Case Events documents.
48.4.1.1.2. Review scope and business problem related documentation.
48.4.1.1.3. Identify the Use Case Events that are defined and captured.
48.4.1.1.4. Identify the Use Case Events related work products.
48.4.1.2. For each Use Case Events related work product assessment:
48.4.1.2.1. Identify the relevant component.
48.4.1.2.2. Identify the description for each interrelated Use Case Event component.
48.4.2. Perform the assessment.
48.4.2.1. Assess each Use Case Event.
48.4.2.1.1. Assess the accuracy, quality and completeness of each Use Case Event with respect to the business requirements.
48.4.2.1.2. Assess whether Use Case Events are able to be inferred from business requirements, and if not whether business requirements or Use Case Events need to be enhanced.
48.4.2.1.3. Assess whether each Use Case Event hierarchy is properly specified, and that all Use Case Event names and descriptions are well defined, non-overlapping, and have been formally approved.
48.4.2.2. Assess whether the Use Case Events are properly identified and are appropriately engineered to address a Use Case Event project.
48.4.2.2.1. Assess whether all the Use Case Events have been delivered in terms of components, instances, and stored metadata work products.
48.4.2.2.2. Assess whether all the Use Case Events have been properly detailed as to content, description, methodology, evaluation, presentation, and delivery work steps.
48.4.2.2.3. Assess whether all the Use Case Events have been properly allocated sufficient unit effort estimates.
48.4.2.2.4. Assess whether all the Use Case Events have been properly allocated sufficient quantity of units that have to be developed.
48.4.2.2.5. Assess whether all the Use Case Events have been properly allocated work environment factors to determine an accurate estimate of required

Use Case Events.

48.4.2.2.6. Assess whether all the Use Case Events have been properly allocated work accomplishment and recording functions necessary to support earned value reporting.

48.4.2.2.7. Assess whether all the Use Case Events have been properly allocated metadata recording effort to ensure that all interrelationships are properly recorded into the Metabase System database.

48.4.2.3. Assign the risk level associated with each Use Case Event not properly constructed.

48.4.3. Determine the findings and create draft assessment report.

48.4.4. Present the findings and revise draft assessment report.

48.4.5. Create final assessment report and deliver to the auditing organization.

48.5. Assess Use Case Event Actor.

48.5.1. Identify artifacts that bear on the assessment.

48.5.1.1. Identify the appropriate set of Use Case Event Actor documents.

48.5.1.1.1. Review Use Case Event Actors documents.

48.5.1.1.2. Review scope and business problem related documentation.

48.5.1.1.3. Identify the Use Case Event Actors that are defined and captured.

48.5.1.1.4. Identify the Use Case Event Actors related work products.

48.5.1.2. For each Use Case Event Actors related work product assessment:

48.5.1.2.1. Identify the relevant component.

48.5.1.2.2. Identify the description for each interrelated Use Case Event Actor component.

48.5.2. Perform the assessment.

48.5.2.1. Assess each Use Case Event Actor.

48.5.2.1.1. Assess the accuracy, quality and completeness of each Use Case Event Actor with respect to the business requirements.

48.5.2.1.2. Assess whether Use Case Event Actors are able to be inferred from business requirements, and if not whether business requirements or Use Case Event Actors need to be enhanced.

48.5.2.1.3. Assess whether each Use Case Event Actor pair properly associates one or more Use Case Events with one or more Use Case Actors, that are turn typed by a Use Case Actor Role.

48.5.2.1.4. Assess whether each Use Case Event Actor pair is properly named and described.

48.5.2.2. Assess whether the Use Case Event Actors are properly identified and are appropriately engineered to address a Use Case Event Actor project.

48.5.2.2.1. Assess whether all the Use Case Event Actors have been delivered in terms of components, instances, and stored metadata work products.

48.5.2.2.2. Assess whether all the Use Case Event Actors have been properly detailed as to content, description, methodology, evaluation, presentation, and

delivery work steps.

48.5.2.2.3. Assess whether all the Use Case Event Actors have been properly allocated sufficient unit effort estimates.

48.5.2.2.4. Assess whether all the Use Case Event Actors have been properly allocated sufficient quantity of units that have to be developed.

48.5.2.2.5. Assess whether all the Use Case Event Actors have been properly allocated work environment factors to determine an accurate estimate of required Use Case Event Actors.

48.5.2.2.6. Assess whether all the Use Case Event Actors have been properly allocated work accomplishment and recording functions necessary to support earned value reporting.

48.5.2.2.7. Assess whether all the Use Case Event Actors have been properly allocated metadata recording effort to ensure that all interrelationships are properly recorded into the Metabase System database.

48.5.2.3. Assign the risk level associated with each Use Case Event Actor not properly constructed.

48.5.3. Determine the findings and create draft assessment report.

48.5.4. Present the findings and revise draft assessment report.

48.5.5. Create final assessment report and deliver to the auditing organization.

48.6. Assess Use Case Pre Test.

48.6.1. Identify artifacts that bear on the assessment.

48.6.1.1. Identify the appropriate set of Use Case Pre Test documents.

48.6.1.1.1. Review Use Case Pre Tests documents.

48.6.1.1.2. Review scope and business problem related documentation.

48.6.1.1.3. Identify the Use Case Pre Tests that are defined and captured.

48.6.1.1.4. Identify the Use Case Pre Tests related work products.

48.6.1.2. For each Use Case Pre Tests related work product assessment:

48.6.1.2.1. Identify the relevant component.

48.6.1.2.2. Identify the description for each interrelated Use Case Pre Test component.

48.6.2. Perform the assessment.

48.6.2.1. Assess each Use Case Pre Test.

48.6.2.1.1. Assess the accuracy, quality and completeness of each Use Case Pre Test with respect to the business requirements.

48.6.2.1.2. Assess whether Use Case Pre Tests are able to be inferred from business requirements, and if not whether business requirements or Use Case Pre Tests need to be enhanced.

48.6.2.2. Assess whether the Use Case Pre Tests are properly identified and are appropriately engineered to address a Use Case Pre Test project.

48.6.2.2.1. Assess whether all the Use Case Pre Tests have been delivered in terms of components, instances, and stored metadata work products.

48.6.2.2.2. Assess whether all the Use Case Pre Tests have been properly detailed as to content, description, methodology, evaluation, presentation, and delivery work steps.
48.6.2.2.3. Assess whether all the Use Case Pre Tests have been properly allocated sufficient unit effort estimates.
48.6.2.2.4. Assess whether all the Use Case Pre Tests have been properly allocated sufficient quantity of units that have to be developed.
48.6.2.2.5. Assess whether all the Use Case Pre Tests have been properly allocated work environment factors to determine an accurate estimate of required Use Case Pre Tests.
48.6.2.2.6. Assess whether all the Use Case Pre Tests have been properly allocated work accomplishment and recording functions necessary to support earned value reporting.
48.6.2.2.7. Assess whether all the Use Case Pre Tests have been properly allocated metadata recording effort to ensure that all interrelationships are properly recorded into the Metabase System database.
48.6.2.3. Assign the risk level associated with each Use Case Pre Test not properly constructed.
48.6.3. Determine the findings and create draft assessment report.
48.6.4. Present the findings and revise draft assessment report.
48.6.5. Create final assessment report and deliver to the auditing organization.

48.7. Assess Use Case Post Test.
48.7.1. Identify artifacts that bear on the assessment.
48.7.1.1. Identify the appropriate set of Use Case Post Test documents.
48.7.1.1.1. Review Use Case Post Tests documents.
48.7.1.1.2. Review scope and business problem related documentation.
48.7.1.1.3. Identify the Use Case Post Tests that are defined and captured.
48.7.1.1.4. Identify the Use Case Post Tests related work products.
48.7.1.2. For each Use Case Post Tests related work product assessment:
48.7.1.2.1. Identify the relevant component.
48.7.1.2.2. Identify the description for each interrelated Use Case Post Test component.
48.7.2. Perform the assessment.
48.7.2.1. Assess each Use Case Post Test.
48.7.2.1.1. Assess the accuracy, quality and completeness of each Use Case Post Test with respect to the business requirements.
48.7.2.1.2. Assess whether Use Case Post Tests are able to be inferred from business requirements, and if not whether business requirements or Use Case Post Tests need to be enhanced.
48.7.2.2. Assess whether the Use Case Post Tests are properly identified and are appropriately engineered to address a Use Case Post Test project.

48.7.2.2.1. Assess whether all the Use Case Post Tests have been delivered in terms of components, instances, and stored metadata work products.
48.7.2.2.2. Assess whether all the Use Case Post Tests have been properly detailed as to content, description, methodology, evaluation, presentation, and delivery work steps.
48.7.2.2.3. Assess whether all the Use Case Post Tests have been properly allocated sufficient unit effort estimates.
48.7.2.2.4. Assess whether all the Use Case Post Tests have been properly allocated sufficient quantity of units that have to be developed.
48.7.2.2.5. Assess whether all the Use Case Post Tests have been properly allocated work environment factors to determine an accurate estimate of required Use Case Post Tests.
48.7.2.2.6. Assess whether all the Use Case Post Tests have been properly allocated work accomplishment and recording functions necessary to support earned value reporting.
48.7.2.2.7. Assess whether all the Use Case Post Tests have been properly allocated metadata recording effort to ensure that all interrelationships are properly recorded into the Metabase System database.
48.7.2.3. Assign the risk level associated with each Use Case Post Test not properly constructed.
48.7.3. Determine the findings and create draft assessment report.
48.7.4. Present the findings and revise draft assessment report.
48.7.5. Create final assessment report and deliver to the auditing organization.

48.8. Assess Use Case Special Test.
48.8.1. Identify artifacts that bear on the assessment.
48.8.1.1. Identify the appropriate set of Use Case Special Test documents.
48.8.1.1.1. Review Use Case Special Tests documents.
48.8.1.1.2. Review scope and business problem related documentation.
48.8.1.1.3. Identify the Use Case Special Tests that are defined and captured.
48.8.1.1.4. Identify the Use Case Special Tests related work products.
48.8.1.2. For each Use Case Special Tests related work product assessment:
48.8.1.2.1. Identify the relevant component.
48.8.1.2.2. Identify the description for each interrelated Use Case Special Test component.
48.8.2. Perform the assessment.
48.8.2.1. Assess each Use Case Special Test.
48.8.2.1.1. Assess the accuracy, quality and completeness of each Use Case Special Test with respect to the business requirements.
48.8.2.1.2. Assess whether Use Case Special Tests are able to be inferred from business requirements, and if not whether business requirements or Use Case Special Tests need to be enhanced.

48.8.2.2 Assess whether the Use Case Special Tests are properly identified and are appropriately engineered to address a Use Case Special Test project.

48.8.2.2.1. Assess whether all the Use Case Special Tests have been delivered in terms of components, instances, and stored metadata work products.

48.8.2.1.2. Assess whether all the Use Case Special Tests have been properly detailed as to content, description, methodology, evaluation, presentation, and delivery work steps.

48.8.2.2.3. Assess whether all the Use Case Special Tests have been properly allocated sufficient unit effort estimates.

48.8.2.2.4. Assess whether all the Use Case Special Tests have been properly allocated sufficient quantity of units that have to be developed.

48.8.2.2.5. Assess whether all the Use Case Special Tests have been properly allocated work environment factors to determine an accurate estimate of required resources.

48.8.2.2.6. Assess whether all the Use Case Special Tests have been properly allocated work accomplishment and recording functions necessary to support earned value reporting.

48.8.2.2.7. Assess whether all the Use Case Special Tests have been properly allocated metadata recording effort to ensure that all interrelationships are properly recorded into the Metabase System database.

48.8.2.3. Assign the risk level associated with each Use Case Special Test not properly constructed.

48.8.3. Determine the findings and create draft assessment report.

48.8.4. Present the findings and revise draft assessment report.

48.8.5. Create final assessment report and deliver to the auditing organization.

48.9. Assess Use Case Fact.

48.9.1. Identify artifacts that bear on the assessment.

48.9.1.1. Identify the appropriate set of Use Case Fact documents.

48.9.1.1.1. Review Use Case Facts documents.

48.9.1.1.2. Review scope and business problem related documentation.

48.9.1.1.3. Identify the Use Case Facts that are defined and captured.

48.9.1.1.4. Identify the Use Case Facts related work products.

48.9.1.2. For each Use Case Facts related work product assessment:

48.9.1.2.1. Identify the relevant component.

48.9.1.2.2. Identify the description for each interrelated Use Case Fact component.

48.9.2. Perform the assessment.

48.9.2.1. Assess each Use Case Fact.

48.9.2.1.1. Assess the accuracy, quality and completeness of each Use Case Fact with respect to the business requirements.

48.9.2.1.2. Assess whether Use Case Facts are able to be inferred from business requirements, and if not whether business requirements or Use Case Facts need to be enhanced.

48.9.2.2. Assess whether the Use Case Facts are properly identified and are appropriately engineered to address a Use Case Fact project.

48.9.2.2.1. Use Case Facts whether all the Use Case Facts have been delivered in terms of components, instances, and stored metadata work products.

48.9.2.2.2. Assess whether all the Use Case Facts have been properly detailed as to content, description, methodology, evaluation, presentation, and delivery work steps.

48.9.2.2.3. Assess whether all the Use Case Facts have been properly allocated sufficient unit effort estimates.

48.9.2.2.4. Assess whether all the Use Case Facts have been properly allocated sufficient quantity of units that have to be developed.

48.9.2.2.5. Assess whether all the Use Case Facts have been properly allocated work environment factors to determine an accurate estimate of required Use Case Facts.

48.9.2.2.6. Assess whether all the Use Case Facts have been properly allocated work accomplishment and recording functions necessary to support earned value reporting.

48.9.2.2.7. Assess whether all the Use Case Facts have been properly allocated metadata recording effort to ensure that all interrelationships are properly recorded into the Metabase System database.

48.9.2.3. Assign the risk level associated with each Use Case Fact not properly constructed.

48.9.3. Determine the findings and create draft assessment report.

48.9.4. Present the findings and revise draft assessment report.

48.9.5. Create final assessment report and deliver to the auditing organization.

48.10. Assess Use Case Fact View Column.

48.10.1. Identify artifacts that bear on the assessment.

48.10.1.1. Identify the appropriate set of Use Case Fact View Column documents.

48.10.1.1.1. Review Use Case Fact View Column documents.

48.10.1.1.2. Review scope and business problem related documentation.

48.10.1.1.3. Identify the Use Case Fact View Columns that are defined and captured.

48.10.1.1.4. Identify the Use Case Fact View Columns related work products.

48.10.1.2. For each Use Case Fact View Columns work product assessment:

48.10.2. Perform the assessment.

48.10.2.1. Assess each Use Case Fact View Column.

48.10.2.1.1. Assess the accuracy, quality and completeness of each Use Case Fact View Column with respect to the business requirements.

48.10.2.1.2. Assess whether Use Case Fact View Columns are able to be inferred from business requirements, and if not whether business requirements or Use Case Fact View Columns need to be enhanced.

48.10.2.1.3. Assess whether each Use Case Fact View Column pair properly associates one or more Use Case Facts with one or more View Columns.

48.10.2.1.4. Assess whether each Use Case Fact View Columns pair is properly named and described.

48.10.2.2. Assess whether the Use Case Fact View Columns are properly identified and are appropriately engineered to address a Use Case Fact View Column project.

48.10.2.2.1. Assess whether all the Use Case Fact View Columns have been delivered in terms of components, instances, and stored metadata work products.

48.10.2.2.2. Assess whether all the Use Case Fact View Columns have been properly detailed as to content, description, methodology, evaluation, presentation, and delivery work steps.

48.10.2.2.3. Assess whether all the Use Case Fact View Columns have been properly allocated sufficient unit effort estimates.

48.10.2.2.4. Assess whether all the Use Case Fact View Columns have been properly allocated sufficient quantity of units that have to be developed.

48.10.2.2.5. Assess whether all the Use Case Fact View Columns have been properly allocated work environment factors to determine an accurate estimate of required resources.

48.10.2.2.6. Assess whether all the Use Case Fact View Columns have been properly allocated work accomplishment and recording functions necessary to support earned value reporting.

48.10.2.2.7. Assess whether all the Use Case Fact View Columns have been properly allocated metadata recording effort to ensure that all interrelationships are properly recorded into the Metabase System database.

48.10.2.3. Assign the risk level associated with each Use Case Fact View Column not properly constructed.

48.10.3. Determine the findings and create draft assessment report.

48.10.4. Present the findings and revise draft assessment report.

48.10.5. Create final assessment report and deliver to the auditing organization.

48.11 Assess Use Case Fact Use Case Pre Test.

48.11.1. Identify artifacts that bear on the assessment.

48.11.1.1. Identify the appropriate set of Use Case Fact Use Case Pre Test documents.

48.11.1.1.1. Review Use Case Fact Use Case Pre Test documents.

48.11.1.1.2. Review scope and business problem related documentation.

48.11.1.1.3. Identify the Use Case Fact Use Case Pre Tests that are defined and captured.

48.11.1.1.4. Identify the Use Case Fact Use Case Pre Tests related work products.

48.11.1.2. For each Use Case Fact Use Case Pre Tests work product assessment:

48.11.2. Perform the assessment.

48.11.2.1. Assess each Use Case Fact Use Case Pre Test.

48.11.2.1.1. Assess the accuracy, quality and completeness of each Use Case Fact Use Case Pre Test with respect to the business requirements.

48.11.2.1.2. Assess whether Use Case Fact Use Case Pre Tests are able to be inferred from business requirements, and if not whether business requirements or Use Case Fact Use Case Pre Tests need to be enhanced.

48.11.2.1.3. Assess whether each Use Case Fact Use Case Pre Test pair properly associates one or more Use Case Facts with one or more Use Case Pre Tests.

48.11.2.1.4. Assess whether each Use Case Fact Use Case Pre Test pair is properly named and described.

48.11.2.2. Assess whether the Use Case Fact Use Case Pre Tests are properly identified and are appropriately engineered to address a Use Case Fact Use Case Pre Test project.

48.11.2.2.1. Assess whether all the Use Case Fact Use Case Pre Tests have been delivered in terms of components, instances, and stored metadata work products.

48.11.2.2.2. Assess whether all the Use Case Fact Use Case Pre Tests have been properly detailed as to content, description, methodology, evaluation, presentation, and delivery work steps.

48.11.2.2.3. Assess whether all the Use Case Fact Use Case Pre Tests have been properly allocated sufficient unit effort estimates.

48.11.2.2.4. Assess whether all the Use Case Fact Use Case Pre Tests have been properly allocated sufficient quantity of units that have to be developed.

48.11.2.2.5. Assess whether all the Use Case Fact Use Case Pre Tests have been properly allocated work environment factors to determine an accurate estimate of required resources.

48.11.2.2.6. Assess whether all the Use Case Fact Use Case Pre Tests have been properly allocated work accomplishment and recording functions necessary to support earned value reporting.

48.11.2.2.7. Assess whether all the Use Case Fact Use Case Pre Tests have been properly allocated metadata recording effort to ensure that all interrelationships are properly recorded into the Metabase System database.

48.11.2.3. Assign the risk level associated with each Use Case Fact Use Case Pre Test not properly constructed.

48.11.3. Determine the findings and create draft assessment report.

48.11.4. Present the findings and revise draft assessment report.

48.11.5. Create final assessment report and deliver to the auditing organization.

48.12 Assess Use Case Fact Use Case Post Test.

48.12.1. Identify artifacts that bear on the assessment.

48.12.1.1. Identify the appropriate set of Use Case Fact Use Case Post Tests documents.

48.12.1.1.1. Review Use Case Fact Use Case Post Tests documents.

48.12.1.1.2. Review scope and business problem related documentation.

48.12.1.1.3. Identify the Use Case Fact Use Case Post Tests that are defined and captured.

48.12.1.1.4. Identify the Use Case Fact Use Case Post Tests related work products.

48.12.1.2. For each Use Case Fact Use Case Post Tests work product assessment:

48.12.2. Perform the assessment.

48.12.2.1. Assess each Use Case Fact Use Case Post Test.

48.12.2.1.1. Assess the accuracy, quality and completeness of each Use Case Fact Use Case Post Test with respect to the business requirements.

48.12.2.1.2. Assess whether Use Case Fact Use Case Post Tests are able to be inferred from business requirements, and if not whether business requirements or Use Case Fact Use Case Post Tests need to be enhanced.

48.12.2.1.3. Assess whether each Use Case Fact Use Case Post Test pair properly associates one or more Use Case Facts with one or more Use Case Post Tests.

48.12.2.1.4. Assess whether each Use Case Fact Use Case Post Test pair is properly named and described.

48.12.2.2. Assess whether the Use Case Fact Use Case Post Tests are properly identified and are appropriately engineered to address a Use Case Fact Use Case Post Test project.

48.12.2.2.1. Assess whether all the Use Case Fact Use Case Post Tests have been delivered in terms of components, instances, and stored metadata work products.

48.12.2.2.2. Assess whether all the Use Case Fact Use Case Post Tests have been properly detailed as to content, description, methodology, evaluation, presentation, and delivery work steps.

48.12.2.2.3. Assess whether all the Use Case Fact Use Case Post Tests have been properly allocated sufficient unit effort estimates.

48.12.2.2.4. Assess whether all the Use Case Fact Use Case Post Tests have been properly allocated sufficient quantity of units that have to be developed.

48.12.2.2.5. Assess whether all the Use Case Fact Use Case Post Tests have been properly allocated work environment factors to determine an accurate estimate of required resources.

48.12.2.2.6. Assess whether all the Use Case Fact Use Case Post Tests have been properly allocated work accomplishment and recording functions necessary to support earned value reporting.

48.12.2.2.7. Assess whether all the Use Case Fact Use Case Post Tests have been properly allocated metadata recording effort to ensure that all interrelationships are properly recorded into the Metabase System database.

48.12.2.3. Assign the risk level associated with each Use Case Fact Use Case Post Test not properly constructed.

48.12.3. Determine the findings and create draft assessment report.

48.12.4. Present the findings and revise draft assessment report.

48.12.5. Create final assessment report and deliver to the auditing organization.

48.13 Assess Use Case Fact Use Case Event.

48.13.1. Identify artifacts that bear on the assessment.

48.13.1.1. Identify the appropriate set of Use Case Fact Use Case Event documents.

48.13.1.1.1. Review Use Case Fact Use Case Event documents.

48.13.1.1.2. Review scope and business problem related documentation.

48.13.1.1.3. Identify the Use Case Fact Use Case Event that are defined and captured.

48.13.1.1.4. Identify the Use Case Fact Use Case Event related work products.

48.13.1.2. For each Use Case Fact Use Case Event work product assessment:

48.13.2. Perform the assessment.

48.13.2.1. Assess each Use Case Fact Use Case Event.

48.13.2.1.1. Assess the accuracy, quality and completeness of each Use Case Fact Use Case Event with respect to the business requirements.

48.13.2.1.2. Assess whether Use Case Fact Use Case Event are able to be inferred from business requirements, and if not whether business requirements or Use Case Fact Use Case Event need to be enhanced.

48.13.2.1.3. Assess whether each Use Case Fact Use Case Event pair properly associates one or more Use Case Facts with one or more Use Case Events.

48.13.2.1.4. Assess whether each Use Case Fact Use Case Event pair is properly named and described.

48.13.2.2. Assess whether the Use Case Fact Use Case Event are properly identified and are appropriately engineered to address a Use Case Fact View Column project.

48.13.2.2.1. Assess whether all the Use Case Fact Use Case Event have been delivered in terms of components, instances, and stored metadata work products.

48.13.2.2.2. Assess whether all the Use Case Fact Use Case Event have been properly detailed as to content, description, methodology, evaluation, presentation, and delivery work steps.

48.13.2.2.3. Assess whether all the Use Case Fact Use Case Event have been properly allocated sufficient unit effort estimates.

48.13.2.2.4. Assess whether all the Use Case Fact Use Case Event have been properly allocated sufficient quantity of units that have to be developed.

48.13.2.2.5. Assess whether all the Use Case Fact Use Case Event have been properly allocated work environment factors to determine an accurate estimate of required resources.

48.13.2.2.6. Assess whether all the Use Case Fact Use Case Event have been properly

allocated work accomplishment and recording functions necessary to support earned value reporting.

48.13.2.2.7. Assess whether all the Use Case Fact Use Case Event have been properly allocated metadata recording effort to ensure that all interrelationships are properly recorded into the Metabase System database.

48.13.2.3. Assign the risk level associated with each Use Case Fact Use Case Event not properly constructed.

48.13.3. Determine the findings and create draft assessment report.

48.13.4. Present the findings and revise draft assessment report.

48.13.5. Create final assessment report and deliver to the auditing organization.

48.14 Assess Use Case Events Business Information System.

48.14.1. Identify artifacts that bear on the assessment.

48.14.1.1. Identify the appropriate set of Use Case Events Business Information System documents.

48.14. Review Use Case Events Business Information System documents.

48.14.1.1.2. Review scope and business problem related documentation.

48.14.1.1.3. Identify the Use Case Events Business Information System that are defined and captured.

48.14.1.1.4. Identify the Use Case Events Business Information System related work products.

48.14.1.2. For each Use Case Events Business Information System work product assessment:

48.14.2. Perform the assessment.

48.14.2.1. Assess each Use Case Events Business Information System.

48.14.2.1.1. Assess the accuracy, quality and completeness of each Use Case Events Business Information System with respect to the business requirements.

48.14.2.1.2. Assess whether Use Case Events Business Information System are able to be inferred from business requirements, and if not whether business requirements or Use Case Events Business Information System need to be enhanced.

48.14.2.1.3. Assess whether each Use Case Events Business Information System pair properly associates one or more Use Case Facts with one or more Business Information Systems.

48.14.2.1.4. Assess whether each Use Case Events Business Information System pair is properly named and described.

48.14.2.2. Assess whether the Use Case Events Business Information System are properly identified and are appropriately engineered to address a Use Case Fact View Column project.

48.14.2.2.1. Assess whether all the Use Case Events Business Information System have been delivered in terms of components, instances, and stored metadata work products.

48.14.2.2.2. Assess whether all the Use Case Events Business Information System have been properly detailed as to content, description, methodology, evaluation, presentation, and delivery work steps.

48.14.2.2.3. Assess whether all the Use Case Events Business Information System have been properly allocated sufficient unit effort estimates.

48.14.2.2.4. Assess whether all the Use Case Events Business Information System have been properly allocated sufficient quantity of units that have to be developed.

48.14.2.2.5. Assess whether all the Use Case Events Business Information System have been properly allocated work environment factors to determine an accurate estimate of required resources.

48.14.2.2.6. Assess whether all the Use Case Events Business Information System have been properly allocated work accomplishment and recording functions necessary to support earned value reporting.

48.14.2.2.7. Assess whether all the Use Case Events Business Information System have been properly allocated metadata recording effort to ensure that all interrelationships are properly recorded into the Metabase System database.

48.14.2.3. Assign the risk level associated with each Use Case Events Business Information System not properly constructed.

48.14.3. Determine the findings and create draft assessment report.

48.14.4. Present the findings and revise draft assessment report.

48.14.5. Create final assessment report and deliver to the auditing organization.

48.15 Assess Use Case Events Mission-Organization-Function.

48.15.1. Identify artifacts that bear on the assessment.

48.15.1.1. Identify the appropriate set of Use Case Events Mission-Organization-Function documents.

48.15.1.1.1. Review Use Case Events Mission-Organization-Function documents.

48.15.1.1.2. Review scope and business problem related documentation.

48.15.1.1.3. Identify the Use Case Events Mission-Organization-Function that are defined and captured.

48.15.1.1.4. Identify the Use Case Events Mission-Organization-Function related work products.

48.15.1.2. For each Use Case Events Mission-Organization-Function work product assessment:

48.15.2. Perform the assessment.

48.15.2.1. Assess each Use Case Events Mission-Organization-Function.

48.15.2.1.1. Assess the accuracy, quality and completeness of each Use Case Events Mission-Organization-Function with respect to the business requirements.

48.15.2.1.2. Assess whether Use Case Events Mission-Organization-Function are able to be inferred from business requirements, and if not whether business requirements or Use Case Events Mission-Organization-Function need to be enhanced.

48.15.2.1.3. Assess whether each Use Case Events Mission-Organization-Function pair properly associates one or more Use Case Events with one or more Mission-Organization-Functions.

48.15.2.1.4. Assess whether each Use Case Events Mission-Organization-Function pair is properly named and described.

48.15.2.2. Assess whether the Use Case Events Mission-Organization-Functions are properly identified and are appropriately engineered to address a Use Case Fact View Column project.

48.15.2.2.1. Assess whether all the Use Case Events Mission-Organization-Functions have been delivered in terms of components, instances, and stored metadata work products.

48.15.2.2.2. Assess whether all the Use Case Events Mission-Organization-Functions have been properly detailed as to content, description, methodology, evaluation, presentation, and delivery work steps.

48.15.2.2.3. Assess whether all the Use Case Events Mission-Organization-Functions have been properly allocated sufficient unit effort estimates.

48.15.2.2.4. Assess whether all the Use Case Events Mission-Organization-Functions have been properly allocated sufficient quantity of units that have to be developed.

48.15.2.2.5. Assess whether all the Use Case Events Mission-Organization-Functions have been properly allocated work environment factors to determine an accurate estimate of required resources.

48.15.2.2.6. Assess whether all the Use Case Events Mission-Organization-Functions have been properly allocated work accomplishment and recording functions necessary to support earned value reporting.

48.15.2.2.7. Assess whether all the Use Case Events Mission-Organization-Functions have been properly allocated metadata recording effort to ensure that all interrelationships are properly recorded into the Metabase System database.

48.15.2.3. Assign the risk level associated with each Use Case Events Mission-Organization-Function not properly constructed.

48.15.3. Determine the findings and create draft assessment report.

48.15.4. Present the findings and revise draft assessment report.

48.15.5. Create final assessment report and deliver to the auditing organization.

49. External Data Interfaces

49.1. Assess External Data Interface.
49.1.1. Identify artifacts that bear on the assessment.
49.1.1.1. Identify the appropriate set of External Data Interface documents.
49.1.1.1.1. Review External Data Interface documents.
49.1.1.1.2. Review scope and business problem related documentation.
49.1.1.1.3. Identify the External Data Interface requirements that are defined and captured.
49.1.1.1.4. Identify the External Data Interface requirements related work products.
49.1.1.2. For each External Data Interface requirements related work product assessment:
49.1.1.2.1. Identify the relevant components, that is, Business Information Systems, Views, View Columns.
49.1.1.2.2. Identify the description for each interrelated External Data Interface component.
49.1.2. Perform the assessment.
49.1.2.1. Assess each External Data Interface.
49.1.2.1.1. Assess the accuracy, quality and completeness of each External Data Interface with respect to the business requirements.
49.1.2.1.2. Assess whether External Data Interfaces are able to be inferred from business requirements, and if not whether business requirements or External Data Interfaces need to be enhanced.
49.1.2.1.3. Assess whether the External Data Interface is sufficiently identified and specified to the level that an Extract, Transform, and Load process can be expertly constructed.
49.1.2.1.4. Assess whether there is sufficient detail to the External Data Interface to unambiguously address issues related to granularity of both sides of the interface, precision of the various values for the data fields, and an exact matching of the values for any data fields that is to be imported.
49.1.2.1.5. Assess whether there is sufficient information to be able to fill out audit trail information and to be able to back out data once it has been imported.
49.1.2.2. Assess the adequacy of each View Data Model with respect to the External Data Interface requirements.
49.1.2.2.1. Assess whether the External Data Interface is sufficiently identified and specified to the level that a set of Views can be constructed to directly import the data from a connected source.
49.1.2.2.2. Assess whether there is sufficient detail to the External Data Interface to unambiguously construct Views that address the granularity of both sides of the interface, precision of the various values for the data fields, and an exact matching of the values for any data fields that is to be imported.

49.1.2.2.3. Assess whether there is sufficient information to be able to fill out audit trail information built into Views.

49.1.2.3. Assess the adequacy of each XML data model with respect to the External Data Interface requirements.

49.1.2.3.1. Assess whether the External Data Interface is sufficiently identified and specified to the level that a set of XML Schemas can be constructed to process data that is exported from external sources.

49.1.2.3.2. Assess whether there is sufficient detail to the External Data Interface to unambiguously construct XML schemas that address the granularity of both sides of the interface, precision of the various values for the data fields, and an exact matching of the values for any data fields that is to be imported.

49.1.2.3.3. Assess whether there is sufficient information to be able to fill out audit trail information built into the XML schemas.

49.1.2.4. Assess whether each External Data Interface requirements is addressed by one or more Business Information Systems as may be appropriate.

49.1.2.4.1. Assess whether the External Data Interface requirements Business Information System component is sufficiently detailed to assure coverage of the requirement.

49.1.2.4.2. Assess whether the performance Requirements from the External Data Interface is acceptable for the resources currently allowed for the operation of the Business Information Systems.

49.1.2.4.3. If External Data Interfaces are able to be inferred from Business Information Systems, determine whether External Data Interfaces and/or Business Information Systems need to be enhanced.

49.1.2.5. Assess whether each External Data Interface requirements is addressed by one or more Data Integrity Rules as may be appropriate.

49.1.2.5.1. Assess whether the External Data Interface requirements Data Integrity Rule is specified to such an extent that it can be executed and will result in a pass/fail result in addition to any data value calculation or transformation.

49.1.2.5.2. If External Data Interfaces are able to be inferred from Data Integrity Rules, determine whether External Data Interfaces and/or Data Integrity Rules need to be enhanced.

49.1.2.6. Assess whether each External Data Interface requirements is addressed by one or more Database Objects as may be appropriate.

49.1.2.6.1. Assess whether each External Data Interface Database Object Data Structure is clearly identified and satisfies the needs of the External Data Interface requirement.

49.1.2.6.2. Assess whether an under specified External Data Interface Database Object Data Structure needs to be enhanced to meet the needs of the External Data Interface requirement.

49.1.2.6.3. Assess whether each External Data Interface Database Object Primitive Data Transformation is sufficiently specified to carry out the required data acquisition, transformation and storage of the data represented by the External Data Interface.

49.1.2.6.4. Assess whether each External Data Interface requirement Database Object State is sufficiently set out and exists within a sequence such that it can be achieved when the Database Object is properly Created, or if the Creation fails that the Database Object returns to a prior state.

49.1.2.6.5. Assess whether each External Data Interface requirement Database Object Business Information System is sufficiently specified that when executed the specified ending state is achieved through the proper execution of the Database Object Table processes.

49.1.2.6.6. If External Data Interfaces are able to be inferred from Database Objects, determine whether External Data Interfaces and/or Database Objects need to be enhanced.

49.1.2.7. Assess whether each External Data Interface requirements is addressed by one or more external quality standards as may be appropriate.

49.1.2.7.1. Assess whether the data interface requirement is expressed within an external quality standard such as ANSI SQL and/or WC3 so that it can be ported from one technology to the next without major recreation.

49.1.2.7.2. If External Data Interfaces are able to be inferred from external quality standards, determine whether External Data Interfaces and/or External Data Interfaces inventory need to be enhanced.

49.1.2.8. Assess whether each External Data Interface requirements is addressed by one or more Mission-Organization-Functions as may be appropriate.

49.1.2.8.1. Assess whether the External Data Interface requirement is discoverable from within Mission-Organization-Functions.

49.1.2.8.2. If External Data Interfaces are able to be inferred from Mission-Organization-Functions, determine whether External Data Interfaces and/or Mission-Organization-Functions need to be enhanced.

49.1.2.9. Assess whether each External Data Interface requirements is addressed by one or more resource life cycles as may be appropriate.

49.1.2.9.1. Assess whether each External Data Interface requirement resource life cycle is clearly identified and that through its execution fulfills a needed action that contributes to the achievement of the resource life cycle node.

49.1.2.9.2. If External Data Interfaces are able to be inferred from resource life cycles, determine whether External Data Interfaces and/or resource life cycles need to be enhanced.

49.1.2.10. Assess whether each External Data Interface requirements is addressed by one or more Use Case is addressed by one or more Value Domains and management as may be appropriate.

49.1.2.12.1. Assess External Data Interface requirement Value Domain to ensure that it is sufficiently specified to meet the needs of both the External Data Interface requirement and the needs of the database in terms of data transformation between an externally defined value and an internally defined value.

49.1.2.10.2. If External Data Interfaces are able to be inferred from more Use Cases, determine whether External Data Interfaces and/or more Use Cases need to be enhanced.

49.1.2.11. Assess whether each External Data Interface requirements is addressed by one or more User Acceptance Tests as may be appropriate.

49.1.2.11.1. Assess each External Data Interface requirement User Acceptance Test to ensure that it is valid, reliable, repeatable, and discriminating.

49.1.2.11.2. Assess each External Data Interface requirement User Acceptance Test to ensure that its results are pass or fail.

49.1.2.11.3. If External Data Interfaces are able to be inferred from User Acceptance Tests, determine whether External Data Interfaces and/or User Acceptance Tests need to be enhanced.

49.1.2.12. Assess whether each External Data Interface requirements is addressed by one or more Value Domains as may be appropriate.

49.1.2.12.1. Assess each External Data Interface to ensure that it is completely represented through an appropriate set of Value Domains.

49.1.2.12.2. If External Data Interfaces are able to be inferred from Value Domains, determine whether External Data Interfaces and/or Value Domains need to be enhanced.

49.1.2.13. Assess whether the External Data Interfaces are properly identified and are appropriately engineered to address a External Data Interface project.

49.1.2.13.1. Assess whether all the External Data Interfaces have been delivered in terms of components, instances, and stored metadata work products.

49.1.2.13.2. Assess whether all the External Data Interfaces have been properly detailed as to content, description, methodology, evaluation, presentation, and delivery work steps.

49.1.2.13.3. Assess whether all the External Data Interfaces have been properly allocated sufficient unit effort estimates.

49.1.2.13.4. Assess whether all the External Data Interfaces have been properly allocated sufficient quantity of units that have to be developed.

49.1.2.13.5. Assess whether all the External Data Interfaces have been properly allocated work environment factors to determine an accurate estimate of required resources.

49.1.2.13.6. Assess whether all the External Data Interfaces have been properly allocated work accomplishment and recording functions necessary to support earned value reporting.

49.1.2.13.7. Assess whether all the External Data Interfaces have been properly allocated metadata recording effort to ensure that all interrelationships

are properly recorded into the Metabase System database.

49.1.2.14. Assign the risk level associated with each External Data Interface not properly constructed.

49.1.3. Determine the findings and create draft assessment report.

49.1.4. Present the findings and revise draft assessment report.

49.1.5. Create final assessment report and deliver to the auditing organization.

Index

www.ingramcontent.com/pod-product-compliance
Lightning Source LLC
LaVergne TN
LVHW082005200926
848481LV00010B/2805
9780978996871